Assessment of
Family Violence

Assessment of Family Violence

A Clinical and Legal Sourcebook

Second Edition

Edited by

Robert T. Ammerman

and

Michel Hersen

John Wiley & Sons, Inc.

New York • Chichester • Weinheim • Brisbane • Singapore • Toronto

This publication is designed to provide accurate and authoritative information in regard to the subject
matter covered. It is sold with the understanding that the publisher is not engaged in rendering
professional services. If legal, accounting, medical, psychological or any other expert assistance is
required, the services of a competent professional person should be sought.

Library of Congress Cataloging-in-Publication Data:

Assessment of family violence : a clinical and legal sourcebook /
   edited by Robert T. Ammerman and Michel Hersen. — 2nd ed.
       p.   cm.
    Includes bibliographical references and index.
    ISBN 0-471-24256-X (cloth : alk. paper)
    1. Family violence. 2. Family violence—Law and legislation—
United States. I. Ammerman, Robert T. II. Hersen, Michel.
   RC569.5.F3A87   1999
   616.85'822—dc21   98-53412

Printed in the United States of America.

10   9   8   7   6   5   4   3   2   1

To Eleanor Thompson and the memory of Bernard Thompson—RTA

To Zoltan Gold—MH

Contributors

Ronald D. Adelman, M.D.
Associate Professor of Medicine
Division of Geriatrics and Gerontology
Cornell University Medical College
New York, New York

Robert T. Ammerman, Ph.D.
Professor of Pediatrics
Children's Hospital Medical Center
University of Cincinnati School of
    Medicine
Cincinnati, Ohio

Sandra T. Azar, Ph.D.
Associate Professor of Psychology and
    Director of Clinical Training
Frances L. Hiatt School of Psychology
Clark University
Worcester, Massachusetts

Ronet Bachman, Ph.D.
Associate Professor
Department of Sociology and Criminal
    Justice
University of Delaware
Newark, Delaware

Pamela M. Berlin, M.S.
Psychologist
Department of Psychology in Education
University of Pittsburgh
Pittsburgh, Pennsylvania

Risa Breckman, M.S.W.
Director of Social Services/Wright
    Center on Aging
Division of Geriatrics and Gerontology
New York, New York

Laura S. Brown, Ph.D.
Psychologist
Seattle, Washington

Jessica A. Card, Ph.D.
Assistant Director, Child Abuse
    Services
Child and Family Guidance Center
Panorama City, California

Linda L. Damon, Ph.D.
Director, Child Abuse Services
Child and Family Guidance Center
North Hills, California

John W. Fantuzzo, Ph.D.
Diana R. Riklis Professor of
    Education
Graduate School of Education
Psychology in Education Division
University of Pennsylvania
Philadelphia, Pennsylvania

Ronit M. Gershater-Molko, M.A.
Behavior Change Associates
Marina del Rey, California

Steven N. Gold, Ph.D.
Professor, Center for Psychological
    Studies
Director, Trauma Resolution Integration
    Program
Nova Southeastern University
Fort Lauderdale, Florida

David J. Hansen, Ph.D.
Associate Professor, Director of Clinical
    Training
University of Nebraska-Lincoln
Department of Psychology
Lincoln, Nebraska

Jeffrey J. Haugaard, Ph.D.
Associate Professor
Department of Human Development
Cornell University
Ithaca, New York

Michel Hersen, Ph.D.
Professor and Dean
School of Professional Psychology
Pacific University
Forest Grove, Oregon

Peter G. Jaffe, Ph.D.
Executive Director and Associate
    Professor (Adjunct)
London Family Court Clinic
Department of Psychology and
    Psychiatry
University of Western Ontario
London, Ontario, Canada

Mark S. Lachs, M.D.
Associate Professor of Medicine
Division of Geriatrics and
    Gerontology
Cornell University Medical College
New York, New York

Megan Noone Lutz
Graduate School of Education
Psychology in Education Division
University of Pennsylvania
Philadelphia, Pennsylvania

John R. Lutzker, Ph.D.
Ross Professor and Chair; Director of
    Graduate Training
Department of Psychology
University of Judaism
Los Angeles, California

Paul McDermott, Ph.D.
Professor of Education
Graduate School of Education
Psychology in Education Division
University of Pennsylvania
Philadelphia, Pennsylvania

Susan V. McLeer, M.D.
Professor and Chair
Department of Psychiatry
State University of New York at Buffalo
Buffalo, New York

Christopher Murphy, Ph.D.
Associate Professor
University of Maryland at Baltimore
    County
Baltimore, Maryland

William D. Murphy, Ph.D.
Professor of Psychiatry
Department of Psychiatry
University of Tennessee, Memphis
Memphis, Tennessee

K. Daniel O'Leary, Ph.D.
Distinguished Professor
Department of Psychology
State University of New York at Stony
    Brook
Stony Brook, New York

I. Jacqueline Page, Psy.D.
Instructor
Department of Psychiatry
University of Tennessee, Memphis
Memphis, Tennessee

Mimi Rose, J.D.
Chief Assistant District Attorney
Office of the District Attorney
Philadelphia, Pennsylvania

Daniel Rosen
Doctoral Candidate
University of Michigan
School of Social Work
Ann Arbor, Michigan

Daniel G. Saunders, Ph.D.
Associate Professor
University of Michigan
School of Social Work
Ann Arbor, Michigan

Georganna Sedlar, M.A.
Clinical Psychology Graduate Student
Department of Psychology
University of Nebraska-Lincoln
Lincoln, Nebraska

Champika K. Soysa, M.A.
Doctoral Student in Clinical Psychology
Frances L. Hiatt School of Psychology
Clark University
Worcester, Massachusetts

Marlies Sudermann, Ph.D.
Psychological Services
Thames Valley District School Board
London, Ontario, Canada

Roberta K. Thyfault, J.D.
Attorney at Law
San Diego, California

Richard M. Tolman, Ph.D.
Associate Professor
University of Michigan
School of Social Work
Ann Arbor, Michigan

Joan I. Vondra, Ph.D.
Associate Professor
Department of Psychology in Education
University of Pittsburgh
Pittsburgh, Pennsylvania

Jody E. Warner-Rogers, Ph.D.
Clinical Psychology
Children's Department
Maudsley Hospital
London, England

Gillian Cara Wood, J.D., M.S.W.
Attorney at Law
Washington, DC

Preface

WHEN THE first edition of this book was published in 1991, research on family violence was in its early stage, and comparatively little information was available on clinical assessment. At this point, family violence research has matured considerably, and the core features and requirements of clinical assessment in this field have been identified. Accordingly, we made the decision to revise and update this volume to take into account the conceptual and procedural advances that have occurred in the past 9 years. It is heartening to see that, in contrast to a decade ago, several assessment measures have been developed that are specifically designed for use with victims and perpetrators of family violence. Moreover, there is greater appreciation for the role of abuse and neglect in the etiology of psychopathology, thus necessitating careful assessment by clinicians working with diverse populations. An established and empirically based assessment approach is essential to the development of effective interventions. The purpose of this book, then, is to document state-of-the-art assessment practices in the field.

Assessment of Family Violence: A Clinical and Legal Sourcebook, Second Edition, is divided into four major sections. Part One, General Issues, begins with an overview of assessment issues in family violence, followed by four chapters on clinical or legal and systems issues encountered in the assessment of family violence involving children and adults. Part Two, Epidemiology, presents two chapters on the epidemiology of family violence directed toward children and adults. Part Three, Types of Family Violence, consists of chapters on the assessment of different forms of maltreatment, including child abuse and neglect, incest in young children, extrafamilial child sexual abuse, spouse battering, elder abuse and neglect, psychological abuse of children, and psychological abuse of adults. Part Four, Special Issues, encompasses chapters on more recently recognized areas of concern, such as child witnesses of family violence, adolescent perpetrators of incest, and adult survivors of sexual abuse. Chapters in Parts Three and Four are presented in the following parallel format: introduction, description of the problem, assessment approaches, legal and systems consideration, case illustration, and conclusion.

We acknowledge the support and assistance provided by a number of individuals. Foremost, we thank the eminent contributors for sharing their expertise. We are grateful to Jennifer Simon, our editor at John Wiley & Sons, for supporting our efforts to bring this second edition to fruition. Finally, we extend our appreciation to those who assisted us at various stages of compiling this book: Cindy DeLuca, Eleanor Gill, Carol Londeree, and Erika Qualls.

ROBERT T. AMMERMAN
MICHEL HERSEN

Cincinnati, Ohio
Forest Grove, Oregon

Contents

PART ONE   GENERAL ISSUES

1   Current Issues in the Assessment of Family Violence: An Update   3
    Robert T. Ammerman and Michel Hersen

2   Clinical Issues in the Assessment of Family Violence
    Involving Children   10
    John W. Fantuzzo, Paul McDermott, and Megan Noone Lutz

3   Clinical Issues in the Assessment of Partner Violence   24
    K. Daniel O'Leary and Christopher Murphy

4   Legal and Systems Issues in the Assessment of Family Violence
    Involving Children   48
    Sandra T. Azar and Champika K. Soysa

5   Legal and Systems Issues in the Assessment of Family Violence
    Involving Adults   73
    Roberta K. Thyfault

PART TWO   EPIDEMIOLOGY

6   Epidemiology of Family Violence Involving Children   91
    Jeffrey J. Haugaard

7   Epidemiology of Intimate Partner Violence and Other Family
    Violence Involving Adults   107
    Ronet Bachman

PART THREE   TYPES OF FAMILY VIOLENCE

8   Child Physical Abuse   127
    David J. Hansen, Georganna Sedlar, and Jody E. Warner-Rogers

9   Child Neglect   157
    Ronit M. Gershater-Molko and John R. Lutzker

10   Incest in Young Children   184
    Linda L. Damon and Jessica A. Card

xiii

11 Extrafamilial Child Sexual Abuse 210
    Susan V. McLeer and Mimi Rose

12 Woman Battering 243
    Daniel G. Saunders

13 Elder Abuse and Neglect 271
    Ronald D. Adelman, Mark S. Lachs, and Risa Breckman

14 Psychological Maltreatment of Children 287
    Pamela M. Berlin and Joan I. Vondra

15 Psychological Maltreatment of Women 322
    Richard M. Tolman, Daniel Rosen, and Gillian Cara Wood

PART FOUR   SPECIAL ISSUES

16 Child Witnesses of Domestic Violence 343
    Marlies Sudermann and Peter G. Jaffe

17 Adolescent Perpetrators of Sexual Abuse 367
    William D. Murphy and I. Jacqueline Page

18 Adult Survivors of Sexual Abuse 390
    Steven N. Gold and Laura S. Brown

Author Index 413

Subject Index 431

PART ONE

GENERAL ISSUES

Current Issues in the Assessment of Family Violence: An Update

ROBERT T. AMMERMAN and MICHEL HERSEN

EVEN BY conservative estimates, family violence is endemic in society. Although not a new problem, only in the last 20 years has family violence been subjected to empirical scrutiny. However, determining accurate prevalence and incidence rates of abuse and neglect is extremely difficult, due largely to the fact that domestic mistreatment is a private event, rarely open to public observation. Further impediments to accurate epidemiological research on family violence include failure to arrive at consensus definitions of the different forms of maltreatment (Gelles, 1997; National Research Council, 1993), and methodological limitations of the data gathering strategies that are typically employed (see Ammerman, 1998). Nevertheless, official reporting agencies and population surveys reveal the pervasiveness of family violence. For example, about 970,000 children in the United States were found by child protective agencies to have been abused or neglected in 1996 (U.S. Department of Health and Human Services, 1998). It is likely that the official reporting statistics underestimate the true incidence of child maltreatment. Spouse battering is also widespread, estimated to occur in up to two million households per year (Straus & Gelles, 1986).

More recently, research has focused on previously overlooked victims of domestic violence, such as child and adult targets of psychological abuse, child witnesses of spouse battering, and ritually abused children. Epidemiological data on these forms of mistreatment are only now emerging, although it is widely viewed that psychological or emotional abuse (Brassard, Hart, & Hardy, in press) and child witnessing of interparental violence (Fantuzzo, Boruch, Beriama, Atkins, & Marcus, 1997) are relatively common. Finally, the maltreatment of elderly family members also occurs at alarming rates. Up to one million elderly persons are believed to be mistreated each year (see Goldstein, 1996; Straus & Gelles, 1986).

Equally impressive are data documenting the prevalence of mistreatment in clinic populations. Retrospective studies of psychiatrically hospitalized patients reveal that between 40% and 70% have experienced abuse and/or neglect at some point in their lives (e.g., Ammerman, Hersen, Van Hasselt, Lubetsky, & Sieck, 1994; Monane, Leichter, & Lewis, 1984). High levels of mistreatment have been documented in various types of psychopathology encompassing such diverse psychiatric conditions as conduct disorder, borderline personality disorder, personality disorder, major depression, and substance use disorders (see Malinoski-Rummell & Hansen, 1993). Taken together, these findings highlight the fact that a history of family violence is a concomitant feature of many patients seeking treatment. The likelihood of a clinician encountering past or current mistreatment is overwhelming, and it behooves all mental health professionals to be familiar with the detection, assessment, and treatment of family violence.

Evidence is accruing that establishes a casual link between maltreatment and short- and long-term psychopathology in victims. In children, physically abused and neglected infants typically have insecure attachments with caregivers (see Cicchetti & Toth, 1995). This, in turn, places these children at high risk for further disruptions and lags in social, emotional, and cognitive development. Disturbances during this crucial period in the formation of trusting relationships are viewed as important to adult interpersonal functioning and the intergenerational transmission of abuse (Belsky, 1993). Child victims of sexual abuse also suffer a variety of consequences secondary to molestation. Depression, anxiety, and symptoms of posttraumatic stress disorder (e.g., nightmares, flashbacks, excessive vigilance) are possible sequelae. Survivors of incest and sexual abuse also suffer and often carry these problems into adulthood. Posttraumatic stress syndrome is also found in victims of spouse battering and elder abuse. Low self-esteem, depression, and anxiety are relatively common in these individuals. When combined with the increased risk of physical injury, the consequences of family violence for its victims are varied and often severe.

The etiology of family violence is equally complex. It is universally acknowledged that the abuse and neglect of children and adults are multidetermined, incorporating causal influences from individual, family system, and societal sources (see Ammerman & Galvin, 1998; Belsky, 1993). Their onset is insidious. Moreover, family violence almost never occurs in isolation and is inextricably linked with events, situations, and states (e.g., unemployment, crowding, alcoholism, poverty, poor parenting skills, and psychiatric disorders) that can by themselves lead to deleterious consequences. The assessment of family violence must take into account the multifaceted influences that may play causative roles in, or be effects of, maltreatment. Assessment strategies need to be comprehensive and thorough. Moreover, there is no unique and specific constellation of symptoms for victims or perpetrators of any form of family violence. As such, assessment should be broad in scope. As the chapters in this volume indicate, there are few measures or approaches that are *specifically* designed for assessing family violence.

PRACTICAL CONSIDERATIONS

A number of issues interfere with the assessment process. The first and most difficult step in assessment is identification. There are at least two obstacles in recognizing family violence. Much of the difficulty stems from the fact that mistreatment is a private event. Victims are often reluctant to disclose abuse. Some fear retribution from the perpetrator. This fear is most clearly exemplified in spouse battering, in which abused women's fear for their lives is understandable given the alarming incidence of happened, and how long it has been occurring. Several interviews and questionnaires have been developed to assist the clinician in this endeavor (e.g., Ammerman, Hersen, & Van Hasselt, 1988).

A complete physical examination of the victim is needed to rule out physical injury and to provide medical treatment if needed (Wissow, 1995). Physical documentation of maltreatment may also be used in criminal prosecution or other legal intervention. Medical complications and illness appear to be quite common among victims of elder abuse (Goldstein, 1996) and maltreatment in infancy.

Assessment of psychosocial functioning must be individually tailored to the needs of the victim and family. The length and breadth of the assessment are determined largely by the clinical interview, which should reveal the range of difficulties exhibited by family members. Within this context, it should be recognized that maltreatment is but a symptom of other problems and difficulties of the perpetrator and/or family system.

In children, emotional, social, and cognitive functioning should be examined, with particular attention to lags in development. As the few extant treatments (see Fantuzzo, 1990) for maltreated children primarily emphasize acquisition of skills, assessment should also focus on specific social and communication skills that may subsequently be addressed in treatment. For adults, assessment should involve emotional and social functioning, as well as examination of personality domains that may be important for treatment. Evaluation for posttraumatic stress disorder is important for victims of mistreatment. Likewise, the assessment of perpetrators should emphasize examination of skills deficits, impulse control problems, and (for abusive and neglectful parents) parent deficits.

LEGAL AND SYSTEMS CONSIDERATIONS

Interfacing with the legal system is inevitable in working with family violence cases. All states in the United States and provinces in Canada have laws requiring that professionals report suspected incidents of child maltreatment. Many states also obligate the reporting of mistreatment of the elderly. Frequently, clinicians see individuals and families after they have become involved with a protective service, or after they have had contact with some aspect of the legal system (e.g., the police).

More extensive involvement with the legal system occurs if criminal prosecution is pursued, or if child custody is an issue. Thus, assessment must be conducted with the courts in mind. Testimony may be required, during which clinicians must defend their choice and use of various measures. It is imperative that they be well versed in the empirical literature on these instruments, and on accepted standards of practice and limitations of their use.

An additional area of considerable importance in the assessment of family violence is *duty to warn*. Clinicians are obliged to alert potential victims of threats made toward them by individuals being assessed and/or treated. The precise circumstances under which clinicians must warn others continues to evolve as the duty to warn is evaluated by the courts (see Koocher, 1988).

CONCLUSION

Recent empirical research has more clearly defined the role of assessment in the treatment of family violence. Although still in the early stages of development, guidelines for practice have emerged for diverse forms of family violence, including spouse battering, child abuse and neglect, elder mistreatment, and psychological maltreatment of children and adults. Nevertheless, significant practical and methodological impediments to assessment await further investigative attention. It is evident, however, that a comprehensive approach addressing multiple aspects of individual and family functioning is the *sine qua non* of assessment. While the measures employed will no doubt be further refined, the complexity of family violence ensures that a multidimensional assessment will be required.

REFERENCES

Ammerman, R.T. (1998). Methodological issues in child maltreatment research. In J.R. Lutzker (Ed.), *Handbook of child abuse research and treatment* (pp. 117–132). New York: Plenum Press.

Ammerman, R.T., & Galvin, M.R. (1998). Child maltreatment. In R.T. Ammerman & J.V. Campo (Eds.), *Handbook of pediatric psychology and psychiatric* (pp. 31–69). Needham Heights, MA: Allyn & Bacon.

Ammerman, R.T., Hersen, M., & Van Hasselt, V.B. (1988). *The child abuse and neglect interview schedule (CANIS).* Unpublished instrument, Western Pennsylvania School for Blind Children, Pittsburgh.

Ammerman, R.T., Hersen, M., Van Hasselt, V.B., Lubetsky, M.J., & Sieck, W.R. (1994). Maltreatment in psychiatrically hospitalized children and adolescents with developmental disabilities: Prevalence and correlates. *Journal of the American Academy of Child and Adolescent Psychiatry, 33,* 567–576.

Belsky, J. (1993). Etiology of child maltreatment: A developmental-ecological analysis. *Psychological Bulletin, 114,* 413–434.

Bradley, R.H., & Whiteside-Mansell, L. (1997). Children in poverty. In R.T. Ammerman & M. Hersen (Eds.), *Handbook of prevention and treatment with children and adolescents: Intervention in the real world context* (pp. 13–58). New York: Wiley.

Brassard, M.R., Hart, S.N., & Hardy, D.B. (in press). Psychological and emotional abuse of children. In R.T. Ammerman & M. Hersen (Eds.), *Case studies in family violence* (2nd ed.). New York: Plenum Press.

Cicchetti, D., & Toth, S.L. (1995). A developmental psychopathology perspective on child abuse and neglect. *Journal of the American Academy of Child and Adolescent Psychiatry, 34,* 541–565.

Fantuzzo, J.W. (1990). Behavioral treatment of the victims of child abuse and neglect. *Behavior Modification, 14,* 316–339.

Fantuzzo, J.W., Boruch, R., Beriama, A., Atkins, M., & Marcus, S. (1997). Domestic violence and children: Prevalence and risk in five major US cities. *Journal of the American Academy of Child and Adolescent Psychiatry, 36,* 116–122.

Goldstein, M.Z. (1996). Elder maltreatment. In S.J. Kaplan (Ed.), *Family violence: A clinical and legal guide* (pp. 181–208). Washington, DC: American Psychiatric Press.

Gelles, R.J. (1997). *Intimate violence in families.* Thousand Oaks, CA: Sage.

Koocher, G.P. (1988). A thumbnail guide to "duty to warn" cases. *Clinical Psychologist, 41,* 22–25.

Malinoski-Rummell, R., & Hansen, D.J. (1993). Long-term consequences of childhood physical abuse. *Psychological Bulletin, 114,* 68–79.

Milner, J.S. (1986). *The child abuse potential inventory manual* (2nd ed.). Webster, NC: Psytec.

Monane, M., Leichter, D., & Lewis, D.O. (1984). Physical abuse in psychiatrically hospitalized children and adolescents. *Journal of the American Academy of Child Psychiatry, 23,* 653–658.

National Research Council. (1993). *Understanding child abuse and neglect.* Washington, DC: National Academy Press.

Saunders, D.G., & Browne, A. (in press). Domestic homicide. In R.T. Ammerman & M. Hersen (Eds.), *Case studies in family violence* (2nd ed.). New York: Plenum Press.

Straus, M.A. (1979). Measuring family conflict and violence: The conflict tactics scale. *Journal of Marriage and the Family, 41,* 75–88.

Straus, M.A., & Gelles, R.J. (1986). Societal change and change in family violence from 1975 to 1985 as revealed by two natural surveys. *Journal of Marriage and the Family, 48,* 465–479.

U.S. Department of Health and Human Services. (1998). *Child maltreatment 1996: Reports from the states to the National Child Abuse and Neglect Data System.* Washington, DC: U.S. Government Printing Office.

Wissow, L.S. (1995). Child abuse and neglect. *New England Journal of Medicine, 332,* 1425–1431.

Wolfe, D.A., & McEachran, A. (1997). Child physical abuse and neglect. In E.J. Mash & L.G. Terdal (Eds.), *Assessment of childhood disorders* (pp. 523–568). New York: Guilford Press.

CHAPTER 2

Clinical Issues in the Assessment of Family Violence Involving Children

JOHN FANTUZZO, PAUL MCDERMOTT, and MEGAN NOONE LUTZ

FAMILY VIOLENCE seriously threatens the stability of families and the health and psychological development of children (National Research Council, 1993, 1998). Current research on the effects of family violence on children makes a distinction between children who are directly victimized by abusive acts and children who are affected indirectly by exposure to maternal abuse. Over the past three decades there has been an intense focus on direct victims of maltreatment. This intensity has resulted in laws, statewide definitions, mandatory reporting, local procedures to investigate reports of maltreatment, and empirical research. The extent of what we know about the indirect victims of family violence is much less than what we know about children who are direct victims. Only in the past decade have researchers addressed the plight of children who witness their mothers being physically abused by a partner. For this category of child victims, our inquiry is less advanced. We currently have no systematic ways of substantiating accounts of child exposure, no national prevalence data, and no conclusive body of controlled studies on the effects of exposure (Fantuzzo, Boruch, Beriama, Atkins, & Marcus, 1997).

Our need for high-quality assessment information that can inform the development of effective intervention strategies for direct and indirect child victims is acute. There is a tremendous amount of pressure on mental health professionals to understand the impact of these traumatic events more precisely and to translate this understanding into effective responses for child victims and their families. This urgency underscores the importance of examining ways to enhance our assessment capacity in this area. The purpose of this chapter is to consider how attention to guiding principles and standards in the assessment literature can improve the accuracy and usefulness of assessment for child victims of family violence. Two critical questions provide the

Work on this chapter was supported in part by a grant received by the first author from the U.S. Department of Health and Human Services' Head Start Bureau.

framework for understanding the significance of these principles and standards: (a) What do we need to measure? and (b) How well do we measure?

WHAT DO WE NEED TO MEASURE?

The magnitude and complexity of this problem necessitate theories of "risk" and "change" to guide our search for information to understand the impact of family violence on children. The merit of these theoretical systems is a function of how comprehensively they address the phenomena of the traumatic effects of family violence. Reviews of the family violence literature conducted by the National Research Council (1993, 1998) have identified developmental-ecological theory as the best suited conceptual framework to address the causes, consequences, and treatment formulations for child victims of family violence.

The developmental-ecological perspective emphasizes the importance of human development in the context in which the development occurs, and seeks to understand human development in terms of changes in multifaceted functions over time. Development is multifaceted in that it is understood by looking at the central tasks that children are expected to perform involving their physiological, cognitive, emotional, and social capacities (Cicchetti & Lynch, 1993). The focus of this approach is studying what constitutes competent, normal performance in these areas of functioning and understanding how this development occurs along various courses or pathways across time.

Understanding the role that context plays in development is an essential feature of this model. In this approach, context is the larger sphere in which development takes place. Interaction with context affects how and when persons manifest psychological competencies. Context includes spheres of influence (e.g., family, peers, school, and community) that create the expectations for performance, and hence, impact that person throughout development (Belsky, 1993). Various influences can alter the course of development creating different pathways for children attempting to adapt within their context. These systems or spheres of influence can enhance or impede development in many ways. It is the child's transactions with multiple contexts over time that influence which pathways, and subsequently which outcomes, the child experiences (Jensen & Hoagwood, 1997).

According to this perspective, it is meaningless to interpret a child's behavior apart from its context, since the behavior is a manifestation of a child's ability to adapt to contextual demands or expectations. An increased exposure to family violence and other risk factors makes the successful resolution of developmental issues more problematic for children, resulting in an increased likelihood of negative developmental outcomes and psychopathology (Cicchetti & Toth, 1995). Conversely, such an ecological model of violence and its effects also helps to account for resilient outcomes in some children. The presence of protective factors at any level of the ecology may help to explain why some children display successful adaptation in the face of high levels of violence within their families (Cicchetti & Lynch, 1993). Therefore, understanding problem behaviors related to family violence requires a thorough understanding of how multiple contextual influences and multiple areas of functioning combine to shape developmental outcomes (Cicchetti & Lynch, 1993).

Multivariate risk, multidimensionality, and nomothesis are three assessment principles that emanate from a developmental ecological perspective. These principles guide the nature and scope of assessment of child victims of family violence.

MULTIVARIATE RISK

Developmental research on the impact of social and family risk factors on children's psychological adjustment has documented the harmful effects of exposure to multiple simultaneous risk factors (Pellegrini, 1990). Longitudinal studies conducted in England (Rutter, 1979) and the United States (Luster & McAdoo, 1994; Sameroff, Seifer, Baldwin, & Baldwin, 1993) have found that the number of contextual risk factors that a child is exposed to is a more salient predictor of negative developmental outcomes than the particular type of risk factors. Moreover, they found that the combination of risk factors had a greater effect than the sum of effects of each risk factor (Weiss, 1997).

Professionals concerned with the well-being of children involved in family violence can no longer be satisfied with an understanding of "family violence" as a univariate risk factor. It is well recognized that children are exposed to many types of family violence (e.g., physical abuse, sexual abuse, neglect, emotional abuse, witnessing of interparental violence), as well as multiple variations within and overlap among these categories (National Research Council, 1998). Moreover, research indicates that each form of family violence occurs more frequently in the context of other risk factors that threaten children's healthy development (National Research Council, 1998). Therefore, in many cases, children must not only overcome direct attacks on their own or their caretaker's well-being, but they must do this in the face of other potential pathogens.

According to the Third National Incidence Study of Child Abuse and Neglect (NIS-3; Sedlak & Broadhurst, 1996), both the incidence and severity of child maltreatment are highest in large families, families living in poverty, and single-parent families. These are family contexts with multiple stressors associated with poverty, parental social isolation, and insufficient social support (National Research Council, 1993, 1998). This pattern is similar for children exposed to domestic violence. A recent investigation explored the prevalence of children's exposure to substantiated cases of maternal assault in five U.S. cities (Fantuzzo, Boruch, et al., 1997). Results of this study identify the most at-risk children to be those living in low-income, female-headed households, and whose primary caregivers did not complete high school. Furthermore, this study identified the youngest children as the highest risk group, as these children were most likely to be exposed to multiple incidents of violence, and the incidents were most likely to involve substance abuse. Therefore, family violence assessment must move beyond simple categorical indications of exposure to violence and determine the child's exposure to additional risk and protective factors across the multiple levels of the child victim's context. These data are necessary to obtain a more precise understanding of how these factors contribute to various negative and resilient outcomes. This comprehensive multivariate assessment of operative contextual influences is essential to the formulation of effective treatment plans.

MULTIDIMENSIONALITY

Consistent with the multifaceted and dynamic conceptualization of child functioning set forth in developmental-ecological theory, multidimensional assessment has been advanced as a viable alternative to traditional, unidimensional approaches. The concept emerges from the observation that all children share certain comparable aspects, or dimensions, of functioning important to psychological and educational development. The broadest and principal dimensions include intellectual functioning (ability), academic functioning (achievement), physical/developmental adaptation (adaptive behavior), and social-emotional functioning (adjustment). As Cromwell, Blashfield, and Strauss (1975) have argued and McDermott and Watkins (1987) demonstrated, more useful dimensions permit both qualitative and quantitative distinctions among levels of functioning. Thus, for example, a more informative measure of social-emotional maladjustment tells us what qualitative aspect of behavioral abnormality is evident ("avoidant" or "oppositional" or "diffident") and the quantitative severity of the pathology (mild, extreme).

Perhaps the most salient feature of multidimensionality is its tendency to provide more comprehensive and generalizable assessments. The literature is replete with evidence pointing to the vicissitudes of alternative unidimensional approaches. Prominent examples are the exclusive dependence on global IQ in diagnosing mental deficiency (Grossman, 1983), inattention to academically relevant skills in classifying learning disabilities (Klatt, 1991), and the extensive categorical system used to diagnose children's mental disorders, the *Diagnostic and Statistical Manual of Mental Disorders,* fourth edition (*DSM-IV;* American Psychiatric Association, 1994).

For example, the *DSM* provides lists of mental disorders that fail to take into account the unique dimensions of human capacity to adapt, regenerate, differentiate, or reorganize. The decontextualized *DSM* categories are unidimensional, isolated conglomerates of behaviors that fail to consider human beings as open systems contiguous with their environment (Jensen & Hoagwood, 1997). Furthermore, despite its putative attempts to give the categories more dimensionality by its multiaxial system of diagnostics, the axial approach fails to provide a detailed taxonomy of the child's competencies. Its contextual and cross-sectional nature renders it unable to account for the human capacity to exhibit similar patterns of functioning resulting from qualitatively different structures (equifinality) and for different patterns of overt functioning that stem from similar processes (multifinality). Neglecting these capacities means that any attempt at explanation assumes that people react in similar ways for similar reasons.

In contrast, multidimensional models offer comprehensive evaluations of child functioning across time. Cicchetti and his colleagues have advanced a multidimensional framework to conceptualize developmental consequences of family violence (Cicchetti & Toth, 1995). This framework provides an organizational perspective on development that focuses on the quality of integration within and among the biological, social, emotional, cognitive, representational, and linguistic systems of human functioning. Numerous investigations have used this framework to assess how family violence uniquely affects the emergence of both competencies and maladaptions throughout childhood.

NOMOTHESIS

Behavioral science and clinical tradition have long appreciated both ideographic and nomothetic approaches to child assessment (e.g., Meehl, Tiedeman, & McArthur, 1956). Ideography focuses on a particular child's developmental and social history, and on those personal and situational factors that help make each child unique. Attention is given to typical and representative features of the child's health, family life, neighborhood, aptitudes, fears, and aspirations, in hopes of answering questions about individual pathogeneses, common manifestations of coping and maladaptation, and probable prognosis.

Modern clinical psychology and psychiatry offer a rich ideographic tradition, as illustrated by the volumes of case studies on child trauma and victimization. In each case study, a specialist strives to comprehend pathology by building a dynamic causal model linking pathogens and sequelae in the life of a given child. It is, as Meehl (1956) depicted, the art of forming little special theories that help to explain the experiences of one child.

Nevertheless, ideographic inquiry, however intuitively appealing or ostensibly sensitive to children's experiences, has a serious inherent disadvantage. Without a much broader understanding of experiences and consequences across *many* children, we have no way to judge their relative significance in the life of any one child. The search for broader understanding is called *nomothesis*.

Nomothesis defines the systematic study of relevant factors across the lives of many children. Inquiry is not limited to youth at risk or to those suffering some disturbance. Rather, it is deemed important to study pertinent experiences and consequences across representative samples of the entire child population. Thus, nomothesis, as the prefix *nomo* implies, means discovery of what is normal or natural variation. By knowing what is commonplace, or normal, within the child population, we are able to recognize and appreciate more fully what is truly rare, or abnormal. Indeed, nomothesis enables one to learn not only whether pathology exists, but also how comparatively common and severe its sequelae are.

A timely illustration of the principle comes with the advent of nomothesis in child psychopathology. We have long been advantaged by the availability of norm-reference tests for assessing childhood cognitive functioning and academic performance (Sattler, 1988) and more recently for competency in basic self-care, motility, and communication (Lambert, 1981; Sparrow, Balla, & Cicchetti, 1984). Nomothesis is brought to the assessment process by grounding each type of technology through stratified national samples of appropriately representative child populations. Thus, we are afforded the necessary information for normative studies of respective functioning both across and within children.

Appreciation of nomothesis in the assessment of child psychopathology is relatively recent. This appreciation is best illustrated by the Adjustment Scales for Children and Adolescents (ASCA; McDermott, 1993, 1994), which is a nationally standardized, teacher report measure of the emotional and behavioral adjustment of children and youth aged 5 through 17 years. The stratified random standardization sample for the ASCA ($N = 1,400$) was blocked on age, gender, race/ethnicity, parent education, national region, community size, and handicapping condition according to the 1988–1989 U.S. Census (U.S. Bureau of the Census, 1988). Subsequent research found the ASCA to be generalizable across demographics (McDermott, 1994), as well as across developmental level, sex, ethnicity, and age (McDermott & Schaefer, 1996). Moreover, in addition to normative information for each of its six core syndromes, the ASCA offers information about normative typologies of behavior, or profiles across the syndromes (McDermott & Weiss, 1995). This allows for an understanding of the variations of *adjustment* (not just maladjustment), and how a child's profile of adjustment compares with typical patterns.

The nomothetic principle is not only relevant to understanding the impact of violence on children's development, but also to an understanding of the scope of the problem. Both child maltreatment and exposure to interparental violence must be understood in terms of a population base. Sensitivity to the broad population of child victims is in contrast to a narrow focus on "who shows up" in clinics, shelters, or hospitals. Such groups of children and families, while in need of attention and services, cannot be assumed to be representative of the universe of victims. Neglecting children and families who fall outside the pipeline of service delivery has implications not only for those specific children (i.e., they do not receive needed attention), but also for the broader knowledge base about the needs of children living with family violence. Information learned from clinical, nonrepresentative samples cannot be automatically generalized to all victims. The assessment of children's psychological adjustment in unique settings, such as shelters, may be associated with factors particular to the setting. For example, uprooting children from their home, separating them from their father, or having them experience their mother under conditions of great stress may contribute significantly to assessment results (Spaccarelli, Sandler, & Roosa, 1994). Fantuzzo et al. (1991) found that children who were living with their mothers in temporary domestic violence shelters evidenced significantly higher levels of psychological distress and different types of distress than carefully matched children who witnessed the same level and type of violence but were living at home.

Attention to pipeline problems and attempts to reach representative samples of children are more advanced for child maltreatment than for exposure to domestic violence. Mandated reporting of child maltreatment to child protective services (CPS) across the country has established the capacity to document and track large numbers of children who have been abused or neglected. Although CPS agencies constitute the largest, most representative source of investigated and substantiated cases of abuse or neglect, not all maltreated children come to the attention of CPS agencies. To address this problem, the NIS-3 established a network of sentinel agencies such as schools and hospitals to detect children outside the CPS pipeline. In this way, a more accurate and representative sample was obtained to estimate the scope of the problem.

In contrast to child maltreatment, the knowledge base about children exposed to interparental violence is largely restricted to what we know about children in domestic violence shelters, both in terms of the extent of their exposure and the impact of exposure on development. Although these children are certainly in need of services, shelter samples are only the "tip of the iceberg," and it is unknown how representative they are of the entire population of battered women and their children (Fantuzzo et al., 1991; Spaccarelli et al., 1994). Using the field of child maltreatment as a model in strategizing ways to reach more children, the parallel agency to child protective services must be identified. The community agency authorized to investigate and to intervene when women are assaulted in their homes is the police department. Therefore, through partnerships with police departments, professionals concerned with children exposed to family violence are more likely to reach the largest, most representative groups of children possible. This will not only improve our understanding of the nature of exposure, the impact of exposure on children's development, and the prevalence of the problem, but it will also enable us to provide services to the previously "invisible" victims of domestic violence.

HOW WELL DO WE MEASURE?

The ethical obligation of researchers and practitioners to attend to issues of quality in assessment is not a recent development. Minimum requirements for high-quality assessment are set forth in the *Standards for Educational and Psychological Testing*

(American Psychological Association, 1985). This document, better than any other document, explicitly defines the criteria by which development and use of assessment instruments and techniques must be evaluated. Standards with particular importance to family violence involving children relate to construct validity (Standard 1.8), cultural validity and contextual relevance (Standard 3.5), and consequential validity (Standard 9.1). The following sections identify important issues regarding the application of these standards to assessment of the diverse groups of child victims of family violence.

CONSTRUCT VALIDITY

Construct validity is primarily concerned with a "test score as a measure of the psychological characteristic of interest" (American Psychiatric Association, 1994). It is critical to appreciate the importance of theory in the establishment of construct validity (American Psychiatric Association, 1994; Clark & Watson, 1995; Silva, 1991). Measures do not define, nor are they equivalent to constructs (Messick, 1995). Rather, measures are imperfect indicators of theoretically derived characteristics. Therefore, construct validity is unattainable unless there is a sound theoretical framework guiding the definition of the target construct. This fundamental issue is of ultimate importance since construct validity is at the core of all other types of evidence for validity (Clark & Watson, 1995; Messick, 1995).

Given the value of the developmental ecological perspective to guide inquiry about family violence involving children, this model must be used to guide the development and use of assessment instruments. One of the basic tenets of the developmental perspective is that specific constructs are expressed differently according to the developmental stage of the child (Cicchetti & Lynch, 1993). Therefore, it is necessary but not sufficient to identify important constructs to assess. It is also essential to employ measurement instruments that reflect these age-appropriate manifestations of the given construct. For example, a researcher interested in exploring the impact of child maltreatment on the social competence of preschool children must first understand that peer interaction in play is a primary stage-salient issue. Therefore, only when an assessment instrument is sensitive to a child's peer play interactions, will it adhere to the developmental model and therefore adequately reflect the construct of social competence in preschool children.

Although it is essential to use the developmental ecological perspective to guide selection of constructs to assess, the malleability of selected constructs is also an important consideration. Our theoretical framework helps us to understand child development in the context of complex environmental influences, but it does not provide clear direction regarding intervention. There is little comfort in knowing that to improve a victimized child's present or future condition, we must change the immediately unchangeable. How, then, can we hope to make a difference in outcomes for children? We cannot pretend an easy answer; one does not exist. But we do believe the wisest course is to concentrate on discovery of childhood characteristics that are most potentially malleable (changeable) and, within that domain, to concentrate primarily on characteristics that are prosocial, resilient, or adaptive—ones that would be regarded as competencies rather than pathologies. Most elements of a child's intellectual ability are relatively resistant to change (Brody, 1985; Glutting & McDermott, 1990). In contrast, constructs such as social skills, communication, and learning styles are promising targets of intervention since they lend themselves more easily to enhancement (Fantuzzo, Coolahan, & Weiss, 1997; Stott, McDermott, Green, & Francis, 1988; Strain, Guralnick, & Walker, 1986). Focusing assessments on malleable constructs establishes the potential for intervention.

CULTURAL VALIDITY

A concern that has been raised in the assessment literature is a widespread lack of understanding that validity is not a property of an assessment instrument itself. It is the specific applications or interpretations of the instrument that require validation (Clark & Watson, 1995; Messick, 1995; Silva, 1991). This important distinction was made over 30 years ago (Cronbach & Meehl, 1955), and is clearly discussed in the *Standards for Educational and Psychological Testing* (Standard 1.2) (American Psychiatric Association, 1994), but professionals continue to discuss the validity of measures without regard for the specific uses of the measures (Clark & Watson, 1995). In the area of family violence involving children, this principle has particular relevance to issues of cultural sensitivity. Validity is not absolute. It is conditional, contingent on the use or function of the assessment instrument, which changes when the instrument is used with different populations (Haynes, Richard, & Kubany, 1995).

An investigation of the construct validity of a popular measure for use with urban Head Start children illustrates the importance of this issue (Fantuzzo, McDermott, Manz, Hampton, & Burdick, 1996). In this study, the Pictorial Scale of Perceived Competence and Social Acceptance for Young Children was administered to 476 African American children in a large, urban, Head Start program. Exploratory factor analyses of these data failed to produce psychologically meaningful constructs. These results demonstrate that assumptions of validity of a measure for use with diverse populations are misguided. Furthermore, when these assumptions go unquestioned, a false sense of security in the knowledge base is perpetuated.

The impact of culture on validity occurs on different levels, and affects all types of evidence for validity. Factors that threaten valid assessment with culturally diverse populations include language barriers, different cultural meanings of a particular construct, and varied interpretations of an observed behavior based on cultural norms (Coll et al., 1996; Foster & Martinez, 1995; Okazaki & Sue, 1995). Furthermore, relevant content to be included in an assessment instrument varies from culture to culture, which greatly impacts content validity (Foster & Martinez, 1995). These issues are especially salient when assessments of children involve reports from adults, which is often the case when working with children exposed to family violence. The cultural similarity or dissimilarity of the informant to the child can profoundly influence reporters' perceptions of relevant behaviors. Winetsky (1978) found that parents' expectations for their children's behavior varied as a function of both social class and ethnicity. Such expectations influence perceptions and interpretations of children's behaviors. Similarly, families living in neighborhoods characterized by high levels of violence are more likely to encourage children to physically defend themselves (Gilkerson & Stott, 1997), which impacts interpretation of aggressive behavior.

Several strategies for enhancing cultural sensitivity in assessment have been recommended in the literature. First, in developing an assessment battery, measures with adequate representation of the target population in the standardization sample should be selected (American Psychiatric Association, 1985). However, such measures are not always available for all constructs and all cultures. In this case, selecting multiple measures and multiple methods for a single construct can increase the likelihood of accurately tapping that construct (Okazaki & Sue, 1995). Moreover, using measures that operationalize broad constructs by describing specific behaviors can minimize the potential for diverse interpretations of behavior (Foster & Martinez, 1995). Finally, when using measures with linguistically diverse populations, the process of back-translation has been recommended to enhance equivalence of the measures (Foster & Martinez, 1995). This technique first involves translating the measure from one language to another. Subsequently, an independent translator translates the new version back into the original language. This process is repeated until acceptable similarity of versions is achieved (Foster & Martinez, 1995).

Although the preceding strategies can help to achieve culturally sensitive assessment practices, they are not sufficient. Empirical evidence supporting the use of a particular measure with a given cultural group is essential. Such evidence can be gathered by testing the measure with the target population, and conducting exploratory factor analyses. Factor-matching strategies should then be applied to ensure that latent structures converge with published or expected results (see Gorsuch, 1983, for a discussion of such strategies).

If equivalence of measures is not established, it is necessary to develop new measures that are appropriate for that culture. To do this, coconstruction of measures with members of the target culture can ensure that all relevant content is included, irrelevant content is not, and mutual understanding of the construct has been achieved (Foster & Martinez, 1995). "Expert" review of assessment content (which includes items, response format, and instructions) is the traditional and standard method for establishing content validity (Haynes et al., 1995). However, the definition of "expert" is open to interpretation. When developing measures for use with a particular cultural group, the expert panel should include members of that culture, as well as individuals who represent the intended reporter (e.g., parents and teachers). Coconstructing measures with indigenous members of the children's natural environment maximizes cultural sensitivity (Fantuzzo, Mendez, & Tighe, in press).

CONTEXTUALLY RELEVANT ASSESSMENT

As discussed earlier, the developmental-ecological perspective underscores the importance of context in influencing a child's development. Contextual risk factors are salient to the development of children living in violent homes, or who are victims of violence themselves. Therefore, to understand a child's functioning, it is essential to use assessment strategies that take into account these spheres of contextual influence (Cicchetti & Lynch, 1993). Furthermore, the context in which a child is developing largely determines whether that child's functioning is adaptive or maladaptive. The same behavior in one context may be seen as pathological, whereas it is quite adaptive given another contextual reality. An understanding of contextual issues is necessary to obtain a true assessment of a salient constructs. This principle is linked closely with cultural validity since culture largely defines the contexts in which a child develops.

An important component to enhancing contextual relevance in assessment is the capacity for cross-informant reports. Multiple informants close to the child (e.g., parents and teachers) should be enlisted to provide information about a child's functioning across multiple natural settings (e.g., home and school). In this way, different perspectives of the child's behavior in different contextual spheres can be compared and integrated into a complete assessment. Obtaining reports of child functioning from multiple informants is particularly important when working with children living with family violence (Sternberg, Lamb, & Dawud-Noursi, 1998). Similarly, assessing behavior across situations within a relevant, natural context can enhance contextual validity. For example, a child's behavior at school may be different with peers than in structured classroom activities. Assessment tools that are sensitive to these different situations provide rich information about a child's strengths and needs.

However, an instrument's capacity for cross-informant reports of child constructs must be considered carefully and established empirically. The mere fact that a measure of child functioning offers both parent and teacher forms does not guarantee that the same constructs are tapped by each form. For example, an examination of the relationship between the parent and teacher versions of the Social Skills Rating System did not support the authors' claims that these versions are parallel forms with matching social competence constructs (Manz, Fantuzzo, & McDermott, 1998). Multivariate analyses did not yield any significant relationships between hypothesized like parent and teacher factors. Moreover, higher order analyses of the factors from both versions of the SSRS yielded a one-factor solution composed of just teacher factor loadings. None of the parent SSRS factors contributed to this single overall social competence factor. The lack of correspondence between parent and teacher constructs of the SSRS impedes its use as a cross-informant indicator of important social competency constructs.

In contrast, parent and teacher versions have been developed and empirically compared for the Penn Interactive Peer Play Scale (PIPPS). Exploratory analyses of each of these versions yielded three factors: Play Interaction, Play Disruption, and Play Disconnection. Multivariate analyses support the congruence of the two versions, indicating that both parents and teachers are reporting on the same constructs (Fantuzzo et al., in press). Sound cross-informant rating systems should empirically demonstrate that hypothesized teacher and parent constructs match, thereby providing the capacity to report common information about these constructs across multiple, natural contexts.

CONSEQUENTIAL VALIDITY

The concept of consequential validity is at the core of high-quality assessment. The motivation behind improving our assessment technology for use with young, vulnerable victims of family violence is so that we, as professionals, know how to respond. Assessment solely for the sake of knowledge is static; vitality lies in knowledge with a meaningful purpose. Unless an assessment practice leads to demonstrated positive social consequences, other types of validity are meaningless (Messick, 1995). However, close attention to sensitive and responsive assessment issues discussed earlier can help ensure the success of an instrument in informing responsible action.

Measures that provide information about age-appropriate manifestations of a given construct provide more precise information about a child's competencies and targeted needs for intervention. When these measures are coconstructed with individuals familiar with the cultural and contextual realities of the child, information obtained is more likely to be relevant and useful to important people in the child's life. Similarly, when multiple reporters close to the child are also involved in or are agents of intervention, there is a seamless flow from assessment to intervention. Finally, instruments that provide extensive information about a child's functioning across situations enable professionals to target more precisely the situational influences on the problem.

The link between developmentally sensitive, contextually relevant assessment and effective intervention has been demonstrated in Head Start with maltreated children (Fantuzzo & Mohr, in press). Using measures coconstructed with Head Start parents and teachers, information was gathered about children's peer play interactions in their natural settings. Because the data collected were both valid for the Head Start population of children, and relevant to the context of the Head Start classroom, they were able to inform a very successful intervention for socially withdrawn maltreated children. The effectiveness of the intervention was largely attributable to its context of intervention: treatment took place in the child's natural classroom ecology, and treatment agents were natural helpers from the child's immediate experience (parents and peers). This context of intervention grew directly from the context of assessment. Information collected was relevant to parents and teachers, and therefore proved to be useful in pairing socially competent children with withdrawn, maltreated children. This pairing resulted in increased interactive peer play for the withdrawn children. The success of this intervention illustrates how sensitive and responsive assessment logically leads to sensitive and responsive action.

CONCLUSION

The purpose of this chapter was to indicate how principles derived from a developmental ecological model and sound psychometric research could improve assessment methods for child victims of family violence. Using these principles to produce sensitive and responsive assessment will require practitioners to widen the scope of their assessment to attend to a multitude of developmental and ecological factors with greater precision for more diverse populations. Principles of multivariate risk and multidimensionality necessitate including multiple child and contextual variables at multiple points in time. Nomothesis requires a population level understanding of the impact of violence and associated pathogens on child development. Attempts to view the impact of family violence through the broadest possible lens will ensure a more authentic account of the nature and extent of this social problem.

To effect these three assessment principles family violence professionals must promote greater interagency coordination and strategic use of integrated information systems to inform policy and practices. In the public health and epidemiology literatures, there are excellent examples of how researchers and practitioners have created comprehensive, longitudinal record histories of children by linking computerized records across multiple agencies (Boussy, 1992, Lilienfeld & Stolley, 1994). For example, a study conducted by Weiss and Fantuzzo (1997) successfully linked records from Departments of Public Health and Human Services, and the school district for a large urban center to study the impact of child maltreatment and other known environmental risk factors on the school adjustment of an entire cohort of first-grade students (over 15,000 students). Data linkage technology should be cultivated by the family violence research community. These data-sharing efforts are viable means of providing longitudinal data on multiple child health and caregiving variables at a population level.

Achieving acceptable levels of psychometric precision in assessments of child victims of family violence has posed a considerable challenge to concerned professionals. Contextually relevant measures that are sensitive to age-salient manifestations of important, malleable constructs are rare. Furthermore, low-income children from highly stressed families are least likely to be represented in the development, standardization, and norms of available instruments. These are the children who are at disproportionate risk for victimization. There is an urgent press to assess the needs of our most vulnerable child victims. However, reliance on inappropriate measurement to respond to this need is a misguided use of available resources. These children deserve high-quality assessments that can lead to effective service delivery. The most sensitive response to child victims of family violence requires that the research community focus attention on developing an appropriate and useful measurement technology for these vulnerable victims.

In this chapter, we have outlined a set of principles to enhance our ability to understand more precisely the effects of family violence on children and to ensure that our knowing will have beneficial results. Establishing and maintaining partnerships among practitioners, community agencies, and researchers offers the best hope of advancing this assessment agenda.

REFERENCES

American Psychiatric Association. (1994). *Diagnostic and statistical manual of mental disorders* (4th ed.). Washington, DC: Author.

American Psychological Association. (1985). *Standards for educational and psychological testing.* Washington, DC: Author.

Belsky, J. (1993). Etiology of child maltreatment: A developmental-ecological analysis. *Psychological Bulletin, 114,* 413–434.

Boussy, C.A. (1992). *Record linkage methodology: The key to epidemiological surveillance.* Florida Department of Health and Rehabilitative Services, Interagency Office of Disability Prevention.

Brody, N. (1985). The validity of tests of intelligence. In B.B. Wolman (Ed.), *Handbook of intelligence: Theories, measurements, and applications* (pp. 353–389). New York: Wiley.

Cicchetti, D., & Lynch, M. (1993). Toward an ecological/transactional model of community violence and child maltreatment: Consequences for children's development. Children and violence [Special issue]. *Psychiatry: Interpersonal and Biological Processes, 56,* 96–118.

Cicchetti, D., & Toth, S. (1995). A developmental psychopathology perspective on child abuse and neglect. *Journal of the American Academy of Child and Adolescent Psychiatry, 34,* 541–565.

Coll, C., Lamberty, G., Jenkins, R., McAdoo, H., Crnic, K., Wasik, B., & Vazquez, G.H. (1996). An integrative model for the study of developmental competencies in minority children. *Child Development, 67,* 1891–1914.

Clark, L.A., & Watson, D. (1995). Constructing validity: Basic issues in objective scale development. *Psychological Assessment, 7,* 309–319.

Cromwell, R.L., Blashfield, R.K., & Strauss, J.S. (1975). Criteria for classification systems. In N. Hobbs (Ed.), *Issues in the classification of children* (Vol. 1, pp. 4–25). San Francisco: Jossey-Bass.

Cronbach, L.J., & Meehl, P.E. (1955). Construct validity in psychological tests. *Psychological Bulletin, 52,* 281–302.

Fantuzzo, J., Boruch, R., Beriama, A., Atkins, M., & Marcus, S. (1997). Domestic violence and children: Prevalence and risk in five major US cities. *Journal of the American Academy of Child and Adolescent Psychiatry, 36,* 116–122.

Fantuzzo, J., Coolahan, K., & Weiss, A. (1997). Resiliency partnership-directed intervention: Enhancing the social competencies of preschool victims of physical abuse by developing peer resources and community strengths. In D. Cicchetti & S.L. Toth (Eds.), *Rochester*

Symposium on Developmental Psychopathology: Vols. 8 & 9. The effects of trauma on the developmental process (pp. 463–490). Rochester, NY: University of Rochester Press.

Fantuzzo, J., DePaola, L., Lambert, L., Martino, T., Anderson, G., & Sutton, S. (1991). Effects of interparental violence on the psychological adjustment and competencies of young children. *Journal of Consulting and Clinical Psychology, 59,* 1–8.

Fantuzzo, J., McDermott, P., Manz, P., Hampton, G., & Burdick, N. (1996). The pictorial scale of perceived competence for young children: Does it work with low-income urban children? *Child Development, 67,* 1071–1084.

Fantuzzo, J., Mendez, J., & Tighe, E. (in press). Parental assessment of peer play: Development and validation of the parent version of the Penn interactive peer play scale. *Early Childhood Research Quarterly.*

Fantuzzo, J., & Mohr, W. (in press). Pursuit of wellness in Head Start: Making beneficial connections for children and families. In D. Cicchetti, J. Rapapport, I. Sandler, & R. Weissberg (Eds.), *The promotion of wellness in children and adolescents.* New York: Sage.

Foster, S.L., & Martinez, C.R., Jr. (1995). Ethnicity: Conceptual and methodological issues in child clinical research. *Journal of Clinical Child Psychology, 24,* 214–226.

Gilkerson, L., & Stott, F. (1997). Listening to the voices of families: Learning through caregiving consensus groups. *Zero to Three,* 9–16.

Glutting, J.J., & McDermott, P.A. (1990). Principles and problems in learning potential. In C.R. Reynolds & R.W. Kamphaus (Eds.), *Handbook of psychological and educational assessment of children* (pp. 296–347). New York: Guilford Press.

Gorsuch, R.L. (1983). *Factor analysis.* Hillsdale, NJ: Erlbaum.

Grossman, H.J. (Ed.). (1983). *Classification in mental deficiency.* Washington, DC: American Association on Mental Deficiency.

Haynes, S.N., Richard, D.C.S., & Kubany, E.S. (1995). Content validity in psychological assessment: A functional approach to concepts and methods. *Psychological Assessment, 7,* 238–247.

Jensen, P.S., & Hoagwood, K. (1997). The book of names: *DSM-IV* in context. *Development and Psychopathology, 9,* 231–249.

Klatt, H.J. (1991). Learning disabilities: A questionable construct. *Educational Theory, 41,* 47–60.

Lambert, N.M. (1981). *AAMD adaptive behavior scale.* Monterey, CA: Publishers Test Service.

Luster, T., & McAdoo, H.P. (1994). Factors related to the achievement and adjustment of young African American children. *Child Development, 65,* 1080–1094.

Manz, P., Fantuzzo, J., & McDermott, P. (1998). The parent version of the preschool social skills rating scale: An analysis of it use with low-income, ethnic-minority children. *School Psychology Review, 36,* 199–214.

McDermott, P.A. (1993). National standardization of uniform multisituational measures of child and adolescent behavior pathology. *Psychological Assessment, 5,* 413–424.

McDermott, P.A. (1994). *National profiles in youth psychopathology: Manual of adjustment scales for children and adolescents.* Philadelphia: Edumetric and Clinical Science.

McDermott, P.A., & Schaefer, B.A. (1996). A demographic survey of rare and common problem behaviors among American students. *Journal of Clinical Child Psychology, 25,* 352–362.

McDermott, P.A., & Watkins, M.W. (1987). *McDermott multidimensional assessment of children: IBM version.* San Antonio: Psychological Corporation.

McDermott, P.A., & Weiss, R.V. (1995). A normative typology of healthy, subclinical, and clinical behavior styles among American children and adolescents. *Psychological Assessment, 7,* 162–170.

Meehl, P.E., Tiedeman, D.V., & McArthur, C. (1956). Symposium on clinical and statistical prediction. *Journal of Counseling Psychology, 3,* 163–173.

Messick, S. (1995). Validity of psychological assessment: Validation of inferences from persons' responses and performances as scientific inquiry into score meaning. *American Psychologist, 50,* 741–749.

National Research Council. (1993). *Understanding child abuse and neglect.* Washington, DC: National Academy Press.

National Research Council. (1998). *Violence in families.* Washington, DC: National Academy Press.

Okazaki, S., & Sue, S. (1995). Methodological issues in assessment research with ethnic minorities. *Psychological Assessment, 7,* 367–375.

Rutter, M. (1979). Protective factors in children's responses to stress and disadvantage. In M. Whalen Kent & J.E. Rolf (Eds.), *Primary prevention of psychopathology: Social competence in children* (Vol. 3, pp. 49–74). Hanover, NH: University Press of New England.

Sameroff, A.J., Seifer, R., Baldwin, A., & Baldwin, C. (1993). Stability of intelligence from preschool to adolescence: The influence of social and family risk factors. *Child Development, 64,* 80–97.

Sattler, J.M. (1988). *Assessment of children* (3rd ed.). San Diego: Author.

Sedlak, A.J., & Broadhurst, D.D. (1996). *Third national incidence study of child abuse and neglect: Final report.* Washington, DC: U.S. Department of Health and Human Services.

Silva, F. (1991). *Psychometric foundations and behavioral assessment.* Newbury Park, CA: Sage.

Spaccarelli, S., Sandler, I.N., & Roosa, M. (1994). History of spouse violence against mother: Correlated risks and unique effects in child mental health. *Journal of Family Violence, 9* 79–98.

Sparrow, S.S., Balla, D.A., & Cicchetti, D.V. (1984). *Vineland social maturity scale.* Circle Pines, MN: American Guidance.

Sternberg, K.J., Lamb, M.E., & Dawud-Noursi, S. (1998). Using multiple informants to understand domestic violence and its effects. In G.W. Holden & R. Geffner (Eds.), *Children exposed to marital violence: Theory, research, and applied issues.* Washington, DC: American Psychological Association.

Stott, D.H., McDermott, P.A., Green, L.F., & Francis, J.M. (1988). *Learning behaviors scale and study of children's learning behaviors.* San Antonio: Psychological Corporation.

Strain, P., Guralnick, M., & Walker, H. (1986). *Children's social behavior: Development, assessment and modification.* Orlando, FL: Academic Press.

Weiss, A.D. (1997). *The unique and combined impact of health and caretaking risk factors on the school adjustment of urban first grade students.* Unpublished doctoral dissertation, University of Pennsylvania, Philadelphia.

CHAPTER 3

Clinical Issues in the Assessment of Partner Violence

K. DANIEL O'LEARY and CHRISTOPHER MURPHY

THE PURPOSES AND GOALS OF CLINICAL ASSESSMENT OF PARTNER ABUSE

BUILDING RAPPORT AND DEVELOPING A WORKING ALLIANCE

OFTEN OVERLOOKED in the technical literature on assessment of victims and perpetrators of domestic abuse is the need to develop a working alliance with the client(s). For over a decade, psychotherapy researchers have recognized the crucial importance of developing an alliance with their clients, and in fact, the alliance has been conceptualized as one of the most important ingredients of therapeutic change (Raue & Goldfried, 1994; Rogers, 1957; Strupp & Binder, 1984). According to Borodin (1979), the alliance consists of three factors: (1) the therapy bond (mutual liking or attachment), (2) agreement on goals of the therapy, and (3) agreement of therapeutic tasks used to reach the goals. Those who regard the therapy alliance as a central component of therapy have assigned high priority to development of the therapeutic bond and working toward an agreement of therapeutic goals and tasks. Yet, this issue has been almost totally ignored in the assessment and treatment of individuals in abusive relationships. We believe that it is time to change the way in which the assessment process is perceived in this literature.

Approximately 50% of the men who enter treatment for partner abuse drop out from treatment (see reviews by Hamberger & Hastings, 1994; Pirog-Good & Stets, 1986). These dropout rates are much higher than dropout rates from other types of individual or marital treatment (Brown, O'Leary, & Feldbau, 1997). With these data in mind, Brown and O'Leary (1998) found that the therapeutic alliance or bond between the male partner and the therapist was associated with decreased psychological and physical aggression. Contrary to our expectations, alliance was not related to dropout.

Nonetheless, it seems important to address the kinds of relationships established between the therapist and client in treatment for abuse, as the study of Brown and O'Leary is the first of its kind, and the clients were all seeking treatment services voluntarily.

Court-ordered clients present the added complexity of coerced assessment, including fear of legal reprisals for a negative clinical evaluation and the wish for legal exoneration from a positive clinical evaluation. Similarly, many victims have concerns about their mental health and the choices they have made to remain in an abusive relationship. They often fear negative evaluation from the clinician or insensitivity to the complexity of their relationship, life situation, and choices. Abusive males, in particular, and males with hostile dispositions more generally, tend to make external attributions for the causes of their problem behaviors (Holtzworth-Munroe, 1988; Holtzworth-Munroe & Hutchinson, 1993; Smith, Sanders, & Alexander, 1990). The more an individual makes such attributions, the more difficult it may be to work with him or her to bring about therapeutic change. Thus, based both on dispositional and situational factors, many domestic abuse clients are suspicious about having their behavior and thoughts scrutinized in a clinical assessment.

The clinical implications of these observations are quite important. Careful handling of client concerns during the assessment process may influence both retention of clients in treatment and eventual outcome, particularly with court-mandated clients. Whenever possible, an open-ended discussion about client concerns with an empathic assessor should precede introduction of structured assessments. Ideally, clients should consent to the assessment procedures and plan, they should see some possible benefits from completing the assessment, and they should come to see themselves as active participants in the assessment process rather than passive recipients of an evaluation.

From both ethical and clinical perspectives, it is very important to be straightforward about the nature, length, and purposes of the assessment. This openness should include providing information and answering questions about the assessment procedures, who will have access to the assessment data, and for what purposes. With court-mandated clients, it is crucially important to delineate the clinician's role vis-à-vis the court and probation system, including the types of information that will be reported back to legal authorities, and the frequency and nature of contact with prosecutors, probation agents, and judges. Even if it is not required legally, we suggest obtaining written informed consent from court-mandated clients about the limits of confidentiality and the nature of communications between the clinician and legal authorities. With clients who have sought services voluntarily, it is also important to address issues of confidentiality, for in such a context, confidentiality may be compromised in several ways, such as the need to warn a potential victim or to address a subpoena regarding an individual in a custody battle.

Clinically, it is also helpful to anticipate concerns that clients may have about the nature and use of assessment data and the clinician's relationship to the spouse and to other systems. Court-ordered clients are often relieved by an honest discussion about the difference between punitive criminal sanctions and supportive counseling toward behavior change and relationship enhancement. Victims may be preoccupied with whether the abusive spouse will gain access to assessment data or clinical information. For someone whose partner has intrusively monitored her activities and successfully isolated her from social contact for many years, the confidentiality discussion may need to go well beyond simple assurances.

ENHANCING MOTIVATION TO CHANGE

There is a growing tradition, particularly within the substance abuse field, to view clinical assessment not only as information gathering, but also as intervention (Miller & Rollnick, 1991). Before making a commitment to active behavior change, individuals usually evaluate the risks and negative consequences associated with the problem behavior, the likely benefits of behavior change, and the difficulty of change (Prochaska, DiClemente, & Norcross, 1992). Reevaluation of the self, life circumstances, and problem behaviors are important aspects of this process. Motivational enhancement therapies include structured feedback sessions that provide assessment data to clients to facilitate contemplation of behavior change, and subsequent commitment to change (Miller & Rollnick, 1991; Miller, Zweben, DiClemente, & Rychtarik, 1992). The feedback is provided in a supportive, empathic fashion, and is designed to facilitate clients' expressions of concerns and motivations for change.

Use of assessment feedback to motivate clients carries implications for choice of assessment instruments. It is easier to provide feedback about problem behaviors and associated risks and consequences when normative data are available on an instrument so the individual can be informed about where they stand relative to population or peer group norms. In the absence of population or group norms, local, clinic-specific norms can be used. Second, feedback is likely to be more motivating if clear implications for risk can be drawn using predictively valid instruments. Brief motivational interventions with problem drinkers use individualized feedback about neuropsychological impairment and liver functioning in addition to information about the quantity and frequency of drinking, reasons for drinking, and negative consequences of drinking (Miller et al., 1992). Such brief interventions, particularly if delivered in an empathic fashion, have been shown to significantly reduce alcohol consumption among problem drinkers (Miller, Benefield, & Tonigan, 1993). It remains to be seen whether similarly salient feedback can be provided with regard to domestic abuse, and whether brief motivational interventions will be successful with this population.

FACILITATING TREATMENT PLANNING

One widely accepted goal of clinical assessment involves treatment planning. Later in the chapter, we cover assessment of abusive behavior, and problems associated with abuse, such as substance dependence, depression, and personality disturbances. A good assessment, however, should not only identify the range and severity of presenting problems, but should also aid in the formulation of goals and strategies for change by assessing strengths and resources. These may include coping strategies that have been helpful in the past, behaviors and values that are incompatible with relationship abuse, and the availability and use of social support. Most domestic abuse clients present a complex picture, involving both remarkable resilience and remarkable skills deficits. Many of these individuals, for example, survived histories of childhood abuse or other severe trauma (Caesar, 1988; Murphy, Meyer, & O'Leary, 1993). Ideally, the intervention plan should build on preexisting strengths, values, and coping strategies, and should enhance opportunities for social support and skill acquisition.

ASSESSING THE FREQUENCY, SEVERITY, AND CHRONICITY OF ABUSIVE BEHAVIOR

The last general goal of clinical assessment in cases of domestic violence is also the most obvious; it involves the frequency, severity, and chronicity of abuse, including considerations about lethality. It bears mention here that abuse can have many dimensions, including physical assault, injuries, sexual coercion and sexual assault, destruction of property, and psychological aggression of various forms. Most of the chapter is devoted to strategies for assessing these aspects of abuse through clinical interview and self-report questionnaires. In discussing aspects of assessment and treatment, we address issues as they relate to three dominant theoretical/professional perspectives in the partner abuse field: (1) the feminist perspective, (2) the systemic or marital therapy perspective, and (3) the individual psychopathology perspective.

WHO IS ASSESSED AND IN WHAT FORMAT?

The feminist, sociohistorical perspective highlights the importance of gender-specific therapeutic issues. The overriding assumption is that wife battering is a reflection of a sexist culture and the sexist institutions that control and oppress women (Dobash & Dobash, 1979). In practice, this perspective generally implies that male and female partners should be assessed and treated separately with different clinical goals. Using this perspective, in many settings services for battered women are provided primarily by females, and services for male batterers are provided primarily by males.

From this vantage point, clinicians assessing battered women must first address the women's safety. Depending on the setting, clinicians may also assess the women's needs for legal assistance, economic assistance, job training, housing, child care, and social support. In addition, stress- and trauma-related symptoms may be evaluated, along with depression, self-esteem, and alcohol or substance abuse problems. The overriding clinical concern motivating assessment is to help empower abused women.

From the profeminist perspective, assessment of abusive husbands should be oriented toward breaking down the minimizations and denial of abuse (to promote taking responsibility). It should also focus on the sexist attitudes and beliefs used to justify the need to control and abuse the partner. Assessment of abusive husbands should foster the clinical goal of ending men's violence through helping them become less sexist, dominating, and controlling in intimate relationships with women.

From the feminist perspective, clinical assessment is commensurate with (and part of) social action on a larger scale designed to alter the sexist ideology and sexist institutions of power that promote and sanction abuse. Indeed, many clinicians operating within this perspective argue that conjoint therapy is virtually always contraindicated while violence is present (e.g., Ganley, 1981; McMahon & Pence, 1996).

In contrast, the systemic perspective (e.g., Everstein & Everstein, 1983) takes a couple-specific or relational view of the violence, rather than a gender-specific view. Most family or marital therapists would see both members of a couple together at some point in the therapeutic process, often from the outset of the assessment (Neidig & Friedman, 1984). Before his death, Neidig changed his view about the assessment process, and we argued that the couple should only be seen together after initial assessments conducted individually and after safety can be maximized (O'Leary, 1996; O'Leary, Neidig, & Heyman, 1995). Specific goals of assessment vary depending on the approach taken (e.g., structural, strategic, cognitive-behavioral). For example, a cognitive-behavioral clinician might attempt to identify patterns of anger arousal, problem-solving deficits, and miscommunication that lead to violence. From the systemic perspective, responsibility for controlling conflict is generally placed on both partners, and, as noted earlier, husbands and wives are usually treated conjointly rather than separately.

Finally, from the individual psychopathological perspective, assessment focuses primarily on the abusive partner (usually the husband). Some potential areas of clinical assessment include self-esteem; jealousy; personality disorder; aggressive, impulsive, and/or explosive personality style; co-occurring problems, such as drug and alcohol abuse; and personal history with violence and abuse (usually in childhood). Assessment might also focus on cognitive and affective components of anger arousal and aggression. The goal of such assessment is to identify psychological sources of violence for the individual abuser and to suggest appropriate treatment strategies, such as individual or group therapy.

The assessment need not be addressing only an individual or the individuals involved in a physically abusive relationship from whatever theoretical perspective one adopts. The assessment could cover individual as well as relationship issues from various vantage points. It is important, however, to keep a woman's safety as a paramount issue, and the initial assessment should always be done individually to allow the woman to discuss her concerns without fear of intimidation and reprisal. Thus, individual assessment always seems in order, and we have taken that stance in all forms of marital assessment for years (O'Leary, 1987).

WHO IS TO BE TREATED AND IN WHAT FORMAT?

If one goal of assessment is to determine appropriate treatment strategies, professionals using the overarching perspectives introduced earlier also make different recommendations to deal with this question. Those with the primarily feminist, sociohistorical approach suggest that men's and women's groups are the most expedient and most helpful vehicle for fostering psychosocial change (at the same time that efforts are to be pursued to foster social change in other ways). Because men and women are seen to occupy different roles, as well as different spheres vis-à-vis power dynamics in the relationship and the broader culture (e.g., Murphy & Meyer, 1991), gender-specific treatment formats allow for battered women and batterers to explore common themes among themselves. In particular, some therapists have emphasized the need for battered women to have a group experience that promotes mutual support in an environment free from the dominating and often intimidating presence of males (e.g., NiCarthy, Merriam, & Coffman, 1984). Likewise, batterers' groups allow group leaders to challenge sexist assumptions of power and control that often underlie physical violence (e.g., Adams & McCormick, 1982).

In contrast, individuals with a systemic perspective recommend treating husbands and wives conjointly, for optimal impact on the relational factors associated with violence. Couple or family treatment can be provided to one couple or to a group of couples. From this perspective, the escalating cycles of negative interchanges or anger involve both partners, and maximally effective treatment will explore and change both partners' roles in the conflicts that lead to violence.

The individual psychopathological perspective suggests that, to end their violence, batterers require special treatment, either individually or in groups. Depending on the specific theoretical orientation (e.g., cognitive-behavioral vs. psychodynamic), treatment may emphasize anger control skills; alternative relationship skills, such as assertiveness; or resolution of the underlying conflicts and motivations that led to violent outbursts.

As was the case for assessment, treatment options offered to the client will depend on the theoretical orientation of the professional. Like assessment methods, however, we suggest that the options offered need not be one or the other. For example, individual treatment or group treatment for anger problems could precede couple treatment (Johannson & Tutty, 1998). In addition, treatment for certain addiction problems like alcoholism could precede marital therapy (O'Farrell & Murphy, 1995).

ARE THERE CLEAR AGGRESSOR AND VICTIM ROLES?

In general, this issue separates the systemic perspective from the other two perspectives. Feminists generally maintain that factors such as the following make women the clear victims (or survivors) of aggression by their partners: (1) the historically and culturally rooted inequalities in power; (2) the greater height, weight, and strength of men; and (3) the longer histories of training in physically aggressive behavior, in sports and the military. In turn, these factors render men to be the perpetrators of violence in marriage. Much of the feminist scholarship on the topic attempts to isolate the effects of abuse on women and the causes of abuse in a sexist society and in individual men most affected by sexist and patriarchal ideology and practices.

Those who hold an individual psychopathology perspective usually suggest that one person has problems that led to violent behavior. In such cases, roles of violent perpetrator and victim generally apply. However, there is nothing inherent in this perspective that would lead one to believe that there should always be one person with psychopathology. In fact, because of the assortative mating data, those using a psychopathological model would often assume that both members in a marriage might have psychopathology (see O'Leary & Smith, 1991), and there is some intriguing evidence from longitudinal follow-up of children with conduct disorders/aggression into young adulthood that they have partners with problems of conduct and aggression (Capaldi & Crosby, 1995). Using this perspective, whether there is a clear victim or perpetrator, depends on the level of psychopathology in each spouse.

In contrast, from some couple or systemic perspectives, there is generally no clear victim or perpetrator. Systems-oriented theorists believe that causality is circular rather than linear. Whether one is seen as victim or as abuser depends on the point at which a sequence of interpersonal events is punctuated (Neidig & Friedman, 1984). At one point in an argument, the wife may have seemed like the perpetrator (e.g., the wife moved close to her husband who was seated in a chair reading the paper and verbally demanded that the husband address an issue), whereas only minutes later, the wife may have seemed like the victim (the husband disagreed with the wife, got angry at her for even addressing the issue, jumped out of his chair, and slapped her). The argument continued as the husband said they had to resolve the matter verbally once and forever. (He now appears to be the perpetrator of a new argument that could lead to more violence.) Some professionals who offer a couple perspective argue that the female partner is likely to be the primary victim because the woman is more likely to be injured as a result of the abuse and the woman is the more likely to be fearful of her partner. Based on initial assessments prior to treatment, we have found that women were five times more likely to sustain injuries than men (21% vs. 4%) (Cantos, Neidig, & O'Leary, 1994). Related research on injuries in a representative community sample shows that injuries are more likely for women than men although the absolute rate of injury of women and men is very small. Only 3% of the women and 0.4% of the men were injured (Stets & Straus, 1990).

Whether there is a victim and perpetrator will depend on the level or severity of violence in a relationship. In some couples, there is slapping by each partner, and the husband and the wife report no injury or fear of the other. Based on representative sampling, this type of aggression is by far the most common in relationships (Stets & Straus, 1990), and has been called "common couple violence" to contrast it with the more controlling and severely injurious violence called "patriarchal terrorism" (Johnson, 1995). The more severe physical aggression is less common, but it is more likely to be seen in centers for domestic violence and, we believe, is more likely to be unilateral (i.e., male to female) though we do not know of data on this issue. As we have argued elsewhere, it seems critical to assess for the level and severity of violence as well as the fear of the partner because such factors should be part of the assessment and treatment engagement process (O'Leary, Neidig, & Heyman, 1995). Stress on safety and fear of partner may seem totally illogical and iatrogenic in treatments for partners in relationships characterized by lower level forms of physical aggression that are infrequent and that do not lead to fear of a partner. But the issues should always be addressed in some fashion, though with sensitivity to the level of aggression being reported.

IS VIOLENCE THE PRIMARY TARGET OF TREATMENT OR A SECONDARY TARGET?

One feminist critique of traditional psychotherapeutic approaches to spouse abuse is that these approaches tend to interpret violence as resulting from some other, more primary disturbance. Feminists argue that this position in essence allows mental health professionals to collude with batterers in denying that abuse is the problem (e.g., Adams, 1988).

Theories about the primary problem range from psychodiagnostic categories, such as personality disorder or delusional jealousy; to psychological factors, such as emotional dependency or low self-esteem; to substance abuse; to relationship factors, such as poor communication or bad problem-solving skills. Thus, depending on the specifics of a given theory, both the systemic and individualistic perspectives at times render the violence as a secondary problem to some more basic psychological or relational problem. As practitioners and researchers have become more sensitized to the specific clinical issues related to spouse abuse, the tendency to deny violence as a primary target of treatment has decreased. There is considerable debate, however, about whether violence is merely a symptom of a more underlying disorder, personality pattern, or relational problem. As noted later, there is now evidence that treating alcoholism and marital problems without a specific focus on violence often leads to significant decrease in partner violence (O'Farrell & Murphy, 1995). Although there are differences of emphasis regarding what problem or problems to treat, even if physical violence is the first order of business, it is unclear how successful one can be in reducing violence without addressing individual or relationship problems at some point in the treatment.

SOME RECOMMENDATIONS

We just addressed four questions that we feel illustrate the central importance of theory and values in determining assessment or treatment choices: (1) Who is to be assessed? (2) Who is to be treated? (3) Who is the victim and who is the aggressor? (4) What should be the primary target of treatment? We do not claim to have captured the subtlety or diversity of different approaches to spouse abuse; instead, we tried to illustrate that vastly different assessment strategies and treatment options can arise from different theoretical and political stances.

As yet, no data support a view with simple, binary answers to the questions examined, and very little empirical evidence exists to guide treatment for spouse abuse. The different perspectives outlined may be more or less useful depending on the clinical settings and population served. Colleagues who work in treatment settings dealing specifically with spousal violence, or in shelter programs for battered women, may encounter quite different clinical issues from those working in couple and family treatment settings. Court-mandated treatment programs may differ in important respects from voluntary treatment programs.

Some of the more acrimonious debates in the field, especially surrounding the propriety or impropriety of couple treatment for spouse abuse, may have resulted from overgeneralization of experience with one or another type of setting and population. Though both of us have conducted research with mandated and voluntary populations, our primary personal experiences have come from work in outpatient marriage or family treatment settings (KDO) and in treatment centers for physically abusive men in an inner city (CM) . Although physical aggression is common in these marital clinic populations, violence is seldom labeled as a presenting problem by the clients (O'Leary, Vivian, & Malone, 1992). The modal forms of violence are grabbing, slapping, pushing, and throwing things at one another. To our surprise, fewer than 10% of the couples in which questionnaires and clinical interviews reveal physical aggression report physical aggression or violence as a problem in their initial intake assessment (Ehrensaft & Vivian, 1996; O'Leary et al., 1992). More specifically, when given an open-ended prompt to list the four major problems in their relationship, only 6% of women presenting at a university-based marital therapy clinic listed physical aggression as a problem (O'Leary et al., 1992). These behaviors are rarely labeled as abuse or violence by spouses coming to a marital clinic facility, and, depending on the population, for approximately half or more of the cases, the aggressive behaviors generally do not result in any injury, such as bruises or lacerations (e.g., Cascardi, Langhinrichsen, & Vivian, 1992). As long as such violence is carefully assessed and addressed directly in treatment, couple therapy appears to be a safe and effective modality of treatment for many of these cases. However, before embarking on a program of couple therapy, the clinician needs to make a judgment about the suitability of such treatment, in light of evidence that abuse is commonly minimized by spouses (discussed below), that further violence escalation is possible, and that there is potential danger in discussing difficult issues conjointly. The clinician should never collude with minimization or denial by failing to address acts such as slapping or pushing directly as abuse.

Where violence has become more severe, more potentially injurious, and often more unilaterally male perpetrated, couple therapy may perpetuate or implicitly sanction a severe imbalance of power. Until the individual has assumed responsibility for the violence and has learned to control it, couple therapy may be counterproductive, and gender-specific treatment approaches may be indicated in such cases. This latter situation appears to be much more common for clinicians working in court-mandated treatment programs, agencies specializing in domestic violence, or shelters. As yet, no data directly address the issues raised in this paragraph (i.e., comparisons of the frequency and level of physical aggression against a partner across different assessment and treatment settings).

Our recommendations is for all involved in the assessment and treatment of spouse abuse to examine the values implicit in their work and to consider the possible utility of alternative approaches where appropriate. In addition, we strongly urge researchers to study different assessment and treatment strategies in the effort to refine work in this area.

TECHNIQUES FOR THE ASSESSMENT OF PSYCHOLOGICAL AND PHYSICAL ABUSE

SELF-REPORT QUESTIONNAIRES

By far, the most widely used instrument in research on spouse abuse is the Conflict Tactics Scale (CTS), developed by Straus (1979). The original scale, which has been modified by researchers to fit specific assessment purposes, contains 18 items that assess the use of reasoning, verbal aggression, and physical aggression during conflicts with a family member or dating partner. Items at the beginning of the scale are about verbal reasoning, and items progress toward the most severe forms of physical aggression as a means of conflict resolution. For example, the physical aggression items range from pushing or slapping the partner, through hitting with a fist or beating up the spouse, to using a knife or gun. Respondents are asked to report the frequency of each behavior in the past year. Often, individuals are asked to report both on their own aggression as well as their partner's aggression.

A revision of the Conflict Tactics Scale has been published by Straus and colleagues (Straus, Hamby, Boney-McCoy, & Sugarman, 1996). The revised CTS has 78 items, and it is more comprehensive in its assessment of psychological, physical, and sexual abuse than the original CTS. Since it has more items assessing each of these domains, frequency comparisons with the original CTS will have to be made item by item. In addition to frequency of behaviors, the CTS measures self-reported injury.

A scale that was developed to assess controlling behaviors and psychological abuse of women is Tolman's 1989's Psychological Maltreatment of Women Scale (Tolman, 1989, 1999). This scale was validated with batterers, and factor analyses of the scale yield two factors, emotional/verbal abuse and a dominance/isolation factor. Although the factors are highly correlated, as might be expected, they measure different behaviors, and both scales have high internal consistency. The scale can be used as a self-report by men or as a report by women about their partners. It is particularly useful in assessing the more extreme forms of control of partners.

Another scale used to assess the psychological (but not physical) aspects of abuse is the Spouse Specific Aggression Scale (O'Leary & Curley, 1986). This scale contains 12 items that assess behaviors and reactions to the spouse. The items can generally be characterized as reflecting passive-aggressive behavior and active-aggressive (primarily verbal) behavior. The respondent rates how characteristic of himself or herself each behavior is (rather than how frequently each behavior occurs). The scale correlates highly with the verbal aggression subscale of the original CTS, but has the advantage of containing more items that assess a somewhat wider array of aggressive or coercive behaviors.

The widely used self-report inventories of spouse abuse have some interesting advantages and disadvantages for clinicians. First, they allow for a relatively quick and confidential screening for verbal and physical abuse. Their brevity can be very helpful in couple and family therapy, where abuse is rarely articulated as a presenting problem even though it may be present in the relationship. For practicing clinicians who may not want to give a self-report questionnaire that is 78 items long (e.g., the revised CTS), we recommend that at a minimum all clients be assessed individually for the presence of partner aggression with a simple rating scale that takes no longer than 3 to 5 minutes to complete (e.g., O'Leary et al., 1995; Vivian & Heyman, 1996).

Another advantage of these self-report inventories is that they provide prompts for highly specific behaviors that may not be assessed during a typical clinical interview. Furthermore, modifications of the CTS, such as that by Neidig (1986), assess behaviors that clinicians working for many years with abusive couples found to be common, such as choking the spouse, abusing pets, and driving recklessly.

There are numerous scales to assess physical and psychological abuse, and the purpose of this chapter is not to review all measures of aggression. For a discussion of measurement of physical aggression, consult the chapter by Straus (1996) and for a review of the measurement of psychological aggression consult the article by O'Leary (1999).

There are some often cited disadvantages to the existing self-report scales. Behavior checklist instruments such as the CTS may lead clinicians and research investigators to suggest that wives are equally aggressive as, or sometimes even more aggressive than husbands in general populations (O'Leary et al., 1989; Straus, Gelles, & Steinmetz, 1980). However, self-report measures of frequencies of behaviors per se fail to capture the ways in which aggression and abuse translate into control and power in relationships. In some cases, the impact (both psychological and physical) of such aggressive acts is not assessed or reported. Results from studies of community samples have yielded results that seem discrepant or at odds with the observations of those working in domestic violence centers and shelters where men clearly predominate as the aggressors and women as the victims of such assaults (Murphy & Meyer, 1991). These discrepancies can be real and may simply reflect population differences. In any case, differences in the severity and impact of violence must be addressed if this field is to move forward.

INTERVIEWS

Some shortcomings of structured self-report measures can be overcome by a careful and thorough clinical interview. In particular, the interview can begin to address the history, relational context, motivation, and effects of abuse, as well as enabling a detailed assessment of the severity, frequency, and types of abusive acts. In settings where abuse is not likely to be openly presented as a problem (e.g., marriage or family clinics), it is often helpful to review the client's responses to a structured self-report measure such as the CTS as a starting point for a more comprehensive interview assessment.

The interview should assess the range and types of abuse present. It is essential for the clinician to be familiar with types of abuse. Four commonly described categories are physical violence, sexual violence, property violence, and psychological abuse (Sonkin, Martin, & Walker, 1985; Walker, 1979). Each has myriad forms of expression. Physical violence can include hitting with objects, throwing objects at the partner, slapping, pushing, grabbing, kicking, punching, restraining, choking, and using weapons, among other acts. Clinicians may fail to detect physical violence because it is phrased by the client in euphemistic terms (e.g., "I put my hands on her shoulders" rather than "I grabbed her or shoved her"), or because it is placed in a positive or neutral motivational context (e.g., "I held her to stop her from going berserk and breaking things"). Partners often disagree widely when describing incidents. For example, the husband might say he placed his arms around the partner to calm her down, whereas the wife says he choked her to the point of collapse.

Sexual violence can include both physical coercion (e.g., holding partner down, twisting her arm) and mental coercion (e.g., threats of violence, continual arguments and pressure, threats to end the relationship) (Koss, Gidycz, & Wisniewski, 1987). The clinician needs to proceed cautiously in assessing sexual violence, because it is often not labeled as such by clients (Kelly, 1988; Russell, 1982). In abusive husbands, sexual assault is often accompanied by extreme jealousy (Sonkin et al., 1985). The partner is often forced to engage in unwanted or bizarre sexual acts to "prove" her faithfulness or love.

Examples of property violence are punching walls, breaking down doors, pounding tables, breaking objects, or destroying treasured possessions. One might also include threatened or actual abuse of pets in this category. These behaviors are common and often not considered abusive; however, they can have serious psychological consequences, and they often serve to intimidate the partner, serving as an all-too-real threat of physical attack.

Psychological abusive behaviors often go undetected or unlabeled by clinicians. Sonkin et al. (1985) listed the following six types: explicit threats of violence, implicit threats of violence, extreme controlling behavior, pathological jealousy, mental degradation, and isolating behavior. If not carefully assessed, some of these acts can appear to reflect concern or insecurity, rather than abuse. For example, a need to know where the partner is at all times, coupled with attempts to check up on the partner or to "chaperone" the partner, often represents extremely controlling behavior.

In addition to assessing the frequency and forms of abuse, the interview can begin to assess the widespread, and often subtle, effects of abuse. Abused women are often clinically depressed or markedly dysphoric, displaying very little positive self-regard. Their profiles on the Minnesota Multiphasic Personality Inventory (MMPI) often appear psychotic if not understood in the context of stress and trauma induced by long-term exposure to a life-threatening relationship (Rosewater, 1985). Alcohol abuse also appears to be relatively common in abused women, and it may mask other psychological effects of victimization. Stress and trauma symptoms, such as sleep disruption, nightmares, headaches, anxiety attacks, stomach problems, uncontrollable crying, and irritability may also result from abuse (see Briere & Runtz, 1989, for measure of trauma symptoms). Presence of such symptoms should be cause to assess the possibility of relationship abuse and/or sexual victimization. Conversely, presence of abuse should be cause to assess a range of possible consequences. Finally, during the interview assessment, the clinician needs to make some initial judgments about the potential for lethality, a topic discussed later in the chapter.

MINIMIZATION AND DENIAL OF ABUSE

Many clinicians working in the area have observed a tendency to minimize or deny abuse on the part of assaultive husbands (e.g., Ptacek, 1988; Sonkin et al., 1985) and abused wives (Ferraro, 1983). The tendency to minimize or deny abuse presents difficult problems for assessment. Some empirical evidence suggests that reports of interspousal aggression on structured questionnaires, such as the CTS, may be affected by the tendency to distort responses in a socially desirable direction (Arias & Beach, 1987; Riggs, Murphy, & O'Leary, 1989). Not surprisingly, some evidence also suggests that victim reports are likely to be more valid than perpetrator reports (Riggs et al., 1989). Heyman and Schlee (1997) provided data on the extent of minimization in different samples and offered guides for correcting the minimization. As might be expected, as the frequency and severity of the physical aggression increases, the greater the likelihood of minimization (or at least disagreement between partners about the acts of physical aggression). Using an assumption that the woman's reports of violence are the more accurate reports, Heyman and Schlee provided correction factors to estimate the prevalence of violence in a couple when only one partner's data can be obtained.

Dutton (1986) delineated three areas often minimized by wife abusers: frequency of assault, severity of assault, and effects on the victim. His study compared incident descriptions provided by wife assaulters with a composite description derived from reports by their partners, social worker, probation officers, police, court records, and hospital records. Two-thirds of the men minimized one or more aspects of the assault, providing support for the clinical observation that batterers downplay their assaults. In particular, men who blamed their wives for causing the violence were more likely than men who blame themselves or the situation to minimize the frequency, severity, or effects of the violence.

Clinicians and researchers should be aware of this common tendency to minimize or deny abuse. In particular, even those who admit to physically abusing a partner may minimize the severity and effects of the aggression, or the risk of future episodes. The opposite tendency also needs to have the attention of the clinician, for example, the possibility that either parent is overreporting abusive behavior for various reasons, especially to make a negative impression in a custody case. One of the authors (KDO) faces this thorny issue weekly in his forensic evaluation for custody and visitation recommendations.

CO-OCCURRENCE OF PSYCHOLOGICAL PROBLEMS

Clinical experience suggests that as the severity of abuse increases, other psychological problems increase. Indeed, in severely violent men in county facilities, such as probation department programs for spouse abuse, the likelihood of alcohol and substance abuse is about 65% (personal communication, Vincent Iaria, Director of Probation, Suffolk County Probation Office, May 20, 1998). In addition, a report highlighted by the National Institute of Justice in 1997 about men arrested for domestic violence assault in Memphis indicated that "almost all assailants had used drugs or alcohol during the day of the assault (Brookoff, 1997). Similarly, for abusive men in public treatment facilities, the likelihood of both personality problems and substance abuse is much higher than in community controls (Hamberger, Hastings, & Lohr, 1988). In victims of physical abuse, as the severity of violence increases, the likelihood of other problems also increases (e.g., depression, low self-esteem, and feelings of being inferior to the partner (Cascardi & O'Leary, 1992).

ALCOHOL ABUSE

As Kantor and Straus (1990) noted, the "drunken bum" theory has been a major conceptualization of wife abuse since the temperance movement. They noted that images of drunken men beating their wives, such as the scene in Tennessee Williams's play *A*

Streetcar Named Desire, where Stanley Kowalski beats his pregnant wife, have ramifications for public conceptualizations of spousal violence. The images are of lower-class families in which drunkenness and violence are expected or scripted behaviors. Moreover, the images portray drinking as a major cause of violence.

Kantor and Straus (1990) provided evidence for a strong link between alcohol and physical aggression against a partner from a nationally representative sample of over 5,000 couples. More specifically, alcohol use by the husband or wife immediately preceded instances of physical aggression in about 25% of the cases. In addition, there was a clear increase in alcohol use as the severity of violence increased. On the other hand, 80% of "high-frequency" and binge drinking men had not hit their wives once in the past year.

To return to the issue of public images of wife abusers, Kantor and Straus (1990) found that blue-collar men who drink heavily and approve of physical aggression have the highest rate of wife abuse, providing some support of the drunken bum notion of violence. Yet, looked at individually or even in terms of averages, we cannot conclude that blue-collar status is a good predictor of violence. Although the overall data can be used to provide some evidence for the notion that drunken wife beaters come from lower socioeconomic classes, it is important to emphasize that only 13% of blue-collar men engage in physical aggression against their partners. Moreover, there was only a 3% difference between the blue-collar and the white-collar men's use of physical aggression (10% of the latter group engaged in physical aggression).

With young engaged and married couples, the association of alcohol use and aggression is statistically significant but small. Furthermore, results in young samples are not even consistent across dependent measures. For example, Leonard and Senchak (1993) found that women's problem use of alcohol (drinking alone or drinking when the husband was not drinking) was associated with frequency of premarital aggression for the couple. On the other hand, frequency of alcohol use by the women was not associated with the couple's frequency of premarital physical aggression.

Another way to look at the association between alcohol and physical aggression is to assess prevalence of physical aggression in alcoholic samples. One study of this phenomenon indicates that about 50% of married male alcoholics in a Veterans Administration hospital program had been physically aggressive toward their partners in the year prior to a marital treatment program for alcoholics and their spouses (O'Farrell & Murphy, 1995). This rate could implicate alcohol use as a factor in spousal violence, but because marital discord in the absence of severe drinking problems is also associated with spousal violence in about 65% of the marital cases assessed at our university marital clinic, it may be that marital discord is the more important associated factor for this population (O'Leary & Vivian, 1990).

In a review of the alcohol/physical aggression link in both community and clinical samples, Schumacher and O'Leary (1998) reached the following conclusions:

1. One of the most important points to be drawn from this review is that the association between alcohol use and physical aggression against an intimate partner depends on the sample to which one refers. More specifically, there is a small or nonsignificant association between alcohol use and partner aggression in community/nonclinical samples. However, when one examines trends within these samples, it appears that those men with the highest rates of partner aggression are often also the men with the highest rates of alcohol consumption and vice versa.

2. In community samples, binge drinking is associated with partner aggression not absolute amount of alcohol consumed per week or month.
3. Use of alcohol at the time of a physically aggressive incident more strongly implicates the causal role of alcohol. That is, in community samples, use of physical aggression is associated with alcohol use approximately 25% of the time. In samples of batterers, physical aggression co-occurs with alcohol use between 50% and 60% of the time. Between 39% and 71% of men in treatment for alcoholism report having engaged in partner aggression, with 20% to 56% of these men reporting severe partner aggression.
4. There are multiple determinants of physical aggression against a partner; alcohol alone is not a sufficient cause. Other important variables that interact with alcohol use to produce partner aggression include attitudes that condone violence, past history of physical aggression, having an aggressive personality style, being psychologically aggressive, and being controlling.
5. Even with the acceptance that partner aggression is multidetermined, in a large sample of military men, alcohol use was one of the most important predictors of partner aggression.

DEPRESSION

Depression is a commonly observed clinical symptom in abused women and their partners. For example, Cascardi and O'Leary (1992) found that 53% of a sample of severely abused women were depressed (Beck Depression Inventory scores > 20). In a sample of couples assessed at a university marital therapy clinic, 34% of the severely abused women were depressed (O'Leary & Vivian, 1990). Further studies suggest that abusive husbands evidence higher levels of depression and lower self-esteem than comparison group men (Goldstein & Rosenbaum, 1985; Hamberger et al., 1988). In a sample of women whose husbands were physically aggressive, the women had a mean BDI score of 14.5, which was clearly higher than that of a control group of women (mean = 4) though it was not different from women in maritally discordant relationships (Cascardi et al., 1992). Using odds ratios, Pan, Neidig, and O'Leary (1994) showed that depressive symptomatology was a significant risk factor for mild and severe partner aggression in a sample of 11,700 military men. Further, Feldbau, Heyman, and O'Leary (1998) assessed men who were physically aggressive toward their wives and who had sought treatment for their aggression. Almost one-third of the men had moderate levels of depressive symptomatology (BDI > 14), but only 11% met criteria for clinical depression (SCID). We found that depressive symptomatology and physical aggression had a small but significant correlation, but that when anger was controlled for, the association between depressive symptomatology and physical aggression became nonsignificant, suggesting that the depression/physical aggression link may be mediated by anger.

PERSONALITY DISTURBANCES

An often-cited early study portrayed battered women as controlling, masculine, and masochistic (Snell, Rosenwald, & Robey, 1964). Indeed, battered women were thought to provoke violence from an inherent self-defeating or masochistic need. The author argued that the violent behavior of alcoholic husbands satisfies the wives' masochistic needs and the violence behavior is necessary to maintain the "working equilibrium" of the marriage. This view was dominant in the field until challenged by activists and scholars (e.g., Dobash & Dobash, 1979). Most importantly, without longitudinal studies of spouse abuse, it is unclear whether any personality differences observed between battered women and nonbattered women are effects, correlates, or causes of abuse. However, there is some evidence with partners of young men who were originally given the diagnosis of conduct disorder as a child of 9 to 10 years of age that they find female partners who have high levels of antisocial behavior (Capaldi & Crosby, 1995).

Nonetheless, as recently as 1984, Gellen, Hoffman, Jones, and Stone reached a conclusion with some similarities to that of Snell et al. (1964). They compared MMPI profiles of abused and nonabused women and found that abused women had elevated scores on the Depression, Hysteria, and Psychopathic Deviancy scales. They acknowledged that abuse may contribute to a woman's inability to act in a logical manner, but they stated that the abused woman may fail to learn from past experience and project onto her husband "bad" elements of her personality. They stated that the "disordered personalities" of the abused women "must be treated in conjunction with the abuse to bring about change in the relationship" (Gellen et al., 1984, p. 604).

The masochism concept of abuse was strongly challenged by Kuhl (1984), who assessed 115 women and found that they did not have strong masculine identification. Rather, they had inadequate coping skills and, in fact, had a need to avoid confrontations. In a similar vein, Launius and Jensen (1987) found that battered women had deficient problem-solving skills. They lack the ability to generate options to solve a problem and lacked skill in generating effective solutions. These differences were evident even after anxiety and depression were statistically controlled.

Hamberger and Hastings (1986) examined personality correlates of 99 men who attended a domestic violence abatement program. Most importantly, they found no *single* personality profile of the spouse abuser. Using the Millon Clinical Multiaxial Inventory, three profiles of these men were identified: (1) schizoid/borderline, (2) narcissistic/antisocial, and (3) passive/dependent/compulsive. In a related vein, Coates, Leong, and Lindsey (1987) compared abusive men voluntarily entering treatment with those who were court ordered for treatment. Using the MMPI, they concluded that both groups were clinically disturbed with character disorder syndromes, although the voluntary group had higher depression and sociopathic scores. Finally, Hamberger and Hastings (1989) extended their previous work with batterers and compared them with a nonbattering group. The batterers scored higher than the nonbatterers on Avoidant, Aggressive, and Negativistic scales. Dutton (1988) has developed a model of abuse that is grounded in personality, especially borderline personality organization (BPO). This conceptualization is not synonymous with borderline personality. He stated that the BPO is characterized by identity problems that become salient in intimate relationships. Among the central characteristics are an unstable sense of self, intense and phasic anger, and impulsivity. Self-reports of BPO are predictive of domination and isolation. While no single unifying theme cuts across the studies by different investigators, there is certainly increasing recognition that personality factors cannot be ignored in the assessment of partner abuse. In addition, there is evidence from one laboratory that physiological assessment of batterers may reveal different subtypes of batterers (Gottman et al., 1995), and that such subtypes may be associated with certain personality correlates.

Although it is easy to criticize any study assessing correlates of abuse in men and/or women, a large body of literature on personality patterns of married partners has some relevance to abusive relationships. Basically, this research indicates that personality similarities, rather than personality differences, are the rule among married partners (O'Leary & Smith, 1991). Although many researchers believed that they would find married partners to have complementary needs or personality styles, similarity between partners is far the more common finding. Furthermore, when one looks at areas of psychopathology, such as sociopathy, alcoholism, and depression, some evidence of assortative mating or of "likes marrying likes" is evident (Merikangas, 1982). As evidence accumulates from severe abusers and their partners, varied types of psychopathology may become evident in both spouses. Thus, it may not be surprising to find that some drug-abusing wife assaulters have spouses with drug problems. Similarly, as noted earlier, young men with histories of conduct disorders often have partners with elevated rates of antisocial behavior (Capaldi & Crosby, 1995). Traditionally, clinicians may have erred in the direction of blaming victims for their abuse. However, clinicians can also err by assuming that only one member of the relationship (i.e., the abusive husband) has problems that require treatment or by assuming that all the problems displayed by an abused woman resulted from the abuse.

THE DIAGNOSTIC DEBATE REGARDING *DSM-IV*

Diagnostic issues in the area of spouse abuse and marital violence are only beginning to receive serious research attention. Some of the issues relate to those questions discussed at the beginning of the chapter, such as who is to be assessed, who is to be treated, and whether there are clear aggressor and victim roles. Diagnostic evidence is just beginning to be gathered systematically on men and women in physically abusive relationships, but in this section we review the existing material to provide some guides for addressing the diagnosis, if any, of men and women in abusive relationships.

POSTTRAUMATIC STRESS DISORDER

The diagnosis of self-defeating personality disorder had been used by some professionals to diagnose abused women. This practice was severely criticized by Walker (1989), who argued that the *DSM-III-R* diagnosis of Posttraumatic Stress Disorder (PTSD) is more relevant. The *DSM-IV* eliminated the self-defeating personality disorder, and thus it cannot be used as a diagnosis for abused women. PTSD, a subclassification of anxiety disorders, is diagnosed when (1) an individual has experiences outside the range of usual human endeavor (e.g., a serious threat to his or her life), (2) a traumatic event is persistently reexperienced by the person, (3) the person persistently avoids stimuli associated with the trauma or experiences numbing of general responsiveness, (4) the person experiences persistent symptoms of increased arousal, and (5) the symptoms last for at least one month.

Posttraumatic Stress Disorder has been studied in severely victimized samples of abused women who sought refuge at battered women's shelters because they feared that their lives were in danger. These women met diagnostic criteria for PTSD; rates at time of admission ranged from 33% to 47% (Gleason, 1993; Housecamp & Foy, 1991; West, Fernandez, Hillard, Schoof, & Parks, 1990). Housecamp and Foy (1991) reported a significant relationship between the intensity of violence, as assessed by the frequency of aggression and injury, length of time in a violent relationship, and severity of PTSD symptoms. They also found that women who sustained an injury from spousal violence requiring medical care, those who perceived their lives to be in danger, or those who had a knife or gun used against them three or more times during the relationship were significantly more likely to meet full or partial symptom criteria for PTSD than women who had not experienced such violence (93% vs. 43%). Of women in physically abusive marriages presenting for treatment, 33% met criteria for PTSD (Cascardi, O'Leary, Lawrence, & Schlee, 1995).

BATTERED WOMAN SYNDROME

The battered woman syndrome is a description of what happens to battered women. The syndrome was championed by Walker (1989), who described it with two essential features: (1) fear of unavoidable physical aggression, and (2) unpredictable physical aggression. The syndrome has recently been recognized and allowed in court in all states in legal cases of murder of husbands by women (Pesce, 1990). Its exact status in court, however, is not clear, as reflected in the Faigman (1986) legal and empirical dissent. This syndrome basically results from repeated victimization by one's partner. It has special social and legal significance because it makes clear that a plea of self-defense for the murder of a partner may occur not only in situations of imminent danger, but in situations where one's life has been repeatedly threatened and where one may *assume* that the threat might occur again. Use of the battered woman syndrome in legal defense cases is based in part on the notion that justified murder in self-defense was written for cases of male versus male aggression in which the physical powers of the individuals are relatively equal. In contrast, in cases of spouse abuse, there is not equal physical power. Thus, there need not be immediate physical danger; instead the danger is held to be ever present if a wife has been beaten repeatedly over many years. Indeed, Browne (1989) found that women who murder their husbands in self-defense can be distinguished from other abused women based on severity of the attacks and other husband factors, such as substance abuse and previous arrests. In contrast, such women were not generally distinguishable on the basis of their own behavior or background from women who did not murder their husbands.

In brief, the battered woman syndrome has been used in many legal cases in which women kill their partners. The extent to which the defense has been used successfully, however, is not documented, though according to Faigman (1986), several appellate courts have upheld the admissibility of battered woman syndrome evidence or "have remanded cases to the trial courts for failure to examine adequately the relevance of such evidence" (p. 334). Without going into detail about the critiques of the syndrome, any practitioner dealing with such issues should be aware of the serious questions raised by Faigman about the admissibility of the scientific evidence for the syndrome, especially the argument about the tenuousness of the learned helplessness research and the absence of control groups in Walker's research, and the fact that most of Walker's subjects did not kill anyone.

RELATIONSHIP DISORDERS

Individual diagnoses based on categories in the *DSM-IV* are the only legitimate insurance codes for which a client or patient can be legitimately reimbursed; marital and/or family problems are not diagnostic categories that insurance companies recognize for reimbursement. Thus, a movement was in place by some members of the American Psychological Association to ensure that *relationship disorders* become a part of

DSM-IV (Kaslow & Olson, 1990). Twelve companion organizations from psychiatry, marital and family therapy, nursing, and social work banded together to lobby for this diagnostic change. Under the heading, "Other Conditions That May Be a Focus of Clinical Attention," *DSM-IV* now includes Relational Problems, a category that contains various V codes, and there is a category, "Problems Related to Abuse or Neglect," with five V code categories. One of those codes includes Physical Abuse of Adult, V61.1, (p. 682). A related chapter, Partner Relational Problems with Physical Abuse, appears in the *DSM- IV, Sourcebook, Volume 3* (O'Leary & Jacobson, 1997). Thus, there now is an explicit diagnosis which applies to partner abuse (for perpetrators and victims).

Private corporations and small businesses also need to recognize the problems that marital discord causes in terms of productivity. The Ohio State Psychological Association, in conjunction with the association of small businesses, conducted a survey and found that supervisors believe that marital discord has more negative effects on the productivity of workers than problems of drug and alcohol abuse (American Psychological Association, 1990). When such facts are made clear, the business community may aid mental health care providers in prompting insurance companies to recognize the need for coverage of marital problems, especially in cases of potential wife abuse (O'Leary & Smith, 1991).

INTERMITTENT EXPLOSIVE DISORDER

Although we have discussed the co-occurrences of various psychological problems in men who physically abuse their partners, we have not presented any single diagnosis of the man who engages in such behaviors. No single diagnosis for these men parallels the battered woman syndrome. One possible diagnosis from the *DSM-III-R* and *DSM-IV* is Intermittent Explosive Disorder. As it exists, however, the diagnosis does not fit the facts about spouse abusers. The defining features of this disorder are as follows:

> Discrete episodes of failure to resist aggressive impulsive impulses that result in serious assaultive acts or destruction of property. The degree of aggressiveness expressed during an episode is grossly out of proportion to any provocation or precipitating psychosocial stressor. The individual may describe the aggressive episodes as "spells" or "attacks" in which the explosive behavior is preceded by a sense of tension or arousal and is followed immediately by a sense of relief. (American Psychiatric Association, 1994, p. 610)

Of special interest is that the following criterion in *DSM-III-R* was dropped. "There are no signs of generalizing impulsivity or aggressiveness between the episodes." In fact, the statement is now, "Signs of generalized impulsivity or aggressiveness may be present between explosive episodes" (p. 610). Most men who abuse their partners have been verbally aggressive periodically, and verbal aggressiveness and aggressiveness as a personality style are clear precursors of physical aggression (O'Leary, Malone, & Tyree, 1994). According to *DSM-IV*, a diagnosis of Intermittent Explosive Disorder should be considered only after all other disorders that are associated with aggressive impulses or behavior are ruled out. Thus, consideration should be given to disorders like Antisocial Personality Disorder. One statement regarding "purposeful behavior" indicates that purposeful behavior is distinguished from Intermittent Explosive Disorder (IED) by the presence of motivation and gain in the aggressive act (p. 611). There is no clear guide regarding the extent to which the act(s) should be purposeful or not in rendering a diagnosis of Intermittent Explosive Disorder, but it appears that if the acts are purposeful, IED should not be used. Given that many men use physically aggressive behavior to control their partners, IED would not be appropriate for them.

ETHICAL ISSUES

Based on the legal decision in *Tarasoff v. Regents of the University of California* (1976), a clinician has a duty to warn the potential victim and legal authorities if any individual is likely to do serious physical harm to another. States have recently begun to incorporate psychotherapists' duty to protect potential victims into law. Even in states where the rule has yet to be formally adopted, experts generally advise clinicians to act as if the *Tarasoff* rule were in effect (Appelbaum & Rosenbaum, 1989). Thus, if a husband or boyfriend is likely to harm his partner, the clinician is both ethically and legally bound to act, and confidentiality must be violated. In group programs for spouse abusers, a clinician may have to violate a confidence and alert the wife or girlfriend of impending danger. Although psychologists and psychiatrists may have wished to hide behind a cloak of ignorance about the predictability of future violence, this contention has been essentially rejected by the courts (Wettstein, 1984).

In all cases of actual or potential spouse abuse, the clinician must be prepared to assess the likelihood of lethal action by an individual. As noted earlier, use of multiple assessment sources regarding both the husband and the wife appears to be the best way to detect spouse abuse. In research described previously in this chapter, interviews with each spouse individually, use of a standardized measure of physical abuse, and spontaneous reports of the major problems in one's marriage yielded considerably different information about rates of physical aggression in spouse abuse (O'Leary, Vivian, & Malone, 1992). Most importantly, it seems helpful and perhaps necessary to use both a standardized self-report measure and a separate interview with each partner. Even if one generally conducts conjoint marital assessment interviews, some type of individual assessment also seems critical because spouse abuse has been minimized by the public as well as professionals. Comparisons of conjoint interviews with self-reports by individuals also appear to support this practice, as conjoint interviews seem to yield less reporting of physical aggression, especially by the wife (Cantos et al., 1994).

CONCLUSION

Assessment of spouse abuse is influenced by one's theoretical position. Three general approaches to the problem—(1) feminist (sociohistorical), (2) systemic, and (3) individual psychopathological—offer different opinions regarding issues such as who is to be assessed and treated (husbands, wives, or couples) and what format of treatment should be used (gender-specific groups, couple groups, or individual therapy). These three theoretical positions were presented to depict the differences among theoretical positions, but we recognized that individual clinicians can adopt aspects of these positions that complement each other.

We recommend a multimethod approach to the clinical assessment of spouse abuse. Standardized self-report questionnaires tend to elicit the highest reporting rates of physical and verbal aggression. These measures can offer a helpful screening for the purpose of abuse, particularly in clinical situations where abuse is not a common presenting problem. Careful interviewing, conducted with spouses individually rather than conjointly, can begin to uncover the forms, frequency, context, motivations, and consequences of abuse. Assessors should be acutely aware of the tendency of both the abusers and the abused to minimize or deny abuse.

Spouse abuse often exists concurrently with other psychological problems, such as alcoholism, depression, and personality disorders or disturbances. Diagnosis of the abuser and the victim remains the subject of continuing debate. Relatively little empirical data exist to help resolve this question. Practically, however, the battered woman syndrome has had important legal implications for protecting abused women. Whether the diagnosis of posttraumatic stress disorder is more descriptive of the abused woman than the battered woman syndrome is unclear. At present, no adequate diagnosis or classification of abusive individuals can be found in the psychiatric nomenclature though for the first time, the APA *Diagnostic and Statistical Manual* contains diagnostic categories and sourcebook material on partner abuse (American Psychiatric Association, 1994).

Ethical concerns in the assessment and treatment of spouse abuse include the importance of safety, the need to address lethality, and the duty to warn potential victims. Clinicians have a special responsibility to detect abuse, not to collude with the denial of abuse, and not to condone abuse in overt or subtle ways. We recommend that clinicians consider the possible utility of various treatment approaches and that researchers begin to address the success of different psychological treatments for abusers and survivors of abuse.

REFERENCES

Adams, D. (1988). Treatment models of men who batter: A profeminist analysis. In K. Yllo & M. Bograd (Eds.), *Feminist perspectives on wife abuse* (pp. 176–199). Newbury Park, CA: Sage.

Adams, D., & McCormick, A. (1982). Men unlearning violence: A group approach. In M. Roy (Ed.), *The abusive partner* (pp. 170–197). New York: Van Nostrand-Reinhold.

American Psychiatric Association. (1994). *Diagnostic and statistical manual of mental disorders* (4th ed.). Washington, DC: Author.

American Psychological Association. (1990). *Practitioner Focus, 4,* 47.

Appelbaum, P.S., & Rosenbaum, A. (1989). Tarasoff and the researcher: Does the duty to protect apply in the research setting? *American Psychologist, 44,* 885–894.

Arias, I., & Beach, S.R.H. (1987). Validity of self-reports of marital violence. *Journal of Family Violence, 2,* 82–90.

Borodin, E.S. (1979). The generalizability of the psychoanalytic concept of the working alliance. *Psychotherapy: Theory, Research and Practice, 16,* 252–260.

Briere, J., & Runtz, M. (1989). The trauma symptom checklist (TSC-33): Early data on a new scale. *Journal of Interpersonal Violence, 4,* 151–163.

Brookoff, D. (1997, October). *Drugs, alcohol, and domestic violence in Memphis.* Washington, DC: National Institute of Justice Research Preview.

Brown, P.D., & O'Leary, K.D. (1998). *Therapeutic alliance: Predicting continuance and success in group treatment for spouse abuse.* Unpublished manuscript, State University of New York, Stony Brook.

Brown, P.D., O'Leary, K.D., & Feldbau, S.R. (1997). Drop-out in a treatment program for self-referring wife abusing men. *Journal of Family Violence, 12,* 365–387.

Browne, A. (1989). Family homicide: When victimized women kill. In V.B. Van Hasselt, R.L. Morrison, A.S. Bellack, & M. Hersen (Eds.), *Handbook of family violence* (pp. 271- 288). New York: Plenum Press.

Caesar, P.L. (1988). Exposure to violence in the families-of-origin among wife abusers and maritally nonviolent men. *Violence and Victims, 3,* 49–63.

Cantos, A.L., Neidig, P.H., & O'Leary, K.D. (1994). Injuries of women and men in a treatment program for domestic violence. *Journal of Family Violence, 9,* 113–124.

Capaldi, D.M., & Crosby, L. (1995, November 16–19). *The association of partners' characteristics with observed and reported aggression for at-risk dating couples.* Paper presented at the annual conference of the Association for the Advancement of Behavior Therapy, Washington, DC.

Cascardi, M., Langhinrichsen, J., & Vivian, D. (1992). Marital aggression: Impact, injury, and health correlates for husbands and wives. *Archives of Internal Medicine, 152,* 1178–1184.

Cascardi, M., & O'Leary, K.D. (1992). Depressive symptomatology, self-esteem, and self-blame in battered women. *Journal of Family Violence, 7,* 249–259.

Cascardi, M., O'Leary, K.D., Lawrence, E.E., & Schlee, K.A. (1995). Characteristics of women physically abused by their spouses and who seek treatment regarding marital conflict. *Journal of Consulting and Clinical Psychology, 63,* 616–623.

Coates, C.L., Leong, D.J., & Lindsey, M. (1987). *Personality differences among batterers voluntarily seeking treatment and those ordered to treatment by the court.* Paper presented at the Third National Family Violence Research Conference, Durham, NH.

Dobash, R.E., & Dobash, R.P. (1979). *Violence against wives: A case against the patriarchy.* New York: Free Press.

Dutton, D.G. (1986). Wife assaulter's explanations for assault: The neutralization of self-punishment. *Canadian Journal of Behavioral Science, 18,* 381–390.

Dutton, D.G. (1988). *The domestic assault of women.* Boston: Allyn & Bacon.

Ehrensaft, M.K., & Vivian, D. (1996). Spouses reasons for not reporting existing physical aggression as a marital problem. *Journal of Family Psychology, 10,* 443–453.

Everstein, D., & Everstein, L. (1983). *People in crisis: Strategic therapeutic interventions.* New York: Brunner/Mazel.

Faigman, D.L. (1986). The battered woman syndrome and self-defense: A legal and empirical dissent. *Virginia Law Review, 72,* 619–647.

Feldbau, S., Heyman, R.E., & O'Leary, K.D. (1998). Major depressive disorders and depressive symptomatology as predictors of husband to wife physical aggression. *Violence and Victims, 13,* 1–14.

Ferraro, K.J. (1983). Rationalizing violence: How battered women stay. *Victimology, 8,* 203–212.

Ganley, A. (1981). *Court-mandated counseling for men who batter: A three day workshop for mental health professionals.* Washington, DC: Center for Women's Policy Studies.

Gellen, M.I., Hoffman, R.A., Jones, M., & Stone, M. (1984). Abused and non-abused women: MMPI profile differences. *Personnel and Guidance Journal, 62,* 109–119.

Gleason, W.J. (1993). Mental disorders in battered women: An empirical study. *Violence and Victims, 8,* 53–68.

Goldstein, D., & Rosenbaum, A. (1985). An evaluation of the self esteem of maritally violent men. *Family Relations, 34,* 425–428.

Gottman, J.M., Jacobson, N.S., Rushe, R.H., Shortt, J.W., Babcock, J., La Taillade, J.J., & Waltz, J. (1995). The relationship between heart rate reactivity, emotionally aggressive behavior, and general violence in batterers. *Journal of Family Psychology, 9,* 227–248.

Hamberger, L.K., & Hastings, J.E. (1986). Personality correlates of men who abuse their partners: A cross validation study. *Journal of Family Violence, 1,* 323–341.

Hamberger, L.K., & Hastings, J.E. (1989). *Psychopathology differences between batterers and non-batterers: Psychosocial modifiers.* Paper presented at the meeting of the American Psychological Association, New Orleans.

Hamberger, L.K., & Hastings, J.E. (1994). Court-mandated treatment of men who batter their partners: Issues, controversies, and outcomes. In Z. Hilton (Ed.), *Legal responses to wife assault* (pp. 188–193). Newbury Park, CA: Sage.

Hamberger, L.K., Hastings, J.E., & Lohr, J.M. (1988). *Cognitive and personality correlates of men who batter: Some continuities and discontinuities.* Paper presented at the Association for the Advancement of Behavior Therapy, New York.

Heyman, R.E., & Schlee, K.A. (1997). Toward a better estimate of the prevalence of partner abuse: Adjusting rates based on the sensitivity of the Conflict Tactics Scale. *Journal of Family Psychology, 11,* 331–338.

Holtzworth-Munroe, A. (1988). Causal attributions in marital violence: Theoretical and methodological issues. *Clinical Psychology Review, 8,* 331–344.

Holtzworth-Munroe, A., & Hutchinson, G. (1993). Attributing negative intent to wife behavior: The attributions of maritally violent versus nonviolent men. *Journal of Abnormal Psychology, 102,* 206–211.

Housecamp, B.M., & Foy, D.W. (1991). The assessment of post traumatic stress disorder in battered women. *Journal of Interpersonal Violence, 6,* 367–375.

Johannson, M.A., & Tutty, L.M. (1998). An evaluation of after-treatment couples' groups for wife abuse. *Family Relations, 47,* 27–35.

Johnson, M.P. (1995). Patriarchical terrorism and common couple violence: Two forms of violence against women. *Journal of Marriage and the Family, 57,* 283–294.

Kantor, G.K., & Straus, M.A. (1990). The drunken bum theory of wife beating. In M.A. Straus & R.J. Gelles (Eds.), *Physical violence in American families* (pp. 203–224). New Brunswick, NJ: Transaction Books.

Kaslow, F., & Olson, D. (1990). Diagnostic and classification task force. *The Family Psychologist, 6,* 10.

Kelly, L. (1988). How women define their experiences of violence. In K. Yllo & M. Bograd (Eds.), *Feminist perspectives on wife abuse* (pp. 114–132). Newbury Park, CA: Sage.

Koss, M.P., Gidycz, C.A., & Wisniewski, N. (1987). The scope of rape: Incidence and prevalence of sexual aggression and victimization in a national sample of higher education students. *Journal of Consulting and Clinical Psychology, 55,* 162–170.

Kuhl, A.F. (1984). Personality traits of abused women: Masochism myth refuted. *Victimology, 9,* 450–463.

Launius, M.H., & Jensen, B.L. (1987). Interpersonal problem solving skills in battered, counseling, and control women. *Journal of Family Violence, 2,* 151–162.

Leonard, K.E., & Senchak, M. (1993). Alcohol and premarital aggression among newlywed couples. *Journal of Abnormal Psychology, 105,* 369–380.

McMahon, M., & Pence, E. (1996). Replying to Dan O'Leary. *Journal of Interpersonal Violence, 11,* 452–456.

Merikangas, K.R. (1982). Assortative mating for psychiatric disorders and psychological traits. *Archives of General Psychiatry, 39,* 173–180.

Miller, W.R., Benefield, R.G., & Tonigan, J.S. (1993). Enhancing motivation for change in problem drinking: A controlled comparison of two therapist styles. *Journal of Consulting and Clinical Psychology, 61,* 455–461.

Miller, W.R., & Rollnick, S. (Eds.). (1991). *Motivational interviewing: Preparing people to change addictive behaviors.* New York: Guilford Press.

Miller, W.R., Zweben, A., DiClemente, C.C., & Rychtarik, R.G. (1992). *Motivational enhancement therapy manual: A clinical research guide for therapists treating individuals with alcohol abuse and dependence* (NIAAA Project MATCH Monograph, Vol. 2, DHHS Publication No. (ADM) 92-1894). Washington, DC: Government Printing Office.

Murphy, C.M., & Meyer, S.L. (1991). Gender, power, and violence in marriage. *The Behavior Therapist, 14,* 95–100.

Murphy, C.M., Meyer, S.L., & O'Leary, K.D. (1993). Family of origin violence and MCMI-II psychopathology among partner assaultive men. *Violence and Victims, 8,* 165–176.

Neidig, P. (1986). *The modified conflict tactics scale.* Beaufort, SC: Behavioral Science Associates.

Neidig, P., & Friedman, D.H. (1984). *Spouse abuse: A treatment program for couples.* Champaign, IL: Research Press.

NiCarthy, G., Merriam, K., & Coffman, S. (1984). *Talking it out: A guide to groups for abused women.* Seattle, WA: Seal Press.

O'Farrell, T.J., & Murphy, C.M. (1995). Marital violence before and after alcoholism treatment. *Journal of Consulting and Clinical Psychology, 63,* 256–262.

O'Leary, K.D. (1987). *Assessment of marital discord.* Hillsdale, NJ: Erlbaum.

O'Leary, K.D. (1996). Physical aggression in intimate relationships can be treated within a marital context under certain circumstances. *Journal of Interpersonal Violence, 11,* 450–453.

O'Leary, K.D. (1999). Psychological abuse: A variable deserving critical attention in domestic violence. *Violence and Victims, 14,* 1–21.

O'Leary, K.D., Barling, J., Arias, I., Rosenbaum, A., Malone, J., & Tyree, A. (1989). Prevalence and stability of physical aggression between spouses: A longitudinal analysis. *Journal of Consulting and Clinical Psychology, 57,* 263–268.

O'Leary, K.D., & Curley, A.D. (1986). Assertion and family violence: Correlates of spouse abuse. *Journal of Marital and Family Therapy, 12,* 281–289.

O'Leary, K.D., & Jacobson, N.S. (1997). Partner relational problems with physical abuse. In American Psychiatric Association, *Diagnostic statistical manual: Sourcebook* (4th ed., Vol. 3, pp. 673–692). Washington, DC: Author.

O'Leary, K.D., Malone, J., & Tyree, A. (1994). Physical aggression in early marriage: Prerelationship and relationship effects. *Journal of Consulting and Clinical Psychology, 62,* 594–602.

O'Leary, K.D., Neidig, P.H., & Heyman, R.E. (1995). Assessment and treatment of partner abuse: A synopsis for the legal profession. *Albany Law Review, 58,* 1215–1234.

O'Leary, K.D., & Smith, D.A. (1991). Marital interactions. *Psychological Review, 42,* 191–212.

O'Leary, K.D., & Vivian, D. (1990). Physical aggression in marriage. In F.D. Fincham & T.N. Bradbury (Eds.), *The psychology of marriage: Basic issues and applications* (pp. 323–348). New York: Guilford Press.

O'Leary, K.D., Vivian, D., & Malone, J. (1992). Assessment of physical aggression against women in marriage: The need for multimodal assessment. *Behavior Assessment, 14,* 5–14.

Pan, H.S, Neidig, P.H., & O'Leary, K.D. (1994). Predicting mild and severe husband to wife physical aggression. *Journal of Consulting and Clinical Psychology, 62,* 975–981.

Pesce, C. (1990, October 4). Inmates' hope for freedom to start over. *USA Today,* pp. 1–2.

Pirog-Good, J., & Stets, J. (1986). Programs for abusers: Who drops out and what can be done. *Response, 9,* 17–19.

Prochaska, J.O., DiClemente, C.C., & Norcross, J.C. (1992). In search of how people change: Applications to addictive behaviors. *American Psychologist, 47,* 1102–1114.

Ptacek, J. (1988). Why do men batter their wives? In K. Yllo & M. Bograd (Eds.), *Feminist perspectives on wife abuse* (pp. 133–157). Newbury Park, CA: Sage.

Raue, P.J., & Goldfried, M.R. (1994). The therapeutic alliance in cognitive-behavior therapy. In A.O. Horvath & L.S. Greenberg (Eds.), *The working alliance: Theory, research, & practice* (pp. 131–152). New York: Wiley.

Riggs, D.S., Murphy, C.M., & O'Leary, K.D. (1989). Intentional falsification in reports of interpartner aggression. *Journal of Interpersonal Violence, 4,* 220–232.

Rogers, C.R. (1957). The necessary and sufficient conditions for therapeutic personality change. *Journal of Consulting Psychology, 22,* 95–103.

Rosewater, L.B. (1985). Schizophrenic, borderline, or battered? In L.B. Rosewater & L.E.A. Walker (Eds.), *Handbook of feminist therapy: Women's issues in psychotherapy* (pp. 215–225). New York: Springer.

Russell, D.E.H. (1982). *Rape in marriage.* New York: Macmillan.

Schumacher, J., & O'Leary, K.D. (1998). *The link between alcohol and physical abuse of partner*. Unpublished manuscript, State University of New York at Stony Brook.

Smith, T.W., Sanders, J.D., & Alexander, J.F. (1990). What does the Cook and Medley hostility scale measure? Affect, behavior and attributions in the marital context. *Journal of Personality and Social Psychology, 58,* 699–708.

Snell, J.E., Rosenwald, R.J., & Robey, A. (1964). The wife-beater's wife: A study of family interaction. *Archives of General Psychiatry, 11,* 107–113.

Sonkin, D.J., Martin, D., & Walker, L.E.A. (1985). *The male batterer: A treatment approach.* New York: Springer.

Stets, J.E., & Straus, M.A. (1990). Gender differences in reporting marital violence and its medical and psychological consequences. In M. Straus & R. Gelles (Eds.), *Physical violence in American families: Risk factors and adaptations in 8,145 families* (pp. 151–165). New Brunswick, NJ: Transaction Books.

Straus, M.A. (1979). Measuring intrafamily conflict and violence: The conflict tactics scale. *Journal of Marriage and the Family, 41,* 75–88.

Straus, M.A. (1996). The conflict tactics scales and its critics: An evaluation and new data on validity and reliability. The conflict tactics (CT) scales. In M.A. Straus & R.J. Gelles (Eds.), *Physical violence in American families* (pp. 49–73). New Brunswick, NJ: Transaction Press.

Straus, M.A., Gelles, R.J., & Steinmetz, S.K. (1980). *Behind closed doors: Violence in the American family.* Garden City, NY: Anchor/Doubleday.

Straus, M.A., Hamby, S.L., Boney-McCoy, S., & Sugarman, D.B. (1996). The revised conflict tactics scales (CTS2): Development and preliminary psychometric data. *Journal of Family Issues, 17,* 283–316.

Strupp, H.H., & Binder, J.L. (1984). *Psychotherapy in a new key: A guide to time-limited dynamic psychotherapy.* New York: Basic Books.

Tolman, R.M. (1989). The validation of a measure of psychological maltreatment of women by their male partners. *Violence and Victims, 4,* 159–178.

Tolman, R.M. (1999). The validation of the psychological maltreatment of women inventory. *Violence and Victims, 14.*

Vivian, D., & Heyman, R.E. (1996). Is there a place for conjoint treatment of couple violence? *In Session: Psychotherapy in Practice, 25,* 25–48.

Walker, L. (1979). *The battered woman.* New York: Harper & Row.

Walker, L. (1989). *Terrifying love: Why battered women kill and how society responds.* New York: Harper & Row.

West, C.G., Fernandez, A., Hillard, J.R., Schoof, M., & Parks, J. (1990). Psychiatric disorders of abused women at a shelter. *Psychiatric Quarterly, 61,* 295–301.

Wettstein, R.M. (1984). The prediction of violent behavior and the duty to protect third parties. *Behavioral Sciences and the Law, 2,* 291–317.

CHAPTER 4

Legal and Systems Issues in the Assessment of Family Violence Involving Children

SANDRA T. AZAR and CHAMPIKA K. SOYSA

WHEN MENTAL health professionals become involved in legal procedures, they typically do so with mixed emotions. Their training has often not prepared them for the roles they will be asked to play or even the "language" of the legal process. They may experience particular uneasiness regarding their expertise when confronted with child abuse and neglect cases,[1] given limitations in both the knowledge base in child maltreatment and in family and parenting risk assessment methods (Azar, Fantuzzo, & Twentyman, 1984; Azar, Benjet, Fuhrmann, & Cavallero, 1995; Budd & Holdsworth, 1996; Grisso, 1986; Heinze & Grisso, 1996; National Research Council, 1993).

The material presented here is designed to sensitize professionals to issues encountered in child abuse and neglect cases and the current level of our field's capacity to respond. It begins with a general overview of the epistemological conflicts and terminology that may confuse us and divert us from carrying out our work when we enter the legal arena. With this foundation, the sections that follow highlight specific assessment roles that we are asked to play in family violence cases involving children and the related legal issues, ending with a discussion of future concerns facing the field.

This chapter is aimed at professionals new to this work, but elaborates on recent issues that more experienced clinicians may find useful. Entering this work should not be done naively. Specialized training and legal consultation are essential. Also, since

---

[1] This chapter deals with child maltreatment primarily. However, such cases often involve another form of family violence, domestic violence and, therefore, such cases are touched on briefly. Domestic violence issues affecting children, however, can also occur in divorce cases. Although issues may be similar (e.g., potential for harm should the child continue to be exposed to such a violent parent), the reader is referred to Chapter 12 for more information.

statutes constantly change and differ by state, readers are warned that they should not rely solely on the material presented, but become aware of current local standards.

GENERAL LEGAL ISSUES

The relationship between mental health professionals and the legal system has been called an "uneasy alliance." At best, clinicians are seen as providing the court with data that is crucial to its decision making (Lanyon, 1986; Melton, Petrila, Poythress, & Slobogin, 1987; Myers, 1993). At worst, they have been viewed by legal scholars as "crystal ball" readers, adding little to the legal process or even detracting from its validity (Faust & Ziskin, 1988; Morse, 1978; Smith, 1989).

Although the reality probably lies somewhere between these two perspectives, an appreciation of the two fields' differences is critical for facilitating a collaborative effort that serves the best interest of children. Conflicts arising out of such differences can be a source of tension and of distraction in carrying out professional duties (e.g., raising issues regarding the limits of expertise). Two points of conflict/confusion are outlined here: (1) conflicting epistemologies and overlapping roles, and (2) confusion regarding the meaning and significance of specific legal terms.

Epistemological Conflicts and Boundary Issues

Although forensic texts have outlined many points of conflict, probably the most basic occurs around goals. Generally, the mental health system's goal is to be helpful to those seeking its assistance.[2] The legal system on the other hand has as its primary goal "truth seeking" (i.e., answering the *ultimate issue* before the court). It seeks to identify wrongdoing, to assign blame, and to engage in decision making as part of a restitution process (e.g., Did sexual abuse occur? Who was the perpetrator?). In some abuse cases, it also may seek to determine whether a child's "rights" under the law have been violated to such an extent that society may rightfully intrude in family life and take action (e.g., remove the child). Clinicians rarely attempt to arrive at such black-and-white pictures of the families they encounter. Rather, they are trained to be comfortable with approximations to "truth" through understanding family members' perceptions of reality. They also do not see themselves as agents of change, but rather strive to create an environment where individuals can take actions for themselves. On these bases alone, clashes are inevitable.

These goal discrepancies are most clearly reflected in the discourse of the two professions. Clinicians are concerned with children's "needs," but these do not always coincide with children's "rights" under the law (Rodham, 1979). Even the use of the term "abuse" itself has been shown to differ between the two professions (Giovanonni & Becerra, 1979). These differing emphases can lead to misunderstandings and frustration as clinical testimony is considered and legal actions are taken. For example, an attorney might want a psychologist to assert that a parent *lied* regarding an event; whereas the psychologist may want to describe the parent's *misperception* of the event or "cognitive distortion." The latter leads to an intervention (e.g.,

---

[2] Indeed, it has been pointed out that child abuse experts' commitment to child advocacy may call into question their credibility and objectivity (Levy, 1989).

using cognitive restructuring; Azar, 1989), while the former leads to decision making regarding culpability (Melton et al., 1987).

Contrasts also exist in how information is treated. The legal system is essentially an adversarial one, where "truth" comes out of a debate. Lawyers, therefore, want to highlight data supporting their position and attempt to block that which does not. In addition, once a legal ruling is made, it stands as reality. Clinicians, on the other hand, seek as much information as possible, even if it leads to ambiguity. Indeed, they are willing to consider some information as credible that courts might not (e.g., child victim reports; Saunders, 1988). Moreover, the picture that is presented is always subject to revision. Clinicians, therefore, are uncomfortable when asked to make blanket statements (e.g., this parent is "unfit"). Lawyers may be restless with clinicians' inability to give anything but judgments laced with qualifiers and may press for clinicians to comment on *ultimate issues* before the court (e.g., based on our expertise, whether children should be permanently removed from parents) or want them to respond in ways that violate ethical standards or guidelines put forth by our professional organizations (American Psychological Association, 1991, 1994).

Some writers have questioned this stark picture of goal discrepancy. As Stromberg et al. (1988) put it, "Beneath the legal garb lies a profound process of resolving human relationships, which after all is the province of psychology" (p. 598). The legal system must grapple with the competing legal *interests* of the parties involved in such cases (e.g., children's need to be protected versus their need to live with their family) (Brooks, Perry, Starr, & Teply, 1994; Fraser, 1976). In addition, Melton and Wilcox (1989) describe a recent move toward "legal realism" in family law, that is, a philosophical shift toward striving for congruence between law and social welfare. This shift, however, has been lamented by some as detracting from the already difficult role of the legal system, calling for limits on clinicians' roles in the process (Morse, 1978).

These conflicting views are played out within court sessions around the level of inference allowed in clinical testimony (i.e., how close it may come to commenting on the "ultimate legal issue" [the question before the court]). In outlining the debate, Slobogin (1989) delineated seven levels of inference that might be included in testimony. Understanding the distinctions he has outlined is crucial in identifying at what level testimony may be subject to challenge and the level at which clinicians might remain within the limits of their expertise. Level 1 involves testimony given as a behavioral observer (e.g., "the parent was observed to touch the child roughly"). Level 2 involves a progression to a higher level of inference by providing a label to the behavior that has psychological meaning (e.g., "the parents were intrusive in their responses to the child"). Going further would be testimony making general statements about mental state and assigning a "diagnosis" (Levels 3 and 4) (e.g., "the parent's responses are consistent with a generally aversive parenting style and are similar to those displayed by abusive parents"). Levels 5 through 7 address issues that lead to greater and greater focus on the *ultimate* legal question and might include statements such as "this parent is likely to abuse the child again and appears not to have responded to treatment provided" to "the parent is not likely to benefit from treatment and further contact with the child should be terminated (Level 7)." Some clinicians believe that testimony should be allowed at all levels, while the American Bar Association would bar testimony at Level 7; legal writers have suggested more severe limitations (only through Level 4). At the extreme, Morse (1978) would limit clinicians' testimony to only Level 1 statements, arguing that legal and moral decision making are issues around which clinicians do not have specialized knowledge. In contrast, other legal scholars argue that the setting will rectify any problems in the data presented (i.e., adversarial testing). That is, the legal process will work as it should in theory, that the participants are competent, and that the limitations of the inferences will be clearly delineated (Slobogin, 1989). As is highlighted later, a similar debate also exists in the mental health field (Azar et al., 1995). For example, it has been argued that ultimate legal questions never correspond to specific psychological functions (e.g., diagnosis; Hoge & Grisso, 1992). In practice, however, mental health professionals continue to be asked questions at all levels. Moves are underway within the profession to clarify this issue (APA, 1998).

Whatever the final outcome of this debate, it highlights the need for sensitivity to role boundary issues, particularly for caseworkers who work very closely with lawyers in child abuse cases. Practices in many communities have blurred the lines between the work of lawyers and that of social service personnel. For example, Russel (1988) noted that in many locations, due to a scarcity of attorney time, caseworkers actually draft sections of petitions that are later filed in court. In addition, the caseworkers and attorneys she surveyed disagreed on ll of 28 task areas as to who should have primary responsibility, including deciding whether a child should testify or be placed outside the home and referring a case for criminal prosecution. Such "jurisdictional disputes," as they have been called in the sociological literature (Moore, 1970), can lead to friction.

Role strain can also develop between mental health professionals as they transact with the legal system. For example, once child protective services decides to take the drastic step of moving to terminate parental rights, a psychological process of dissonance reduction may take place within caseworkers whereby every piece of data elicited is viewed within the light of that decision. When an independent evaluation by a clinician outside the system is ordered, it may then be *assumed* that the clinician's opinion will confirm the caseworkers' views (i.e., that the parent is "unfit" and cannot "be fixed"). Any "hope" noted in the evaluation may, therefore, be viewed with dismay. The referral "agenda" needs to be clarified before such an evaluation is undertaken, to short-circuit the potential for later conflict (Azar & Wolfe, 1998). As noted later, this "agenda" may change in the course of the evaluation and thus, the assessment question(s), as the evaluator understood it (them) to be, may need to be outlined in any report written and shifts in purposes for which a report will be used may need to be anticipated and any limitations outlined.

Internal role conflict can also occur. The roles of therapist and that of forensic evaluator are not the same. In therapy, for example, one is concerned with timing one's interpretations to client's readiness to benefit from them, placing them in context, and providing information in a nurturant environment. In forensic work, one does not have control over the flow of information in the court setting, and information can be presented out of context, and thus may cause harm.

Fortunately, attempts at working through the difficulties inherent in these goal and role discrepancies in myriad legal domains are being carried out on a systemwide level as evidenced by recent publications (Grisso, 1986; Matarazzo, 1990; Melton et al., 1987) and professional guidelines (APA, 1991, 1994, 1998). Since the previous edition of this book, joint law/psychology programs and workshops to provide training in such work have increased (e.g., APA, 1997, lists 14 programs with specializations in law and psychology). A spectrum of models of training in forensic work have recently been outlined from specializations to pre- and postdoctoral training, to joint degree programs (see Bersoff et al., 1997).

Despite strains, successful collaboration among professionals is particularly important in cases involving family violence and children. Designing ways in which to respond to legal questions, minimizing child trauma and, when possible, keeping families intact are major issues with which the law continually grapples and ones in which the mental health field is specially equipped to play a role. If some level of mutual understanding can be gained, facilitating interactions can occur.

BASIC LEGAL TERMS AND DISTINCTIONS

Along with being sensitive to differences in assumptions, clinicians need to be knowledgeable about basic aspects of the law . This may require ongoing legal consultation. Without such knowledge and consultation, clinicians may make errors in presentation of materials or misinterpret the goals of lawyers' questions during testimony resulting in harm. For example, data that may be meaningless in psychological terms (e.g., an increase of 3 points in IQ from pre- to posttreatment) may be used by a lawyer inappropriately to fit some element of a statute (e.g., that the parent did in fact make "progress" in treatment). Some basic terms and distinctions are crucial in legal cases (see Melton et al., 1987; Stromberg et al., 1988, for more details).

First, testimony may be provided by clinicians as either a "fact" witness or as an "expert" witness. In the former instance, clinicians deal with facts (thoughts or perceptions) that are within their experience. Expression of opinions, with some exceptions, are not allowed. An expert, on the other hand, provides the decision maker (typically a judge in abuse cases) with facts and opinions beyond the experience of average people (Stromberg et al., 1988). A person is "qualified" as an expert by virtue of knowledge, skill, experience, training, or education specific to the question under consideration (Bolocofsky, 1989). In child abuse cases, this would mean experience with child or adult assessment, especially around parenting and child abuse issues. Since judges often have limited background in mental health, these criteria may be interpreted rather liberally in child custody cases (Hirsch, 1985).

As "experts," clinicians should be prepared to be questioned on a variety of basic professional topics (e.g., diagnostic criteria, the validity of instruments), as well as the material collected on the individuals involved in the case (Matarazzo, 1990). Indeed, their provision of scientific evidence is admissible only if the methods and procedures that contributed to their opinions meet professional and scientific standards (the so-called *Frye* test, *Frye v. United States,* 1923). While it has been suggested by some that the *Frye* test has been taken to mean the accuracy of the expert's opinion (Faust & Ziskin, 1988), it has been argued that it merely refers to whether the evidence from which the clinician's deduction has been made is sufficiently established to have gained general acceptance in the field (Hoge & Grisso, 1992). Given the adversarial process, attempts may also be made to discredit expert testimony and volumes have been published to aid lawyers here[3] (Ziskin, 1981). For example, a lawyer may quote a recent article in an obscure journal that refutes conclusions made. A well-prepared evaluator can respond with the scientific evidence supporting his or her views with due

---

[3] Mental health experts are also employed by lawyers as consultants for this purpose. While the typical parent involved in child abuse cases is not likely to have the resources to do this, evaluators may still be asked by a parent's lawyer for advice regarding the interpretation or validity of another clinician's evaluations or, in testifying, may be questioned regarding this issue.

consideration of its limitations. Clinicians must be cautious, however, to resist responding to what has been described in some cases as the judicial system's "unquenchable thirst" for the input of mental health professionals. This may lead them to go beyond the limits of generally accepted knowledge (Azar & Benjet, 1994; Hoge & Grisso, 1992).

A second set of distinctions occurs around *rules of evidence.* The law may have very different views on what is credible or even allowable evidence for consideration and for taking action. This varies with the type of court in which a case is heard. In criminal court, where perpetrators of abuse are typically prosecuted, the criterion for action is evidence "beyond a shadow of a doubt"; whereas in family or juvenile court, where child custody decisions are usually made, actions may be taken when the "preponderance of the evidence" favors it (i.e., a lower standard of proof). Thus, more challenging of testimony may occur in the former court.

There is also special handling of information that is *prejudicial* to a defendant. For example, restrictions may be placed on how much historical information is available to the evaluator (e.g., parents' past psychiatric records). The clinician may decide she cannot carry out a valid evaluation under such conditions. Parts of the report or the entire report may also be blocked from being entered into evidence for similar reasons.

Rules regarding *hearsay* may be invoked in such cases. (i.e., exclusion of testimony that involves statements by a person not available to the court). For instance, statements from agency records may be blocked if the persons making them (e.g., past caseworkers) are not present for questioning or the record itself is not available in the courtroom for entering into evidence.

A final area of importance involves *confidentiality* and *privilege.* Confidentiality refers to the ethical and sometimes legal duty to maintain the secrecy of client's communications. Privilege refers to protection from being required by the legal system to reveal confidences (Blau, 1984). Protection varies with conditions in the legal system. While communications in therapy are typically protected by statute, the law requires that confidentiality be violated when suspicions of abuse occur. Purely evaluative relationships created by third parties (courts) typically are not protected. The exact protections accorded evaluations depend on who the client is. If the person's lawyer is requesting the evaluation, then some protection of the use of this evaluation is provided. This lawyer may decide to use the report material or not. Thus, the prosecution or agency attorney may not have access to the report. If the court has ordered the evaluation, with the court's permission,[4] all attorneys involved may have access to the material and any of it may find itself read in open court. This raises ethical dilemmas (i.e., the mandate not to do harm).

Limits to confidentiality must be stated to the person being evaluated clearly before beginning, otherwise the report may be invalid for legal use. If the evaluation is being conducted for the courts, the individual should be informed that in consenting to the evaluation, he or she is consenting to disclosure of the evaluation's findings in the context of the forthcoming litigation and in any other proceedings deemed necessary by the courts (the so-called *Lamb* warning). The APA guidelines for divorce custody

---

[4] Clinicians need to be knowledgeable regarding rules for releasing reports. For example, although all attorneys may ultimately have access to evaluations ordered by judges for the courts' use, release of the report may only be done with the judge's permission. Thus, the clinician cannot supply a copy on his or her own to an attorney who requests one.

evaluations (APA, 1994) require that a waiver of confidentiality be obtained from all adult participants or from their authorized legal representatives and this may be a wise practice in all circumstances.[5] Opportunities should also be provided for the person who is to be evaluated to withdraw. Legal constraints, however, may make this an empty offer (e.g., sanctions may be in place for failure to comply with a court-ordered evaluation). Assessment material may still be tainted by the legal process and judgments regarding the extent to which this is true must be stated in reports or testimony. The confidentiality of minors in abuse cases (e.g., investigatory interviews with child victims) has not received much attention, although discussions have occurred in the child therapy literature (Knapp & Vandercreek, 1985; Taylor & Adelman, 1989).

The material in this section merely touches the surface of the complexity of the legal process. When required in the following sections, further clarifications are provided. Extra training and consultation are crucial to ensure an adequate understanding for participation in these cases.

MENTAL HEALTH PROFESSIONALS AND THE LEGAL PROCESS IN CHILD ABUSE CASES

Figure 4.1 provides a flowchart of the typical movement of child abuse cases through the social service and court systems indicating the points at which clinicians' work may interface with the legal process. Three major phases (Reporting, Investigation, and Disposition) are delineated in the sections that follow, and the assessment roles that mental health professionals play within each are described. Standards for answering the legal questions in each phase are provided where appropriate. It must be reiterated that legal statutes vary. For example, different laws exist in military and American Indian communities (Fischler, 1985; Miller, 1976). In addition, statutes are constantly changing and the material provided may become obsolete before this chapter even goes to print. For example, at the time of the first edition of this book, states were enacting various statutes allowing child victims of sexual abuse to be spared from having to be face to face with their alleged perpetrators (e.g., use of depositions, allowing them to testify behind screens). Initially, some court decisions did not support many of these strategies, favoring the constitutional rights of defendants to face their accusers (Gordon, 1992). More recent decisions have held that *some* children may be traumatized by testifying and, therefore, direct testifying in the presence of the defendant in these cases may not be required by the court (Small & Melton, 1994). Hearsay exceptions also may be allowed, whereby therapists, pediatricians, and others are permitted under certain circumstances to describe what a child has said to them (Ceci & Bruck, 1995). There has also been experimentation with mandated videotaping of interviews (Child Victim Witness Investigative Pilot Projects, 1994), allowing alternatives for children unable to testify.

It must also be noted that we have artificially separated the phases in the process. In practice, multiple questions are put before most clinicians by the courts. Indeed, the initial referral question may change in the midst of an evaluation or a legal proceeding. Prior to accepting a case and to report writing or testifying, clinicians should delineate clearly the areas of knowledge on which they can legitimately comment to the court

---

[5] See the *Specialty Guidelines for Forensic Psychologists* (APA, 1991) for further information regarding informed consent.

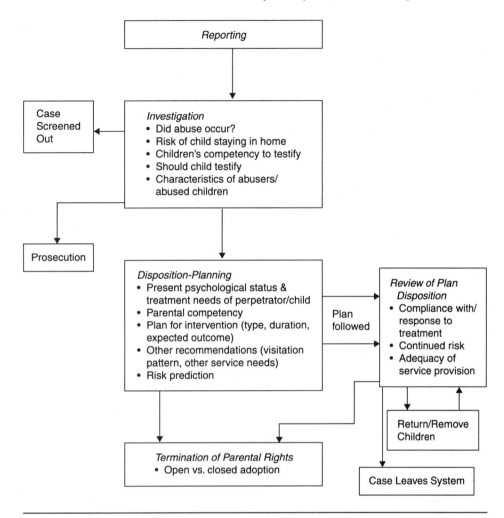

Figure 4.1   Movement of Child Abuse Cases through Social Service and Legal Systems.

or referral agent at the outset, in written reports, and during testimony. Resisting efforts to comment on areas outside this *territory* of expertise is essential. If "educated" comments are possible, limits to their validity should be stated. Even with this, testimony may be used in a manner not intended (e.g., a report done for treatment planning being used as baseline for terminating parental rights). Forensic clinicians should be aware of the potential uses of their data and where possible, they should note limitations to its use.

ENTRANCE INTO THE SYSTEM: REPORTING

Since 1964, all states have enacted laws that require reporting of suspected child abuse or neglect. In the authors' state, abuse is defined as the nonaccidental commission of an act by a caretaker that causes or creates a substantial risk of serious physical or emotional injury to a child. Abuse may be physical or sexual. Neglect is defined as the intentional withholding of necessary food, clothing, shelter, or medical care by a care-taker (Mass. Gen. L., ch. 119, 51A). These legal definitions cite individuals in the role of "caretaker," thus abuse by a noncaretaker (e.g., adult or other child/teenager not in this role) would be covered under assault statutes and not abuse statutes in Massachu-setts. Reporters' anonymity is typically protected in abuse laws and "good faith" re-porters are generally immune from civil liability and criminal penalty.

Over the years, the professionals required to report have expanded from only physi-cians to include teachers, nurses, social workers, psychologists, and staff in out-of-home settings (e.g., residential care). In Massachusetts, mandated reporters include psycholo-gists, physicians, dentists, osteopaths, chiropractors, podiatrists, nurses, school person-nel, social workers, police officers, and any other person responsible for the care of children. Laws indicate who must report, to whom abuse must be reported, and the form and content of the report. It is important to note that the fact the parent might be seeking treatment for his or her child does not absolve the professional of the duty to report (Brant, 1991). Because of diversity in the wording of laws and local practices, profes-sionals must be familiar with their own state's procedures.

Laws also have provisions for individuals who refuse to accept this obligation to protect children, most carrying specific criminal penalty and a number establishing civil liability (Besharov, 1987). Potential fines range from $100 up to $1,000 and im-prisonment from 5 days to 1 year.

Key in most statutes are words like "suspected" or "risk" of harm. Definitive proof is not required. Prompt reporting can be crucial, in that documentation of abuse is dif-ficult and if physical evidence is not present at the time of investigation, action may not be taken. Even if proof is not strong, reporting is recommended as subsequent reports may be taken more seriously. In many cases, it is only after multiple reports that ac-tions to protect a child can be taken. Indeed, reports made after one has already been substantiated have a higher substantiation rate (Wells, 1985).

Over the past few decades, reporting has continued to increase (e.g., overall in-crease of 331% in the rate of substantiated reports since 1976, with the majority of this increase in reporting of physical abuse, up 58%, and sexual abuse, up 300%; NCCAN, 1995). Underreporting, however, is still a problem (Burgdorf, 1980, 1988; Garbarino, 1989). A national survey estimated that only 44% of the cases found through community settings (e.g., hospital, schools) that met criterion for abuse were known to child protective services (Burgdorf, 1988). Many reasons have been given for failures to report. First, the professional status of the reporter (Giovanonni & Becerra, 1979), the minority and/or socioeconomic status of the family (Turbett & O'Toole, 1980), the social attractiveness of the potential perpetrator and victim child (Jensen & Nicholas, 1984), and the age of the child (Pagelow, 1989) have been shown to affect re-porting. Fears of legal entanglement (e.g., testifying in court and being questioned regarding expertise), loss of the therapeutic relationship with the family, and the po-tential for trauma to the child and parents may also prevent it (Zellman, 1990). Seeking knowledge about what happens once a report is made before the occasion arises may help to allay some such fears. Another obstacle to reporting may be the reaction of other professionals. A supervisor or administrator may discourage reporting. Particu-larly vulnerable to such biases is abuse discovered in an institutional setting. While a few states now have statutes protecting employees from retaliation for reporting (Besharov, 1987), they are still not widespread. This fact may deter reports.

Over the past few decades, the mandate of protective service agencies and the legal system has been to keep families intact, protect the child, and provide help to the family (e.g., support services, therapeutic help). For many parents, therefore, being reported may be seen as a relief that someone has noticed that they are at the end of their rope. As numbers have increased and resources decreased, however, there have been recent reports in the media that the social service system has begun to move back toward quicker prosecution of parents and removal of children from the home (Swarns, 1997). If this trend continues, we may see an impact on reporting.

Despite potential positive outcomes of reporting maltreatment, the possibility for negative impact on families has received some discussion in recent professional publications (Denton, 1987; Emery & Billings, 1998). Concerns include the iatrogenic impact of labeling (e.g., increasing resistance to intervention), failures of the system to provide real interventions to families once they are identified, and subjecting already traumatized children to further trauma (e.g., foster care). Some evidence supports such concerns. For example, Schene (1991) noted that despite an increase of 55% in abuse reporting between 1980 and 1985, there was only a 2% increase in resources at federal, state and local levels combined (U.S. House of Representatives Select Committee, 1987). More recent surveys have suggested a dearth of services in most states (Berkowitz & Sedlak, 1993). Despite these concerns, however, the impact of failing to report and the possibility of further injury to the child should take precedence. Not reporting may mean a vulnerable child is left unprotected. In cases where a reporter feels the outcome is unsatisfactory (e.g., not enough was done to protect a child), he or she may speak with the CPS supervisor in charge and in some states procedures exist whereby any adult may bring the case to the attention of juvenile court where further actions to protect a child may be ordered (McKittrick, 1981).

A final word of warning regarding failure to report is needed for clinicians working with already identified abusive families. Recidivism rates in maltreatment are high (from 20% to 70% of cases; Cohn & Daro, 1986). It is easy to become "desensitized" to potential maltreatment when abusive families are one's entire caseload. Treatment teams may safeguard against such failures to report.

What happens once the report is made? In some states, the police are immediately involved; in others, except where a perpetrator is charged (e.g., rape of a child), only child welfare staff are involved. Reporters are typically interviewed over the phone to determine children's immediate risk, with a more detailed follow-up interview at a later time. (Some cases are "screened out" at this juncture as not fitting "mandated reporting" or outside agency's jurisdiction, e.g., rape of a child by a stranger may be a police matter. A record, however, is often still made in case another report should occur.) After the verbal report, many states require reporters to file a written one stating briefly the cause for suspicion. Only information pertinent to the maltreatment suspicions should be shared. It is only here that confidentiality can be breached within legal and ethical mandates.

Most states require an investigation within a specified time period and in extreme cases, the response is immediate (e.g., temporary removal of the child from the home with a more long-term arrangement made when additional data has been elicited). Removal typically involves the legal system, but it is uncommon for clinicians to be involved in investigations or removal decision making. A recent exception is a role played in the investigation of sexual abuse. Clinicians are providing testimony based either on their own investigation and/or the literature on the effects of abuse. While the old roles in the dispositional phase (e.g., evaluation of parental fitness for termination of parental rights) have limitations and pitfalls to be discussed later, this new investigatory role has even more difficulties (Melton & Limber, 1989). Further, substantiation of abuse does not mean it will lead to a court action (e.g., a prosecution of a perpetrator). Fewer than one half of cases result in criminal prosecution (Portwood, Reppucci, & Mitchell, 1997). Alternative or mandatory treatment is often substituted for criminal penalties such as probation or incarceration (Fridell, 1991; Tjaden & Thoennes, 1992). Whether prosecution will occur, however, is not known at the time a clinician is asked to conduct an evaluation. Thus, any attempt to substantiate the occurrence of abuse needs to meet legal criteria. This role in the legal process is described next.

THE INVESTIGATION AND PROSECUTION—INTERVIEWER AND EXPERT WITNESS TESTIMONY

While children's divulging sexual abuse may precipitate the entrance into the legal system, it is a rare case where their word alone is enough to take legal actions to protect them. First, a portion of sexual abuse occurs to children under the age of ten. Until recently, the credibility of young children was open to question by most legal standards. Although some relaxing of these criteria has occurred, young children's testimony still presents difficulties that may need to be addressed by the clinician. Also, unlike physical abuse (i.e., battering), visible evidence of maltreatment is often lacking or inconclusive in sexual abuse. For example, in many cases "lower" levels of abuse have occurred (e.g., fondling, showing pornographic pictures, photographing), leaving no physical evidence. Even with older children and teenagers, buttressing their testimony may, therefore, be helpful. Finally, the trauma of testifying may be too great for children and if they are unable to testify, it may only be with clear psychological testimony that a case may proceed (e.g., in *White v. Illinois,* 1992, cited in Kermani, 1993, the testimony of a 4-year-old made to a physician immediately following an incident of abuse was used to support that of the child, when the child broke down in the courtroom on two occasions).

Of the multitude of issues that might be discussed in doing investigatory assessments, only a few areas will be highlighted here, including: (1) professional preparation (e.g., understanding pediatricians' reports on physical evidence); (2) the conducting of legally valid interviews; (3) assessing children's trauma should they testify; and (4) assessing their competency to testify.

Preparation Issues

Assessment should always be restricted to areas within one's expertise, but as part of drawing conclusions regarding molestation, clinicians may have access to findings from a physical examination. Failure to understand the meaningfulness of such findings can bias the manner in which further psychological information is collected and interpreted (e.g., taking physical findings as strong evidence may lead to a more firmly stated question to the child than would occur otherwise). For physical abuse and neglect, physical findings have historically played a major part in substantiation (e.g., evidence of poor growth, atypical injury patterns; Schmitt, 1980). With increases in sexual abuse reports, doctors have experienced pressure to discover analogous abnormalities that might document children's claim of molestation (i.e., evidence of penetration).

Physical findings, or lack thereof, may not provide definitive evidence. For example, initially some studies indicated increased hymen diameter among sexually abused children. With later findings, however, it was found that using this indicator at least one in four girls in the general population would have a positive test with only a small of percentage of these having actually experienced penile penetration (Paradise, 1989). This has prompted work to establish normal hymen appearance across development and changes over time to provide normative information against which to judge physical findings (Berenson, 1993; Berenson, Heger, & Andrews, 1991; Berenson, Heger, Hayes, Bailey, & Emans, 1992). Such work will provide some assistance in this area.

Along with understanding physical findings, clinicians need to consider the experience of the physician who carried out the examination. Family physicians continue to be the ones most likely to do such examinations and they typically do not have legal expertise. If involved in making recommendations, physicians with expertise in identifying sexual abuse should be selected to minimize children's trauma (Madansky & Santora, 1989) and to provide the information necessary for testimony. Finally, it must also be noted that physical findings are not required to corroborate sexual assault even under the stringent standards of proof in criminal proceedings (Paradise, 1989).

Careful developmental knowledge of children's memory abilities, their ability to conceptualize complex events, understand moral dilemmas, and potential for suggestibility is crucial in conducting valid assessments, as well as to withstand legal challenges to conclusions reached (Bruck, Ceci, & Hembrooke, 1998; Ceci & Bruck, 1995; Goodman, 1984; Melton & Limber, 1989). Goodman (1984) gives the useful example of a 3-year-old boy who gave in great detail the events surrounding his molestation by a stranger when asked about what happened in the perpetrator's "apartment," but whose case was not pursued because he denied the abuse when the questioning officer used the descriptor "house." At this age, a "house" and an "apartment" are not interchangeable. A better prepared interviewer might have been sensitive to this issue, allowing the prosecution to take place. Unfortunately, while research in this area has been steadily improving, all that is required to respond to challenges may not be available as yet, reducing clinical judgments at times to "informed speculation" (Melton & Limber, 1989). Ceci and Bruck (1995) go so far as to argue that few practicing clinicians have the level of expertise to do such interviews and be expert witnesses.

Interviewing Children Regarding Abuse for Legal Purposes

While clinicians have expertise in interviewing children, the need for such interviews to meet legal standards of evidence adds new dimensions. "Mistakes" made from the legal standpoint may have major repercussions in terms of the system's ability to protect vulnerable children.[6] For this reason, there has been a growth in special clinical teams with expertise in conducting these interviews. Unfortunately, such teams may not be available everywhere, which means that individual practitioners may need to develop the necessary skills. As noted earlier, this may be very difficult for the average clinician.

Adaptations of clinical practice are needed to accommodate the legal process. Because multiple interviews of children are often required (from deposition taking to trials), videotaping has become common to protect them from trauma, as well as to aid in the legal process. Children's emotional reaction to "telling their story" may become more neutral over multiple interviews and thus, less believable in court. Early studies also indicated that recanting allegations in sexual abuse cases was common (Sorenson

---

[6] Ceci and Bruck (1995) persuasively argue for the idea that harm can also be done to children by poorly prepared interviewers' overly zealous questioning.

& Snow, 1991), although a recent review of the literature argues that it may not be as common as first thought (as few as 3% to 5% of cases; Bruck et al., 1998). Since perpetrators are often family members, children may experience pressure to recant or feel concerned at testifying against someone they love. In such cases, the initial videotaped interviews may be entered into evidence. They may also be used to reduce the children's time on the witness stand (i.e., entered as their testimony with opportunities for live cross-examination).

Investigatory interviews with sexually abused children and adolescents should cover five content areas: (1) who was involved, (2) what happened, (3) when the abuse occurred, (4) where the incident occurred, and (5) whether the perpetrator coerced the victim. The interview may also establish children's ability to act as witnesses, although this may be done in a separate situation (discussed in a later section). Important issues from a legal standpoint include the setup of the interview (e.g., who is present) and quality of questions asked. It has been recommended that no contact with the child occur prior to the interview to prevent defense attorneys challenging that the child was rehearsed or coached. Whereas the interviewer should develop a knowledge base about known facts in the case and the important people in the child's life (e.g., names of people in the child's environment such as relatives, friends, or teachers) to facilitate building rapport with the child, care should be taken to avoid leading questions (i.e., ones that are directive and lead, suggest, or encourage a child's answer) (Powell & Thomson, 1994). Colby and Colby (1987) give the example of asking, "Has anyone ever touched you? Who?" rather than "Did your daddy touch you?" Leading questions may invalidate the child's allegations for legal purposes. If videotaping is used, its technical qualities can also lead to challenging of data (e.g., who the tape shows, whether a timer is present on the film to document that the film has not been edited).

Anatomically correct dolls have been used in interviews investigating sexual abuse. Such dolls are believed to allow children to talk more freely about abuse or show the interviewer what they cannot articulate in words. If responses to dolls are used to supplement other information, the child's names for body parts should be established early in the interview, justifying later interpretations regarding statements made by the child. There is debate as to the utility of such doll procedures. To respond to challenges made to both the content of material collected and how it was collected, the interviewer should be well versed in the data regarding normal and abused children's responses to such dolls (e.g., August & Forman, 1989; Boat & Everson, 1988b; Sivan, Schor, Koeppl, & Noble, 1988). Whether this scientific literature is strong enough to meet legal standards is still open to question (the *Frye* test). First, the dolls being utilized in clinical practice are not standardized. Levy (1989), for example, noted that in 1987 the dolls being used in one state (North Carolina) were manufactured by 15 different companies and over half of the professionals using them relied on homemade dolls. More importantly, normative data regarding children's behavior with such dolls is limited (Jampole & Weber, 1987; White, Strom, Santilli, & Halpin, 1986). Finally, the doll interviews are not standardized. In fact most professionals using such dolls (CPS workers, police officers, clinicians, and physicians) have little training in their use (Boat & Everson, 1988b). Some efforts have been made to develop standardized protocols (Boat & Everson, 1988a; White et al., 1986). Until these problems are remedied, the evidence gathered through doll interviews may not meet the scientific standards needed for admissibility in court.

Knowledge as to developmental differences in children's ability to describe events, suggestibility, and the characteristics of the most reliable interviews has been amassed over the past decade (Bruck et al., 1998; Ceci & Bruck, 1995; Goodman, 1984; Melton, 1981). For example, even preschoolers have been shown to be able to provide accurate reports of events, although details may be sparse. Such young witnesses, however, may also be the most susceptible to suggestibility (Bruck et al., 1998). Nevertheless, all age groups have been shown to be subject to impairments in the reliability of their reports through suggestive interviewing.

Along with conducting interviews, psychologists may be asked to testify as to the child's exhibiting the "sexually abused child syndrome," a collection of symptoms allegedly associated with the experience of abuse as evidence of its occurrence, or the alleged perpetrator's sharing characteristics that are common among sexual offenders. While information bearing on the child's current psychological symptoms and evidence of trauma or the perpetrator's psychological characteristics may be well within psychologists' expertise, evidence supporting a unique syndrome associated with sexual abuse or characterizing perpetrators of abuse is weak and testimony of this sort may be without strong scientific foundation (Melton & Limber, 1989; Sagatun, 1991).

A better use of experts may be to provide data as to children's ways of coping with abuse that may be used to challenge validity of their reports. For example, a defense attorney may cite the child's delay in reporting of the incident(s) or recanting of an earlier allegation as evidence of the abuse not having occurred. Debate exists as to the interpretation of recanting. Some studies suggest that recanting is common (Gonzales, Waterman, Kelly, McCord, & Oliver, 1993; Sorenson & Snow, 1991). Other work, that may be more methodologically sound, suggests that among validated cases, only a very small percentage of children recant abuse (Bradley & Wood, 1996; Jones & McGraw, 1987). The expert witness needs to be familiar with this evidence.[7]

Evaluation for sexual abuse that occurs in the context of divorce proceedings warrants a special discussion. Such cases are emotionally charged and produce tension for all participants. Clinically based guidelines for conducting such evaluations have been provided (Benedek & Schetky, 1985; Bresee, Stearns, Bess, & Packer, 1986), but empirical work is limited. Such cases may be heard in different courts than abuse cases and involve different standards for custody decisions (i.e., "best interests of children"). Clinicians should be familiar with these criteria (Weithorn, 1987).

Should the Child or Adolescent Victim Testify?

The defendant in any trial has the constitutional right to face his or her accusers (the Sixth Amendment). Yet, asking children to face the perpetrator of violence against them has been a major concern for both legal and mental health professionals. Various alternatives have been tried, such as employing special courtrooms where the child's testimony is observed through a one-way mirror or via a closed circuit television setup, having the child testify on videotape with only cross-examination taking place in the courtroom, and using a partition blocking the child's view of the perpetrator as they testify (Libai, 1969; Small & Melton, 1994). As noted earlier, there has been much legal debate around such changes.

---

[7] This chapter does not deal with legal issues involved in civil actions being taken by adult survivors of sexual abuse. The many legal intricacies in such cases are beyond the scope of our discussion. For example, some statutes prohibit such civil actions after a certain time frame. In the case of "recovered" memories, there is now case law regarding the time frame being counted taken from the time of recovering the memories of the abuse, rather than from the time of the abuse itself ("tolling") (see Whitehead, 1992; Zoltek-Jick, 1997).

Clinicians may be asked to testify about potential damage of forcing a child to testify (i.e., to get a ruling of "psychological unavailability" freeing them from appearing) or to justify the use of special procedures. Several factors are needed for such a ruling for a *particular* child: probability of psychological injury; degree and duration of such injury; and whether expected psychological injury is substantially greater than the reaction of the average victim of rape, kidnapping, or terrorist act (Whitcomb, Shapiro, & Stellwagen, 1985). In *Maryland v. Craig* (1990), it was ruled that the emotional distress the child might experience be more than *de minimus* (i.e., more than "mere nervousness or excitement or some reluctance to testify") and that it be a reaction to the defendant's presence, not just the courtroom. Empirically based evidence for establishing these factors are limited. Clinicians must make a compelling case to protect a child from testifying.

Information is now available on the impact of testifying in court. Although potential positive outcomes have been discussed (e.g., providing the child with a sense of self-efficacy and psychological closure; Pynoos & Eth, 1984), data are lacking. More evidence has emerged for negative effects. This data prompted the APA in the *Maryland v. Craig* case (1990) to file an *amicus curiae* brief arguing that stronger research has begun to appear suggesting that child witnesses could suffer trauma as a result of confrontation in criminal trials (Small & Melton, 1994). Findings, however, are complex. One study by Gibbens and Prince (1963) found that victims who testified experienced greater trauma than those who did not. It was, however, the more severe cases that were seen in court. Goodman et al. (1992) also found more disturbance in children who had testified than matched controls, but only after seven months (controls had improved, whereas those who had testified did not). Factors associated with poorer outcome include the number of times testifying, severity of abuse, the level of maternal support, history of violence in the home, and level of fear during the testimony (Goodman et al., 1992; Sas, 1997). It has been argued that these findings should not be used to prevent children from testifying, but rather to prompt courts to make it less stressful. With more studies, testimony in this area will have a stronger scientific basis.

Assessment of Child Competency to Testify

Until recently, only children above the age of 14 were presumed competent to act as witnesses by courts (Whitcomb et al., 1985). More liberal Federal and Uniform Rules have been enacted to allow younger children to testify and their testimony to be weighed as to credibility. Many states have adopted comparable statutes. Ability to testify typically requires the establishment of the following qualities/abilities: (1) understanding of the difference between truth and falsity and an appreciation of the obligation or responsibility to speak the truth; (2) mental capacity at the time of the occurrence in question to observe or receive accurate impressions of the occurrence; (3) memory sufficient to retain an independent recollection of the observations; and (4) capacity to communicate or translate into words the memory of such observations and the capacity to understand simple questions about the occurrence. Experts must know the developmental research addressing these areas to be able to comment on the validity of children's testimony and when appropriate, to defend against attempts to question their competency (Ceci & Bruck, 1995; Goodman, 1984; Melton, 1981). This work is still experimental in nature and instruments assessing these abilities have either not been developed or do not meet professional standards for psychological tests as yet.

DISPOSITIONAL PHASE: PARENTING COMPETENCE, PREDICTION OF RISK, AND
TERMINATION OF PARENTAL RIGHTS

Once abuse is substantiated, CPS typically makes a response (e.g., removal of children). A service plan is often drawn up. This plan can be a voluntary one between the agency and the parent(s) (e.g., when abuse was minimal). When children are placed in foster care, this plan is a legal agreement stating the conditions under which consideration of returning a child will occur. [In some cases, a parent may retain physical custody, but legal conditions are put in place that, if violated, may entail loss of custody (e.g., the mother may be required to have no contact with an alleged perpetrator boyfriend)]. In this plan, an evaluation of the psychological status and treatment needs of the parent or child may be requested to identify the services needed to reunify the family. More often, formal evaluations only occur when parents fail to comply with an agency devised plan of services. The goal, then, is to set the stage for termination of parental rights (TPR) and documentation of parental unfitness and unamenability to treatment. In extreme abuse, this goal may occur earlier (at the point abuse is substantiated and children are removed). Given the legal system's adversarial nature, in TPR cases, more than one assessment may be carried out (i.e., one for each side in the dispute). Validity issues raised by this practice have not been discussed.

Interestingly, many state statues do not have provisions for mandating evaluations (Grisso, 1986). Also, although the court may appoint a lawyer for indigent parents, it may not pay for an independent evaluation on their behalf (even when it has ordered one). The conditions of payment (e.g., who will pay, reimbursement of court time), therefore, must be agreed on in advance.

Evaluators may be asked to provide data and recommendations based on their own evaluation or the literature regarding a nested set of legal questions:

1. Can the child be returned safely to the parent's custody (parental fitness/child risk) and if not, what can be done, if anything, to effect a return (e.g., services—types, duration, and expected outcome)?
2. Has the parent complied with the service plan and profited enough from the treatment and/or services offered such that the child can now be safely returned home?
3. If not, has CPS done all it could to effect the required changes?
4. If they have, should parental rights be terminated?

These dispositional questions ultimately require determinations of parental competency or "fitness" in legal terms, and prediction of risk for violence and maladaptive parenting behavior. Such questions are problematic given our current knowledge base and the availability of valid family/parenting assessment methods (Azar, Lauretti, & Loding, 1998; Budd & Holdsworth, 1996; Grisso, 1986). The defining qualities of "competent" parenting have only recently been addressed in the child development and family literature (Azar, 1989; Belsky & Vondra, 1989; Epstein, Bishop, & Baldwin, 1982). Belsky and Vondra (1989), for example, have outlined a complex model specifying parent and child characteristics and social contextual factors contributing to parenting competence. They neither assign weights to these factors nor designate valid ways to assess them. In another more systemic effort, Epstein, Bishop, and Baldwin (1982) outlined three major task areas that are crucial for optimal family functioning:

basic tasks (provisions of food, shelter), developmental tasks (meeting of the developmentally based needs of its members), and hazardous tasks (dealing with emergency situations that befall family members (e.g., illness). Six dimensions were also described on which to evaluate family functioning: behavioral control, problem solving, affective involvement, roles, affective responsiveness, and communication. The legal system has developed its own criterion for custody decision making in divorce cases (i.e., "best interests of the child"), that have pointed to similarly broad capacities within the parent and child, as well as situational factors, including the child's emotional ties between competing parties, capacity to provide food, clothing, and medical care, and the child's adjustment and wishes (Grisso, 1986). While such theoretical models and legal criteria are helpful in conducting evaluations with child abuse cases, they typically delineate qualities of optimal parenting, not minimally adequate ones (the more important question in maltreatment cases). For example, criteria for neglect, a common element of such cases (e.g., lack of supervision), are not well developed as yet (Zuravin, 1991). These criteria also do not lead directly to specification of interventions to reunify families. Thus, they address neither the development of viable service plans nor child risk and parental fitness.

Some theorists have attempted to address factors predictive of child risk that concurrently specify areas for intervention. Taking a skills approach, Azar and Twentyman (1986) outlined five areas of skill deficits associated with abuse: (1) specific parenting skills (e.g., a wide repertoire of discipline strategies, emergency skills), (2) cognitive disturbances (e.g., unrealistic expectations of children, poor problem solving, negative attributional bias toward children), (3) poor stress coping, (4) anger control problems, and (5) social skills deficits. Wolfe (1988) has also done a similar list of skills to be assessed in determining risk for abuse. An attempt to apply such approaches to court evaluations has occurred (Azar et al., 1998), although it did not address the prediction of violence, instead focusing on assessment of parenting capacities. The prediction of risk for violence has been generally difficult to achieve (Menzies, Webster, & Sepejak, 1985; Monahan, 1981, 1984), and only limited efforts have been directed at child abuse in particular (Milner, 1986, 1994), with no attempts aimed at neglect. Validity of such efforts has been questioned.

A combination of traditional instruments (e.g., MMPI) and more behaviorally based techniques (e.g., observations, child behavior problem checklists) has been suggested in evaluating abusive parents and their children (Azar & Twentyman, 1986; Wolfe, 1988). The utility of traditional assessment techniques in decision making in child abuse cases has been questioned. Aside from long-standing concerns regarding reliability and validity for court-related purposes (Lanyon, 1986), their utility for "transactional" and basic skills questions typical in abuse cases has been doubted (Azar et al., 1995; Azar et al., 1998; Grisso, 1986). For example, the relevance of intellectual ability, diagnostic status, and personality factors to those functions crucial to parenting has not been well documented, thus limiting the predictive utility of such instruments as the sole strategy. In addition, these measures' ability to predict future use of violence has long been questioned (Monahan, 1981) and most work has dealt primarily with male, not female violence, making them less relevant in assessing mothers' violence risk.

Newer behavioral techniques, while more relevant, have not as yet been standardized and normed to the extent required for court use (see Mash, 1991, for discussion of behavioral observation strategies in child abuse). Parenting instruments found in the research literature, while having potential, were not designed for legal or clinical use. They also fail to address the functions of parenting (e.g., nurturance capacities, medical care capacities) and do not have corresponding instruments for measuring the child's needs (Grisso, 1986). Finally, they were not designed for culturally or racially diverse parents (Azar & Benjet, 1994).

There has been a recent growth of custody evaluation instruments (primarily for divorce cases). Although they may provide a structure for doing evaluations, they lack evidence for their claims of validity and reliability (Heinze & Grisso, 1996). The best ones were those developed for limited purposes (e.g., parental stress). Even scales designed to measure risk for abuse, however, do not show strong enough predictive validity (e.g., high false positive rates; Caldwell, Bogat, & Davidson, 1988) (see Chapter 8 for a more detailed discussion of evaluations).

Ability to parent is always child specific. Children's needs and how parents' abilities interface with these needs must be addressed. This entails firsthand evaluations of the child(ren) individually and in interaction with the parent. In addition, the development of a database from other sources is crucial, including reports from caseworkers, teachers, foster parents, and extended family members. Testimony regarding parental psychological status without such information may have little utility in custody decision making. Empirically valid ways to assess "congruency" between parental abilities and child needs, however, have not been devised as yet (Azar et al., 1998; Grisso, 1986), making any comments here more speculative.

Along with a lack of instruments, scientific data for making recommendations regarding types and duration of treatment, visitation schedules, and support services is still limited. Although behavioral treatments have shown success (Abel, Blanchard, & Becker, 1978; Azar, 1989; Marshall, Laws, & Barbaree, 1990), data are limited and they appear less effective with more severe cases (Szykula & Fleischman, 1985). Similarly, information regarding considerations in determining placement and visitation of children is also limited. Nonetheless, highly specific questions are asked of clinicians by courts (e.g., how often does a 2-year-old "need" to visit parents to maintain the bond?). Testimony here must be approached with extreme caution.

Compliance with service plans is often seen as a critical indicator of parental investment (e.g., therapy attendance; making visits with the child) and evaluators are often asked to comment regarding such indicators. Empirically based data regarding their meaning, however, is limited (Famularo, Kinscherff, Bunshaft, Spivak, & Fenton, 1989; Hess, 1988; Meddin & Hansen, 1985) and these factors may be colored by systems-based factors. For example, parental visitation may hinge on caseworkers' efforts to provide transportation, distance to the child's placement, and foster parents' cooperation (Azar et al., 1995). Evaluators who are unaware of these circumstances might be cautious in interpreting the meaning of parental noncompliance.

Similarly, services for child abuse cases are not available in many localities or available for only a small number of parents (Berkowitz & Sedlak, 1993; Meddin & Hansen, 1985). Knowledge of effective treatments (Azar & Wolfe, in press; Becker et al., 1995; Wolfe & Wekerle, 1993), their availability in the community, and non-parent-based obstacles to their being utilized become essential when evaluators are asked to comment on whether the state made "diligent" efforts to rehabilitate the parent.

If it is judged that the parent has failed to make use of provided services or has not benefited from them (i.e., no evidence of improved parental competency or decreased potential for violence) or that the child's needs (either produced by the abuse itself or constitutional handicaps) are so great that the parent's capacities are exceeded, the social service agency involved may file for TPR, freeing the child for adoption. In most states, the parent will no longer have contact with the child if a such ruling occurs. In some cases, parents can have some contact or information (e.g., receiving yearly pictures). An extended family member may adopt the child and there may more ongoing contact. Children may also recontact parents once they reach adulthood.

Termination of parental rights typically involves two questions: whether parental "unfitness" exists that has shown itself not to be amenable to intervention and whether TPR is in the "best interests" of the child(ren) (Melton et al., 1987). Grisso (1986) outlined five categories of parental conditions that allow courts to terminate parental rights: (1) conditions constituting abandonment of the child (desertion), (2) conditions of neglect or abuse, (3) conditions of behavior or lifestyle that constitute an extreme threat to the child (e.g., drug abuse), (4) conditions of mental deficiency or mental illness of parents, and (5) conditions of loss of civil rights the exercise of which are necessary to meet the needs of the child (e.g., imprisonment, found "incompetent" in legal standards). Cases often involve more than one of these conditions. Their mere presence alone, however, is not enough to constitute legal grounds for TPR (Grisso, 1986). How the parent's condition significantly affects the child's welfare, if at all, must be documented. For example, abuse of drugs must be shown to impinge on the ability to parent. To accomplish this, the question of how the parents' abilities fit with children's present and future needs must be addressed.

Determining whether termination is in the child's best interest has other components. First, how long has the child been out of care and what will be the effect of removing him or her from a foster or preadoptive home and returning him or her to the parent? Second, what are the alternatives to returning children to their parents (does the state have an adequate preadoptive home willing to take the child)? Finally, what will be the long-term impact of termination of parental rights? The scientific literature does not have much to say regarding these issues and commenting on them may again be in the realm of informed speculation, rather than scientific fact.

CONCLUSION

This chapter has overviewed mental health professionals' participation in cases involving violence toward children. Since the first edition of this book, substantial new information has emerged in selected issues within this area of practice (e.g., child witness data), highlighting the need for vigilance regarding changes in our field's knowledge base. Despite these advances, many basic and specific theoretical and applied issues continue to face the field. First, clinicians continue to grapple with how much of a role they should play in such proceedings. The epistemology and actions of the legal system at times strain the limits of the field's knowledge and ethical standards. Second, if they are to play a role in such cases, the scientific community needs to continue to address the questions that are raised in legal context. For example, operational definitions of parental competency need to be developed that have valid instruments associated with them and that take into consideration different cultural and ethnic perspectives (Azar et al., 1998). The defining qualities of minimally adequate parenting might also be addressed, given the field's traditional emphasis on the optimal meeting of children's needs. Discussions of this dilemma need to take place in professional circles and work done to advance practice and social policy in this area.

Methods for doing evaluations that provide valid responses to legal questions need continued development (e.g., interview protocols, data regarding whether and how to use doll interviews; normative data regarding doll interviews). Finally, if clinicians are going to make recommendations regarding treatment and visitation schedules, then further study is needed to address these areas. Unfortunately, over the past decade, research funding has actually decreased in child abuse and this has prompted a recent National Academy of Science report (National Research Council, 1993) to outline a research agenda in this area, but the needs of the legal process were not detailed in this report. More attention is needed here to place expert testimony on stronger ground.

Several other issues have begun to be discussed. For example, our field has already drafted guidelines for practice in child custody disputes in divorce (APA, 1994). Similar criteria are in the midst of being devised by APA for child protection cases. Discussions regarding the effectiveness of our legal solutions to the problem of child abuse have also begun to take place. In the 1960s when these laws were enacted, they were thought of as the best way to protect vulnerable children and help stressed families. This has been questioned. One suggestion is for the use of mediation as is done in divorce custody cases (Palmer, 1989), although this may be controversial. Emery and Billings (1998) argued for differential responses depending on level of abuse and the family's cooperation with treatment, including (1) clinicians not having to report maltreatment while a family is engaged in therapy, (2) greater attention to treatment by social service agencies (what they call "rediscovering their roots") for moderate level maltreatment, and (3) swift and decisive legal intervention for cases of serious family violence. Identifying level of risk, however, is still a difficult task and the assumption that treatment is effective may not be true. Social policy level discussions such as these will act to advance this forensic field.

REFERENCES

Abel, G.E., Blanchard, E.B., & Becker, J.V. (1978). An integrated treatment program for rapists. In R.T. Rada (Ed.), *Clinical aspects of the rapist* (pp. 161–214). New York: Grune & Stratton.

American Psychological Association. (1994). *Guidelines for child custody evaluations in divorce proceedings.* Washington, DC: Author.

American Psychological Association. (1997). *Graduate study in psychology 1996, with 1997 addendum.* Washington, DC: Author.

American Psychological Association. (1998). *Draft of guidelines in CPS cases.* Washington, DC: Author.

American Psychological Association, Committee on Ethical Guidelines for Forensic Psychologists. (1991). Specialty guidelines for forensic psychologists. *Law and Human Behavior, 15,* 655–665.

August, R.L., & Forman, B.D. (1989). A comparison of sexually abused and nonsexually abused children's behavioral responses to anatomically correct dolls. *Child Psychiatry and Human Development, 20,* 39–47.

Azar, S.T. (1989). Training parents of abused children. In C.E. Schaefer & J.M. Briesmeister (Eds.), *Handbook of parent training* (pp. 414–441). New York: Wiley.

Azar, S.T., & Benjet, C.L. (1994). A cognitive perspective on ethnicity, race and termination of parental rights. *Law and Human Behavior, 18,* 249–268.

Azar, S.T., Benjet, C.L., Fuhrmann, G., & Cavallero, L. (1995). Child maltreatment and termination of parental rights: Can behavioral research help Solomon? *Behavior Therapy, 26,* 599–623.

Azar, S.T., Fantuzzo, J., & Twentyman, C.T. (1984). An applied behavioral approach to child maltreatment. Back to basics. *Advances in Behaviour Research & Therapy, 6,* 3-11.

Azar, S.T., Lauretti, A., & Loding, B. (1998). The evaluation of parental fitness in termination of parental rights cases: A functional-contextual perspective. *Clinical Child and Family Psychology Review, 1,* 77–100.

Azar, S.T., & Twentyman, C.T. (1986). Cognitive behavioral perspectives on the assessment and treatment of child abuse. In *Advances in cognitive-behavioral research and therapy* (Vol. 5, pp. 237–267). New York: Academic Press.

Azar, S.T., & Wolfe, D.A. (1998). Child abuse and neglect. In E.G. Mash & R.A. Barkley (Eds.), *Behavioral treatment of childhood disorders* (2nd ed., pp. 501–544). New York: Guilford Press.

Becker, J.V., Alpert, J.L., BigFoot, S.S., Bonner, B.L., Geddie, L.F., Henggeler, S.W., Kaufman, K.L., & Walker, C.E. (1995). Empirical research on child abuse treatment: Report by the child abuse and neglect working group, APA. *Journal of Clinical Child Psychology, 24,* 23–46.

Belsky, J., & Vondra, J. (1989). Lessons from child abuse: The determinants of parenting. In D. Cicchetti & V. Carlson (Eds.), *Child maltreatment* (pp. 153–202). New York: Cambridge University Press.

Benedek, E.P., & Schetky, D.H. (1985). Allegations of sexual abuse in child custody and visitation disputes. In D.H. Schetky & E.P. Benedek (Eds.), *Emerging issues in child psychiatry and the law* (pp. 145–156). New York: Brunner/Mazel.

Berenson, A.B. (1993). Appearance of the hymen at birth and one year of age: A longitudinal study. *Pediatrics, 91,* 820–825.

Berenson, A.B., Heger, A.H., & Andrews, S. (1991). Appearance of the hymen of newborns. *Pediatrics, 87,* 458–465.

Berenson, A.B., Heger, A.H., Hayes, J.M., Bailey, R.K., & Emans, S.J. (1992). Appearance of the hymen of prepubertal girls. *Pediatrics, 89,* 387–394.

Berkowitz, S., & Sedlak, A.J. (1993). *Study of high risk: Child abuse and neglect groups. State survey report.* Washington, DC: National Center on Child Abuse and Neglect.

Bersoff, D.N., Goodman-Delahunty, J., Grisso, T., Hans, V.P., Poythress, N.G., & Roesch, R.G. (1997). Training in law and psychiatry: Models from the Villanova conference. *American Psychologist, 52,* 1301–1310.

Besharov, D.J. (1987). Reporting out-of-home maltreatment: Penalties and protections. *Child Welfare, 66,* 399–408.

Blau, T.H. (1984). *The psychologist as expert witness.* New York: Wiley.

Boat, B.W., & Everson, M.D. (1988a). Interviewing young children with anatomical dolls. *Child Welfare, 62,* 337–352.

Boat, B.W., & Everson, M.D. (1988b). Use of anatomical dolls among professionals in sexual abuse evaluations. *Child Abuse & Neglect, 12,* 171–179.

Bolocofsky, D.N. (1989). Use and abuse of mental health experts in child custody determinations. *Behavioral Sciences & the Law, 7,* 197–213.

Bradley, A., & Wood, J. (1996). How do children tell? The disclosure process in child sexual abuse. *Child Abuse & Neglect, 20,* 881–891.

Brant, J. (1991). *Law and mental health professionals: Massachusetts.* Washington, DC: American Psychological Association Press.

Bresee, P., Stearns, G.B., Bess, B.H., & Packer, L.S. (1986). Allegations of child sexual abuse in child custody disputes: A therapeutic assessment model. *American Journal of Orthopsychiatry, 56,* 560–569.

Brooks, C.M., Perry, N.W., Starr, S.D., & Teply, L.L. (1994). Child abuse and neglect reporting laws: Understanding interests, understanding policy. *Behavioral Sciences and the Law, 12,* 49–64.

Bruck, M., Ceci, S.J., & Hembrooke, H. (1998). Reliability and credibility of young children's reports. *American Psychologist, 53,* 136–151.

Budd, K.S., & Holdsworth, M.J. (1996). Issues in clinical assessment of minimal parenting competence. *Journal of Clinical Child Psychology, 25,* 2–14.

Burgdorf, K. (1980). *Recognition and reporting of child maltreatment: Findings from the national study of the incidence of child abuse and neglect.* Washington, DC: NCCAN.

Burgdorf, K. (1988). *Study of the national incidence and prevalence of child abuse and neglect: 1988.* Washington, DC: NCCAN.

Caldwell, R.A., Bogat, G.A., & Davidson, W.S. (1988). The assessment of child abuse potential and the prevention of child abuse and neglect: A policy analysis. *American Journal of Community Psychology, 16,* 609–624.

Ceci, S.J., & Bruck, M. (1995). *Jeopardy in the courtroom.* Washington, DC: American Psychological Association.

Child Victim Witness Investigative Pilot Projects. (1994, July). *Research and evaluation final report.* Sacramento: California Attorney General's Office.

Cohn, A., & Daro, D. (1986). *Is treatment too late? What ten years of evaluation research tells us.* Chicago: NCPCA.

Colby, I., & Colby, D. (1987). Videotaping the child sexual abuse victim. *Social Casework, 68,* 117–121.

Denton, L. (1987). Child abuse reporting laws. Are they a barrier to helping troubled families? *APA Monitor, 18,* 1–23.

Emery, R.E., & Billings, L.L. (1998). An overview of the nature, cases, and consequences of abusive family relationships. *American Psychologist, 53,* 121–135.

Epstein, N.B., Bishop, D.S., & Baldwin, L.M. (1982). McMaster model of family functioning. In F. Walsh (Ed.), *Normal family processes* (pp. 115–141). New York: Guilford Press.

Famularo, R., Kinscherff, R., Bunshaft, D., Spivak, G., & Fenton, T. (1989). Parental compliance to court-ordered treatment interventions in cases of child maltreatment. *Child Abuse & Neglect, 13,* 507–514.

Faust, D., & Ziskin, J. (1988). The expert witness in psychology and psychiatry. *Science, 241,* 31–35.

Fischler, R.S. (1985). Child abuse and neglect in American Indian communities. *Child Abuse & Neglect, 9,* 95–106.

Fraser, B.G. (1976). The child and his parents: A delicate balance of rights. In R.H. Helfer & C.H. Kempe (Eds.), *Child abuse and neglect: The family and the community* (pp. 315–333). Cambridge: Ballinger.

Fridell, L.A. (1991). Intrafamilial sexual abuse treatment: Prosecution following expulsion. *Child Abuse & Neglect, 15,* 587–592.

Frye v. United States, 293 F. 1013 (D.C.Cir., 1923).

Garbarino, J. (1989). The incidence and prevalence of child maltreatment. In L. Ohlin & M. Tonry (Eds.), *Family violence* (pp. 219–261). Chicago: University of Chicago Press.

Gibbens, T.C., & Prince, J. (1963). *Child victims of sex offenses.* London: The Institute for the Study and Treatment of Delinquency.

Giovanonni, J.M., & Becerra, R.M. (1979). *Defining child abuse.* New York: Free Press.

Gonzales, L., Waterman, J., Kelly, R., McCord, L., & Oliver, M. (1993). Children's patterns of disclosures, and recantations of sexual and ritualistic abuse allegations in psychotherapy. *Child Abuse & Neglect, 17,* 281–289.

Goodman, G.S. (1984). The child witness: Conclusions and future directions for research and legal practice. *Journal of Social Issues, 40,* 157–175.

Goodman, G.S., Taub, E.P., Jones, D.P., England, P., Port, L., Rudy, L., & Prado, L. (1992). Testifying in criminal court: Emotional effects on child sexual abuse victims. *Monographs of the Society for Research in Child Development, 57*(5, Serial No. 229).

Gordon, M.A. (1992). Recent Supreme Court rulings on child testimony in sexual abuse cases. *Journal of Child Sexual Abuse, 1,* 61–73.

Grisso, T. (1986). *Evaluating competencies.* New York: Plenum Press.

Heinze, M.C., & Grisso, T. (1996). Review of instruments assessing parenting competencies used in child custody evaluations. *Behavioral Science and the Law, 14,* 293–313.

Hess, P. (1988). Case and context: Determinants of planned visit frequency in foster care family care. *Child Welfare, 67,* 311–325.

Hirsch, R.A. (1985). Expert witnesses is child custody cases. *Family Law Quarterly, 19,* 207–243.

Hoge, S.K., & Grisso, T. (1992). Accuracy and expert testimony. *Bulletin of the American Academy of Psychiatry & the Law, 20,* 67–76.

Jampole, L., & Weber, M.K. (1987). An assessment of the behavior of sexually abused and non-sexually abused children with anatomically correct dolls. *Child Abuse & Neglect, 11,* 187–192.

Jensen, R.F., & Nicholas, K.B. (1984). Influence of the social characteristics of both father and child on the tendency to report child abuse. *Professional Psychology, 15,* 121–128.

Jones, D., & McGraw, J.M. (1987). Reliable and fictitious accounts of sexual abuse in children. *Journal of Interpersonal Violence, 2,* 27–45.

Kermani, E.J. (1993). Child sexual abuse revisited by the U.S. Supreme Court. *Journal of the American Academy of Child and Adolescent Psychiatry, 32,* 971–976.

Knapp, S.J., & Vandercreek, L. (1985). Psychotherapy and privileged communications in child custody cases. *Professional Psychology: Research and Practice, 16,* 398–407.

Lanyon, R.I. (1986). Psychological assessment procedures in court related settings. *Professional Psychology: Research and Practice, 17,* 260–268.

Levy, R. (1989). Using "scientific" testimony to prove child sexual abuse. *Family Law Quarterly, 23,* 383–411.

Libai, D. (1969). The protection of the child victim of sexual offence in the criminal justice system. *Wayne Law Review, 15,* 971–1032.

Madansky, D., & Santora, D. (1989, March). *Pediatrician-therapist cooperation in the treatment of sexually abused children.* Paper presented at the National Child Abuse Conference, Philadelphia.

Marshall, W.L., Laws, D.R., & Barbaree, H.E. (1990). *Handbook of sexual assault: Issues, theories and treatment of the offender.* New York: Plenum Press.

Maryland v. Craig, 110 S.Ct. 3157 (1990).

Mash, E.H. (1991). Measurement of parent-child interaction in studies of maltreatment. In R. Starr & D.A. Wolfe (Eds.), *The effects of child abuse and neglect* (pp. 203–255). New York: Guilford Press.

Massachusetts General Law, Ch. 119, 51A.

Matarazzo, J.D. (1990). Psychological assessment versus psychological testing: Validation from Binet to the school, clinic and courtroom. *American Psychologist, 45,* 999–1017.

McKittrick, C.A. (1981). Child abuse: Recognition and reporting by health professionals. *Nursing Clinics of North America, 16,* 103–115.

Meddin, B.J., & Hansen, I. (1985). The services provided during child abuse and neglect case investigations and the barriers that exist to service provision. *Child Abuse & Neglect, 9,* 175–182.

Melton, G.B. (1981). Children's competency to testify. *Law and Human Behavior, 5,* 73–85.

Melton, G.B., & Limber, S. (1989). Psychologists' involvement in cases of child maltreatment: Limits of role and expertise. *American Psychologist, 44,* 1225–1233.

Melton, G.B., Petrila, J., Poythress, N.G., & Slobogin, C. (1987). *Psychological evaluations for the courts: A handbook for mental health professionals.* New York: Guilford Press.

Melton, G.B., & Wilcox, B.L. (1989). Changes in family law and family life. Challenges for psychology. *American Psychologist, 44,* 1213–1216.

Menzies, R.J., Webster, C.D., & Sepejak, D.S. (1985). Hitting the forensic sound barrier: Predictions of dangerousness in a pretrial psychiatric clinic. In C.D. Webster, M.H. Ben-Aron, & S.J. Hucker (Eds.), *Dangerousness* (pp. 115–144). New York: Cambridge University Press.

Miller, J.K. (1976). Perspectives on child maltreatment in the military. In R.E. Helfer & C.H. Kempe (Eds.), *Child abuse and neglect* (pp. 267–291). Cambridge: Ballinger.

Milner, J.S. (1986). *The child abuse potential inventory: Manual* (2nd ed.). Webster, NC: Psytec.

Milner, J.S. (1994). Assessing physical child abuse risk: The child abuse potential inventory. *Clinical Psychology Review, 14,* 547–583.

Monahan, J. (1981). *Predicting violent behavior: An assessment of clinical techniques.* Beverly Hills, CA: Sage.

Monahan, J. (1984). The prediction of violent behavior: Toward a second generation of theory and policy. *American Journal of Psychiatry, 141,* 10–15.

Moore, W.E. (1970). *The profession: Roles and rules.* New York: Russell-Sage Foundation.

Morse, S.J. (1978). Crazy behavior, morals, and science: An analysis of mental health law. *Southern California Law Review, 51,* 554–560.

Myers, J.E. (1993). Expert testimony regarding child sexual abuse. *Child Abuse & Neglect, 17,* 175–185.

National Center on Child Abuse and Neglect. (1995). *Child maltreatment 1995. Reports from the states to the National Center on Child Abuse and Neglect.* Washington, DC: U.S. Department of Health and Human Services.

National Research Council. (1993). *Understanding child abuse and neglect.* Washington, DC: National Academy Press.

Pagelow, M.D. (1989). The incidence and prevalence of criminal abuse of other family members. In L. Ohlin & M. Tonry (Eds.), *Family violence* (pp. 263–314). Chicago: University of Chicago Press.

Palmer, S.E. (1989). Mediation in child protective cases: An alternative to the adversary system. *Child Welfare, 68,* 21–31.

Paradise, J.E. (1989). Predictive accuracy and the diagnosis of sexual abuse: A big issue about a little tissue. *Child Abuse & Neglect, 13,* 169–176.

Portwood, S.G., Reppucci, N.D., & Mitchell, M.S. (1997). Balancing rights and responsibilities: Legal perspective on child maltreatment. In J.R. Lutzker (Ed.), *Handbook of child abuse research and treatment* (pp. 31–52). New York: Plenum Press.

Powell, M.B., & Thomson, D.M. (1994). Children's eye-witness memory research: Implications for practice. *Families in Society: The Journal of Contemporary Human Services, 75,* 204–216.

Pynoos, R.S., & Eth, S. (1984). The child as witness to homicide. *Journal of Social Issues, 40,* 87–108.

Rodham, H. (1979). Children's rights: A legal perspective. In P.A. Vardin & I.N. Brody (Eds.), *Children's rights: Contemporary perspectives* (pp. 21–360). New York: Teachers College Press.

Russel, R. (1988). Role perceptions of attorneys and caseworkers in child abuse cases in juvenile court. *Child Welfare, 62,* 205–216.

Sagatun, I.J. (1991). Expert witnesses in child abuse cases. *Behavioral Sciences and the Law, 9,* 201–215.

Sas, L. (1997). Sexually abused children as witnesses: Progress and pitfalls. In D.A. Wolfe, R.J. McMahon, & R.D. Peters (Eds.), *Child abuse: New directions in prevention and treatment across the lifespan* (pp. 248–267). Thousand Oaks, CA: Sage.

Saunders, E.J. (1988). A comparative study of attitudes toward child sexual abuse among social work and judicial system professionals. *Child Abuse & Neglect, 12,* 83–90.

Schene, P.A. (1991). Intervention in child abuse and neglect. In J.C. Westman (Ed.), *Who speaks for the children?* (pp. 205–220). Sarasota, FL: Professional Resources Exchange.

Schmitt, B.D. (1980). The child with nonaccidental trauma. In C.H. Kempe & R.E. Helfer (Eds.), *The battered child* (pp. 128–146). Chicago: University of Chicago Press.

Sivan, A.B., Schor, D.P., Koeppl, G.K., & Noble, L. (1988). Interaction of normal children with anatomical dolls. *Child Abuse & Neglect, 12,* 295–304.

Slobogin, C. (1989). The "ultimate issue" issue. *Behavioral Science & the Law, 7,* 259–266.

Small, M.A., & Melton, G.B. (1994). Evaluation of child witnesses for confrontation by criminal defendants. *Professional Psychology: Research and Practice, 25,* 228–233.

Smith, S.R. (1989). Mental health expert witnesses: Of science and crystal balls. *Behavioral Science & the Law, 7,* 145–180.

Sorenson, T., & Snow, B. (1991). How children tell: The process of disclosure of child sexual abuse. *Child Welfare, 70,* 3–15.

Stromberg, C.D., Haggarty, D.J., Leivenluft, R.F., McMillian, M.H., Mishkin, B., Rubin, B.L., & Trilling, H.R. (1988). *The psychologist's legal handbook.* Washington, DC: The Council for the National Register of Health Service Providers in Psychology.

Swarns, R.L. (1997, October 25). In a policy shift, more parents are arrested for child neglect. *New York Times, 5157,* p. 1.

Szykula, S.A., & Fleischman, M.J. (1985). Reducing out-of-home placements of abused children. *Child Abuse & Neglect, 9,* 277–284.

Taylor, L., & Adelman, H.S. (1989). Reframing the confidentiality dilemma to work in children's best interests. *Professional Psychology: Research and Practice, 20,* 79–83.

Tjaden, P.G., & Thoennes, N. (1992). Predictors of legal intervention in child maltreatment cases. *Child Abuse & Neglect, 16,* 807–821.

Turbett, J.P., & O'Toole, R. (1980, August). *Physicians' recognition of child abuse.* Paper presented at the annual meeting of the American Sociological Association, New York.

U.S. House of Representatives Select Committee on Children, Youth, and Families. (1987). *Victims of official neglect.* Washington, DC: U.S. Congress.

Weithorn, L.A. (1987). *Psychology and child custody determinations.* Lincoln: University of Nebraska Press.

Wells, S.J. (1985). Decision-making in Child Protective Services intake and investigation. *Protecting Children,* 3–8.

Whitcomb, D., Shapiro, E.R., & Stellwagen, L.D. (1985). *When the victim is a child: Issues for judges and prosecutors.* Washington, DC: NIJ.

White, S., Strom, G.A., Santilli, G., & Halpin, B.M. (1986). Interviewing young sexual abuse victims with anatomically correct dolls. *Child Abuse & Neglect, 10,* 519–529.

Whitehead, T.M. (1992). Application of the delayed discovery rule: The only hope for justice for sexual abuse survivors. *Law and Psychology Review, 16,* 153–170.

Wolfe, D.A. (1988). Child abuse and neglect. In E.J. Mash & L.G. Terdal (Eds.), *Behavioral assessment of childhood disorders* (pp. 627–699). New York: Guilford Press.

Wolfe, D.A., & Wekerle, C. (1993). Treatment strategies for child physical abuse and neglect: A critical progress report. *Clinical Psychology Review, 13,* 473–500.

Zellman, G.L. (1990). Report decision-making patterns among mandated reporters. *Child Abuse & Neglect, 4,* 325–336.

Ziskin, J. (1981). *Coping with psychiatric and psychological testimony.* Venice, CA: Law & Psychology Press.

Zoltek-Jick, R.R. (1997). For whom does the bell toll? Repressed memory and challenges for the law. Getting beyond the statute of limitations. In P.S. Applebaum, L.A. Uyehara, & M.R. Elin (Eds.), *Trauma and memory: Clinical and legal controversies* (pp. 445–476). New York: Oxford University Press.

Zuravin, S.J. (1991). Research definitions of child physical abuse and neglect. In R.H. Starr & D.A. Wolfe (Eds.), *The effects of child abuse and neglect* (pp. 100–128). New York: Guilford Press.

CHAPTER 5

Legal and Systems Issues in the Assessment of Family Violence Involving Adults

ROBERTA K. THYFAULT

MEDIA REPORTS and political rhetoric suggest that many Americans are afraid to walk the streets of their neighborhoods because of the violence in our cities. Because of their fear, citizens retreat into their homes, lock windows, draw the shades, and bolt doors. For many, however, locked windows and bolted doors do not provide a safe refuge. Contrary to popular belief, we actually run the greatest risk of assault, physical injury, and even murder, not from a stranger on the street, but from members of our own families in our own homes (Straus, Gelles, & Steinmetz, 1980).

Traditionally, domestic violence has remained "behind closed doors" (Straus et al., 1980). Slowly, however, we have recognized the toll domestic violence takes on individuals and society. Society's recognition of the seriousness of domestic violence has been reflected within the criminal justice system. Congress passed the Violence Against Women Act of 1994 (Public Law 103-322, Title IV), expressly recognizing that domestic violence is a serious crime. States have enacted legislation affecting the prosecution of batterers and the admissibility of evidence about battering. Police departments have changed their responses to domestic violence calls. Special domestic violence units have been established in some prosecutors' offices to ensure that batterers are prosecuted and punished, by incarceration in jail or prison or, when appropriate, diversion and counseling (Parrish, 1996; Soler, 1987).

As a result of these changes, increasingly more women are able to escape the violence and start new lives. For many women, however, even those who have left the violent relationship, these changes have not ended the violence in their lives. For these women, violence does not end until they kill their abusive partner. This chapter addresses some of the legal issues associated with the defense of a battered woman charged with the murder of her abusive mate. Some case law is cited to provide examples of the problems battered women face in establishing a legal defense or mitigation for their actions. This chapter also addresses issues associated with presenting expert testimony about battering and its effects. Most of the issues are discussed in the context of the woman who is charged with the murder of her batterer. Many battered women find themselves involved in the criminal justice system charged with crimes they committed at the behest of their batterer and under fear of another battering. These women face many of the same hurdles in defending themselves as the battered woman charged with murder.

LEGAL ISSUES

A battered woman who kills her abuser often does so in circumstances that do not comport with traditional male-defined concepts of self-defense. Instead of defending herself during a violent face-to-face confrontation, a battered woman may act to protect herself when it appears to her that a violent episode is about to occur (Bochnak, Krauss, Macpherson, Sternberg, & Wiley, 1981; Crocker, 1985). For example, the woman may kill her batterer while he is sleeping because the man threatened to kill her when he awakens [e.g., *People v. Aris,* 215 Cal.App.3d 1178, 264 Cal.Rptr. 167 (1989)]. A battered woman may kill her abuser while he is sitting in a chair, after he makes a gesture or statement she knows from past experiences means a beating is about to occur [e.g., *People v. Scott,* 97 Ill.App.3d 899, 424 N.E.2d 70 (1981)]. A battered woman may respond with force the law deems excessive when she uses a gun or other weapon to defend herself against a violent man's fists (Gillespie, 1989).

When the battered woman acts outside traditional definitions of self-defense, she faces a number of hurdles in attempting to convince a judge and jury that she was justified in defending herself. A California case, *People v. Aris,* 215 Cal.App.3d 1178, 264 Cal.Rptr. 167 (1989), highlights some of the problems facing a battered woman charged with the murder of her abusive partner.

At the time of the homicide, Ms. Aris and her husband had been married for 10 years. Ms. Aris was beaten frequently, and often severely, throughout the marriage. Although not reflected in the court's opinion, evidence was presented at the trial showing that Ms. Aris had sustained a broken jaw, a black eye, and fractured ribs. Ms. Aris made several attempts to leave the relationship. Her husband found her each time and persuaded her to return, either through promises to change his behavior or threats to harm her or to take away their three daughters. On one occasion, Ms. Aris secretly moved from the area where they had been living, only to have her husband find her and threaten to harm her if she did not return to him. Several witnesses corroborated Ms. Aris' testimony about the beatings, including members of her husband's family.

Frequency of the beatings increased prior to the homicide. Mr. Aris became so jealous that Ms. Aris was afraid to venture out of the house, even to take her daughters to the park or to go to a relative's house to do the family laundry.

On the night of the homicide, a party was being held at the house the Aris family shared with a friend. During the party, Mr. Aris became angry and began beating his wife in the bathroom. Later, another beating occurred in the couple's bedroom, during which Mr. Aris told his wife he did not think he was going to let her live until morning. He then fell asleep. Ms. Aris waited about ten minutes, then went next door to get some ice to ease the pain from the blows to her face. While at the neighbors, she saw a gun on top of the refrigerator and took it for protection. When she returned to the house, she sat on the bed and began thinking that she had to shoot her husband because she felt that when he awakened he was going to hurt her very badly or kill her. Ms. Aris fired a shot at her husband, which caused him to jump. She thought he was coming after her and fired four more times. After firing the shots, Ms. Aris ran out of the house, past the party guests, and hid behind a car because she thought her husband would be chasing her. She waited there until police arrived and arrested her.

Ms. Aris was charged with murder. During her trial, the judge allowed the jury to hear testimony about battered women and the "battered woman syndrome." However, he precluded testimony about the expert's psychological evaluation of Ms. Aris. The trial judge also would not allow the expert to render an opinion that Ms. Aris was a battered woman experiencing "battered women syndrome" at the time of the shooting. Although Ms. Aris testified that she killed her husband because she believed her life was in imminent danger, the trial judge refused to instruct the jury on self-defense because Mr. Aris was sleeping when he was shot.

Ms. Aris was convicted of second degree murder and sentenced to a term of 15 years to life in state prison. Her conviction and sentence were upheld on appeal. Later, a clemency petition was filed with the governor of California. The governor granted a partial clemency in that he authorized the Parole Board to consider Ms. Aris for parole a few years earlier than allowed by law. Ms. Aris was finally released from prison in February 1997.

LEGAL ISSUES RELATING TO THE ESTABLISHMENT OF A DEFENSE

The Myth of a "Battered Woman Syndrome" Defense

The term "battered woman syndrome" has been used by the courts, attorneys, experts, and others, to identify common characteristics of women who are abused (Gordon, 1996; *People v. Humphrey,* 13 Cal.4th 1073, 1083-1084, 56 Cal.Rptr.2d 142, 921 P.2d 1). The term has also been used to suggest that there is a separate defense for battered women, commonly referred to as the "battered woman defense" or "battered woman syndrome defense."

A woman who kills her abuser can assert any number of legal defenses, some of which will be discussed later. Evidence of the violent relationship is used to show the effect of battering on her perceptions and her state of mind. The evidence may help to prove an element of a legal defense or to negate an element of the charged offense. It does not, however, establish a separate defense. There is no "battered woman defense" or "battered woman syndrome defense" (Bochnak et al., 1981; Thyfault, 1984).

Concerns have been raised about the use of the term "battered woman syndrome" (Gordon, 1996; Schneider, 1986). The California Supreme Court, referring to a brief filed by the California Alliance against Domestic Violence and others, stated that the preferred term is "expert testimony on battering and its effects" or "expert testimony on battered woman's experiences" (*People v. Humphrey,* 13 Cal.4th 1073, 1083, fn.3, 56 Cal.Rptr.2d 142, 921 P.2d 1). The court noted that the term "battered woman syndrome" has been criticized "because it implies that there is one syndrome which all battered women develop, (2) it has pathological connotations which suggest that battered women suffer from some sort of sickness, (3) expert testimony on domestic violence refers to more than woman's psychological reactions to violence, (4) it focuses attention on the battered woman rather than on the batterer's coercive and controlling behavior and (5) it creates an image of battered women as suffering victims rather than as active survivors" *(Ibid.).*

These concerns must be taken into consideration in selecting a defense for a battered woman. As discussed later, they must also be considered in deciding whether to present expert testimony.

Self-Defense

A defense of self-defense requires proof that the defendant reasonably believed her life was in imminent danger of death or great bodily harm at the time of the homicide. The requirements of reasonableness and imminent danger have proved to be difficult, and in some cases insurmountable, hurdles for battered women charged with the murder of their mates (Crocker, 1985; Fiora-Gormally, 1978; Kinports, 1988).

As mentioned, in the *Aris* case, the trial judge refused to instruct the jury on self-defense. The court reasoned that Ms. Aris's life was not in imminent danger because her husband was sleeping when he was shot. The Court of Appeal upheld this ruling. Similar rulings have been made by the other courts [e.g., *State v. Norman,* 324 N.C. 253, 378 S.E.2d 8 (1989); *State v. Stewart,* 243 Kan. 639, 763 P.2d 572 (1988)].

Other courts have been more willing to allow the issue of imminence to be decided by the jury. In *State v. Gallegos,* 104 N.M. 247, 719 P.2d 1268 (Ct.App. 1986), the trial judge refused to give self-defense instructions in a case involving a battered woman who shot and stabbed her former husband as he was lying in bed. The conviction was reversed on appeal. The appellate court ruled that the jury should have been allowed to decide the question of imminence. The court reasoned that the repeated and often severe violence the man had inflicted on the defendant in the past, including a threat to kill her on the day of the homicide, could have caused her to reasonably believe her life was in imminent danger when he called her into the bedroom.

A similar decision was reached in *People v. Scott,* 97 Ill.App.3d 899, 424 N.E.2d 70 (1981). In *Scott,* the defendant shot her abusive mate as he was talking on the telephone. While talking, the man motioned to Ms. Scott to get his handcuffs by tapping on his wrists. In the past, Ms. Scott had been handcuffed and then beaten. Fearing another beating, she obtained a .357 magnum, closed her eyes, and fired six shots at her batterer as he sat in the chair.

The courts in *Gallegos* and *Scott* each showed a clear understanding of the impact a history of battering can have on a battered woman's perception of danger. *Gallegos* and *Scott* recognize that behaviors or communications that appear nonthreatening to the outside observer can cause a battered woman to reasonably believe her life is in imminent danger.

A successful defense of self-defense also requires proof that the defendant acted reasonably. In some states, the reasonableness of the defendant's actions is judged solely from her subjective experiences: Did the woman honestly believe her life was in danger [e.g., *State v. Koss,* 49 Ohio.St.3d 213, 551 N.E.2d 970 (1990); *State v. Leidholm,* 334 N.W.2d 811 (N.D. 1983); *State v. Wanrow,* 88 Wash. 22, 559 P.2d 548 (1988)]?

Other states utilize a two-part test. First, the evidence must show that the defendant honestly believed her life was in imminent danger. This belief is assessed from the woman's subjective viewpoint. Second, the evidence must show that the woman's subjective belief of imminent danger was objectively reasonable. The jury must find that the ordinary, reasonable person in a similar situation would have believed his or her life was in imminent danger [e.g., *State v. Gallegos,* 104 N.M. 247, 719 P.2d 1268 (Ct.App. 1986); *People v. Humphrey,* 13 Cal.4th 1073, 56 Cal.Rptr.2d 142, 921 P.2d 1

(1996); *State v. Kelly,* 97 N.J. 178, 478 A.2d 364 (1984); *State v. Norman,* 324 N.C. 253, 378 S.E.2d 8 (1989)].

Requirement of objective reasonableness can be particularly difficult for battered women. The requirement grew out of traditional concepts of self-defense, which generally involve face-to-face confrontations between men. These traditional concepts of self-defense do not allow for the situation facing the battered woman who finds herself repeatedly beaten and terrorized by a larger and stronger man. They also fail to take into consideration sex role socialization, which does not value strength and aggressiveness in women, nor teach women how to defend themselves [Gillespie, 1989; Schneider, Jordan, & Arguedas, 1981; *State v. Wanrow,* 88 Wash. 521, 559 P.2d 548 (Wash. 1988)].

Imperfect Self-Defense

In some states a defendant can be convicted of manslaughter, a lesser offense than murder, on a theory of imperfect self-defense. Imperfect self-defense acknowledges the battered woman's subjective belief that she was in imminent danger, but rejects that belief as being objectively unreasonable. In other words, the reasonable person would not have believed they were in imminent danger (Fiora-Gormally, 1978). Although the defense presents an alternative to a murder conviction and lengthy imprisonment, and may be appropriate in some cases, for many women it discounts the reality of living in a violent relationship and the impact the violence has had on them.

Other Defenses

Self-defense may not be an appropriate plea in every case in which a battered woman kills a battering spouse (Bochnak et al., 1981). In some cases, it may be more appropriate for the woman to present another defense to a murder charge, such as insanity or temporary insanity. In other cases, it may be best to try to mitigate the murder charge to manslaughter. Like self-defense, each of these defenses present their own unique problems for the battered woman.

When a woman asserts that she acted in self-defense, she is asking a jury to find that she acted reasonably under the circumstances. In other words, her actions were "normal" and justified. A defense of insanity or temporary insanity says that the woman was insane and thus not responsible for her actions. The woman asks the jury to excuse her actions because of her insanity (Schneider et al., 1981). Perhaps the best known case of a battered woman gaining an acquittal by reason of temporary insanity is that of Francine Hughes, whose life was documented in the movie *The Burning Bed* (Gillespie, 1989; Jones, 1980).

Until recently, an impaired mental state defense was often the first choice of defense for a battered woman (*Id.,* p. 29). This choice may have been supported by clinicians who misdiagnosed battered women as suffering from mental disorders. The symptoms of mental illness were confused with the effects of a violent relationship (Rosewater, 1981).

The effects of living in a violent relationship may leave some battered woman mentally ill (Rosewater, 1981; Schneider et al., 1981). For these women, an impaired mental state defense may be the best choice of defense. A decision to present an impaired mental state defense should not be made lightly, however, because of the severe consequences facing the woman. An acquittal by reason of insanity or temporary insanity may lead to a mandatory commitment to a mental hospital that can last anywhere from a few months to several years (Jones, 1980; Schneider et al., 1981).

When the facts of a particular case preclude a woman charged with murder from asserting a defense that could result in an outright acquittal, the evidence may support a verdict on the lesser offense of manslaughter. Manslaughter may be an appropriate verdict for the battered woman who kills out of anger or "in the heat of passion" rather than out of fear for her life (Kinports, 1988). In many states, a manslaughter conviction can mean the difference between probation and a mandatory sentence of life in state prison.

Like self-defense, the concept of "heat-of-passion" is based in male traditions. In fact, the classic example of a heat-of-passion killing involves a man who kills his wife after finding her in bed with another man. A woman who claims that she acted in the heat-of-passion must show that she was provoked by her abuser, under circumstances which would have provoked the reasonable person, and that there was no "cooling off" period between the provocation and the homicide (Fiora-Gormally, 1978).

Provocation and lack of cooling-off time are not difficult to show when the woman kills during a battering. However, some battered women kill during a break in the violence (Browne, 1987). When this happens, the prosecutor argues that the woman was not provoked because she was not being battered at the time. If the killing occurs sometime after a battering, the argument is made that the reasonable person would have "cooled off" between the battering and the killing.

These arguments fail to account for the effects battering has on a woman. The fear a battered woman lives with everyday becomes the provocation. Because the fear is always present and intensifies over time, there may not be a cooling-off period or there may be a considerably longer interval between the provocation and the cooling-off period than in the typical heat-of-passion case (Fiora-Gormally, 1978). Like insanity or temporary insanity, heat-of-passion manslaughter suggests that the woman's actions were not justified under the circumstances (Schneider et al., 1981).

Because of the difficulty a battered woman faces in proving that her use of lethal force against her abuser was justifiable, or at least excusable, expert testimony about battering and its effects may be useful in persuading judges and juries that a battered woman acted reasonably when she defended herself against further violence (Gillespie, 1989; Macpherson, Ridolfi, Sternberg, & Wiley, 1981; Thyfault, 1984). For many women, however, getting this expert testimony before the jury presents another difficult hurdle to overcome.

LEGAL ISSUES RELATING TO THE ADMISSIBILITY OF EXPERT WITNESS TESTIMONY

Trial courts may admit only evidence that is relevant to the issues in a case. Thus, courts have faced the task of determining whether expert testimony about battering and its effects is relevant when the woman asserts that she acted in self-defense or that the prior abuse played some role in the circumstances leading to the homicide. Currently, expert testimony on battering and its effects is admissible, to some, degree in every state and the District of Columbia (Parrish, 1996).

Most courts considering the issue have concluded that evidence about battering and its effects is helpful to jurors in assessing the reasonableness of the woman's actions. Some courts have found that the testimony would dissuade jurors about the myths of violent relationships and help jurors understand why the woman was unable to get away from the batterer, why she may not have told anyone or sought help, and why she would fear further violence from the man [*Id.,* pp. 5–6; e.g., *People v. Humphrey,* 13 Cal.4th

1073, 56 Cal.Rptr.2d 142, 921 P.2d 1 (1996); *Smith v. State,* 247 Ga. 612, 277 S.E.2d 678 (1981); *State v. Allery,* 101 Wash. 591, 682 P.2d 312 (1984); *State v. Kelly,* 97 N.J. 178, 478 A.2d 364 (1984); *State v. Koss,* 49 Ohio.St.3d 213, 551 N.E.2d 970 (1990)]. In addition, several states have passed or are considering passage of legislation allowing for the admission of expert testimony on battering and its effects (Parrish, 1996).

Although most courts allow for some form of expert testimony, a court may exclude the testimony based on the specific facts of the case. The Mississippi Supreme Court upheld the exclusion of expert testimony in *Lentz v. State,* 604 So.2d 243 (Miss. 1992). The court noted that the decedent had been shot twice, once in the back, and that one shot had been fired in the bedroom and a second one as he walked to a relative's house. The court ruled that these facts did not require expert testimony about "battered women syndrome" to assist the jury in deciding whether the defendant reasonably believed her life was in imminent danger.

Assuming a court determines that evidence of the effects of battering is relevant, the battered woman still faces hurdles in getting the evidence before the jury. In some states, the proponent of expert testimony must show that the state of the art of the expert witness methodology has gained general acceptance within the scientific community and permits a reasonable opinion to be asserted by the expert. This requirement is based on criteria set forth in *Dyas v. United States,* 376 A.2d 827 (D.C.App. 1977) and *Frye v. United States,* 293 F. 1013 (D.C. Cir. 1923). Critical here is that it is the expert's methodology that must be scrutinized for general acceptance, not the conclusions the expert draws from those methods. In federal courts and some state courts, the proponent of expert testimony must only show that the testimony will assist the jury. The stricter standards of *Dyas* and *Frye* are no longer required [e.g., *Daubert v. Merrill Dow Pharmaceuticals, Inc.,* 509 U.S. 579, 113 S.Ct. 2786, 125 L.Ed.2d 469 (1993)].

Ibn-Tamas v. United States, 407 A.2d 626 (D.C.App. 1979), affm'd on remand 455 A.2d 893 (D.C.App. 1983) and *Hawthorne v. State,* 408 So.2d 801 (Fla.App. 1982), affm'd on remand 470 So.2d 770 (Fla. App. 1985) were two of the first courts to rule that testimony about battering and its effects would be of assistance to the jury in understanding the defendant's situation. However, these courts also upheld the exclusion of the expert testimony after the trial courts found that the state of the art of the study of battered women did not permit an expert opinion. Both courts indicated that a different result could be reached in a later case.

The American Psychological Association (APA) filed an amicus brief on behalf of Gladys Kelly when her case was pending before the New Jersey Supreme Court. The APA took the position that the state of the art of the study of battered women was generally accepted by the scientific community in which it was developed and thus allowed for an expert opinion about battered women and battered woman syndrome. A similar brief had been filed in *Hawthorne* (Kinports, 1988). Although one justice in *Kelly* was prepared to rule that the state of the art of the study of battered women would support an expert opinion, the majority of the court remanded the case for a hearing on the issue [*State v. Kelly,* 97 N.J. 178, 478 A.2d 364 (1984)]. More recently, many courts have concluded that "battered woman syndrome" is accepted within the scientific community (Parrish, 1996).

As a final requirement, the party offering expert testimony must show that the witness is truly an expert in the field. This is a legitimate requirement because it ensures that opinions will be rendered only by those who have demonstrated experience in working with battered women. Generally, this poses few problems when the expert has studied and worked in the field for a period of time and has received some recognition and acceptance from peers for that work. Any prior experience as an expert witness can also be helpful (Thyfault, 1984).

However, battered women have been precluded from presenting expert testimony because courts have determined that their expert did not have significant experience in the field. In *People v. White,* 90 Ill.App.3d 1067, 414 N.E.2d 196 (1980), the testimony of an internist who had "occasion to treat battered women" was found to be irrelevant. On the other hand, in *State v. Anaya,* 438 A.2d 892 (Me. 1981), the Maine Supreme Court ruled that a specialist in internal medicine who had occasionally seen battered women, including the defendant, should have been permitted to offer an opinion that the defendant was a battered woman.

Even when a witness has a wealth of practical experience in the field, some trial court judges are hesitant to allow them to testify as an expert unless they also have academic credentials (Macpherson et al., 1981). In some courts, only psychiatrists or psychologist are allowed in give expert opinions. A trio of cases from Kentucky illustrate this issue.

In *Commonwealth v. Rose,* 725 S.W.2d 558 (Ky. 1987), the court ruled that a registered nurse was not qualified to give an opinion that the defendant was a battered woman. The court suggested that only a psychiatrist or psychologist could give such an opinion. *Rose* was overruled in *Commonwealth v. Craig,* 783 S.W.2d 387 (Ky. 1990). There, the court ruled that the director of a local shelter for battered women, with a Master's degree in counseling, five years of experience working with battered women, and prior experience as an expert witness was qualified to give an opinion that a woman was a battered woman. However, in *Dyer v. Commonwealth* (1991) 816 S.W.2d 647 (Ky. 1991), the same court overruled *Craig* and reaffirmed the ruling in *Rose.* Although *Dyer* did not involve testimony about battered women, the court held that expert testimony, such as "battered woman syndrome" testimony, can only be given by persons qualified to render an opinion about the defendant's mental state.

Expert testimony about battering and its effects can be useful to the jury's understanding of the woman's state of mind and her perceptions of danger at the time of the homicide (Macpherson et al., 1981). The expert can also diffuse the myths, stereotypes, and misconceptions raised by the prosecution and answer the question on many jurors' minds: Why didn't she leave? (Gillespie, 1989). If the woman did leave, expert testimony is helpful in explaining why leaving the relationship did not end the abuse. The expert can serve as an educator in the courtroom, teaching the judge and jury about the experiences of battered women and the effects of repeated abuse (Schneider, 1986).

The use of expert testimony has not been limited to cases where battered woman are the defendants. In *Commonwealth v. Kacsmar,* 421 Pa.Super. 64, 617 A.2d 725 (1992), a male defendant's conviction was reversed because the trial court precluded him from presenting expert testimony about battering and its effects. In addition, experts are often called on to assist in the prosecution of cases involving domestic violence, such as when a batterer is being tried for assault on or murder of a battered woman. In these circumstances, the witness can offer assistance should the woman become reluctant to testify in an assault case, or provide corroboration for the woman's testimony [Sonkin & Fazio, 1987; *People v. Humphrey,* 13 Cal.4th 1073, 56 Cal.Rptr.2d 142, 921 P.2d 1 (1996)]. In *State v. Baker,* 424 A.2d 171 (N.H. 1980), the prosecutor used expert witness testimony about battering to refute the insanity defense of a man on trial for the attempted murder of his wife. Experts also may be helpful in formulating and providing a treatment plan for the batterer participating in a pretrial diversion program, or following his conviction (Gangley, 1987; Sonkin, 1987).

Many of the issues just discussed are resolved by the trial judge before trial begins. Even if the testimony is ultimately rejected, or if a decision is made not to present expert witness testimony, an expert still can be of tremendous assistance to the trial team. Before trial, the expert can provide the defense attorney with information that may be useful in obtaining a dismissal or reduction of the charges. The expert can provide crisis intervention to the woman and her family, and even to defense attorneys who find themselves representing a client very different from their other clients. In the event the woman is convicted, the expert may be able to provide information at sentencing that will result in a lesser sentence (Gillespie, 1989; Thyfault, Browne, & Walker, 1987). For example, in *United States v. Ramos-Oseguera,* 120 F.3d 1028 (9th Cir. 1997) and *United States v. Johnson,* 956 F.2d 894 (9th Cir. 1992), evidence that the defendants were battered was relied on to impose mitigated sentences.

Once a decision is made to use the expert's testimony, additional issues concerning the content and scope of the testimony must be resolved before the witness takes the stand.

LEGAL ISSUES RELATING TO THE PRESENTATION OF EXPERT TESTIMONY AT TRIAL

A thorough psychological evaluation of the defendant should be conducted as early as possible by a clinician experienced in working with battered women (Hutchinson, 1992). An early evaluation helps the defense attorney select the most appropriate theory of defense and ensures that the expert's testimony will complement rather than undermine that defense. This is especially important because, as mentioned earlier, too often attorneys proceed under the misconception that they will present a "battered woman defense" or "battered woman syndrome defense" when there are no such defenses (Bochnak et al., 1981; Thyfault, 1984).

An early evaluation may identify other factors that could be relevant to the defense and require additional investigation. Factors such as language barriers, immigrant status, and cultural, racial, and ethnic differences may need to be explored (Wang, 1996).

Another benefit of an early evaluation is that the expert may help the woman begin to talk about the violence. It is not uncommon for a battered woman to minimize the abuse and not tell her attorney, and in particular her male attorney, the details of the abuse. This is especially true when the violence includes sexual abuse. Getting the woman to talk about the abuse provides valuable information to the attorney. It also requires the woman to begin to remember specific episodes of violence. This will be critical if she ultimately testifies at a trial. Eventually, a judge and jury will have to be made to understand the fear the woman lived with daily. The best way to build this fear at trial is by providing the jury with as many details about the relationship as possible.

Browne (1987) has identified several factors that distinguish abusive homicide relationships from abusive nonhomicide relationships. These include an escalation in the frequency and severity of the violence and injuries to the woman, increases in the use of alcohol and drugs by the men, and higher levels of sexual abuse. An evaluation interview that combines open-ended and closed-ended questions can be very successful in obtaining the information relevant to these factors (Browne, 1987; Thyfault et al., 1987).

Research suggests that the wording of a question may produce different responses (Frieze & Browne, 1989). For example, the woman's narrative description of a battering may not include specific details. To obtain these details, the woman can be given a list of specific behaviors and asked whether and how often any of them were used by the batterer during the incident (e.g., slap, punch, kick, threats, use of weapons). Likewise, asking a woman if she was ever raped by her mate may produce a negative response. An affirmative response might be forthcoming if the woman is asked whether she was ever forced to have sexual intercourse or to perform sexual acts she did not want to perform. Some women find it difficult to discuss sexual abuse. In those cases, it may be helpful to read a list of sexual acts (vaginal, oral, anal, etc.) and ask the woman to indicate whether she was ever forced to participate in any of them (Browne, 1987; Thyfault et al., 1987).

As mentioned, it is important that the evaluation be conducted by someone who is experienced in the field of domestic violence. This can be a problem for indigent women who must rely on a court to approve funds for an expert.

In *Ledford v. State*, 254 Ga. 656, 333 S.E.2d 576 (1985) and *Lentz v. State*, 604 So.2d 243 (Miss. 1992), the defendants were denied funds to retain experts experienced in working with battered women. In *Ledford*, the court ruled that it was sufficient that the defendant was examined by professionals from the state's Forensic Services Program to determine her competency to stand trial and her degree of criminal responsibility. Similarly, in *Lentz*, the court ruled it was sufficient that the defendant was examined by personnel at the state hospital.

On the other hand, in *Dunn v. Roberts*, 963 F.2d 308 (10th Cir. 1992), the defendant's conviction was reversed because the trial judge had refused to provide funds for the defense attorney to retain an expert to determine whether the defendant was a battered woman. In *Doe v. Superior Court*, 39 Cal.App.4th 538, 45 Cal.Rptr.2d 888 (1995), the defense sought funds to retain a psychologist with an expertise in battering and its effects. The trial judge denied the funds because the expert was not on a list of approved witnesses maintained by the court, even though none of the experts on the list were experienced in working with battered women. The appellate court ruled that the trial court could not deny the defendant funds to retain a domestic violence expert simply because the expert was not on the court's list of approved experts.

The person conducting the evaluation of the woman defendant must keep in mind that the information gathered may eventually be used in court. For this reason, it is important that the evaluation not be allowed to become a therapy session. Therapy may be important at some point, but it should not interfere with the psychological evaluation (Thyfault et al., 1987).

Conclusions reached following an evaluation based on a self-report interview are a prime target for cross-examination because they are based, for the most part, on what the woman has told the interviewer. The prosecutor may suggest that the woman's responses during the evaluation were merely self-serving statements designed to justify her conduct (Macpherson et al., 1981).

Such criticism can be deflected by corroborating the information provided by the woman. Corroboration may be found in the police and medical reports of the homicide and witness statements. Prior incidents of abuse may have been reported to or observed by children, other family members, friends, neighbors, police officers, social service workers, clergy, and coworkers. The expert witness, with approval of the defense attorney, may want to interview some or all of these people or review reports they may have written.

The woman's self-report of abuse can also be corroborated by standardized psychological tests that are familiar to the courts. The Minnesota Multiphasic Personality Inventory (MMPI) has proven to be especially useful since norms were established based on research with women who were currently in abusive relationships (Rosewater, 1987).

Once an evaluation is completed and a decision made to present evidence about battering and its effects, the preparation of that testimony can begin. There is no substitute for thorough preparation. In many states, the woman's testimony serves as part of the foundation for the expert's testimony. Thus, the woman must be thoroughly prepared so she can present the horror of her life to the judge and jury and respond to cross-examination by the prosecutor.

The expert witness must be familiar with the facts of the case as well as the laws of each jurisdiction. The witness must understand the elements of the defense and how the expert testimony will help establish those elements. The expert must also anticipate and be prepared to answer questions posed by the prosecutor on cross-examination.

The subject matter of the expert testimony varies from state to state. In some jurisdictions, an expert may testify about battered women in general, as well as the specific woman who is on trial. In these circumstances, the expert is allowed to testify to the results of any psychological evaluation that was conducted on the woman and express an opinion that the woman is a battered woman experiencing battered woman syndrome [e.g., *People v. Aris,* 215 Cal.App.3d 1178, 264 Cal.Rptr. 167 (1989); *Smith v. State,* 247 Ga. 612, 277 S.E.2d 678 (1981); *State v. Allery,* 101 Wash.2d 591, 682 P.2d 312 (1984); *State v. Anaya,* 438 A.2d 892 (Me. 1981); *State v. Kelly,* 97 N.J. 178, 478 A.2d 364 (1984)].

Although *Kelly* and *Aris* do allow for general and specific testimony, the courts in those cases precluded experts from expressing an opinion on the "ultimate issue" of whether the woman acted reasonably. The court in *Commonwealth v. Craig,* 783 S.W.2d 378 (Ky. 1990), also ruled that a qualified expert could testify that a battered woman is "suffering" from "battered woman syndrome"; however, the expert may not voice an opinion on whether the woman's actions were the result of the syndrome.

In other states, testimony is allowed only about battered women in general on the theory that the determination of whether the woman on trial is a battered woman is an "ultimate issue" to be decided by the jury [e.g., *State v. Hennen,* 441 N.W.2d 793 (Minn. 1989)]. On the other hand, a court might exclude expert testimony because the expert is unfamiliar with the facts of a particular case and unable to identify the defendant as a battered woman [e.g., *Ward v. State,* 470 So.2d 100 (Fla.App. 1985)].

The expert who testifies will probably be required to turn over any notes and reports that were prepared for the case. Prior to the witness's testimony, the expert's notes and reports may fall within the attorney-client or work-product privileges. As such, they are protected from discovery by the opposing side, although this varies from state to state. Once the expert is identified as a potential witness or testifies, he or she may be required to turn over notes and reports of the evaluation. Some courts have also required experts to turn over the actual answer sheets that were completed by the women so they can be evaluated by an expert working for the other party. Failure to produce this "raw data" can result in the striking of the expert's testimony.

As mentioned earlier, it is important to corroborate the woman's information with information from other sources. However, the expert must keep in mind that any documents relied on in reaching an opinion may have to be turned over to the opposing party and may be the target of cross-examination during trial. For example, a defense investigator may prepare a report that the prosecution would ordinarily not be entitled to view, or the police may prepare a report that contains inadmissible evidence. However, if the expert reads the report and relies on it in reaching an opinion, the prosecution may be entitled to a copy of the report and its contents may then be made known to the jury. This same procedure applies to any books or studies the expert relies on in reaching an opinion.

Although expert testimony can be extremely valuable, in some cases it may be more damaging to the woman than helpful. A decision to present expert testimony about battering and its effects may open the door for the prosecution to request that the defendant submit to an examination by the state's expert. The prosecution can then present the results of that examination during trial to rebut the defense evidence (Parrish, 1996).

In some cases, the potential for negative community attitudes about expert testimony must be considered. In other cases, the woman's life history may not fit the patterns research has identified as being common to battering relationships (Macpherson et al., 1981). This does not mean the woman's experiences are unworthy of belief and consideration by a jury. It simply means that the woman herself may be the best person to relate her experiences to the jury.

Concerns have been raised that the case law has created a stereotypical battered woman who is passive and helpless (Crocker, 1985; Schneider, 1986). Consequently, if the woman on trial is not helpless, perhaps because she is not economically dependent on her abusive mate, she may face an argument that she cannot be a battered woman. This argument was made in a case involving a battered woman who worked in a traditional male environment and was perceived by her coworkers as very assertive and in control. The prosecutor argued that she could not possibly have been a battered woman because she had not cowered in fear in the corner of the kitchen!

Expert testimony can be helpful to a battered woman; however, as Schneider persuasively argues, testimony that focuses only on the battered woman's helplessness or victimization is partial and incomplete because it does not address why the woman acted. The testimony must focus on the common experiences of battered women and the reasonableness of the woman's actions (Schneider, 1986). It may also be helpful to show a judge and jury that the battered woman reacted to her violent situation in much the same way as others who have experienced traumatic events in their lives (Frieze & Browne, 1989).

CONCLUSION

The battered woman who comes into a courtroom to defend herself against charges that she murdered her batterer faces many hurdles. The defenses available to her are based on a male perception of the world. She may find that the law does not allow her to present a defense that accounts for her perceptions. She may face a judge and jury who do not understand her situation and blame her because she did not "just leave." Expert testimony may help her persuade the judge and jury that she acted reasonably, but the law also imposes numerous hurdles to her presentation of that evidence. The testimony may harm her if it defines a stereotypical battered woman different from the particular woman on trial.

The most effective way to overcome some of these hurdles is through legislative changes in the law. It has been suggested that more states adopt the Model Penal

Code's definition of self-defense. This would remove the imminence requirement and replace it with a standard that would require the defendant to believe that his or her actions were immediately necessary at the time of the lethal incident (Fiora-Gormally, 1978; Gillespie, 1989). Laws can also be adopted to ensure that a battered woman could present testimony by a qualified expert about battering and its effects on the particular battered woman who is on trial. In addition, expert witnesses can evaluate their testimony to ensure that they are focusing on the experiences of battered women and the reasonableness of the woman's actions.

Many of our laws are rooted in common-law traditions that were carried to this country from England. Changing these laws is a slow and difficult process, but changes are occurring. In the meantime, the battered women charged with killing her abuser should be able to expect that her attorney will listen to her and become educated about battered women, so he or she can, in turn, make a judge and jury understand the fear the woman lived under day after day.

We cannot, however, leave it to the courts and legislatures to end domestic violence in our society. Each of us, men and women, must teach our children that violence is wrong. We must help our daughters develop the skills that will keep them from becoming locked in an abusive relationship. We must support our sisters, coworkers, friends, and others in their efforts to leave abusive relationships. We must encourage our local, state, and federal governments to provide safe havens for women who are escaping violent mates. Perhaps, then, the day will come when women no longer have to fear their own homes or find themselves in a courtroom charged with killing their abuser.

REFERENCES

Bochnak, E., Krauss, E., Macpherson, S., Sternberg, S., & Wiley, D. (1981). Case preparation and development. In E. Bochnak (Ed.), *Women's self-defense cases: Theory and practice* (pp. 41–85). Charlottesville: Michie.

Browne, A. (1987). *When battered women kill.* New York: Free Press.

Commonwealth v. Craig, 783 S.W.2d 387 (Ky. 1990).

Commonwealth v. Kacsmar, 421 Pa. Super. 64, 617 A.2d 725 (1992).

Commonwealth v. Rose, 725 S.W.2d 588 (Ky. 1987).

Crocker, P.L. (1985). The meaning of equality for battered women who kill men in self-defense. *Harvard Women's Law Journal, 8,* 121–153.

Daubert v. Merrill Dow Pharmaceuticals, Inc., 509 U.S. 579, 113 S.Ct. 2786, 125 L.Ed.2d 469 (1993).

Doe v. Superior Court, 39 Cal.App.4th 538, 45 Cal.Rptr.2d 888 (1995).

Dunn v. Roberts, 963 F.2d 308 (10 Cir. 1992).

Dyas v. United States, 376 A.2d 827 (D.C.App. 1977).

Dyer v. Commonwealth (1991) 816 S.W.2d 647 (Ky. 1991).

Fiora-Gormally, N. (1978). Battered wives who kill—double standard out of court, single standard in? *Law and Human Behavior, 2,* 133–165.

Frieze, I.H., & Browne, A. (1989). Violence in marriage. In L. Ohlin & M. Tonry (Eds.), *Family violence* (pp. 163–218). Chicago: University of Chicago Press.

Frye v. United States, 293 F. 1013, 54 App. D.C. 46 (1923).

Gangley, A.L. (1987). Perpetrators of domestic violence: An overview of counseling the court-mandated client. In D.J. Sonkin (Ed.), *Domestic violence on trial: Psychological and legal dimensions of family violence* (pp. 155–173). New York: Springer.

Gillespie, C.K. (1989). *Justifiable homicide: Battered women, self-defense, and the law.* Columbus: Ohio State University Press.

Gordon, M. (1996). Validity of "battered woman syndrome" in criminal cases involving battered women. In the validity and use of evidence concerning battering and its effects in criminal trials: Report responding to Section 40507 of the Violence Against Women Act. In *When battered women are charged with crimes: A resource manual for defense attorneys and expert witnesses.* Produced by the National Clearinghouse for the Defense of Battered Women for the New Jersey Coalition for Battered Women.

Hawthorne v. State, 408 So.2d 801 (Fla.App. 1982), affm'd on remand 470 So.2d 770 (Fla.App. 1985).

Hutchinson, M.A. (1992). I think I may have one of those battered woman cases. In *Defending battered women in criminal cases.* American Bar Association.

Ibn-Tamas v. United States, 407 A.2d 626 (D.C.App. 1979), affm'd on remand 455 A.2d 893 (D.C.App. 1983).

Jones, A. (1980). *Women who kill.* New York: Holt, Rinehart & Winston.

Ledford v. State, 254 Ga. 656, 333 S.Ed.2d 576 (1985).

Lentz v. State, 604 So.2d 243 (Miss. 1992).

Kinports, K. (1988). Defending battered women's self-defense claims. *Oregon Law Review, 67,* 393–465.

Macpherson, S., Ridolfi, K., Sternberg, S., & Wiley, D. (1981). Expert testimony. In E. Bochnak (Ed.), *Women's self-defense cases: Theory and practice* (pp. 87–106). Charlottesville: Michie.

Parrish, J. (1996). Trend analysis: Expert testimony on battering and its effects in criminal cases. In the validity and use of evidence concerning battering and its effects in criminal trials: Report responding to Section 40507 of the Violence Against Women Act. In *When battered women are charged with crimes: A resource manual for defense attorneys and expert witnesses.* Produced by the National Clearinghouse for the Defense of Battered Women for the New Jersey Coalition for Battered Women.

People v. Aris, 215 Cal.App.3d 1178, 264 Cal.Rptr. 167 (1989), disapproved in part in People v. Humphrey, 13 Cal.4th 1073, 56 Cal.Rptr.2d 142, 921 P.2d 1 (1996).

People v. Humphrey, 13 Cal.4th 1073, 56 Cal.Rptr.2d 142, 921 P.2d 1 (1996).

People v. Scott, 97 Ill.App.3d 899, 424 N.E.2d 70 (1981).

People v. White, 90 Ill.App.3d 1067, 414 N.E.2d 196 (1980).

Rosewater, L.B. (1987). The clinical and courtroom application of battered women's personality assessments. In D.J. Sonkin (Ed.), *Domestic violence on trial: Psychological and legal dimensions of family violence* (pp. 86–94). New York: Springer.

Schneider, E.M. (1986). Describing and changing: Women's self-defense work and the problem of expert testimony on battering. *Women's Rights Law Reporter, 9*(3/4), 195–222.

Schneider, E.M., Jordan, S.B., & Arguedas, C.C. (1981). Representation of women who defend themselves in response to physical or sexual assault. In E. Bochnak (Ed.), *Women's self-defense cases: Theory and practice* (pp. 1–39). Charlottesville: Michie.

Smith v. State, 247 Ga. 612, 277 S.E.2d 678 (1981).

Soler, E. (1987). Domestic violence is a crime: A case study—San Francisco family violence project. In D.J. Sonkin (Ed.), *Domestic violence on trial: Psychological and legal dimensions of family violence* (pp. 21- 35). New York: Springer.

Sonkin, D.J. (1987). The assessment of court-mandated male batterers. In D.J. Sonkin (Ed.), *Domestic violence on trial: Psychological and legal dimensions of family violence* (pp. 174–196). New York: Springer.

Sonkin, D.J., & Fazio, W. (1987). Domestic violence expert testimony in the prosecution of male batterers. In D.J. Sonkin (Ed.), *Domestic violence on trial: Psychological and legal dimensions of family violence* (pp. 218–236). New York: Springer.

State v. Allery, 101 Wash.2d 591, 682 P.2d 312 (1984).

State v. Anaya, 438 A.2d 892 (Me. 1981).

State v. Baker, 120 N.H. 773, 424 A.2d 171 (1980).

State v. Gallegos, 104 N.M. 247, 719 P.2d 1268 (Ct.App. 1986).

State v. Hennen, 441 N.W.2d 793 (Minn. 1989).

State v. Kelly, 97 N.J. 178, 478 A.2d 364 (1984).

State v. Koss, 49 Ohio.St.3d 213, 551 N.E.2d 970 (1990).

State v. Leidholm, 334 N.W.2d 811 (N.D. 1983).

State v. Norman, 324 N.C. 253, 378 S.E.2d 8 (1989).

State v. Stewart, 243 Kan. 639, 763 P.2d 572 (1988).

State v. Wanrow, 88 Wash. 221, 559 P.2d 548 (1988).

Straus, M.A., Gelles, R.J., & Steinmetz, S.K. (1980). *Behind closed doors: Violence in the American family.* New York: Doubleday.

Thyfault, R.K. (1984). Self-defense: Battered woman syndrome on trial. *Californian Western School of Law Review, 20,* 485–510.

Thyfault, R.K., Browne, A., & Walker, L.E. (1987). When battered women kill: Evaluation and expert witness testimony techniques. In D.J. Sonkin (Ed.), *Domestic violence on trial: Psychological and legal dimensions of family violence* (pp. 71–85). New York: Springer.

United States v. Johnson, 956 F.2d 894 (9th Cir. 1992).

United States v. Ramos-Oseguera, 120 F.3d 1028 (9th Cir. 1997).

Wang, K. (1996). Comment: Battered Asian American women: Community responses from the battered women's movement and the Asian American community. *Asian Law Journal, 3,* 151–184.

Ward v. State, 470 So.2d 100 (Fla.App. 1985).

PART TWO

EPIDEMIOLOGY

CHAPTER 6

Epidemiology of Family Violence Involving Children

JEFFREY J. HAUGAARD

THIS CHAPTER provides an overview and analysis of the epidemiology of family violence involving children. Issues that will aid in understanding epidemiology research are discussed first. These include the definition of epidemiology, limitations of epidemiology studies, influence of values in epidemiology research, and problems of defining family violence involving children. The research is then reviewed.

EPIDEMIOLOGY

Epidemiology is the study of the distribution and correlates of a disorder within a designated population (Tsuang, Tohen, & Zahner, 1995). It is an important part of the study of any disorder or problem. Revealing the extent of a disorder or problem may help to initiate or galvanize professional and public response to it and can suggest the degree of services needed by those afflicted. Variables associated with higher or lower rates of a disorder can be identified, and this may help in planning efficient distribution of services and developing testable hypotheses about the causal mechanisms of the disorder (see Rutter, 1979). Repeated studies may help gauge the effectiveness of prevention or intervention efforts.

Some authors have cautioned about the limitations inherent in epidemiology studies (e.g., Rutter, 1979). As the result of the apparent objectivity of numerical results, we may form theories based on the variables employed in epidemiology studies and be unaware of doing so. These theories could then influence the way that we conceptualize the problem addressed by the study. For example, reading that there is a higher prevalence of abused children in a particular racial group may lead us to form an informal theory that race has a causal influence on child abuse. This could be incorrect, since the variable of race may only be a marker for other variables associated with the prevalence of abuse (e.g., income, geographic location). Appropriate reading of epidemiology research requires that the reader be cautious of any tendency to attach improper causal explanations to the associations between variables discovered in individual studies. Finally, we must be careful not to become so involved in quantifying a problem that we lack sufficient time, interest, or resources to understand the development of the problem and work toward counteracting or preventing it (see Blackman, 1989).

VALUES AND EPIDEMIOLOGY STUDIES

The apparent objectivity of epidemiology studies may disguise the fact that they, as well as all scientific endeavors, involve values (Rollin, 1985). Recognizing the ways in which societal, professional, and individual values can influence epidemiology research reduces the chance that our vision of the issues being studied will be narrowed inappropriately by these values (Graham, Dingwall, & Wolkind, 1985; Rollin, 1985; Williams, 1986). Values can influence epidemiological research in the following ways.

Topic of Study

To classify family violence as a problem worth studying involves a value judgment. The attention of professionals and the public is drawn to what is being studied, and thus away from an array of other issues. Societal and professional values influence the issues studied, and results of these investigations influence ongoing societal and professional interest in these issues.

Unit of Study

Studying violence within the family represents societal and professional judgments about which unit of analysis is appropriate in violence research. The choice of the family as the unit of study can narrow the way we conceptualize issues relating to violence, and thus divert our attention from other circumstances in which violence occurs. Gil (1970) noted, "The somewhat sensational concern with individual cases of child abuse seems, at times, to have the quality of 'scapegoating,' for it enables the public to express self-righteous feelings of anger, disgust, resentment, and condemnation toward an abusing parent while the entire society is constantly guilty of massive acts of 'social abuse' of millions of children" (p. 174).

Definitions

Societal, professional, and individual values influence which family interactions are defined as violent or abusive. These definitions, in turn, have significant influences on epidemiological studies since they determine which interactions are counted. Broader definitions typically result in higher prevalence and incidence estimates.

Differences between cultures and within cultures over time influence the definition of violent and abusive acts. For example, the painful ritualistic scarring done to improve children's physical attractiveness in some cultures is likely to be viewed as abusive in ours, while the painful procedures that we put our children through to improve their physical attractiveness (e.g., orthodontia) are generally seen as commendable (Starr, 1988). Similarly, corporal punishment that was seen as an important component of discipline 25 years ago is currently seen by many as inappropriate violent behavior.

Values of the profession of the researcher may also influence definitions. Gelles (1982) found that medical professionals were less likely than school counselors, mental health professionals, or social workers to label aggressive acts that did not result in some physical injury to a child as child abuse. This may be a result of their area of intervention (physical injury) or of their need to document observable indications for treatment. Atteberry (1987; cited in Haugaard & Reppucci, 1988) found that social workers and mental health professionals were more likely to label potentially sexual acts between parents and children as sexual abuse than were lawyers. Atteberry suggested that this was due to the different possible outcomes attached to the label of abuse. For the mental health professional it could result in therapy or other forms of potential help for a child and family, while to a lawyer it could result in legal action aimed at punishing an adult.

Within societal and professional parameters, individual values of researchers can influence the definitions of violence or abuse that they use. Experiences that researchers have within their families or in working with child victims or perpetrators of family violence may influence how broadly or narrowly they define violence.

CHOICE OF VARIABLES

Any epidemiology study involves selection of variables that will be used to organize the data (e.g., age, income). Researchers must choose enough variables to avoid undue narrowness, but not so many that the analysis is confusing. Values can influence which variables are included in any study and which are avoided or to go unnoticed. Selection of variables directs the investigation in predetermined directions and consequently limits the available range of information.

OTHER AREAS OF INFLUENCE

Values can also influence researchers' choices regarding whom to ask about the occurrence of violence or whom to believe in the face of conflicting reports. Some research has shown that women are more revealing about sensitive issues than men (Cozby, 1973) and that when couples are asked about marital violence, women say that more has occurred than reported by their male partners (Jouriles & O'Leary, 1985). Thus, the researcher's choice of subjects influence study results. The ways in which studies are presented to potential subjects can reflect a researcher's values and can influence which people participate. For example, Blackman (1989) advertised her study in a newspaper in which she featured "a grotesque drawing of two blood-streaked people clawing at each other's faces" (p. 88).

DEFINITIONAL ISSUES

Defining "family violence involving children" and "child abuse" is not an easy task. Researchers have used a variety of definitions and this is an important source of the diversity of epidemiology study results (Haugaard & Emery, 1989; Knutson, 1995; Wekerle & Wolfe, 1996). Moreover, several studies of violence have not included the specific criteria that they employed, making comparison of the studies impossible and limiting their applicability (Geffner, Rosenbaum, & Hughes, 1988).

DISTINGUISHING FAMILY VIOLENCE FROM CHILD ABUSE

As used in the research literature, family violence and child abuse are two distinct concepts. Although many acts may be considered both family violence and child abuse (e.g., a parent beating or raping a child), other acts only fall into one category or the other. For example, some researchers have included acts under the category of "violence" that many people do not consider to be child abuse, such as spanking a young child (e.g., Straus & Gelles, 1986; Straus, Gelles, & Steinmetz, 1980). Alternately, many nonviolent acts are considered child abuse, such as depriving a child of food or locking a child in a closet for many hours. A consideration of child sexual abuse adds another complication, since most sexual abuse involves fondling (Haugaard & Reppucci, 1988), and much of this fondling is nonviolent. Because of the distinctions between family violence and child abuse, the terms should not be used interchangeably.

CHILD ABUSE

The process of defining child abuse has received considerable attention, in part because defining an act as child abuse often requires an intrusion by the state into the life of a family. Although some acts are seen by almost all people as child abuse, consensus does not exist about many other acts. Several criteria have been proposed for distinguishing abusive from nonabusive acts, including the community standard, the intent of the adult, and the result to the child (Garbarino & Gilliam, 1980; Gelles, 1982; Giovannoni & Becerra, 1979). In child sexual abuse, additional criteria include the ability of the child to consent to the interaction and the type of sexual act (Finkelhor, 1979; Haugaard & Reppucci, 1988). These criteria are not uniformly agreed on, however, and are often difficult to apply in a standard fashion.

Basing the definition of abuse on the intent or the consequences of an act can be problematic. Some parents may insist that a harmful act was never intended to cause harm, and determining the accuracy of their statement may be impossible (Bourne, 1979). The consequences of some acts may be influenced by chance, such as whether a child who is thrown down is bruised, breaks a bone, or is unmarked (Gil, 1970), and reports of many kinds of abuse may not be made until after any demonstrable effects have faded. In addition, some hypothesized consequences of abuse, such as a tendency toward violence in relationships, may not be evident for many years. Defining abuse based on community standards can lead to controversy. Determining which community will be considered (e.g., a commune or the county in which it is located) can be difficult, and the community standard on sensitive issues is often unclear. Consequently, determining the majority standard and the extent to which minority standards will be accommodated are value judgments left to those in the community who are influential in this area.

Further muddling the definition of abuse is the problem of reconciling the opinions of researchers and those experiencing the violent or abusive acts. In a sample of college students, only 27% of those who fell into the researchers' stringent definition of abuse considered themselves to have been abused (Berger, Knutson, Mehm, & Perkins, 1988).

CHILD SEXUAL ABUSE

In describing his research definition of child sexual abuse, Finkelhor (1979) included the "consent standard" and rejected the notion that the child should feel victimized for abuse to have occurred. He and others have argued that children are unable to truly consent to sexual activity with an adult, because of the power differential between adults and children and children's training to follow the instructions of adults who care for them. These researchers rely solely on the type of act and the age of the child and abuser when determining sexual abuse.

Differences have appeared in the criteria for age and sexual act. Some researchers have considered "children" to be those below the age of 18 (Russell, 1983; Wyatt, 1985), below the age of 17 (Finkelhor, 1979; Fromuth, 1986), and below the age of 16 (Wurr & Partridge, 1996). Different criteria for the sexual acts that constitute abuse have been used. Some researchers have included nonphysical contacts such as an encounter with an exhibitionist (Finkelhor, 1979; Russell, 1983; Wurr & Partridge, 1996; Wyatt, 1985), whereas others have not (Fritz, Stoll, & Wagner, 1981; Lodico, Gruber, & DiClemente, 1996).

Atteberry (1987; cited in Haugaard & Reppucci, 1988) surveyed people in several professions involved with sexual abuse victims and found general agreement on the abusiveness of some acts, such as intercourse, but little agreement on others, such as bathing children or sleeping with them. Atteberry also found that gender was an important consideration. Acts such as sleeping together, kissing on the lips, and entering a bathroom while a child was bathing were seen as more likely to be abusive when occurring between fathers and daughters than between mothers and sons.

FAMILY VIOLENCE INVOLVING CHILDREN

This concept has been used in a few research projects. *Family* has generally been defined as the child and any adult caretakers with whom the child lives. Ages of children have generally been between 3 and 17, although some have considered children from birth on. *Involving* has generally been seen to include only acts in which the child is directly involved in some violence. A child who observes violence between parents would not be considered "involved," although it is acknowledged that witnessing violence is often very traumatic for children. The term violence has been used broadly in these studies. Gelles (1979), for instance, defined violence as "an act carried out with the intention, or perceived intention, of physically injuring another person. The injury can range from slight pain, as with a slap, to murder" (p. 78). Gelles (1982) distinguishes violence from child abuse. Abuse includes only violent acts in which "the child was at high risk of injury . . . including punching, biting, kicking, beating, and threatening to use or using a weapon" (p. 28). Although Gelles appears to be using two different definitions for injury, the injury associated with child abuse appears to be of the type that might require medical attention.

SUMMARY

A generally accepted definition of child physical or sexual abuse or family violence remains elusive, even though research in this area has continued for decades. The problems in determining a shared definition of child abuse reflect our societal confusion about what are and are not appropriate ways for parents to interact with and discipline their children. Expecting exact and shared definitions is probably unreasonable. What is required is that we not accept the myth of shared meaning for child abuse. The concept must be defined clearly in each context where it is used. Those who read research must be aware of the definitions used in each study.

FINDINGS OF EPIDEMIOLOGY STUDIES
OF CHILDREN AS VICTIMS

Epidemiology studies of physical and sexual abuse can be grouped into three general categories: those involving (1) community or national samples of households, (2) cases reported to child protective services or other agencies, and (3) college students. Each approach has strengths and weaknesses, and these will be outlined before the study results.

RESEARCH WITH COMMUNITY OR NATIONAL SAMPLES

Methodological Issues

The primary strength of this approach is that it involves a broader range of households than the others. Occurrence of violence among families that have not been identified as problematic can be assessed. Results can impel us toward acknowledging the extent of violence in a wide cross-section of homes.

Among the methodological concerns associated with community surveys are several with particular relevance for family violence research. Rate of participation of potential participants is an important consideration. Cox, Rutter, Yule, and Quinton (1977) showed that families of nonparticipants in several surveys of childhood behavioral problems had higher rates of child behavioral deviance, child or adult psychiatric disorders, and marital discord. This raises concern that studies with a substantial rate of nonparticipation may underestimate the overall prevalence of violence and that dysfunctional families may be the most underrepresented.

A related issue is the honesty of the respondents. Adults may be reluctant to reveal violent acts that they fear will cause the intrusion of governmental agencies into their family. Adults who are asked about abuse they endured as a child may find a discussion of their experiences to be embarrassing or painful, and thus may say that they were not abused (Haugaard & Emery, 1989). These influences may result in a reduction of the estimates of family violence, particularly of the most intense forms.

A final issue is the effect of the choice of whom to interview. As noted in the previous section on values, interviewing women is likely to result in a higher estimate of family violence than interviewing men. Some researchers have argued that violence toward a woman or her children will have more salience for her than her spouse, and thus she will remember its frequency with more accuracy. Although Steinmetz (1978) showed that many husbands are the targets of violence, it may be more difficult for them to admit that they have been either a victim or an aggressor. Interviewing both adults in a family could be a solution. If they are interviewed separately, however, decisions must be made about which report to record if they differ. Gelles (1978) reports that in several joint interviews with a couple, the strength of their disagreements about the extent of family violence raised concerns that the interview might be the cause of additional family violence.

Study Results

Straus and his colleagues (Straus, Gelles, & Steinmetz, 1980; Straus & Gelles, 1986) have completed two surveys with national probability samples of households. The 1975 study involved 1,146 households and the 1985 sample involved 1,428 households that included a parental couple and at least one child between the age of 3 and 17. Thus, single-parent families and those with only young children were not interviewed. As shown in other studies, some of the most severe violence can occur in young and single-parent families (Gil, 1970; NCCAN, 1988). The final number of households represented a 65% and 84% response rate, respectively. The Conflict Tactics Scale was used in both studies. It assesses whether a variety of violent acts had occurred between family members in a situation involving conflict. The study definition of violence was discussed in the previous section on definitional issues and included any purposeful act that caused pain or injury to the child.

Similar levels of family violence were reported in the two studies, with a small reduction in several categories of family violence in the 1985 study. Both studies found that a large majority of families had at least one incident of minor violence between a parent and child in the past year. For example, a parent slapped or spanked a child in about 60% of families and pushed, grabbed, or shoved a child in about 30% of families. More dangerous types of violence happened less frequently, but still occurred in many homes: a parent hit a child with an object in about 12% of families; kicked, bit, or hit a child with a fist in about 2% of families; and beat up a child in about 1% of families.

Boney-McCoy and Finkelhor (1995) reported on a study of 2,000 youths aged 10 to 16 years who were contacted through national random-digit dialing. Eighty-two percent of the youths who were contacted agreed to participate in a telephone interview. The participants came from a broad range of racial and economic backgrounds and family types. Participants were asked about whether they had ever experienced a wide range of physical and sexual assaults. Two categories of assault were *physical assault by a parent* and *physical assault by a family member other than a parent.* Neither category was defined more specifically in the results, except that "spanking" was not included in the category of physical assault by a parent. Among the girls, 2.6% reported a parental assault and 1.9% of the boys reported at least one parental assault. Of those who experienced a parental assault, 59% reported being injured and 24% reported fearing serious injury or death from the assault. Five and one half percent of the girls and 4.7% of the boys reported an assault by a family member other than a parent. Of these youth, 35% reported being injured by the assault and 13% reported fearing serious injury or death.

Studies of the prevalence of child sexual abuse have included community samples of adults from San Francisco (Russell, 1983) and Los Angeles (Siegel, Sorenson, Golding, Burnam, & Stein, 1987; Wyatt, 1985). In face-to-face interviews, participants were asked to describe any sexual abuse experiences they had as a child. Russell and Wyatt interviewed women only, Siegel interviewed both men and women. Russell and Wyatt defined children as those under the age of 18 and included encounters involving physical contact and noncontact (such as an encounter with an exhibitionist). Russell considered only extrafamilial contact that was unwanted and all intrafamilial sexual contact. Wyatt considered all sexual contact with girls under the age of 13, and only unwanted contact with older girls. Siegel included only incidents occurring before the child turned 16 and that involved some force or physical coercion. Sexual contact was defined as, "someone touching your sexual parts, your touching their sexual parts, or sexual intercourse" (p. 1146). Response rates were 79% (Russell), 73% (Wyatt), and 68% (Siegel).

The reporting of the results makes it somewhat difficult to distinguish those abused within their immediate family, but some specific information is available. In Russell's sample of 930 women, 42 (4.5%) women had been abused by a father or father figure,

20 (2.2%) by a brother, 3 by a sister, and 1 by her mother. Approximately one third of those abused by a father or father figure had experienced vaginal, oral, or anal intercourse, one third had experienced genital fondling, and one third had experienced other sexual behavior. In Wyatt's sample of 248 women, 4 (1%) had been abused by their father, 19 (7%) by a stepfather, foster father, or mother's boyfriend, and 10 (4%) had been abused by a brother. None of the women had been abused by a female family member. Among the 3,132 adults interviewed by Siegel, approximately 28 (1%) of the women and none of the men reported sexual abuse by a parent.

Lodico, Gruber, and DiClemente (1996) surveyed 90% of the 9th and 12th graders throughout Minnesota about heath-related behaviors. One question was whether "any older or stronger member of your family ever touched you sexually or had you touch them sexually" (p. 212). Based on a random sample of all responses, 6.8% of the girls and 1.9% of the boys responded positively to this question. Approximately half these students had experienced both intrafamilial and extrafamilial sexual abuse. There were no differences in the percentage of affirmative reports from White, African American, and Native American students.

Discussion

Comparing the studies of physical assault is complicated by their use of different methods and definitions of assault. However, there is some consistency in their results, even though the studies were conducted over a 20-year period. It appears that about 2% to 3% of children are seriously assaulted by a parent. Although these percentages may be small, they do represent a very large number of children who are seriously assaulted by their parents. Consistency across the studies raises concerns that serious assault by parents on their children has not diminished over the past two decades, despite many efforts to prevent child abuse. Comparing sexual abuse investigations is difficult because of the different definitions and results categories that they employed. The Wyatt and Russell results suggest that approximately 6% of women had been abused by a father figure and about 3% by a brother. Both results were higher than those reported by Siegel, and this may be because Siegel only considered cases involving physical coercion. The study by Lodico et al. reported somewhat lower rates for girls than Wyatt's and Russell's studies. This is likely because many of Lodico's participants were in the 9th grade, and some girls who have not experienced sexual assault by the 9th grade will experience it before becoming an adult.

RESEARCH WITH SAMPLES OF IDENTIFIED VICTIMS

Methodological Issues

An advantage of using of samples of identified victims is that larger numbers of abused children can be studied in a more efficient and cost-effective manner. Also, these studies allow us to focus on children whose abuse places them at greater risk for long- and short-term impairment.

Two methodological issues concern the accuracy with which the prevalence of child abuse can be estimated by examining reported cases, and whether reported cases accurately represent the characteristics of all abused children. Only a minority of abused children come to the attention of official agencies (NCCAN, 1988). Others are known to other professionals, such as physicians or therapists, or to nonprofessionals, such as neighbors. Many others remain unknown. Thus, a counting of officially reported cases will result in a prevalence rate that is much lower than the actual.

If there is some bias that influences which suspected cases are reported to official agencies, then reported cases would inaccurately represent the distribution of child abuse. Minority and low-income families appear to be at greater risk for being reported to an official agency for child abuse (Gil, 1970; Hampton, 1987; Lindholm & Willey, 1986). In sexual abuse, several factors appear to influence which cases are reported more frequently. Comparing studies of community samples with those of reported victims shows that children who were younger, experienced more physically invasive abuse, or were abused by a member of their family were more likely to be reported (Haugaard & Reppucci, 1988).

Study Findings

One of the first major epidemiology studies of child abuse was conducted by Gil (1970). His study raised the standard of epidemiology studies by gathering data nationwide, rather than from individual hospitals or locales. Gil defined physical abuse as "the intentional, nonaccidental use of physical force, or intentional, nonaccidental acts of omission, on the part of a parent or other caretaker interacting with a child in his care, aimed at hurting, injuring, or destroying that child" (p. 6). He did not include child sexual abuse unless force was involved. Each state submitted information on every reported case of child abuse during 1967 and 1968. At that time, however, the states used different criteria when defining a case.

Gil found an overall abuse rate of about 9 reports per 100,000 children across the United States. Reports ranged from 31 reports per 100,000 in Texas to zero reports from Rhode Island. Injuries were primarily bruises, welts, and lacerations; however, 35% of the children experienced burns, fractures, or internal injuries. Severe injuries were more likely to occur to children living with a single mother and to children from very low-income homes. Boys were abused more often than girls under the age of 12, with teenage girls being abused at about 1½ times the rate of teenage boys. The highest percentage of abused children occurred between 6 and 12 years. Non-White children were reported at a rate three times higher than White children. The percentage of children from low-income homes was higher than that from more affluent homes.

In response to a mandate from Congress, the National Center for Child Abuse and Neglect (NCCAN) has collected data from each state on the number of cases of child maltreatment reported to their child protection system for the past 6 years. Each report involves maltreatment by a parent or other caregiver (maltreatment by others is reported through other agencies). The latest report covers reports submitted in 1995 (NCCAN, 1997). Nearly two million cases of suspected maltreatment were investigated and 58% of these cases were substantiated, resulting in a total of 1,000,502 victims of substantiated maltreatment in 1995 (some substantiated cases involved more than one victim). This represents a rate of 15 per 1,000 children in the United States experiencing substantiated maltreatment in 1995. Twenty-five percent of these cases were of physical abuse (for a rate of 4 victims per 1,000 children) and 13% of the cases were of sexual abuse (for a rate of 2 victims per 1,000 children) (as is typical, most of the cases were for a form of neglect).

Rates of substantiated cases of child maltreatment reported to NCCAN have remained fairly stable since 1992, when there were 1,002,288 substantiated victims (NCCAN, 1996). The first year that the total number of substantiated victims declined from the prior year was 1994 (with 1,018,692 victims in 1993 and 1,011,628 victims in 1994).

Because of concerns about data on child maltreatment collected solely from state child protective service agencies, Congress has commissioned three broader studies of the incidence of child abuse and neglect. All of the studies have been sponsored by NCCAN, and data were collected in 1980, 1986, and 1993 (see Sedlak & Broadhurst, 1996, for a full report). Physical abuse was defined in 1980 as any parent's or parental substitute's act that caused demonstrable physical harm to the child. In 1986 and 1993 a second category of maltreatment was added that included all those with demonstrable harm and all those who were judged by a professional to be in danger of experiencing harm at some point in the future. Sexual abuse was categorized into intercourse, other genital contact, and nongenital contact (such as exposing genitals or fondling). Reports of abuse were gathered from child protection service agencies, schools, day-care centers, hospitals, police departments, mental health agencies, probation departments, and public health agencies. Thus, information was gathered that eluded child protective service agencies. Reports were screened to assure compliance with the definition of abuse and to eliminate duplicate reports on the same child.

Based on reports from selected counties throughout the country for a one-year period (42 counties were used in 1993), estimates of the incidence of child maltreatment during that year throughout the United States were made. The estimated number of children experiencing physical and sexual abuse by a parent or parental substitute are reported in Table 6.1. As can be seen, using the stricter harm standard resulted in far fewer reports than the use of the endangerment standard. Still, even with the harm standard, almost 600,000 children in the United States were physically or sexually abused in 1993 and became known to some professional. The percentage of the total number of cases of physical or sexual abuse that this represents is unknown.

Table 6.1
Results of the National Incidence Studies of Child Abuse and Neglect

		NIS-3 1993		NIS-2 1986		NIS-1 1980	
		Total Number of Children	Rate per 1,000 Children	Total Number of Children	Rate per 1,000 Children	Total Number of Children	Rate per 1,000 Children
Total[1]	(Harm[2])	1,553,800	23.1	931,000	14.8	625,100	9.8
	(Danger[3])	2,815,600	41.9	1,424,400	22.6	*	
Physical Abuse	(Harm)	381,700	5.7	269,700	4.3	199,100	3.1
	(Danger)	614,100	9.1	311,500	4.9	*	
Sexual Abuse	(Harm)	217,700	3.2	119,200	1.9	42,900	0.7
	(Danger)	300,200	4.5	133,600	2.1	*	

[1] All forms of physical, sexual, and emotional abuse and physical, emotional, and educational neglect.

[2] Using the "harm standard" requiring that some type of demonstrable harm to the child is apparent.

[3] Using the "endangerment standard," which includes all children counted in the harm standard *and* children who were judged to be in danger of experiencing harm from the maltreatment in the future.

* Data using the endangerment standard was not collected in NIS-1.

There has been a steady increase in the number of incidents known to professionals. The number of sexual abuse cases has increased the most, with nearly a tripling of known cases between 1980 and 1986, and nearly a further doubling of cases between 1986 and 1993.

Among sexual abuse victims in 1980 (using the harm standard), 50% had experienced intercourse, 30% had experienced some other genital contact, and 20% another form of sexual abuse. In 1986, the percentages were 32, 45, and 23 respectively (types of sexual abuse were not reported in 1993).

The amount of harm to the children was divided into several levels, including fatal, serious, and moderate. Serious harm resulted from either abuse or neglect that involved a life-threatening condition, a condition resulting in long-term impairment of physical or emotional functioning, or a condition that required professional intervention to prevent long-term impairment. Examples included loss of consciousness, broken bones, and diagnosed cases of failure to thrive. Moderate harm resulted from abuse or neglect that involved injuries or impairments that persisted in observable form for at least 48 hours. Examples included bruises and depressed mood. The amount of harm is described in Table 6.2.

Child Fatalities

One of the most disturbing aspects of child maltreatment is the number of cases of fatal child maltreatment each year. In 1995, 996 child fatalities were reported to NCCAN (NCCAN, 1997), and in 1994, 1,111 cases were reported (NCCAN, 1996). The number of fatalities has remained relatively steady during the 6 years of data collection by NCCAN, with less than a 10% difference reported from year to year (NCCAN, 1996). Most victims of fatal child maltreatment are very young, with about half the cases involving children less than 1 year of age, and about 75% of cases involving children less than 3 years (NCCAN, 1997). Rates of fatalities in the three National Incidence Studies are higher than those in the yearly NCCAN reports (see Table 6.2).

The U.S. Advisory Board on Child Abuse and Neglect (ABCAN) argues that the number of fatalities reported to NCCAN is an underestimation (ABCAN, 1995), and NCCAN acknowledges that child fatalities that occur in families not already involved in the child protection system are unlikely to be reported to NCCAN (NCCAN, 1997). ABCAN estimates that 2,000 children die from child maltreatment each year, or approximately 5 children each day (ABCAN, 1995). If this estimate is correct, then about

Table 6.2
Severity of Outcomes under the Harm Standard[1]

	NIS-3 1993		NIS-2 1986		NIS-1 1980	
	Total Number of Children	Rate per 1,000 Children	Total Number of Children	Rate per 1,000 Children	Total Number of Children	Rate per 1,000 Children
Fatal	1,500	0.02	1,100	0.02	1,000	0.02
Serious	565,000	8.4	141,700	2.3	131,200	2.1
Moderate	822,000	12.2	682,700	10.8	393,400	6.2

[1] Includes cases of abuse and cases of neglect.

4 children per 100,000 children are killed each year through child maltreatment. This is just under half the murder rate in the United States, which was estimated at 10 people per 100,000 population in 1995 (ABCAN, 1995).

Discussion

Incidence of reported child abuse has increased dramatically since 1970, although it appears to have leveled off since 1992. The extent to which the dramatic increase was due to an increase in the occurrence of abuse and neglect rather than increased reporting is impossible to say. It is notable that in 1980 there were about 4½ times as many reported cases of physical abuse than sexual abuse. By 1986, this difference was reduced to about twice as many cases of physical abuse. This suggests an increased vigilance for sexual abuse across the various agencies and possibly more refined methods for detecting sexual abuse.

Reported cases continue to show the vulnerability of young children to maltreatment, particularly to fatal child maltreatment. Children from low-income homes also are at greater risk for maltreatment.

STUDIES OF COLLEGE STUDENTS

Methodological Issues

The primary strength of these studies is the easy availability of college undergraduates for many researchers. Consequently, theories about abuse may be tested initially with relative ease. As well as the methodological issues previously mentioned, one other meaningful concern is that college students are generally not representative of either the general population or others their age. Colleges are often selective in the students they accept. Ongoing or severe family violence may adversely affect some children to the point where they cannot successfully compete for college admission. Therefore, results of college surveys may underestimate the prevalence of abuse in the general population, and may especially underestimate the most severe forms of abuse.

Study Findings

Berger et al. (1988) surveyed 4,695 undergraduates about "punitive childhood experiences" using anonymous questionnaires. One section contained questions about punitive experiences at the hands of their parents. Percentages of students who reported that the following experiences occurred at least once were: spanked, 80%; hit other than spanking, 20%; hit with an object, 35%; punched, 6%; kicked, 5%; choked 3%; and severely beaten, 2%. Twelve percent of the sample said that they had been injured as the result of punishment. Most of the injuries involved bruises or cuts; however, 7% were broken bones, 8% were burns, 5% were dental injuries, and 11% were head injuries. Despite the types of punishments and number of injuries, only 2.9% of the sample reported that they had been physically abused as a child.

Finkelhor (1979) and Haugaard and Emery (1989) were among researchers who investigated the prevalence of child sexual abuse in college samples. Both included abuse occurring before a child's 17th birthday. Finkelhor included noncontact abuse experiences and experiences that were both wanted and unwanted. Haugaard included only unwanted experiences that involved physical contact. Each study involved anonymous questionnaires. Finkelhor had a response rate of 90%, Haugaard and Emery had a response rate of 61%.

Haugaard and Emery found that 6% of the undergraduates had experienced sexual abuse with a father or father figure, and Finkelhor found that 8% had such an experience. These prevalence rates are similar but slightly lower than those reported in the community samples by Russell (1983) and Wyatt (1985).

FINDINGS OF STUDIES OF CHILDREN AS AGGRESSORS TOWARD PARENTS

Studies of the prevalence of children acting violently toward a parent are scarce. Parents might be reluctant to discuss situations in which they were assaulted by one of their children, and these parents have no group to advocate their situation in the public forum. It may be assumed that these parents are getting what they deserve, a position similar to that of many a few decades ago regarding child abuse. Two nationally based studies have shown that violence acts by children toward their parents are not isolated events.

Using the Straus et al. (1980) study discussed in a previous section, Cornell and Gelles (1982) examined the data from the 608 families that had at least one child between the ages of 10 and 17 living at home. Mothers or fathers were asked about violent acts toward them by a designated child in their family. The Conflict Tactics Scale was used, which gave an *overall violence* rating—including everything from slaps to using a gun or a knife—and a *severe violence* rating—including whether the child had kicked, punched, bit, hit with an object, beaten up, or threatened to use or used a gun or a knife.

Nine percent of the parents reported that a child had used one form of violence on them during the year before the interview, and 3% reported some type of severe violence. Daughters and sons had a similar likelihood of being violent. The amount of severe violence from boys steadily increased as they got older. Girls' violence increased between ages 10 and 13, and then decreased between the ages of 14 and 17. Mothers were more often victims than fathers of both overall violence (11% and 7%) and severe violence (5% and 1%). There was no association between the amount of child-initiated violence and family income, race, or family structure—a finding different from that regarding adult-initiated violence. Children who were more violent came from homes in which there was a higher incidence of parent-to-parent and parent-to-child violence.

Agnew and Huguley (1989) used data from the 1972 National Survey of Youth, conducted by the University of Michigan. A total of 1,395 adolescents between the ages of 11 and 18 were interviewed. One question they were asked was whether they had hit one of their parents in the previous 3 years. Approximately 9% of the adolescents had hit a parent in those 3 years. The authors classified 21% of these incidents as "trivial" in that the hit either was accidental, made in a playful way, or was so light that it was not detected by the parent. Five percent of the adolescents had hit a parent in a nontrivial manner. Similar percentages of females and males had hit a parent. Mothers were twice as likely to have been hit as fathers (6% and 3%). The amount of hitting for females increased steadily with age, and more White than Black females hit a parent. There was no association between age or race and hitting for males.

Discussion

These two studies are difficult to compare because of their many methodological differences. The discrepancy in overall amounts of violence may be due to the identity of the survey respondent (parent versus adolescent), definitions of violence employed, or types of families involved in the research. Similarities in the studies suggest that girls and boys hit their parents with similar frequency, and that mothers are more likely to be victims. Further study is needed, specifically about whether children who hit their parents are recipients of, or witnesses to, other forms of family violence.

CONCLUSION

Despite the type of sample examined, it is clear that prevalence of family violence involving children is very high in the United States. About 600,000 children in the United States are physically or sexually abused and then became known to some professional each year (Sedlak & Broadhurst, 1996). At least 1,000 children are killed by their parents each year (NCCAN, 1996) and the figure may be closer to 2,000 (ABCAN, 1995). Given that there are approximately 64 million children under the age of 18 in the United States (Department of Commerce, 1990), the results from Straus and Gelles's (1986) study suggests that 670,000 children may have been the victims of some severe form of violence within the past year. Results from college studies suggest that 12% of children who enter college have been physically injured by a parent before reaching college. Sexual abuse surveys suggest that 6% to 10% of children have been sexually abused by a parental figure, and that many encounters involve intercourse. Family violence is a problem of great magnitude.

The methodological issues discussed throughout this chapter could generally be expected to result in an underestimation of the actual prevalence of violence and abuse. Therefore, it seems reasonable to expect that the results of the studies reveal only some of the violence that has occurred. It also appears reasonable to assume that the most violent forms of abuse may be underestimated, particularly in studies involving general samples of households and college students.

Although some room for disagreement exists, it appears that children from low-income homes are at greater risk for physical and sexual abuse and that girls are at a higher risk during their teens and boys at a higher risk during their school-age years. This information may be valuable in directing prevention and intervention efforts.

The continuing greater amount of interest in the professional community and the public regarding children who have been sexually abused rather than physically abused seems incorrect, given that many more children are the victims of physical abuse than sexual abuse. Part of the difference in interest may be due to the more recent "emergence" of the problem of sexual abuse or a concern that sexually abused children may sustain more serious long- and short-term consequences. Another explanation is that the difference in interest reflects our society's greater abhorrence of those who are sexual with children than those who beat them. This may reflect our continuing ambivalence about the good or harm that can come from hitting a child, and a deeply rooted belief that children should remain shielded from sexuality.

REFERENCES

ABCAN (US Advisory Board on Child Abuse and Neglect). (1995). *A nation's shame: Fatal child abuse and neglect in the United States.* Washington, DC: U.S. Government Printing Office.

Agnew, R., & Huguley, S. (1989). Adolescent violence toward parents. *Journal of Marriage and the Family, 51,* 699–711.

Berger, A.M., Knutson, J.F., Mehm, J.G., & Perkins, K.A. (1988). The self-report of punitive childhood experiences of young adults and adolescents. *Child Abuse & Neglect, 12,* 251–262.

Blackman, J. (1989). *Intimate violence.* New York: Columbia University Press.

Boney-McCoy, S., & Finkelhor, D. (1995). Psychosocial sequelae of violent victimization in a national youth sample. *Journal of Consulting and Clinical Psychology, 63,* 726–736.

Bourne, R. (1979). Child abuse and neglect: An overview. In R. Bourne & E. Newberger (Eds.), *Critical perspectives on child abuse* (pp. 1–25). Lexington, MA: Lexington Books.

Department of Commerce. (1990). *Statistical abstracts of the United States.* Washington, DC: U.S. Government Printing Office.

Cornell, C.P., & Gelles, R.J. (1982). Adolescent-to-parent violence. *Urban Social Change Review, 15,* 8–14.

Cox, A., Rutter, M., Yule, B., & Quinton, D. (1977). Bias resulting from missing information: Some epidemiological findings. *British Journal of Preventive and Social Medicine, 31,* 131–136.

Cozby, P.C. (1973). Self disclosure: A literature review. *Psychological Bulletin, 79,* 73–91.

Finkelhor, D. (1979). *Sexually victimized children.* New York: Free Press.

Fritz, G.S., Stoll, K., & Wagner, N.N. (1981). A comparison of males and females who were sexually molested as children. *Journal of Sex and Marital Therapy, 7,* 54–59.

Fromuth, M.E. (1986). The relationship of childhood sexual abuse with late psychological and sexual adjustment in a sample of college women. *Child Abuse & Neglect, 10,* 5–15.

Garbarino, J., & Gilliam, G. (1980). *Understanding abusive families.* Lexington, MA: Lexington Books.

Geffner, R., Rosenbaum, A., & Hughes, H. (1988). Research issues concerning family violence. In V. Van Hasselt, R. Morrison, A. Bellack, & M. Hersen (Eds.), *Handbook of family violence* (pp. 457–481). New York: Plenum Press.

Gelles, R.J. (1978). Methods for studying sensitive family topics. *American Journal of Orthopsychiatry, 48,* 408–424.

Gelles, R.J. (1979). *Family violence.* Beverly Hills, CA: Sage.

Gelles, R.J. (1982). Child abuse and family violence: Implications for medical professionals. In E. Newberger (Ed.), *Child abuse* (pp. 25–41). Boston: Little, Brown.

Gil, D.G. (1970). *Violence against children.* Cambridge, MA: Harvard University Press.

Giovannoni, J.M., & Becerra, R.M. (1979). *Defining child abuse.* New York: Free Press.

Graham, P., Dingwall, R., & Wolkind, S. (1985). Research issues in child abuse. *Social Science in Medicine, 21,* 1217–1228.

Hampton, R.L. (1987). Race, class and child maltreatment. *Journal of Comparative Family Studies, 18,* 113–126.

Haugaard, J.J., & Emery, R.E. (1989). Methodological issues in child sexual abuse research. *Child Abuse & Neglect, 13,* 89–100.

Haugaard, J.J., & Reppucci, N.D. (1988). *The sexual abuse of children.* San Francisco: Jossey-Bass.

Jouriles, E.N., & O'Leary, K.D. (1985). Interspousal reliability of reports of marital violence. *Journal of Consulting and Clinical Psychology, 53,* 419–421.

Knutson, J.F. (1995). Psychological characteristics of maltreated children. *Annual Review of Psychology, 46,* 401–431.

Lindholm, K.J., & Willey, R. (1986). Ethnic differences in child abuse and sexual abuse. *Hispanic Journal of Behavioral Sciences, 8,* 111–125.

Lodico, M.A., Gruber, E., & DiClemente, R.J. (1996). Childhood sexual abuse and coercive sex among school-based adolescents in a Midwestern state. *Journal of Adolescent Health, 18,* 211–217.

National Center on Child Abuse and Neglect (NCCAN). (1988). *Study of national incidence and prevalence of child abuse and neglect.* Washington, DC: U.S. Department of Health and Human Services.

NCCAN. (1996). *Child maltreatment in 1994: Reports from the states to the National Center on Child Abuse and Neglect.* Washington, DC: U.S. Government Printing Office.

NCCAN. (1997). *Child maltreatment in 1995: Reports from the states to the National Center on Child Abuse and Neglect.* Washington, DC: U.S. Government Printing Office.

Rollin, B.E. (1985). The moral status of research animals in psychology. *American Psychologist, 40,* 920–926.

Russell, D. (1983). The incidence and prevalence of intrafamilial and extrafamilial sexual abuse of female children. *Child Abuse & Neglect, 7,* 133–146.

Rutter, M. (1979). Surveys to answer questions. *Acta Psychiatrica Scandinavica, 65*(Suppl. 296), 64–76.

Sedlak, A.J., & Broadhurst, D.D. (1996). *The third national incidence study of child abuse and neglect.* Washington, DC: U.S. Government Printing Office.

Siegel, J.M., Sorenson, S.G., Golding, J.M., Burnam, M.A., & Stein, J.A. (1987). The prevalence of childhood sexual assault. *American Journal of Epidemiology, 126,* 1141–1153.

Starr, R.H. (1988). Physical abuse of children. In V. Van Hasselt, R. Morrison, A. Bellack, & M. Hersen (Eds.), *Handbook of family violence* (pp. 119–155). New York: Plenum Press.

Steinmetz, S.K. (1978). The battered husband syndrome. *Victimology, 2,* 499–509.

Straus, M.A., & Gelles, R.J. (1986). Societal change and change in family violence from 1975–1985. *Journal of Marriage and the Family, 48,* 465–479.

Straus, M.A., Gelles, R.J., & Steinmetz, S.K. (1980). *Behind closed doors: Violence in the American family.* Garden City, NY: Anchor Books.

Tsuang, M.T., Tohen, M., & Zahner, G. (Eds.). (1995). *Textbook in psychiatric epidemiology.* New York: Wiley.

Wekerle, C., & Wolfe, D. (1996). Child maltreatment. In E. Mash & R. Barkley (Eds.), *Child psychopathology.* New York: Guilford Press.

Williams, D.H. (1986). The epidemiology of mental illness in Afro-Americans. *Hospital and Community Psychiatry, 37,* 42–49.

Wurr, C.J., & Partridge, I.M. (1996). The prevalence of a history of childhood sexual abuse in an acute adult inpatient population. *Child Abuse & Neglect, 20,* 867–872.

Wyatt, G.E. (1985). The sexual abuse of Afro-American and White-American women in childhood. *Child Abuse and Neglect, 9,* 507–519.

CHAPTER 7

Epidemiology of Intimate Partner Violence and Other Family Violence Involving Adults

RONET BACHMAN

TWO PRIMARY questions are addressed in this chapter: (1) How many adults in the United States experience intimate-perpetrated violence and other forms of family violence annually? (2) Are particular subgroups of the population more likely to experience these types of violence? The answers to these questions are very important, but not altogether straightforward. For many reasons, including the historical stigma attached to intimate perpetrated violence, fear of retaliation from their perpetrators, and other safety concerns, estimating incidence rates of these victimizations has always been a difficult task. Not surprisingly, research employing diverse methodologies and definitions of these victimizations has yielded different estimates.

The most enduring source of statistical information about violent crime in the United States is the Uniform Crime Reporting (UCR) program compiled by the Federal Bureau of Investigation (FBI). The UCR collects information about criminal incidents of violence that are reported to the police. However, using police reports to estimate incidence rates of violence between intimates and family members is problematic for several reasons. Perhaps foremost of these is that large percentages of these crimes are never reported to police. Based on comparisons with national survey data, it is estimated that only about 40% to 50% of crimes become known to police, and reporting percentages for violent crimes committed by intimates and other family members may be much lower (Reiss & Roth, 1993). In addition, except for the crime of homicide, the current UCR program does not include information on the victim/offender relationship within its reports.

Because of the weaknesses of the UCR program for estimating rates of violence within families, random sample surveys of the population have begun to be used as the social science tool of choice for uncovering incidents of violence within families. However, as can be imagined, surveys employing diverse methodologies and different definitions of violence have resulted in tremendously diverse estimates. Studies of how many women experience violence by an intimate partner annually range from 9.3 per 1,000 women (Bachman & Saltzman, 1995) to 116 per 1,000 women (Straus & Gelles, 1990). Further, the differences across survey methodologies often preclude direct comparison across studies.

Estimates of family violence cannot be appropriately discussed without adequate attention given to the methodologies on which these estimates are based. Thus, the purpose of this chapter is actually twofold: to highlight what is known about the extent of family and intimate perpetrated violence between adults and to discuss the methodological foundations from which this information was obtained. The chapter begins with a discussion on the most extreme form of violence, homicide. It then reviews what is known about nonfatal forms of this violence from representative sample surveys. Finally, because there has been so much controversy about the magnitude and scope of intimate-perpetrated violence, the chapter concludes with a discussion of the methodological differences which may account for the differences in estimates between two of the largest survey attempts to measure this violence against women: the redesigned National Crime Victimization Survey and National Family Violence Survey.

DEFINING TERMS

Definitions of violence in the research literature vary widely. For example, Gelles and Straus (1979) define violence as an "act carried out with the intention or perceived intention of physically hurting another person" (p. 20). This "hurt" can range from the slight pain caused by a slap, to harm that results in severe injury or even death. In contrast, the Committee on Family Violence of the National Institute of Mental Health (1992) included in its definition of violence "acts that are physically and emotionally harmful or that carry the potential to cause physical harm . . . [and] may also include sexual coercion or assaults, physical intimidation, threats to kill or to harm, restraint of normal activities or freedom, and denial of access to resources." As can be seen in operationalizing conceptual definitions of violence, some include psychological and emotional abuse, financial abuse, and sexual coercion, as well as physical and sexual assault as legally defined. In addition, some investigators include acts that were intended to cause physical harm or injury while others argue that intentionality, because it is difficult to ascertain, should also include acts that are perceived as having the intention of producing physical harm (Crowell & Burgess, 1996). Such diversity in definitions has not surprisingly produced a wide array of estimates of intimate partner and family violence.

This chapter focuses exclusively on acts of physical violence, which refer to behaviors that threaten, attempt, or actually inflict physical harm. The focus on physical violence does not imply that physical acts are the only types of abuse that intimates and family members can inflict on each other. Verbal aggression and emotional abuse can be just as harmful; however, these forms of maltreatment are beyond the scope of this chapter and are discussed in detail elsewhere in this book.

In addition, intimate partner violence is used in this chapter to refer to violent behaviors by intimate partners: spouses, ex-spouses, boyfriends, and girlfriends, and ex-boyfriends and ex-girlfriends. Violent incidents perpetrated by other family members such as parents, siblings, children, and grandparents are referred to as forms of other family violence.

FATAL VIOLENCE

As mentioned earlier, data on homicides in the United States that include characteristics of both the victim and offender are collected by the FBI and termed the Supplementary Homicide Reports (SHR), which are part of the larger UCR program. The victim/offender relationship information for homicides occurring in 1992 against male and female victims is presented in Table 7.1.

It should be noted that in 41% of male homicides and 31% of female homicides, the victim-offender relationship was never identified. Thus, readers are urged to use caution in interpreting these estimates. Nonetheless, it can be seen that patterns of vulnerability across types of homicide offenders significantly differ for men and women. As shown in Table 7.1, female victims of homicide were significantly more likely to be killed by a husband, ex-husband, or boyfriend than male victims were to be killed by their wife, ex-wife, or girlfriend. In 1992, approximately 28% of female victims of homicide (1,414 women) were known to have been killed by their husband, ex-husband, or boyfriend. In contrast, just over 3% of male homicide victims (637 men) were known to have been killed by their wife, ex-wife, of girlfriend. Men were significantly more likely to be killed by strangers and acquaintances compared with intimates and other family members.

Unlike rates of nonfatal violence for intimate partner violence, trends in homicide between intimates can be more reliably tracked. Figure 7.1 displays the trends in the rate per 100,00 population aged 16 and over of homicide victimization for wives or girlfriends and of husbands or boyfriends. As this figure illustrates, the rates of homicide by an intimate has remained very stable for women, but has declined for men. The rate for female victims killed by their boyfriends or husbands has remained between 1.5 and 1.7 per 100,000 for the entire time period between 1977 and 1992. However, for men, the rate has dropped from 1.5 in 1977 to 0.7 in 1992. Many researchers have speculated about this differential decline, with some suggesting that the availability of

Table 7.1
Percentage of Homicides in 1992 by Sex of Victim
and Victim/Offender Relationship

	Female Victims	Male Victims
Victim/Offender Relationship		
Spouse/ex-spouse	18.0%	2.2%
Boy/girlfriend	10.3	1.4
Other relative	10.2	5.5
Acquaintance/friend	22.0	34.6
Stranger	8.6	15.0
Relationship not identified	30.9	41.3
Number of Incidents		
Relationship identified	3,454	10,351
Relationship not identified	1,547	7,824
Total number of incidents	5,001	17,635

Note. Adapted from Bachman & Saltzman (1995).

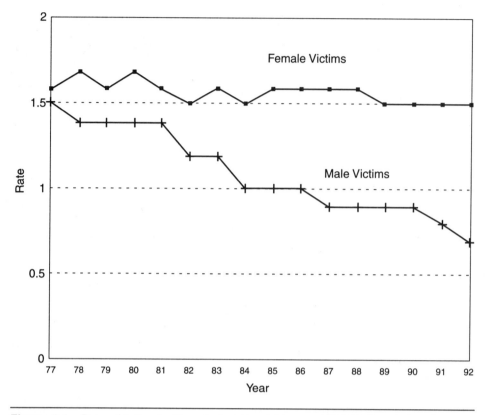

Figure 7.1   Rate of Intimate Perpetrated Homicide per 100,000 Population Aged 16 and Over by Sex of Victim, 1977–92.

services for battered women may be playing a role in the decrease in males killed by intimates by offering women shelters and other means of escaping violent situations (Browne & Williams, 1989).

NONFATAL VIOLENCE: ESTIMATES FROM SURVEYS

Ideally, the most accurate and reliable method of measuring the incidence of family violence would be to interview all individuals within a given population about their past victimization experiences. For obvious reasons, however, this is not feasible. A method which is currently used to estimate rates of victimization within a given population is called a random sample survey. Most researchers agree that a sample of the population that is selected randomly from among all eligible respondents will produce estimates of a given phenomenon that are accurate within a measurable range. Random selection helps to ensure that those who respond are statistically representative of everyone in the population and that the results can be generalized to the population as a whole. This is important because many studies of family violence do not rely on random samples, but rather on what are termed "clinical" or "convenience" samples. In fact, the earliest attempts to study family violence involved case studies of female victims who had been in contact with helping agencies such as shelters for battered women or counseling facilities. These samples have the advantage to researchers of being readily available and inexpensive to acquire. However, the major problem with these samples is that respondents are not representative of the entire population of people who experience forms of intimate and family-perpetrated violence. Therefore, generalizations made from these samples about patterns of family violence within the population as a whole are precarious at best. For this reason, the remainder of this chapter will rely on information about intimate and family-perpetrated violence obtained from large representative and random sample surveys of the population. The first to be discussed is the National Family Violence Survey.

THE 1985 NATIONAL FAMILY VIOLENCE SURVEY

The National Family Violence Survey, conducted in 1976 and in 1985, was sponsored by the National Institute of Mental Health. For simplicity of presentation, this survey will be referred to as the "Family Violence Survey" in this chapter. The primary investigators for this study were Murray Straus, from the University of New Hampshire, and Richard Gelles, from the University of Rhode Island. The most recent 1985 survey was done by telephone with a nationally representative sample of 6,002 persons aged 18 and over who were married or cohabiting with a person of the opposite sex.

As noted earlier, violence, as defined by Gelles and Straus (1990), is an act carried out with the intention or perceived intention of physically hurting another person. To obtain incidents of violence from respondents, the survey utilized what is known as the *Conflict Tactics Scale* (CTS) (Gelles & Straus, 1990). Introduction to the CTS asks respondents to think of situations in the past year when they had a disagreement or were angry with a specified family member and to indicate how often they engaged in each of the acts included in the CTS. The list of acts covered in the CTS spans many tactics, including reasoning, verbal aggression, and physical aggression or violence. Physical violence by the CTS index is often subdivided into two categories: (1) minor violence, and (2) severe violence. These categories consist of the following acts:

Minor Violence

- Threw something.
- Pushed, grabbed, or shoved.
- Slapped.

Severe Violence

- Kicked, bit, or hit with a fist.
- Hit or tried to hit with something.
- Beat up.
- Choked.
- Threatened with a knife or gun.
- Used a knife or fired a gun.

Annual incidence rates for violence perpetrated by both men and women against their partners obtained from the 1985 Family Violence Survey are displayed in Table 7.2.

As Table 7.2 indicates, the rate of 116 per 1,000 couples shows that almost 1 out of 8 husbands carried out 1 or more violent acts during the year of this study. Further, the

Table 7.2

Percentage of Women and Men Who Had Experienced Violence
Perpetrated by a Partner as Operationalized by the CTS,
National Family Violence Survey, 1985

	Acts of Violence Committed Annually		
	Percent of Couples	Annual Rate per 1,000	Number Assaulted*
Any Violence Perpetrated by Husband	11%	116	6,250,000
Severe Violence Perpetrated by Husband	3%	34	1,800,000
Any Violence Perpetrated by Wife	12%	124	6,800,000
Severe Violence Perpetrated by Wife	4%	48	2,600,000

Note. Adapted from Straus & Gelles (1990), Table 6.1, p. 97. Any violence includes both minor and severe items, while severe violence includes only those items specified as severe. These violence rates were computed by reclassifying the violence subscales into violent and nonviolent categories, scored 0 and 1. As such, any act of minor violence by the husband would result in the "Any Violence" scale to be coded as 1. Similarly, any act of severe violence by the husband would result in the "Severe Violence" scale to be coded as 1.

*The number assaulted was computed by multiplying the rates in this table by the 1984 population figures as given by the 1986 Statistical Abstract of the United States. The population figure (rounded to millions) was 54 million couples.

rate of severe violence perpetrated by husbands indicates that about 1.8 million women were beaten by their partner that year.

Notice that rates of violence perpetrated by wives against husbands are very similar to rates of violence perpetrated by husbands against wives. Herein lies one of the most frequent criticisms of the CTS methodology, that it measures acts of violence in isolation from the circumstances under which the acts were committed. As critics point out, the CTS ignores who initiates the violence, the relative size and strength of the persons involved, and the nature of the participant's relationship (Dobash, Dobash, Wilson, & Daly, 1992; Saunders, 1986). Straus and Gelles (1990) themselves, however, are quick to point out that the meaning behind these estimates is often misunderstood. They acknowledge, "To understand the high rate of intrafamily violence by women, it is also important to realize that many of the assaults by women against their husbands are acts of retaliation or self-defense. One of the most fundamental reasons why women are violent within the family (but rarely outside the family) is that for a typical American woman, her home is the location where there is the most serious risk of assault (p. 98)." This remains only conjecture since the CTS methodology does not account for the sequence of events which precipitate an act of violence. The other nationally representative sample survey to be addressed in this chapter is the redesigned National Crime Victimization Survey.

THE REDESIGNED NATIONAL CRIME VICTIMIZATION SURVEY

Before reviewing the rates of intimate-perpetrated assault obtained by the National Crime Victimization Survey, this section first provides a brief description of the survey's methodology. Again, for ease of interpretation, this survey is referred to as the

"NCVS." Sponsored by the Bureau of Justice Statistics (BJS), the NCVS is the second largest ongoing survey sponsored by the U.S. government. In the sample design used for the survey, housing units (e.g., addresses) are selected from a stratified, multistage cluster sample. When a sample unit is selected for the survey, all current residents of that unit are interviewed by an interviewer from the U.S. Bureau of the Census. Those eligible for the sample include individuals 12 years of age or older living in the United States; group quarters such as dormitories, rooming houses, and religious dwellings are permissible housing units, but correctional quarters such as prisons are excluded. The current sample consists of approximately 50,000 housing units and 101,000 persons. These households are interviewed every six months for three years; the first and fifth interviews are conducted in person, and the remainder are held by telephone whenever possible. The NCVS obtains an average annual response rate of over 96%.

Since its inception in 1972, the NCVS has collected information about the following types of crimes including attempts: rape, robbery, assault, larceny, burglary, and motor vehicle theft. Detailed information about each victimization is recorded; so are the characteristics of the offender, insofar as the victim can report them. Beginning in 1979, BJS began an extensive 10-year redesign project of the NCVS. An important goal of the redesign was to estimate more accurately the incidents of rape and violence perpetrated by intimates and other family members. The new survey screening instrument began a phase-in process in 1989 and was incorporated into the entire NCVS sample by 1993.

Before the redesign, no specific questions asked respondents directly about attacks that were perpetrated by relatives or offenders known to them. If a respondent revealed, however, that he or she had been attacked or otherwise victimized by someone who was known, the incident was recorded as such. The relationship of the victim to the offender then would have been placed in one of the following categories: known by sight only, casual acquaintance, spouse at time of incident, ex-spouse at time of incident, parent or stepparent, own child or stepchild, brother/sister, other relative, boy/girlfriend, ex-boy/girlfriend, friend or ex-friend, roommate or boarder, schoolmate, neighbor, someone at work, or other nonrelative.

After extensive deliberations, it was decided that although it would not be feasible to change the focus of the NCVS to include a section on tactics of conflict resolution between spouses or partners, the current instrument could incorporate questions that would estimate more accurately the incidents of violence by relatives and intimates.

Accordingly, after the general questions about acts of violence or theft, the screener instrument for uncovering victimizations now includes the following questions:

Other than any incidents already mentioned, has anyone attacked or threatened you in any of these ways:

    a. With any weapon, for instance, a gun or knife—
    b. With anything like a baseball bat, frying pan, scissors, or a stick—
    c. By something thrown, such as a rock or bottle—
    d. Include any grabbing, punching, or choking,
    e. Any rape, attempted rape or other type of sexual attack—
    f. Any face to face threats—

        OR

    g. Any attack or threat or use of force by anyone at all?

Please mention it even if you are not certain it was a crime.

2) Incidents involving forced or unwanted sexual acts are often difficult to talk about. Have you been forced or coerced to engage in unwanted sexual activity by—

    a. Someone you didn't know before—
    b. A casual acquaintance OR—
    c. Someone you know well—

If respondents reply affirmatively to one of these questions, interviewers next ask *"Do you mean forced or coerced sexual intercourse?"* to determine whether the incident should be recorded as rape or as another type of sexual attack. The definition from the NCVS interviewer's manual for rape is as follows: "Rape is forced sexual intercourse and includes both psychological coercion as well as physical force. Forced sexual intercourse means vaginal, anal, or oral penetration by the offender(s). This category also includes incidents where the penetration is from a foreign object such as a bottle."

To further cue respondents about incidents of victimization that are not committed by strangers, they are then asked:

3) People often don't think of incidents committed by someone they know. Did you have something stolen from you OR were you attacked or threatened by—

    a. Someone at work or school—
    b. A neighbor or friend—
    c. A relative or family member—
    d. Any other person you've met or known?

Not surprisingly, estimates of violence against women using this new screening instrument almost doubled the rates of intimate-perpetrated violence (by husband, ex-husband, boyfriend, or ex-boyfriend) against women estimated by the NCVS. Using the redesigned screening instrument, estimates reveal that nearly 5 million violent victimizations are experienced by females over the age of 12 every year. Of those victimizations involving lone offenders, the NCVS estimates that 29% are perpetrated by intimates, 9% are perpetrated by other relatives such as siblings, parents, and children, 40% are committed by other known offenders, and only 23% are perpetrated by strangers. The rates of lone-offender victimization per 1,000 males and females aged 12 and over are presented in Table 7.3.

From Table 7.3, it can be seen that rates of intimate-perpetrated violence estimated using the NCVS are lower than those obtained from the Family Violence Survey. Also notice, however, that unlike estimates from the Family Violence Survey, the NCVS indicates that women are much more likely to experience an act of intimate-perpetrated violence than are men (9.3 per 1,000 vs. 1.4 per 1,000).

In addition, unlike the Family Violence Survey, the sample for the NCVS includes all persons, regardless of their marital or living status. Thus, the NCVS can also estimate rates of intimate-perpetrated violence for single, divorced, and never married women. This is important because rates of intimate perpetrated violence for these women have been found to be significantly higher than those for married women. For example, as shown later in this chapter, rates of intimate perpetrated violence for separated women are over 8 times higher than rates for married women: a rate of 2.7 per 1,000 married women versus a rate of 82.2 per 1,000 separated women (Bachman & Saltzman, 1995).

Table 7.3

Average Annual Rate and Number of Violent Victimizations Committed
by Lone Offenders by Sex of Victim and Victim/Offender Relationship,
National Crime Victimization Survey 1992–1994

	Intimate	Other Relative	Acquaintance/ Friend	Stranger
FEMALE VICTIMS				
Average annual rate per 1,000 females age 12 or older	9.3	2.8	12.9	7.4
Average annual number of victimizations against females	1,008,000	304,500	1,402,500	802,300
MALE VICTIMS				
Average annual rate per 1,000 males age 12 or older	1.4	1.2	17.2	19.0
Average annual number of victimizations against males	143,400	122,000	1,754,000	1,933,100

Note. Adapted from Bachman & Saltzman (1995).

WHY ARE THE INCIDENCE ESTIMATES SO DIFFERENT ACROSS THE FAMILY VIOLENCE SURVEY AND THE NCVS?

The most obvious explanation for the rate differentials across the Family Violence survey and the NCVS pertains to the manner in which information about these victimizations was solicited. The Family Violence Survey is guised as a survey interested in a number of family-related issues including tactics used in "conflict resolution." The National Crime NCVS, as the name clearly conveys, is a survey interested in obtaining information about "crimes." Some survey participants still may not view assaults by intimates and other family members as criminal acts. Even though many of the behaviors conveyed in the screening instruments (e.g., kicking, punching) are the same for both surveys, the context in which these questions are asked must inevitably play a role in the extent of disclosure respondents are willing to provide.

Related to the issue of disclosure is that, for the NCVS, all respondents within a selected household are interviewed. Thus, all family members are asked the same set of screening questions regarding their victimization experiences with both known and unknown offenders. Even though respondents are instructed that they can reschedule a telephone or personal interview for a more "convenient" time (e.g., when the respondent can be interviewed without others being present), this situation may nevertheless prevent some respondents from disclosing incidents of violence to interviewers, particularly those incidents perpetrated by intimate partners within the same household.

Another difference has to do with the universe from which the samples of each survey are taken. The Family Violence Survey, as stated earlier, interviewed married or cohabiting heterosexual couples over the age of 18 only. The NCVS includes *all* individuals age 12 and over in its sample. Since rates of intimate perpetrated violence are highest for those between the ages of 19–29 (Bachman & Saltzman, 1995), the inclusion of those aged 12–18 in the NCVS sample may serve to deflate overall rates of violence generated by this survey relative to the Family Violence Survey. In addition, widowed women who are typically over the age of 65 are also included in the NCVS sample. These women are the least likely to experience intimate perpetrated violence, yet because they are also included in the sample, this also serves to deflate the overall rates of intimate-perpetrated violence produced by the NCVS compared with the Family Violence Survey.

A more fundamental reason why estimates may vary, which is rarely acknowledged, has to do with the way in which incidents of violence are counted by the NCVS. This issue is related to "bounding," that is, placing the incident within a particular time frame, and is best explained through example. During each interview, respondents are asked about any victimization they may have experienced within the past 6 months. Interviews then focus on the specific period in which the incident occurred. Incidents reported in that interview are compared with incidents reported in a previous interview. When a report appears to be a duplicate of an earlier reported incident, respondents are reminded of that report and are asked whether the new report represents the incident mentioned previously or a different incident. The sole purpose of the first interview, then, is to set an initial time reference (bounding). Data collected at the first interview are not included in NCVS estimates. Since respondents in the Family Violence Survey sample were interviewed only once, incidents were not bounded. Because tests have found unbounded interviews to produce significantly higher victimization rates than bounded interviews (Backman & Taylor, 1994), this is another likely reason why Family Violence Survey estimates are higher compared with NCVS estimates.

MEN'S AND WOMEN'S USE OF VIOLENCE

A more perplexing issue concerning rate differentials between the Family Violence Survey and the NCVS has to do with the extent of gender "symmetry" in male-to-female violence versus female-to-male violence as indicated by estimates from the Family Violence Survey. Rates of victimization from the Family Violence Survey indicate that women use violence against men as much as men use violence against women. Because this issue comes up again and again in critiques among advocates and researchers, the methodological foundations for this perplexing finding are worth reiterating. Recall that the basic methodology of the Conflict Tactics Scale (CTS) used in the Family Violence Survey is to simply count the raw number of violent acts committed by individuals. It does not provide us with any information on why these acts of violence took place, such as how many of these acts occurred because a woman was using physical violence in self-defense against her attacker. In general, research demonstrates that estimates using the CTS methodology will usually find gender symmetry, that is, men and women engaging in similar rates of violence. The context of the violence is not taken into account, however, making this symmetry somewhat erroneous primarily because women commonly use violence to defend themselves. Research employing the CTS, but including qualifying questions after each act (e.g., "What percentage of these times do you estimate that in doing these actions you were primarily motivated by acting in self-defense, that is, protecting yourself from immediate physical harm?") has shown that a substantial number of women reported that their violence was in self-defense or fighting back (DeKeseredy, Saunders, Schwartz, & Alvi, 1997; Saunders, 1986).

In contrast to this gender symmetry, the NCVS clearly demonstrates that women are more often the victims of intimate-perpetrated violence compared with men. In fact, the NCVS estimates that rates of intimate violence against women perpetrated by men are almost 8 times higher than rates of intimate violence against men perpetrated by women. These differential patterns of intimate-perpetration are also found when homicide statistics from the Supplementary Homicide Reports compiled by the Federal Bureau of Investigation are analyzed. As discussed earlier, women are significantly more likely to be killed by intimates such as husbands and boyfriends compared with men. Thus, other data and research findings lend no support for the gender symmetry thesis.

DEMOGRAPHIC CHARACTERISTICS OF INTIMATE AND FAMILY VIOLENCE AGAINST WOMEN

Debates about the magnitude of family violence sometimes divert attention from the fact that survey research shows a number of consistent patterns. For example, the highest rates of intimate partner violence are experienced by young women, particularly those who may be living in conditions of economic deprivation and poverty. Table 7.4 provides average annual rates of intimate and other family perpetrated violent victimization against women from the NCVS for 1992–1993 by various demographic characteristics.

As Table 7.4 indicates, violence against women perpetrated by intimates was consistent across both racial and ethnic boundaries. No statistically significant differences exist between African American and White women or between Hispanic and non-Hispanic women. Compared with other age groups, women aged 19 to 29 experienced more violence by intimates while women aged 12 to 18 reported more incidents of violence by other family members and relatives. Compared with all other age groups, women aged 65 and older were the least likely to experience an act of violence perpetrated by either intimates or other family members.

Regarding income, women with an annual family income under $10,000 were more likely to report having experienced acts of violence perpetrated by both intimates and other family members than those with an income of $10,000 or more. Among female victims of violence committed by an intimate, the victimization rate of women separated from their husbands was about 3 times higher than that of divorced women and about 25 times higher than that of married women. However, because the NCVS reflects a respondent's marital status at the time of the interview, not necessarily at the time of the victimization, it is not possible to determine whether a woman was separated or divorced at the time of the incident or whether separation or divorce followed the incident. Regarding location of residence, there was little variation in the extent to which women living in urban, suburban, and rural locations experienced violence by intimates.

There is paucity of research exploring violence against women of color. Although the findings from the NCVS fail to demonstrate significant differences in intimate partner violence between White and African American women and Hispanic and non-Hispanic women, other surveys have found such differences (Cazenave & Straus, 1990; Sorenson, Upchurch, & Shen, 1996; Straus & Smith, 1990). However, it remains unclear how much of the differences found in these studies may be explained by socioeconomic factors and how much by cultural factors. Moreover, even less is known

Table 7.4

Average Annual Rate per 1,000 of Violent Victimizations of Women
by a Lone Offender by Victim Characteristics and Victim/Offender
Relationship, National Crime Victimization Survey 1992–1993

	Intimate Violence	Other Family/ Relative Violence
Race		
White	9.1	2.6
Black	10.9	3.6
Other	6.5	4.5
Ethnicity		
Hispanic	7.3	3.2
Non-Hispanic	9.4	2.8
Age		
12–18	9.6	6.1
19–29	21.3	4.7
30–45	10.8	2.8
46–64	2.2	1.2
65 or older	1.2	0.3
Annual Family Income		
$9,999 or less	19.9	6.1
$10,000–$14,999	13.3	4.0
$15,000–$19,999	10.9	3.1
$20,000–$29,999	9.5	2.7
$30,000–$49,999	5.4	1.8
$50,000 or more	4.5	1.8
Marital Status		
Married	2.7	1.6
Widowed	1.9	0.6
Divorced	23.1	4.2
Separated	82.2	10.0
Never Married	12.0	4.6
Location of Residence		
Urban	10.7	3.0
Suburban	9.2	2.7
Rural	7.7	2.7

Note. Adapted from Bachman & Saltzman (1995).

about other minority groups such as Asian American and American Indian women (Bachman, 1992; Malcoe, Montgomery, & Lee, 1997).

SEXUAL VIOLENCE

Like the measurement of other violence, estimating the incidence rates of rape and sexual assault continues to be problematic. Why include a discussion of rape and sexual assault in this chapter? Because it will be seen that as with other forms of violence, disaggregated rates of rape reveal that intimate offenders perpetrate a significant proportion of these victimizations against women.

Also like research investigating the extent of other violence, many methodological factors influence who will be counted as a rape victim in surveys including the definition of rape used, the type of screening questions used, and the use of the word rape versus the use of behavioral descriptions to name but a few. The only two nationally representative surveys to attempt to measure the incidence rates of rape to date are the redesigned NCVS and the National Women's Study (Kilpatrick, Edmunds, & Seymour, 1992).

To reiterate, the redesigned NCVS now asks respondents: "Incidents involving forced or unwanted sexual acts are often difficult to talk about. (Other than any incidents already mentioned), have you been forced or coerced to engage in unwanted sexual activity by (1) Someone you didn't know before, (2) A casual acquaintance, or (3) Someone you know well." If a respondent replies yes, the interviewer completes an incident report. At this time, the interviewer is asked to clarify exactly what type of sexual activity occurred by asking the respondent, "Do you mean forced or coerced sexual intercourse?" Again, if the answer is affirmative, the incident is coded as a rape. If there is some confusion about the meaning of "sexual intercourse," interviewers are provided with a very explicit definition of rape adopted by the NCVS. This definition can be used for reference or can be read to respondents at any time during the interview and states:

> Rape is forced sexual intercourse and includes both psychological coercion as well as physical force. Forced sexual intercourse means vaginal, anal, or oral penetration by the offender(s). This category also includes incidents where the penetration is from a foreign object such as a bottle.

Depending on the respondent's reply, an incident can be categorized into one of several specific types of victimization including completed rape, attempted rape or another form of sexual attack. Both males and females can be classified as rape victims according to this methodology; however, average annual rates of victimization indicate that women are significantly more likely to be victimized than men (Bachman & Saltzman, 1995, reported rates of 4.6 and 0.5 for women and men respectively). An analysis of lone-offender rape and sexual assault victimizations against women from the NCVS in 1992–1993 revealed that only 18% of all victimizations were perpetrated by strangers; 26% of all rapes and sexual assaults were committed by intimate partners, 3% by other family members and relatives, and 53% by friends and other acquaintances.

The National Women's Study was supported by the National Institute on Drug Abuse and conducted by Dean Kilpatrick and colleagues at the Medical University of South Carolina (Kilpatrick et al., 1992). The survey was obtained through a random digit dialing telephone survey and resulted in a national household probability sample of 4,008 women 18 years of age or older. The sexual assault screening questions were much more specific and were preluded by the following introduction:

> Another type of stressful event that many women have experienced is unwanted sexual advances. Women do not always report such experiences to the police or discuss them with family or friends. The person making the advances isn't always a stranger, but can be a friend, boyfriend, or even a family member. Such experiences can occur anytime in

a woman's life—even as a child. Regardless of how long ago it happened or who made the advances . . .

1) Has a man or boy ever made you have sex by *using force* or threatening to harm you or someone close to you? Just so there is no mistake, by sex we mean putting a penis in your vagina.
2) Has anyone ever made you have oral sex by force or threat of harm? Just so there is no mistake, by oral sex we mean that a man or boy put his penis in your mouth or someone penetrated your vagina or anus with their mouth or tongue?
3) Has anyone ever made you have anal sex by force or threat of harm?
4) Has anyone ever put fingers or objects in your vagina or anus against your will by using force or threats?

It should not be surprising that multiple, behaviorally specific questions such as these were associated with greater disclosure by survey respondents compared to the NCVS. The estimated rate of rape per 1,000 women from this survey was 7–1. However, when the composition of these rapes was examined by victim/offender relationship, patterns similar to the NCVS emerged. Results from the National Women's Study indicate that 41% of the rape victimizations were perpetrated by husbands or boyfriends, 10% by other relatives, 25% by friends and other acquaintances, and 24% by strangers. As data from both the NCVS and the National Women's Study reveal, a chapter discussing the epidemiology of violence perpetrated by intimates and other family members would not be complete without a discussion of rape and sexual assaults.

ELDER ABUSE

Elder abuse has been the most recent form of family violence to receive national attention by researchers and policy makers alike. The methodological obstacles in obtaining accurate estimates of this type of violence are even more daunting. Gioglio and Blakemore (1983) questioned a random sample of 342 elders in the state of New Jersey about experiences of abuse. Only five respondents reported some form of maltreatment, which yielded an estimate of 15 per 1,000 elders. This figure, however, included no reports of violence; only financial abuse was uncovered.

Perhaps the most ambitious study to uncover incidents of elder abuse was carried out by Pillemer and Finkelhor (1988). These investigators conducted a stratified random sample of community-dwelling elderly persons (65 or older) in the Boston metropolitan area. Under Massachusetts law, each municipality in the state is required to publish an annual listing of the residents of every dwelling, including residents' birth dates. Potential respondents were randomly selected from persons on the lists who were 65 years of age or older.

All interviews of the selected sample were conducted either by telephone or in person. If a telephone number could not be obtained for the respondent, if the respondent had obvious difficulty using the telephone, or if the respondent preferred it for any reason, an interviewer was sent to the household to conduct the interview. Of the 2,813 eligible respondents selected for the study from the city and town lists, 72% were interviewed for a total of 2,020 interviews.

Respondents were administered a modified form of the CTS regarding their relationships with their spouse, one coresident child (if present), and one other member of their social network with whom they reported significant conflict. Physical abuse was defined as at least one act of physical violence against the respondent since he or she had turned 65 years of age. If any reference person had been violent toward the respondent at least once since he or she had turned 65, the respondent was placed in the physically abused category.

Results indicated that 40 elderly persons reported having experienced physical violence. This yielded a rate of 20 victims per 1,000 elderly persons. The severity of the violent incidents varied: 45% of the victims reported having something thrown at them; 63% had been pushed, grabbed, or shoved; 42% had been slapped; and 10% had been hit with a fist, bitten, or kicked.

CONCLUSION

Over the past two decades, our society has moved beyond the antiquated view that violence between intimates and family members is a private matter to an acceptance of this behavior as a serious social problem that should fall within the purview of the criminal justice system. This growing awareness has been accompanied by significant improvements to the methods used to quantify and study this violence; however, even the most sensitive survey techniques fail to capture the full magnitude of the problem. The estimates obtained to date almost certainly represent an undercount of the true prevalence of violence between intimates and family members in our society.

As this chapter has illustrated, research definitions of violence have been inconsistent, not only making epidemiological findings difficult to compare, but also contributing to the controversy over the magnitude of the problem. Different research designs and samples will continue to produce disparate findings. In fact, the field is currently awaiting findings from another nationally representative survey investigating violence against women and men that was funded by the National Institute of Justice and the Centers for Disease Control and Prevention (Tjaden & Thoennes, 1996). This survey, which was conducted in 1994 through 1995, utilized somewhat different questioning techniques to estimate rates of violence perpetrated by both known and unknown offenders.

What is clear, however, is that regardless of the estimates relied on, all nationally representative surveys indicate that violence perpetrated by intimates and other family members affects thousands of individuals annually in this country, particularly women. This violence represents a serious threat to the safety of our population. Further, despite differences in magnitude, several consistent findings about intimate partner and other family violence go beyond issues of magnitude. The following list highlights a few of these consistencies:

- Except for research employing the Conflict Tactics Scale, research indicates that women are significantly more likely than men to experience violence committed by an intimate such as a husband or a boyfriend.
- Women of all races and ethnic backgrounds are equally vulnerable to violence by an intimate. However, families living in conditions of economic deprivation, regardless of race, are more likely to experience violence by both intimates and other family members.
- Women who are separated and/or divorced from their husbands appear particularly vulnerable to violence perpetrated by their partners. The victimization rate of women separated from their husbands is about 3 times higher than that of divorced women and about 25 times higher than that of married women. It is

important to keep in mind, however, that because of survey methodology, it is difficult to determine whether the violence occurred before or after a couple's separation.

- As patterns of nonfatal violence, women are more likely to be killed by an intimate compared with men. In fact, while rates of intimate perpetrated homicide against men have declined over the past decade, rates of women killed by intimate partners have remained relatively stable.

Will researchers ever obtain the magic number that reveals the true rates of intimate and family-perpetrated violence experienced by men and women in our society? Some contend that, regardless of this elusive goal, policy makers and researchers alike should move beyond the debate about scope and magnitude to more intense research efforts at understanding, preventing, and ameliorating the consequences of this violence. Many factors inhibit women from reporting their victimizations not only to police, but to researchers as well, including the private nature of the event, the perceived stigma associated with one's victimization, the belief that no purpose may be served in reporting it, and even fear of retaliation from the offender. Increased efforts should be directed at eradicating stereotypical notions and antiquated myths regarding these acts of violence that linger in our society. Our understanding of the nature and magnitude of this violence and our ultimate attempts to prevent it depend, in part, on such enlightened awareness.

REFERENCES

Bachman, R. (1992). *Death and violence on the reservation: Homicide, family violence, and suicide in American Indian populations.* New York: Auburn House.

Bachman, R., & Saltzman, L.E. (1995). *Violence against women: Estimates from the redesigned national crime victimization survey* (NCJ-154348). Bureau of Justice Statistics, U.S. Department of Justice.

Bachman, R., & Taylor, B. (1994). The measurement of family violence and rape by the redesigned national crime victimization survey. *Justice Quarterly, 11,* 499–512.

Browne, A., & Williams, K.R. (1989). Exploring the effects of resource availability and the likelihood of female-perpetrated homicides. *Law and Society Review, 23*(1), 75–94.

Cazenave, N.A., & Straus, M.A. (1990). Race, class, network embeddedness, and family violence: A search for potent support systems. In M.A. Straus & R.J. Gelles (Eds.), *Physical violence in American families: Risk factors and adaptations to violence in 8,145 families.* New Brunswick, NJ: Transaction Books.

Crowell, N.A., & Burgess, A.W. (1996). *Understanding violence against women.* Washington, DC: National Academy Press.

DeKeseredy, W.S., Saunders, D.G., Schwartz, M.D., & Alvi, S. (1997). The meanings and motives for women's use of violence in Canadian college dating relationships: Results from a national survey. *Sociological Spectrum, 17,* 199–222.

Dobash, R.P., Dobash, R.E., Wilson, M., & Daly, M. (1992). The myth of sexual symmetry in marital violence. *Social Problems, 39,* 71–91.

Gelles, R.J., & Straus, M.A. (1979). Determinants of violence in the family: Towards a theoretical integration. In W.R. Burr, R. Hill, F.I. Nye, & I.L. Reiss (Eds.), *Contemporary theories about the family.* New York: Free Press.

Gelles, R.J., & Straus, M.A. (1990). *Physical violence in American families: Risk factors and adaptations to violence in 8,145 families.* New Brunswick: Transaction Books.

Gioglio, G., & Blakemore, P. (1983). *Elder abuse in New Jersey: The knowledge and experience of abuse among older New Jerseyans.* Unpublished manuscript. Trenton: New Jersey Division on Aging.

Kilpatrick, D.G., Edmunds, C.N., & Seymour, A.K. (1992). *Rape in America: A report to the nation.* Arlington, VA: National Victim Center.

Malcoe, L.H., Montgomery, J., & Lee, A. (1997). *Prevalence and correlates of partner violence and injury in Native American women.* Paper presented at the 1997 annual meeting of the American Society of Criminology, San Diego.

Pillemer, K., & Finkelhor, D. (1988). The prevalence of elder abuse: A random sample survey. *Gerontologist, 28,* 51–57.

Reiss, A.J., Jr., & Roth, J.A. (1993). *Understanding and preventing violence.* Washington, DC: National Academy Press.

Saunders, D.G. (1986). When battered women use violence: Husband-abuse or self-defense? *Violence and Victims, 1,* 47–60.

Sorenson, S.B., Upchurch, D.M., & Shen, H. (1996). Violence and injury in marital arguments. *American Journal of Public Health, 86,* 35–40.

Straus, M.A., & Gelles, R.J. (1990). *Physical violence in American Families: Risk factors and adaptations to violence in 8,145 families.* New Brunswick, NJ: Transaction Books.

Straus, M.A., & Smith, C. (1990). Violence in Hispanic families in the United States: Incidence rates and structural interpretations. In M.A. Straus & R.J. Gelles (Eds.), *Physical violence in American families: Risk factors and adaptations to violence in 8,145 families.* New Brunswick: Transaction Books.

Tjaden, P., & Thoennes, N. (1996). *National survey of violence against women: Findings and implications.* Paper presented at the 1996 American Society of Criminology meeting, Chicago.

PART THREE

TYPES OF FAMILY VIOLENCE

CHAPTER 8

Child Physical Abuse

DAVID J. HANSEN, GEORGANNA SEDLAR, and JODY E. WARNER-ROGERS

DESCRIPTION OF THE PROBLEM

EVEN THOUGH acts of child abuse have been committed throughout history (Zigler & Hall, 1989), widespread concern over child abuse as a significant social problem began as recently as the 1960s. Maltreated children have been an increasing focus of protection efforts, which may be due to frequent and intense attention from the media, general public, legislators, and health, mental health, and social service professionals (Hansen, Conaway, & Christopher, 1990). Increased attention to child maltreatment is evident in the research literature, which has grown rapidly since the 1970s. Much of the initial focus was on identification and remediation of deficits in parental functioning, whereas current emphases seem to be on identification of the correlates and consequences of maltreatment (Hansen & MacMillan, 1990; Warner-Rogers, Hansen, & Hecht, 1999; Wolfe, 1988; Wolfe & McEachran, 1997).

Several excellent reviews have provided detailed summaries of the more established assessment procedures specifically for use with physically abusive parents and their children, including newly developed measures (e.g., Hansen & MacMillan, 1990; Lutzker, Van Hasselt, Bigelow, Greene, & Kessler, 1998; Milner, 1991; Wolfe & McEachran, 1997). The present chapter supplements the previous literature by providing additional evaluation of current procedures and issues, as well as further discussion of practical issues, legal and system considerations, and a case illustration. The chapter provides information relevant for identifying and preventing additional maltreatment, selecting and formulating treatment goals, and monitoring treatment effectiveness.

Prior to discussing specific assessment techniques, a brief description of the problem of physical abuse is needed.

DEFINITIONS

Operational, practical definitions of physical abuse have been difficult to develop because of problems in specifying what is excessive discipline or inappropriate treatment

127

of children. Physical abuse has commonly been defined as an act of commission by the parent and is characterized by presence of nonaccidental injury and infliction of overt physical violence (e.g., Kelly, 1983; National Center on Child Abuse and Neglect [NCCAN], 1988; Wolfe, 1988). Physical abuse usually occurs in discrete, low-frequency episodes and is often accompanied by frustration and anger toward the child (Kelly, 1983). Physical abuse may include beating, squeezing, burning, lacerating, suffocating, binding, poisoning, exposing to excessive heat or cold, sensory overload (e.g., excessive light, sound, stench, aversive taste), and prevention of sleep. Although evidence of physical injury of the child has been a critical factor in identifying abusive behavior, especially for legal purposes, increasing emphasis is being placed on the circumstances and nature of the act, as opposed to the consequences on the child (Wolfe, 1988). There is not a clear distinction between acceptable forms of physical punishment and abuse.

Definitions of abuse in state statutes vary significantly in terms of specificity (Besharov, 1990; Kalichman, 1993), and information on state laws and procedures are available from local child protective services offices. Often the legal definitions are too vague to have applied research implications, but are sufficiently general to help prevent cases from slipping through the legal system on technicalities.

ETIOLOGY OF ABUSE

A brief discussion of potential causes of physical abuse is important for understanding the maltreating environment and the rationale for the various assessment procedures (for further information, see Ammerman, 1990; Wolfe, 1987; Wolfe & McEachran, 1997). The value of valid and objective assessment techniques stems from their ability to screen at-risk parents, identify suspected child abusers, and evaluate child abuse intervention and prevention efforts. Because a reliable diagnostic profile of the abusive parent has yet to be empirically validated beyond those that include concerns related to parenting role and stressful family circumstances, and the wide range of characteristics observed in abusive families, singular perspectives of etiology are discouraged. It is recommended that greater attention be placed on the bases of parenting and parent-child relationships and the environmental conditions that lead to extreme responses along a continuum of parenting experiences (Kolko, 1996).

Early conceptualizations proposed that child abuse results from severe parental psychopathology (Spinetta & Rigler, 1972). It is estimated, however, that few abusive parents are diagnosed with a psychiatric condition or exhibit significant psychopathology (Ammerman, 1990; Kelly, 1983). Etiological models have now emerged that attempt to integrate findings on the many variables correlated with abuse (Ammerman, 1990; Lutzker et al., 1998). Belsky (1980) proposed an ecological model of maltreatment with four levels of influence that bring about maltreatment: ontogenetic (personal characteristics), microsystem (family characteristics), ecosystem (community and social forces), and macrosystem (cultural determinants). Similarly, the transitional model proposed by Wolfe (1987) emphasized the importance of multiple causes and destabilizing and compensatory factors in physical abuse. There are three stages in the transition from milder to more harmful interactions: (1) reduced tolerance for stress and disinhibition of aggression, (2) poor management of acute crises and provocation, and (3) habitual patterns of arousal and aggression with family members.

The work of Cicchetti and colleagues builds on these models by focusing on the transactions among risk factors for the occurrence of maltreatment (Cicchetti &

Lynch, 1993; Cicchetti & Rizley, 1981). Under this model, risk factors are divided into two broad categories: potentiating and compensatory factors. Potentiating factors increase the probability of maltreatment and compensatory factors mitigate against the risk of maltreatment. Within these two broad categories, both short (i.e., transient) and long-term (i.e., enduring) factors may be identified. Enduring vulnerability factors include relatively long-lasting factors, conditions, or attributes that serve to increase maltreatment risk (Cicchetti & Lynch, 1993). These include parental, child, or environmental characteristics. Such vulnerability factors may be biological, historical, psychological, and sociological. Short-term vulnerability factors include current life stressors or conditions such as loss of a job, loss of a loved one, physical injury or illness, legal difficulties, marital and family problems, and the child's reaching a new developmental stage. Enduring protective factors comprise stable conditions that protect against maltreatment risk (e.g., parent's history of good parenting, positive relationship between parent figures). Transient buffers (i.e., short-term protective factors) that may decrease maltreatment risk include sudden improvement in financial or living conditions, periods of marital harmony, and a child's successful resolution of a difficult developmental period.

In general, a behavioral, social-learning perspective, consistent with the ecological (Belsky, 1980), transitional (Wolfe, 1987, 1988), and developmental-transactional (Cicchetti & Lynch, 1993; Cicchetti & Rizley, 1981) models of physical abuse, is adopted for this chapter. Child abuse may be seen as the result of complex maladaptive interactions and/or lack of essential caretaking behaviors that are influenced by parental skill or knowledge deficits and other stress factors (Hansen et al., 1990; Hansen, Warner-Rogers, & Hecht, 1998; Kelly, 1983). Maltreatment may be related to the limited ability of parents to control their child's, as well as their own, behavior. Parental skill deficits may be found in areas such as child management and parent-child interaction, anger and stress control for child and non-child-related stressors, or problem solving for familial or other stressors. Maltreating parents may also have unrealistic expectations and distorted judgments of child behavior. In addition, a lack of motivation may interfere with adequate parenting behavior (e.g., due to personal values, cultural standards). Abuse is not usually the result of a specific event or single parent or child characteristic (Warner-Rogers et al., 1999; Wolfe & McEachran, 1997), but rather the product of multiple risk factors that interact or "potentiate" one another in the absence of protective factors or buffers (Cicchetti & Lynch, 1993; Cicchetti & Rizley, 1981; Wolfe & McEachran, 1997).

EPIDEMIOLOGY

The Third National Incidence Study of Child Abuse and Neglect (NIS-3) was recently completed by the National Center on Child Abuse and Neglect (NCCAN, 1996). The NIS-3 surveyed a wide range of community professionals and agencies in a national probability sample of 42 counties. Abuse was defined according to two standards: (1) the Harm Standard, in which children were considered maltreated if they had already experienced harm (e.g., physical injury); and (2) the Endangerment Standard, a more inclusive standard in which children were considered maltreated if they experienced abuse that put them at risk of harm or if they had already experienced harm. Under the Harm Standard, 5.7 children per 1,000 (for an estimated 381,700 children nationwide) experienced physical abuse in the United States in 1993. Under the less stringent Endangerment Standard, 9.1 children per 1,000 (for an estimated 614,100 children nationwide) experienced physical abuse. In 1993, an estimated 1,500 children died from maltreatment (NCCAN, 1996). The results likely underestimate the extent of the problem because they include only cases known to relevant agencies.

As child maltreatment definitions have evolved and changes in the identification and handling of cases taken place, estimates of the number of children physically abused in the United States have increased greatly over the past several years. According to the NIS-3 (NCCAN, 1996), from 1986 to 1993 the incident rate of physical abuse rose by 33% (from 4.3 to 5.7 per 1,000), while the total number of identified physically abused children increased by 42% (from 269,700 to 381,700). It is unclear whether the figures reflect an actual increase in incidence or an increase in reporting due to growing public awareness, or both.

Several demographic correlates of physical abuse were identified in the NIS-3 (NCCAN, 1996), including the following: boys showed a 24% higher risk for serious injury than girls; boys had higher incidence of fatal injuries than girls; disproportionate increases in the incidence of maltreatment among children under age 12 were seen, with children ages 6–8 having the highest incidence of physical abuse and the highest rate of moderate injuries from abuse and neglect; younger children (ages 0–2) had the lowest incidence rate of abuse; single-parent households, especially father-only households, appear to be at greater risk for physical abuse than dual-parent households; families with four or more children had marginally higher incidence rates of maltreatment in general; children from low-income families (less than $15,000 per year) are significantly more likely to be physically abused; and the majority of cases (72%) involved the natural parents as perpetrators of physical abuse, and the next largest group (21%) consisted of other parents or parent substitutes (e.g., parent's boyfriend). No racial differences in maltreatment incidence were reported in the NIS-3. Other research has indicated that fathers are more likely to be reported for physical abuse, whereas mothers are more likely to be reported for neglect; that abusive parents are often younger than the average parent at the birth of their first child, with many being teenagers; and that parents with intellectual disabilities are at increased risk for being physically abusive (Ammerman, 1990; Lutzker, 1998; Walker, Bonner, & Kaufman, 1988; Wolfe, 1988). Although beyond the scope of this chapter, overlap exists among the forms of maltreatment within individual families, such that neglect, psychological maltreatment, and/or sexual abuse of children often are present in physically abusive families (Garbarino, Guttmann, & Seeley, 1986; Hansen et al., 1998).

Consequences

Child physical abuse warrants clinical and empirical attention because of the risks to children's immediate safety and long-term developmental course and psychological adjustment. Several research studies have examined the characteristics of abused children. The literature often confuses correlates of maltreatment status with consequences of maltreatment (i.e., causation is inferred from correlational findings) (Conaway & Hansen, 1989; Malinosky-Rummell & Hansen, 1993). Little can be said confidently about the consequences of maltreatment; however, several correlates have been identified. Maltreated children have been found to evidence greater perceptual-motor deficits; lower scores on measures of general intellectual functioning; lower scores on academic achievement tests; insecure attachments; internalizing psychological problems, such as feelings of hopelessness, depression, and low self-esteem; and negative social behavior, such as more aggression with adults and peers (Ammerman, Cassisi, Hersen, & Van Hasselt, 1986; Conaway & Hansen, 1989; Fantuzzo, 1990; Kolko, 1996; Malinosky-Rummell & Hansen, 1993). Long-term correlates of a history of maltreatment include familial and nonfamilial violence, including abuse of their own children; conduct problems and criminal behaviors; substance abuse; self-injurious and suicidal behavior; emotional problems; and interpersonal problems (Kolko, 1996; Malinosky-Rummell & Hansen, 1993).

ASSESSMENT APPROACHES

There are unique aspects to the assessment of maltreating families, including that participation in services may be involuntary or under duress; the target behavior of abuse cannot be readily observed; and abusive families are a heterogeneous group of multiproblem families (Lundquist & Hansen, 1998; Lutzker et al., 1998; Wolfe, 1988). Assessment may include collecting information to validate the occurrence of maltreatment (e.g., for the judicial system), but is usually done to identify target areas for intervention and monitor progress throughout treatment. As child abuse is a multidetermined phenomenon, assessment of abusive situations and families should parallel such a perspective and occur across multiple domains. A scientist-practitioner approach to assessment and intervention is always important, but the empirical selection and evaluation of treatment procedures is especially beneficial when under the scrutiny of the court and child protective services.

A functional analytic perspective is helpful for conducting a complete, treatment-relevant assessment (Hansen et al., 1998; Hansen & MacMillan, 1990). Potential antecedents of maltreatment include child misbehavior, developmental problems, conflict between parents, unrealistic expectations or lack of knowledge regarding child development and behavior, substance abuse, and other stressors or interaction problems. There may be many positive consequences for abusive behavior. Maltreating behavior may remove an aversive event, such as noncompliance and tantruming. It may bring praise or approval to the maltreating parent from others who perceive the actions as appropriate child-rearing practices. Absence of negative consequences may also contribute to continued maltreatment.

The following sections discuss some of the most commonly used or promising measures for the assessment of target behaviors related to the occurrence of maltreatment and improved family functioning. Because of the extensive number of relevant measures, most are presented briefly. Unless otherwise noted, measures discussed have psychometric properties that support their use. Other reviews of the assessment of maltreating parents and their children (e.g., Hansen & MacMillan, 1990; Lutzker et al., 1998; Milner & Chilamkurti, 1991; Walker et al., 1988; Wolfe, 1988; Wolfe & McEachran, 1997) or more general assessment resources (e.g., Bellack & Hersen, 1998; Mash & Terdal, 1997) may be useful because of the wide variety of problems that occur in maltreating families.

HISTORY AND RISK OF ABUSE

Interviewing is an essential procedure for identifying circumstances associated with maltreatment and assessing risk. Interviews with a variety of individuals may be needed, including parents, children, and caseworkers. Wolfe and McEachran (1997) present a helpful Parent Interview and Assessment Guide, which addresses identification of general problem areas and assessment of parental responses to child-rearing demands. Ammerman, Hersen, and Van Hasselt (1988) developed the Child Abuse and Neglect Interview Schedule, an extensive semistructured interview, to assess presence of maltreatment behaviors (e.g., corporal punishment, physically abusive behavior) and factors related to abuse and neglect (e.g., history of maltreatment). The whole interview is lengthy (approximately 45 minutes); however, a portion can be used to obtain information related to detection of abuse.

A widely researched measure for detection of at-risk status is Milner's (1986) Child Abuse Potential Inventory (CAP Inventory). The Abuse Potential Scale can be divided into six factor scales: Distress, Rigidity, Unhappiness, Problems with Child and Self, Problems with Family, and Problems from Others. Distortion indexes of Fake-Good, Fake-Bad, and Random Responding are derived from the validity scales of Lie, Random Response, and Inconsistency. Two special scales, the Ego-Strength scale (Milner, 1988, 1990) and the Loneliness scale (Mazzuacco, Gordon, & Milner, 1989; Milner, 1990) have been developed from existing CAP Inventory items (Milner, 1991). The measure has substantial promise for screening, but it should not be used in isolation as a predictor of abuse because of the possibility of misclassification (Hansen & MacMillan, 1990; Kaufman & Walker, 1986).

Excellent resources are available for professionals who are seeking practical guidance in identifying and reporting child abuse (Lutzker, 1998; Milner, 1991; Wolfe & McEachran, 1997). Kalichman (1993) and Besharov (1990) have published books that can serve as practical guides to help professionals recognize and respond to suspicions of child maltreatment. The books examine important topics, including the child protection and legal systems, the various forms of maltreatment, signs or symptoms that may indicate maltreatment, and the reporting process.

PSYCHOPATHOLOGY AND SUBSTANCE ABUSE

In addition to clinical interviewing, other commonly used measures may be useful for screening for the presence of psychopathology and alcohol or drug abuse, as well as assessing their role in maltreatment and other family dysfunction. Because clients may not report honestly about substance use, it may also be helpful to get collateral information from caseworkers or family members.

The Symptom-Checklist-90-Revised (Derogatis, 1994) is a 90-item questionnaire that assesses self-report of a variety of problems. It has nine primary symptom scales (Somatization, Obsessive-Compulsive, Interpersonal Sensitivity, Depression, Anxiety, Hostility, Phobic Anxiety, Paranoid Ideation, Psychoticism) and three global indices of stress (Global Severity, Positive Symptom Distress, Positive Symptom Total).

The Minnesota Multiphasic Personality Inventory-2 (MMPI-2) (Butcher, Dahlstrom, Graham, Tellegen, & Kaemmer, 1989; Butcher & Williams, 1992) may also be helpful. This update of the widely used MMPI has continued its predecessor's popularity with clinicians and the courts. The validity scales include Lie *(L)*, Infrequency *(F)*, and Correction *(K)*, and the three new validity scales of Back Page Infrequency *(Fb)*, which is for items in the latter part of the measure, Variable Response Inconsistency *(VRIN)*, and True Response Inconsistency *(TRIN)*. The basic clinical scales, essentially the same as the original MMPI, except for some new items, are Hypochondriasis *(Hs)*, Depression *(D)*, Conversion Hysteria *(Hy)*, Psychopathic Deviate *(Pd)*, Masculinity-Femininity

(MF), Paranoia *(Pa)*, Psychasthenia *(Pt)*, Schizophrenia *(Sc)*, Hypomania *(Ma)*, and Social Introversion *(Si)*. Several of the available supplementary scales may also be useful, such as Anxiety, Repression, Ego Strength, MacAndrew Alcoholism Scale-Revised, Overcontrolled Hostility, Dominance, and Social Responsibility. The Content scales that seem particularly promising with maltreating parents include Anxiety, Fears, Obsessiveness, Depression, Health Concerns, Bizarre Mentation, Anger, Cynicism, Antisocial Practices, Low Self-Esteem, Social Discomfort, Family Problems, Work Interference, and Negative Treatment Indicators. As with the original MMPI, analysis of critical items and Harris-Lingoes Subscales may also prove important. The first 370 items must be administered for the basic scales, and all 567 items must be administered for the additional scales. An eighth-grade reading level is required to comprehend the content of all MMPI-2 items (Butcher et al., 1989).

More specific measures for screening for alcohol and drug abuse may also be necessary, and several instruments are available (Allen & Columbus, 1995; National Institute on Drug Abuse, 1994). Useful screening instruments for parents include the short version of the Michigan Alcohol Screening Test (SMAST; Selzer, Moskourtz, Schwartzman, & Ledingham, 1991) and the Drug Abuse Screening Test (DAST; Skinner, 1982).

KNOWLEDGE AND EXPECTATIONS REGARDING CHILD DEVELOPMENT AND BEHAVIOR

Parental knowledge and expectations about child development and behavior are particularly difficult areas of assessment because normative levels and timing of developmental milestones are so varied. The Parent Opinion Questionnaire (POQ; Azar & Rohrbeck, 1986) is an 80-item questionnaire that requires subjects to rate appropriateness of expecting a variety of child behaviors. In addition to the total score, six subscales are scored: Self-Care, Family Responsibility and Care of Siblings, Help and Affection to Parents, Leaving Children Alone, Proper Behavior and Feelings, and Punishment.

The Adult-Adolescent Parent Inventory (AAPI; Bavolek, 1984, 1989) is a 32-item self-report measure that assesses attitudes of adult and adolescent parents in four areas of parenting: (1) parental expectations of children, (2) empathetic awareness of children's needs, (3) belief in corporal punishment, and (4) view of parent-child roles. The content of the AAPI is specific to parenting expectations and attitudes toward child rearing and is particularly useful when these constructs are the target of intervention (Bavolek, 1984, 1989). Holden and Edwards (1989) provide a detailed review and discussion of approximately 100 measures of parental attitudes toward child rearing, although these measures have not been specifically developed or evaluated for use with abusive parents.

The Family Beliefs Inventory (Roehling & Robin, 1986) is a useful measure of adherence to unreasonable beliefs in parent-adolescent conflict. For parents, the beliefs measured are ruination, perfectionism, approval, obedience, self-blame, and malicious intent. For adolescents, the beliefs are ruination, unfairness, autonomy, and approval. Agreement with these beliefs is assessed for 10 vignettes of conflict.

CHILD MANAGEMENT AND PARENT-CHILD INTERACTION SKILLS

A variety of assessment approaches may be utilized for child management and parent-child interaction skills. Parent-report measures of child behavior problems are commonly used in clinical settings. Two of the most common and useful are the Child Behavior Checklist (CBCL; Achenbach, 1991) and the Eyberg Child Behavior Inventory (ECBI; Eyberg, 1992; Eyberg & Ross, 1978). The CBCL consists primarily of ratings of 118 items describing specific behavior problems. In addition, several questions are included to evaluate the child's social strengths. Behavior Problem scales of the CBCL vary according to the age and sex of the child, but may include Schizoid or Anxious, Depressed, Uncommunicative, Obsessive-Compulsive, Somatic Complaints, Social Withdrawal, Ineffective, Aggressive, and Delinquent. Social Competence scales include Activities, Social, and School.

The ECBI (Eyberg, 1992; Eyberg & Ross, 1978) is brief and can be readily used as a repeated measure for monitoring changes in child behavior. Thirty-six behavior problems are rated on a 7-point scale for frequency (or "intensity"). Parents are also asked to indicate which behaviors they consider a problem. Example behaviors include refusal to do chores when asked, temper tantrums, hitting parents, short attention span, and verbally or physically fighting with siblings or friends.

A measure developed to assess parental knowledge about child management is the Knowledge of Behavioral Principles as Applied to Children (KBPAC; O'Dell, Tarler-Benlolo, & Flynn, 1979). The KBPAC is a 50-item multiple-choice measure. Although it may be useful as a pre/post measure of parent training for some parents, its use is limited because substantial reading skills are apparently needed.

Direct observations of parent-child interactions and parenting behavior are essential for a complete assessment. Videotaping can be an informative, integral part of assessment, especially given the availability and portability of videorecording equipment. Several direct observation codes have been developed for assessing the quality and content of parent-child interactions (McMahon & Estes, 1997), such as the Dyadic Parent-Child Interaction Coding System II (DPICS-II; Eyberg, Bessmer, Newcomb, Edwards, & Robinson, 1994; Eyberg, Edwards, Bessmer, & Litwins, 1994), the Interpersonal Process Code (Rusby, Estes, & Dishion, 1991), or the Behavioral Coding System (Forehand & McMahon, 1981). The DPICS-II, for example, has 26 specific behaviors in five categories for comprehensive assessment of parent-child interactions. The five categories and example behaviors are (1) verbalizations (e.g., labeled praise, direct or indirect command, criticism), (2) vocalizations (e.g., laugh, whine), (3) physical behaviors (e.g., physical positive or negative, destructive), (4) responses following commands (e.g., compliance, noncompliance), and (5) responses following commands (e.g., answer, no answer). The behaviors may be coded for both parents and children. The DPICS-II is flexible in that fewer categories can be used for clinical purposes or specific research questions (Eyberg, Bessmer, et al., 1994; Eyberg, Edwards, et al., 1994).

The Behavioral Coding System (Forehand & McMahon, 1981) has fewer categories, and is particularly useful in the context of parent training (McMahon & Estes, 1997). The appropriateness of child behavior is recorded, as well as the parental antecedents (command, warning, question, attend, reward), child responses (compliance, noncompliance), and parental consequences (attend, reward).

Tuteur, Ewigman, Peterson, and Hosokawa (1995) developed two clinic-based observational screening instruments that focus on the qualitative aspects of parent-child interactions. The first instrument, the Maternal Observation Matrix (MOM) takes approximately 10 minutes to complete and can be used in a clinic setting. Mother-child interactions are coded along 11 behavior categories (description of child, description of child's behavior, request, affect, nonphysical promise, tone, intense head touch, intense body touch, uncharged head touch, uncharged body touch and control) in 20 intervals of 30-second duration.

The Mother-Child Interaction Scale (MCIS; Tuteur et al., 1995) is an observer rated checklist consisting of eight qualitative categories for which each dyad is rated along a 3-point scale ranging from *negative* (1) to *positive* (3). These categories include degree of positive or negative parental direction of child, names mother called child, maternal touch, maternal observation of child, maternal expression, manner in which child approached mother, quality of control and manner in which mother physically moved child. Preliminary analyses support the instruments' discriminant utility in correctly classifying abusers and nonabusers. The useful features of the MOM and MCIS measures are that they are cost-effective, may be used by nonclinically trained observers, and may be used as a preliminary screening device after which more intensive instruments, interviews or home visits could be used to perform further assessment of the possibility of risk of abuse (Tuteur et al., 1995).

While behavioral coding approaches possess more objectivity, reliability, and descriptive power, major drawbacks include that they can be time-consuming and training-intensive (King, Rogers, Walters, & Oldershaw, 1994). A "judgment observation approach," in which an observer encodes and interprets information in terms of a given categorization system, may provide greater generalizability to opinions and judgments of others and is less expensive and time-consuming (King et al., 1994). King and colleagues have used the judgment observation approach in establishing preliminary evidence of the reliability and validity of a series of rating scales for assessing abusive maternal behavior. Observers rate videotaped mother-child interactions along the following categories of maternal behavior: approval, intrusiveness, responsiveness, humiliation, negative physical, and cooperation. The instrument does not require resources for full-scale direct observation and coding, and may be useful for tailoring interventions to the specific needs of particular mothers (King et al., 1994).

In terms of variables associated with physical child abuse, cognitive and affective factors are an important domain. Recently, a factor that includes both cognitive and affective components, parental empathy, has drawn attention in risk assessment for child abuse. The small amount of research performed to date suggests that physically abusive parents are less able to empathize with their children than their nonabusive counterparts (Rosenstein, 1995). Empathy (both cognitive and affective) has also been found to predict two risk factors of abuse—perceived loss of control and parental depression. Rosenstein found a negative correlation between empathy and stress in the parent-child relationship (i.e., higher levels of stress associated with lower levels of empathy) to be predictive of child abuse. Thus, empathy seems to be a potential mediating variable between stress and physical abuse. While this area is in need of further exploration with sound empirical studies (e.g., use of larger sample sizes, detailed examination of constructs, etc.), Rosenstein states that a complete assessment of the risk of child physical abuse must include a measure of parental empathy. Although relatively few standardized, objective measures of empathy exist, the following measures seem to be appropriate: the Mehrabian and Epstein Emotional Empathy Scale (Letourneau, 1981; Mehrabian & Epstein, 1972), which consists of 33 items that measure emotional responsiveness to various situations; and the Parent/Partner Empathy Scale (Feshbach, 1989), a 40-item self-report inventory designed to specifically assess a parent's empathy toward his/her child and his/her spouse or partner. The Parent/Partner Empathy

Scale is based on Feshbach's conceptual model of empathy and provides information across the following factors: cognitive, affective, spouse/partner empathy, and empathic distress (Feshbach, 1989). Additionally, one of the four constructs on the AAPI (Bavolek, 1984, 1989) discussed in a previous section relates to parental empathy and has been used in abusive parenting research (e.g., East, Matthews, & Felice, 1994; Rosenstein, 1995).

Situations in which discipline is attempted are high risk for physical abuse and should be an assessment priority (Hansen & MacMillan, 1990). Because directly observing actual discipline is often difficult (Lutzker et al., 1998), an assessment utilizing an adult actor to present deviant child behavior was developed by MacMillan, Olson, and Hansen (1991). The Home Simulation Assessment (HSA) measures parent ability to apply child management skills in realistic problem situations. During the assessment, parents are provided with 10 tasks (e.g., dry the dishes) and asked to "do their best" at prompting the actor to complete the tasks. "Deviant" scripted behaviors are exhibited by the actor in response to each of four types of control or parental discipline efforts: instructions, prediscipline warnings, initiation of timeout, and maintenance of timeout (i.e., efforts to keep the actor in a timeout chair). A high-deviance segment of the HSA can also be utilized to examine anger and stress responses to child behaviors. The high-deviance assessment uses an additional actor and increases the frequency of deviant actor behaviors. Following the 10 tasks, parent ratings of stress, anger, and anxiousness are also collected. The assessment introduces costs of time, equipment, and human resources, but may be especially useful when children are not available to participate in assessment of parent-child interactions.

The quality of stimulation and affection provided within parent-infant interactions may also be a focus of assessment. For example, Dietrich, Starr, and Kaplan (1980) coded tactile, auditory, vestibular, and visual stimulation provided by abusive parents. In a maltreatment prevention project, Lutzker, Lutzker, Braunling-McMorrow, and Eddleman (1987) assessed and trained several parent-infant affection behaviors, including smiling, affectionate words, eye-to-face behavior, affectionate physical, passive physical, leveling (i.e., putting parent on same plane as infant), speech, guided play, and vocalizations.

STRESS AND ANGER CONTROL

General measures of stress may be helpful in examining recent stressful experiences of maltreating families. Such measures include the Life Experiences Survey (Sarason, Johnson, & Siegel, 1978), which assesses occurrence and impact of major life events, and the Hassles Scale (Kanner, Coyne, Schaefer, & Lazarus, 1981), which assesses occurrence and impact of minor, commonly occurring stressors.

The Parenting Stress Index (Abidin, 1995) was developed specifically for assessing dysfunctional parent-child relationships and stress associated with parenting. The Child Domain scales (based on 47 items) are Adaptability, Acceptability, Demandingness, Mood, Distractibility/Hyperactivity, and Reinforces Parent. The Parent Domain scales (based on 54 items) are Parent Health, Depression, Attachment, Restrictions of Role, Sense of Competence, Social Isolation, and Relationship with Spouse. Life Stress is an optional 19-item scale. A 36-item short form of the PSI (Abidin, 1995) has subscales of Total Stress, Parental Distress, Parent-Child Dysfunctional Interaction, Difficult Child.

Anger specifically related to child behavior should be an assessment priority with abusive parents. The Parental Anger Inventory (PAI; Hansen & Sedlar, 1998; MacMillan, Olson & Hansen, 1988) was developed to assess anger experienced by maltreating parents in response to child misbehavior and other child-related situations. For a child between 2 and 12 years of age, parents rate 50 child-related situations (e.g., child refuses to go to bed, child throws food) as problematic or nonproblematic and rate the degree of anger evoked by each situation. It may be used for identifying anger control problems and evaluating the effects of treatment. Research has supported the internal consistency, temporal stability, content, and construct validity of the measure; however, like many self-report measures, it may be influenced by socially desirable response patterns (Sedlar, Hecht, & Hansen, 1997). Research efforts are underway to further document the psychometric and evaluative properties of the PAI.

The Issues Checklist (IC) (Robin & Foster, 1989) is valuable for assessment of anger specifically related to parent-adolescent conflict. The IC is a 44-item self-report measure of conflict issues and intensity of anger during interactions about these issues. Example issues are telephone calls, doing homework, cleaning up bedroom, cursing, lying, and sex. A brief 17-item version of the IC has also been developed (e.g., Fuhrman & Holmbeck, 1995). Other, more general measures of adult anger may also be useful, such as the State-Trait Anger Scale (STAS; Spielberger, Jacobs, Russel, & Crane, 1983) or the Multidimensional Anger Inventory (Siegel, 1986).

A disadvantage of utilizing self-report ratings of negative affect with maltreating parents is that these parents might underreport negative responses (Hansen & MacMillan, 1990; Warner-Rogers et al., in press). Although not often practical, it may be of value to record physiological measurements of arousal (e.g., heart rate, electromyographic activity, galvanic skin response, blood pressure, and peripheral temperature) during exposure to audiorecorded or videorecorded stimuli (e.g., child-deviant behavior) or in vivo exposure to child deviance warranting discipline (Hansen & MacMillan, 1990; Wolfe, 1988).

Self-report procedures, such as monitoring of responses associated with arousing events, are also useful for assessing stress and anger-control deficits. The parent may be instructed to record a description of each incident that led to feelings of anger, frustration, or tension, the manner in which he or she dealt with the problems, the way it was resolved, and the feelings he or she had afterward.

PROBLEM-SOLVING AND COPING SKILLS

An area of assessment receiving increasing attention is the problem-solving skill of abusive parents (Azar, Robinson, Hekimian, & Twentyman, 1984; Hansen et al., 1998). The Parental Problem-Solving Measure (PPSM) (Hansen, Pallotta, Christopher, Conaway, & Lundquist, 1995; Hansen, Pallotta, Tishelman, Conaway, & MacMillan, 1989) measures problem-solving skill for child-related as well as non-child-related areas. Problem situations for the PPSM are classified into one of five problem areas: (1) child behavior and child management, (2) anger and stress control, (3) finances, (4) child care resources, and (5) interpersonal problems. Responses are rated for the number of solutions generated and effectiveness of the chosen solution. An initial 25-item version (Hansen et al., 1989) and a subsequent 15-item version (Hansen et al., 1995) have been evaluated. Although such measures assess skill levels based on parent verbal report, it is not yet clear to what degree such reports are related to in vivo behavior.

Self-report problem-solving measures that have shown promise with other populations may also be helpful (Hansen & MacMillan, 1990). For example, the Social Problem-Solving Inventory (D'Zurilla & Nezu, 1988) is a measure of multiple components of problem-solving ability, and the Problem-Solving Self-Monitoring Form (D'Zurilla, 1986) is a measure of handling of problems that occur in the natural environment.

Assessment of coping styles may also be evaluated (Hansen & MacMillan, 1990). As coping skills deficits may be detected in several areas (e.g., anger control, general life stressors), multimodal measures that assess a broad range of functioning should be utilized (Kolko, 1996). The Ways of Coping Checklist-Revised (Lazarus & Folkman, 1984) is a 66-item inventory comprising of eight scales (problem-focused coping, wishful thinking, detachment, seeking social support, focusing on the positive, self-blame, tension reduction, keeping to self). It is completed for a particular, single stressor, and has been used with adult populations (Hansen & MacMillan, 1990; Lazarus & Folkman, 1984). Another measure that has utility with maltreating parents is the Parental Locus of Control Scale (Campis, Lyman, & Prentice-Dunn, 1986), a 47-item self-report scale that provides an overall score and five subscale scores (parental efficacy, parental responsibility, child control of parents, parental belief in fate/chance, parental control of child behavior).

Adaptive Social Contacts and Social Support

Presence and quality of social contacts and social support may be assessed through interview and self-monitoring. The Community Interaction Checklist (Dumas & Wahler, 1983; Wahler, Leske, & Rogers, 1979) is an easy-to-use semistructured interview that examines the frequency and nature of social contacts. Availability and use of types of social support such as guidance and advising, emotional support, socializing, tangible assistance, self-disclosure, and support related to child problems (e.g., advice on how to handle tantrums, emotional support for handling child-related stressors) should also be evaluated.

Measures developed with nonmaltreating adults may prove useful. Cohen, Mermelstein, Kamarck, and Hoberman (1985) developed the Interpersonal Support Evaluation List, a 40-item inventory to assess the degree to which social support fulfills the following functions: tangible support (i.e., concrete or material aid), appraisal support (i.e., opportunities to assess or evaluate the problem), self-esteem support (i.e., positive evaluation), and belonging support (i.e., opportunities to socialize with others). The Perceived Social Support Questionnaire (Procidano & Heller, 1983) is a 40-item measure of the extent to which needs for support, information, and feedback are fulfilled by friends and family. If social support and social interaction measures reveal deficits, then social skill inventories and role-play measures should also be considered for use (Kelly, 1982, 1983).

Marital Functioning and Parenting Cooperation

Assessment of marital interaction, including conflict, aggression, and cooperation in child-rearing efforts can be valuable. Self-report measures commonly used in the assessment of marital problems include the Marital Adjustment Scale (MAS; Kimmel & van der Veen, 1974; Locke & Wallace, 1959) and the Dyadic Adjustment Scale (DAS; Spanier, 1976). The DAS, which is similar to the MAS, is a 32-item questionnaire using primarily Likert-style rating scales to assess the quality of dyadic relationships.

The DAS yields a standard score that represents the degree of dissatisfaction in the relationship, which can be compared with distressed and nondistressed norms.

The Conflict Tactics Scale (Straus, 1979) is a 19-item measure designed to assess individual responses to situations involving conflict within the family. It can be used to assess conflict resolution tactics between adults or between a parent and a child, and can be administered in interview or questionnaire fashion. Subscales are Reasoning, Verbal Aggression, Minor Violence, and Severe Violence. Items assess a wide range of tactics, from "discussed the issue calmly" to "kicked, bit, or hit with a fist." Respondents are asked to report on their own and their significant other's behavior. The more thorough Revised Conflict Tactics Scales (CTS2; Straus, Hamby, Boney-McCoy, & Sugarman, 1996) has 39 items that are designed to be asked about both the participant and the partner, for a total of 78 questions. The CTS2 has a simplified format, increased clarity and specificity of items, better distinction between minor and severe levels of psychological and physical aggression, replacement of the Reasoning scale by an improved Negotiation scale, and addition of new scales to address sexual coercion and physical injury.

Direct observation coding procedures are available, such as versions of the Marital Interaction Coding System (MICS; Heyman, Weiss, & Eddy, 1995; Weiss & Summers, 1983; Weiss & Tolman, 1990). The MICS-III includes 32 behavior codes that assess functions including problem description, blame, proposal for change, validation, invalidation, and facilitation (Weiss & Summers, 1983). The MICS-IV (Heyman et al., 1995) includes 36 behavior codes and addresses more nonverbal affect during interactions than the MICS-III. The MICS-IV hierarchical rules for creating sequences produce stronger negative codes (e.g., blame) and more subtle positive codes (e.g., facilitation) than the MICS-III. There is also a MICS-G (Weiss & Tolman, 1990), a global rating system based on the MICS-III. The MICS-G consists of six global rating categories, five of which are derived from the MICS-III summary categories: Conflict, Problem Solving, Validation, Invalidation, and Facilitation. A sixth category, Withdrawal, was included because it is considered a potential mediating factor in spouse abuse and a predictor of marital satisfaction. Thus, the MICS-G has the advantages of being derived from the empirically valid and widely used MICS, a microanalytic coding system, but is less costly in training and time required for making ratings (Weiss & Tolman, 1990).

Specific measurement of parenting-related conflict can also be valuable (McMahon & Estes, 1997). The 20-item Parenting Alliance Inventory (Abidin & Brunner, 1995) is designed to measure the degree of parental collaboration in child rearing. Each partner is asked to rate the other parent's involvement with the child and parenting competence, as well as the degree of agreement-discord between parents over child-rearing issues. Extensive discussions of assessment of marital interaction in the context of the family (e.g., Grotevant & Carlson, 1989; Touliatos, Perlmutter, & Straus, 1990), and more specifically as it relates to parenting (e.g., McMahon & Estes, 1997) and marital violence (e.g., Holtzworth-Munroe, Beatty, & Anglin, 1995), are available for interested readers.

PRACTICAL ISSUES IN THE ASSESSMENT OF ABUSIVE FAMILIES

Practical issues arise in the assessment of maltreating families, and a few warrant discussion here. Interacting with child protective services (CPS) workers is important for a coordinated, multidisciplinary effort. Prompt initial contact with the relevant CPS worker, followed by regular contact by phone or periodic written updates, may facilitate communication. It is also important to clarify the goals of all parties (i.e., therapists, client, CPS workers) and to clarify with the client the distinction from and relationship with CPS.

Although most states have mandatory reporting laws requiring physicians, psychologists, teachers, and other professionals to report suspected instances of child maltreatment, as many as one-third of possible child physical abuse cases remain unidentified or unreported (NCCAN, 1988, 1996). Much research attention has been directed toward factors that influence or bias judgments of the presence, severity, and reporting of child abuse (e.g., Hansen, Bumby, Lundquist, Chandler, Le, & Futa, 1997; Howe, Herzberger, & Tennen, 1988; Kalichman & Brosig, 1993; Warner-Rogers, Hansen, & Spieth, 1996). Factors that may influence judgments about whether an event is abusive and should be reported, include the gender of the child victim, the perpetrator, or the person making the judgment; one's own personal history of maltreatment; the age of the victim; socioeconomic status and race of the perpetrator; the severity of the abuse; and familiarity with reporting laws and procedures. The impact of such factors is complex and still not well understood, as their influence varies across professional groups (e.g., psychologists, social workers) and types of maltreatment (Hansen et al., 1997). Reviews of the influence of such variables on the ability to recognize and willingness to report abuse are available (e.g., Kalichman, 1993; Warner & Hansen, 1994).

An issue in need of further evaluation is to inform parents of a decision to report them for child maltreatment (Lundquist & Hansen, 1998). Indeed, some argue that not informing parents of suspicion or intent to report is deceptive and may be unethical (Racusin & Felsman, 1986). The impact of such actions on the assessment and treatment process likely varies with different parents, but little is known at this time.

Significant attention has been directed toward acceptability of treatment procedures by abusive parents (e.g., Kelley, Grace, & Elliott, 1990; Lundquist & Hansen, 1998); however, the acceptability of assessment procedures has been neglected (Hansen & McMillan, 1990). Maltreating parents, often mandated and reluctant to participate in therapy, may be hypersensitive to negative evaluation and prone to make inaccurate interpretations of assessment procedures if they are not explained thoroughly (e.g., videotaping parent-child play behavior may be viewed as an attempt to show that the child does not like the parent). Research is needed that examines acceptability of various assessment procedures for maltreating parents and the conditions that may make procedures more or else acceptable (Hansen & McMillan, 1990; Lundquist & Hansen, 1998).

Maltreating parents often do not identify themselves as having a problem and are usually not self-referred for evaluation or treatment (Kelly, 1983; Wolfe, 1988). It is not surprising, then, that research indicates that session attendance and homework completion are problems with maltreating families (e.g., Hansen & Warner, 1994; Warner, Rummell, Ellis, & Hansen, 1990). Use of strategies to improve attendance, as well as participation within and after the session (e.g., homework), may be essential and should begin in the early phases of contact. Professionals must be sensitive to the factors that may contribute to noncompliance, such as inadequate instructions, lack of skills or motivation to perform the assignment, and competing contingencies that may reinforce noncompliance or punish compliance (Lundquist & Hansen, 1998; Hansen & Warner, 1994). Antecedent, prompting strategies include establishing attendance policies, providing additional stimuli (e.g., reminders), getting written commitments, and training parents in tasks assigned. Consequent strategies include reinforcement (e.g., praise), tangibles (e.g., clothing, movie tickets, money), and attention to nonadherence responses (e.g., open discussion). Combined antecedent and consequent strategies include contingency contracting and involving significant others (e.g., children, partners) in assignments to be carried out in the home. Results on the effectiveness of court orders, which may or may not specify positive or negative consequences (e.g., return child to home or remove child from home) for participation in assessment or therapy, have been inconclusive (Lundquist & Hansen, 1998). In addition to antecedent and consequent strategies, it can be valuable to address contextual or environmental factors that may impact compliance, such as providing stress-management training or intervention for other problems that interfere, such as substance abuse, emotional problems, or marital difficulties (Hansen et al., 1998; Kolko, 1996). Although many of these procedures are used in clinical and research endeavors with maltreating families, the effectiveness of these and other procedures to enhance compliance of abusive parents has not specifically evaluated (Lundquist & Hansen, 1998).

An in-depth discussion of the role of cultural and ethnic factors extends beyond the scope of this chapter, but some general considerations warrant attention. Just as parental acts and child-rearing practices should be evaluated within the context of the immediate family and community environment as well as the developmental stages of the child, such behavior should also be examined from the perspective of the culture in which they happen. Evaluators and practitioners should possess an awareness and sensitivity about another culture's attitudes, beliefs and values which in turn may influence child-rearing practices. For example, a traditional value of the Hispanic culture, *familism,* strongly emphasizes family unity and encourages a sense of familial obligation among members (Zayas, 1992). Without such sensitivity and understanding, misinterpretation of events or decision making based on personal biases rather than on empirical information about the effect of specific parent behaviors is possible (Sternberg, 1993). Additionally, when professionals target areas for intervention and monitor progress of those interventions, they should consider culturally relevant factors throughout the process. These cultural factors may interact with child abuse risk factors such as distress, social isolation, family conflict, and stressful life events (Derezotes & Snowden, 1990; Rubin, 1992). Clinicians have been found to be more successful at engaging minority families by demonstrating cultural sensitivity (Sue & Sue, 1977; Tsui & Schultz, 1985). Miscommunication and language barriers between English-speaking professionals and families who speak another language may present obstacles to providing needed and most appropriate services. Finally assessment and intervention should include an individualized evaluation of the family's strengths as well as weaknesses (Rubin, 1992).

LEGAL AND SYSTEMS CONSIDERATIONS

LEGAL AND CHILD PROTECTION ISSUES

Professionals who work with physically abusive families can expect to have interactions with the legal system. These interactions can be with the local child protective services agency, law enforcement officials, lawyers, or the judicial system. Although most states and Washington, DC, have laws requiring certain professionals (e.g., psychologists, physicians, teachers) to report suspected child maltreatment, these laws vary from state to state (Besharov, 1990; Kalichman, 1993). Many professionals are reluctant to report, possibly due to fear of getting involved in the legal system, as well as concern about harming a therapeutic relationship (Besharov, 1990; Wolfe, 1988). As noted previously, many professionals may also fail to report abuse because they do not recognize the abuse or because they make a judgment that reporting is not appropriate or necessary for a particular situation (Kalichman, 1993; Hansen et al., 1997; Warner & Hansen, 1994). Not reporting is a crime, usually a misdemeanor, and civil liability is also possible. Those who report are immune from criminal and civil liability.

There are two general areas of legal involvement regarding child maltreatment. The first, the protection of children, is typically addressed through civil procedures. The second, the criminal prosecution of the child abuser, occurs when abuse is severe. Thus, professionals must be aware of the current laws and practices in their state as to definitions of abusive and neglectful acts, as well as reporting procedures and requirements. In addition, they should be cognizant of the local and national norms for appropriate parenting behavior.

In most cases, reports of suspected maltreatment reach the local child protective services (CPS) office for substantiation. Practitioners may be asked by CPS to assist in any of the ensuing procedures: report taking, screening, investigation, initial risk assessment, crisis intervention, report disposition, case planning and implementation, and eventually case closure (Besharov, 1990). If maltreatment is substantiated, the legal system may become involved more formally. Examples of more formal involvement include mandating the family to participate in therapy, temporary removal of the child from the home and, in rare cases, termination of parental rights or criminal prosecution of the perpetrator. Clinicians may participate in courtroom proceedings, giving expert testimony or preparing children for testimony.

When working with a family, it is important for practitioners to confine their part in the legal process to either investigator, evaluator, or therapist (Melton & Limber, 1989; Melton, Petrila, Poythress, & Slobogin, 1997). Adoption of more than one role may result in conflict of interest or require a breach of confidentiality that could be detrimental to the therapeutic relationship. The clinician should be clear about the nature of his or her role at the outset of any legal case. To offset any potential misunderstanding by individuals being evaluated, professionals should explicitly state their roles, the scope and nature of the services, who requested the services, who will have access to assessment information, and limits of confidentiality.

Additional System Considerations

Cicchettti, Toth, and Hennessy (1993) note that, given federal legislative efforts that allocate money for demonstration and service programs which work in conjunction with preschool, elementary and secondary schools, "educators and other professionals are being called upon to become more active in efforts to identify and treat victims of child abuse" (p. 304). These federal efforts point to a recognition that abuse must be dealt with through an integration of social service, health, mental health, education, and substance abuse agencies (Cicchetti et al., 1993). Such recognition necessitates a strong working alliance between the school system, health and mental health practitioners, and social service agencies regarding the assessment of child physical abuse.

Americas's educators and school personnel spend a significant amount of time with children and consequently are able to witness patterns of behavior across time. Not surprisingly, more reports are provided from schools than any other systems (e.g., hospitals, day-care centers, mental health systems) (NCAAN, 1988, 1996). Maltreating families may fail to provide proper or consistent health care (e.g., medical, dental, mental health) for their children, and therefore many possible instances of abuse may escape observation by medical and other professionals. Thus, teachers are a primary source for reports of frequent or suspect injuries. These facts carry important implications for school systems with regards to identifying and assessing children who may have experienced physical abuse. Educators are in a prime position to encourage timely and suitable assessment and intervention services for these children and their families. In addition, teachers are important sources of information pertaining to a child or family that may warrant attention in the assessment of abuse, including the child's academic, behavioral, emotional, and social functioning. Comprehensive and integrative assessments in school settings can be valuable for identification of intervention goals for the child and family, especially when assessment across the multiple domains of development is conducted (e.g., cognitive, socioemotional, and linguistic/representational) (Cicchetti et al., 1993).

In recognition of the presence of child abuse across various systems (e.g., health, education, social services, legal), many states have developed multidisciplinary teams for investigation, assessment, and intervention (Melton et al., 1997). These teams consist of professionals from settings such as health, judicial, mental health, and social service systems. Here the clinician serves as a team member, often serving an advisory role concerning decisions about legal issues. The clinician may be looked on as an expert in interviewing and evaluating the allegedly abused child or abusive parent. When the clinician is obtaining information that may be used in prosecution of a case, however, the potential exists for confusion regarding the clinician's role by both the clinician and the child or parent being interviewed.

CONSIDERATIONS AT VARIOUS STAGES OF ASSESSMENT

The goal of mandatory reporting laws is to promote child protection, not to punish the perpetrators. After a report of suspected maltreatment is received, the child protection system may request an assessment of the likelihood that the child is in danger of being maltreated. Any assessment conducted during this disposition phase must focus on ensuring the safety and welfare of the children, as well as determining the parent's need and willingness to participate in intervention. Historically, clinicians have rarely been involved in the validation of abuse; however, this trend is changing (Melton & Limber, 1989). Mental health professionals are not only becoming more involved in addressing forensic issues in child abuse cases, they are getting involved at earlier stages (e.g., prior to adjudication) as well (Melton et al., 1997). Clinicians may become involved at any of the following phases of a child maltreatment case: investigation, emergency decision making, adjudication, disposition and postdispositional review, and mediation and other alternative processes.

Typically, answers to two questions are sought in abuse investigations: (1) whether abuse occurred and (2) if so, what can be done to mediate its harmful effects in the immediate and long term (which may involve prevention and intervention decisions). Because clinicians may assume the roles of decision maker, initiator, and objective expert for one case, there is increasing opportunity for confusion to arise concerning professional roles and boundaries. It is important for the professional to be aware of the constraints of their role within the legal system. Mental health practitioners should avoid dispensing ultimate issue opinions concerning disposition (e.g., whether risk is so great that the child requires out-of-home placement) (Melton et al., 1997).

Assessment information may be used in a court hearing or trial. Especially in cases where criminal charges are pending, practitioners must ensure that the parents had an opportunity to consult with their counsel prior to the onset of assessment (Melton & Limber, 1989). Legal proceedings are adversarial in nature; thus, cross-examination, including questioning of professional credibility or choice of assessment devices, can be expected. Practitioners must be extremely familiar with any assessment devices they used, including its psychometric properties. They should formulate opinions and judgments on clear, well-defined databases and make cautious use of clinical observations (Guyer & Ash, 1985). The reliability of subjective opinions may be questioned rather easily in the courtroom.

Those involved in the evaluation of maltreatment may have more information concerning use and interpretation of assessment procedures than the legal and other professionals. Thus, it is important to confirm that the assessment procedures and their results are neither misconstrued nor misused (Melton & Limber, 1989). While mental health practitioners should avoid answering ultimate opinion issues or making legal determinations, they can provide valuable assistance to the court by focusing clinical assessments on prevention of further abuse and amelioration of the psychological harm that may already be present (Melton et al., 1997). The purposes and appropriate uses of formal assessment instruments are often delineated clearly in accompanying manuals. For example, the Child Abuse Potential Inventory (Milner, 1986) was designed to assess maltreatment potential by comparing characteristics of the parent with those of known abusers; practitioners must prevent its use as a determining measure of whether the parent did or did not maltreat a child.

Assessment throughout intervention is critical for monitoring treatment effectiveness. This information may be required for hearings, or relayed to the CPS workers and used for decisions regarding case closure. At these times, evaluation of changes in the home environment and the impact of services received by the family are of primary interest (Melton & Limber, 1989). In many cases, following an initial hearing, families will be granted an improvement period. Several states require clear documentation that the state has tried repeatedly to provide assistance to the family (Melton et al., 1997). If this assistance has not proved beneficial, there may be grounds for more intense legal involvement (e.g., court mandation for services, removal of children, termination of parental rights).

GENERAL CAVEATS REGARDING ASSESSMENT

Some general concerns must be considered at every point in the legal process. At all times, it is critical that everyone involved is knowledgeable about who will be receiving the results of the assessments (Guyer & Ash, 1985; Melton & Limber, 1989). In addition, during any assessment procedure, parental rights, as well as the child's welfare, must be protected. Unless there is a court order stating otherwise, information gathered during assessment is confidential. The parents control their own records, as well as those of children in their legal custody. Nevertheless, these clients should be warned that their records may be subpoenaed by the court and that the clinician cannot guarantee unconditional confidentiality (Guyer & Ash, 1985).

If the assessment is ordered by the court, assessment material is not considered privileged, even initially. All data acquired throughout assessment will be given to the court and the attorneys. Clients, when assessed in this context, must be informed of this lack of confidentiality. Records should document that information about confidentiality has been related to the clients (Guyer & Ash, 1985). It must be clear that all parties understand their role in the process prior to the onset of assessment (Melton & Limber, 1989).

In many cases, information gathered during these assessment phases eventually will be included in reports to CPS and possibly to the courts or other members of the legal community. At the minimum, these reports should include the dates of assessment, pertinent background information regarding the clients, the reason and source for the referral to the clinician, the names of all assessment devices used, the scores on the devices as appropriate, interpretation of scores and other assessment data, and a summary and recommendations. These reports should be as free as possible from psychological jargon and readable by other professionals involved in the case. A lawyer, for example, may not understand or appreciate the meaning of an elevated T-score on the Rigidity Scale of the CAPI.

An important caveat about assessment is that conclusions and recommendations should be based on relevant, objective data and not on unfounded speculation. In addition, it is important that professionals avoid reliance on any one measure and look for converging evidence across various measures when attempting to understand parental behavior. Practitioners must also be careful not to overstep their professional roles or training and make decisions best made by others (Melton & Limber, 1989; Melton et al., 1997). Although they may be more knowledgeable about the etiology and epidemiology of maltreatment, and more familiar with the tools of assessment, they are probably less familiar with the legal issues and proceedings.

The growing involvement of mental health professionals in the legal system has not been without controversy or problems (Melton & Limber, 1989; Melton et al., 1997). Faust and Ziskin (1988), in a controversial article, noted, "Studies show that professionals often fail to reach reliable or valid conclusions and that their accuracy does not necessarily surpass that of laypersons, thus raising substantial doubt that psychologists or psychiatrists meet legal standards for expertise" (p. 31). However, research on the collaboration of child welfare, mental health, and judicial systems suggests a good working relationship among the systems, with placement recommendations and decisions being highly correlated (Butler, Atkinson, Magnatta, & Hood, 1995).

CASE ILLUSTRATION

As illustrated in the following case description, evaluation and treatment planning for a physically abusive parent can be a lengthy and challenging process.

BACKGROUND INFORMATION

Sharon Reed was referred to a university-based treatment program for physically abusive and neglectful parents by her CPS caseworker. On a referral checklist, her caseworker identified the following as "highly important" targets for treatment: child management skills, knowledge of child development, anger control, financial management, social isolation, emotional neglect, and medical care.

Ms. Reed was a 21-year-old woman who described herself as a "recovering alcoholic" with a "horrible temper." She reported a history of three hospitalizations for depression and substance abuse. Ms. Reed indicated that she left two of these hospitalizations against medical advice. She was not currently on any medications and denied all use of alcohol and drugs. She denied current suicidal ideation, though she reported that she attempted suicide by overdosing on prescribed medication approximately 11 months earlier, which resulted in her most recent hospitalization.

Her daughter, Samantha, was 26 months old at the time of the referral. Ms. Reed reported that she had no current contact with Samantha's biological father. Ms. Reed indicated that she voluntarily placed Samantha in foster care approximately 19 months earlier because the child was suffering from "failure-to-thrive." Samantha was returned to her mother approximately 2 months later after gaining weight at the foster placement.

Ms. Reed was referred for the current assessment by CPS for suspected physical abuse of Samantha. The CPS investigation and concerns about possible physical abuse were initiated when Ms. Reed brought Samantha to the University hospital emergency room for a high fever, and at that time medical personnel reported to CPS that Samantha had "unexplainable bruises" on her face and "apparent burn marks" on the palms of her hands. CPS also reported concerns about Ms. Reed leaving her daughter with various caregivers over extended periods of time (e.g., several weeks) without contact from Ms. Reed.

CPS requested a psychological evaluation of Ms. Reed to determine her capacity to care for Samantha and her potential for abuse. They also requested that Ms. Reed receive parent training and other interventions as needed (e.g., anger control). At the time of referral, Samantha had been in foster care for approximately 3 months, and Ms. Reed had weekly 48- to 72-hour visits with her daughter.

Ms. Reed and Samantha lived in a rented house with Ms. Reed's boyfriend, Tony Blake. Mr. Blake was 29 years old. They were engaged and had plans to marry following Ms. Reed's divorce from her previous husband. Because Mr. Blake planned to take an active role in parenting Samantha and he was a source of financial and emotional support for Ms. Reed and Samantha, he was included in assessment and subsequent treatment as much as possible. At the time of assessment, he worked in a nearby city (approximately 75 miles away) and was primarily home on weekends.

Ms. Reed completed high school and had not worked outside of the home since that time. Ms. Reed reported that she was attending computer classes at a community college; however, soon after the intake interview she stopped attending these classes. Mr. Blake held a variety of jobs in recent years, and was currently employed as a mechanic for a trucking company.

Ms. Reed and Mr. Blake expressed a strong desire to have Samantha returned to their custody. At the time of the referral, Ms. Reed had been receiving services from a variety of professionals and agencies (e.g., CPS, the community mental health center, and others). Ms. Reed reported that she and Mr. Blake were very dissatisfied with the services they had received thus far in their improvement period since the removal of Samantha from their care. They did not take any responsibility for the problems they had in attempting to work with the various helping agencies (e.g., not attending scheduled appointments, lack of transportation to sessions) and tended to complain about the professionals and the various agencies (e.g., that these professionals were not interested in helping them get Samantha returned to their custody).

OVERVIEW OF CURRENT ASSESSMENT

The goal of assessment was to select target areas for intervention, with special attention to parenting skill and discipline style. Procedures used to gather the following information took place over a period of approximately 4 months. At onset of assessment, there were two clinic sessions, and subsequently nine sessions took place in the home. In general, sessions were approximately one hour long. For the clinic visits, Ms. Reed arrived on time or early. She was usually at home when the therapist arrived for scheduled home sessions, though she missed and canceled a couple of sessions over the 4-month period. Much of the assessment was intermingled with intervention and instruction (e.g., about child management strategies or child care) throughout these sessions. Often, the initial portion of a session was dedicated to the completion of assessment procedures and the latter portion to treatment-related issues.

ASSESSMENT OF PARENT BEHAVIOR AND FUNCTIONING

On the Wechsler Adult Intelligence Scale-III (Wechsler, 1997), her Full Scale IQ fell in the low average range of functioning. No significant difference was noted between the Verbal and Performance IQ scores, suggesting that her verbal comprehension and perceptual organizational skills were comparable.

The MMPI-2 (Butcher et al., 1989; Butcher & Williams, 1992) was completed in valid fashion. The profile was characteristic of individuals who are low in self-confidence and have feelings of inadequacy, are lacking in energy, and are irritable and moody. Ms. Reed's responses on the Symptom- Checklist-90-Revised (Derogatis, 1994) did not suggest significant psychopathology, but did reflect symptoms of depression.

Ms. Reed identified a moderate number of daily hassles on the Hassles Scale (Kanner et al., 1981), with an average severity in the mild range. Responses indicated that her primary hassles or concerns were over not having enough money (e.g., for basic necessities, housing, entertainment) and having too much to do (e.g., too many responsibilities, not enough time to do things that need to be done).

As indicated on the Community Interaction Checklist (Wahler, 1980), with the exception of occasional contact with one female friend, the majority of Ms. Reed's social contacts were with members of her family and professionals from helping agencies, such as her therapist or CPS workers. She generally viewed these contacts as neutral in nature. Ms. Reed's verbal report throughout the assessment period indicated she was experiencing social isolation.

On the Parental Anger Inventory (Hansen & Sedlar, 1998), Ms. Reed identified many child-related situations that were sources of mild to moderate anger (e.g., child makes messes around the house, child screams and yells when you say "no" to a request, child misbehaves after you have had a bad day, child demands something immediately, child breaks things on purpose). Overall, her scores on the Parent Opinion Questionnaire (Azar & Rohrbeck, 1986) were unremarkable, with the exception of the subscales of Help and Affection to Parents and Proper Behavior and Feelings, where her scores suggested that her expectations regarding what to expect from her child were possibly inappropriate and unrealistic. Ms. Reed's responses on the Knowledge of Behavioral

Principles as Applied to Children Inventory (O'Dell et al., 1979) indicated that she had limited knowledge of basic child-management skills. Interview of Ms. Reed further supported that she had limited knowledge of child development, particularly regarding communication and self-help skills of young children, and a limited repertoire and understanding of child-management skills.

Ms. Reed's score on the Abuse Scale of the Child Abuse Potential Inventory (Milner, 1986) was elevated, indicating that she may have characteristics similar to parents who have abused their children. In addition, her scores on the Distress and Unhappiness scales were elevated suggesting that she might be experiencing some emotional difficulties that could impact her parenting ability. When questioned about any distress or unhappiness, she indicated that her unhappiness was primarily related to not having custody of her daughter.

Ms. Reed's scores on the Child subscales of the Parenting Stress Index (Abidin, 1995) were within normative range with the exception of a high score on the Reinforces Parent subscale. A high score on this subscale indicates that Ms. Reed may not view Samantha as a source of positive reinforcement. Her elevated Parent Domain scales were Depression and Social Isolation.

Given his engagement to Ms. Reed and his stated commitment to parenting Samantha, Mr. Blake was asked to complete the CAP Inventory and the Parenting Stress Index. Mr. Blake's score on the Abuse scale and the six other scales of the CAP Inventory were all within normal limits. His scores on the PSI were not elevated on any Child or Parent subscales.

Assessment of Child Behavior and Parent-Child Interaction

On the Eyberg Child Behavior Inventory (Eyberg & Ross, 1978), Ms. Reed reported that she considered a variety of Samantha's behaviors to be problems, and that these behaviors occurred fairly regularly. For example, problem behaviors included dawdling at mealtime, refusing to eat food presented, getting angry when she doesn't get her own way, having temper tantrums, whining, crying easily, yelling or screaming, and constantly seeking attention.

Direct observation of Ms. Reed's interactions with her daughter were done on three separate occasions during home visits. In general, her behavior with Samantha appeared appropriate and positive. She verbally prompted Samantha away from dangerous situations, such as telling her to move away from the door to the stairway and locking it, and instructing her to remove a pen from her mouth, then physically removing it when she did not comply. She also allowed Samantha to sit next to her, put her arm around Samantha, and talked with her while she completed some forms. Ms. Reed's language was age-appropriate for Samantha. Samantha complied with her mother's instructions most of the time, and when she did, Ms. Reed thanked her and praised her for "doing a good job." There were no angry or physically abusive incidents during the observations.

Both Ms. Reed and Mr. Blake reported that Samantha was a difficult child to feed. The therapist observed Ms. Reed feed Samantha on one occasion, and although she had several appropriate strategies (e.g., verbally reinforcing Samantha for sitting down and taking a bite), Ms. Reed appeared to become very frustrated when Samantha was noncompliant. Ms. Reed reported frustration that Samantha was a "picky eater" and that she did not know what foods her daughter liked. On the morning of one session, Ms. Reed attempted to feed refried beans to Samantha, although she did switch to applesauce when Samantha did not eat the beans.

It was reported by Ms. Reed and her CPS worker that some visits with Samantha had been terminated early for a variety of reasons (e.g., Ms. Reed not feeling well or having another commitment, such as spending time with her fiancee in the nearby city where he worked). The inability to regularly complete 48 to 72 hour visitations raised concerns whether Ms. Reed had the personal commitment and resources to care for Samantha on a full-time basis.

ADDITIONAL ASSESSMENT OF THE HOME ENVIRONMENT

Given Samantha's young age, the safety and cleanliness of the home environment was a concern of the therapist. The therapist initially requested to conduct an assessment of the home, which would have involved viewing each room of the house for safety and cleanliness issues that may have been harmful to the child, and providing suggestions for improving the environment. During the first three home visits, Ms. Reed indicated that the house was "messier than usual" and promised to clean it for viewing by the next session. Eventually, despite her concerns that the house was still "too messy," Ms. Reed allowed the therapist to briefly look at each room of the house, but did not permit a detailed inspection (e.g., opening cupboards under sinks or viewing other areas the child may access, such as closets). The house was cluttered, with a variety of items strewn throughout on the floors and furniture (e.g., clothing, dirty dishes). The ashtrays were full of cigarette butts and lighters were observed on the tables. With the exception of a few books and one doll, very few age-appropriate toys for Samantha were in the house. Samantha did not have a baby bed or high chair. Samantha did have a small table and chairs and Ms. Reed was attempting to teach Samantha to eat her meals at this table. Establishment of good rapport and providing a rationale was important for gaining access to viewing the various rooms of their home. Overall, Ms. Reed recognized potential hazards in the home environment and took some necessary precautions (e.g., blocking access to the staircase). She reported always utilizing a car seat when traveling with Samantha.

CASE SUMMARY AND RECOMMENDATIONS

Several possible treatment targets have been identified for Ms. Reed. It appears that she is continuing to experience problems of mild depression, as well as feelings of social isolation and stress (e.g., regarding financial concerns). Therapy to address these issues will likely be necessary to facilitate her ability to participate and implement additional interventions to improve parenting and child-care abilities. Intervention to improve parenting skills is considered important, with an emphasis on gaining knowledge and acquiring skills to enhance parent-child interaction and improve child management techniques, and improving her knowledge of child care and child development. Alternatives to physical discipline (e.g., time out) and increasing child compliance (e.g., via more appropriate and effective commands, praise and reinforcement) are considered priorities to reduce likelihood of abuse in the context of excessive physical discipline. In particular, improving anger and stress control during child-management and child-care situations is viewed as essential. Improving the parent-child relationship through increasing the occurrence of positive parent-child interactions will also be valuable (e.g., via increased compliance as well as increased opportunities for appropriate play between mother and child). As much as possible it will be important to include Mr. Blake in the intervention activities, to improve his skills as needed and further support and reinforce changes made by Ms. Reed.

Continued assessment throughout the course of treatment is warranted, and several of the devices mentioned previously will be used as dependent measures. For example, the Eyberg Child Behavior Inventory, the Parental Anger Inventory, the Parent Opinion Questionnaire, and the Parenting Stress Index are examples of relevant measures that are easily completed and may be used repeatedly to identify treatment effects. In addition, repeated direct observation in the home (e.g., of parent-child interactions and child care situations such as feeding) will be invaluable for monitoring and implementing treatment. As Ms. Reed and Samantha become more accustomed to being observed, it may be found that the interactions are more representative of what normally occurs (e.g., possibly more problems and conflicts may arise). Additional measures that directly assess treatment procedures and effects will be added as treatment progresses (e.g., via parent-monitoring of child management procedures, anger control skills, child-care activities, or child behavior). Mr. Blake will be included when possible in assessment and information gathering, and input will be sought from other professionals and agencies also involved with the family (e.g., CPS, the community mental health center).

CONCLUSION

Widespread attention to the problem of child physical abuse has increased dramatically in recent decades. Extensive research evidence has described child physical abuse as a complex, multidimensional phenomenon that is best assessed by procedures using multiple modalities (e.g., interview, self-report, direct observation) that address multiple content areas. Comprehensive assessment is essential for identifying risk and occurrence of abuse, guiding the focus or direction of treatment, as well as monitoring treatment efficacy and outcome, all of which may be disseminated to interested parties as appropriate (e.g., CPS, judicial system, school, other treatment providers). Increasingly specific and relevant procedures have become available for many of the commonly targeted areas of assessment. In general, recent advances have been especially significant in the development of self-report and analogue assessments to measure parental responses in a variety of contexts (Hansen & MacMillan, 1990; Lutzker, 1998; Lutzker et al., 1998; Wolfe & McEachran, 1997).

The complex, multiproblem nature of maltreating families and child physical abuse presents many assessment difficulties for both clinicians and researchers. The assessment of physically abusive families is complicated by issues such as mandatory reporting and other legal considerations, the potential unwillingness of parents to cooperate, and contextual factors and stressors that interfere with a family's ability to participate (e.g., social isolation, relationship problems, financial difficulties). Although there are many suggested strategies, further research on the most effective and appropriate methods of addressing these issues and conducting comprehensive and accurate assessments is needed.

REFERENCES

Abidin, R.R. (1995). *Parenting Stress Index* (3rd ed.). North Tonawanda, NY: Multi-Health Systems.

Abidin, R.R., & Brunner, J.F. (1995). Development of a parenting alliance inventory. *Journal of Clinical Child Psychology, 24,* 31–40.

Achenbach, T.M. (1991). *Manual for the Child Behavior Checklist/4–18 and 1991 profile.* Burlington: University of Vermont.

Allen, J.P., & Columbus, M. (Eds.). (1995). *Assessing alcohol problems: A guide for clinicians and researchers* (NIAAA Treatment Handbook No. 4, DHHS Publication No. NIH 95-3745). Washington, DC: U.S. Government Printing Office.

Ammerman, R.T. (1990). Etiological models of child maltreatment: A behavioral perspective. *Behavior Modification, 14,* 230–252.

Ammerman, R.T., Cassisi, J.E., Hersen, M., & Van Hasselt, V.B. (1986). Consequences of physical abuse and neglect in children. *Clinical Psychology Review, 6,* 291–310.

Ammerman, R.T., Hersen, M., & Van Hasselt, V.B. (1988). *The Child Abuse and Neglect Interview Schedule (CANIS).* Unpublished instrument. Western Pennsylvania School for Blind Children, Pittsburgh.

Azar, S.T., Robinson, D.R., Hekimian, E., & Twentyman, C.T. (1984). Unrealistic expectations and problem-solving ability in maltreating and comparison mothers. *Journal of Consulting and Clinical Psychology, 52,* 687–691.

Azar, S.T., & Rohrbeck, C.A. (1986). Child abuse and unrealistic expectations: Further validation of the Parent Opinion Questionnaire. *Journal of Consulting and Clinical Psychology, 54,* 867–868.

Bavolek, S.J. (1984). *Adult-Adolescent Parenting Inventory.* Eau Claire, WI: Family Development Resources.

Bavolek, S.J. (1989). Assessing and treating high-risk parenting attitudes. In J.T. Pardeck (Ed.), *Child abuse and neglect: Theory, research and practice* (pp. 97–110). New York: Gordon and Breach.

Bellack, A.S., & Hersen, M. (Eds.). (1998). *Behavioral assessment: A practical handbook* (4th ed.). New York: Allyn & Bacon.

Belsky, J. (1980). Child maltreatment: An ecological integration. *American Psychologist, 35,* 320–335.

Besharov, D.J. (1990). *Recognizing child abuse: A guide for the concerned.* New York: Free Press.

Butcher, J.N., Dahlstrom, W.G., Graham, J.R., Tellegen, A., & Kaemmer, B. (1989). *Minnesota Multiphasic Personality Inventory-2 (MMPI-2): Manual for administration and scoring.* Minneapolis: University of Minnesota Press.

Butcher, J.N., & Williams, C.L. (1992). *Essentials of MMPI-2 and MMPI-A interpretation.* Minneapolis: University of Minnesota Press.

Butler, S., Atkinson, L., Magnatta, M., & Hood, E. (1995). Child maltreatment: The collaboration of child welfare, mental health, and judicial systems. *Child Abuse & Neglect, 19,* 355–362.

Campis, L.K., Lyman, R.D., & Prentice-Dunn, S. (1986). The parental locus of control scale: Development and validation. *Journal of Clinical Child Psychology, 15,* 260–267.

Cicchetti, D., & Lynch, M. (1993). Toward an ecological/transactional model of community violence and child maltreatment: Consequences for children's development. *Psychiatry, 56,* 96–118.

Cicchetti, D., & Rizley, R. (1981). Developmental perspectives on the etiology, intergenerational transmission, and sequelae of child maltreatment. In D. Cicchetti & R. Rizley (Eds.), *New directions for child development: No. 11. Developmental perspectives on child maltreatment* (pp. 31–55). San Francisco: Jossey-Bass.

Cicchetti, D., Toth, S.L., & Hennessy, K. (1993). Child maltreatment and school adaptation: Problems and promises. In D. Cicchetti & S.L. Toth (Eds.), *Child abuse, child development, and social policy* (pp. 301–330). Norwood, NJ: ABLEX.

Cohen, S., Mermelstein, R., Kamarck, T., & Hoberman, H.M. (1985). Measuring the functional components of social support. In I.G. Sarason & B.R. Sarason (Eds.), *Social support: Theory, research, and applications* (pp. 73–94). The Hague, Netherlands: Martinus Nijhoff.

Conaway, L.P., & Hansen, D.J. (1989). Social behavior of physically abused and neglected children: A critical review. *Clinical Psychology Review, 9,* 627–652.

Derezotes, D.S., & Snowden, L.R. (1990). Cultural factors in the intervention of child maltreatment. *Child and Adolescent Social Work, 7,* 161–175.

Derogatis, L.R. (1994). *SCL-90-R: Administration, scoring, and procedures manual* (3rd ed.). Minneapolis: National Computer Systems.

Dietrich, K.N., Starr, R.H., & Kaplan, M.G. (1980). Maternal stimulation and care of abused infants. In T.M. Field, S. Goldberg, D. Stern, & A.M. Sostek (Eds.), *High-risk infants and children: Adult and peer interactions* (pp. 25–41). New York: Academic Press.

Dumas, J.E., & Wahler, R.G. (1983). Predictors of treatment outcome in parent training: Mother insularity and socioeconomic disadvantage. *Behavioral Assessment, 5,* 301–315.

D'Zurilla, T.J. (1986). *Problem-solving therapy: A social competence approach to clinical intervention.* New York: Springer.

D'Zurilla, T.J., & Nezu, A.M. (1988, November). *Development and preliminary evaluation of the Social Problem-Solving Inventory.* Paper presented at the Association for the Advancement of Behavior Therapy Convention, New York.

East, P.L., Matthews, K.L., & Felice, M.E. (1994). Qualities of adolescent mothers' parenting. *Journal of Adolescent Health, 15,* 163–168.

Eyberg, S.M. (1992). Parent and teacher behavior inventories for the assessment of conduct problem behaviors in children. In L. VandeCreek, S. Knapp, & T.L. Jackson (Eds.), *Innovations in clinical practice: A source book* (Vol. 11, pp. 261–270). Sarasota, FL: Professional Resource Exchange.

Eyberg, S.M., Bessmer, J., Newcomb, K., Edwards, D.L., & Robinson, E.A. (1994). *Dyadic Parent-Child Interaction Coding System-II: A manual.* Social and behavioral sciences documents (Ms. No. 2897). San Rafael, CA: Select Press.

Eyberg, S.M., Edwards, D., Bessmer, J., & Litwins, N. (1994). *The workbook: A coder training manual for the Dyadic Parent-Child Interaction Coding System-II.* Social and behavioral sciences documents (Ms. No. 2898). San Rafael, CA: Select Press.

Eyberg, S.M., & Ross, A.W. (1978). Assessment of child behavior problems: The validation of a new inventory. *Journal of Clinical Child Psychology, 7,* 113–116.

Fantuzzo, J.W. (1990). Behavioral treatment of the victims of child abuse and neglect. *Behavior Modification, 14,* 316–339.

Faust, D., & Ziskin, J. (1988). The expert witness in psychology and psychiatry. *Science, 241,* 31–35.

Feshbach, N.D. (1989). The construct of empathy and the phenomenon of physical maltreatment of children. In D. Cicchetti & V. Carlson (Eds.), *Child maltreatment: Theory and research on the causes and consequences of child abuse and neglect* (pp. 349–373). New York: Cambridge University Press.

Forehand, R.L., & McMahon, R.J. (1981). *Helping the noncompliant child: A clinician's guide to parent training.* New York: Guilford Press.

Fuhrman, T., & Holmbeck, G.N. (1995). A contextual-moderator analysis of emotional autonomy and adjustment in adolescence. *Child Development, 66,* 793–811.

Garbarino, J., Guttmann, E., & Seeley, J.W. (1986). *The psychologically battered child.* San Francisco: Jossey-Bass.

Grotevant, H.D., & Carlson, C.I. (1989). *Family assessment: A guide to methods and measures.* New York: Guilford Press.

Guyer, M.J., & Ash, P. (1985). Law and clinical practice in child abuse and neglect cases. In C.P. Ewing (Ed.), *Psychology, psychiatry and the law* (pp. 305–330). Sarasota, FL: Professional Resource Exchange.

Hansen, D.J., Bumby, K.M., Lundquist, L.M., Chandler, R.M., Le, P.T., & Futa, K.T. (1997). Factors that influence identification and reporting of child maltreatment: A study of licensed psychologists and certified Masters social workers. *Journal of Family Violence, 12,* 313–332.

Hansen, D.J., Conaway, L.P., & Christopher, J.S. (1990). Victims of child physical abuse. In R.T. Ammerman & M. Hersen (Eds.), *Treatment of family violence: A sourcebook* (pp. 37–49). New York: Wiley.

Hansen, D.J., & MacMillan, V.M. (1990). Behavioral assessment of child abusive and neglectful families: Recent developments and current issues. *Behavior Modification, 14,* 255–278.

Hansen, D.J., Pallotta, G.M., Christopher, J.S., Conaway, R.L., & Lundquist, L.M. (1995). The Parental Problem-Solving Measure: Further evaluation with maltreating and nonmaltreating parents. *Journal of Family Violence, 10,* 319–336.

Hansen, D.J., Pallotta, G.M., Tishelman, A.C., Conaway, L.P., & MacMillan, V.M. (1989). Parental problem-solving skills and child behavior problems: A comparison of physically abusive, neglectful, clinic, and community families. *Journal of Family Violence, 4,* 353–368.

Hansen, D.J., & Sedlar, G. (1998). *The Parental Anger Inventory: A guide for practitioners and researchers.* Lincoln, NE: Clinical Psychology Training Program.

Hansen, D.J., & Warner, J.E. (1994). Treatment adherence of maltreating families: A survey of professionals regarding prevalence and enhancement strategies. *Journal of Family Violence, 9,* 1–19.

Hansen, D.J., Warner-Rogers, J.E., & Hecht, D.B. (1998). Effectiveness of individualized behavioral intervention for maltreating families. In J.R. Lutzker (Ed.), *Handbook of child abuse research and treatment* (pp. 133–158). New York: Plenum Press.

Heyman, R.E., Weiss, R.L., & Eddy, J.M. (1995). Marital interaction coding system: Revision and empirical evaluation. *Behaviour Research and Therapy, 33,* 737–746.

Holden, G.W., & Edwards, L.A. (1989). Parental attitudes toward child rearing: Instruments, issues, and implications. *Psychological Bulletin, 106,* 29–58.

Holtzworth-Munroe, A., Beatty, S.B., & Anglin, K. (1995). The assessment and treatment of marital violence. In N.S. Jacobson & A.S. Gurman (Eds.), *Clinical handbook of couple therapy* (2nd ed., pp. 317–339). New York: Guilford Press.

Howe, A.C., Herzberger, S., & Tennen, H. (1988). The influence of personal history of abuse and gender on clinicians' judgments of child abuse. *Journal of Family Violence, 3,* 105–119.

Kalichman, S.C. (1993). *Mandated reporting of suspected child abuse: Ethics, law, and policy.* Washington, DC: American Psychological Association.

Kalichman, S.C., & Brosig, C.L. (1993). Practicing psychologists' interpretations of and compliance with child abuse reporting laws. *Law and Human Behavior, 17,* 83–93.

Kanner, A.D., Coyne, J., Schaefer, C., & Lazarus, R.S. (1981). Comparison of two modes of stress measurement: Daily hassles and uplifts versus major events. *Journal of Behavioral Medicine, 4,* 1–39.

Kaufman, K.L., & Walker, C.E. (1986). Review of the Child Abuse Potential Inventory. In J.D. Keyser & R.C. Sweetland (Eds.), *Test critiques* (Vol. 6, pp. 55–64). Kansas City, MO: Westport.

Kelley, M.L., Grace, N., & Elliott, S.N. (1990). Acceptability of positive and punitive discipline methods: Comparisons among abusive, potentially abusive, and nonabusive parents. *Child Abuse & Neglect, 13,* 219–226.

Kelly, J.A. (1982). *Social skills training: A practical guide for intervention.* New York: Springer.

Kelly, J.A. (1983). *Treating child-abusive families: Intervention based on skills training principles.* New York: Plenum Press.

Kimmel, D.C., & van der Veen, F. (1974). Factors of marital adjustment in Locke's marital adjustment test. *Journal of Marriage and the Family, 36,* 57–63.

King, G.A., Rogers, C., Walters, G.C., & Oldershaw, L. (1994). Parenting behavior rating scales: Preliminary validation with intrusive, abusive mothers. *Child Abuse & Neglect, 18,* 247–259.

Kolko, D.J. (1996). Child physical abuse. In J. Briere, L. Berliner, J.A. Bulkley, C. Jenny, & T. Reid (Eds.), *The APSAC handbook on child maltreatment* (pp. 21–50). Thousand Oaks, CA: Sage.

Lazarus, R.S., & Folkman, S. (1984). *Stress, appraisal, and coping.* New York: Springer.

Letourneau, C. (1981). Empathy and stress: How they affect parental aggression. *Social Work, 26,* 383–390.

Locke, H.J., & Wallace, K.M. (1959). Short marital adjustment and prediction tests: Their reliability and validity. *Journal of Marriage and Family Living, 21,* 251–255.

Lundquist, L.M., & Hansen, D.J. (1998). Enhancing treatment adherence, generalization, and social validity of parent-training with physically abusive and neglectful families. In J.R. Lutzker (Ed.), *Handbook of child abuse research and treatment* (pp. 449–471). New York: Plenum Press.

Lutzker, J.R. (Ed.). (1998). *Handbook of child abuse research and treatment.* New York: Plenum Press.

Lutzker, J.R., Van Hasselt, V.B., Bigelow, K.M., Greene, B.F., & Kessler, M.L. (1998). Child abuse and neglect: Behavioral research, treatment, and theory. *Aggression and Violent Behavior, 3,* 181–196.

Lutzker, S.Z., Lutzker, J.R., Braunling-McMorrow, D.B., & Eddleman, J. (1987). Prompting to increase mother-baby stimulation with single mothers. *Journal of Child and Adolescent Psychotherapy, 4,* 3–12.

MacMillan, V.M., Olson, R.L., & Hansen, D.J. (1988, November). *The development of an anger inventory for use with maltreating parents.* Paper presented at the Association for the Advancement of Behavior Therapy Convention, New York.

MacMillan, V.M., Olson, R.L., & Hansen, D.J. (1991). Low and high stress analogue assessment of parent-training with physically abusive parents. *Journal of Family Violence, 6,* 279–301.

Malinosky-Rummell, R., & Hansen, D.J. (1993). Long-term consequences of childhood physical abuse. *Psychological Bulletin, 114,* 68–79.

Mash, E.J., & Terdal, L.G. (Eds.). (1997). *Assessment of childhood disorders* (3rd ed.). New York: Guilford Press.

Mazzuacco, M., Gordon, R.A., & Milner, J.S. (1989, April). *Development of a loneliness scale for the Child Abuse Potential Inventory.* Paper presented at the meeting of the Southeastern Psychological Association, Washington, DC.

McMahon, R.J., & Estes, A.M. (1997). Conduct problems. In E.J. Mash & L.G. Terdal (Eds.), *Assessment of childhood disorders* (3rd ed., pp. 130–193). New York: Guilford Press.

Mehrabian, A., & Epstein, N. (1972). A measure of emotional empathy. *Journal of Personality, 40,* 525–543.

Melton, G.B., & Limber, S. (1989). Psychologists' involvement in cases of child maltreatment. *American Psychologist, 44,* 1225–1233.

Melton, G.B., Petrila, J., Poythress, N.G., & Slobogin, C. (1997). *Psychological evaluations for the courts: A handbook for mental health professionals and lawyers* (2nd ed.). New York: Guilford Press.

Milner, J.S. (1986). *The Child Abuse Potential Inventory: Manual* (2nd ed.). Webster, NC: Psytec.

Milner, J.S. (1988). An ego-strength scale for the Child Abuse Potential Inventory. *Journal of Family Violence, 3,* 151–162.

Milner, J.S. (1990). *An interpretive manual for the Child Abuse Potential Inventory.* Webster, NC: Psytec.

Milner, J.S. (1991). Physical child abuse perpetrator screening and evaluation. *Criminal Justice and Behavior, 18,* 47–63.

Milner, J.S., & Chilamkurti, C. (1991). Physical child abuse perpetrator characteristics: A review of the literature. *Journal of Interpersonal Violence, 6,* 3, 345–366.

National Center on Child Abuse and Neglect. (1988). *Study of national incidence and prevalence of child abuse and neglect: 1986.* Washington, DC: U.S. Department of Health and Human Services.

National Center on Child Abuse and Neglect. (1996). *Third national incidence study of child abuse and neglect.* Washington, DC: U.S. Department of Health and Human Services.

National Institute on Drug Abuse. (1994). *Assessing drug abuse among adolescents and adults: Standardized instruments* (DHHS Publication No. NIH 94-3757). Washington, DC: U.S. Government Printing Office.

O'Dell, S.L., Tarler-Benlolo, L., & Flynn, J.M. (1979). An instrument to measure knowledge of behavioral principles as applied to children. *Journal of Behavior Therapy and Experimental Psychiatry, 10,* 29–34.

Procidano, M., & Heller, K. (1983). Measures of perceived social support from friends and from family: Three validation studies. *American Journal of Community Psychology, 11,* 1–24.

Racusin, R.J., & Felsman, J.K. (1986). Reporting child abuse: The ethical obligation to inform parents. *Journal of the American Academy of Child Psychiatry, 25,* 485–489.

Robin, A.L., & Foster, S.L. (1989). *Negotiating parent-adolescent conflict: A behavioral-family systems approach.* New York: Guilford Press.

Roehling, P.V., & Robin, A.L. (1986). Development and validation for the family beliefs inventory: A measure of unrealistic beliefs among parents and adolescents. *Journal of Consulting and Clinical Psychology, 54,* 693–697.

Rosenstein, P. (1995). Parental levels of empathy as related to risk assessment in child protective services. *Child Abuse & Neglect, 19,* 11, 1349–1360.

Rubin, G.B. (1992). Multicultural considerations in the application of child protection laws. *Journal of Social Distress and the Homeless, 1,* 249–271.

Rusby, J.C., Estes, A., & Dishion, T. (1991). *The interpersonal process code (IPC).* Unpublished manuscript, Oregon Social Learning Center, Eugene.

Sarason, I.G., Johnson, J.H., & Siegel, J.M. (1978). Assessing the impact of life change: Development of the life experiences survey. *Journal of Consulting and Clinical Psychology, 46,* 932–946.

Sedlar, G., Hecht, D.B., & Hansen, D.J. (1997, November). *Parental Anger Inventory: Further evaluation with maltreating and nonmaltreating parents.* Paper presented at the Association for the Advancement of Behavior Therapy, Miami Beach, FL.

Selzer, M.L., Moskowitz, D.S., Schwartzman, A.E., & Ledingham, J.E. (1991). A self-administered short Michigan alcoholism screening test. *Journal of Studies on Alcohol, 36,* 117–126.

Siegel, J.M. (1986). The Multidimensional Anger Inventory. *Journal of Personality and Social Psychology, 51,* 191–200.

Skinner, H.A. (1982). The drug abuse screening test. *Addictive Behaviors, 7,* 363–371.

Spanier, G.B. (1976). Measuring dyadic adjustment: New scales for assessing the quality of marriage and similar dyads. *Journal of Marriage and the Family, 38,* 15–28.

Spielberger, C.D., Jacobs, G., Russel, S., & Crane, R.S. (1983). Assessment of anger: The state-trait anger scale. In J.N. Butcher & C.D. Spielberger (Eds.), *Advances in personality assessment* (Vol. 2, pp. 159–187). Hillsdale, NJ: Erlbaum.

Spinetta, J.J., & Rigler, D. (1972). The child abusing patent: A psychological review. *Psychological Bulletin, 77,* 296–304.

Sternberg, K.J. (1993). Child maltreatment: Implications for policy from cross-cultural research. In D. Cicchetti & S.L. Toth (Eds.), *Child abuse, child development, and social policy.* Norwood, NJ: ABLEX.

Straus, M.A. (1979). Measuring intrafamily conflict and violence: The Conflict Tactics (CT) Scales. *Journal of Marriage and the Family, 41,* 75–88.

Straus, M.A., Hamby, S.L., Boney-McCoy, S., & Sugarman, D.B. (1996). The revised Conflict Tactics Scales (CTS2): Development and preliminary psychometric data. *Journal of Family Issues, 17,* 283–316.

Sue, D.W., & Sue, D. (1977). Barriers to effective cross-cultural counseling. *Journal of Counseling Psychology, 24,* 420–429.

Touliatos, J., Perlmutter, B.F., & Straus, M.A. (1990). *Handbook of family measurement techniques.* Newbury Park, CA: Sage.

Tsui, P., & Schultz, G.L. (1985). Failure of rapport: Why psychotherapeutic engagement fails in the treatment of Asian clients. *American Journal of Orthopsychiatry, 55,* 561–569.

Tuteur, J.M., Ewigman, B.E., Peterson, L., & Hosokawa, M.C. (1995). The Maternal Observation Matrix and the Mother-Child Interaction Scale: Brief observational screening instruments for physically abusive mothers. *Journal of Clinical Child Psychology, 24,* 55–62.

Wahler, R.G. (1980). The insular mother: Her problem in parent-child treatment. *Journal of Applied Behavior Analysis, 13,* 207–219.

Wahler, R.G., Leske, G., & Rogers, E.S. (1979). The insular family: A deviance support system of oppositional children. In L.A. Hamerlynck (Ed.), *Behavioral systems for the developmentally disabled: I. School and family environments.* New York: Brunner-Mazel.

Walker, C.E., Bonner, B.L., & Kaufman, K.L. (1988). *The physically and sexually abused child: Evaluation and treatment.* New York: Pergamon Press.

Warner, J.E., & Hansen, D.J. (1994). Identification and reporting of child abuse by medical professionals: A critical review. *Child Abuse & Neglect, 18,* 11–25.

Warner, J.E., Rummell, R.M., Ellis, J.T., & Hansen, D.J. (1990). *An examination of demographic and treatment variables associated with session attendance of maltreating families.* Paper presented at the Association for the Advancement of Behavior Therapy Convention, San Francisco.

Warner-Rogers, J.E., Hansen, D.J., & Hecht, D.B. (1999). Child physical abuse and neglect. In V.B. Van Hasselt & M. Hersen (Eds.), *Handbook of psychological approaches with violent criminal offenders* (pp. 329–355). New York: Plenum Press.

Warner-Rogers, J.E., Hansen, D.J., & Spieth, L.E. (1996). The influence of case and professional variables on identification and reporting of physical abuse: A study with medical students. *Child Abuse & Neglect, 20,* 851–866.

Wechsler, D. (1997). *WAIS-III administration and scoring manual.* San Antonio, TX: Psychological Corporation.

Weiss, R.L., & Summers, K.J. (1983). Marital Interaction Coding System-III. In E.E. Filsinger (Ed.), *Marriage and family assessment: A sourcebook for family therapy* (pp. 65–84). Beverly Hills, CA: Sage.

Weiss, R.L., & Tolman, A.O. (1990). The Marital Interaction Coding System—Global (MICS-G): A global companion to the MICS. *Behavioral Assessment, 12,* 271–294.

Wolfe, D.A. (1987). *Child abuse: Implications for child development and psychopathology.* Newbury Park, CA: Sage.

Wolfe, D.A. (1988). Child abuse and neglect. In E.J. Mash & L.G. Terdal (Eds.), *Behavioral assessment of childhood disorders* (2nd ed., pp. 627–666). New York: Guilford Press.

Wolfe, D.A., & McEachran, A. (1997). Child physical abuse and neglect. In E.J. Mash & L.G. Terdal (Eds.), *Assessment of childhood disorders* (3rd ed., pp. 523–568). New York: Guilford Press.

Zayas, L.H. (1992). Childrearing, social stress, and child abuse: Clinical considerations with Hispanic families. *Journal of Social Distress and the Homeless, 1*(3/4), 291–309.

Zigler, E., & Hall, N.W. (1989). Physical child abuse in America: Past, present and future. In D. Cicchetti & V. Carlson (Eds.), *Child maltreatment: Theory and research on the causes and consequences of child abuse and neglect* (pp. 38–75). New York: Cambridge University Press.

CHAPTER 9

Child Neglect

RONIT M. GERSHATER-MOLKO and JOHN R. LUTZKER

CHILD MALTREATMENT (in the forms of child abuse and neglect) is not a new problem, but it was only formally recognized as a significant social issue with the publication of Kempe and colleagues' 1962 article "The Battered Child Syndrome," sparking widespread public and professional awareness (Kempe, Silverman, Steele, Droegemueller, & Silver, 1962). Despite this enlightenment, however, the public and professional focus has been on the impact of child physical abuse, even though the consequences of neglect are as serious (Erickson & Egeland, 1996; Erickson, Egeland, & Pianta, 1989). This disparate focus exists partly because abuse generally leaves highly visible signs such as scars, burns, bruises, and can be fatal. Although neglect can also result in visible evidence, such as malnutrition and even death, it is more difficult to assess and observe than abuse. It is also sometimes difficult to discriminate between abuse and neglect, and the two are often comorbid in families.

Child neglect is the mostly frequently reported type of child maltreatment. In 1993, neglect constituted 47% of all reported and substantiated cases of child maltreatment (McCurdy & Daro, 1994). Since 1993, neglect has comprised more than half of the reported cases of child maltreatment (U.S. Department of Health and Human Services [DHHS], 1996). However, researchers and policy makers have continued to devote far less attention to neglect than abuse.

Generally, the literature has referred to child abuse and neglect together, and most interventions have treated them similarly. Researchers now are beginning to examine and treat neglect as a phenomenon that is conceptually different from abuse and that warrants specific attention. Zuravin and DiBlasio (1996) identified certain risk factors that are specific to either abusive parents or neglectful parents, thereby differentiating

This chapter was funded in part through a grant to Project SafeCare from the California Wellness Foundation (TCWF). Created in 1992 as a private and independent foundation, TCWF's mission is to improve the health of the people of California through proactive support of health promotion and disease prevention programs.

The authors gratefully acknowledge the assistance of Holly Minear.

between these forms of maltreatment. They identified 11 characteristics associated with neglect and 4 characteristics associated with abuse that enabled them to correctly categorize the child's parent into either the abuse group or the neglect group 80% of the time. Characteristics such as a history of sexual abuse as a child, running away from home, having committed a crime, being placed in foster care, having had abortions and premature babies, having more than two children before age 18, suffering from depression, and having low levels of education were associated with neglect. On the other hand, abusive mothers were more likely to have had a mother with emotional problems, more likely to have been antisocial as a child, more likely to be receiving AFDC support, and less likely to be positively attached to their own mothers.

Of particular importance, and with serious implications for researchers and service providers, was the finding that different correlates were identified for abusive versus neglectful mothers. If the factors that cause an act of commission (abuse) versus an act of omission (neglect) are indeed different, this research confirms that these types of maltreatment need to be assessed and treated differently.

This chapter provides an overview of the scope of child neglect and the issues that clinicians and researchers have to face when assessing neglect. First, we describe the problem and discuss the impact that the lack of a specific definition of neglect has had on the ability to conduct well-controlled research on this issue. Second, we provide information on the assessment of child neglect, as well as the legal and systems issues that impact assessment by clinicians and service providers. Finally, we present a case illustration of a woman who was reported for severe neglect of her children.

DESCRIPTION OF THE PROBLEM

The incidence of child maltreatment continues to rise dramatically; in 1994 there were 1,012,000 children in the United States for whom reports of maltreatment were substantiated (DHHS, 1996). Of these victims, 53% suffered general neglect and 3% suffered medical neglect, while 44% were involved in one of (or a combination of) the following types of maltreatment: physical abuse (26%); sexual abuse (14%); emotional abuse (5%); and, other types of maltreatment (19%). Forty-seven percent of those children were 6 years old or younger.

Neglect is generally defined as an act of omission, committed by parents or caregivers, that results in harm to children (Zuravin, 1991). As a result of this lack of adequate physical care, nutrition, and shelter, neglected children are often malnourished, lack adequate hygiene, and are prone to accidents due to an unsafe environment (Erickson & Egeland, 1996). Severely neglected homes with major cleanliness problems and unsanitary conditions may contribute to numerous developmental and health problems in children (Watson-Perczel, Lutzker, Greene, & McGimpsey, 1988). Children who are neglected often suffer from disorders such as anxiety disorders, avoidant behavior, and challenging behaviors (Lutzker, Bigelow, Swenson, Doctor, & Kessler, in press). Other long-term sequelae of child maltreatment are withdrawal, avoidance of adults or overdependence of adults, and sexual acting out and sexually verbal behavior (Lutzker et al., in press). Emotional neglect, which is far less visible, can also be extremely damaging, and sometimes fatal. Many of these victims suffer from "failure to thrive" as a result of the lack of human contact and nurturance (Erickson & Egeland, 1996). Research has suggested that the lasting damage from psychological and emotional maltreatment can be far more devastating than physical injury (Claussen &

Crittenden, 1991). The physical injury that a child may sustain will heal with time; however, psychological maltreatment leaves lasting damage to the child's self-esteem and may result in social, emotional and cognitive impairment (Claussen & Crittenden, 1991). Thus, the long-term effects of this type of maltreatment can be extremely damaging, and often irreparable.

Azar, Vera, Lauretti, and Pouquette (1998) suggest that neglect has been considered a less serious form of child maltreatment and does not arouse societal rage as much as child physical or sexual abuse. In addition, neglect is often only visible when it has reached quite severe proportions and the child is visibly suffering from malnutrition is or extremely unkempt. These factors may account, in part, for the relative lack of research on neglect compared with abuse.

The lack of a clear definition of child neglect is also considered a contributing factor to the dearth of adequate research in this area (Dubowitz, Black, Starr, & Zuravin, 1993). Historically, there have been different proposed definitions of neglect. Conceptual definitions have varied, focusing specifically on the parents or the child, often blaming either the child or the parent for the neglect (DHHS, 1996). Definitions have also varied depending on whether a legal, medical, psychological, or lay perspective is taken (Erickson & Egeland, 1996).

Neglect is broadly defined as an act of omission and is viewed as a continuum of inaction on the part of the parents (DHHS, 1996; Dubowitz et al., 1993; Peterson & Gable, 1998). When raising a child, parents assume the responsibility of providing food, clothing, shelter, education, and protection from danger, as well as fostering a sense of morality and love. Parents are also largely responsible for promoting their child's social, emotional and intellectual development. To protect a child from danger (slipping in the bathtub, falling down the stairs), the parent needs to be in close proximity to the child and in almost constant supervision, which is often extremely difficult to maintain. Thus, it is as important that parents take precautions to protect their children from household hazards such as poisonous substances. There are no standards of agreement on what constitutes sufficient supervision of children, and the requirements for adequate supervision change as the child grows older. Therefore, neglect is viewed as inaction on a continuum rather than a dichotomy between acceptable and neglectful parenting (Peterson & Gable, 1998).

Responding to the need for a definition of neglect, the United States Department of Health and Human Services (1996) conducted a study designed to compile a standardized definition of child neglect. Different types of neglect were explored: physical neglect, child abandonment and expulsion, medical neglect, inadequate supervision, emotional neglect, and educational neglect by parents or other adult caretakers of children.

Physical neglect involves the child being left under inadequate supervision and/or parental inattention, as well as child exposure to hazards such as inadequate nutrition, hygiene and clothing; driving the child while intoxicated; or leaving the child unattended in the car. Physical neglect also includes refusal or delay in health care, abandonment, expulsion from the home, inadequate supervision, and inattention to avoidable hazards in the home.

Emotional neglect is marked by indifference to the child's needs for affection, attention, and emotional support. Included in this definition is chronic or extreme spousal abuse in the child's presence, permitted drug and alcohol abuse by the child, and permitted maladaptive behavior such as assaultiveness. It also includes the parent's failure to seek and provide, or the outright refusal of treatment for the child's behavioral or emotional impairment (depression), as well as other inattention to the child's developmental and emotional needs.

Educational neglect includes permitted and habitual truancy, failure to enroll the child in a school or educational program, as well as failure to allow or inattention to obtain necessary remedial educational services for a child's diagnosed learning disorder or other special education need.

Research in child neglect (Dubowitz et al., 1993) emphasizes that neglect needs to be viewed from a social ecological perspective. This perspective incorporates child, parental, societal, and environmental variables as all playing a role. For example, a poverty-stricken family might experience stress as a result of the lack of resources, inadequate nutrition, and insufficient health care. The combination of these factors may result in a neglectful situation where the needs of the children are not sufficiently met (Dubowitz et al., 1993). The social ecological model recognizes the shared responsibility among the individuals, families, communities, and society, thereby enabling a more constructive approach and targeting interventions on multiple levels. This model, which focuses on the child's entire social ecology, illustrates the need for a broad perspective of child neglect; it would be far less effective to focus on one factor alone. Programs that adhere to this model offer parental support, and emphasize teaching parenting and other skills that are necessary for adequate child care (Lutzker & Rice, 1984).

Dubowitz et al. (1993) offer a conceptual definition of neglect based on the ecological approach which states that neglect occurs when "the basic needs of children are not met, regardless of care." These basic needs include shelter, food, health, care, clothing, education, protection, and nurturing that is adequate and sufficient to allow for optimal health, growth, and development. This definition also includes the roles of the parent, the society, and the environment. Neglect is understood to exist on a continuum ranging from optimal to extremely harmful. It is also viewed as a heterogeneous phenomenon ranging in type, severity, and chronicity. This definition of neglect is not based on who or what is responsible for the neglect, thereby assuming that the effect on the child is the same, regardless of the cause. The approach, however, does emphasize that an evaluation of the specific contributory factors is crucial for the development of appropriate treatment strategies. Thus, a treatment program may include parent education only, or may necessitate the involvement of child protective services if the neglect is chronic.

Another area of concern is unintentional injury. Unintentional injuries affect 16 million children each year, of which 600,000 require extended medical care and hospitalization, and at least 30,000 will experience permanent disability (Peterson & Gable, 1998). These injuries often occur as a result of neglect such as failing to put up a barrier at the top of a stairway to prevent the child from falling. Unintentional injuries are not easily distinguishable from injuries caused by neglect and abuse. In fact, compelling evidence suggests that child maltreatment fatalities are often misclassified as unintentional injury (Ewigman, Kivlahan, & Land, 1993; National Research Council, 1993; Peterson & Gable, 1998).

Early treatment of child maltreatment focused on either parent training or stress reduction (Gilbert, 1976; MacMillan, Olson, & Hansen, 1991; Wolfe, Edwards, Manion, & Koverola, 1988). More recently, programs based on cognitive-behavioral approaches have used a combination of parenting skills training, anger management, and general stress management to successfully improve the abilities of parents, as well as reduce recidivism rates of abuse and neglect (Peterson, Gable, Doyle, & Ewigman, 1997; Wolfe, 1994). Despite the successes of these programs, the multifaceted nature of child abuse and neglect requires a more comprehensive behavioral approach to ensure improved long-term outcomes (Lutzker, Van Hasselt, Bigelow, Greene, & Kessler, 1998). The ecobehavioral model of treatment involves a multifaceted treatment model that focuses on the child's entire social ecology (Lutzker, Van Hasselt, et al., 1998). Treatment services include behavioral strategies (that are delivered in-situ) such as parent-child interaction training, planned activities training, stress reduction, job finding, money management, nutrition counseling, home cleanliness, infant stimulation, and health care skills (Harrold, Lutzker, Campbell, & Touchette, 1992; Lutzker, Bigelow, Doctor, Gershater, & Greene, 1998; Lutzker & Campbell, 1994; Lutzker & Rice, 1984). Although several treatments appear promising and helpful, there is still a paucity of evaluation data, as well as a lack of direct behavioral treatment of the victims.

ASSESSMENT APPROACHES

Assessment in child maltreatment is used to determine whether or not parents possess sufficient knowledge, skills, and competence to adequately care for their children (Budd & Holdsworth, 1996). Professionals are often called upon by child protective services or legal authorities to conduct assessments, to testify in court regarding the adequacy of parents involved in custody cases, and to make treatment recommendations based on assessments. However, the existing psychological methods and assessment measures have created controversy regarding whether they are appropriate and sufficiently sensitive to address issues of parental competence and adequacy (Azar, 1992; Brodzinsky, 1993).

One of the major factors affecting the ability to perform appropriate assessments is the lack of standards of minimal parenting competence (Azar & Benjet, 1994; Greene & Kilili, 1998). Most states provide a list of parenting standards (e.g., income and money management standards, physical care standards, shelter, clothing, and personal hygiene standards) that describe minimally adequate parenting. These parenting standards have no operational definitions, no quantitative criteria, and lack established assessment procedures to indicate whether parents meet the minimum parenting standards or not (Greene & Kilili, 1998). In addition, many of these standards refer to minimum parenting standards that are not equivalent to competency and competent parenting (Azar & Benjet, 1994).

In the absence of standards of parenting competence, evaluators are left to establish and employ their own criteria for judging adequate parenting (Azar & Benjet, 1994). The assessment devices that are available, some of which are valid and reliable, assess specific areas of skill level and functioning as well as dimensions of parenting, and not parental adequacy. These assessments focus on aspects of the families' life: substance abuse, intellectual functioning, disorders, violence within the home, child behavior problems, the social network of the family and the state of the physical living environment. They do not measure how the existence of these variables within the child's social ecology affects the child's ability to develop and thrive. There is some research evidence to suggest a link between parental and demographic factors and child maltreatment (Ammerman, 1990; Starr, Dubowitz, & Bush, 1990); however, researchers also caution that the presence of these factors does not imply the existence of child maltreatment within the home (Budd & Holdsworth, 1996; Greene & Kilili, 1998).

The assessment of child maltreatment is necessary prior to implementation of a treatment program. In addition to providing valuable insight into the family's situation, assessment measures also provide data to help determine prevalence rates and outcomes. The process of assessment involves examining the potential risk to the child or children, as well as documenting behaviors and characteristics of the parents that can subsequently be targeted for intervention. A comprehensive assessment allows the development of effective treatment plans and the evaluation of those treatments (Lutzker, Van Hasselt, et al., 1998).

In the past, assessment of child maltreatment focused on the child's intellectual, emotional, physical, behavioral, and social characteristics with limited attention paid to the role of the parents in incidents of maltreatment (Fox, 1994). More recently, multiple measurement devices have been developed that enable the assessment of many characteristics of the target family, focusing on the children and the parents. A comprehensive assessment involves examining the child's social ecology and can be divided into four specific areas of focus: risk assessment, parent factors, child factors, and environmental factors (Lutzker, Van Hasselt, et al., 1998).

Risk assessment involves an examination of the risk for maltreatment and the degree to which this risk is present in the child's environment. An assessment of parental factors includes an examination of parental psychopathology, parenting skills, the quality of parent-child interactions, parental stress, anger, depression and physiological arousal, expectations of the child, knowledge of child development and behavior, problem-solving skills, and the social support system. Child factors are examined by assessing child development and the presence of any challenging behaviors. An environmental assessment would involve an examination of the living environment of the child and family and an assessment of the level of cleanliness and the presence of any hazards that may pose a potential harm to the child (Lutzker, Van Hasselt, et al., 1998). Many of the structured assessment devices that are available are geared toward an assessment of child abuse, not neglect. However, these devices are still useful in an assessment of neglect in an assessment of neglect as they are used to examine many factors related to neglect.

Structured assessment measures are a necessary component of the assessment process as the information they yield provides specific indications about the characteristics of the family as well as specific variables that may indicate a propensity for child maltreatment. It is important, however, to use structured assessments in combination with self-report ratings, direct observations by trained observers, and interviews to yield a well-rounded assessment (Lutzker, 1998; Milner, Murphy, Valle, & Tolliver, 1998). Some of these measurement techniques pose problems. Self-report can be biased or unreliable (Hansen & MacMillan, 1990), as many parents may misrepresent their situation. Direct observation can result in reactivity as individuals become aware that they are being watched. Parents may attempt to portray their home life and their relationships with their family members in an inaccurate light.

It is important to conduct a measure of risk assessment. Structured assessment devices are available. The Childhood Level of Living Scale (CLLS; Hally, Polansky, & Polansky, 1980) provides a quantifiable measure of the quality of physical and emotional/cognitive care for young children aged 4 through 7 years. Nine factors are assessed; five are descriptive of physical care and four are descriptive of emotional/cognitive care. The scale consists of 99 items that require a yes/no answer, indicating the presence or absence of the behavior of the parent toward the child. These items were selected on the basis that they are observable indicators of the quality of care to be used in discriminating between neglectful care and high-quality care of children. The assessment is conducted by a caseworker, or someone else who is familiar with the parents' patterns of behavior toward the target child or children.

When completed, the scale yields a total score between 1 and 99. The higher the score, the better the quality of child care. Separate scores can be calculated for physical care, emotional/cognitive care, and nine other subscales. Validity and reliability of the scale have been well established, and norms for neglectful, severely neglectful, marginally adequate, adequate, and excellent levels of care have been empirically documented. This scale is useful for measuring change in the quality in care over time.

Another widely used risk assessment device that has demonstrated adequate psychometric characteristics (Kaufman & Walker, 1986) is the Child Abuse Potential Inventory (CAP-Inventory; Milner, 1986, 1994). This measure was developed in response to the lack of reliable and valid objective measures for protective service workers to use in screening parents for potential child abuse. The CAP-Inventory contains a total of 10 scales and is designed to have a readability level of 3rd grade. The primary clinical scale is the 77-item physical abuse potential scale. The scale is made up of six factor scales (Distress, Rigidity, Unhappiness, Problems with Child and Self, Problems with Family, and Problems from Others), and three validity scales (Random Responding, Inconsistency, and Lie). These validity scales are used in various combinations to produce three response distortion indices: faking-good, faking-bad, and random-response index. This measure provides an abuse potential score that has a cut-off score of 166. Milner (1986) cautions users of this measure that the CAP-Inventory should be used in conjunction with other assessment tools such as interviews, a case history, direct observations, and other test data.

The assessment of parental factors should include demographic information, as well as a complete examination of parental characteristics. The recognition of specific parental characteristics may indicate parental problems that may contribute to insufficient child care and neglect. The Symptom-Checklist-90-Revised (Derogatis, 1983) is a self-report device that measures adult psychopathology. It includes 90 items with primary symptoms scales including Somatization, Obsessive-Compulsive, Interpersonal Sensitivity, Depression, Anxiety, Hostility, Phobic Anxiety, Paranoid Ideation, and Psychoticism. In addition, there are three global stress indices: Global Severity, Positive Symptom Distress, and Positive Symptom Total. The presence of depression or anxiety, for example, may illuminate the need for parental psychiatric treatment focusing on the psychopathologies to improve the overall home situation for the children.

The assessment of parent behavior and parenting skills is also crucial to a comprehensive assessment. The Parent Behavior Checklist (PBC; Fox, 1994) is appropriate if the child for whom reports of maltreatment were made is between the ages of 1 and 4 years. This checklist, which consists of 100 items and 3 subscales, assesses parental discipline, nurturing, and expectations of child behavior. The PBC helps professionals identify parenting strengths and weaknesses to adequately address these deficits during intervention. The PBC also illuminates parenting styles, such as a parent with a high Discipline or a low Nurturing profile.

Another measurement device that assesses the adequacy and quality of child care is the Child Well-Being Scale (Magura & Moses, 1986). This scale is designed to be administered by someone who is familiar with the family, such as a caseworker. The scale assesses the quality of child care on 43 separate dimensions ranging from the appropriateness of the primary care provider's expectations for the child to the provision of nutritious meals and physical safety of the home. Each anchored scale measures a dimension of care related to one or more physical, social, and/or psychological needs of the children. The status of the child's overall well-being is defined by the degree to which these needs are being met (U.S. Department of Health and Human Services [DHHS], 1993). Three primary factors are measured: household adequacy, parental disposition, and child performance. Application of this assessment device has demonstrated its reliability and validity (Gaudin, Polansky, & Kilpatrick, 1992).

The Home Simulation Assessment (HSA; MacMillan et al., 1991) evaluates the parent's child behavior management skills, as well as the effects of training. It is appropriate for use with parents whose children are placed outside the home or as an alternative to in-home assessment (MacMillan, Olson, & Hansen, 1988). During this assessment, a simulated child behavior management scenario is created and parents are given 10 tasks that they are to prompt an adult actor to complete. The adult actor portrays deviant child behavior and the parent's application of child-management skills is evaluated. The actor's behavior is monitored by a clinician who observes the behavior from behind a one-way mirror. The parent's percentage of correct instructions and responses to the behaviors is calculated.

It is preferable to use direct observation of parent-child interactions to assess the relationship between the family members and the parenting skills of the parents. However, it may be unethical or impractical to conduct such an assessment. In addition, parents may be reluctant to behave as they naturally would with their own children if an observer is present. Under such conditions, the HSA provides the necessary information without the risk of child endangerment or misrepresentation (MacMillan et al., 1991).

Parental characteristics such as stress and anger can contribute to child maltreatment. The Parental Stress Index/Short Form (PSI/SF; Abidin, 1990; Loyd & Abidin, 1985) assesses the level of stress in the parent's and child's life, as well as in the parent-child relationship. This assessment, which includes 36 items with a high total stress score of 90, was derived directly from the long form. Three domains are assessed: parent characteristics, child characteristics, and situations that are directly related to the parenting role. The assessment is well validated and reliable, and includes Child and Parent Domain Scales that measure the parent's total stress level. The subscales were developed to assess the child's temperament (e.g., adaptability, mood, attention-seeking behavior, hyperactivity, distractibility). A measure of parent characteristics examines the presence of depression, the parent's level of competence regarding her parenting role, and the degree of parental commitment to fulfilling their responsibilities toward their child. Two subscales measure child characteristics that affect parent-child interaction, and four subscales measure situational variables that contribute to parental stress (such as degree of spousal support and perceived isolation).

The Parental Anger Inventory (PAI; DeRoma & Hansen, 1994) is a 50-item, yes/no, and 1–5 rating system that measures the parents' levels of anger in response to their child's disruptive behaviors. Parents are presented with 50 child-related situations and are asked to rate the degree of anger that this situation elicits. Content validity has been established and the PAI is recommended for identifying anger-control problems, as well as measuring the effectiveness of anger-control interventions.

There are a number of ways of measuring the quality and nature of parent-child interactions. Direct observations are typically conducted while a parent and child are interacting (Lutzker et al., in press). There are structured assessment tools such as the Dyadic Parent-Child Interaction Coding System (Eyberg, Bessmer, Newcomb, Edwards, & Robinson, 1994; Eyberg & Robinson, 1981) and the Behavioral Coding System (Forehand & McMahon, 1981) designed for this purpose. The Dyadic Parent-Child Interaction Coding System assesses positive and negative child and parent behaviors. Child behaviors include whining, crying, shouting, compliance, noncompliance, and destructive behaviors. Parent behaviors include the use of instructions, commands, labeled praise, critical statements, and descriptive/reflective statements of questions. The Behavioral Coding System evaluates the appropriateness of commands, warnings, questions, and attention given by the parents, the use of consequences and rewards, and child compliance or noncompliance.

The quality of affective behaviors demonstrated by parents toward their children was assessed by Lutzker, Lutzker, Braunling-Morrow, and Eddleman (1987). Specific parent behaviors such as smiling, guided play, leveling (assuming the physical level of the child so that eye contact is possible), affectionate words, affectionate touch, and eye contact were assessed using direct observation. The quality of parent-infant and parent-child interactions have been assessed using direct observation of parent and child behaviors during activities such as play, bathing, meals, and dressing (Lutzker, Bigelow, Doctor, & Kessler, 1998). The parent behaviors that were observed included smiling, looking, verbal statements, touch, play, imitation, leveling, attending, and giving instructions. The infant and child behaviors included smiling, looking, crying, touch, play, imitation, verbalizations, sleeping, affect, aggression, and following instructions. These behaviors were validated by experts as important behaviors for appropriate and effective parent-child interactions.

Planned Activities Training (PAT; Lutzker et al., in press; Lutzker, Huynen, & Bigelow, 1998; Sanders & Dadds, 1982) is a training technique that teaches parents to plan for play and daily living activities such as grocery store shopping in advance. Parents are taught to organize and manage time effectively and to prepare their child for these activities by providing rules and discussing consequences, and engaging the child in the activities using affective interaction skills and incorporating incidental teaching. This technique prevents challenging behaviors from occurring and promotes positive interactions.

Effective adult-child interaction skills have also been taught to professionals working in child abuse treatment, as well as to parents referred for child abuse and neglect (Lutzker, Megson, Webb, & Dachman, 1985; McGimsey, Lutzker, & Greene, 1994). The skills taught were content and socially validated by early childhood specialists, teachers, and experts. Criterion-based training with feedback resulted in criterion performance of the skills by both parents and professionals (Lutzker et al., 1985). The participants also showed generalization of these skills to settings other than those in which they were trained (McGimsey et al., 1994).

Parental expectations of child development and child behavior is another domain for assessment. Studies comparing nonabusive parents with abusive parents have noted that abusive parents have unrealistic expectations of their children. Many abusive or neglectful parents have unrealistic expectations of their children both in terms of their cognitive abilities at young ages and their behavior. For example, Azar (1986) demonstrated that effective parents appear to have a sensitivity to their child's developmental level and adjust their interactions accordingly, whereas abusive parents have unrealistic expectations and view their children as possessing adult capabilities and skills (Azar & Rohrbeck, 1986; Azar & Siegel, 1990). These misperceptions can foster child maltreatment as the parent expects the child to behave in an adultlike fashion.

The Parent Opinion Questionnaire (Azar, Robinson, Hekimian, & Twentyman, 1984) assesses the level of parents' unrealistic expectations of appropriate child behavior. It is an 80-item questionnaire on which parents are asked to rate (agree/disagree) the appropriateness of expecting a variety of child behaviors. There are six subscales: self-care, help and affection to parents, family responsibility and care of siblings, leaving children alone, proper behavior and feelings, and punishment. It has demonstrated that it is possible to discriminate between abusive and neglectful mothers from control group mothers, as well as abusive mothers from control group mothers with abusive partners (Azar et al., 1984).

The majority of child factor assessments are obtained through the parent's report or rating of the child's behavior. Two of the most commonly used measures for assessing child behavior problems are the Eyberg Child Behavior Inventory (ECBI; Eyberg & Colvin, 1994; Eyberg & Ross, 1978) and the Child Behavior Checklist (CBCL; Achenbach & Edelbrock, 1983). Designed for parents with children over the age of 2, the ECBI is a 36-item assessment that rates problem behavior on a 7-point scale of intensity. The assessment provides a measure of disruptive child behavior on an Intensity Scale and a Problem Scale. It is designed for children between the ages of 2 and 16 and can be used repeatedly to measure behavior change. The CBCL is also designed for children between the ages of 2 and 16 years. Specific behavior problems are described in 118 items that are rated by the parent. The domains that are assessed, which are derived separately based on age and gender, include Schizoid/ Anxious, Depressed, Uncommunicative, Obsessive-Compulsive, Somatic Complaints, Social Withdrawal, Ineffective, Aggressive, and Delinquent.

The living conditions within a home can pose a threat to the health and safety of its inhabitants. The Home Observation for Measurement of the Environment Inventory (HOME, Caldwell & Bradley, 1984) is an observation/interview assessment that evaluates the safety and quality of the child-rearing environment. It provides separate rating scales for infants, toddlers, and 3- to 6-year-olds so that the living environment can be assessed. The assessment items include parent-child interactions, discipline and emotional nurturing, and activities with the child that provide intellectual stimulation. The presence of affordable, age-appropriate toys and books is also evaluated. The scale correlates significantly with measures of socioeconomic status and has bias toward middle- and upper-income families.

The Home Accident Prevention Inventory (HAPI; Tertinger, Greene, & Lutzker, 1984) and the Home Accident Prevention Inventory-Revised (HAPI-R; Mandel, Bigelow, & Lutzker, 1998) was developed to directly assess the number of hazards present in the home. The checklist divides hazards into six categories: suffocation by ingestible objects, suffocation by mechanical objects, fire and electrical hazards, firearms, hazardous sharp objects, and poisonous solids and liquids. Falling hazards such as balconies, steps and windows are also examined for accessibility and potential accidents. The observers search through every section of the home in which the parents have consented and record the number of accessible hazards in each room. Accessibility is defined by the height that the child can reach when standing on the floor and reaching upward. In addition, surfaces onto which the child can pull him- or herself are included. The HAPI-R has adequate interrater reliability and content validity in identifying hazards and evaluating the effects of training to reduce accessible hazards (Lutzker et al., in press).

For families' homes that present a health hazard, an assessment of filth and clutter is necessary. The Checklist for Living Environments to Assess Neglect (CLEAN; Watson-Perczel et al., 1988) evaluates the cleanliness of sections of the home on three dimensions: objects not belonging in a certain area or room; clothes and linen not belonging in an area; and, the presence of organic or nonorganic decaying matter. This measure has demonstrated interrater reliability and is also effective at assessing the effects of intervention. Typically, the assessment of the effects of child maltreatment and its impact on the child's life has been obtained primarily from parent reports and structured assessments (Fantuzzo et al., 1991).

In addition to assessments of child maltreatment, a comprehensive assessment of other parental circumstances, health, and skills should be conducted. A comprehensive assessment of the child's entire social ecology is important, even if some of the measures are not directly related to potential child maltreatment. A parent who is suffering from severe depression, for example, is more likely to feel that her parenting skills are inadequate. These feelings of inadequacy and inability to cope can drastically affect the quality of child care.

The Beck Depression Inventory (BDI; Beck & Steer, 1993), assesses the presence of symptoms of depression in the parent. It incorporates 21 items that generate one score that reflects the level of depression as being minimal, mild, moderate, or severe. The BDI is used to indicate any reduction in depression after treatment is completed.

Research has demonstrated that families that experience social isolation, loneliness, and a lack of social support may be more prone to neglect than comparison families (DePanfilis, 1996). The ecological models of Belsky (1980; Belsky & Vondra, 1989) and Garbarino (1981) emphasize the need for sufficient social support in parental adequacy. Some researchers have suggested that a strong social network may decrease the incidence of neglect as members of the family's social network may express disapproval of certain practices and neglectful behaviors (Thompson, 1992).

Various measures are available for the assessment of the quality and quantity of the social network surrounding the family, as well as the family's association with formal supportive resources (DePanfilis, 1996). The Eco Map (Hartman, 1978) examines the family's complete social ecology on a one-page circular chart. The Social Network Map (Tracy & Whittaker, 1990) assesses the composition of the family's informal social network, as well as the nature of the support provided by these individuals. The Interpersonal Support Evaluation List (Cohen, Mermelstein, Kamarck, & Hoberman, 1985) examines the extent to which the family is receiving acknowledgment, self-esteem, and a sense of belonging from their social network. The Perceived Social Support Questionnaire (Procidano & Heller, 1983) also evaluates the degree to which the family's needs for support are being met by their social group. The nature of social interactions and the frequency with which they occur can be assessed using the Community Interaction Checklist (Wahler, Leske, & Rogers, 1979). Other assessment measures that examine the social network of families and identify targets for intervention to strengthen these connections are the Social Network Form (Wolf, 1983, cited in DePanfilis, 1996) and the Index of Social Network Strength (Gaudin, 1979, cited in DePanfilis, 1996).

If parents cannot cope with everyday stressors and are unable to solve these problems, they are more likely to feel inadequate and frustrated. The Parent Problem Solving Instrument assesses the ability of parents to problem-solve 10 different child-rearing problems that are presented in story form (Wasik, Bryant, & Fishbein, 1980, cited in Azar et al., 1984). This measure differentiates between maltreating and nonmaltreating mothers. The Parent Problem Solving Measure (Hansen, Palotta, Tishelman, Conaway, & MacMillan, 1989) also assesses problem-solving skills in child-related and non-child-related scenarios that are presented to the parent. The parent is asked to provide all possible solutions to the problem and then describe which one she would use. The responses are rated on a 7-point scale. Coping skills can be assessed using the Ways of Coping Checklist-Revised (Lazarus & Folkman, 1984). This measure comprises eight scales including problem focused coping, wishful thinking, detachment, seeking social support, focusing on the positive, self-blame, tension reduction, and keeping to oneself.

Only recently has the field of child maltreatment research moved toward gaining an empirical perspective on home violence from children's reports, as well as their parents (Kolko, Kazdin, & Day, 1996). As a result of the increasing frequency with which children's reports are assessed, the factor structure, and intercorrelations of the children's reports needs to be evaluated to ensure congruency with constructs developed for parent report measures (Kolko et al., 1996). In addition, the content of child reports needs to be assessed to determine whether they are reporting events and violent behavior beyond that of the parents' reports. If this were the case, the information yielded from these reports would hold significant implications for prevalence rates and treatment outcome (Kolko et al., 1996).

Considerable research supports the need for the evaluation of child reports in addition to parental reports of incidents of maltreatment. Victims and perpetrators of abuse and neglect involved in the same incident have reported different levels of maltreatment (Kolko et al., 1996). For example, the individuals who perpetrated the violent act tend to report less severe violence than the individuals against which the violence was inflicted (Sariola & Uutela, 1992). Kolko et al. discovered that children reported higher rates of mother-to-child violence than did mothers. Conversely, the children reported less child-to-mother violence than did the mothers. This study also suggested that children's reports of child maltreatment can provide information that parent reports do not. Further investigation into the situations in which children's reports are more informative than parents' reports warrants attention.

As is evident from the measures described here, there is not a singular measure that should be used independently to assess parental capabilities or adequacy, and none of the measures is undeniably better than others. All of the assessment measures described measure aspects and characteristics of child maltreatment that identify abusive/neglectful situations and are helpful in developing treatment programs. Most researchers recommend a multi-method evaluation utilizing multiple assessment measures over multiple sessions (Brodzinsky, 1993; Wolfe, 1988). The disadvantage of this approach is the impracticality and the level of intrusiveness that goes along with the use of multiple measures. Since assessment plays such a critical role in examining and treating child neglect, the key is for the interventionist to choose the assessment measures that best evaluate each family's specific situation and needs. Careful selection of the most appropriate assessment measures can minimize the length of the assessment process while still enabling the interventionist to gain the necessary information. The cautionary use of these measures can provide the necessary information to compile a comprehensive, relevant, and effective intervention package.

LEGAL AND SYSTEMS CONSIDERATIONS

As a direct result of Kempe et al.'s (1962) seminal article on child maltreatment, a statute requiring that specific individuals report known cases of child maltreatment was created (Nelson, 1984). Since the development of that statute, other statutes developed mandating the reporting of child maltreatment have been developed (Fraser, 1986). Mandated reporting laws were quickly adopted by all states in the United States. These laws were created to enable the protection of the victims of maltreatment and the prosecution of the perpetrators. Despite these laws, research indicates that underreporting still exists and many cases do not result in formal reports (Zellman & Faller, 1996).

All states in the United States consider child abuse and neglect to be both a civil and a criminal offense. Reporting of suspected child maltreatment is mandated by law in all states (Bulkley, Feller, Stern, & Roe, 1996). Anyone who suspects child maltreatment may make a report; however, professionals and other individuals (identified in specific laws) who have regular contact with children are mandated by law to report any suspicion they might have. All states in the United States require the following individuals to make a report: teachers, day-care personnel, law enforcement personnel, physicians, nurses, dentists, emergency room personnel, medical examiners, coroners, social workers, and other mental health professionals. Some states also require camp counselors, clergy, attorneys, foster parents and film processors to report any suspicion of child maltreatment. Only in about 20 states is it mandated by law that anyone is required to report a suspicion of abuse (Bulkley et al., 1996).

Generally, many state reporting laws only require mandated reporting of maltreatment by primary care providers such as a parent, a guardian, a custodian, or another individual responsible for the child's care. Some states also include others who reside in the child's home such as siblings and relatives, as well as out-of-home settings such as day care, foster homes, or other residential settings (Bulkley et al., 1996). Mandated reporters are not required to have specific knowledge about child maltreatment. Their responsibility is to make a report if they suspect any form of child abuse or neglect. Once a report has been made, provided the report was not made maliciously or recklessly, the reporter is immune from any civil or criminal liability. If, however, a mandated reporter knowingly failed to report a suspicion of child maltreatment, he or she may be subject to civil or criminal liability. Such failure to report is considered a misdemeanor in all states (Bulkley et al., 1996).

The main objective of mandated reporting is to bring the case to the attention of child protective services (CPS) to assist the victims, as well as provide the necessary protection from future incidences of abuse. The immediacy of the response and the type of assistance offered depends on the nature of the report and the severity of the maltreatment (Zellman & Faller, 1996). CPS will first decide whether or not the allegation is justified and whether to investigate the situation. After investigation, a decision is made regarding the validity of the report and whether services should be rendered. In addition, CPS makes a decision regarding placement of the child in foster care, if necessary, under what conditions the parents may visit the child, and, whether the family's progress is sufficient progress to warrant returning the child to the home or permanent placement outside the home is indicated (Greene & Kilili, 1998).

Reports of child abuse and neglect may lead to civil or criminal court proceedings. It is the responsibility of the courts to balance the rights of the parents and the child with those of the state. Under the legal doctrines of parens patriae and the "best interests of the child," the court is required to intervene when the physical or mental health of a child is jeopardized and to act in the best interests of the child when deciding whether to place a child in foster care, or return him home (Bulkley et al., 1996; *Prince v. Massachusetts,* 1944).

In the early 1900s, child civil protection court proceedings were influenced by two legal doctrines: *parens patriae* and the "best interests of the child" (Bulkley et al., 1996). The doctrine of *parens patriae* limited the power of a child's parents and allowed the government to intervene when the physical or mental health of a child was jeopardized (Bulkley et al., 1996; *Prince v. Massachusetts,* 1944). The "best interests of the child" doctrine stated than when deciding whether to remove children from, or return children to, their homes, the courts should consider the children's best interests. In 1967, a decision made by the Supreme Court *(In re Gault)* changed the nature of the juvenile court system by once again limiting their power. This decision stated that the court was failing to meet the needs of the child. Children in the juvenile court system were given rights to due process. The court was still required to act in the best interests of the child, however, they were forced to recognize the right of parents to raise their children as they see fit. With this new ruling, the courts and the judges were no longer viewed as compassionate caretakers with unlimited discretion in their protection of children. The Supreme Court did not impose the duty on the State to protect a child from his parents *(DeShaney vs. Winnebago County Department of Social Services,* 1989). This ruling has made it more difficult for professionals to intervene in maltreatment cases.

Finkelhor (1993) suggests that despite the strict reporting laws, overall reporting rates are low. Some have suggested that this may be due to an overall lack of knowledge about reporting, intimidation regarding the implications of making a report, the misbelief that solid evidence of maltreatment should exist, and misconceptions regarding reporting requirements (Portwood, Reppucci, & Mitchell, 1998). The research on rates of reported and mandated reporting suggests that training of professionals on reporting requirements is required (Portwood et al., 1998).

One of the factors complicating the process of reporting and assessing cases of maltreatment is the lack of precise and standardized definitions of child maltreatment (Portwood et al., 1998). The current definitions, specifically statutory definitions, include terminology that is subject to multiple interpretations (Portwood et al., 1998). This issue becomes even more complicated when dealing with neglect alone. The common definitions of neglect describe harm to a child as a result of failing to provide necessary conditions for health and safety (Roscoe, 1990). These acts of omission cannot be quantified using direct observation. Research that has examined the attitudes of mental health professionals, legal professionals, and laypersons indicates that there is very little consensus as to whether intent should be considered when deciding whether a particular act constitutes maltreatment (Portwood et al., 1998). In addition, the legal field also lacks a standardized behavioral definition of adequate parenting (Portwood et al., 1998), which may result in subjective assessments of whether a case of child maltreatment should be reported. In general, there is dissatisfaction in the professional communities regarding the imprecise definitions of child maltreatment (Barnett, Manly, & Cicchetti, 1993; Portwood et al., 1998).

Many obstacles need to be overcome by caseworkers and treatment providers in the child maltreatment arena. Attrition and recalcitrance are prevalent issues in most treatment programs (McCurdy, Hurvis, & Clark, 1996). Some reported attrition rates as high as 75%, with the majority of dropouts occurring before or during assessment. This suggests that assessment procedures and measures are too cumbersome, too lengthy, and too invasive, leaving families withdrawn and lacking the motivation to complete the training program. Most of the current assessments such as the Beck Depression Inventory (BDI; Beck & Steer, 1993) ask intrusive questions about feelings and parents' sex lives. Given that most assessments are conducted at the initial meetings when counselors have had little time to build a rapport with the families, these questions may be inappropriate and impertinent. It is presumptuous for us to believe that parents would answer such questions willingly and honestly at this stage of intervention. It has been suggested that more open and honest responses on these assessments might be elicited if these assessments were conducted after a relationship has been secured with the family. Families have also reported a preference for assessments that evaluate skills and not parenting deficits (Fantuzzo, DeoGaudio Weiss, & Coyle Coolahan, 1998).

Other systemic issues involving child protective services have arisen. Most caseworkers carry extremely heavy case loads which prevents them from maintaining frequent contact with families, and from providing constant encouragement to families to continue with the treatment program. As a result of their case loads, many caseworkers can only attend to the very severe cases of child maltreatment. This lack of support from child protective service workers may discourage many families from persevering with exerting the effort that is required when making major changes in their lifestyles and parenting attitudes.

Great strides have been made in attempting to protect children who are victims of child maltreatment (Lutzker, 1998). Nationwide mandated reporting laws, child protective services, and the laws governing court proceedings are intended to protect current victims and prevent future incidence of child abuse and neglect. However, the lack of a standardized definition of neglect, as well as inadequate standards of adequate parenting prevent the system from working effectively. Much change is needed to create a system that is effective at ameliorating the current state of child neglect prevention and treatment. This change could begin in the court system: instead of relying on expert opinions, the courts should be requesting data and basing their decisions on the results of empirical research.

CASE ILLUSTRATION

Alexis, a 27-year-old woman, was reported to a Department of Child and Family Services (DCFS) for child neglect. DCFS referred her case to Project SafeCare, an intervention program based on the ecobehavioral model that serves families reported for child abuse and neglect (CAN), and families determined to be at-risk for child maltreatment. The ecobehavioral approach to CAN has been demonstrated by Project 12-Ways, which offers numerous services designed to ameliorate the social and ecological factors that contribute to CAN (Lutzker, Bigelow, Doctor, & Kessler, 1998). Project

SafeCare is a systematic replication of Project 12-Ways and is designed to examine three service components: child/infant health, home safety, and parent-child interactions (bonding). After Alexis's referral to Project SafeCare, a thorough assessment was conducted and intervention was implemented.

Alexis had reportedly taken her 2-year-old son to a nearby hospital and passed her son to a nurse saying that she could no longer handle taking care of him. At the time, she was pregnant with her third child. Alexis was enthusiastic about the training program that was offered by Project SafeCare to her and was eager and willing to participate and learn. She attended 22 of the 25 scheduled in-home training sessions.

When conducting the assessment, the Project SafeCare counselor requested that Alexis focus on her 2-year-old son when giving her answers on both the indirect and direct assessment measures. This child was considered the target child for assessment and intervention as she had tried to give him up at the hospital. The first assessment device that was used was an extensive demographic form that requested information regarding variables such as race, age, and history of abuse. From the completion of this form it was determined that Alexis, a single mother of Mexican-Irish descent, had two children and was pregnant with her third child. Her oldest son was 8 years old. Alexis reported that she had completed high school and had received a college AA degree. She was not in school at the time, but intended to return to college to complete her bachelor's degree.

Alexis lived with her two sons in a two-bedroom rented apartment. There were many toys and more than five television sets in Alexis's home. There were a few children's storybooks and a few games. Alexis was unemployed and reported that she received AFDC (federal) support, food stamps, Medicaid, parental financial support and unemployment that totaled approximately $1,000 per month.

She reported that she had never been abused by a boyfriend or any other individual as an adult and that there had been no violence directed toward her children in her home. She reported that she felt extreme stress because of recent events in her life, having recently moved to Los Angeles and recently separated from her boyfriend who was a heroin addict. She had also lost her job, was in debt from moving, and was feeling depressed because she had left her close friends and family from her recent move. She reported that she had been using cough syrup to help fall asleep at night.

In addition to these stressors, Alexis was suffering from chronic depression and anxiety. She had been taking antidepressant medications; however, she stopped when she discovered that she was pregnant. She reported that she had been pregnant four times. She had one abortion.

Alexis reported being abused and neglected during her childhood. She reported consistent and chronic neglect by her mother, as well as severe and regular (weekly) physical, emotional, and sexual abuse by her father. She reported substance abuse in her home by her siblings and other close relatives and also reported that her father abused her siblings and her mother. Her parents divorced when she was 18 years old.

She reported that her ex-boyfriend (her 2-year-old son's father and the father of her unborn child) was also abused as a child. His stepmother had physically abused him on a regular basis. The abuse was considered moderate (cuts and bruises). He had been separated from his parents at the age of 16. His stepfather abused his siblings as well as his mother. Alexis also reported that there had been substance abuse in his home by his stepfather.

This mother admitted neglecting her children. She reported giving them cough mixture to make them sleep. She also described how depressed and anxious she felt and that she wanted the hospital staff to take her children from her as she felt she could no longer care for them. She felt that her only method of requesting help was to go to the hospital and attempt to give up her children. Alexis reported feeling alone; her only sources of social support were her siblings and friends, from some of whom she was separated.

Several standardized assessment measures were conducted. She scored 33 on the Beck Depression Inventory, indicating severe depression. She reported being extremely worried and concerned about physical problems, feeling tired most of the time, lacking an appetite, and having sleeping problems.

Alexis also scored extremely high on the Parenting Stress Index which has a total stress cutoff (percentile) score of 90+. A parent who scores higher than 90 is experiencing a clinically significant level of stress. Alexis' total stress score was 138. She also scored above the clinical cutoff (36+) on the Parental Distress Scale (56). The components that are highlighted by this scale are an impaired sense of parenting, incompetence, stresses associated with the restrictions placed on other life roles, conflict with the child's other parent, lack of social support, and presence of depression, which is known to correlate with dysfunctional parenting (Abidin, 1990). The Parent-Child Distress Scale has a clinical cutoff of 27; Alexis scored 29. This scale indicates that the parent has expectations of the child that the child does not meet and that the parent-child interactions are not reinforcing to the parent. This also suggests that parents do not feel strongly bonded to their child or feel alienated from their child. The Difficult Child Scale has a cutoff score of 39; Alexis scored 53. This scale focuses on the basic behavior characteristics of children that make dealing with them easy or difficult. These characteristics include temperament, compliance, noncompliance, and demanding behavior (Abidin, 1990).

An interpretable score on the Child Abuse Potential Inventory was yielded from Alexis, meaning that she was not lying or faking her answers. The clinical cutoff score is 166; Alexis scored 331. She also scored extremely high on the Distress Scale (228) which has a cutoff of 150, the Unhappiness Scale, and the Problems with Family Scale.

The Eyberg Child Behavior Inventory was also administered. The cutoff scores on the ECBI are 11 for the Problem Scale and 127 for the Intensity Scale. Alexis scored 27 on the Problem Scale and 173 on the Intensity Scale. These scores indicated that Alexis viewed her child's behaviors as being inappropriate and had a low tolerance level for the behaviors. The scores also revealed Alexis' depression and anxiety level, as well as the high intensity that the behaviors bothered her.

The Parent Behavior Checklist has three main scales: Expectations, Discipline, and Nurturing. Alexis scored low on expectations of her child, in normal range on discipline, and in the normal range for nurturing.

The last structured indirect assessment that Alexis completed was the Parental Anger Inventory. She scored 33 on the Problem Scale and 159 on the Severity Scale (clinical cutoff = 148) indicating that she had difficulty coping with many child behaviors, and that she was easily angered by these behaviors.

In addition to these structured indirect assessments, three direct observation assessments were conducted by the counselor. The first assessment, the Home Accident Prevention Inventory-Revised was used to assess the number of hazards present in the home. Baseline HAPI-R data indicated that there were (on average) 100 hazards in the bedroom, 70 hazards in the kitchen, 27 hazards in the bathroom, and 4 hazards in the living room. At the beginning of intervention, Alexis watched training videos that described how to maintain a safe home environment; however, she did not reach training criterion using the video training alone. Therefore, a five-session training intervention phase implemented by a counselor was introduced. Staff trained Alexis (one room at a time) using instruction, modeling, practice with feedback, and homework assignments to reduce the number of hazards and create a safe environment for her children. Alexis was taught that her child could climb onto any surface that was at his eye level, that he could drown in an inch of water and that cosmetic products were poisonous. Staff demonstrated how children could easily access hazards even if they were stored in high closets by climbing onto shelves and drawers. Alexis was given cabinet locks to secure closets that had dangerous or poisonous items stored in them. She was asked to check all the door and window screens to ensure that they were secure, to check all electrical appliances and outlets for loose covers or exposed wires, and to remove all poisonous substances. As shown in Figure 9.1, Alexis demonstrated posttraining maintenance of zero hazards in all the rooms of her apartment.

The quality of parent-child interactions was assessed by the staff member who observed the interactions between Alexis and her son during bathtime, mealtime, and playtime. Dressing was used as a generalization action by both parent and child. Behaviors were scored separately. The final score was a percentage of positive interaction that was based on leveling, appropriate touch, appropriate instructions, incidental teaching, and smiling (parent behaviors), and eye contact, smiling or crying, following instructions, and the presence or lack of aggression (child behaviors). The baseline data showed 70% positive parent interactions and 55% positive child interactions. Alexis used some Planned Activities Training (PAT; Lutzker et al., in press; Sanders & Dadds, 1982) skills (30%). After baseline data were collected, PAT training which included training in the use of incidental teaching during activities was conducted. The results of this training are depicted in Figure 9.2. Alexis was provided with activity cards that depicted various activities that she could conduct with her children.

Alexis also participated in health care training (adapted from Delgado & Lutzker, 1988) which was designed to train parents to prevent illnesses, to use reference materials appropriately, and to follow the steps of a task analysis to identify, treat, and report children's illnesses (Lutzker et al., in press). She was given health-related scenarios of child illnesses (chicken pox, a fever, a broken arm) during which she had to describe whether it was appropriate for her to self-treat her child, call the doctor, or go to the emergency room. If her choice was self-treat, she had to explain and demonstrate exactly what she would do.

During baseline, Alexis demonstrated 40% correct responses for these scenarios. She was provided with subsequent training in child health care and maintenance. She received a health manual that the staff member reviewed with her over five training sessions. The health manual included an index of symptoms of childhood illnesses, as well as the appropriate treatment for the illness. The manual also described symptoms that warranted calling the doctor or going directly to the emergency room. Alexis's knowledge of health care was tested after each session with additional scenarios describing symptoms of illnesses. As shown in Figure 9.3, she demonstrated 100% correct responding after 1 session of training by a research assistant and maintained 100% correct responses across all phases of the health training. She was also provided with basic first aid and health care supplies and was required to demonstrate correct use of these devices.

Posttreatment assessments of the CAPI, BDI, and PSI were conducted, showing that Alexis demonstrated a significant reduction in scores across all three measures (see Table 9.1). Her baseline CAPI score dropped from 331 to 93 at posttreatment and 71 at

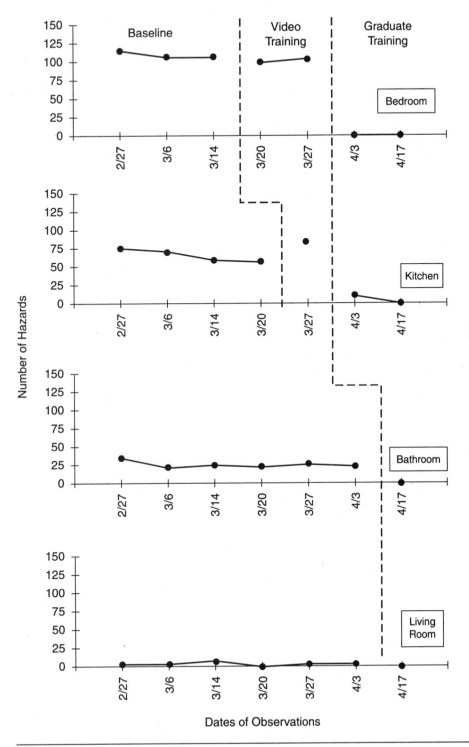

Figure 9.1 Number of Hazards Per Room for One Family That Completed Safety Training.

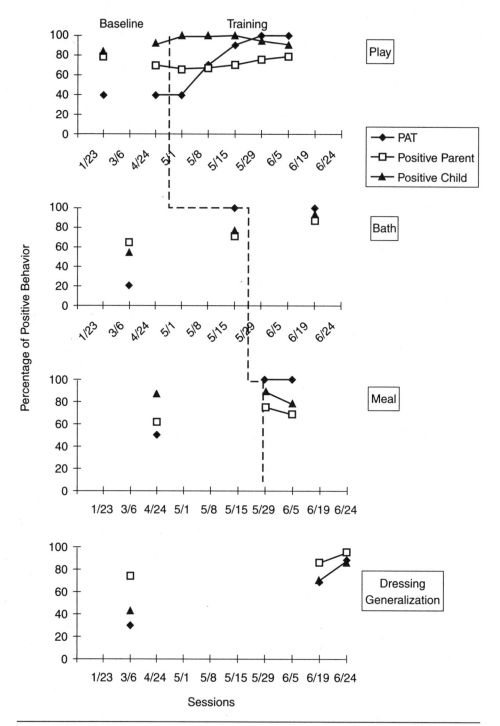

Figure 9.2 Percentage of Steps Correct on PAT Checklist, and Percentage of Positive Parent and Positive Child Behavior during Parent-Child Interactions.

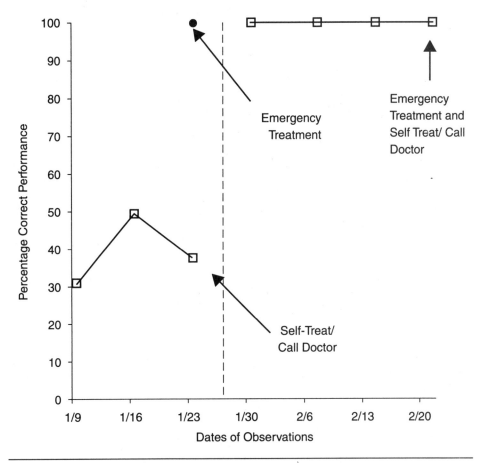

Figure 9.3 Percentage of Steps Correct on Self-Treat/Call the Doctor or Emergency Room Treatment Health Role Play Senarios for One Family Completing Health Training.

Table 9.1
Parent's Scores on Three Indirect Measures during Baseline
Post Treatment and at 3-Month Follow Up

	Baseline	Post Treatment (final treatment session)	3-month Follow Up
Child Abuse Potential Inventory	331	93	71
Beck Depression Inventory	31	0	4
Parental Stress Index	138	66	84

follow-up. These scores are well below the cut-off of 166. Her baseline BDI score of 31 indicated moderate/severe depression: at posttreatment she scored 0; and at follow-up she scored 4 (mild depression). Her score on the PSI dropped from a baseline score of 138 to 66 at posttreatment and 84 at follow-up. After intervention, Alexis described a reduction in her feelings of anxiety and frustration with her children. She felt more competent and adequately prepared to care for her children, as well as enthusiastic about engaging them socially. Alexis has since returned to college and is very close to obtaining her BA degree.

These results demonstrate that direct intervention by a staff member with a family reported for child neglect can be extremely effective in causing durable change. The results yielded by Project SafeCare thus far have suggested that the training package is effective at reducing the high BDI and PSI scores that are common in negligent mothers (Lutzker et al., in press). In general, the families that have participated in Project SafeCare show many reading and writing skill deficits, and perform far better on simple quizzes than in role-play situations. This emphasizes the need for direct training, as opposed to the use of reading materials only.

CONCLUSION

Neglect is the most common form of child maltreatment, yet it has received much less attention in the research and treatment literature than abuse. This chapter has included data on the incidence and prevalence of neglect, theories relating to its correlates, assessment of child maltreatment risk and other variables associated with maltreatment (and neglect in particular), legal and systems issues pertaining to neglect, and a case illustration of direct behavioral assessment and treatment with another referred for neglect.

Research and treatment in child neglect remains a dicey area. Attention and funding goes to abuse, which appears more acute to service and legal authorities, despite all the known serious sequelae of neglect. Parents involved in neglect are often more difficult to treat than those involved in abuse because the patterns of neglect are more long-standing and the parent may lack the feelings of guilt that a parent involved in abuse may feel. These issues notwithstanding, child neglect can be assessed and treated. A broad-spectrum or wraparound method appears to be the most effective approach.

REFERENCES

Abidin, R.R. (1990). *Parenting stress index* (2nd ed.). Charlottesville: Pediatric Psychology Press.

Achenbach, T.M., & Edelbrock, C.S. (1983). *Manual for the child behavior checklist and revised child behavior profile.* Burlington, VT: Author.

Ammerman, R.T. (1990). Etiological models of child maltreatment: A behavioral perspective. *Behavior Modification, 14,* 230–254.

Azar, S.T. (1986). A framework for understanding child maltreatment: An integration of cognitive behavioral and developmental perspectives. *Canadian Journal of Behavioral Science, 18,* 340–355.

Azar, S.T. (1992). Legal issues in the assessment of family violence. In R.T. Ammerman & M. Hersen (Eds.), *Assessment of family violence: A clinical and legal sourcebook* (pp. 47–70). New York: Wiley.

Azar, S.T., & Benjet, C.L. (1994). A cognitive perspective on ethnicity, race, and termination of parental rights. *Law and Human Behavior, 18,* 249–268.

Azar, S.T., Robinson, D.R., Hekimian, E., & Twentyman, C.T. (1984). Unrealistic expectations and problem-solving ability in maltreating and comparison mothers. *Journal of Consulting and Clinical Psychology, 52,* 687–691.

Azar, S.T., & Rohrbeck, C.A. (1986). Child abuse and unrealistic expectations: Further validation of the parent opinion questionnaire. *Journal of Consulting and Clinical Psychology, 54,* 867–868.

Azar, S.T., & Siegel, B.R. (1990). Behavioral treatment of child abuse: A developmental perspective. *Behavior Modification, 14,* 279–300.

Azar, S.T., Vera, T.Y., Lauretti, A.F., & Pouquette, C.L. (1998). The current status of etiological theories in intrafamilial child maltreatment. In J.R. Lutzker (Ed.), *Handbook of child abuse research and treatment* (pp. 3–20). New York: Plenum Press.

Barnett, D., Manly, J.T., & Cicchetti, D. (1993). Defining child maltreatment: The interface between policy and research. In D. Cicchetti & S.L. Toth (Eds.), *Child abuse, child development, and social policy* (pp. 7–73). Norwood, NJ: ABLEX.

Beck, A.T., & Steer, R.A. (1993). *Beck depression inventory: Manual.* San Antonio, TX: Psychological Corporation.

Belsky, J. (1980). Child maltreatment: An ecological integration. *American Psychologist, 35,* 320–335.

Belsky, J., & Vondra, J. (1989). Lessons from child abuse: The determinants of parenting. In D. Cicchetti & V. Carlson (Eds.), *Child maltreatment theory and research on the causes and consequences of child maltreatment* (pp. 153–202). Cambridge, MA: Cambridge University Press.

Brodzinsky, D.M. (1993). On the use and misuse of psychological testing in custody evaluations. *Professional Psychology: Research and Practice, 24,* 213–219.

Budd, K.S., & Holdsworth, M.J. (1996). Issues in clinical assessment of minimal parenting competence. *Journal of Clinical Child Psychology, 25,* 2–14.

Bulkley, J.A., Feller, J.N., Stern, P., & Roe, R. (1996). Child abuse and neglect laws and legal proceedings. In J. Briere, L. Berliner, J.A. Bulkley, C. Jenny, & T. Reid (Eds.), *The APSAC handbook on child maltreatment* (pp. 4–20). Thousand Oaks, CA: Sage.

Caldwell, B.M., & Bradley, R.H. (1984). *Administration manual: Home observation for measurement of the environment* (Rev. ed.). Little Rock: University of Arkansas.

Claussen, A.H., & Crittenden, P.M. (1991). Physical and psychological maltreatment: Relations among the types of maltreatment. *Child Abuse & Neglect, 15,* 5–18.

Cohen, S., Mermelstein, R., Kamarck, T., & Hoberman, H.M. (1985). Measuring the functional components of social support. In I.G. Sarason & B.R. Sarason (Eds.), *Social support: Theory, research and application* (pp. 73–94). The Hague: Martinus Nijhoff.

Delgado, L.E., & Lutzker, J.R. (1988). Training young parents to identify and report their children's illnesses. *Journal of Applied Behavior Analysis, 21,* 311–319.

DePanfilis, D. (1996). Social Isolation of neglectful families: A review of social support assessment and intervention models. *Child Maltreatment, 1,* 37–52.

Derogatis, L.R. (1983). *SCL-90-R: Administration, scoring, and procedures manual–II.* Towson, MD: Clinical Psychometric Research.

DeRoma, V.M., & Hansen, D.J. (1994, November). *Development of the parental anger inventory.* Poster presented at the Association for the Advancement of Behavior Therapy Convention, San Diego, CA.

DeShaney vs. Winnebago County Department of Social Services, 489 U.S. 189 (1989).

Dubowitz, H., Black, M., Starr, R.H., & Zuravin, S. (1993). A conceptual definition of child neglect. *Criminal Justice and Behavior, 20,* 8–26.

Egeland, B., & Erickson, M.F. (1987). Psychologically unavailable caregiving. In M. Brassard, B. Germain, & S. Hart (Eds.), *Psychological maltreatment of children and youth* (pp. 110–120). Elmsford, NY: Pergamon.

Erickson, M.F., & Egeland, B. (1996). Child neglect. In J. Briere, L. Berliner, J.A. Bulkley, C. Jenny, & T. Reid (Eds.), *The APSAC handbook on child maltreatment* (pp. 4–20). Thousand Oaks, CA: Sage.

Erickson, M.F., Egeland, B., & Pianta, R.C. (1989). The effects of maltreatment on the development of young children. In D. Cicchetti & V. Carlson (Eds.), *Child maltreatment: Theory and research on the causes and consequences of child abuse and neglect* (pp. 647–684). New York: Cambridge University Press.

Ewigman, B., Kivlahan, C., & Land, C. (1993). The Missouri child fatality study: Underreporting of maltreatment fatalities among children under five years of age, 1983–1986. *Pediatrics, 91,* 330–337.

Eyberg, S.M., Bessmer, J., Newcomb, K., Edwards, D., & Robinson, E. (1994). *Dyadic parent-child interaction coding system–II: A manual.* Unpublished manual, University of Florida, Gainesville.

Eyberg, S.M., & Colvin, A. (1994, August). *Restandardization of the Eyberg child behavior inventory.* Poster presented at the annual meeting of the American Psychological Association, Los Angeles.

Eyberg, S.M., & Robinson, E.A. (1981). *Dyadic parent-child interaction coding system: A manual.* Unpublished manuscript, Oregon Health Sciences University.

Eyberg, S.M., & Ross, A.W. (1978). Assessment of child behavior problems: The validation of a new inventory. *Journal of Clinical Child Psychology, 7,* 113–116.

Fantuzzo, J.W., DeoGaudio Weiss, A., & Coyle Coolahan, K. (1998). Community-based partnership-directed research: Actualizing community strength to treat child victims of physical abuse and neglect. In J.R. Lutzker (Ed.), *Handbook of child abuse research and treatment* (pp. 213–238). New York: Plenum Press.

Fantuzzo, J.W., DePaola, L.M., Lambert, L., Martino, T., Anderson, G., & Sutton, S. (1991). Effects of interparental violence on the psychological adjustment and competencies of young children. *Journal of Consulting and Clinical Psychology, 59,* 258–265.

Finkelhor, D. (1993). The main problem is still underreporting, not overreporting. In R.J. Gelles & D.R. Loseke (Eds.), *Current controversies on family violence* (pp. 273–287). Newbury Park, CA: Sage.

Forehand, R., & McMahon, R. (1981). *Helping the noncompliant child: A clinician's guide to parent training.* New York: Guilford Press.

Fox, R.A. (1994). *Parent behavior checklist.* Brandon, VT: Clinical Psychology.

Fraser, B. (1986). A glance at the past, a gaze at the present, a glimpse at the future: A critical analysis of the development of child abuse reporting statutes. *Journal of Juvenile Law, 10,* 641–686.

Garbarino, J. (1985). An ecological approach to child maltreatment. In L. Pelton (Ed.), *The social context of child maltreatment* (pp. 228–267). New York: Human Sciences Press.

Gaudin, J.M. (1933). *Child neglect: A guide for intervention.* Washington, DC: National Center on Child Abuse and Neglect.

Gaudin, J.M., Polansky, N.A., & Kilpatrick, A.C. (1992). The child well being scales: A field trial. *Child Welfare, 61,* 319–328.

Gilbert, M.T. (1976). Behavioral approach to the treatment of child abuse. *Nursing Times, 72,* 140–143.

Greene, B.F., & Kilili, S. (1998). How good does a parent have to be? In J.R. Lutzker (Ed.), *Handbook of child abuse research and treatment* (pp. 53–72). New York: Plenum Press.

Hally, C., Polansky, N.F., & Polansky, N.A., (1980). *Child neglect: Mobilizing services* (DHHS Publication No. OHDS 80-30257). Washington, DC: U.S. Government Printing Office.

Hansen, D.J., & MacMillan, V.M. (1990). Behavioral assessment of child abusive and neglectful families: Recent developments and current issues. *Behavior Modification, 14,* 255–278.

Hansen, D.J., Palotta, G.M., Tishelman, A.C., Conaway, L.P., & MacMillan, V.M. (1989). Parental problem-solving skills and child behavior problems: A comparison for physically abusive, neglectful, clinic, and community families. *Journal of Family Violence, 4,* 353–368.

Harrold, M., Lutzker, J.R., Campbell, R.V., & Touchette, P.E. (1992). Improving parent-child interactions for families of children with developmental disabilities. *Journal of Behavior Therapy and Experimental Psychiatry, 23,* 89–100.

Hartman, A. (1978). Diagrammatic assessments of family relationships. *Social Casework, 59,* 465–476.

In re Gault 387 U.S. 1 (1967).

Kaufman, K.S., & Walker, C.E. (1986). Review of the child abuse potential inventory. In J.D. Keyser & R.C. Sweetland (Eds.), *Test critiques* (pp. 55–64). Kansas City, MO: Westport.

Kempe, C.H., Silverman, F.N., Steele, B.F., Droegemueller, W., & Silver, H.K. (1962). The Battered-child syndrome. *Journal of the American Medical Association, 181,* 17–24.

Kolko, D.J., Kazdin, A.E., & Day, B.T. (1996). Children's perspectives in the assessment of family violence: Psychometric characteristics and comparison to parent reports. *Child Maltreatment, 1,* 156–167.

Lazarus, R.S., & Folkman, S. (1984). *Stress, appraisal, and coping.* New York: Springer.

Loyd, B.H., & Abidin, R.R. (1985). Revision of the parenting stress index. *Journal of Pediatric Psychology, 10,* 169–177.

Lutzker, J.R. (Ed.). (1998). *Handbook of child abuse research and treatment.* New York: Plenum Press.

Lutzker, J.R., Bigelow, K.M., Doctor, R.M., Gershater, R.M., & Greene, B.F. (1998). An ecobehavioral model for the prevention and treatment of child abuse and neglect: History and applications. In J.R. Lutzker (Ed.), *Handbook of child abuse research and treatment* (pp. 239–266). New York: Plenum Press.

Lutzker, J.R., Bigelow, K.M., Doctor, R.M., & Kessler, M.L. (1998). Safety, health care, and bonding, within an ecobehavioral approach to treating and preventing child abuse and neglect. *Journal of Family Violence, 13,* 163–185.

Lutzker, J.R., Bigelow, K.M., Swenson, C.C., Doctor, R.M., & Kessler, M.L. (in press). Problems related to child abuse and neglect. In S. Netherton, C.E. Walker, & D. Holmes (Eds.), *Comprehensive handbook of child and adolescent disorders.* Oxford, England: Oxford University Press.

Lutzker, J.R., & Campbell, R.V. (1994). *Ecobehavioral family interventions in developmental disabilities.* Pacific Grove, CA: Brooks/Cole.

Lutzker, J.R., Huynen, K.B., & Bigelow, K.M. (1998). In V.B. Van Hasselt & M. Hersen (Eds.), *Handbook of psychological treatment protocols for children and adolescents* (pp. 467–500). Hillside, NJ: Erlbaum.

Lutzker, J.R., Megson, D.A., Webb, M.E., & Dachman, R.S. (1985). Validating and training skills to professionals and to parents indicated for child abuse and neglect. *Journal of Child and Adolescent Psychotherapy, 2,* 91–104.

Lutzker, J.R., & Rice, J.M. (1984). Project 12-ways: Measuring outcome of a large-scale in-home service for the treatment and prevention of child abuse and neglect. *Child Abuse and Neglect: The International Journal, 8,* 519–524.

Lutzker, J.R., Van Hasselt, V.B., Bigelow, K.M., Greene, B.F., & Kessler, M.L. (1998). Child abuse and neglect: Behavioral research, treatment, and theory. *Aggression and Violent Behavior, 3,* 181–196.

Lutzker, S.Z., Lutzker, J.R., Braunling-Morrow, D., & Eddleman, J. (1987). Prompting to increase mother-baby stimulation with single mothers. *Journal of Clinical and Adolescent Psychiatry, 4,* 3–12.

MacMillan, V.M., Olson, R.L., & Hansen, D.J. (1988, November). *The development of an anger inventory for use with maltreating parents.* Paper presented at the Association for the Advancement of Behavior Therapy Convention, New York.

MacMillan, V.M., Olson, R.L., & Hansen, D.J. (1991). Low- and high-deviance analogue assessment of parent-training with physically abusive parents. *Journal of Family Violence, 6,* 279–301.

Magura, S., & Moses, B.S. (1986). *Outcome measures for child welfare services.* New York: Child Welfare League of America.

Mandel, U., Bigelow, K.M., & Lutzker, J.R. (1998). Using video to reduce home safety hazards with parents reported for child abuse and neglect. *Journal of Family Violence, 13,* 147–162.

McCurdy, D., & Daro, D. (1994). *Current trends in child abuse reporting and fatalities: The results of the 1993 annual fifth state survey.* Chicago, IL: National Committee to Prevent Child Abuse, National Center on Child Abuse Prevention Research.

McCurdy, K., Hurvis, S., & Clark, J. (1996). Engaging and retaining families in child abuse prevention programs. *APSAC Advisor, 9,* 1–9.

McGimsey, J.F., Lutzker, J.R., & Greene, B.F. (1994). Validating and teaching affective adult-child interaction skills. *Behavior Modification, 18,* 198–213.

Milner, J.S. (1986). *The child abuse potential inventory: Manual* (2nd ed.). Webster, NC: Psytec.

Milner, J.S. (1994). Assessing physical child abuse risk: The child abuse potential inventory. *Clinical Psychology Review, 14,* 547–583.

Milner, J.S., Murphy, W.D., Valle, L.A., & Tolliver, R.M. (1998). Assessment issues in child abuse evaluations. In J.R. Lutzker (Ed.), *Handbook of child abuse research and treatment* (pp. 75–115). New York: Plenum Press.

National Research Council. (1993). *Understanding child abuse and neglect.* Washington, DC: National Academy of Sciences.

Nelson, B. (1984). *Making an issue of child abuse.* Chicago: Chicago University Press.

Peterson, L., & Gable, S. (1998). Holistic injury and prevention. In J.R. Lutzker (Ed.), *Handbook of child abuse research and treatment* (pp. 291–318). New York: Plenum Press.

Peterson, L., Gable, S., Doyle, C., & Ewigman, B. (1997). Beyond parenting skills: Battling barriers and building bonds to prevent child abuse and neglect. *Cognitive and Behavioral Practice, 4,* 53–74.

Portwood, S.G., Reppucci, N.D., & Mitchell, M.S. (1998). Balancing rights and responsibilities: Legal perspectives on child maltreatment. In J.R. Lutzker (Ed.), *Handbook of child abuse research and treatment* (pp. 31–52). New York: Plenum Press.

Prince v. Massachusetts, 321 U.S. 158 (1944).

Procidano, M., & Heller, K. (1983). Measures of perceived social support from friends and from family: Three validation studies. *American Journal of Community Psychology, 11,* 1–24.

Roscoe, B. (1990). Defining child maltreatment: Ratings of parent behaviors. *Adolescence, 99,* 517.

Sanders, M.R., & Dadds, M.A. (1982). The effects of planned activities training and child management procedures in parent training: An analysis of setting generality. *Behavior Therapy, 13,* 452–461.

Sariola, H., & Uutela, A. (1992). The prevalence and context of family violence against children in Finland. *Child Abuse & Neglect, 16,* 823–832.

Starr, R.H. Jr., Dubowitz, H., & Bush, B.A. (1990). The epidemiology of child maltreatment. In R.T. Ammerman & M. Hersen (Eds.), *Children at risk* (pp. 23–53). New York: Plenum Press.

Starr, R.H. Jr., MacLean, D.J., & Keating, D.P. (1991). Life-span developmental outcomes of child maltreatment. In R.H. Starr, Jr. & D.A. Wolfe (Eds.), *The effects of child abuse and neglect: Issues and research* (pp. 1–26). New York: Guilford Press.

Tertinger, D.S., Greene, B.F., & Lutzker, J.R. (1984). Home safety: Development and validation of one component of an ecobehavioral treatment program for abused and neglected children. *Journal of Applied Behavior Analysis, 17,* 159–174.

Thompson, R.A. (1992). *Social support and the prevention of maltreatment.* Paper prepared for the U.S. Advisory Board on Child Abuse and Neglect, University of Nebraska, Department of Psychology.

Tracy, E.M., & Whittaker, J.K. (1990). The social network map: Assessing social support in clinical practice. *Families in Society, 7,* 461–470.

U.S. Department of Health and Human Services, National Center on Child Abuse and Neglect. (1993). *Child neglect: A guide for intervention.* Washington, DC: Westover Consultants.

U.S. Department of Health and Human Services, National Center on Child Abuse and Neglect. (1996). *Child maltreatment 1994: Reports from the states to the national center on child abuse and neglect.* Washington, DC: U.S. Government Printing Office.

Wahler, R.G., Leske, G., & Rogers, E.S. (1979). The insular family: A deviance support system of oppositional children. In L.A. Hamerlynck (Ed.), *Behavioral systems for the developmentally disabled: I. School and family environments* (pp. 102–127). New York: Brunner/Mazel.

Watson-Perczel, M., Lutzker, J.R., Greene, B.F., & McGimpsey, B.J. (1988). Assessment and modification of home cleanliness among families adjudicated for child neglect. *Behavior Modification, 12,* 57–81.

Wolfe, D.A. (1994). The role of intervention and treatment services in the prevention of child abuse and neglect. In G.B. Melton & F.D. Barry (Eds.), *Protecting children from abuse and neglect: Foundations for a new national strategy* (pp. 182–223). New York: Guilford Press.

Wolfe, D.A., Edwards, B., Manion, I., & Koverola, C. (1988). Early intervention for parents at risk of child abuse and neglect: A preliminary investigation. *Journal of Consulting and Clinical Psychology, 56,* 40–47.

Zellman, G.L., & Faller, K.C. (1996). Reporting of child maltreatment. In J. Briere, L. Berliner, J.A. Bulkley, C. Jenny, & T. Reid (Eds.), *The APSAC handbook on child maltreatment* (pp. 4–20). Thousand Oaks, CA: Sage.

Zuravin, S.J. (1991). Research definition of child physical abuse and neglect: Current problems. In R.H. Starr, Jr. & D.A. Wolfe (Eds.), *The effects of child abuse and neglect: Issues and research* (pp. 101–127). New York: Guilford Press.

Zuravin, S.J., & DiBlasio, F.A. (1996). The correlates of child physical abuse and neglect by adolescent mothers. *Journal of Family Violence, 11,* 149–166.

CHAPTER 10

Incest in Young Children

LINDA L. DAMON and JESSICA A. CARD

THE GENERAL public usually views incest as sexual intercourse between a father and daughter. Child abuse clinicians employ a more comprehensive psychosocial definition of incest, which encompasses any form of sexual activity between a child and a parent, parental figure, or extended family member (Sgroi, 1982). This broader definition includes not only a wide range of activity, but also a more general designation of the perpetrator, including mothers, siblings, cousins, and other family members. Most experts would not consider noncoercive exploratory sexual play between siblings or cousins of similar age to be incest.

The psychological dynamics present in an incest situation include the issues of power differential and coercion, the need to keep the secret to preserve the family, the breaking of a cultural taboo, and the fear of being caught in a criminal act. The victim usually feels responsible and guilty and, not wanting to feel more shame, keeps the secret. Other family members may deny existence of incest to avoid facing painful issues, as well as legal action and criminal charges. All these factors mitigate against disclosure. Mothers of incest victims are particularly subject to scrutiny as they may be accused of failing to protect the child or of making unsubstantiated allegations to secure sole custody.

Because medical evidence is present in only a small proportion of young sexual abuse victims (Muram, 1989), mental health assessment assumes substantial importance in the validation of allegations. The evaluator must consider a wide range of data from various sources before forming an opinion.

Clinical assessment in the validation of alleged sexual abuse requires an approach that is sensitive to new research findings and legal implications. The approach we are presenting has emerged during our 15 years of specialization in the evaluation and treatment of child sexual abuse. Our approach has evolved, influenced by our clinical experience, based on research findings and legal decisions that impact the tools and techniques we use.

DESCRIPTION OF THE PROBLEM

There is no consensus among social scientists regarding the prevalence and incidence of sexual abuse in young children (Finkelhor et al., 1986). Prevalence studies, which estimate the proportion of a population that has experienced childhood sexual abuse, vary from 6% to 62% for females. The variability in the studies results from differences in definitions of sexual abuse, questions asked, and methodologies. Incidence studies, which estimate the number of new cases occurring in any given time period, are derived either from data on reported cases or from retrospective self-reports.

Assessment of sexual abuse of young children is a complicated and challenging responsibility. No syndrome or set of symptoms clearly identifies a sexually abused child. In fact, abused children are sometimes asymptomatic, appearing to function normally at school and with peers (Jones & McQuiston, 1986). Other children exhibit symptoms such as age-inappropriate sexualized behaviors, bed-wetting, nightmares, age-inappropriate separation anxiety, aggression, depression, psychosomatic complaints, self-destructive thoughts and behaviors, fire setting, and fearfulness. Likewise, there is no evidence that perpetrators can be identified by their behavior, symptoms, or any currently available psychological test (Williams & Finkelhor, 1990). Lack of a clear profile or syndrome, coupled with the fact that both perpetrators and victims often deny incest, increases the difficulty in conducting sexual abuse evaluations.

Furthermore, the dynamics of incest involve secrecy, fear, guilt, shame, and coercion. The interviewer has the task of obtaining accurate information from a child who has been raised in an atmosphere of secrecy and shame, repeatedly abused, and pressured not to tell the secret. The interviewer is faced with the dilemma of trying to obtain information from a victim who is reluctant to talk. The interviewer's dilemma is exacerbated by the need to be directive and structured to help the child understand the task and disclose the secret, without giving suggestions or coercing the child.

These difficulties are compounded when the assessment process is challenged in the adversarial court arena. Evaluators may be accused of having led highly suggestible children into making false allegations even when they have been very careful not to contaminate the interview with leading questions. Despite empirical evidence that children are not very suggestible regarding abuse, the suggestibility of children remains extremely controversial and is likely to be raised in court. Attorneys will challenge the credibility of the evaluator and the interviewing techniques because the legal process relies heavily on confrontation and cross-examination as methods of assessing the reliability and validity of information.

DISCLOSURE OF A SECRET

The family is supposed to provide children with protection, nurturance, the basis of reality, and a blueprint for relationships. Children in incestuous families are not protected or appropriately nurtured. They learn that, to have their needs met, they must first meet the needs or conditions dictated by the caregiver. The child fuses affection and sexuality and believes one is conditional on the other. Very young children (under 4 years of age) may not be aware that the sexual activities are wrong. Confusion and betrayal impact these children once they become aware that these acts are wrong. This then undermines their development of a basic sense of trust and leads them to question their relationships. Sexually abused children do not have the basis for trust required for them to disclose the secret. Before they can begin to disclose, children must often confront their shame, guilt, and fears about telling the secret. Some children must be in therapy for an extended period of time before they can disclose their abuse.

Fears and Threats

Threats by the perpetrator can range from relatively benign statements (e.g., "I won't be your friend if you don't do what I say"; "No one will believe you if you tell") to threats on a child's life. Ceci and Bruck (1995) state that threats do not adversely affect a child's ability to disclose information. However, Lyon (1996) provides a persuasive argument that threats will, in fact, diminish the likelihood of a child revealing abuse, especially if the relationship between the offender and the child is familial. For some children, the relationship with the perpetrator is the only relationship they have that gives them a sense of closeness and affection. Loss of that relationship, in their view, would create more pain than the continuation of sexual abuse.

Fear that the perpetrator will go to jail and be unable to support the family is a common concern for all members of the family. Because perpetrators are usually the dominant or most powerful member of the family, the burden of financial support typically rests on them. The child's fear of abandonment is frequently actualized when the secret is exposed. The mother may align with the father, as may the siblings, even if they too have been victimized.

Guilt and Shame

When self-destructive or suicidal behaviors are present, interviewers should consider the possibility that the child or adolescent is exhibiting these behaviors due to a deep sense of shame. Most young children experience guilt or shame related to the incest (Sgroi, 1982). Many perpetrators rationalize their actions (e.g., "I only do this because you like it") in a way that makes it even more difficult for a child to disclose the abuse. In addition, the guilt of young children is further reinforced by their tendency to blame themselves, due to egocentric thinking, for causing the incest. As the young child becomes more aware of social prohibitions, shame becomes an obstacle to disclosure. The child may feel shame for either having participated in or not having stopped the molestation.

Coercion

The perpetrator in incest families usually wields a great deal of power, expressed through the use of physical force, intimidation, withdrawal of love, or any combination of these strategies. While physical coercion leads to fears of bodily harm, threat of withdrawal of affection may be equally effective in eliciting compliance with the perpetrator's demands.

Children in such families learn that people in power meet their own needs first, frequently at the expense of those less powerful, and have the right to take, use, or abuse the less powerful person's body, belongings, or personal space (Sgroi, 1982). This lesson may, in turn, lead sexually abused children to victimize younger or less powerful children.

RETRACTION

Children commonly retract or refuse to "remember" a painful event because they are unable to defend against the strong emotions accompanying the memory. Young children may attempt to avoid experiencing their emotions by denying that the events actually happened. The presence of posttraumatic stress disorder (PTSD) symptomatology (avoidance and numbing) offers an explanation for a child's retraction or inability to recall specific details of the abuse (Koverola & Foy, 1993).

Retraction by the victim sometimes occurs while a child is being assessed or treated (Summit, 1983). Although the clinical literature is replete with case examples of retraction, there is surprisingly little research to document the frequency of this phenomenon and the circumstances under which it occurs. Waterman, Kelly, Oliveri, and McCord (1993) found a 23% recantation rate during therapy in young children molested in a daycare setting by a perpetrator who had confessed. Sorenson and Snow (1991) studied the recantation rate of children molested either in or out of the home whose sexual abuse was supported by medical evidence, perpetrator confession, or criminal conviction. Twenty-two percent of these children retracted their previous disclosures over the course of therapy (and 39% of them later re-affirmed their initial disclosures).

The recantation rate for children during the time frame of the initial assessment is lower, ranging from 3% (Bradley & Wood, 1996) to 8% (Jones & McGraw, 1987). Gries, Goh, and Cavanaugh (1996) studied a large sample of foster children who either had disclosed or were suspected of having been molested and found a 15% recantation rate between the first and the second interview (occurring one week later). Recantation rates of children during the initial assessment phase appear to be significantly lower than rates that occur at a later point in time, during the psychotherapy process.

Although there is no research to support this hypothesis, the authors suspect that the recantation rate would be higher for intrafamilial abuse due to the profound impact disclosure has on the family in this situation. Also, in most of the preceding studies, the selection criteria for molestation required some actual "proof" of sexual abuse for the children to be included in the research. Whereas this kind of "proof" is the exception rather than the norm in intrafamilial abuse, the authors suspect that recantation rate would be higher still in those victims without strong external validation (such as medical evidence, etc.) to further convince the child's support system that molestation had actually occurred.

Retractions occur for many reasons. When a child has disclosed the secret of incest, families are besieged with intrusions by police and social workers, and the child feels responsible for these actions. The father may be required to move out of the home, causing the mother to fear loss of economic support. Anger and disbelief exhibited by parents and siblings may precipitate retraction. The guilt-ridden victim often feels shame, a realistic fear of abandonment by the family, and embarrassment at having to continue to repeat the details of the sexual abuse to investigative agencies. Victims may retract their statements to return the situation to "normal." Victimized children may also retract in an effort to protect their parents from being punished. Such retractions may occur right before or during legal or investigative processes.

FAMILY SUPPORT OF DISCLOSURE

Caretaker's willingness to accept the possibility of abuse is a major factor in facilitating if a child will disclose. For example, Lawson and Chaffin (1992) studied the disclosure rate of children who had been treated for sexually transmitted diseases. The children in the study had not disclosed sexual abuse prior to their medical treatment for the STD. When interviewed, 63% of children with supportive caretakers (i.e., were willing to accept the possibility that the child was molested) were able to disclose their abuse, whereas only 17% of children with unsupportive caretakers were able to disclose. The authors pointed out that almost half of the children in this study were asymptomatic, and therefore would not have been identified as molested were it not for the presence of the STD. Family support has reportedly been found to influence initial disclosure rate.

DEVELOPMENTAL LIMITATIONS OF THE YOUNG CHILD

A number of developmental limitations affect the young child's ability to provide a comprehensive and clear description of sexual victimization. The limitations of expressive and receptive language skills affect children's ability to describe what has occurred. Cognitive limitations influence their ability to understand the interviewer's questions, making it often necessary to rephrase and repeat them. Thus, descriptions of sexual abuse by children are fraught with problems of clarity, consistency, and certainty, all of which raise serious difficulties for assessment. However, the child's ability to provide information about the allegations has been considered by practitioners to be one of the 10 most important criteria for sustaining allegations of sexual abuse (see Conte, Sorenson, Fogarty, & Rosa, 1988).

ASSESSMENT APPROACHES

An evaluation for suspected sexual abuse may be requested by a parent, a law enforcement officer, a child protective service worker, or the court. One or more of the following prompts a referral:

- Age-inappropriate sexual behavior or knowledge.
- A disclosure of incest by the child.
- Medical evidence suggestive of abuse.
- A report that a sibling was sexually abused, raising the possibility that other children in the family could also have been sexually abused.

When the court requests an evaluation, it is important that all relevant family members participate in the assessment to make recommendations about custody. A complete clinical assessment of incest should include four specific areas of inquiry: physical evidence, psychological tests, outside sources of information, and clinical interviews with the family and child. This chapter focuses on how to conduct the family and child interviews, but the other areas of inquiry are briefly examined here.

Physical evidence includes all data from medical evaluations. Although positive physical signs of abuse are highly suggestive of sexual abuse, lack of medical evidence does not establish that incest has not occurred. Enos, Conrath, and Byer (1986, cited in Meyers, Bays, Berlinger, Corwin, & Saywitz, 1989) suggested that physical evidence of sexual abuse is found in only 10% to 50% of sexual abuse cases. Levitt (1986, cited in Meyers et al., 1989) reported that if disclosure of abuse is delayed (as is usually the case for incest victims), physical findings are present in only 10% to 20% of cases. Even when perpetrators admit to penetration, children do not always exhibit positive physical findings. Muram (1989) did not find positive medical evidence of vaginal penetration in 39% of his sample of 31 female children, even though all the perpetrators had admitted to penetration. In court, negative findings are embraced by the defense, but positive findings are also challenged and alternative explanations for the injury are sought. It is essential that the evaluator keep abreast of current literature about the findings on medical evaluations, because this information needs to be considered in the complete clinical assessment. Furthermore, evaluators should question the training and experience of physical examiners to ascertain that they are qualified to render an opinion. Heger (1992) provides information about the format of a medical-legal examination.

Psychological testing of parents and children may be conducted for custody evaluations. Data from adult personality tests can sometimes be helpful to the examiner in formulating opinions about custody recommendations, but they do not provide a profile for the perpetrator of incest (Williams & Finkelhor, 1990). At present, no tests, including the polygraph test and the penile plethysmograph, validly identify perpetrators or rule out the possibility of penetration (Meyers et al., 1989). Hall, Proctor, and Nelson (1988) found that 80% of admitted male offenders in their study were able to voluntarily completely inhibit their sexual arousal to pornography as measured by a penile plethysmograph. Absence of psychiatric problems does not indicate that an offense was not committed. Williams and Finkelhor (1990) concluded that one-fourth to one-third of incestuous fathers appear quite normal. Similarly, no psychological test substantiates or rules out victimization in children (Friedrich, 1990).

It is important to examine outside sources of information on child behavior, including schools and day-care providers. Although not all incestuously abused children exhibit age-inappropriate sexual behaviors, these symptoms are among the indications of possible molestation. Included are such behaviors as masturbating with an object and asking others to engage in sex acts (Friedrich et al., 1991). A recently developed instrument, the Child Sexual Behavior Inventory (Friedrich, 1990), is a very useful tool for obtaining information about a wide range of sexualized behaviors. This inventory will soon provide age and diagnostic norms against which the abused child's behavior can be compared, and is available through PAR (Friedrich, 1997).

In addition, the evaluator should gather information about indicators of stress, including anxiety and fearfulness, such as bed-wetting, nightmares, and age-inappropriate separation anxiety. Other symptoms and behaviors of concern are anger, fire setting, psychosomatic complaints, depression, and self-destructive thoughts and behaviors (see Lusk & Waterman, 1986). In addition to interviews, the Child Behavior Checklist (Achenbach & Edelbrock, 1983) can be utilized to obtain information about a child's symptoms and behaviors from parents, teachers, and day-care providers. A commonly used research instrument, this measure assesses social functioning and behavioral disturbances.

INTERVIEW PROTOCOLS AND PROCEDURES

A variety of interview techniques and procedures have been developed for assessment of sexual abuse allegations. These protocols vary in purpose, thoroughness, structure, and degree of specificity regarding which procedures and techniques to utilize. Evaluators may be challenged in court for not following a specific protocol or for deviating in any way from the one followed. In these cases, it is important to educate judges and lawyers that no protocol has been proven to be superior to the others, and there is no "correct way" to conduct sexual abuse evaluations.

Guidelines for evaluation of suspected sexual abuse in young children have been published by the American Professional Society on Abused Children (APSAC Task Force, 1990). Evaluators who conduct sexual abuse evaluations will benefit from familiarizing themselves with the APSAC guidelines and the protocols and interview guidelines published in this field and discussed in this chapter. Our own clinical interview, also discussed here, utilizes some of the techniques described in these protocols.

In their manual and videotape on the clinical interview, Mac Farlane and Feldmeth (1988) provided an excellent summary of issues and techniques involved in child sexual abuse evaluations. The manual includes a thorough discussion of developmental issues, building rapport, the interview environment, obstacles to disclosure, the resistant child, interviewing techniques, common indicators, obtaining the psychosocial history, termination and follow-up, responding to parents, and legal issues.

Friedman and Morgan (1985) and Jones and McQuiston (1986) describe numerous techniques in addition to anatomical dolls that can be used to interview young children suspected of having been molested. For example, they suggested using drawings, puppets, and play techniques in helping a young child disclose.

Hewitt and Arrowood (1994) have described an interview format utilizing simple drawings that review both positive and negative forms of touching and screen for physical, sexual, and emotional abuse. In their study comparing abused with nonabused children, they found an underreporting of abuse with no fabricated allegations. Although the method is very conservative it does present a systematic way in which to proceed in interviews. Saywitz describes an experimental technique, *narrative elaboration,* designed to assist school-age children to elaborate without the use of leading questions (Dorado & Saywitz, 1997; Saywitz & Snyder, 1996). Her technique teaches a memory enhancement strategy, using pictorial category cues, that represent four categories of information (participants, setting, actions, and conversation/affective states). Children trained in the technique demonstrated a 53% increase in accurate information through a free-recall narrative of a previous activity, than did children without the training. The narrative elaboration technique promises to be a viable technique when interviewing children about possible sexual molestation.

Gardner (1987) claimed that his Child Sexual Abuse Legitimacy Scale can differentiate between true and false allegations in custody dispute cases. The scale contains a number of items that are scored if "yes" answers are given. The higher the score, the greater the likelihood of molestation. Gardner's scale is not sensitive to developmental limitations of very young children, for they tend to lose points on many of the items (e.g., whether they expressed guilt about the abuse or indicated that they felt betrayed). We do not recommend this scale be used until normative data indicate that it is, in fact, valid. An additional problem with this approach is that Gardner recommended, in most cases, interviewing the accused individual and accusing child together. Doing so allows the accused individual a chance to cross-examine the child about the accusations. In our experience, most children are unable to confront an offending parent about molestation unless they have had extensive therapy.

THE CLINICAL INTERVIEW

A single chapter cannot cover everything an interviewer needs to know about how to conduct an assessment or evaluation for sexual abuse, and this section focuses on pointing out issues that require specialized knowledge on the part of the evaluator.

Thorough training in clinical interviewing and a basic knowledge of developmental psychology are required. Even experienced professionals may be surprisingly ignorant about sexual abuse. For example, Hibbard and Zollinger (1990) found that 20% of a sample of 900 professionals working in the sexual abuse area were not knowledgeable about some important issues in child sexual abuse, such as that an abused child may have positive feelings about the molestation experience.

Clinical interviews can be utilized for evidentiary purposes or solely for clinical needs. Determination of the purpose of the assessment should occur prior to a decision regarding how to obtain needed data. However, assessments conducted for clinical purposes may end up being used as evidence. Interviewers should conduct all assessments with the possibility in mind that some type of litigation may result. If information is needed for evidentiary purposes, it is essential that current legal decisions are kept in mind so that data will not be contaminated and unusable (see the following major section on legal considerations).

Ideally, evaluators conducting sexual abuse assessments will have specialized academic training and professional experience relevant to sexually abused children. Knowledge of current professional literature on sexual abuse and experience in providing court testimony are also important. (For more specific guidelines regarding qualifications of individuals conducting sexual abuse evaluations, see the guidelines by APSAC, 1990.) If the evaluator does not have such training or experience, an evaluator who meets the preceding criteria must closely supervise him or her. The criteria may seem extensive, yet an error in either direction can have profound implications for members of the family: Failure to identify abuse can leave a child unprotected, whereas an accusation that proves erroneous can destroy an individual's personal and professional life. Because of the magnitude of the consequences, this area demands great skill and rigor from practitioners.

It is essential to remember that incest occurs in secret. When the secret has been disclosed, it is important to try to understand the child's motivation for disclosure (e.g., the child was hurt, or feels safer to disclose because there has been a change in custody due to divorce). Disclosure of sexual abuse can be deliberate or accidental. Deliberate disclosures are usually attempts by young children to obtain assistance in stopping the sexual abuse, often because they are being hurt. Accidental disclosures occur when a child inadvertently makes statements that alert an adult to the problem, even though the child may or may not feel it is a problem. Some children might boast to peers about the special things they do with their parents. Children who do this are usually fairly young and unaware of social prohibitions against the activities they consider to be positive and special. Children also accidentally "disclose" when they are caught in sexual activities with peers and are asked who taught them this activity.

The overall format of the sexual abuse evaluation involves an interview with the referring parent to obtain background information prior to the interview of the child. The sexual abuse evaluation of the child should be conducted without the parents present; however, an additional interview with the child and parents present may assist in assessing the overall quality of the relationships.

Gries et al. (1996) found that 20% of their disclosures would not have been made had there not been a second interview. Furthermore out of their sample of foster children in which molestation had been suspected, over 36% of the sample failed to disclose during either session. These results are consistent with our clinical experience and support the need for more than one or two interviews with the child. Children may disclose abuse in one or two interviews. However, to ensure a child has not been traumatized by the interview and is able to disclose sufficient information, four to six one-hour sessions may be necessary to rule out all alternative explanations in a thorough manner.

Interview with the Parent

The following information is sought from the referring parent: child's developmental history, family history, list of persons with access to the child, list of names the child uses for family members and pets, words used by family and child for genitals and bodily elimination, child's daily routine, and symptomatic behaviors.

Several factors operate within incestuous families that affect how the interview must be conducted to obtain the necessary information. Denial, one of the most prevalent defenses in incestuous families, is frequently the only coping mechanism available to family members (Sgroi, 1982). Pervasive denial may interfere with a parent's ability to understand questions and lead to an inability to perceive or reveal examples of the type of behavior about which the evaluator is asking. Therefore, specific and concrete questions are required about family boundaries, including family rules regarding intimacy, sexuality, sleeping arrangements, and hygiene. For example, when asked whether she ever uses babysitters, a mother may answer "No." However, it is necessary to question such a statement further by asking "You mean you never go out?" which may lead to an explanation that the parents leave the child with the maternal grandfather, who had molested the mother.

Because of their denial and repression, many parents are unable to give accurate information about their own childhood. A common response to a question regarding their own childhood is "It was good." If asked to describe family relationships or to give specific examples of "how good," they often give a different impression. Questions regarding whether anyone in their family was physically or sexually abused are often answered "No," but when asked specifically whether anyone ever tried to touch them inappropriately or exposed themselves, they may then give information about sexual abuse. However, some parents do not recall having been molested until after they enter treatment. Asking how discipline was administered will provide more accurate descriptions of possible physical abuse than a more general question.

Whether accused individuals should be included in the assessment and interview is controversial. Some argue that doing so may contaminate court proceedings in various ways. To maintain an unbiased position, evaluators may include accused individuals; however, it is usually best to postpone interviewing the accused individual (without the child present) until after the child abuse report is filed and acted on by the authorities. This may avoid the possibility that the accused will pressure the child to retract. The evaluator's goal is to obtain the information listed earlier, whereas the accused's goal is to prove his or her innocence. Accused individuals frequently bring other data and documents, such as character references or previous custody evaluations, to defend themselves. It is important to review and consider these data and all sources of information.

At the close of the interview with the referring parent, the evaluator should provide instructions on how the parent can prepare the child for the interview. The parent should tell the child that he or she will be talking to someone who asks lots of questions about a lot of different things and that the child will know some answers and not others, but either way it is okay. The parent should be instructed to avoid discussing the alleged sexual abuse with the child.

INTERVIEW WITH THE CHILD

The importance of the evaluator's training and experience in both child development and child sexual abuse cannot be overstated. Limitations of language and cognition in young children require that the interviewer have special knowledge and training to conduct an assessment. Faller (1990) and Saywitz (1990) offered some excellent suggestions about how to talk to young children in language they can understand. In addition to the limitations of language and cognition in younger children, issues unique to sexual abuse determine how to both conduct the evaluation and interpret the findings.

The interview with the child can begin with the referring parent present for a few minutes to reduce the child's anxiety. If the child has separation difficulties, the parent may be present in the beginning phase of the interview. The parent can be warned in advance that discussion of the alleged sexual abuse will not be allowed in the parent's presence. Verbal and nonverbal communications of the accusing or the referring parent may interfere with obtaining information about the alleged sexual abuse and can best be avoided by not having him or her present.

Interviewing the child and accused individual together for the purpose of assessing the veracity of the allegations is not recommended by 98% of experts in the field of sexual abuse evaluation (Conte et al., 1988). If asked to confront the alleged perpetrator, the victim will frequently deny or refuse to talk about the allegations due to the dynamics typically present in incest. One cannot assume that children who demonstrate a warm, positive, or fearless relationship with the accused individual have not been molested, since the incest is only part of their overall relationship (Sgroi, 1982).

The interview with the child should be conducted in an environment that facilitates a child's ability to communicate freely and comfortably. The evaluator should schedule enough time to allow for a complete evaluation. A minimum of two interviews is preferable, with up to a maximum of six sessions of focused evaluation. Gries et al. (1996) found that 20% of younger children disclosed in the second interview. If the child does not disclose abuse within six sessions and the evaluator is unable to give an opinion, the child can be referred for extended evaluation/therapy if the evaluator has concerns about the possibility of molestation or other psychological problems. Extended evaluation/therapy is less directive but diagnostically focused and should continue to address the possible obstacles to disclosure, as well as alternative hypotheses to account for the original sexual abuse assessment referral.

The beginning phase should be used to orient the child to the structure of the interview, including the child and evaluator's roles. The evaluator's role is to "ask a lot of questions," to assist in "getting to know" the child better. Children assume adults know more about what a child is thinking or is remembering. Therefore, the interviewer should make it very clear to the child he does not know what happened to the child since he was not present during the events the child might describe. Mulder and Vrij (1996) found that children who were told that interviewers did not have knowledge about an event the children were describing provided more information that was accurate about the event. In addition to telling children that the interviewer has no knowledge of what happened to them, they should be instructed as to the different options they have when they answer questions, such as "I don't know," "I don't remember," "I don't understand the question," or "I don't want to answer." It should be stressed to the child that all information they provide should be truthful, and they should tell only "what really happened." These options allow the child to respond in a truthful manner to the evaluator's questions. For example, a child who is embarrassed about details about the sexual activities has the option to say "I don't want to talk about it" and avoid discussing details without having to be untruthful and deny that any sexual activity occurred. It also is useful to ask the child about his or her understanding of the purpose of the meeting to gain some sense of the child's perspective.

The next phase of the evaluation should establish rapport while assessing the child's developmental level. The Denver Developmental Screening Test will provide a rough estimate of cognitive, social, and motor functioning. Saywitz and Damon (1988) and Waterman (1986) described other useful tools for the assessment of developmental functioning.

The child's language level, affect, anxiety, and avoidance should be monitored throughout the evaluation, because age-inappropriate language or sudden changes in affect may indicate areas that require further exploration. For example, a sudden escalation of anxiety and avoidance may signify fear of disclosure, guilt about the secret, or even discomfort with sexual talk.

The following information can be obtained from the child during this beginning phase: names of all family members and their relationships to the child; names of the child's friends; names of family member's friends with whom the child has contact; names of pets, names of teachers or caretakers; and a description of his or her daily routine, including who assists the child in the morning and evening routine. Other questions include where the child sleeps, where other family members sleep, with whom the child plays, and what the child's favorite and least favorite games are. The child's style and ability to provide such information can be compared with information provided about the alleged sexual molestation.

Unstructured projective play, although helpful for building rapport, has been found to be an ineffective technique to elicit disclosure. Gries et al. (1996) found only a 1% disclosure rate during projective play. Furthermore younger children were found to need the additional structure and focus offered by the identification of body parts and learning about the three types of touching. These two procedures accounted for one-third of all disclosures.

Faller (1990) described five types of questions that follow a continuum from general to specific: (1) general, (2) focused, (3) multiple choice, (4) yes/no, and (5) leading. General questions are those about an individual's state of mind or circumstances asked in a nonspecific manner (e.g., "Is anything troubling you?"). Children usually need more specific information to respond to such an open-ended question in a useful way.

Focused questions are open-ended, but are directed to possible sexual abuse scenarios. They can be specific to people, body parts, or circumstances related to possible abuse. For example, a set of person-focused questions might be, "Tell me some fun things you do with mom/dad," "Tell me about some things you don't like that mom/dad do," or "Tell me about that." The line of questioning starts with positive statements and relationships and then proceeds to possible perpetrators.

Focused questions also can elicit information about the child's knowledge and experiences with body parts. This line of questioning flows more easily when children are asked to draw a body and add the different parts, naming and identifying their use and function as they go. Or the interviewer can provide them with an outline of a person or a gingerbread man drawing. Sexually abused children will draw genitalia in the body outline more often than nonabused children (Hibbard, Roghmann, & Hoekelman, 1987), and the interviewer is then presented with an opportunity to explore their experience and knowledge about genitalia. In studies when children who have not been sexually abused add genitalia to their drawings, the quality of the drawings are not phallic (Hibbard et al., 1987) or the drawings can be explained by other factors such as medical problems with genitalia (Steward, 1991). Using the words the child gives for body parts, evaluators can then ask, "Have you ever seen one of these?" "What is it for?" "Does it do anything else?" More specific questions include, "Have you touched one of these?" "Has anyone ever touched [kissed, licked, pinched, hurt, tickled] yours?"

Questions focusing on the circumstances of sexual abuse include queries about secrets, bathing, bedtime, special games, or other circumstances about which the interviewer may have knowledge. Examples include, "What kinds of things do you do with dad when mom is at work?" "Do you have secrets in your family?" "What secrets?"

Multiple-choice questions should allow for all possible choices. This may not work well with young children, because complex questions are difficult for them to understand, and they may select one choice because of their inability to keep the other possible options in mind. On the other hand, limiting choices may force a child to pick an untrue answer because the correct alternative was not presented. Young children can be asked, however, who had hurt their genital area and presented with several options, such as mother, father, and all others with access to the child. In this way, the evaluator avoids bias and explores all possible alternatives.

Yes-no questions limit the information obtained, but can sometimes be helpful to the fearful or anxious child. When using yes-no questions, the evaluator should ask questions that have both affirmative and negative responses to control for response bias. In addition, yes-no questions can be used to eliminate alternative possibilities (e.g., "Did your dad ever touch you there? Did your mom?"). It is always important to follow up close-ended questions with open-ended questions, thus raising the level of confidence regarding the responses given. For example, if a child responds with a "Yes" when asked if anyone has ever touched his "pee-pee," the evaluator must revert to a more open-ended question to elicit details, such as "Can you show me how?" or "Tell me about it."

When there are allegations of sexual abuse, relatives and/or professionals in the system may wonder if a child is lying or fantasizing about sexual acts. Although young children sometimes try to lie, it is important to remember that the concrete, egocentric, preoperational thinking of the young child under 7 years precludes logical or abstract thinking. Therefore, lies told by young children must be based on actual experiences, including those that the child participated in, observed, read about, or listened to (de Young, 1986; Sivan, 1991). A national survey of 212 recognized experts in evaluating suspected cases of child sexual abuse were asked to rank order 41 criteria used to validate reports of sexual abuse (Conte et al., 1988). Age-inappropriate sexual knowledge was the most commonly reported (99%) indicator used to substantiate reports of sexual abuse. As children become older, their ability to think in more complex and abstract ways, as well as their greater knowledge of sexual matters, increase the difficulty of ruling out deliberate fabrication. Because older children are able to abstract or generalize, they may, in rare cases, fabricate allegations with the motive of retaliation, or the desire to live apart from the alleged perpetrator (Goodwin, Sahd, & Rada, 1980).

Coaching consists of attempts to persuade children to describe allegations of incest or to encourage them to retract these allegations. An angry parent who wants the child to accuse another parent can carry out coaching. On the other hand, a perpetrator may have coached children who retract a previous disclosure of sexual abuse or other family member invested in keeping the family together. Some parents may unconsciously influence a child to retract an allegation because of their difficulties in believing the child. Some young children are enmeshed with a parent, and "mirror" or "parrot" that parent's statements. They will assume their parent's description and feelings regarding experiences and situations (Blush & Ross, 1986). Children under 7 years who allege incest in these situations are unable to manifest the behavioral symptoms and describe their abuse with the affect and kinesthetic details characteristic of substantiated incest victims. For example, a 5-year-old boy may state that his father touches him in his privates, but when asked for details about when, how, or where, the boy refuses to elaborate. Instead, he angrily retorts, "That's all Mom told me."

To assess the plausibility of sexual abuse, and especially for legal requirements, it is important to obtain information about the dates and/or times that abusive incidents occurred. The ability to give this information is highly dependent on the developmental level of the child, as discussed later under assessments with specific age groups.

In addition, disassociating during sexual abuse is a common defense mechanism employed by victims, creating a memory more like a dream. The child may make a statement about a dream in which daddy put his penis in his or her mouth. The more the child can describe feelings and a sensation of tastes or smells in the dream, the higher the likelihood is that the dream was a real experience. Movies do not provide taste or olfactory information about sexual actions.

During assessment of the child, it is important that evaluators continually evaluate their own performance. Are questions structured in a way that the child can conceptually understand? Are questions referring to concepts beyond the child's abilities? How is the child perceiving the questions and the reason the questions are being asked? When a child is resistant to talking or answering questions, the evaluator needs to explore the resistance. If the child denies any possible sexual abuse, but there is evidence that sexual abuse has occurred, focused questions are necessary, along with exploration of resistance to disclosure to ensure protection of the child.

Although most children resist disclosing the secret of incest, some children find it impossible to talk. The evaluator should still have concerns when a nondisclosing child has given a previous disclosure, displayed age-inappropriate sexual behaviors, and had medical evidence and/or anxiety during the interview, especially when talking about sexual matters of family members. In these cases, it is necessary to retreat from trying to obtain a disclosure and begin to deal with obstacles to revealing the incest. Especially useful might be exploring what children fear will happen to them or their family if they talk by making a list of fears, drawing a picture of what will happen, or asking them how to help another child who is afraid to talk. Conerly (1986) and Mac Farlane and Krebs (1986) have described techniques to lessen children's anxieties and fears.

ASSESSMENT OF THE CHILD UNDER FIVE YEARS OF AGE

Children under 5 years of age perform very differently from older children in assessment interviews because of limitations in their attention, cognition, and language. Children in this age range do not respond well to open-ended questions. They are frequently not successful in producing information about specific events. Their ability to recall events improves dramatically when they are given specific cues to activate their recognition memory. In most cases, they are unable to provide specific information regarding times or dates of abuse incidents. Hierarchical conceptual categories, such as touch, may not be recognized as an inclusive category for more specific forms of touching such as tickling, licking, pinching, or stroking. Therefore a child might deny being touched but acknowledge having been licked. The child does not conceptualize that the specific term licking would fall in the wider category of touch.

They frequently mix up personal pronouns, so that "he" and "she" may be used interchangeably to refer to the same individual. They need frequent breaks due to their limited attention span and ability to remain focused. A comfortable relationship with the interviewer and the use of encouragement for remaining focused will increase the frequency of correct responses as demonstrated in research (Dorado & Saywitz, 1997). They may have difficulty in showing what has happened to them without using their bodies to demonstrate what happened to them. Goodman and Saywitz (1994) and Myers, Saywitz, and Goodman (1997) offer valuable suggestions concerning interview techniques with very young children.

ASSESSMENT OF THE FIVE- TO SEVEN-YEAR-OLD CHILD

Although the 5-year-old may be able to produce more relevant and accurate details when asked open-ended questions, the narrative will be limited and specific questions will be needed to elicit more extensive information. Interviewers should proceed from general questions to more specific questions and only utilize closed questions (e.g., yes/no, multiple choice) when more specific detail is needed prior to ending the interview.

The 5-year-old child may begin to develop feelings of shame or acute embarrassment about sexual abuse. As children grow older, these feelings grow more intense. The child becomes more reluctant to disclose the abuse for various reasons. These may include the guilt of having experienced pleasurable feelings from sexual contact; benefits they may have received from participating in the abuse, such as gifts or special privileges; or guilt from having not followed through with sexual abuse prevention instructions (e.g., say "No," run away, and tell someone). The interviewer may ask "what if" questions to address these issues (e.g., "What if a child was touched by someone in a way that wasn't okay and she knew she should tell, but didn't. Do you think the child would get in trouble for not telling?").

More mature 6- and 7-year-old children may be able to provide more precise information about time, frequency, or other specific details relating to the abuse. To address the question of time, the interviewer may ask questions about other time-related events (e.g., what was on television; what was the season of the year; was it dark or light outside; was it before school, during the school break, or during a school holiday).

Children may be able to give simplistic definitions of reproduction, but they do not have the knowledge to describe the kinesthetic details that accompany the sexual act (Berstein, 1976). Children do not have knowledge of oral or anal sexual activity, unless they have been exposed to pornographic materials or have been engaged in or observed sexual activities. The interviewer needs to keep in mind that children may have knowledge of adult foreplay as depicted in movies and television, yet are still unable to describe the kinesthetic details that accompany the sexual act.

ASSESSMENT OF THE EIGHT- TO ELEVEN-YEAR-OLD CHILD

Older children understand most of the questions the interviewer may ask. It is very important to encourage them to tell everything, even the little things they might think are not important. They can provide information about time, place, and frequency more readily than younger children will. Older children also have the ability to reason, abstract, and predict outcomes, which enables them to fabricate allegations and makes it difficult for the interviewer to ascertain their veracity. They also have access to information about sexual actions from older peers and media that allows them to provide some sensory details about events they may have read about or heard their peers describe.

CONSIDERING ALTERNATIVE EXPLANATIONS

To avoid "interviewer bias" (Ceci & Bruck, 1995), the evaluator's mind-set should be that of a scientist ruling out all other possible explanations for behaviors or statements that suggest sexual abuse. The evaluator must consider all alternative hypotheses to incest during the assessment and when interpreting the data. Sufficient information needs to have been gathered to assist in ruling out alternative hypotheses, such as contact during normal hygiene or information obtained from watching pornography. For example, if a child indicates that she was touched during a bath, the evaluator needs to gather sufficient additional information to determine whether the incident was part of hygiene or molestation. Furthermore, it is important to explore the likelihood of multiple perpetrators, as well as the possibility of the child's naming another person to protect the actual perpetrator.

Sibling Incest

Sibling incest is the least studied yet probably the most common form of incest and is approximately three to five times more common than father-daughter incest (Caffaro & Conn-Caffaro, in press). Sibling incest (as well as sexually reactive behavior) should always be ruled out whenever there are substantiated allegations of parent-child incest, since sexual boundaries are permeable and sexuality is confounded with other needs in these families. It is the authors' opinion that individual evaluations of each child should be conducted whenever there are allegations of incest due to the frequency with which sibling incest occurs in these families.

Caffaro and Conn-Caffaro identify two types of sibling incest. The first type is nurturance oriented and is usually not coercive in nature but indicative of high levels of neglect within the family. They believe that removal of the offending child may not be warranted in these cases if successful family interventions can be made. However, the second type of incest, which is labeled sexually reactive abuse, is coercive and usually indicates removal of the offender.

Gender of the Offender

Although it is commonly assumed that the offender is male, the evaluator must entertain the possibility that the offender may be female. Strong cultural and societal belief that women are asexual with children may cause the interviewer to not consider the possibility that the offender could be a female. Jennings (1994) cites an unpublished document by Mathew and Speltz stating that the view of females as perpetrators challenges traditional cultural stereotypes in the same manner as the viewing of males as victims. Typically, females are viewed as mothers, nurturers, and caretakers, and as the receivers (not the instigators) of sexuality. For example, if a child discloses fondling done by a parent figure prior to bedtime, would you be less likely to consider the possibility of sexual abuse if the parent were a mother rather than a father? It is important for us as interviewers to entertain all possible persons having access to the child when conducting our assessments.

Interpretation of Assessment Results

Often it is not possible to arrive at a simple yes or no opinion about allegations of sexual abuse. Currently, there are three options in assessing the validity of allegations (Conte et al., 1988). Allegations judged to be true by the data, such as convincing disclosure, medical evidence, or confession from a perpetrator, are termed substantiated.

The second choice, unsubstantiated, is used for cases in which there is insufficient confirmation of the allegations to indicate clearly and unequivocally that there was or was not abuse. Unsubstantiated does not imply that the allegations are false. Despite a comprehensive assessment, the evaluator may be unable to determine unequivocally whether the allegations are true, or he or she may be certain that abuse occurred but be uncertain about the perpetrator. In one study, approximately 45% of allegations were described as unsubstantiated (Jones & McGraw, 1987).

The third option is that the allegations are judged to be unfounded or false. The child's disclosure is not deemed credible and there are no additional data to support an opinion of unsubstantiated allegations. There may be indications that the allegations were fabricated either by the adult requesting the sexual abuse evaluation or the child. Unfounded allegations also include those reports believed to be based on misinterpretations of the events by the parent, child, or interviewer. False allegations are unusual. In a review of studies of allegations, Everson and Boat (1989) found that only 2% of allegations were considered to be unfounded for children under 6 years, and the rate was only slightly higher for older children.

In addition to providing an opinion about the allegations, the clinician can provide a psychosocial assessment of the child, including the impact of the allegations on the child and the family system. These results can then guide treatment and may be used to formulate a treatment plan for the child, as well as other family members. Treatment is recommended for all families whenever there are allegations of incest, even in cases where the interviewer does not believe the incest occurred. Even if the allegations were unfounded, clinical intervention should address the dynamics contributing to the initial allegations and the impact of the allegations on the family.

LEGAL AND SYSTEMS CONSIDERATIONS

The clinical process is designed to delineate and alleviate symptoms. The legal process is an adversarial procedure designed to make decisions about the innocence or guilt of an accused person. These two processes may work at cross-purposes, so that the demands of the legal system may be nontherapeutic for the child.

Those who work in the family law and children's courts may erroneously assume that allegations of sexual abuse are false when there is lack of even an attempt of criminal prosecution. These professionals may not understand that the lack of prosecution may be due to the child's inability to qualify as a reliable witness in a criminal court setting. The average age of the victims in child sexual abuse criminal proceedings is 10 years (Whitcomb, 1994), whereas the average age of the child in children's court would be significantly younger. The standard of proof of a crime in criminal court is beyond a shadow of a doubt (99%), whereas children's court requires a preponderance of the evidence.

Changing statutes and appellate decisions affect the evidence that may be put before the court. For example, in California, current legal rulings (Meyers et al., 1989) preclude the use of anatomical dolls in assessments as a diagnostic or interpretive tool to aid in determining whether sexual abuse occurred. Each state or jurisdiction has legal rulings regarding assessment tools and techniques that may create problematic situations. It is imperative that clinicians who conduct sexual abuse assessments keep abreast of the current legal rulings in their jurisdiction to avoid problems with their assessments in the legal arena. An excellent resource for interviewers is found in the Nebraska Law Review (Meyers et al., 1989), and in an article by Myers et al. (1997).

Video- or audiotaping is highly controversial. Each state or local district attorney's office has a preference regarding the use of these tools. Before deciding to use either method, clinicians should determine the stance of the local district attorney's office and judicial systems on video- and audiotaping. Most importantly, if a tape is made it cannot subsequently be destroyed, because the destruction of evidence is a criminal offense.

Audio- or videotaping can be helpful to avoid the necessity of multiple interviews by various agencies, as well as to obtain confessions from perpetrators. Each subsequent interview can lead to the following: a decrease in affect in the child; reluctance or retraction of the allegations due to having to "tell it one more time"; increased suggestibility of the child due to a need for compliance; or a feeling that he or she did not "tell it right the first time."

Problems with audio- or videotaping include impeaching a child's later testimony when that testimony differs from the original video- or audiotaped disclosure. This is not an uncommon situation, because a child may not tell about every incident that happened during the incest period, and may thus appear to be contradicting himself or herself at a later point in time. Another area of concern is that there are no guidelines delineating who owns or has access to the tapes. Therefore, a child may or may not give permission to be taped and may not be aware that the tape may be reviewed by others, including the perpetrator, during the investigative process. An additional factor to consider is whether a child can give informed consent to allow taping, and if a parent gives consent, can a child at a later time sue the person for surrendering his or her right to confidentiality. Mac Farlane and Krebs (1986) have provided excellent information about the issues related to taping, including purposes, uses, and technical considerations.

CURRENT ISSUES IN ASSESSMENT

The attorney representing the accused will challenge the assessment approach, medical findings, and data reviewed in arriving at an opinion. The evaluator must be aware of research and current literature regarding the areas that may be challenged in the legal system. Memory and suggestibility of young children, and the effects of leading questions, are some areas that attorneys frequently address. Furthermore, attorneys often challenge the techniques and qualifications of the evaluator. Evaluators must be aware of their rationale for their choice of assessment techniques or protocols and know the strengths and weaknesses of each. An evaluator who has taken care to preserve his or her objectivity and who has made a careful assessment will be able to explain that the assessment was conducted without assumptions about the probable outcome.

RESEARCH ON FALSE ALLEGATIONS

Although false allegations are rare (Everson & Boat, 1989), assessing for them is an important part of the evaluation. Areas to investigate include age-inappropriate language; inconsistency, lack of affect, and lack of details; willingness to discuss the molestation only when the nonoffending parent is present; and continuously looking for approval from that parent. However, children who have been sexually abused may also display these behaviors. When children have been interviewed several times, their report of the molestation can be without affect and appear rote. Very young children may be unable to give details or remain consistent due to developmental limitations discussed previously. Age-inappropriate language may be learned from the perpetrator or from another adult to whom the child disclosed.

ALLEGATIONS DURING CUSTODY DISPUTES

Many professionals, even those who work with children, assume that a sexual abuse allegation made in the context of a divorce is most likely false. However, Thoennes and Tjaden (1990) found that, among a sample of 9,000 families in 12 court systems throughout the United States, less than 2% of contested custody cases involved sexual abuse allegations. They stated that allegations of sexual abuse among families in dispute over custody and visitation are no more likely to be determined false than are allegations of child sexual abuse in the general population. Furthermore, mothers are no more likely than fathers to make false allegations (p. 161).

Claims of incest may arise during divorce proceedings or custody battles. Assessments of allegations in these situations are extremely difficult. A parent who is highly disturbed may believe the child is being sexually abused by the other parent due to his or her own pathology rather than anything the child has said or done. In these situations, which are rare, the child is usually very young with verbal abilities that are not consistent with what the parent states the child had said to him or her. Faller and DeVoe (1995) studied legal outcomes of 215 cases in which there were allegations of sexual abuse in divorcing families. They found that child disclosure after marital breakup is more common. Children report the reason for the delay in reporting prior to the marital breakup was due to several fears. These fears included that disclosures would lead to marital breakup, stress to the nonabusing parent, or loss of love or punishment by the abuser. The prospect of unprotected exposure during unsupervised visitation precipitated the disclosure in some of the victims. In cases where divorce preceded the onset of sexual abuse, the authors identify several contributing factors to the onset of the sexual abuse. Marital disruption may increase the risk of sexual abuse. The emotional upheaval caused by the loss can lead the offender to substitute the child for the role of the lost spouse. The child may be used as an object for need gratification and/or retaliation against the spouse, leading to sexual abuse.

Monitored visitation of a suspected parent during a sexual abuse evaluation many times can give a child the sense of protection from ongoing sexual abuse, yet not deprive the child of the contact with that parent. The parties who monitor the visitation must always have visual and auditory ability to monitor anything said to the child to prevent the possibility of threats or pressure, which may lead to retraction. Blick (1989) has outlined a visitation plan for children in these situations. Hewitt (1991) describes how to therapeutically manage alleged, but unsubstantiated cases of sexual abuse with preschool children. Excellent guidelines for monitoring in cases with sexual abuse allegations have been developed by the California Professional Society on the Abuse of Children (CAPSAC, 1993).

Leading Questions and Suggestibility

There is controversy as to what constitutes leading questions. We define a leading question as one that suggests its own answer (e.g., "Daddy touched your pee pee, didn't he?) Despite cited evidence that children resist leading questions, we recommend avoiding them. However, it may be necessary to ask children very specific questions, which may then be attacked as leading.

Research indicates that children need specific questions to provide details of an event (Saywitz, Goodman, Nicholas, & Moan, 1989). For example, Saywitz et al. found that of 36 girls who had undergone a genital exam, 28 (64%) failed to report that any genital touching had occurred during the examination. However, when specifically asked a yes-no question about whether they had been touched in the vagina, all but five of the girls reported the experience. This study supports that children need to be provided with a context for them to know what events the interviewer is asking about. Focused or specific questions may also assist the child in overcoming embarrassment about sexual matters. The study also indicated that some children will deny embarrassing events even when they are asked focused questions.

Goodman (1990) found that by the age of 4 or 5 years, children are resistant to false suggestions of details or behaviors relevant to abuse cases. Even when children are asked misleading questions (e.g., "How many times did the doctor kiss you?" in the Saywitz et al., 1989, study), they are quite resistant to suggestion.

On the other hand, Ceci and Bruck (1995) have cited numerous studies in which they have been able to manipulate young children to agree that nonexistent events occurred when repeatedly interviewed over a period of time. However, there are limitations in generalizing from their research paradigm to that of the real-world interview of a possibly traumatized child. First of all, Ceci and others commonly *tell* rather than *ask* the child what has occurred. When the questions asked presuppose the truth of the suggested material, it makes sense that children as well as adults will be more apt to accept the interviewer's account of the event. Another feature of this research is that the children may be asked the same questions over multiple (up to 11) interviews, thereby increasing their feelings that the examiner must be correct and that they are incorrect in their answers. Their research certainly cautions against the use of coercive, repeated interviews and lends examples of inappropriate interview strategies. Their research also points out problems that could occur when the defense attorney asks children leading questions during cross-examination.

Memory

Children's memory of core events can be as good as that of adults, but their memory for peripheral events is not as good as that of older children or adults. This causes children to give less detailed reports of events than adults. Young children are more likely to display errors of omission, which may be more related to ambiguity of questions or the child's limited language skills than to memory failure or lying (Saywitz et al., 1989).

Sexual abuse is a traumatic event that usually recurs over an extended period. A child's recall of sexual abuse may appear to be inconsistent because the events blur and memory of the events elicits strong and disruptive emotional affect. Indeed, an adult would also experience blurred memories if asked to recall specific sexual events with the same partner over a period of time. An adult would similarly be inconsistent if asked to provide details about a single event in the way that a child is required to do in a sexual abuse evaluation.

Inconsistency in a child's reporting of abuse may be related to difficulties with chronological order of complex events, inability to recognize and correct inconsistency in reporting, and contradictions or unbelievable comments about an event. These inconsistencies are explained by developmental limitations in cognition and language and are not to be judged to be a lie or fantasy, unless there is ample evidence to the contrary.

ASSESSMENT OF CHILDREN'S TESTIMONIAL COMPETENCE

A child's developmental competence to understand the difference between the truth and lies is sometimes assessed during an evaluation, especially those conducted in the context of a court proceeding. Assessment of young children's understanding of the concept of truthfulness requires sensitivity to their language capabilities. An interviewer's method of assessment may underestimate a child's ability to understand the difference between a truth and a lie.

Saywitz and Lyon (1997) have conducted important research, which finds that the manner in which competency questions are asked has a substantial effect on the child's ability to demonstrate knowledge of the difference between truth and lies. They conducted research with 475 4- to 7-year-olds in determining the most sensitive way to assess children's competency for oath taking. Their major findings were:

- Young maltreated children who are dependents of a children's court exhibited serious delays in receptive and productive vocabulary when compared with a nonreferred university preschool group of children, performing at least one year behind nationwide averages.
- Their apparent understanding of the meaning and morality of lying seems to be dependent on the manner in which they are asked to demonstrate their understanding. Among the children who could *identify* statements that were truthful or a lie, 60% to 70% were unable to either define "truth" or "lie" or to explain the difference between the terms. For example, a child is more easily able to demonstrate understanding of these concepts if asked "Is it the 'truth' or a 'lie' that this crayon is red?"
- Younger children seem reluctant to identify a lie as such if doing so requires them to indicate that the interviewer is a liar.
- Young children find it easier to discuss the negative consequences of lying if they are shown pictures about a story character rather than being asked about themselves.
- Most 5-year-old maltreated children demonstrated an understanding of the meaning and morality of lying. In contrast, the nonreferred university preschool children demonstrated substantial understanding as young as 3 years of age.

ANATOMICAL DOLLS

The arguments against the use of anatomical dolls—that the dolls cause children to make false allegations or act out sexual fantasy—have not been supported by research (see APSAC Guidelines, 1995). There is general agreement that the dolls can stimulate memory and allow the child to demonstrate what they are unable to verbalize. However, they should be used with caution with children under age 5 and the interviewer should be aware of the general acceptance of their use within their legal community.

ROLE OF THE EVALUATOR WITHIN THE LEGAL SYSTEM

Thorough preparation is essential for any court appearance. In addition to reviewing the material from the assessment, the evaluator must be prepared to explain the theoretical and scientific rationale for the approach used and conclusions drawn. If the evaluator is testifying as an expert witness, a review of the literature relevant to sexual abuse is essential, because an expert opinion arises from theory, research, or practice. During a court appearance, the opposing counsel will attempt to discredit the evaluator's qualifications and testimony, an unsettling and difficult process that feels like a personal attack. Preparation and experience help the evaluator make an effective witness. Also, an understanding of the legal process and the reason for its rules and traditions, with due process and presumption of innocence, can provide a more positive perspective of the cross-examination experience.

CASE ILLUSTRATION

The children services worker referred Amber, who had just turned 5, for an evaluation of possible sexual abuse, as the result of two child abuse reports filed within the previous 3 months. Her mother had recently filed a report, and a sexual abuse report had been filed 3 months before by the preschool. Amber had told her teachers that her father "kissed my 'Teddy.'" When interviewed by a police officer, Amber denied every making the statement, so the investigation was dropped. Amber's mother and father had divorced when she was 3, and she had visitations with her father on alternate weekends and one night each week.

The first appointment with Amber's mother revealed a history of depression after Amber's birth. She was unable to recall any of her childhood, even though she stated it was "good." Although initially denying a history of either physical or sexual abuse, with more direct questioning, she revealed that an uncle frequently babysat and, when he bathed her, he would insert his finger inside her vagina to "clean her." She also recalled an instance when her uncle asked her to touch his penis while they were showering together. However, the mother adamantly denied having ever been molested. When asked about her marriage, she acknowledged that her sexual relationship with Amber's father was practically nonexistent. Upon further questioning, she revealed that Amber's father had asked her to shave her pubic hair, indicating that the father might have a preference for genitalia resembling those of prepubescent children.

Amber's sexual abuse evaluation consisted of three interviews. Her developmental level was assessed to be within the normal range, with verbal skills slightly above average. Scores on the teacher's report form of the Child Behavior Checklist (CBCL) indicated that Amber had an externalizing profile, with elevated scales on aggression, inattention, self-destruction, and sex problems. This was consistent with the CBCL profile her mother completed. When asked to draw a picture of a person, she became hesitant and stated she didn't know how to draw. This was inconsistent with her spontaneous drawing she had completed in the waiting room. The interviewer drew an outline of a gingerbread person and asked Amber to fill in all the body parts. Although she was able to quickly and easily fill in the facial characteristics, she hesitated before deliberately and forcefully shading in the genital area of the gingerbread person. When the interviewer inquired as to if the drawing was of a boy or girl, Amber ripped the paper up as she loudly stated "None of your business." When the interviewer inquired as to who had said that it was none of his business, she got up to leave the room. The interviewer then suggested that they just play and Amber involved herself in doll play in which the Barbie and Ken dolls started kissing and moaning. She then had to go to the bathroom. When she returned to the room, the interviewer queried her about Ken and Barbie's activity with each other, and Amber responded "They were fooling around." When asked who she knew that "fooled around," Amber reported that Mommy and Bob fool around. When asked how she knew that's what it was, she stated that "It's a secret." Since the time was up, the interviewer arranged a second session. At this point, the interviewer had several hypotheses about Amber's sexualized behaviors leading to the reports: (1) that Amber witnessed sexual activity between Mother and her boyfriend; (2) that Amber was a participant in such activity; (3) and/or that Amber had been involved in some yet undisclosed activity. The high degree of anxiety and resistance present initially in Amber, which dissipated when she began to talk about her mother's sexual activity, had contributed to the speculations.

At the beginning of her second interview, the interviewer inquired more about the statements made by Amber the previous session. Amber indicated that her mother had told her that it was none of her business when Amber once observed her mother and Bob in sexual activity. Deciding to explore her resistance to disclosure, the interviewer asked with whom Amber had secrets. When she said that she had secrets with Bob and Daddy, the interviewer realized she would need to explore Amber's secrets with both persons mentioned. Amber revealed that if she told the secret she would get in trouble. Empathizing with her difficulty, the interviewer gave Amber a puppet, which seemed to free Amber to disclose in a less threatening manner. She stated that Bob was her 7-year-old friend from whom she had stolen some candy. The secret with Daddy involved "fooling around." When exploring what she meant by "fooling around" with Daddy, she indicated that she "fooled around" with her daddy the same way that Mom and Bob had "fooled around." Amber then angrily said that Daddy said that she was better at "fooling around" than Mommy. As the interviewer built an alliance, Amber went on to describe oral copulation and fondling of and by Dad, mutual masturbation and digital penetration of her vagina. When asked if Amber "fooled around" with anyone else, Amber stated that Daddy said that only he could "fool around" with her.

The Department of Children's Services filed a petition in juvenile court on the sexual abuse allegation. The interviewer testified in court as to the assessment procedures used and the findings, and the conclusion that Amber had been molested. The father's attorney asked the interviewer to report verbatim the questions and responses made during the evaluations. He challenged the interviewer's techniques and conclusions, asking if alternative hypotheses could account for Amber's statements. When the attorney also challenged the interviewer's conclusion because of negative medical findings, the interviewer was able to cite references about the low incidence of medical findings in sexual abuse cases.

The petition of sexual abuse was sustained, and the judge ordered monitored visitation. Both parents and the child were court-ordered to treatment, and the next hearing was scheduled six months later. The father never admitted to molesting his daughter and attended therapy sporadically. However, Amber and her mother continued to make great progress in treatment, as they both acquired skills in expressing their feelings, asserting themselves, and communicating with others. Due to the progress of mother and child in treatment, the Department of Children's Services closed their case with the recommendation to the family law court that the mother be awarded full custody and the father allowed only monitored visitation.

CONCLUSION

Assessment of incest allegations in young children is a complicated and formidable task. Special skills are required of the evaluator who is conducting the assessment. The evaluator must have knowledge of child development and be able to use age-appropriate language and build rapport with children. Even with highly skilled evaluators, however, children's developmental limitations may interfere with their ability to understand the questions and to describe what occurred.

Professionals who evaluate allegations of incest are imbued with a tremendous responsibility. These evaluators must keep abreast of the literature about theory and research on memory, suggestibility, medical findings, and dynamics of sexual abuse. They must continuously update their knowledge of the legal ramifications of the interview format, and must consult with other professionals to coordinate and facilitate the process of protecting the child and cooperating with law enforcement and the legal system in their attempts to prosecute. The evaluator also must assess the impact of the allegations on the family and child, and provide recommendations about how to ameliorate their effect.

The evaluation may lead to decisions about custody and legal proceedings that will significantly affect the child and family. It is of the utmost importance that evaluators proceed cautiously and weigh all information carefully before forming an opinion. Evaluators must remain unbiased and eliminate all other possible alternative explanations when there are allegations of incest.

REFERENCES

Achenbach, T., & Edelbrock, C. (1983). *Manual for the Child Behavior Checklist and Revised Child Behavior Profile.* Burlington: Department of Psychiatry, University of Vermont.

American Professional Society on the Abuse of Children (APSAC). (1995). *Use of anatomical dolls in child sexual abuse evaluations.* Chicago: Author.

APSAC Task Force. (1990). *APSAC guidelines for evaluation of suspected sexual abuse in young children.* Chicago: Author.

Berstein, A.C. (1976). How children learn about sex and birth. *Psychology Today, 46,* 31–36.

Blick, L.C. (1989). *The APSAC Advisor, 2,* 11–12.

Blush, G., & Ross, K. (1986). *Sexual allegations in divorce: The SAID syndrome.* Unpublished manuscript.

Bradley, A.R., & Wood, J.M. (1996). How do children tell? The disclosure process in child sexual abuse. *Child Abuse & Neglect, 20,* 881–891.

Caffaro, J., & Conn-Caffaro, A. (1988). *Sibling abuse trauma.* Binghamton, NY: Haworth Maltreatment and Trauma Press.

California Professional Society on the Abuse of Children (CAPSAC). (1993). *Guidelines for monitored visitation.* South Pasadena, CA: Author.

Ceci, S.J., & Bruck, M. (1995). *Jeopardy in the courtroom: A scientific analysis of children's testimony.* Washington, DC: American Psychological Association.

Conerly, S. (1986). Assessment of suspected child sexual abuse. In K. MacFarlane, J. Waterman, S. Connerly, L. Damon, M. Durfee, & S. Long (Eds.), *Sexual abuse of young children: Evaluation and treatment* (pp. 30–51). New York: Guilford Press.

Conte, J., Sorenson, E., Fogarty, L., & Rosa, J. (1988). *Evaluating children's report of sexual abuse: Results from a survey of professionals.* Unpublished manuscript, University of Chicago, School of Social Service Administration.

de Young, M. (1986). A conceptual model for judging the truthfulness of a young child's allegations of sexual abuse. *American Journal of Orthopsychiatry, 56,* 550–559.

Dorado, J., & Saywitz, K. (1997). Interviewing preschoolers: A test of an innovative technique. In B. Clark (Chair.), *Assessment of Child Maltreatment Symposium.* Chicago, IL.

Everson, M.D., & Boat, B.W. (1989). False allegations of sexual abuse by children and adolescents. *Journal of the American Academy of Child and Adolescent Psychiatry, 28,* 230–235.

Faller, K. (1990). Types of questions for children alleged to have been sexually abused. *The APSAC Advisor, 3,* 3–5.

Faller, K.C., & DeVoe, E. (1995). Allegations of sexual abuse in divorce. *Journal of Child Sexual Abuse, 4,* 1–25.

Finkelhor, D., Araji, S., Baron, L., Browne, A., Peters, S.D., & Wyatt, G.E. (1986). *A sourcebook on child sexual abuse.* Newbury Park, CA: Sage.

Friedman, V.M., & Morgan, M.H. (1985). *Interviewing sexual abuse victims using anatomical dolls: The professional's guidebook.* Eugene, OR: Shamrock Press.

Friedrich, W. (1990). *Psychotherapy of sexually abused children and their families.* New York: Norton.

Friedrich, W. (1997). *The Child Sexual Behavior Inventory.* Odessa, FL: Psychological Assessment Resources.

Friedrich, W., Grambsch, P., Damon, L., Hewitt, S., Koverola, C., Lang, R., Wolfe, V.H., & Broughton, D. (1991). The Child Sexual Behavior Inventory: Normative and clinical comparisons. *Journal of Consulting and Clinical Psychology, 4,* 303–311.

Gardner, R. (1987). *The parental alienation syndrome and the differentiation between fabricated and genuine child sex abuse.* Cresskill, NJ: Creative Therapeutics.

Goodman, G. (1990). Child sexual abuse: The search for professional agreement and "relevant" research on children's reports. *The APSAC Advisor, 13,* 14–15.

Goodman, G.S., & Saywitz, K.J. (1994). Memories of abuse. Interviewing children when sexual victimization is suspected. *Child & Adolescent Psychiatric Clinics of North America, 3,* 645–661.

Goodwin, J., Sahd, D., & Rada, R.T. (1980). Incest hoax: False accusations, false denials. In W.M. Holder (Ed.), *Sexual abuse of children* (pp. 37–45). Englewood, CO: The American Humane Association. (Reprinted from *The Bulletin of the American Academy of Psychiatry and the Law, 6*(3), 1979)

Gries, L.T., Goh, D.S., & Cavanaugh, J. (1996). Factors associated with disclosure during child sexual abuse assessment. *Journal of Child Sexual Abuse, 5,* 1–19.

Hall, G., Proctor, W., & Nelson, G. (1988). Validity of physiological measures of pedophilic sexual arousal in a sexual offender population. *Journal of Consulting & Clinical Psychology, 56,* 118–122.

Heger, A.H. (1992). *Evaluation of the sexually abused child.* New York: Oxford Press.

Hewitt, S.K. (1991). Therapeutic management of preschool cases of alleged but unsubstantiated sexual abuse. *Child Welfare League of America, 70,* 59–67.

Hewitt, S.K., & Arrowood, A.A. (1994). Systematic touch exploration as a screening procedure for child abuse: A pilot study. *Journal of Child Sexual Abuse, 3,* 31–43.

Hibbard, R.A., Roghmann, K., & Hoekelman, R.T. (1987). Genitalia in children's drawings in association with sexual abuse. *Pediatrics, 79,* 129–137.

Hibbard, R.A., & Zollinger, T.W. (1990). Patterns of child sexual abuse knowledge among professionals. *Child Abuse & Neglect, 14,* 347–355.

Jennings, K.T. (1994). Female child molesters: A review of the literature. In M. Elliott (Eds.), *Female sexual abuse of children* (pp. 219–234). New York: Guilford Press.

Jones, D.P., & McGraw, J.M. (1987). Reliable and fictitious accounts of sexual abuse of children. *Journal of Interpersonal Violence, 2,* 27–45.

Jones, D.P., & McQuiston, M. (1986). *Interviewing the sexually abused child* (2nd ed.). Denver, CO: The C. Henry Kempe National Center for the Prevention and Treatment of Child Abuse and Neglect.

Koverola, C., & Foy, D. (1993). Posttraumatic stress disorder symptomatology in sexually abused children: Implications for legal proceedings. *Journal of Child Sexual Abuse, 2,* 119–128.

Lawson, L., & Chaffin, M. (1992). False negatives in sexual abuse disclosure interviews. Incidence and influence of caretaker's belief in abuse in cases of accidental abuse discovery by diagnosis of STD. *Journal of Interpersonal Violence, 7,* 532–542.

Lusk, R., & Waterman, J. (1986). Effects of sexual abuse on children. In K. Mac Farlane, J. Waterman, S. Connerly, L. Damon, M. Durfee, & S. Long (Eds.), *Sexual abuse of young children: Evaluation and treatment* (pp. 101–118). New York: Guilford Press.

Lyon, T. (1995). False allegations and false denials in child sexual abuse. *Psychology, Public Policy, and Law, 1,* 429–437.

Lyon, T. (1996). The effect of threats on children's disclosure of sexual abuse. *The APSAC Advisor, 9,* 9–14.

Mac Farlane, K., & Feldmeth, J. (1988). *Response to child sexual abuse: The clinical interview.* New York: Guilford Press.

Mac Farlane, K., & Krebs, S. (1986). Techniques for interviewing and evidence gathering. In K. Mac Farlane, J. Waterman, S. Connerly, L. Damon, M. Durfee, & S. Long (Eds.), *Sexual abuse of young children evaluation and treatment* (pp. 67–100). New York: Guilford Press.

Meyers, L.E.B., Bays, J., Berlinger, L., Corwin, D.L., & Saywitz, K.J. (1989). Expert testimony in child sexual abuse litigation. *Nebraska Law Review, 68,* 1–145.

Mulder, M.R., & Vrij, A. (1996). Explaining conversation rules to children: An intervention study to facilitate children's accurate responses. *Child Abuse & Neglect, 20,* 623–631.

Muram, D. (1989). Child sexual abuse: Relationship between sexual acts and genital findings. *Child Abuse & Neglect, 13,* 211–216.

Myers, J., Saywitz, K., & Goodman, G. (1997). Psychological research on children as witnesses: Practical implications for forensic interviews and courtroom testimony. *Pacific Law Journal, 28,* 3–91.

Saywitz, K. (1990). Developmental considerations for forensic interviewing. *The Advisor, 3,* 15.

Saywitz, K., & Damon, L. (1988). Developmental considerations for interviewers. In K. Mac Farlane & J. Feldmeth (Eds.), *Response to child sexual abuse: The clinical interview* (pp. 5–14). New York: Guilford Press.

Saywitz, K., Goodman, G.S., Nicholas, E., & Moan, S. (1989). *Children's memory for a genital examination: Implications for child sexual abuse cases.* Paper presented at the Society for Research on Child Development, Kansas City.

Saywitz, K., & Lyon, T.D. (1997). *Sensitively assessing children's testimonial competence* (Final report to the National Center on Child Abuse and Neglect, Grant no. 90-CA-1553).

Torrance: University of California, Los Angeles, Harbor-UCLA Medical Center, Department of Psychiatry.

Sgroi, S. (Ed.). (1982). *Handbook of clinical intervention in child sexual abuse*. Lexington, MA: Lexington Books.

Sivan, A.B. (1991). Preschool child development: Implications for investigation of child abuse allegations. *Child Abuse & Neglect, 15,* 485–493.

Sorenson, T., & Snow, B. (1991). How children tell: The process of the disclosure in child sexual abuse. *Child Welfare, 70,* 3–15.

Summit, R. (1983). The child sexual abuse accommodation syndrome. *Child Abuse & Neglect, 7,* 177–193.

Thoennes, N., & Tjaden, P.G. (1990). The extent, nature, and validity of sexual abuse allegations in custody/visitation disputes. *Child Abuse and Neglect, 14,* 151–163.

Waterman, J. (1986). Developmental considerations. In K. Mac Farlane, J. Waterman, S. Connerly, L. Damon, M. Durfee, & S. Long (Eds.), *Sexual abuse of young children: Evaluation and treatment* (pp.15–29). New York: Guilford Press.

Waterman, J., Kelly, R., Oliveri, M.K., & McCord, J. (1993). *Behind the playground wall: Sexual abuse in preschools*. New York: Guilford Press.

Whitcomb, D. (1994). *The child victim as a witness*. Washington, DC: Office of Juvenile Justice and Delinquency Prevention.

Williams, L., & Finkelhor, D. (1990). The characteristics of incestuous fathers. In W.L. Marshall (Ed.), *Handbook of sexual assault* (pp. 231–255). New York: Plenum Press.

CHAPTER 11

Extrafamilial Child Sexual Abuse

SUSAN V. MCLEER and MIMI ROSE

FAMILY VIOLENCE usually refers to the victimization of a family member by another within the family system and encompasses the areas of the intrafamilial physical and sexual abuse of children and adolescents, adult domestic violence, and the familial abuse of the elderly. Sometimes, the domain is extended to include child neglect and the emotional or psychological abuse of children. The focus of this chapter, however, will be somewhat unconventional and address the sexual abuse of children and adolescents by individuals outside the family system, an event that is experienced not only by the child as traumatic, but that reverberates throughout the entire family affecting many aspects of functioning.

DESCRIPTION OF THE PROBLEM

Russell (1984) defines extrafamilial sex abuse as follows:

> One or more unwanted sexual experiences with persons unrelated by blood or marriage ranging from attempted petting (touching of breasts or genitals or attempts at such touching) to rape, before the victim turned 14 years and completed or attempted forcible rape experiences from ages of 14 to 17 years (inclusive). (p. 180)

This definition includes the sexual abuse of children by known adults outside the family as well as by strangers. It includes the sexual assault of teenagers by peers and abuse that occurs in relatively private settings as well as that in day-care centers. Extrafamilial abuse can involve a solitary perpetrator or multiple perpetrators. It can be a one-time occurrence or involve systematic and persistence abuse that extends across time. The abuse can be motivated by paraphiliac interests or can be ritualistic or cult motivated. The definition extends across the wide range of behaviors that by necessity have a differential impact on the child and her/his family. This heterogeneity of extrafamilial child sexual abuse hinders the collection and generalization of data for estimating the incidence and prevalence of this form of child sexual abuse (CSA).

210

EXTENT OF EXTRAFAMILIAL CHILD SEXUAL ABUSE

Data estimating incidence and prevalence of extrafamilial CSA are derived from three sources: (1) studies of adult populations who retrospectively report having been sexually abused during childhood, (2) studies utilizing data culled from official records of reported CSA, and (3) studies of nonrepresentative populations of children and adolescents. All of these are methodologically problematic; hence, the true incidence and prevalence of these heterogenous forms of CSA are unknown.

In the first national telephone survey of 2,626 adult men and women, CSA was reported by 27% of women and 16% of men (Finkelhor, Hotaling, Lewis, & Smith, 1990). Of those abused, 40% of the men had been abused by a stranger compared with 21% of women. Fifty percent of the abused girls and 49% of the abused boys had been sexually abused by a known person outside the family. Only 29% of females and 11% of males had been abused by a family member, indicating that the majority reported being abused by someone outside the family. These statistics reflect higher levels of extrafamilial CSA than any previously reported, possibly secondary to people being more willing to report abuse outside the family than abuse from within on a telephone survey.

Russell (1984), in a representative sample of 930 women living in the San Francisco area, found that 31% reported at least one experience of sexual abuse by a nonrelative before the age of 18 as compared with 16% reporting at least one episode of intrafamilial abuse, again, reflecting that the majority were abused by individuals outside the family. In Russell's study, 15% of extrafamilial perpetrators were strangers, 47% acquaintances, and 41% were more intimately related to the victims (e.g. friends of the family or victim, dates, boyfriends, and lovers). Of known perpetrators, 40% of those in the Russell Study were classified as authority figures compared with the National Telephone Survey, which found 49% of all abusers to be authority figures.

The statistics derived from both the National Telephone Survey and the San Francisco study are markedly dissimilar from those reported in studies based on data culled from official records of reported cases, which indicate that 29% of victims are abused by natural parents and an additional 25% are abused by parent substitutes, some of whom may be extrafamilial (e.g., day care, baby sitters). Forty-six percent of children are sexually abused by other than parents (Sedlak & Broadhurst, 1996). This disparity reflects a sampling bias with official records being derived from child protective service agencies and police departments. Cases of extrafamilial CSA are not usually investigated by child protective service agencies which have statutory responsibility for investigating abuse in the child's home or under conditions where there is a surrogate caretaker. Extrafamilial cases, instead, are referred to police departments and prosecutors for investigation and criminal charging decisions. Data derived from police reports indicate an unusually high comorbidity of CSA with physical injury, suggesting that only the most serious cases of extrafamilial CSA are reported to the police (Sedlak & Broadhurst, 1996). This also suggests that many extrafamilial cases are handled informally. Consequently, many incidents of CSA go unreported, resulting in officially derived statistics that reflect a smaller percentage of extrafamilial CSA than other data sources.

While studies utilizing random sampling of representative populations are preferred for determining the prevalence of specific forms of CSA, there are two areas where it becomes necessary to look at more targeted studies of specific population groups, mainly, (1) the extrafamilial sexual assault of teenagers and (2) CSA in day-care centers. The former is underrepresented in prevalence studies since the individual respondent must perceive herself, or himself, as having been abused in order to report (Mynatt & Allgier, 1990; Parrot, 1989). CSA in day-care centers is an event of high visibility causing great concern among parents regarding their child's risk of exposure, with media coverage creating an impression that sexual abuse in day care is a high-frequency event. Finkelhor and Williams (1988), in a national study of CSA in day care settings, have determined that while the duration and severity of sexual abuse in day care is of great concern, the risk of exposure is less than that in the child's own home. However, since abuse in this setting persists for significant periods of time without disclosure, since the threats and coercion directed toward minimizing disclosure are often times extreme and the level of abuse to children may be severe, evaluators must modify techniques in working with both children and parents when allegations surface in day-care settings. Similarly, modifications and assessment techniques are needed with adolescents when there is a suspicion of sexual assault by a peer.

The literature indicates that adolescents are frequently assaulted by those outside the family and that rape is more frequent among adolescents than any other age group (Bureau of Justice, 1984; Hall & Flannery, 1984). Among sexual assault victims who present to rape crisis centers, 70% to 80% have been assaulted by acquaintances (Warshaw, 1988), with date rape constituting a substantial subset of this group. However, even these statistics do not reflect the extent of adolescent sexual assault. In a national study of sexual assault, 92% of victims between the ages of 11 and 17 years, had been assaulted by someone they knew. More than half reported they were raped while on a date (Ageton, 1988). Few of these students reported the rape to authorities, an action consistent with findings that only 2% of those sexually abused/assaulted by an extrafamilial acquaintance report their experience (Mynatt & Allgier, 1990). Prevalence studies in high school settings have found that 23.0% to 44.8% of girls report unwanted sexual contact perpetrated by dates or boyfriends (Davis, Peck, & Storment, 1993; Gidycz & Koss, 1989; Vicary, Klingaman, & Harkness, 1995). Between 13% and 25% indicated they had experienced unwanted sexual intercourse (Gidycz & Koss, 1989; Vicary et al., 1995). Mynatt and Allgier (1990) reported that physical force or restraint had been used in 62% of sexually abusive dating incidents. In 32% of these incidents, psychological coercion was used. Studies have additionally indicated that adolescents are uncertain what constitutes sexual assault. Many believe that unwanted sexual activity in certain social situations or without a great deal of force is not rape (Gidycz & Koss, 1989; Parrot, 1989). Additionally, adolescents may fear reporting peer sexual assault or "date rape" because of conflicts about disclosing sexual contact to parents (Belden, 1979; Krasner, Meyer, & Carroll, 1976).

Gidycz and Koss (1989) found that symptoms of clinical depression and anxiety were far more prevalent among peer-assaulted ("date rape") girls than among a matched group of nonvictimized girls. Their findings are consistent with studies of adult survivors of acquaintance rape who report themselves as being less recovered than a matched group of stranger raped victims (B. Katz & Burt, 1988). These women tended to blame themselves and reported experiencing great psychological distress (B. Katz & Burt, 1988; Warshaw, 1988). These studies indicate the need to inquire routinely about experiences of sexual assault when evaluating teenagers.

ASSESSMENT

This section addresses generic issues and outlines protocols for the investigation and assessment necessary for development of effective intervention strategies for children and adolescents who are victims of extrafamilial sexual abuse. Because assessment must address not only the clinical needs of the child, but also be an evidence-gathering process that will stand up to careful scrutiny within the courtroom setting, those involved in the assessment process have a responsibility to be emotionally and developmentally sensitive to the child in her/his family as well as systematic and concise in information gathering. Professionals must become adept in utilizing specialized interview strategies that are developmentally appropriate, and they must have the necessary training to recognize and identify developmental factors that influence the child's perceptions and reports of alleged sexual abuse.

In investigations of alleged extrafamilial CSA, the police and prosecutors determine whether there is sufficient evidence for arrest and prosecution. As with intrafamilial CSA, it is essential for health professionals to be clear regarding two different needs that emerge during this process, the most important need being the protection of the child, the alleged victim. The second need is to determine whether the allegation has sufficient substance to initiate a criminal prosecution of the alleged offender. This latter determination is the responsibility of the police and prosecutors and will depend on many factors, including the presence or absence of witnesses, physical evidence of abuse, and the child's age and verbal skills as they relate to the child's ability to remember and report events reliably. Young children and children with developmental disabilities may be unable to meet criteria used in courtroom settings for determination of credibility and yet still be at considerable risk. The alleged offender may well be prosecuted and acquitted with criteria for guilt being "beyond a reasonable doubt," whereas the child may still be at considerable risk. It is essential that individuals coordinating and/or conducting the assessment process for allegations of extrafamilial sexual abuse keep these two issues in mind and help the family to differentiate between the criteria being used for prosecution and the criteria, they as caretakers, might use for determining the child's risk and need for protection.

DEVELOPMENTAL ISSUES AND ASSESSMENT

The child's level of emotional, cognitive, linguistic, and social development affects the assessment process in several ways. First, and most obviously, developmental age will determine the mode of interaction and materials necessary for interviewing the child. Linguistic skills, both receptive and expressive, will determine the child's ability to understand the examiner and express him- or herself in an understandable way. Critical to this process is the systematic determination of the child's developmental status by obtaining a careful developmental history from the parents beforehand, directly examining the child regarding physical, cognitive, and linguistic skills and specifically determining the words used by the child to describe different anatomical parts of the human body, either by use of drawings or the anatomically correct dolls. Likewise, developmental age has a direct bearing on the child's understanding of time. Inasmuch as references to time are essential in an investigation and assessment of alleged CSA, it will be necessary for the examiner to use concrete markers of time to aid the young child in the temporal placement of events. Young children simply do not have an adequate sense of abstract time, but frequently can relate events to proximity to holidays, TV programs, mealtime, and so on (Friedman, 1982).

Second, consideration of developmental levels will have considerable bearing on the court's assessment of the child's credibility and ability to testify. New findings by developmental researchers regarding children's capacity to remember, differentiate fantasy from reality, and their alleged suggestibility are of great relevance and yet, to date, have not been disseminated widely enough to impact accepted standards for interviewing young children (Ceci & Huffman, 1997; Goodman & Quas, 1996; Goodman & Schwartz-Kenney, 1992).

While jurors' perceptions of child witness credibility have usually been found to reflect a direct correlation with age (Goodman & Schwartz-Kenny, 1992; Leippe & Romanczyk, 1987), and only infrequently an indirect correlation (Ross, Miller, & Moran, 1987), research has indicated that children 4 years of age or older are quite accurate in reporting actions witnessed or experienced in real life (Goodman & Quas, 1996; Gordon & Fullmer, 1994; Orstein, Gordon, & Larus, 1992). Clinical researchers have reported that children who have undergone significant trauma describe the traumatic event in excruciating detail and for years may be troubled by intrusive memories of the event (Pynoos et al., 1987; Terr, 1988, 1990). Neurobiologists have, additionally, found that certain hormones found in high levels under stressful conditions, mainly catecholamines, enhance memory considerably (Gold, 1987; Pitman, Orr, & Shalev, 1993; van der Kolk & van der Hart, 1991), suggesting that, when stressed, both adults and children, may have a greater capacity than usual for biologically encoding the memory of the stress-associated events.

Early studies on memory found lower recall in children than adults (DeLoache, Cassidy, & Brown, 1985; Donaldson, 1978; Nelson, 1986). However, other investigators have indicated that this may not reflect a lack of development of memory itself, but rather of a retrieval strategy (Johnson & Foley, 1984). Johnson and Foley, in summarizing their research, have stated that "in general, memory is improved when the original physical or cognitive context is reinstated. Children especially appear to need such contextual support for remembering." In keeping with these basic research findings, Pynoos and Eth (1986; Pynoos & Nader, 1989) have reported that, by asking children to draw or return physically to the scene of a major trauma, more accurate and complete reports could be obtained than by relying on spontaneous verbal recall. These authors, consequently, have recommended the use of a systematic direct approach for interviewing the traumatized child (Pynoos & Eth, 1986). Their findings have been rigorously tested and confirmed by other investigators (Goodman & Reed, 1986; M. Lamb, Hershkowitz, Sternberg, Boat, & Everson, 1996; M. Lamb, Sternberg, & Esplin, 1996; Miller, Fremorrow, Aljazireh, & Parker, 1996; Tobey & Goodman, 1992).

Interviewing techniques for investigating and assessing sexual abuse allegations have been hotly debated. Many experts and defense attorneys have argued that children are enormously suggestible and that using direct, "leading" questions greatly increases the probability of a false allegation of abuse. This position has been supported by early reports that underestimated children's cognitive and memory abilities (DeLoache et al., 1985; Donaldson, 1978; Nelson, 1986) and by studies where children have been swayed by an authority figure to give false reports of neutral events that they have witnessed (Ceci, Russ, & Toglia, 1987). Others, supported by newer findings, argue that since children do not report abuse readily and recall memory is not as complete as when the child is reminded of the place and context of the stressful event, that the mode of questioning children should be changed from open-ended questions to more direct and focused questioning to facilitate children's disclosures (Goodman, Rudy, Bottoms, & Aman, 1990; M. Lamb, Hershkowitz, et al., 1996; M. Lamb, Sternberg, et al., 1996; Miller et al., 1996; Saywitz, Geiselman, & Bornstein, 1992). The central issue of this debate is how suggestible are children?

Researchers conducting experiments on the relationship of age and suggestibility have now consistently found that actions affecting a child's sense of well-being, safety, and social acceptance are not only remembered remarkably well, but also at least to the age of four, children are surprisingly resistant to suggestions (Goodman et al., 1990; Orstein et al., 1992). Studies conducted by Goodman's research team have been particularly well designed with experimental conditions being sensitive to ecological validity (Goodman & Schwartz-Kenny, 1992). Essentially, Goodman's work confirms and extends that of other investigators who have demonstrated that people have better recall under conditions of active participation and conditions that affect central concerns of involved individuals, such as conditions affecting well-being, safety, and social acceptance (Garcia & Koelling, 1966; Keenan, MacWhinney, & Mayhew, 1977; Linton, 1982; Pullyblank, Bisanz, Scott, & Champion, 1985; Rogers, Kuiper, & Kirker, 1977). These researchers have indicated that laboratory studies of children's memory and cognitive abilities, which have utilized emotionally neutral experimental conditions or have investigated memories of children who have been passive witnesses to relatively innocuous events (DeLoache et al., 1985; Donaldson, 1978; Nelson, 1986), tend to underestimate age-related skills.

Under certain conditions, some younger children have been found to be suggestible and may develop false beliefs. Ceci and Huffman (1997) have indicated that false beliefs may be created by both suggestion and source misattribution. Although their experiments may be of questionable ecological validity when applied to sexually abused children testifying in court, they suggest that three factors may increase the likelihood of a false report and need consideration in determining the veracity of the child's allegation or testimony: (1) suggestive interviewing of the child over a long period of time (several months), (2) having someone in authority tell the child that a particular event was true, and (3) repeatedly asking the child to create mental images of "fictitious" events. The issues raised by these investigators are not of minor importance in criminal proceedings since errors of commission or false beliefs may result in the accused losing his or her civil liberties. On the other hand, in the adversarial atmosphere of a court proceeding, defense attorney tactics are less directed toward examining the child in a developmentally sensitive manner and more directed toward confusing the child and "catching" the child in even peripheral inconsistencies. Additionally, in the United States a significant grassroots effort has been mobilized asserting that "false memories" are being repeatedly created by professionals caring for suspected victims of maltreatment, particularly victims of CSA. Although there are some well-documented reports of false memories being induced by poorly trained professionals, the consequence of the false-memory movement has been to press professionals into using techniques (e.g., free recall) that have been demonstrated to be least effective in helping young children report their experiences. Additionally, the false-memory movement has unleashed an intense effort directed toward finding any possible variance in investigatory and interviewing technique that might "suggest" to the child that he/she was abused. Studies with considerable ecological validity have been conducted that indicate young children (4 years old and 7 years old) are not only accurate in recall of events that they have actively experienced, including painful experiences such as inoculations, but also are enormously resistant to suggestion (Goodman & Quas, 1996; Goodman et al., 1990; Tobey & Goodman, 1992). Studies regarding children's resistance to suggestion have actually simulated a sexual abuse investigation with "leading questions" and despite that condition, have demonstrated that children rarely commit errors of commission, incorporating material that would be construed as legally dangerous (e.g., implying that abuse has occurred when in fact it did not). These findings challenge widely held assumptions about children's reports of abuse and ability to testify as witnesses, assumptions challenging the accuracy of children's memory, and assumptions indicating that children are highly suggestible.

An additional concern emanating from Ceci and Huffman's work (1997) is whether based on their assertion that suggestibility is enhanced by repeated interviewing and by authorities directing children to visualize an event, that children in need of treatment will be denied access to effective treatment because of their involvement in court proceedings. Children who have been sexually abused are at high risk for the development of posttraumatic stress disorder (PTSD) (McLeer, Ruggiero, & Dixon, 1997). PTSD is a condition that persists across time and tends to be unresponsive to traditional talking therapies (McFarlane, 1987; Nader, Pynoos, Fairbanks, & Frederick, 1990; Yehuda, Southwick, Perry, Mason, & Giller, 1990). The treatment that appears to be most efficacious for PTSD in both children and adults is a cognitive behavioral treatment with a desensitization component (Deblinger, McLeer, Atkins, Ralphe, & Foa, 1989; March, Amaya-Jackson, Murray, & Schulte, 1998). Such treatment requires the patient to describe repeatedly the traumatic event in detail as if the event were occurring in the present. The patient is directed to remember and report as much detail as possible. The mechanism for symptom relief appears to be habituation to anxiety stimulated by repeated exposure through imagery to the scenes associated with the trauma. One of the authors (SVM) has already been told that children in a district attorney's office will not be referred for cognitive behavioral treatment because it will jeopardize the court proceedings. The theoretical bickering that is occurring in the professional literature on memory and suggestibility poses a substantial credibility risk not only to children who have, in fact, been sexually abused and are trying to report the events to the best of their ability, but also to those in need of treatment for PTSD subsequent to the abuse. These latter children may, in fact, be denied access to what appears to be an effective treatment pending finalization of court proceedings, a process that can take many months.

DETECTION AND DISCLOSURE OF EXTRAFAMILIAL SEXUAL ABUSE

The literature on both the process of detection and disclosure of sexual abuse rarely differentiates between extrafamilial and intrafamilial CSA, although the variables affecting this process are apt to be quite different. Consequently, by necessity, we must examine studies where both intrafamilial and extrafamilial abuse have been pooled together in order to understand variables associated with detection and disclosure.

In a Boston study of disclosure in 156 sexually abused children (both intra- and extrafamilial), it was reported that the child was first to tell of the abuse 55% of the time. A nonparent suspected abuse 17% of the time, while parents suspected abuse only 9% of the time. Medical evidence indicated abuse in only 5% of the cases (Sauzier, 1989). In the same study, initial disclosure most frequently was made directly to the parents (55%), to siblings or another child (16%), or to an adult relative or friend (10%). School professionals were told first in only 8% of cases; medical or mental health professionals only 6% of the time. Law enforcement personnel were told first only 1% of the time. Sauzier's study, additionally, found that when the relationship of the offender to the victim was examined, 67% of the children told someone about the abuse sooner or later when abuse was perpetrated by someone outside the family. This compares with 47% for children abused by a parent, with disclosure increasing in frequency the more distant the relative. One can conclude that in cases of extrafamilial abuse, disclosure is considerably more likely when the abuse occurs within the family system. The exception to this is when abuse occurs in a day-care setting. In day-care settings, abuse is typically disclosed only after a prolonged period of time (Finkelhor & Williams, 1988).

In Sauzier's (1989) study, factors were identified that mitigated against disclosure. These factors included both severe abuse (intercourse), with 54% of the children never disclosing, and extremely mild abuse (attempts only and nontouching), with 50% never telling. Sexual abuse that was associated with aggressive behavior had a bimodal distribution, with 39% of the children telling immediately following the abuse and 43% never telling. Of children who were threatened or manipulated, 62% to 67% ultimately told someone about being abused.

In a second study on disclosure and detection of sexual abuse in day-care settings, it was also found that abuse was most frequently revealed by the children themselves (37%) and that the children told their parents about the abuse first in 86% of cases (Finkelhor & Williams, 1988). In 63% of cases, an adult noted suspicious behavior or symptoms in the children and questioned the children directly; hence, precipitating disclosure. Most of the time, it was the children's parents who noticed the behavioral changes. Only 7% of the time were day-care staff apt to be sufficiently suspicious to precipitate a disclosure. Once abuse was disclosed, 86% of the time it was reported to the appropriate authorities within a week. However, Finkelhor's team found that day-care abuse could go undetected for significant periods of time. Only in 19% of cases did disclosure occur on the same day as the abuse. Thirty-two percent of the time the abuse had been ongoing for over 6 months. Thirty percent of the time the abuse had been ongoing for less than one month's duration, while in 19% of the cases the abuse had persisted for 1 to 5 months.

When spontaneous disclosure occurred regarding abuse in the day-care setting, it was usually at a point when the child felt safe enough and sufficiently removed from the perpetrator to tell or, conversely, under circumstances where the child felt enormously frightened about the prospect of returning to the site of the abuse. Over 50% of the children studied had been threatened with harm directed, either toward themselves or toward their families; hence, many were very frightened and clearly could not disclose until they felt safely removed from the perpetrator. In some instances, this was particularly difficult when the children's trust in their own parents had been undermined. This occurred specifically in situations where abuse was ritualistic. Ritualistic abuse appears to be a most malignant form of CSA with children being severely abused, threatened, and subjected to a systematic undermining of the child's trust in his or her parents (Finkelhor & Williams, 1988; Kelly, 1989).

In the Finkelhor Study of sexual abuse in day-care settings, one of the most important findings was that in those cases where there was adult-precipitated disclosure, parents or professionals became suspicious on the basis of physical symptoms or behavioral changes noted in the children. Fifty-one percent of adult-prompted disclosure emanated from noting behavioral changes such as fears, nightmares, sexual acting out, or sleep disorders. A frequent symptom that would arouse suspicion in parents and other adults was noting unusual sexual knowledge in the child, or sexual behaviors that were viewed as not appropriate to the child's developmental age. This finding again underscores that inappropriate sexual behavior and/or knowledge may be behavior markers for child sexual abuse (Kendall-Tackett, Williams, & Finkelhor, 1993). In 32% of cases, children presented with physical symptoms such as genital bleeding, persistent rashes and evidence of infection. What has been most surprising in Finkelhor's study was that these physical symptoms were frequently misinterpreted not only by parents, but also by professionals who gave alternate explanations minimizing the possibility of sexual abuse.

What has been demonstrated in this superb study is that parents are a key factor in ensuring early detection of CSA in day-care settings. A similar study for other forms of extrafamilial sexual abuse has not been done, but the development of educational programs for parents which would aid them in identifying the behavioral and physical symptoms associated with sexual abuse would be of enormous importance in providing a system for early detection. Parents need to be knowledgeable about the effects of sexual abuse and be provided with skills for helping their children both when children disclose abuse or present symptomatically without disclosure secondary to being too frightened or ashamed to report.

Following disclosure of extrafamilial CSA, assessing its impact on the family system is essential, and, yet, this process is frequently overlooked. Studies have indicated that disclosure of intrafamilial CSA is enormously disruptive to the family, but what is the impact of extrafamilial sexual abuse? In cases involving close and trusted family friends, feelings of betrayal and loss can be similar to that stimulated by disclosure of abuse from within the family. In a study by Van Scoyk, Gray, and James (1988), almost all families experienced extrafamilial CSA as a violation or breach in the family's "protective shield." The direct impact on the family and the child within the family was variable depending on whether the incident was isolated or repeated; violent, seductive, or coercive; or the perpetrator was a friend or stranger. In almost all cases, the disclosure of abuse was experienced as an existential crisis that derailed the entire family system by changing major belief systems about the family. The most frequent belief that was challenged, and at times shattered, was, "Our family is a safe place. We can protect our children from evil." The beliefs and family myths that were challenged by disclosure of abuse are noted in Table 11.1.

The impact of disclosure of extrafamilial CSA has been more recently studied and the findings of earlier investigators confirmed (Manion et al., 1996; Wolfe & Gentile, 1992). Parents, both mothers and fathers, experience considerable secondary traumatization following their child's disclosure of abuse. However, satisfaction in the parenting role and perceived environmental support have been found to be significantly predictive of positive parental outcome (Manion et al., 1996). Most families need considerable help, support, and opportunity for working through feelings associated with sexual abuse and for reintegrating the experience of having a child hurt and abused by someone else outside the family system. Parents need support and information from

Table 11.1
Parents'/Family Beliefs and Myths

---

1. Our family is a *safe place*.
2. We can protect our children from evil.
3. We can trust our judgment about those to whom we entrust our children's care.
4. If something terrible does happen, "Justice will be done."
5. "Vengeance will be ours"—sayeth the parents.
6. We are law-abiding, ethical citizens.
7. We can live in peace in our community.
8. We can talk about things in our family and leave the problem behind.
9. It will get worse if we talk about it.
10. Children who are sexually abused are somehow ruined for life.

Note. Adapted from Van Scoyk, Grey, and James (1988).

professional staff to provide necessary help to the abused child. Since children frequently experience significant fears regarding their own safety and need for protection, anger directed at parents may occur because children themselves also hold certain myths to be true and valid (e.g., "my parents can always protect and take care of me"). Parents need help in understanding why their child may express so much anger toward them. In the Van Scoyk et al. (1988) study, researchers noted multiple concerns of the children themselves (see Table 11.2).

Working with parents and the entire family system is essential at the point of disclosure. Studies have indicated that the impact of CSA and the course of recovery is positively correlated with the degree of parental responsiveness and support (Wyatt & Mickey, 1988). Parents who believe and support their children by way of helping them understand that the abuse is not their fault are major allies in the recovery process. Working with parents to help reduce inappropriate guilt and provide them with guidance and help in supporting their abused child must be given priority in all cases of extrafamilial CSA.

Table 11.2
Children's Concerns

---

1. Fears regarding safety/protection.
2. Anger at parents for not having been protected.
3. Confused feelings/responses to perpetrator:
     Participant guilt.
     Revenge fantasies.
4. Fear of threats.
5. Fear/feeling of being "damaged goods" or bad.
6. Fear it will happen again.
7. Fear of loss of love/approval from parents.

Note. Adapted from Van Scoyk, Grey, and James (1988).

THE INVESTIGATION PROCESS

Child sexual abuse is a crime in all 50 states in the United States. With intrafamilial CSA, reports of suspected abuse are usually filed by mandated reporters (e.g., teachers, physicians) who, on the basis of a child's disclosure, physical signs and symptoms, or behavioral characteristics, will initiate a report of suspected abuse. The filing of a report of suspected CSA initiates a two-pronged process of investigation with immediate attention being directed first and foremost to protecting the child from the possibility of further abuse while the investigation is pending. The allegation will be investigated by both the child protective service agency to determine whether the abuse has sufficient substance, and whether the child remains at risk of continued abuse and is in need of protection. The police and prosecutor will determine whether the suspect will be charged with the crime, arrested, and prosecuted.

With extrafamilial CSA, the investigation process is often different from that utilized in intrafamilial cases. The most obvious difference is that at the beginning of the process, the disclosure, itself, is most frequently made by the children to a parent or other trusted adult (either spontaneously or in response to questions raised by the adult because of concern about the child's behavior and/or physical signs and symptoms). Rarely is disclosure first made to a mandated reporter. Because of this, the parents or other responsible adults, usually make decisions about what actions are necessary to protect the child and may, or may not, report the suspected abuse. Consequently, many cases of extrafamilial CSA are never reported or officially investigated.

The second major difference in extrafamilial cases involves instances where community agencies, such as school systems, mental health clinics or day-care centers, have been implicated in the abuse allegation. In such cases, an investigation may also be initiated by governmental licensing authorities, either secondary to the police initiating an investigation or the parents or caretakers calling the appropriate licensing bodies and requesting an investigation.

From this brief review of the investigation process, three areas of systemic weakness can be quickly identified that increase the likelihood of serious problems developing:

1. The initiation of a report of suspected CSA is at the discretion of the parent or caretaker. This frequently results in decisions being made to handle the abuse allegation informally outside official channels. Reasons for doing so often include a wish to protect the children from being repeatedly questioned by strangers assigned to investigate the case, the wish to end the abuse immediately and "get on" with life as usual without the burden of an investigation and subsequent criminal prosecution, or feelings of loyalty to the alleged perpetrator, particularly when he or she is a close friend of the family or respected community leader.

The problems with these informal methods of handling extrafamilial CSA are significant. It is rare that a child molester victimizes one child, one time only. The more frequent scenario is that the sex offender has an attraction toward children of a specific sex and age group, and that the drive toward sexual activity with children is strong and repetitive. Therefore, to not report suspected extrafamilial CSA to the authorities and initiate an investigation significantly increases the likelihood that other children will be left at considerable risk. Without an investigation, no paper trail will be established indicating that the alleged perpetrator has been implicated in an abuse allegation, with the result that the alleged perpetrator can continue to have unrestricted access to other children.

Also, for a family to "protect" the alleged perpetrator from police investigation means that the child may be denied access to treatment, for if the child is in treatment and discloses the abuse, the therapist is then mandated to report it; hence, precipitating an investigation. Consequently, families may choose not to bring a child to a therapist even though the child is in need of care.

2. Police, being the primary investigatory unit, are confronted with the task of interviewing abused children of all ages frequently without adequate training in the specialized skills needed for interviewing young children. Throughout the United States, model programs have been established that provide specialized police investigation units with training for investigating sex crimes perpetrated against children. In many parts of the country, however, police officers have not been given the opportunity to acquire needed interviewing skills (Sullivan, Barth, Bhatt, & Gilbert, 1987). This reduces the likelihood of collecting adequate evidence for prosecution, and hence, increases the likelihood of charges either not being brought or the perpetrator being acquitted.

3. The different agencies and professionals involve usually work sequentially or in parallel to each other, but often without any real coordination of effort. This, combined with varying levels of skill, or lack thereof, in different professionals interviewing children during the investigation process, means that children and families will be subjected to multiple interviewers, confused feedback and confronted with a fragmented uncoordinated system.

Additionally, with a lack of coordinated effort during the investigation process in cases involving the systematic abuse of children within day-care settings, including ritualistic abuse or cases where juveniles are involved in sex rings and the production of pornography, one party to the investigation process may inadvertently "tip off" the alleged perpetrator prematurely, thus, providing him or her with the necessary time to dispose of valuable evidence (e.g., photographs, videotapes and sex paraphernalia) needed for prosecution.

What has been demonstrated repeatedly in working with sexually abused children is that using investigators who are knowledgeable regarding child development and interviewing techniques is invaluable to an investigation (Finkelhor & Williams, 1988; Sgroi, 1982). Personnel within police sex crimes unit can be provided with training in the necessary and specialized interviewing skills needed for investigating CSA, or personnel can be hired from outside the agency to serve as consultants. Joint interviewing involving the police, human service agencies, and mental health consultants, are becoming increasingly popular and are helpful in limiting the number of interviews to which the child is subjected. Multiple interviews, particularly with young children, can be problematic in that interviewing techniques and perceived inconsistencies can jeopardize the prosecution of the case.

Coordination between those with statutory responsibility for investigating CSA and licensing agencies is also essential to reduce risk and protect children. Increasingly, child advocacy centers (CAC) are being established in communities throughout the United States to streamline and coordinate the investigation and prosecution of cases involving allegations of CSA (Reichard, 1993). CACs typically include investigators from agencies charged with statutory responsibility for investigating abuse allegations, such as child protection workers and police detectives, pediatricians, mental health professionals, and prosecutors. Team members at the CACs usually undergo extensive training targeted to increase forensic interviewing skills with children, including preschoolers and adolescents. Teams coordinate their activities and minimize repeated interviewing of the child by having one team member interview the child while others watch though one way mirrors or closed circuit TV. Frequently, the interviewer is hooked up to an earphone allowing observing team members to call in and request specific information. If abuse is substantiated, then the team meets together and determines which interventions are required, who will talk with the child and family, and who will provide the actual intervention. Such an approach insures faster delivery of services, minimizes misinformation and ensures coordination of efforts. CACs represent an advance in providing for skilled and sensitive investigation of abuse allegations and coordination of intervention efforts (Westman, 1996).

ASSESSMENT OF THE IMPACT OF ABUSE ON THE CHILD

Following disclosure of extrafamilial CSA, each child and family should have access to services designed to assess the impact of the abuse on both the child and the family system. Evaluation and services need to be provided in a timely manner, and be sensitive to the child's and family's needs. However, there is one instance where services must be provided immediately, and that is when the alleged abuse has occurred within the past 72 hours. In such cases, the child needs to have an immediate, emergency medical examination because physical evidence of sexual abuse may be present. Specifically, there may be evidence of sperm, semen and subtle signs of physical trauma to the genitalia and rectum. If the sexually abusive incident was more than 72 hours before disclosure, the medical examination can then be scheduled on an elective basis.

MEDICAL ASSESSMENT

For medical examination (see Table 11.3), if possible, the child should be taken to a center specializing in the examination of victims of sexual assault. Such facilities are experienced in evidence gathering and are frequently subsidized by public agencies to provide services to crime victims. This approach to medical assessment is recommended since there are many physicians in the community, often excellent in the care of pediatric patients, who have nonetheless had minimal training in the forensic medical examination of the sexually abused child. Because of this, when children are examined by community physicians, the examination is often inadequate for forensic purposes. This is particularly unfortunate when the child has been seen within 24–72 hours of an alleged sexually abusive incident, and the opportunity to collect important evidence may be lost.

The medical examination, itself, has three purposes: (1) to diagnose and treat any medical problems related to the abuse, (2) to gather medical and legal evidence, and (3) to provide the child and family with support and reassurance that he or she is "alright" (Benedek & Schetky, 1987b). Guidelines for the physical examination of sexually abused children have been published by the American Academy of Pediatrics (1991).

Children frequently disclose facts regarding their sexually abusive experience in a gradual sequential manner. Hence, in providing a medical examination of the sexually abused child, one should not make modifications in the examination process based on assumptions about what sexual activities the child has been subjected to based on the child's initial disclosure. Rather the medical examination should be

Table 11.3
Protocol for Medical Examination of
Sexually Abused Child

Forensic Evidence Contribution:
1. Corroboration of history.
2. Determination of sexual contact.
3. Perpetrator identification.

Forensic Evidence:
1. Characteristic traumatic injuries.
2. Evidence of sexually transmitted diseases.
3. Pregnancy.
4. Semen present.
5. Sperm present.
6. Miscellaneous.

Methods of Collection:
1. Clothing.
2. Debris and foreign material.
3. Woods Lamp Examination.
4. Hair sampling.
5. Fingernail scrapings.
6. Saliva.
7. Blood.
8. Photographs.

Laboratory Tests:
A. Sperm detection and motility—
   1. Wet mount.
   2. Gram stain.
B. Semen detection—
   1. Acid phosphatase.
   2. Semen glycoprotein (P30).
C. Offender identification—
   1. ABO typing.
   2. DNA fingerprinting.
   3. Hair and fiber analysis.
D. Pregnancy test—
   1. Urine and serum test.
   2. Chorionic villi/tissue biopsy.
   3. Ultrasonography.
E. Tests for Sexually transmitted diseases:
   1. Gonorrhea.
   2. Syphilis.
   3. Chlamydia.
   4. Trichomonas.
   5. HIV infections.
   6. Other.

Note. Adapted from Kanda (1989).

thorough with visual inspection of the genitalia and rectum. Many professionals now advocate use of colposcopy of both of the vaginal and anal orifice (Clayton, Barth, & Shubin, 1989; Finkel, 1989). Others are less convinced of its value (Paradise, 1989). This issue has yet to be settled. The genitalia, rectum, and pharynx should be examined for presence of semen (Enos & Contrath, 1986; Graves, Sensabaugh, & Blake, 1985). Genital cultures as well as rectal and pharyngeal cultures should be taken for sexually transmitted disease (Enos & Contrath, 1986; J. Glaser, Hammerschlag, & McCormak, 1986; Ingram, Everett, Lyna, White, & Rockwell, 1992). The child should not only be examined and cultured for gonorrhea and chlamydia, but also wet mount examinations should be performed for trichomonas and serology for syphilis (Kramer & Jason, 1982). Pregnancy tests should be performed for pubertal girls and follow-up medical evaluation scheduled, particularly for repeat serology for syphilis and culturing for gonorrhea. The child should, additionally, be examined from head to toe, specifically looking for evidence of violent behavior during the abuse, including trauma to the buttocks, thighs, or breasts as well as grasp marks (American Academy of Pediatrics, 1991).

Physical signs of trauma, both genital and extragenital, can be photographed, with photography through the colposcope being particularly helpful for documenting evidence of sexual abuse. Photographs are helpful, not only for forensic purposes, but additionally provide the opportunity to review or double-check findings or perhaps discover previously unnoticed findings (Ricci, 1988). Photographs are also useful when seeking consultation from colleagues in that the photographs provide a means of avoiding repeating genital and/or rectal examinations of the child. Colposcopy (with its magnification) has been invaluable in detecting previously missed evidence of hymenal scarring, abrasions, and increased vascularization secondary to trauma. In cases of sexual assault where violent behavior has accompanied the sexual abuse, it is essential to collect additional forensic evidence by way of clothing, debris, foreign materials, hair samplings, and fingernail scrapings, and examine materials stained with blood and saliva. Special consideration should be given to HIV testing on follow-up examination of the child when the sexual abuse has been perpetrated by someone at high risk for HIV infection (Gellert & Durfee, 1989; Paradise, 1990).

Although systematic and routine medical examination is essential, absence of physical findings is the rule, not the exception, with physical findings being present between only 5% to 15% of the time (Adams, Harper, Knodson, & Revilla, 1994; American Academy of Child and Adolescent Psychiatry, 1997a). The absence of physical evidence of abuse does not mean abuse has not occurred.

ASSESSMENT OF THE IMPACT OF EXTRAFAMILIAL SEXUAL ABUSE

In the absence of a direct credible witness and physical evidence of abuse, it is difficult, indeed, to "prove" that a child has been sexually abused by an individual or individuals. The validation of the allegation, in fact, rest on the determination of the child's credibility and on corroborating evidence (e.g., behavioral signs and symptoms that have been demonstrated to occur in children who have been sexually abused). The assessment of CSA, becomes a two-phased process of first determining the validity of the allegation, and second of assessing the impact of the abuse on the child and his or her family.

Table 11.4
Sources of Information for Assessment

Interview/s with parents/caretakers.
Interview with child.
Teacher reports regarding academic function and behavior.
Review of available reports from CPS and/or police.
Self, parent, and teacher standardized reports.
Developmental assessment and cognitive testing as needed.

The validation process usually occurs during the initial investigation and is carried out by the agency with statutory responsibility for investigating sexual abuse allegations. However, as has been previously indicated, a mental health professional will occasionally be requested to provide consultation to the investigating agency during the initial investigation. If requested to participate in the determination of whether an abuse allegation can be substantiated or nor, it is essential that the clinician maintain objectivity and do a careful, thorough, and fair evaluation, for to come to the conclusion that abuse has occurred without adequate data, places the alleged abuser at risk of being imprisoned when in fact he or she is innocent. Alternatively, to dismiss prematurely the data supporting the allegation can result in an increased risk to the child of further abuse and, in cases of extrafamilial abuse, place other children at risk. The evaluator must maintain clarity regarding the two issues in abuse investigations: (1) establishing offender accountability, and (2) determining if the child is at risk, a child-protective issue requiring less rigorous criteria than that for establishing criminal guilt.

The process for investigation of an allegation has already been discussed, but it is important to review basic guidelines for assessing the validity of an allegation. A methodical data-gathering process during this phase of the assessment provides a background for the more detailed assessment of the impact of the abuse once investigators determine it probably occurred. The sources of information that should be utilized in assessing extrafamilial CSA are outlined in Table 11.4. The targeted tasks are delineated in Table 11.5.

Table 11.5
Ten Essential Tasks in Assessing Child Sexual Abuse

1. Obtain history of abuse.
2. Assess child's credibility.
3. Determine familial response to disclosure.
4. Assess child's current and past level of functioning.
5. Address other major stressors (current and past).
6. Identify current symptoms causing dysfunction.
7. Identify coexisting psychiatric disorders (current and past).
8. Identify areas of strength and dysfunction in family system.
9. Provide feedback to child and family.
10. Document findings carefully in the medical record.

With extrafamilial CSA, the parents/caretakers should usually be met with first since initial disclosure is almost always made to them. Parental response to the child's disclosure has been demonstrated to be critical: a positive supporting response may be protective, resulting in a lessening of symptoms and dysfunction postabuse (S. Lamb, 1986; Regehr, 1990). On the other hand, negative responses coupled with disbelief or blame or an idiosyncratic response may result in a more distressed and dysfunctional child.

Parents are usually enormously distressed on learning that their child has been sexually abused, particularly since it shatters a commonly held myth that parents can protect their children from bad things happening (Van Scoyk et al., 1988). The family's distress may be even more acute when the abuser is not a stranger, but a close friend of the family or community leader. At such times, the family member may be in considerable conflict regarding reporting the abuse, and blaming and prosecuting the perpetrator. The need to work with parents regarding their conflicting loyalties, feelings of responsibility and guilt is essential if parents are to be free to support and help the abused child through a most troublesome time. Parents, additionally, need to be asked if they, themselves, have ever been sexually abused or assaulted, since feelings about their own experiences may make it difficult for them to be emotionally available to the child.

It is essential during the initial meetings with parents to obtain a careful developmental history covering sensorimotor, socioemotional, cognitive and linguistic domains. In the United States, 12% to 22% of children suffer from moderate to severely handicapping mental disorders, including developmental impairments (Institute of Medicine, 1989). Hence, being aware of specific developmental delays and difficulties is essential in structuring the interview with the child in a manner that will facilitate communication and understanding. Additionally, professionals may need to be aggressive advocates for abused children who also have neurodevelopmental disorder and/or comorbid psychiatric disorders since the criteria used in the criminal justice system for determining competency and credibility frequently are problematic for children with these handicaps. The issue of abused handicapped children will be addressed later in this book.

Often, the institutions working with abused children make an assumption that, if a child is sexually abused, the symptoms and dysfunction manifested by the child are secondary to the abuse. Or, conversely, if the child has a strong history of serious psychiatric disorder or neurodevelopmental disorder, the abused child's credibility may be inappropriately called in to question. The reality is that healthy children, behaviorally and emotionally disturbed children, as well as children with neurodevelopmental delays and disorders, can be sexually abused. It is, therefore, important to conduct a systematic clinical evaluation targeted to identify areas of dysfunction that were present prior to the alleged incident, and to determine which functional problems developed during and/or after the alleged abuse started. It is essential to obtain a clear history of the child's functioning, not only within the family system, but across behavioral domains including with peers, extrafamilial adults, and at school. Parents can provide this information as well as give pertinent details about family psychiatric history, which may be an added risk factor for the child. A history of all major psychiatric disorders in first degree relatives should be obtained systematically, including a history of learning and attentional problems, alcohol and substance abuse as well as difficulties with the law. Other major stressors affecting the family need to be identified, including routine inquiries about adult domestic violence, the witnessing of which is a major stressor for children (Jaffe, Wolf, & Wilson, 1990). Family strengths and resources, as well as the family's ability to mobilize extrafamilial resources, should be assessed as well. The evaluation strategy for the child's parents and caretakers is outlined in Table 11.6.

The interview with the child should obviously be structured based on the developmental age and unique needs of the child. Sexually assaulted adolescents may present with much reluctance and embarrassment, particularly if assaulted by a peer. A significant issue may be that the adolescent may not want the parent to be aware that he or she has been sexually active. Early studies indicated that peer-assaulted adolescents often do not perceive the offender as culpable, and frequently blame themselves (Parrot, 1989). However, more recent investigations of young adults suggest that women do blame the assaultive peer (Kopper, 1996; Stormo, Lang, & Stritake, 1997). These studies have yet to be replicated with an adolescent population. All these issues need to be sensitively addressed in the evaluation of the sexually abuse or assaulted adolescent.

The children who are most difficult for evaluators to assess are those that are younger. Parents can aid the clinician in choosing play materials that will be most helpful as a medium through which the child can discuss the abuse with the examiner. Techniques for working with young children and interviewing young sexually abused children have been elegantly reviewed by Sgroi (1982) and MacFarlane et al. (1986). Guidelines for evaluating infants and toddlers have been issued by the American Academy of Child and Adolescent Psychiatry (1997b). Issues relating to children's memory, suggestibility (or lack thereof), ability to report abuse and other developmental considerations have already been discussed in detail earlier in this chapter.

The use of anatomically correct dolls has been a hotly debated issue, with proponents indicating that sexually abused children use the dolls differently than nonsexually abused children. Others claim the dolls overstimulate the children and cause them to give reports of activities that, in fact, have not occurred. Multiple studies have been conducted regarding the use of the anatomically correct dolls and the data appear to

Table 11.6
Tasks for Meeting with Parents/Caretakers

1. Obtain history of alleged abuse.
2. Assess family response to disclosure.
3. Obtain developmental history including:
   a. Sensory motor development.
   b. Socioemotional development.
   c. Cognitive and linguistic development.
4. Assess child's current and premorbid functioning:
   a. With family.
   b. With peers.
   c. With extrafamilial adults.
   d. At school.
5. Obtain family history of psychiatric disorders.
6. Identify other major stressors (past and current).
7. Identify familial and extrafamilial support and resources.

indicate that sexually abused children are more apt to play in a sexualized manner than nonsexually abused children when left alone with the anatomically correct dolls in free play (August & Forman, 1989; D. Glaser & Collins, 1989; Jampole & Weber, 1987; Leventhal, Hamilton, Rekedal, Tebano-Micci, & Egston, 1989; Siven, Shor, Koepp, & Noble, 1988). Additionally, sexually abused children have been found to use more avoidant behaviors toward the dolls when an observer is present in the room (August & Forman, 1989; Siven et al., 1988). However, Everson and Boat (1990) found that 6% of 223 normal children, ages 2 to 5 years, played in a sexually explicit manner with anatomically correct dolls, indicating that sexualized play is not diagnostic for child sexual abuse. From other studies, anatomically correct dolls do not appear to be a necessary prop for eliciting sexualized behavior, with sexually abused children displaying more sexually explicit behavior with anatomically neutral dolls than children who have not been abused. It certainly appears, that while not diagnostic, sexualized play may be a psychosocial marker for CSA (Kendall-Tackett et al., 1993).

There are no data to support the hypothesis that anatomically correct dolls stimulate the child sexually and increase the child's suggestibility with consequent increased risk of a falsified disclosure of child sexual abuse (August & Forman, 1989; Boat & Everson, 1988; D. Glaser & Collins, 1989; Jampole & Weber, 1987; Simkins & Renier, 1996; Siven et al., 1988). In fact, S. Katz, Schonfeld, Carter, Leventhal, and Cicchetti (1995) have demonstrated that children aged 3 to 7 years provide more accurate reports with fewer omission with direct questioning using dolls, compared with open-ended, free recall interview conditions. No significant differences were found across groups regarding the number of false reports generated. Samra and Yuille (1996) studied the effect of anatomically neutral dolls in reporting accuracy and completeness in 4- to 6-year-old children. They found that accuracy and completeness increased with use of these props, suggesting that anatomic specificity is less important than interview strategies utilizing focused questions versus free recall. As indicated earlier, retrieval strategy, not memory appears to be critical with preschoolers, with free recall being most incomplete. An even more interesting finding was that, with focused interviewing, children interviewed without dolls gave a longer and more detailed report than those who were interviewed with dolls (M. Lamb, Hershkowitz, et al., 1996a; M. Lamb, Sternberg, et al., 1996b). These findings add support to the utilization of interviewing techniques that are focused versus open-ended and unstructured. These studies imply that anatomically correct dolls have less specificity and importance in the evaluation of sexually abused children than was previously thought. It appears that the introduction of dolls into the interview tend to focus the interviewer and, hence, introduce an interview structure that invokes a more efficient and complete retrieval strategy in preschool children.

It is beyond the scope of this chapter to detail interviewing techniques at different ages, a process that has been comprehensively addressed in the practice parameters of the American Academy of Child and Adolescent Psychiatry (1995, 1997b). However, the tasks needing to be addressed in the assessment of the child are outlined in Table 11.7. What is unique to the assessment of the sexually abused child is the importance of assessing the developmental level and determining the words used by the child for naming different body parts. This can be done by the use of drawings or with the anatomically correct dolls. It is also essential to determine what names are used for different people in the family and outside the family. If the abuse was perpetrated by a previously known adult, it is important to be clear as to the child's name for this person

Table 11.7
Tasks for Meeting with Child

1. Establish rapport.
2. Determine level of cognitive and linguistic functioning.
3. Obtain history of abuse.
4. Assess child's perception of family response to disclosure.
5. Assess current and premorbid level of functioning:
   a. Behavioral.
   b. Emotional.
   c. Cognitive.
6. Identify other major stressors (current and past).
7. Perform mental status examination.
8. Assess child's credibility.

and to be certain of the alleged abuser's identity. The child's report of the abuse should be recorded in the medical record using the child's own words for what occurred, where it occurred, and who did it. The timing of the abuse and the duration of the abuse may need to be recorded by the use of concrete markers of time with younger children (e.g., relationship to birthdays, holidays, favorite TV programs).

It is critical to determine the child's perception of his or her parents' response to the abuse disclosure, and to aid the child and parents in resolving any conflicting and discrepant feelings. Systematically assessing the child's functioning based on the child's perceptions regarding behavior, and emotional and cognitive functioning, is also important. If the child's report and parent's report differ, determination of symptom level is dependent on the domain. Parents are usually better reporters for behavioral disorders and academic functioning, whereas children are more reliable in reporting about emotional distress, sleep disorders, and other subjective experiences (Orvaschel, Weissman, Padian, & Lowe, 1981). Identifying other events that have been unduly stressful for the child and family is critical as is determining the child's mental status.

After completion of the evaluation with data from parents, the child, and teachers, the convergence or divergence of abuse history, signs and symptoms, and direct mental status examination of the child will aid in the determination of the child's credibility. Credibility determination and validation of abuse allegations have been discussed extensively in the literature (American Academy of Child and Adolescent Psychiatry, 1997a; Benedek & Schetky, 1987a, 1987b; Goodman et al., 1981; Goodman, Golding, & Haith, 1984; Leippe & Romanczyk, 1987; Ross et al., 1987). Most reports address the issue of credibility in intrafamilial child sexual abuse. The current authors have yet to find a report in the literature regarding extrafamilial child sexual abuse, itself. The child's consistency, clarity, and use of language as well as spontaneous disclosure are all factors that add to the credibility of the child. Consistency and clarity need to be present regarding what happened, who did it, where and when. The presence of details that are described in age-appropriate language add additionally to credibility. Obviously, physical evidence of sexual abuse adds support to the child's story. However, physical evidence of abuse is infrequently present (Adams et al., 1994; American Academy of Child and Adolescent Psychiatry, 1997a). The absence of secondary gain from the allegation of abuse also increases the likelihood that the child's story is credible. While of great importance in intrafamilial abuse allegations in families with custody disputes, it is infrequently an issue in extrafamilial child sexual abuse.

The use of standardized instruments for evaluating behavioral and emotional symptoms cannot be overemphasized as a means of providing a baseline for documenting symptomatology and a means for monitoring behavioral responses to treatment. The following instruments in Table 11.8 have been found helpful in assessing psychopathology in sexually abused children and all have established norms for the general population.

Formal differential diagnosis is essential in determining if a child meets full criteria for a major psychiatric disorder for which specific treatments with demonstrated efficacy exist. Posttraumatic stress disorder (PTSD) is a psychiatric disorder that all too few evaluators screen for systematically, and yet, it is a frequent finding subsequent to sexual abuse. McLeer et al. (1997) reported that 52.5% of nonclinically referred, sexually abused children met full diagnostic criteria for PTSD at some point during a 24-month period following disclosure and termination of abuse. This study clearly indicates that sexually abused children are at significant risk for the development of PTSD. Furthermore, children who met criteria for PTSD had higher symptoms levels at baseline, 12 and 24 months, than those who did not. PTSD status was a highly significant predictor of symptom severity and persistence. These findings confirm those reported for clinical samples of sexually abused children (McLeer, Deblinger, Atkins, Foa, & Ralphe, 1988; McLeer, Deblinger, Henry, & Orvaschel, 1992; Merry & Andrews, 1994; Wolfe, Gentile, & Wolfe, 1989). With the exception of the PTSD subscale of the Child Behavior Check List (CBCL) (Wolfe et al., 1989), standardized rating scales for anxiety, depression, and behavioral disorders do not identify PTSD in children. This, coupled with the lack of systematic interviewing for PTSD symptomatology, suggests that many sexually abused children with this disorder may not be identified during assessment. Routine questioning regarding the symptoms in the PTSD subcategories of reexperiencing phenomena, avoidant behaviors, and signs of autonomic hyperarousal are critical to ensure identification of this subgroup of children in need of targeted, disorder-specific treatment.

Finally, following completion of the evaluation process, it is essential to provide feedback to both the child and the family. It is important to identify areas of dysfunction and

Table 11.8
Standardized Instruments for Assessing Psychopathology

The Child Behavior Checklist (CBCL) (Achenbach, 1991a).

The Teacher Report Form of the Child Behavior Checklist (TRF-CBCL) (Achenbach, 1991b).

The Child Depression Inventory (CDI) (Kovacs, 1977).

The State-Trait Anxiety Inventory for Children (STAIC) (Spielberger, 1973).

The Child Manifest Anxiety Scale-Revised (CMAS-R) (Reynolds & Richmond, 1978).

The Perceived Competence Scale for Children (PCSC) (Harter, 1985).

The Social Support Scale for Children (SSSC) (Harter, 1985).

The Clinician Administered PTSD Scale-Child and Adolescent Version (CAPS-C) (Nader et al., 1996).

make treatment recommendations, as well as review legal considerations for the process which will unfold over the next year following the disclosure of child sexual abuse. Close contact with the family throughout the treatment of the child helps greatly in healing the trauma of extrafamilial child sexual abuse.

LEGAL CONSIDERATIONS

Since sexual contact between adults and children under the age of 14 is a crime in every state, a child victim of extrafamilial sexual abuse may be involved in a criminal prosecution of the offender. The type of contact, ranging from fondling to penetration, and the age of the child at the time of the offense determines the specific crime and the potential penalty imposed for its violation.

A child's disclosure of extrafamilial sexual abuse reaches the criminal justice system in various ways. Sometimes a child tells a parent, guardian, or neighbor who contacts the police. In other cases, discovery of sexually explicit photographs of children may lead police to finding these children. While the creation, distribution, and possession of child pornography is a criminal offense in itself, it is almost certain that the children depicted in child pornography are also victims of sexual abuse.

In other cases, when a child discloses sexual abuse by an adult affiliated with children's group activities such as day care, school, youth groups, clubs or sports teams, disclosure by a child will widen the scope of law enforcement investigation to include interviews with other children having past or present affiliation with the suspect. Additional victims often come forward following a child's disclosure to police.

Occasionally, disclosure of extrafamilial sexual abuse follows the diagnosis of a sexually transmitted disease. In cases involving adolescent males involved in sex rings or prostitution, it is unusual for a victim to reveal abuse unless confronted with conclusive proof or sexual contact.

Extrafamilial sexual abuse usually involves a perpetrator who is known to the child. However, it does happen that children are assaulted by strangers. In the authors' experience, these cases are the most likely to result in physical injury to the victim, and are the most likely to yield physical evidence if the report is quickly made and evidence promptly collected and preserved.

In cases of stranger sexual assault, the identity of the assailant is obviously a critical factor. It is sometimes necessary to have the child victim identify the suspect before police can make an arrest. Suspect identification is conducted by having the child select the assailant's image from several photographs, or by having the child identify the perpetrator at a line-up where the prime suspect stands with other similarly featured persons of the same gender, race and general physique.

While research involving the accuracy of children's eyewitness testimony suggests that under certain conditions children over 6 may be as able as adults to identify their assailant (Goodman & Reed, 1986), it is difficult to convince a jury in a stranger sexual assault case where the only evidence of identity of the assailant is identification by a young child. Physical evidence found on children or their clothes (such as body fluids or hair fibers) which can be linked to the suspect, other witnesses, statements or circumstances corroborating children's testimony are often necessary to secure a conviction when the assailant is a stranger.

While the criminal process varies somewhat from state to state, the procedure from investigation to trial is similar enough to provide the reader with a general overview.

After police have completed their investigation, the prosecutor reviews the facts and decides whether there is sufficient evidence to file criminal charges against the suspect. In some jurisdictions, this function is assumed by a grand jury who hears the evidence and makes its recommendation to the prosecutor. Once charges are filed, the suspect, now called the defendant, is arrested. He is required to hire an attorney, or if he is indigent, legal counsel is appointed at government expense.

The victim of a crime is represented by the prosecutor (also known in some areas as the state's attorney or assistant district attorney). Unlike legal action initiated by private individuals for breach of contract or personal injury, criminal prosecutions are initiated by the state since, theoretically, criminal acts are offenses committed against the community. Although the child victim is certainly a crucial witness in a criminal trial, a crime is an affront to the community at large and the community's interests are represented by the prosecutor.

The criminal trial is an adversarial proceeding designed to determine whether a crime was committed, and if so, whether the defendant was the perpetrator. The prosecutor introduces evidence to prove the defendant's guilt. The defense attorney challenges the evidence through cross examination and sometimes by introducing other evidence. While the adversarial process is designed to arrive at the truth, the prosecution and the defense do not stand at equal footing. The defendant is not required to testify or offer any evidence in support of his innocence; the law presumes his innocence. It is the job of the prosecution to establish guilt beyond a reasonable doubt. A verdict of acquittal is not equivalent to a finding of innocence, it is a conclusion that the state's evidence has failed to persuade a unanimous jury of the defendant's guilt beyond a reasonable doubt.

A criminal case is proved by direct or circumstantial evidence. Direct evidence is testimony from a witness who saw or heard something tending to support or disprove an aspect of a case. The most obvious form of direct evidence in a case of child maltreatment is the testimony of the victim, and there are often difficult legal issues when the witness is a young child.

In many states, before a child witness is permitted to testify in a criminal trial a judge must legally rule that the child is able to give an accurate and truthful account of events. This requirement is called legal competency and it requires that the potential witness demonstrate the ability to recall and relate events, to distinguish the concepts of truth and lie, and that the witness understands the moral duty to testify truthfully. While these competency requirements are minimal, and presumptively satisfied when the witness is older than 14, a child under the age of 4 usually lacks the developmental skills to qualify as a witness. A child who has told her mother and the police that she was sexually molested by her school bus driver for example, may be precluded from telling her story in a criminal court because she cannot meet legal competency requirements. Absent other evidence to support a conviction, the accused child abuser may never go to court if the only eyewitness to his crime is his 3-year-old victim. This problem may also arise when a sexual assault victim is developmentally or cognitively disabled.

Frustrated by this all too frequent dilemma, child advocates from several disciplines proposed the repeal of legal competency requirements, that the child should be permitted to testify whether or not she is developmentally able to articulate the difference between the truth and a lie, and that the accuracy and reliability of her testimony should be evaluated by the jury. Several states and the federal courts have adopted this approach.

There is often considerable delay between disclosure and trial. As weeks and months pass, the child's memory may dim as to details so critical to assessing the credibility of her testimony. In other cases, a child may be so overwhelmed by the courtroom environment that she may not be able to testify. In both of these situations, the child has probably made several prior out-of-court statements concerning the abuse, possibly to parents, police, a physician, or a therapist. Child hearsay laws enacted in many states may enable the jury to hear a child's disclosures about sexual abuse when memory or emotional trauma precludes the child from giving courtroom testimony.

While the introduction of a child's prior statements concerning the abuse may seem the obvious solution, always keep in mind that a criminal trial is an adversarial proceeding where the accused has the legal right to test the credibility of witnesses by cross-examination. The Sixth Amendment to the United States Constitution guarantees, "In all criminal prosecution the accused shall enjoy the right . . . to be confronted with the witnesses against them." Where a child is unable to testify, how does an accused defend himself against allegations of child abuse when the only testimony comes not from the child, but from a third party to whom the child disclosed? Whether child hearsay laws strike a fair balance between a child's right to justice and the accused's right to confront the witness is an evolving and controversial area of criminal law.

Another vexing issue when a child is involved in criminal court proceedings also involves the constitutional requirement of confrontation. In this context, does the legal right of confrontation require the physical presence of the child in the same courtroom with the accused?

Historically, the requirement that an accused shall be in the same room, face to face with the accuser was believed to promote truthful testimony. This notion is premised on the idea that a witness will be compelled to speak the truth under the scrutiny of the defendant's gaze. Leaving aside the validity of this presumption, our ancestors could not have contemplated children as witnesses when fashioning this legal right. To suppose that a frightened young child, threatened with physical harm if she tells about the molestation will testify more truthfully in the presence of the accused is dubious at best. This may be a particular problem when a child victim describes bizarre activity such as supernatural threats, torture, death or mutilation that she witnessed in connection with the abuse. In these cases fear is often the primary controlling tactic to prevent disclosure from child victims. The potential emotional trauma to some of these children if forced to face their assailant in a courtroom is of great concern.

The United States Supreme Court has ruled that in appropriate cases, victims of child abuse may testify by way of one-way closed circuit television rather than in the presence of the abuser (*Maryland vs. Craig,* 1990). The court held that this procedure does not violate the constitutional right of defendants to confront their accusers if the prosecution demonstrates in each case that the child witness would be traumatized by having to testify in the defendant's presence. However, in some jurisdictions, specific procedures for ensuring the right of defendants to confront their accusers preclude the use of closed-circuit TV. Therefore, it is critical to determine what the law stipulates on a state-to-state basis.

In cases of intrafamilial sexual abuse, the attitudes of the nonoffending parent toward protecting her child and the child's participation in the criminal justice system requires close attention by law enforcement, social service and mental health professionals. Often, the child's willingness to disclose sexual abuse and participate in the justice process is largely dependent on the support, protection, and approval offered by the nonoffending parent. Conflicting loyalties, ambivalence, and economic and emotional bonds with the suspect are often present and problematic in these cases.

Although by definition a parent is not a perpetrator in extrafamilial CSA, the parents' role may be different but no less important to the interests of the child and the interests of justice. Where the perpetrator is not a family member, parents may want to assist law enforcement by conducting their own independent investigation. Or, motivated by a sincere desire to have their child remember details of the incident in preparation for trial, parents may repeatedly rehearse their child's testimony as an exercise to improve memory. These parental strategies can do great damage to a criminal case and are to be discouraged. However, it is very important to appropriately involve the parent in both the investigation and in preparation for trial. Information about the progress of an investigation, court dates, and education about the trial permits constructive familial participation in the legal process.

When a child is the alleged victim of a sexual assault, a parent or family member may be called as a witness at trial. If the parent is the first person to whom the child disclosed the abuse, he or she may be asked to tell the jury what the child said and the child's demeanor at the time of disclosure. Sometimes a parent will be asked to testify about observed behavioral changes in the child during or following the abuse such as fear of separation from the parent, or sleep or appetite changes.

Finally, in some cases parents bring civil lawsuits seeking monetary restitution from institutions or agencies who employed the alleged molester. While these legal actions are often appropriate, a criminal defense attorney may attempt to persuade the jury that the parents colluded with the child to fabricate abuse charges for financial gain. When anticipated, parents should be told in advance of trial of this potential attack on their credibility and encouraged not to allow their anger at this often spurious attack interfere with the truthfulness of their testimony.

Professionals who work with children must understand their legal and ethical duties to their clients. In a criminal trial involving charges of CSA, school counselors, physicians and therapist may be subpoenaed to testify by either the defense or the prosecution. These professionals may also be ordered to bring their records concerning their patient or client to the courtroom for inspection by the judge or the attorneys. Privileges such as physician-patient privilege or therapist-client privilege that limit disclosure of confidential information as well as the contents of certain records may be at odds with a court order to produce the child's records or to testify at trial about something the child said.

Absent a waiver of confidentiality authorized by the child, the child's guardian, or both, the professional is well advised to consult with an attorney before releasing confidential information concerning a child.

CASE ILLUSTRATION

Lisa was a 6-year-old female attending the first grade. She was taught by her teacher, Mrs. R., and a teacher aide F.S. who, had begun employment at the school that fall. F.S. had known Lisa since she was born. He lived down the street from her home and occasionally he would come by to share a beer with her father. About the third week of the school term, Lisa told her mother that she didn't like school and no longer wanted to attend. Although a bit concerned about her daughter's attitude, mother concluded that

Lisa was just having some difficulty adjusting and sent her on her way each morning. As weeks went by, Lisa's distress escalated. She became fearful of going to bed each night and would have nightmares 3 to 5 times per week. Occasionally, she would return from school having wet her pants. She would cry and plead not to be sent to school each morning. Her parents spoke with a friend who was a mental health professional working with children; this person indicated that Lisa had a classic school phobia and that the parent should simply insist that she go to school each morning and her symptoms would abate. Her parents followed this advice, but despite their efforts Lisa continued to be considerably distress each morning.

Finally, one morning Lisa returned from the bus stop trembling. On this occasion, Lisa disclosed to her mother that F.S. had been touching her in her private parts when she went into the school bathroom. Lisa told mother of several episodes of digital penetration and fellatio. When mother asked Lisa why she didn't tell her before, Lisa explained that F.S. told her he would have someone climb in her window at night and kill her if she told.

Mother immediately called the police who came to their home and spoke to her and Lisa. Lisa was given a physical examination at the local hospital. The physical examination was normal and testing for sexually transmitted disease was negative. Mother contacted the community mental health center and scheduled an appointment for Lisa with a therapist.

At the time of evaluation, Lisa appeared as an anxious child, clinging to her mother and not wanting to leave her mother's side. Lisa refused to go into the therapist's office alone. She looked anxiously around the room and appeared hyperalert, scanning the environment as if looking for someone. Mother reported that her daughter was having great difficulty going to bed each night and once asleep was having nightmares almost every night. Lisa had started insisting that both her mother and father check all the windows in the house ensuring that each window was locked and secured before going to bed. Although F.S. was immediately suspended from the school pending investigation and that Lisa was repeatedly assured that F.S. was no longer at the school, Lisa continued to cry and scream every morning about going to school. Lisa's teacher reported that she would avoid going to the bathroom and frequently would wet her pants because of waiting too long to go. The teacher, additionally, reported that she refused to go near any male teachers or teacher's aides and would start trembling whenever she saw a male teacher enter the room. Lisa told the therapist that the police were going to arrest F.S. and that she didn't want to talk about what happened anymore. She refused to discuss the abuse for 5 consecutive sessions. Lisa became withdrawn and refused to go outside to play with her friends. She stopped eating her favorite breakfast food, oatmeal, because it was "yucky" and reminded her of F.S. The therapist concluded that Lisa met full diagnostic criteria for posttraumatic stress disorder. A treatment program of gradual exposure by imagery and play was developed and with the parents' help and encouragement, Lisa started gradually to talk about the abuse. Her anxiety and efforts at avoiding talking about the abusive incidents were striking. She needed considerable support and encouragement from her parents even to go to her therapy sessions. The behavioral treatment for her posttraumatic stress symptoms was coupled with a cognitive, educational intervention targeted to increase Lisa's skills in recognizing potentially abusive situations and developing strategies for getting help from trusted adults. Over the course of 20 sessions, Lisa's symptoms gradually abated and she became able to talk about the abusive incident without undo anxiety.

After thorough investigation, police arrested F.S. for sexual assault of Lisa and one of her 6-year-old classmates who disclosed after questioning by trained, experienced child sex crimes police officers. Charges of sexual assault were approved by the prosecutor and the trial date was set for the spring, several months away.

Weeks before trial, the prosecutor met with Lisa and her parents to explain the court process. At this meeting, the family was shown the courtroom where the trial would take place. Lisa was told about the different jobs of the people in a courtroom, especially the job of a witness to tell the truth. When the prosecutor learned that Lisa was in therapy she contacted the therapist to inquire about how to ease Lisa's anxiety about going to court.

A few days before trial, the therapist received a subpoena from the defense attorney ordering the production of Lisa's therapy records at the trial. The therapist promptly contacted the prosecutor with this information. Following a hearing, the judge ruled pursuant to the law in their state that the privileged relationship between therapist and client precluded the inspection of these confidential records.

On the day of the trial, the prosecutor took her into a courtroom and a judge, after asking Lisa some questions, decided she had sufficient communication skills and understanding of her duty to tell the truth to be found legally competent to testify at trial. Lisa was very anxious about going to court and mother was not at all confident that Lisa would be able to testify, particularly with F.S. in the room. However, Lisa did tell the jury what happened. It helped that she had been in the courtroom before and it was less frightening when the judge allowed her to turn her chair away from F.S. so she didn't have him staring at her when she told her story. Mother was also called as a witness to testify about Lisa's behavioral changes and about her eventual disclosure.

The defense attorney told the jury that the only evidence against his client was the testimony of a 6-year-old child and this should create a reasonable doubt in their minds about guilt and therefore they should acquit F.S. The jury deliberated among themselves for a while before arriving at a unanimous verdict of guilty.

Lisa's therapist attended the sentencing hearing along with the child's parents. Each told the judge about the emotional difficulties Lisa suffered as a result of the abuse. The judge then considered the aggravating and mitigating circumstances of the crime as argued to him by the prosecutor and defense attorney. F.S. was sentenced to 15 years of incarceration in the state penitentiary.

CONCLUSION

Extrafamilial child sexual abuse, according to research, appears to be the most prevalent form of sexual abuse affecting children (Finkelhor et al., 1990). Although there are similarities between extrafamilial abuse and that perpetrated by someone within the family, there are differences which impact on the investigation and assessment process. Professionals involved in the evaluation of children who have been abused by someone outside the family system, need to be sensitive both to the child's needs and the needs of the entire family. Knowledge regarding developmental factors affecting the child's ability to report the abuse and participate in the investigatory process as well as the criminal justice system is essential. Assessment of the child should be conducted with a systematic evaluation of not only the factual information surrounding the specific abusive incident/s, but also of specific symptoms and *DSM-IV,* Axis I psychiatric disorders (American Psychiatric Association, 1994), including posttraumatic stress disorder. Many standardized instruments, while helpful in evaluating symptoms, have not been demonstrated to be sensitive to posttraumatic stress disorder (McLeer, Callaghan, Henry, & Wallen, 1994). Hence, their use should be supplemented with a semistructured clinical interview with specific questions about PTSD. Newer rating scales for PTSD have been developed and provide a systematic assessment of this disorder (Nader et al., 1996). Because the criminal justice systems vary on a state-by-state basis, professionals involved in the assessment of children who have been allegedly abused need to familiarize themselves with the criminal justice system in their own states. Finally, some states have established and others are moving toward the development of integrated systems for coordinating the investigation and management of reported cases of suspected child abuse. Such efforts are to be applauded and encouraged.

REFERENCES

Achenbach, T.M. (1991a). *Manual for the Child Behavior Checklist/4–18 and 1991 Profile.* Burlington: University of Vermont, Department of Psychiatry.

Achenbach, T.M. (1991b). *Manual for the Teacher's Report Form and 1991 Profile.* Burlington: University of Vermont, Department of Psychiatry.

Adams, J.A., Harper, K., Knodson, S., & Revilla, J. (1994). Examination findings in legally confirmed child sexual abuse: It's normal to be normal. *Pediatrics, 94,* 310–317.

Ageton, S.S. (1988). Vulnerability to sexual assault. In A.E. Burgess (Ed.), *Rape and sexual assault: II. Gerland reference library of social sciences* (pp. 221–244). New York: Garland.

American Academy of Child and Adolescent Psychiatry. (1995). Practice parameters for the psychiatric assessment of children and adolescents. *Journal of the American Academy of Child and Adolescent Psychiatry, 31,* 1386–1402.

American Academy of Child and Adolescent Psychiatry. (1997a). Practice parameters for the forensic evaluation of children and adolescent who may have been physically or sexually abused. *Journal of the American Academy of Child and Adolescent Psychiatry, 36,* 423–442.

American Academy of Child and Adolescent Psychiatry. (1997b). Practice parameters for the psychiatric assessment of infants and toddlers (0–36 months). *Journal of the American Academy of Child and Adolescent Psychiatry, 36*(Suppl. 10), 21S–36S.

American Academy of Pediatrics. (1991). Guidelines for the evaluation of sexual abuse of children. *Pediatrics, 87,* 254–260.

American Psychiatric Association. (1994). *Diagnostic and statistical manual* (4th ed.). Washington, DC: Author.

August, R.L., & Forman, B.D. (1989). A comparison of sexually abused and non-sexually abused children's behavioral responses to anatomically correct dolls. *Child Psychiatry and Human Development, 20,* 39–47.

Ageton, S.S. (1988). *Sexual assault among adolescents.* Lexington, MA: Heath.

Belden, L. (1979). *Why women do not report sexual assault.* Portland, OR: Portland Women's Crisis Line.

Benedek, E.P., & Schetky, D.H. (1987a). Problems in validating allegations of sexual abuse: Part 1. Factors affecting perception and recall of events. *Journal of the American Academy of Child and Adolescent Psychiatry, 26,* 912–915.

Benedek, E.P., & Schetky, D.H. (1987b). Problems in validating allegations of sexual abuse: Part 2. Clinical evaluation. *Journal of the American Academy of Child and Adolescent Psychiatry, 26,* 916–921.

Boat, B.W., & Everson, M.D. (1988). Interviewing of young children with anatomical dolls. *Child Welfare, 67,* 337–352.

Britten, H.L., & O'Keefe, M.A. (1991). Use of non-anatomical dolls in the sexual abuse interview. *Child Abuse & Neglect, 15,* 567–573.

Bureau of Justice Statistics. (1984). *Criminal victimization in the United States 1982* (Publication # NCJ-92820). Washington, DC: U.S. Department of Justice.

Ceci, S.J., & Huffman, M.L.C. (1997). How suggestible are preschool children? Cognitive and social factors. *Journal of the American Academy of Child and Adolescent Psychiatry, 36,* 948–958.

Ceci, S.J., Russ, D.F., & Toglia, M.P. (1987). Suggestibility of children's memory: Psycholegal implications. *Journal of Experimental Psychology: General, 116,* 38–49.

Clayton, R.N., Barth, K.L., & Shubin, C.I. (1989). Evaluating child sexual abuse: Observations regarding anogenital injury. *Clinical Pediatrics, 28,* 419–422.

Davis, T.C., Peck, G.Q., & Storment, J.M. (1993). Acquaintance rape and the high school student. *Journal of Adolescent Health, 14,* 220–224.

Deblinger, E., McLeer, S.V., Atkins, M.S., Ralphe, D., & Foa, E. (1989). Post-traumatic stress in sexually abused, physically abused, and non-abused children. *Child Abuse & Neglect, 13,* 403–408.

DeLoache, J.S., Cassidy, D.J., & Brown, A.L. (1985). Precursors of mnemonic strategies in very young children's memory. *Child Development, 56,* 125–137.

Donaldson, M. (1978). *Children's minds.* New York: Norton.

Doneck, H.J., Weston, E.A., Filbert, E.A., Beekhuis, R., & Redlich, H. (1997). A child witness advocacy program: Caretakers' and professionals' views. *Journal of Child Sexual Abuse, 6,* 113–132.

Enos, F.W., & Contrath, T.B. (1986). Forensic evaluation of the sexually abused child. *Pediatrics, 78,* 385–398.

Everson, M.D., & Boat, B.W. (1990). Sexualized doll play among young children: Implications for the use of anatomical dolls in sexual abuse evaluations. *Journal of the American Academy of Child and Adolescent Psychiatry, 29,* 736–742.

Finkel, M.R. (1989). Anogenital trauma in sexually abused children. *Pediatrics, 84,* 317–322.

Finkelhor, D., Hotaling, G., Lewis, I.A., & Smith, C. (1990). Sexual abuse in a national survey of adult men and women: Prevalence characteristics and risk factors. *Child Abuse and Neglect, 14,* 19–28.

Finkelhor, D., & Williams, L.M. (1988). *Nursery crimes: Sexual abuse in day care.* Newbury Park: Sage.

Friedman, W.J. (1982). *The developmental psychology of time.* New York: Academic Press.

Garcia, J., & Koelling, R. (1966). Relationship of cue to consequence in avoidance learning. *Psychonomic Science, 4,* 123–124.

Gellert, G.A., & Durfee, M.J. (1989). HIV infection in child abuse. *New England Journal of Medicine, 321,* 685.

Gidycz, C.A., & Koss, M.P. (1989). The impact of adolescent sexual victimization: Standardized measures of anxiety and depression and behavioral deviancy. *Violence and Victims, 4,* 139–149.

Glaser, D., & Collins, C. (1989). The response of young non-sexually abused children to anatomically correct dolls. *Journal of Child Psychology and Psychiatry and Allied Disciplines, 30,* 547–560.

Glaser, J.B., Hammerschlag, M.R., & McCormak, W.M. (1986). Sexually transmitted diseases in victims of sexual assault. *New England Journal of Medicine, 315,* 625–627.

Gold, P.E. (1987). Sweet memories. *American Scientist, 75,* 151–155.

Goodman, G.S., Golding, J.M., & Haith, M.M. (1984). Juror's reactions to child witnesses. *Journal of Social Issues, 40,* 139–156.

Goodman, G.S., & Michelli, J. (1981). Would you believe a child witness? *Psychology Today, 15,* 82–95.

Goodman, G.S, & Quas, J. (1996). Trauma and memory: Individual differences in children's recounting of stressful experience. In N.L. Stein, C. Brainerd, P.A. Orstein, & B. Twersky (Eds.), *Memory for everyday and emotional events* (pp. 267–294). Mahwah, NJ: Erlbaum.

Goodman, G.S., & Reed, R.S. (1986). Age differences in eyewitness testimony. *Law and Human Behavior, 10,* 317–332.

Goodman, G.S., Rudy, L., Bottoms, B.L., & Aman, C. (1990). Children's concerns and memory: Issues of ecological validity in the study of children's eyewitness testimony. In R. Fivush & J. Hudson (Eds.), *Knowing and remembering in young children.* New York: Cambridge University Press.

Goodman, G.S., & Schwartz-Kenney, B.M. (1992). Why knowing a child's age is not enough: Influences of cognitive, social and emotional factors in children's testimony. In H. Dent & R. Flin (Eds.), *Children as witnesses* (pp. 15–32). New York: Wiley.

Gordon, B.N., & Fullmer, A. (1994). Developmental issues in judging the credibility of children's testimony. *Journal of Clinical Child Psychology, 23,* 283–294.

Graves, H.C.B., Sensabaugh, G.F., & Blake, E.T. (1985). Post-coital detection of a male specific semen protein. Application to the investigation of rape. *New England Journal of Medicine, 312,* 338–343.

Hall, E.R., & Flannery, P.J. (1984). Prevalence and correlates of sexual assault experience in adolescents. *Victimology: An International Journal, 9,* 398–406.

Harter, S. (1985). *Manual for the self-perception profile for children.* Denver: University of Denver.

Ingram, D.L., Everett, D., Lyna, P.R., White, S.T., & Rockwell, L.A. (1992). Epidemiology of adult sexually transmitted disease agent in children being evaluated for sexual abuse. *Pediatric Infectious Disease Journal, 11,* 945–950.

Institute of Medicine. (1989). *Research on children and adolescents with mental, behavioral and developmental disorders.* Washington, DC: National Academy Press.

Jaffe, P.G., Wolf, E.D.A., & Wilson, S.K. (1990). *Children of battered women.* Newbury Park, CA: Sage.

Jampole, L., & Weber, M.K. (1987). An assessment of the behavior of sexually abused and non-sexually abused children with anatomically correct dolls. *Child Abuse & Neglect, 11,* 187–192.

Johnson, M.K., & Foley, M.A. (1984). Differentiating fact from fantasy: The reliability of children's memory. *Journal of Social Issues, 40,* 33–50.

Kanda, M.B. (1989, March 17). *Specimen collection and sperm analysis in the sexually abused child.* Presented at the third annual National Child Abuse Conference, Philadelphia.

Katz, B., & Burt, M.R. (1988). Self-blame in recovery from rape. In A.W. Burgess (Ed.), *Rape and sexual assault: II. Garland reference library of social sciences* (Vol. 261, pp.151–190). New York: Garland.

Katz, S.M., Schonfeld, D.J., Carter, A.S., Leventhal, J.M., & Cicchetti, D.V. (1995). The accuracy of children's reports with anatomically correct dolls. *Journal of Developmental and Behavioral Pediatrics, 16,* 71–76.

Keenan, J.M., MacWhinney, B., & Mayhew, D. (1977). Pragmatics and memory: A study of natural conversation. *Journal of Verbal Learning and Verbal Behavior, 16,* 549–560.

Kelly, S.J. (1989). Stress response of children to sexual abuse and ritualistic abuse in day care centers. *Journal of Interpersonal Violence, 4,* 502–513.

Kendall-Tackett, K.A., Williams, L.M., & Finkelhor, D. (1993). Impact of sexual abuse on children: A review and synthesis of recent empirical studies. *Psychological Bulletin, 113,* 164–180.

Klajmer-Diamond, H., Wehrspann, W.H., & Steinhauer, D.D. (1987). Assessing the creditability of young children's allegations of sexual abuse: Clinical issues. *Canadian Journal of Psychiatry, 32,* 610–614.

Kopper, B.A. (1996). Gender, gender identity, rape myth acceptance and time of initial resistance in the perception of acquaintance rape blame and avoidability. *Sex Roles, 34,* 810–893.

Kovacs, M., & Beck, A.T. (1977). An empirical-clinical approach toward a definition of childhood depression. In J.G. Schulterbrandt & A. Raskin (Eds.), *Depression in childhood: Diagnosis, treatment, and conceptual models* (pp. 1–25). New York: Raven Press.

Kramer, D.G., & Jason, M.J. (1982). Sexually abused children and sexually transmitted diseases. *Review Infectious Diseases, 4* (Suppl.), 883–890.

Krasner, W., Meyer, L.C., & Carroll, N.E. (1976). *Victims of rape* (Stock # 017-024-00683-1). Rockville, MD: National Institute of Mental Health, U.S. Government Printing Office.

Lamb, M.E., Hershkowitz, I., Sternberg, K.J., Boat, B., & Everson, M.D. (1996). Investigative interviews of allege sexual abuse victims with and without anatomical dolls. *Child Abuse & Neglect, 20,* 1251–1259.

Lamb, M.E., Sternberg, K.J., & Esplin, P.W. (1996). Making children into competent witnesses. *Psychology, Public Policy, & Law, 1,* 438–449.

Lamb, S. (1986). Treating sexually abused children: Issues of blame and responsibility. *American Journal of Orthopsychiatry, 56,* 303–307.

Leippe, M.R., & Romanczyk, A. (1987). Children on the witness stand: A communication persuasion analog of juror's reactions to child witnesses. In S.J. Ceci, M.P. Toglia, & D.F. Ross (Eds.), *Children's eyewitness memory* (pp. 155–177). New York: Springer-Verlag.

Leventhal, J.M., Hamilton, J., Rekedal, S., Tebano-Micci, A., & Egston, C. (1989). Anatomically correct dolls in interviewing of young children suspected of having been sexually abused. *Pediatrics, 84,* 900–906.

Linton, M. (1982). Transformation of memory in everyday life. In U. Neisser (Ed.), *Memory. observed: Remembering in natural context* (pp.77–91). San Francisco: Freeman.

MacFarlane, K., Waterman, J., Comerly, S., Domon, L., Durfee, M., & Long, S. (1986). *Sexual abuse of young children.* New York: Guilford Press.

Manion, I.G., McIntyre, J., Firestone, P., Ligezinsky, M., Ensom, R., & Wells, G. (1996). Secondary traumatization in parents following the disclosure of extrafamilial child sexual abuse: Initial effects. *Child Abuse & Neglect, 20,* 1095–1109.

March, J.S., Amaya-Jackson, L., Murray, M.C., & Schulte, A. (1998). Cognitive-behavioral psychotherapy for children and adolescents with posttraumatic stress disorder after a single-incident stressor. *Journal of the American Academy of Child and Adolescent Psychiatry, 37,* 585–593.

Maryland vs. Craig, 110 SCT 3175 (U.S. Supreme Court 1990).

McFarlane, A.C. (1987). Post traumatic phenomena in a longitudinal study of children following a natural disaster. *Journal of the American Academy of Child and Adolescent Psychiatry, 26,*764–769.

McLeer, S.V., Callaghan, M., Henry, D., & Wallen, J. (1994). Psychiatric disorders in sexually abused children. *Journal of the American Academy of Child and Adolescent Psychiatry, 33,* 313–319

McLeer, S.V., Deblinger, E., Atkins, M.S., Foa, E.B., & Ralphe, D.L. (1988). Post-traumatic stress disorder in sexually abused children. *Journal of the American Academy of Child and Adolescent Psychiatry, 27,* 650–654.

McLeer, S.V., Deblinger, E., Henry, D., & Orvaschel, H. (1992). Sexually abused children at high risk for post traumatic stress disorder. *Journal of the American Academy of Child and Adolescent Psychiatry, 31,* 875–879.

McLeer, S.V., Ruggiero, K., & Dixon, F. (1997, October 18). *PTSD: Implications for sexually abused children* [Abstract]. Annual meeting of the American Academy of Child and Adolescent Psychiatry, Toronto, Ontario, Canada.

Merry, S.N., & Andrews, L.K. (1994). Psychiatric status of sexually abused children 12 months after disclosure of abuse. *Journal of the American Academy of Child and Adolescent Psychiatry, 33,* 939–944.

Miller, C.M., Fremorrow, W.J., Aljazireh, L., & Parker, B.K. (1996). Two methods of recall enhancement for child and adult eyewitness testimony. *American Journal of Forensic Psychology, 14,* 67–84.

Mynatt, C.R., & Allgier, E.R. (1990). Risk factors, self-attribution and adjustment problems among victims of sexual coercion. *Journal of Applied Sociology, 20,* 120–153.

Nader, K.O., Kriegler, J.A., Blake, D.D., Pynoos, R.S., Newman, E., & Weather, S. (1996). *Clinician administered PTSD scale: Child and adolescent version (CAPS-C).* White River Junction, VT: National Center for PTSD.

Nader, K.O., Pynoos, R., Fairbanks, L., & Frederick, C. (1990). Children's PTSD reactions one year after a sniper attack on their school. *American Journal of Psychiatry, 147,*1526.

Nelson, K. (1986). *Event knowledge: Structure and function in development.* Hillsdale, NJ: Erlbaum.

Orstein, P.A., Gordon, B.N., & Larus, D.M. (1992). Children's memory for a personally experienced event: Implications for testimony. *Applied Cognitive Psychology, 6,* 49–60.

Orvaschel, H., Weissman, M.M., Padian, N., & Lowe, T. (1981). Assessing psychopathology in children of psychiatrically disturbed parents. *Journal of the American Academy of Child Psychiatry, 20,* 112–122.

Paradise, J.E. (1989). Predictive accuracy in the diagnosis of sexual abuse: A big issue about a little tissue. *Child Abuse & Neglect, 13,* 169–176.

Paradise, J.E. (1990). The medical evaluation of the sexually abused child. *Pediatric Clinics of North America, 37,* 839–862.

Parrot, A. (1989). Acquaintance rape amongst adolescents: Identifying risk groups and intervention strategies. In P. Allen-Meares & C.H. Shapiro (Eds.), *Adolescent sexuality: New challenges for social work* (pp. 47–61). New York: Haworth Press.

Pitman, R.K., Orr, S., & Shalev, A. (1993). Once bitten, twice shy: Beyond the conditioning model of PTSD. *Biological Psychiatry, 33,* 145–146.

Pullyblank, J., Bisanz, J., Scott, C., & Champion, M.A. (1985). Developmental invariance in the effects of functional self-knowledge or memory. *Child Development, 56,* 1447–1454.

Pynoos, R.S., & Eth, S. (1986). Witness to violence: The child interview. *Journal of the American Academy of Child Psychiatry, 25,* 306–319.

Pynoos, R.S., Frederick, C., Nader, K., Arroyo, W., Steinberg, A., Eth, S., Nunez, F., & Fairbanks, L. (1987). Life threat and post traumatic stress in school-aged children. *Archives of General Psychiatry, 44,* 1057–1063.

Pynoos, R.S., & Nader, K. (1989). Children's memory and proximity to violence. *Journal of the American Academy of Child and Adolescent Psychiatry, 28,* 236–241.

Regehr, C. (1990). Parental response to extrafamilial child sexual assault. *Child Abuse and Neglect, 14,* 113–120.

Reichard, R.D. (1993). Dysfunctional families in dysfunctional systems? Why child advocacy centers may not be enough. *Journal of Child Sexual Abuse, 2,* 103–109.

Reynolds, C.R., & Richmond, B.O. (1978). What I think and feel: A revised measure of children's manifest anxiety. *Journal of Abnormal Child Psychology, 6,* 271–280.

Ricci, L.R. (1988). Medical forensic photography of the sexually abused child. *Child Abuse & Neglect, 12,* 305–310.

Rogers, T.B., Kuiper, N.A., & Kirker, W.S. (1977). Self-reference and the encoding of personal information. *Journal of Personality and Social Psychology, 35,* 677–688.

Ross, D.F., Miller, B.S., & Moran, P.B. (1987). The child in the eyes of the jury: Assessing mock juror's perceptions of child witnesses. In S.J. Ceci, M.P. Toglia, & D.F. Ross (Eds.), *Children's eyewitness memory* (pp.142–154). New York: Springer-Verlag.

Russell, D.E.H. (1984). *Sexual exploitation: Rape, child sexual abuse, and work place harassment.* Newbury Park, CA: Sage.

Samra, J., & Yuille, J.C. (1996). Anatomically-sexual dolls: Their effects on the memory and suggestibility of 4- to 6-year-old eyewitnesses. *Child Abuse & Neglect, 20,* 1261–1272.

Sauzier, M. (1989). Disclosures of child sexual abuse: For better or worse. *Psychiatric Clinics of North America, 12,* 455–469.

Saywitz, K.J., Geiselman, R.S., & Bornstein, G.K. (1992). Effects of cognitive interviewing and practice on children's recall performance. *Journal of Applied Psychology, 77,* 744–756.

Schwartz-Kenney, B.M., Wilson, M.E., & Goodman, G.S. (1990). An examination of child witness accuracy. In K. Oates (Ed.), *Understanding and managing child sexual abuse* (pp. 293–311). Philadelphia: Saunders.

Sedlak, A.J., & Broadhurst, D.D. (1996). *Third national incidence study of child abuse and neglect–Final report* (p. 6). Washington, DC: National Center on Child Abuse and Neglect.

Sgroi, S.M. (1982). *Handbook of clinical intervention and child sexual abuse.* Lexington, MA: Lexington Books.

Simkins, L., & Renier, A. (1996). An analytic review of the empirical literature of children's play with anatomically detailed dolls. *Journal of Child Sexual Abuse, 5,* 21–45.

Siven, A.B., Shor, D.P., Koeppl, G.K., & Noble, L.D. (1988). Interaction of normal children with anatomically correct dolls. *Child Abuse & Neglect, 12,* 295–304.

Spielberger, C.D. (1973). *Preliminary manual for the state-trait anxiety inventory for children.* Palo Alto, CA: Consulting Psychologists.

Stormo, K.J., Lang, A.R., & Stritake, W.G.K. (1997). Attributions about acquaintance rape and the role of alcohol and individual differences. *Journal of Applied Social Psychology, 27,* 279–305.

Sullivan, R., Barth, R.P., Bhatt, B., & Gilbert, N. (1987). *Coordinating interagency responses to child sexual abuse.* Berkley: School of Social Welfare, University of California.

Terr, L. (1988). What happens to early memories of trauma? A study of 20 children under age at the time of documented traumatic event. *Journal of the American Academy of Child and Adolescent Psychiatry, 27,* 96–104.

Terr, L. (1990). *Too scared to cry: Psychic trauma in childhood.* New York: Harper & Row.

Tobey, A.E., & Goodman, G.S. (1992). Children's eyewitness memory: Effects of participation and forensic context, *Child Abuse & Neglect, 16,* 779–796.

van der Kolk, B.A., & van der Hart, O. (1991). The intrusive past: The flexibility of memory and the engraving of trauma. *American Imago, 48,* 425–454.

van Scoyk, S., Gray, J., & James, D.P.H. (1988). A theoretical framework for evaluation and treatment of the victims of child sexual assault by a non-family member. *Family Process, 27,* 105–113.

Vicary, J.R., Klingaman, L.R., & Harkness, W.L. (1995). Risk factors associated with date rape and sexual assault of adolescent girls. *Journal of Adolescence, 18,* 289–306.

Warshaw, C. (1988). *I never called it rape: The U.S. report on recognizing, fighting and surviving date and acquaintance rape.* New York: Harper & Row.

Westman, J.C. (1996). The child advocacy team in child abuse and neglect matters. *Child Psychiatry and Human Development, 26,* 221–234.

Wolfe, V.V., & Gentile, C. (1992). Psychological assessment of sexually abused children. In W.T. Obonabue & J.R. Geer (Eds.), *The sexual abuse of children: Theory, research & therapy* (pp.143–187). New York: Erlbaum.

Wolfe, V.V., Gentile, C., & Wolfe, D.A. (1989). The impact of sex abuse on children: A PTSD formulation. *Behavior Therapy, 20,* 215–228.

Wyatt, G.E., & Mickey, M.R. (1988). The support by parents and others as it mediates the effects of child sexual abuse. In G.E. Wyatt & G.J. Powell (Eds.), *Lasting effects of child sexual abuse* (pp. 211–226). Newbury Park, CA: Sage.

Yehuda, R., Southwick, S.M., Perry, B.D., Mason, J.W., & Giller, E.L. (1990). Interactions of the hypothalamic-pituitary-adrenal axis and the catecholaminergic symptom in post traumatic stress disorder. In E.L. Giller (Ed.), *Biological assessment and treatment of PTSD* (pp. 117–134). Washington, DC: American Psychiatric Press.

CHAPTER 12

Woman Battering

DANIEL G. SAUNDERS

THE ASSESSMENT of domestic abuse presents many challenges to the practitioner. Abuse takes a wide variety of forms and both the victim and offender are often reluctant to share information. Offenders typically try to minimize the extent of abuse out of shame and fear of punishment. Victims, who are sometimes blamed for their victimization, also may feel shame. They may be reluctant to talk about the abuse because they fear retaliation, have a sense of loyalty to the abuser, or want to avoid painful memories.

Assessment in this area is challenging for other reasons as well. There are complex legal issues with which the practitioner must be familiar, such as providing information for child custody decisions or determining when signs of dangerousness require warning a potential victim. Most assessment tools in the family violence field are not well developed. Some commonly used measures of family violence have been criticized for their inadequacies.

This chapter describes multiple methods for assessing the presence of domestic violence as well as its risk factors and aftereffects. The application of these assessment methods to legal cases is described, followed by a case example to illustrate the evaluation of an actual court case. The chapter focuses primarily on physical abuse.

DESCRIPTION OF THE PROBLEM

The view of the family as "a haven in a heartless world" has been tempered in recent years by the knowledge that all too often it is a place of great cruelty. Domestic violence affects over two million marriages in the United States every year and a comparably high rate of dating and cohabiting couples (Levy, 1991; Plichta, 1996; Straus & Gelles, 1990). Violence frequently continues after separation (Tjaden & Thoennes, 1998). The violence can range from a few slaps to threats with lethal weapons. Its frequency can range from a single occurrence to weekly. Even minor violence must be the focus of concern because it sometimes escalates to severe violence, and in itself can change the power dynamics of the relationship.

The primary focus of intervention has been to aid battered women. This focus is consistent with evidence that the violence is more traumatic physically and psychologically for women (e.g., Stets & Straus, 1990). There is less consensus on the extent to which women's violence is in self-defense, although it is clear that when women kill they are much more likely to do so in self-defense (Saunders & Browne, in press). However, the extent of the problem of husband abuse continues to be debated (McNeely & Robinson-Simpson, 1987; Saunders, 1988b). This chapter focuses on woman abuse because existing evidence shows that they are more likely to be victimized (Saunders, 1989).

Physical abuse usually occurs with sexual and psychological abuse, and these latter forms of abuse usually have the most damaging emotional effects (e.g., O'Leary, in press). Among the common sequelae are depression and posttraumatic stress (e.g., J. Campbell & Lewandowski, 1997). There is increasing awareness of the need to measure sexual and psychological abuse and their emotional aftermath.

Until recently, woman abuse was not viewed as a serious problem. The criminal justice system and helpers in general took a "hands off approach," believing that abuse was part of nonserious "family squabbles." Sexist attitudes, such as "a man's home is his castle," further kept the problem hidden behind closed doors. These trends are being reversed today and, increasingly, domestic violence is regarded as a serious crime. In some ways, it is more serious than other assaults because of the emotional ties between victim and offender and the high rate of recidivism, averaging more than three incidents per year (Straus, Gelles, & Steinmetz, 1980).

Clinical lore 20 years ago presented similar profiles of the offender and victim. They were both said to be from violent homes, to be isolated, deficient in communication skills, and have low self-esteem. More recent reviews of empirical studies make it clear, however, that it is the offender who differs the most from the norm. For example, Hotaling and Sugarman (1986) reviewed many studies of husband-to-wife violence. Out of 15 risk factors, the men had 9 including nonassertiveness, problems abusing alcohol, and a propensity to abuse their children. The women, on the other hand, had only one risk factor.

Despite the existence of general risk factors, there is no single profile of abusers. They can be men who are aggressive and domineering in all situations or only at home (e.g., Holtzworth-Munroe & Stuart, 1994). The family-only aggressor may be meek and nonassertive much of the time. He tends to "stuff" his feelings until he erupts. He is likely to be a "model citizen" and the extent of his violence is easily overlooked. The generally aggressive type may be very adept at convincing himself and others that his partner is to blame for his violence. He is the most likely to have been severely abused in childhood and to abuse drugs and alcohol in adulthood. A third type is emotionally volatile, with borderline and dependent personality traits. He is most likely to seek help voluntarily and to have a history of suicide attempts. Each type of offender presents unique challenges to clinical assessors.

ASSESSMENT APPROACHES

Assessment methods can be used for several purposes. The goal might be restricted to answering a single question posed by a court, or it might involve trying to determine the dangerousness of a client, his level of motivation for treatment, or his appropriateness for treatment (Sonkin, 1987). Assessment can also be used to judge the extent of trauma to the victim. Finally, it can be used to evaluate the effectiveness of intervention programs. Assessment that becomes part of research evaluation is discussed in more depth elsewhere (Gefner, Rosenbaum, & Hughes, 1988; Saunders, 1988a, 1993). Whatever the purpose of the assessment, the practitioner should be aware of his or her own norms and values that may influence the outcome of the assessment (Porter, 1986). Simply holding onto the myth that the family is universally a place of peace and security can prevent practitioners from asking directly about the occurrence of violence in the home. Theoretical orientations can also influence the extent of assessment: little information about violence will be gathered if it is seen as a symptom of a faulty relationship. For example, Harway and Hansen (1993) found that cues about lethal violence in a case description were less likely to be recognized among therapists ascribing to communication theory.

VIOLENT BEHAVIOR

What to Measure

Clinicians have taken the lead of sociologists in asking about a large number of abusive acts. The more questions asked, the greater chance that abuse will be uncovered. This has been found to be true in studies of sexual abuse and is likely to be the case with domestic abuse as well (Peters, Wyatt, & Finkelhor, 1986; Straus, 1990). Naturally, the approach taken by the clinician will also affect the rate of detection. Clinicians have taken the lead of sociologists here also (Brekke, 1987). Rather than asking bluntly "Do you beat your wife?" questioning begins with nonabusive ways the couple relates and progresses to minor and then severe forms of violence. This "funneling" procedure was used by Straus and his associates in their national surveys of family violence (Straus & Gelles, 1990). Their measure, the Conflict Tactics Scales (CTS), normalizes the violent events by placing them within the context of everyday conflict. Much violence, however, is not associated with family conflict. The clinician can normalize the abuse with prefacing remarks about how commonly physical force is used in intimate relationships. For both married and dating couples, factor analysis generally reveals that the CTS has four factors: reasoning, verbal aggression/coercion, physical aggression/threat, and severe aggression (Caulfield & Riggs, 1992).

Many intervention programs have modified the Conflict Tactics Scales for use in assessment (e.g., Saunders, 1995). As in research projects using the CTS, it can be administered over the phone (with the safeguard that the partner is not present), in person, or by self-administration. Most programs have added items to cover sexual abuse and additional forms of physical and psychological abuse that were not in the original CTS. For example, practitioners have discovered that the car can be used as a weapon, and also that many men use nonviolent threats to control their partners (e.g., "I'll take away the kids if you leave me"). Sexual abuse, not part of the original CTS, has also been added. It is usually the most difficult form of abuse for offenders and victims to reveal, and may need to be asked about more than once over the course of treatment. Using neutral language like "forcing you to do something sexual" is more likely to uncover this abuse than using the word "rape." A modified version of the Conflict Tactics Scales, that we call the Woman Abuse Scale, is published elsewhere (Saunders, 1995).

A revised Conflict Tactics Scales (CTS2) was recently constructed (Straus, Hamby, Boney-McCoy, & Sugarman, 1996). It includes two new scales: seven items on sexual coercion, and six on injury; construct validity of these new scales is also provided. In addition, each of the original three scales—reasoning, verbal abuse, and physical abuse—have been changed or augmented. Some items were clarified, for example, "threw something at him/her" was changed to "threw something at my partner that could hurt." The CTS2 contains 39 items compared with 19 in the original CTS. The ordering of the items was also changed. Rather than starting with nonviolent items and then proceeding to violence items of increasing severity, the CTS2 has interspersed the order of minor and severe items. This method may reduce demand characteristics and seems to require respondents to think more about each item. There are now norms available for college students (Straus et al., 1996) and the wording of the instructions and items allow the measure to be used with dating couples.

The Woman Abuse Scale, CTS2, or similar measure can be used to educate clients about behaviors that are considered violent or abusive. Clinicians typically begin by asking clients about the most recent episode of violence. Asking for detailed information about the first and worst episodes in the relationship helps to broaden the picture. It is also important to ask about trends: whether the severity and frequency of violence are increasing or decreasing (e.g., see Campbell's Danger Assessment Instrument, J. Campbell, 1995; and the Appendix in Sonkin, Martin, & Walker, 1985). One of the most complete pictures of the abusive pattern may be obtained by asking about the frequency of each act of abuse within a particular time frame. This more thorough evaluation may be necessary for courtroom applications or program evaluation. The national studies using the original Conflict Tactics Scales asked about frequencies for the past year (Straus & Gelles, 1990). Some outcome studies attempt to obtain a retrospective baseline up to 2 years prior to treatment. There have been no methodological studies to inform us about possible recall distortions for these time periods. The National Crime Survey, focusing primarily on stranger crime, uses a 6-month time frame. The revised CTS (the CTS2) has the same frequency categories as the original, but the authors note that other time periods can be used, for example, since the start of the relationship, since a previous stage of treatment, the previous month, or previous 6 months (Straus et al., 1996). The wording of the CTS2 was simplified to more easily obtain reports on self and partner and violence over the past year or ever in the relationship. Some intervention programs use fairly subjective response categories for the frequency of abuse, for example "sometimes" or "a lot." The original categories of the CTS seem preferable because they give actual frequencies or a range of frequencies (e.g., "twice" or "6–11" times in the past year).

Offender versus Victim Reports

When both offender and victim reports are available, the question is raised about whose should be relied on. In a pilot study for the development of the CTS, Bulcroft and Straus (1975) found a higher level of agreement about the occurrence of violence than for variables like power when comparing the reports of husbands, wives, and children. Because the national studies did not have reports from both partners, it took a series of other studies to show that offenders usually underreport the extent of their violence compared with victims (Browning & Dutton, 1986; Edleson & Brygger, 1986; Jouriles & O'Leary, 1985; Szinovacz, 1983). This is the case even though the correlation between victim and offender reports is strong (e.g., Cascardi, Langhinrichsen, & Vivian, 1992). Browning and Dutton (1986), for example, compared men's and women's reports among men in treatment for wife assault. The men tended to view both of them as violent, while the women viewed the men as the primary aggressor. Szinovacz (1983) also found that husbands tend to underreport the extent of their violence; wives, on the other hand, were somewhat more likely to report their use of violence. There is some evidence that after treatment, the level of agreement between partners improves (Edleson & Brygger, 1986). In a small percentage of cases, police records may indicate violence that neither partner reports (Saunders, 1997). The men and women may both deny any violence, or the man may abuse a new partner who has not yet been interviewed.

METHODS OF DATA COLLECTION

The importance of systematic and detailed questioning about violence is highlighted in a study that compared different methods (O'Leary, Vivian, & Malone, 1992). Only 6% of wives wrote that physical aggression was a problem on a marital clinic intake form asking about the most important marital problems. However, when questioned directly in an interview, 44% reported physical aggression as a problem, and 53% were classified as abused from their responses to the CTS. In a study of 30 battered women, questionnaire and interview responses on frequency were highly correlated but ratings of severity tended to be higher on the questionnaire (Rhodes, 1992). The first national study of family violence used in-person interviews and the second national study used telephone interviews. Straus (Straus & Gelles, 1990) provides evidence that the techniques are comparable. A study in a clinical setting found a high degree of consistency between telephone and written administrations of the CTS (E. Lawrence, Heyman, & O'Leary, 1995). M. Smith (1989) points out the advantages of telephone interviewing. Programs conducting follow-up assessments with battered women or collecting data for program evaluation can probably rely on telephone interviews in place of in-person interviews, providing that steps are taken for the survivor's safety (Gondolf, 1998; Parker & Ulrich, 1990). M. Smith (1994) found that many women who did not disclose abuse to close-ended questions did disclose to this open-ended question after the CTS: "We realize that this topic is very sensitive and that many women are reluctant to talk about their own experiences. But we're also a bit worried that we haven't asked the right questions. So now that you have had a chance to think about the topic, can you tell me anything (anything more) from your own experience that may help us understand this problem?" (p. 119).

INTERVIEWING METHODS

If interviews are chosen for data collection, researchers and clinicians have developed some impressions about useful ways to interview battered women and their partners. In Walker's (1984) research, lengthy interviews were conducted with over 400 battered women. Her interviewers were impressed with the women's apparent ability to recall abusive events over a long period of time. They attributed the accurate recall to the heightened emotional content of the abusive events. The major impediment seemed to be the tendency of many women to try to please the interviewer. For example, they might not report that the interview process became tiring. Walker concluded that "a matter-of-fact attitude on the part of the interviewer that these sorts of things could happen, accompanied with compassion for the woman's pain, was most helpful in eliciting accurate data" (Walker, 1984, p. 231).

Washburn and Frieze (1980) likewise warn that too much sympathy or shock upon hearing about the violence can place the woman in a victim role. Revulsion about the violence directed toward the woman also seemed to inhibit the women from reporting their violence toward their children and partners. The most effective interviewers seemed to be those who could tolerate different lifestyles and values. The authors believe that the "best interviewers are relatively apolitical but they are sensitive and empathetic towards women in general" (p. 18).

M. Dutton (1992) recommends that a combination of an open-ended interview, structured or scenario method, and questionnaires be used to obtain an understanding of the nature and pattern of abuse. She emphasizes active listening and empathic responding. The therapeutic effect for a battered woman in telling her story to a non-judgmental listener can be very powerful. Information from the open-ended interview needs to be compared with information from more structured methods. The scenario method involves women recounting one or more episodes in great detail, as in a movie script. Dutton also recommends gathering information on violence directed at pets and property. The Abusive Behavior Observation Checklist (in an appendix on her book) includes many psychologically controlling behaviors. She also provides cautions about the assessment process, including the importance of titrating the emotional impact of recalling abusive episodes. It is not necessary for women to recall all the episodes.

Not surprisingly, it is more difficult to obtain a history of relationship violence from the men. This is especially true of those who are court-ordered. However, some rapport can be developed even with these men (Murphy & Baxter, 1997). Empathy can be shown toward their anger and sense of powerlessness about being mandated to treatment. In fact, empathy can be shown in particular for the men's fear and hurt and at the same time a strong message can be given that rejects the violence. In essence, the message is: "You are not being judged as a person, I am here to help you change one of your many behaviors." This combination of empathy and confrontation may need to be repeated as the entire history of violence is obtained. Here is excerpt from an assessment session to illustrate the method (from Saunders, 1982, p. 20):

MAN: "I wouldn't have done it if she'd kept her mouth shut."
THERAPIST: "Were you hurt and angry that she brought up your job?" (empathy)
MAN: "You bet!"
THERAPIST: "It's OK to have those feelings (empathy) but it's not OK to hit her" (confront).
MAN: "Well she knows what hurts me and I warned her."
THERAPIST: "You probably both know the weak spots of your partner (empathy), yet you can learn not to let her get to you" (confront).
MAN: "I suppose. I never thought hitting was right."

It often helps to ask about relationship violence after obtaining a history of the men's childhood traumas. The clinician and man can then see that there may still exist a "hurt little child" inside the man that is worthy of understanding and support. The majority of battering men observed their mothers being hit or were severely abused themselves as children (Straus et al., 1980).

Choosing among Measures of Violence

The Conflict Tactics Scales (CTS; Straus & Gelles, 1990; Straus et al., 1996) are the most widely used measures of marital and other forms of family violence, but they are not the only ones. Some of these other measures will be described after outlining the strengths and weaknesses of the CTS.

If the instructions for the original CTS are used, then violence not arising from conflict at home may not be uncovered, because respondents are asked about "ways of trying to settle their differences" in the midst of a "dispute" (Straus et al., 1980, p. 256). Modification of the instructions, however, can be accomplished simply. The Revised Conflict Tactics Scales has an introduction that is broadly worded: "No matter how well a couple gets along there are times when they disagree, get annoyed with the other person, want different things from each other, or just have spats or fights because they are in a bad mood, are tired, or for some other reason" (p. 310). It is also a simple matter to add new items and, as noted earlier, the original CTS has been greatly expanded to include new items of physical, sexual, and psychological abuse. In our treatment program, it proved useful to add the item "Drove recklessly to frighten you," since it is reported quite often. This is in contrast to the item "Burned you," which rarely occurs.

Other limitations of the CTS can be handled similarly, by using it with other measures. For example, the sequence of events, including violence by each partner (if it occurred), could be obtained for the first, worst, and last episode. Items measuring self-defense and initiation of the violence can also be used, as they were in a study showing that help-seeking battered women usually use violence in self-defense (Saunders, 1986).

There have been few attempts to measure the injurious outcomes of violence. Straus (1990) makes the point that whether someone is injured may depend entirely on the accuracy of the assailant's aim or on other such circumstances. Thus, it is actually better to measure violence and injuries separately, because a measure of injuries would greatly underestimate the level of violence (Straus et al., 1996). A few attempts have been made to measure injuries (e.g., Berk, Berk, Loseke, & Rauma, 1983; Rhodes, 1992; Saunders, 1980). More work is needed to validate such measures. The measure used in the latest national study (Straus & Gelles, 1990) is confounded with help-seeking since it asks if the injuries were severe enough to require medical attention. Many battered women do not seek medical help out of shame or fear of retaliation (Dobash & Dobash, 1979). Important questions to ask about injuries include those about head injuries (with or without unconsciousness) and injuries during pregnancy.

The Revised Conflict Tactics Scales contain a separate five-item injury scale. It has an item: "went to doctor for injury," but also one that says: "needed to see a doctor but didn't." In addition, it asks about cuts or bleeding, pain the next day, sprains or bruises, and bleeding in private parts. The injury scale correlated very highly with the physical assault and sexual coercion scales of the CTS2 for men and only slightly for women.

In 1990, Straus (Straus & Gelles, 1990) summarized his responses to the criticisms of the CTS. He also presented new evidence of its reliability and validity. The Revised Conflict Tactics Scales were published in 1996, along with evidence of internal reliability and construct validity. The major drawback in the use of the CTS occurs when conclusions are made about men's and women's violence without taking into account the sequence, motives, and outcomes of the violence (e.g., DeKeseredy, Saunders, Schwartz, & Alvi, 1997). Straus (1990) notes that the distinction he makes between "minor" and "severe" violence has not been tested empirically. Because of the size and strength differences between men and women, the distinctions may underestimate male "minor" violence and overestimate female "severe" violence. What is needed is a way to weight each CTS item for the size and gender of each partner.

In addition to its use as a measure of marital violence, the CTS has also been used to measure violence between other family members. Some or all of the items can be used to detect violence from a client to his or her children and from children to the client. The items can also be used to uncover the client's abuse in the family of origin—abuse between parents or directed by parents or siblings toward the client.

A number of other measures have been developed to measure marital violence. Rhodes (1992) attempted to expand the number of abusive behaviors and injuries measured. Among the abusive behaviors were pulled or dragged, shook, ripped clothing, pulled hair, threw hard object, smothered; among the injuries recorded were vision or hearing loss, and miscarriage. Unfortunately, her sample was small ($n = 30$) and validity information is not provided.

Hudson and McIntosh (1981) factor analyzed a large number of items pertaining to abusive behavior to create the Index of Spouse Abuse. Although they labeled one of the two factors "Physical Abuse," only 4 of its 11 items actually measure physical abuse. It appears to measure "angry" psychological abuse, while the other factor appears to measure nonangry psychological abuse. The two subscales differentiated abused women from nonabused women and correlated in expected directions with measures of depression and fear. The alpha coefficients of the scales were over .90. Attala, Hudson, and McSweeney (1994) revised the Index into two short-form Partner Abuse Scales and clearly separated the physical and nonphysical abuse items. These new scales showed high internal reliability and evidence of discriminant validity in conjunction with measures of stress and general contentment.

A measure developed by Lewis (1983) has a weakness similar to that of the original Index of Spouse Abuse as a measure of physical aggression. Only 2 items on her 31-item Wife Abuse Inventory measure physical abuse. Two items measure power differences in the relationship and several measure psychological abuse. The majority of items reflect the couple's quality of communication, existence of sexual problems, and ability to resolve conflict. Nonabusive characteristics of the husband, such as job satisfaction, are also included. Thus, it seems to measure the causes and consequences of abuse more than actual abuse. The scale differentiated abused and nonabused women and was highly reliable, but its validity as a measure of wife abuse is very questionable. A subsequent factor analysis (Poteat, Gorssnickle, Cope, & Wynne, 1990) revealed six factors: emotional respect, abusiveness, economic stress, instability, sexual adequacy, and emotional flexibility. Five of the six items on the "abusiveness" factor correlated with reports of physical abuse as reflected by Pearson's r's of .30 or greater. All seven of the "emotional respect" items correlated with reports of emotional abuse at .30 or greater. The other three factors were not strongly correlated with abuse. The total score of the Inventory was more highly correlated with emotional abuse ($r = .57$) than with physical abuse ($r = .42$).

Stacey and Shupe (1983) constructed a questionnaire to help victims gauge the degree of violence in their relationship. Items include psychological abuse, such as forcing isolation, being critical and making threats, and several items on physical abuse. No evidence is provided of its reliability or validity. Their interpretation of the scale's scores has no empirical basis and their advice to victims could be extremely misleading and possibly dangerous. For example, they claim that a score below 15 represents strains that "are not unusual in modern homes, and she and the man deal with them nonviolently" (p. 126). Those with the highest scores are told that the violence will not "take care of itself" and that "over time the chances are good that the woman's life will literally be in jeopardy more than once" (p. 127). Because the scale is not validated with a criterion of dangerousness, such interpretations could cause victims to make decisions that are not at all warranted.

Rodenburg and Fantuzzo (1993) developed the Measure of Wife Abuse, containing 60 items and dividing into four scales: physical, sexual, psychological, and verbal abuse. It asks for an absolute frequency of each behavior over the past 6 months. It is designed for survivors of abuse to answer each question beginning with "Your partner . . ." After each behavior, respondents are asked how often they were "hurt or upset" by the behavior (never, rarely, sometimes, often). All internal reliability coefficients were .80 or more except for the sexual abuse scale. The physical aggression scale correlated .63 with the violence scale of the CTS and the verbal aggression scale correlated .38 with the verbal aggression scale of the CTS.

Shepard and Campbell (1992) constructed a 30-item measure that drew heavily from a program for men who batter that focused on their controlling tactics (Pence & Paymar, 1985). Twenty items reflected various types of psychological abuse: emotional, isolation, intimidation, threats, use of male privilege, and economic. Ten other items reflected physical assault including forced sexual activity. A 1–5 rating scale was used, from "no abuse" to "very frequent." The internal reliability coefficients ranged from .70 to .92 depending on the scale (physical vs. psychological) and type of sample (men vs. women; abused and nonabused). The authors present some evidence of convergent and divergent validity. Following a factor analysis, items reflecting threats and violence toward objects were shifted from the psychological abuse scale to the physical abuse scale.

A problem with the tests for criterion validity used in some of the preceding measurement development studies is that comparing battered and nonbattered women on a scale of violence does not actually provide evidence that violence is being measured. Hamby, Poindexter, and Gray-Little (1996) point out that many measures, such as depression, can discriminate between battered and nonbattered women, yet they do not measure violence.

Several attempts have been made to develop severity-weighted measures of violence. Walker (1984) asked 20 shelter staff and research interviewers to rate 16 aggressive acts (about half were similar to CTS items). Ratings were made on a scale from 0 to 100 with 100 meaning the act was "extremely severe." Deschner (1986) asked students to rate the severity of many CTS items. She also used a 100-point scale, with 100 meaning that the partner was killed. Both studies revealed a generally linear increase in severity from "slap, hit, spank" to the use of a knife or gun. There was little variation in severity ratings, with most over 75. Walker suggests that a scale of overall battering severity be developed that is a multiplicative function of duration, frequency, and average severity of acts and injuries. Marshall (1992), in the development of the Severity of Violence Against Women Scales, asked student and community groups to assess the physical and emotional harm of threats and violence toward women. A strength of her scale is its many items of threatened and sexual violence. Her respondents indicated that these behaviors produce severe emotional harm.

Saunders (1989) found that severity ratings differed greatly by gender of the victim. Seven professionals working with victims and offenders rated the probability of severe injuries resulting from acts listed on the CTS. There was about a 40% or greater probability of severe injuries for all acts of violence (even the so-called minor violence) when the man was the aggressor. When the woman was the aggressor, the same likelihood of injury occurred only when a weapon was used.

Very little work has been conducted on developing or adapting measures for diverse cultural groups. A few examples will be given. An oversampling of Hispanic respondents (800 out of about 2,000) was done in a recent national survey on the link between alcohol and family violence (Kaufman, Jasinski, & Aldarondo, 1994). The CTS and other measures were translated into Spanish and then "back translated" into English. The questions were reviewed and pretested with several Hispanic groups in order to reach a consensus of understanding. Respondents had the choice of being interviewed in English or Spanish.

The Index of Spouse Abuse, described earlier, was used with a sample of 504 poor African American women (D. Campbell, Campbell, King, Parker, & Ryan, 1994). A factor analysis revealed three factors rather than two. The new factor focused on isolation, jealousy, sexual abuse, and threats to masculinity. The authors speculate that these issues may be more salient for African American men, who may have more difficulty fulfilling a provider role due to discrimination. Thus, different cultural groups may attach different meanings to items or have such different experiences that the original scales do not fit.

An example of the need to add behaviors not conventionally considered abusive comes from a survey of Japanese women (Yoshihama & Sorenson, 1994). Items such as "overturned a dining room table with food on it," "refused to cooperate with contraceptive use," and throwing water, have special cultural significance that add to their abusiveness.

OFFENDER CHARACTERISTICS

Characteristics of offenders other than their violence are usually of interest for predicting dangerousness, assessing appropriateness and motivation for treatment, and providing a pretest for changes on intervening variables expected from treatment. The most widely used approaches are in-person interviews and self-administered instruments and questionnaires. Observations of the couple's interaction, behavioral role plays, and physiological measures are other possible sources of information.

Predicting Dangerousness

Practitioners have been increasingly concerned about predicting the dangerousness of their clients following a number of lawsuits against therapists for not properly warning homicide victims of the danger they were in (Sonkin & Ellison, 1986). Practitioners are also concerned about the long waiting lists for batterers programs, meaning that the more dangerous men on these lists are not receiving immediate treatment or close monitoring. However, attempts to predict dangerousness in the past have led to disappointing results, with many people falsely identified as dangerous (Gottfredson & Gottfredson, 1988). The more serious the event is the more rare it is, and thus the more difficult it is to predict. Homicide is a good example of such an event. Yet mental health and criminal justice personnel must try to make use of our growing knowledge, as inexact as it is (Monahan, 1996).

Several studies of types of men who batter provide some clues to identify the most severely violent offenders (Gondolf, 1988; Holtzworth-Munroe & Stuart, 1994; Saunders, 1995). These men appear to have been the most severely physically abused in childhood, abuse alcohol and other drugs, and are violent outside as well as inside the home. They report only moderate levels of anger and have antisocial personality traits. Although these men are the most severely violent during the relationship, another type, with borderline traits and an emotionally traumatic childhood, may be at higher risk for homicide. This latter type has a higher fear of abandonment and may stalk and harass their partners after separation (Saunders & Browne, in press).

No large scale studies have been conducted of factors associated with domestic homicide by men. A study using the MMPI found that the profile of men who killed their wives was very similar to that of men who killed strangers (Kalichman, 1988). The Psychopathic Deviate scale was the most elevated in both groups. Those who killed strangers were somewhat higher on impulsivity and psychopathic traits. In another study of men who killed their partners, one group had normal MMPI profiles but an impaired ability to metabolize glucose. Most in this group abused alcohol (Virkkunen & Kallio, 1987). Generally speaking, measures of psychopathology are not very good predictors of violence (Monahan, 1981). Past violent behavior and environmental factors are stronger predictors.

Browne's (1987) study of battered women who killed gives indicators of men at risk to kill because these women were defending their lives. She found the following variables to be higher among the homicide cases: severity of injuries to the woman, frequency of the man's physical and sexual assaults, his frequency of intoxication and drug use, his threats to kill, and the woman's suicide attempts or threats. J. Campbell (1995) used a similar list of factors to assess danger levels for battered women. She added to the list the presence of weapons, total control by the man, and low income. Campbell's Danger Assessment Index has some evidence of validity but needs further psychometric work. Several other measures for predicting danger are being developed. There is some evidence that survivors' intuitions about danger are as accurate as a checklist of other factors (Weisz, Tolman, & Saunders, 1997).

Assessing Motivation for Change

Practitioners are often interested in identifying how strongly offenders are motivated to stop their aggressive behavior. Some practitioners might use this knowledge to claim that the offender is untreatable and requires incarceration or close supervision by a probation officer. Other practitioners would use this knowledge to try to enhance the motivation of the offender.

One strategy for assessing motivation is to compare the CTS scores of the man and his partner. Underreporting by the man can be a sign of poor motivation. On the other hand, discrepancies may not be from a conscious attempt to suppress, since alcoholic blackouts and perhaps states of rage can wipe out memory. Another strategy for assessing motivation is to have the men complete the Marlowe-Crowne Social Desirability Scale. It is an indicator of defensiveness and has been associated with early termination from treatment (Crowne & Marlowe, 1964).

Demaris (1989) took a direct approach and simply asked the men, "How important is it to you to stop being violent with your partner?" Those who answered that it was "very" important to stop being violent were more likely to complete the treatment program.

Gondolf (1987) placed the men on a continuum of moral development according to Kolberg's stages—moving from denial, to behavioral change, and ending with personal transformation. Gondolf contends that multiple forms of intervention are needed to match the level of the men's developmental stages. Men may drop out of treatment if an approach is used that does not match their source of motivation as determined by their developmental stage.

Recent work has focused on empirically testing stages of change based on a transtheoretical model (e.g., Levesque, Gelles, & Velicer, 1998). Identifying each man's stage of change can aid in guiding treatment length and client-treatment matching. A measure developed by Levesque and associates predicted treatment participation and alcohol use. Sample items for each of the four stages are: Precontemplation—"There's nothing I can do to end the violence in my relationship"; Contemplation—"More and more I'm seeing how my violence hurts my partner"; Action—"I'm finally doing something to end the violence"; and Maintenance—"Although I haven't been violent in awhile, I know it's possible for me to be violent again."

Studies identifying risk factors for dropping out of treatment indicate that external barriers may also explain some of the men's resistance. Men who are poorly educated, from minority groups, and who have low incomes tend to drop out (Saunders & Parker, 1989). Characteristics of the programs themselves may deter clients from returning. Programs that emphasize written homework or that do not have culturally diverse staff may unknowingly create "resistant" clients. Many programs lack culturally competent components and same-race groups may be one method for increasing cohesion and reducing attrition (Williams, 1998).

Assessing Correlates of Abuse

Many risk markers or correlates of abuse can be assessed. These are usually used to aid in treatment planning and evaluation. Sometimes they are used to screen men out of routine treatment. A number of areas of assessment are described briefly here. More complete descriptions are provided in Ganley (1981), Saunders (1982), and Sonkin et al. (1985). A number of authors provide detailed interview forms for use at intake (e.g., Mantooth, Geffner, Franks, & Patrick, 1987; Neidig & Friedman, 1984; Sonkin et al., 1985).

Anger

Sometimes, but not always, anger is a precursor of domestic violence. For some men, improved awareness of anger-producing situations can improve their control over anger. Often the awareness of anger leads to awareness of underlying feelings of hurt and fear. Novaco's Anger Index (Novaco, 1975) is a frequently used measure of the anger-arousing potential of various situations. There are numerous other such self-report measures, for example, the Buss-Durkee Hostility Inventory (Buss & Durkee, 1957) and the State-Trait Anger Scale (Spielberger, Russell, & Crane, 1970). None of these measures are specific to marital situations (for a review, see Biaggio & Maiuro, 1985). A solution to this problem is to tailor them to marital conflict, for example, changing the word "other" to "partner" in the Novaco Scale. Saunders & Hanusa (1986) reports results with such a modified scale. All of these self-report measures are highly contaminated with social desirability response bias. To avoid this bias, physiological responses to stress role plays can be measured (Saunders, 1988a). Novaco (1975) found that blood pressure readings were not correlated with response bias.

Depression and Suicide Risk

One cannot assume that anger directed outwardly cannot also be directed inwardly. All family members should be assessed for suicide risk. In addition to the standard interview questions about the certainty and lethality of a suicide plan, some measures of depression might also prove useful. For example, an item on the Beck Depression Inventory (Beck, Ward, Mendelson, Mock, & Erbaugh, 1961) pertains to suicidality and the scale's total score is a good measure of the level of depression. Ganley (1981) provides practical information for responding to the suicidal offender.

Jealousy

This is a common trait of men who batter, but also one they are likely to hide. White (1977) constructed a simple six-item scale of romantic jealousy that has evidence of reliability and validity.

Assertive Skills

Perhaps the most valid, but least efficient way, to measure the men's assertive skills is through a stress role play with a partner surrogate (Novaco, 1975; Saunders, 1988a). Several self-report measures are available, some of which distinguish among different types of assertion and aggression (e.g., Mauger, Adkinson, & Simpson, 1979), and between passive-aggressive and aggressive behavior (P. Lawrence, 1970). O'Leary and Curley (1986) constructed a scale that is specific to marital situations.

Attitudes

Many practitioners are convinced that, for long-term success, fundamental changes are needed in the men's beliefs about patriarchal norms and sex roles. Several measures of sex-role stereotyping are available, the most widely used with men who batter is the Attitudes Toward Woman Scale (Spence & Helmreich, 1978). A scale is also available to measure specific attitudes toward woman abuse, for example whether certain acts justify abuse, whether women gain from the abuse, and what actions should be taken against the abuser (Saunders, Lynch, Grayson, & Linz, 1987). The national surveys of family violence (Straus & Gelles, 1990) used modifications of the Blood and Wolfe (1960) index of decision-making power. Projective techniques are less contaminated by response bias and measures of male power and threat from female competence have been used with offenders (D. Dutton, 1988a; Saunders & Hanusa, 1986). General measures of beliefs about the justifiability of violence are available as well (Blumenthal, Kahn, Andrews, & Head, 1972).

Alcohol and Other Drug Abuse

These forms of abuse are frequently associated with domestic violence. A detailed history should be obtained of current and past patterns of use. A brief version of the Michigan Alcohol Screening Test (Pokorny, Miller, & Kaplan, 1972) is used by some programs, but they often supplement such assessment with specialized assessment at an alcohol and drug abuse agency. During treatment, some programs rely on urine screens ordered by probation officers.

Weapons

Lethality risk for homicide and suicide increases with the presence of guns. Recent legal changes in the United States have responded to this concern by making it illegal for convicted spouse assaulters to own guns.

Support System

Many men who batter are "loners." An assessment of their support system will help to identify who they are likely to turn to in time of a crisis and can indicate if a man needs more intensive help. Support is not always positive, however. Sexist and proviolence norms often find support in men's informal gatherings (DeKeseredy, 1988).

Psychopathology

Contrary to early etiological formulations of family violence, the majority of offenders do not suffer from severe mental disorders. An MMPI study showed many to have personality disorders, with signs of being unpredictable and distrustful of others and having excessive concerns about their masculinity (Bernard & Bernard, 1984). Specific measures of personality disorders show them to be quite heterogeneous, primarily with negativistic, narcissistic, and borderline traits (e.g., Hamberger & Hastings, 1986). Different types of childhood traumas appear to be related to different constellations of abusive behavior (general vs. specific to family), alcohol and drug use, attachment style, and personality disorder (Holtzworth-Munroe & Stuart, 1994).

Child Abuse

Men who batter, and to a lesser extent their partners, are at risk for abusing their children (Hotaling & Sugarman, 1986; Saunders, 1995). Current and potential abuse of all types—physical, emotional, sexual—needs to be assessed. As with violence between the partners, this form of abuse can be approached with less threatening questions at the beginning (e.g., What do you do when the children do not follow directions? Do you have concerns about the way your partner relates to the children?). A standardized measure of child abuse potential is also available to supplement other data sources (Milner, 1986; Milner & Gold, 1986). Evidence of emotional abuse through exposing children to violence between parents is included in mandated child abuse reporting laws but is difficult to substantiate and often receives low priority.

Organic and Physiological Factors

In some instances, these factors will contribute to domestic violence or make it more difficult for the offender to benefit from treatment. Hypoglycemia is a possible contributor. Poor intellectual functioning and a history of head injuries, seizures, and exposure to heavy metals should be checked for (Elliott, 1977; Gearan & Rosenbaum, 1996). If there is a possible link between these factors and violence, then a more thorough neurological exam should be required.

Correcting for Response Bias

Most of the self-report measures mentioned earlier are highly susceptible to response bias. The content of most of the measures is easily detected and clients are likely to answer in a socially desirable manner, or to try to "fake good." Some measures, like the Millon Clinical Multiaxial Inventory, have built-in corrections for response bias. It is also possible to detect the extent of each person's bias by administering a scale such as the Marlowe-Crowne Social Desirability Scale and disguising its purpose by calling it the "Personal Reaction Inventory." Those who have high scores on the measure of response bias can have their self-report scores discarded or their self-report scores can be statistically adjusted (see Saunders, 1991, for formula and examples).

SURVIVORS' STAGES OF CHANGE

Women's struggles to become free of violence have increasingly been seen as a process rather than a single event. Their responses to violence are also increasingly being placed in a social context in combination with the meaning they attach to events (M. Dutton, 1996). Qualitative studies provide some general categories for stages of change. Landenberger (1993), for example, characterizes the stages as "binding," enduring the abuse, disengaging, and recovery. Women are likely to attach different meanings to each of these stages, including the attributions for causing the violence or resolving it, social expectations, and views about help seeking (P. Smith, Earp, & DeVellis, 1995). M. Dutton (1992) recommends open-ended, structured, and questionnaire approaches to gathering this information. She includes items that reflect the woman's attributions about the cause of violence and abuse, expectations of recurrent violence, expectations of lethal violence, attribution of responsibility for safety, and expectations regarding controllability and safety.

SURVIVOR TRAUMA

Abused women and their children sustain both immediate and long-term traumas. Only trauma to the women will be covered here, since the children's trauma is covered in other chapters.

Predicting Lethality

As with assessment of the offender, the first concern in assessment of the victim is her potential for killing her partner. The major risk factors from Browne's study of women who killed were listed in the section "Predicting Dangerousness." In addition to these factors, one can ask directly about the women's fantasies—how strong, certain, and detailed are they regarding a lethal attack on her partner? Does she have weapons? Does she seem to have exhausted all other means of protecting herself?

Depression and Suicide Risk

Depression is common among battered women. Researchers use measures such as the Beck Depression Inventory or CES-D Depression Scale (Radloff, 1977) to measure its extent. Depression and anger may become particularly pronounced once she realizes the children are affected by the violence. Women who feel the most trapped in the relationship are likely to have thoughts of suicide. Again, a thorough suicide risk assessment is necessary. In addition to the practical realities of a lack of resources, lack of effective help and his threats of further harm, symptoms of posttraumatic stress disorder may make her think that she is going "crazy."

Posttraumatic Stress Disorder

Information on the traumatic symptoms experienced by survivors is growing. Depending on the setting, as many as 80% of survivors suffer from posttraumatic stress disorder (J. Campbell & Lewandowski, 1997; Saunders, 1994). Walker (1984) applied the criteria for prisoners of war used by Amnesty International; for example, the forced isolation and sleep deprivation experienced by some battered women. Battered women experience intrusive symptoms, such as flashbacks and nightmares, and also avoidant symptoms, such as avoiding reminders of the abuse. Avoidant symptoms are of concern because victims may suppress the trauma and have decreased social functioning without realizing it. Both self-report questionnaires and structured interviews have been used to gather this data. One standardized measure, the Impact of Event Scale (Horowitz, Wilner, & Alvarez, 1979) indicates the extent of traumatization on two dimensions: avoidant and intrusive symptoms. Foa, Riggs, Dancu, and

Rothbaum (1993) recently published a self-report measure based on *DSM-IV* diagnostic symptoms.

Attributions for Violence

The explanations given by the victim for the violence may determine the course of her recovery. If she blames herself, she may become more depressed and immobilized. However, the type of self-blame may make a difference. If the blame is of one's entire character, then depression is more likely to result than if blame is of one's behavior. Searching for a behavioral explanation may be a healthy phase that victims go through. Studies of victims' generalized beliefs about the locus of control of events—whether internal or external to oneself—have had disappointing results (e.g., Walker, 1984). M. Dutton (1992) provides a questionnaire for assessing women's attributions for causing the violence and for ending it.

COUPLE'S INTERACTION

The major focus for assessment and intervention has been on the man's behaviors, thoughts, and emotions because reviews of the scientific literature indicate that risk factors center on the man's background and traits (Hotaling & Sugarman, 1986). Nonetheless, most practitioners believe that after the man changes, couples counseling is appropriate. Controversy centers largely around whether conjoint assessment and treatment should occur immediately. Woman may feel coerced into couples counseling or are endangered when pushed to reveal further abuse or their intentions to leave.

Standard measures of marital satisfaction and communication style have been applied with violent couples (e.g., Deschner & McNeil, 1986; Neidig, 1986). Research teams have applied laboratory role-play measures to cases of domestic violence in their research (e.g., Jacobson & Gottman, 1998; Margolin, John, & Gleberman, 1988). These measures have the advantage of allowing the practitioner to directly observe the couple's style of communication and its strengths and weaknesses.

LEGAL AND SYSTEMS CONSIDERATIONS

CHILD CUSTODY DECISIONS

Those who must help make child custody decisions in domestic violence cases are faced with a dilemma. They know that men who batter have a propensity for violence, and they may know as well that battered women are at risk for abusing the children. Their tendency might be to recommend joint custody. However, the potential for child abuse by each of these parents is vastly different. Although the women are at higher than normal risk, they are much less likely to abuse the children than the men (Saunders, 1994). Furthermore, women seem to displace some of their anger from their violent husband onto the children, and when in a nonviolent relationship are not nearly as aggressive with the children (Walker, 1984). Children will also reexperience the trauma of being exposed to violence if either partner is in a new violent relationship. The majority of men, but not of women, are likely to be violent in a new relationship (Saunders, 1994, 1998).

Joint custody is appropriate in cases in which the partners have about equal power and are able to communicate well. These are hardly the characteristics of domestic abuse cases. Even those who generally favor joint custody say that it should not be used in these cases (e.g., Emery & Wyer, 1987).

DUTY TO WARN

Practitioners have a duty to warn or protect potential victims when there is imminent danger to their lives. As noted earlier, it is extremely difficult to predict homicide, yet practitioners must make use of the limited knowledge available. The history of past violence remains the best predictor of future violence (Monahan, 1996). In addition to the risk markers described in the section "Predicting Dangerousness," McNeill (1987) offers the following indicators of imminent danger:

- The extent to which the client appears to have a plan as distinguished from fantasy.
- The specificity with which the client describes the plan.
- Whether the client has targeted a victim or a victim is reasonably foreseeable with knowledge in the therapist's possession.
- Whether triggering events are attached to the plan that will cause the client to activate it on the occurrence of some conditions.
- Whether a dramatic or sudden change in the client's circumstances has occurred, such as divorce, loss of job, etc.
- Whether any steps have been taken to execute the plan, such as purchasing a weapon or other dangerous material, buying an airplane ticket to visit the intended victim, saving money toward the objective, sending threats to the victim directly or through third parties, or performing minor acts as a prelude to the intended "grand finale." (p. 201)

Therapists originally feared that recent court rulings and laws mandating the duty to warn would discourage clients from seeking help or deter therapists from working with dangerous clients. Apparently this has not been the case (McNeill, 1987).

BATTERED WOMEN WHO KILL

Assessment information on the history of violence and its aftermath can be invaluable in helping battered women who have killed their partners in self-defense. Laypersons who sit on juries often lack the knowledge necessary to understand the woman's actions (Ewing & Aubrey, 1987). The jury needs to be educated about the practical and psychological ties that keep women in abusive relationships (Strube, 1988), including the immobilization that can occur with depression and PTSD. The jury may have difficulty understanding her "flat affect" while recounting very emotional events or why she forgets parts or all of violent episodes. An explanation of violence-produced PTSD provides the answers.

The expert witness can also summarize the full history of abuse suffered by the woman and explain how it is more severe than the "average" battered woman's. The particular case can be compared with the factors uncovered in research on battered women who killed (Saunders & Browne, in press). The expert can lay the foundation for explaining the woman's fears and sense of helplessness. Most courts, however, will not allow the expert to testify on the "ultimate" issue—whether the woman had a reasonable belief that she was in imminent danger of death or great harm (Thyfault, Bennett, & Hirschhorn, 1987). That must be weighed by the jury. The expert's task is more difficult when there is a time gap between an assault by the man and the woman's act of self-defense. Usually in these cases, the woman tried to escape many times and was always found and punished for her efforts. Her belief in his omnipotence and her pending death becomes so overwhelming that she responds violently even though his last attack occurred hours earlier.

PROSECUTION OF THE OFFENDER

Assessment procedures are sometimes applied in the prosecution of men who batter. Sonkin and Fazio (1987) point out that expert testimony in the prosecution of men who batter is often useful in severe cases where the defendant denies his guilt and the victim is reluctant to testify. The reluctant victim can be assisted by the testimony of the expert in corroborating her testimony and by explaining her reluctance or forgetfulness to the court. The expert is also in a position to explain the abuser's tendency to deny or minimize his violence. This tendency may be from shame, fear of punishment or, in cases of alcohol abuse, from blackouts. A history of alcoholic blackouts is especially difficult to substantiate and may require extensive medical testing.

The expert can also help interpret possible differences in the courtroom demeanor of the man and woman. As described by Sonkin and Fazio (1987), the batterer "may seem controlled, calm, and quite believable. On the other hand, the victim may be agitated, defensive, depressed, or inconsistent, rendering her testimony somewhat questionable" (p. 221). When men who batter describe their partners as angry or as not performing household chores, the expert witness can explain that these may be symptoms of posttraumatic stress and depression caused by the battery. If the men claim that they are also battered, a careful assessment usually reveals that they do not suffer from nearly the same level of fear as their partners.

CASE ILLUSTRATION

The following illustration describes the assessment of a domestic violence case with a court evaluation of a couple who were in a custody dispute. The couple had been awarded joint custody of their 6-year-old adopted daughter four years before the evaluation. The mother had primary physical custody and the father was suing for that right. The author was hired by the mother's attorney to attempt to assess which parent had the greater potential for maltreating the child. The names of family members have been changed to protect their confidentiality.

I interviewed each parent and reviewed numerous reports, including previous psychological evaluations of the parents, family court counseling recommendations, police reports, court findings, physician's reports, and counselor's progress reports. MMPI and MCMI reports of the parents and standardized assessments of the child's behavior were also available to me.

The father, Gary, portrayed the mother as being emotionally unstable and as being dependent on drugs, which he claimed led to child neglect. The mother, Jean, claimed that her ex-husband neglected the child due to his alcohol abuse and that he had used harsh, physical discipline with the child. At the time of the evaluation, Jean was living with her daughter in another state, something for which the judge had criticized her in an earlier hearing as a sign of "impulsiveness" and poor judgment. It also made her appear uncooperative toward the court's preference for joint custody. Gary had remarried and apparently his new wife was pushing hard to gain primary custody. Some courts continue to be biased in favor of financially sound, "stable" families over single-parent families (Chesler, 1987). Fortunately, a model statute is increasingly being adopted by states (National Council of Juvenile & Family Court Judges, 1993). It provides many mechanisms for women and their children to find safety.

My report to the court was intended to educate the judge about the abuse potential of battered women and their partners and to apply this knowledge to this particular family.

CHILDHOOD TRAUMAS OF THE PARENTS

Both parents had experienced child traumas. Jean's father was rigid in his discipline and her mother had hit her with a strap more than once. When she was a teenager, her father objected to her dating and at one point threatened to beat her with a pipe. She took an overdose of aspirin as a help-seeking gesture. She was placed in a mental hospital and then a foster home.

Gary did not reveal any physical abuse from his parents. His childhood traumas related to the drowning death of his brother and his mother's two divorces. He reported some "jostling" and "pushing" between his parents, but Jean reported that he had told her about more extensive abuse. He said his primary fear was of being "unsettled."

This section of my report concluded: "The scientific literature on child abuse potential is clear that, although abuse in childhood places one at risk for being abusive, the majority of the people abused do not become abusive. Other risk factors are more important as indicators of child abuse potential."

PHYSICAL AGGRESSION IN MARRIAGE

My report continued with some statistics showing that the majority of men who batter also physically abuse their children. Other statistics showed that battered women were at a much lower risk, although still higher than the norm. I also reported data that showed that women's risk of directing anger at the children decreases greatly after they leave the abusive relationship.

Gary had admitted to a psychiatrist that he had hit Jean. Both the psychiatrist and Jean's counselor had seen bruises on her. She reported being abused every weekend early in the marriage and less frequently later. She reported being most frightened when he once "played" with a gun in front of her. She reported emotional abuse as well, for example, strict control over her own paycheck, disabling her car, suicidal threats, and threats to kill her. Once when they were separated, she found a note written in his handwriting that said, "I am dead and so are you."

I summarized in the report Jean's attempts to end the abuse, including calling the police, separating temporarily, and going to counseling. She reported that divorce was the most helpful solution.

Gary admitted to very little aggression and denied completely any homicidal or suicidal threats. It was not clear if he was consciously or subconsciously suppressing information or if he had alcoholic blackouts that caused amnesia for violent episodes. In general, the validity of Gary's statements had to be questioned seriously based on a written evaluation conducted by an alcoholism program and the discrepancies between his reports of violence and those of the police and psychiatrist, which gave more detailed accounts of his violence.

ALCOHOL AND DRUG ABUSE

The report included a summary of Gary's statements about his father's abuse of alcohol, and his own history of alcohol abuse and helpseeking. It noted his refusal to obtain followup counseling at the outpatient facility he attended and the counselor's diagnosis of alcohol abuse with possible dependence. A police report described his "belligerence" when arrested for driving while intoxicated.

The psychiatrist had testified in an earlier proceeding that he had prescribed antianxiety medication for Jean to help her avoid nightmares of Gary's beatings. He had also prescribed an antidepressant for her. Jean said that she hoped to be off all psychotropic medication before long. Her history was consistent with that of many battered women who increase their drug use after the battering occurs in the relationship, to fight depression, anxiety, or pain.

PERSONALITY TRAITS OF PARENTS

The report stated, "While personality tests are not very good predictors of wife or child abuse, they can suggest areas for further assessment and corroborate existing evidence. The best predictors of future violence, are not personality profiles, but past behaviors."

The MCMI showed very similar profiles for the two parents on general personality patterns. They both showed a compulsive-conforming style that was within normal limits and a slight elevation on the narcissistic and antisocial scales, revealing some immaturity and competitiveness. Both parents also had elevated depression scores, with Jean's being somewhat higher. The psychiatrist had testified that Jean had been hospitalized for depression as a direct result of Gary's abuse.

Jean had elevated scores on the somatoform, anxiety, paranoid, and borderline scales. The elevations seemed consistent with studies of battered women that showed profiles much like those of chronic schizophrenics or those with borderline personalities (Rosewater, 1987). Jean's history of posttraumatic stress, which was now subsiding, was also consistent with her scores. I stated, "When Jean appears detached from her feelings or becomes irritable, she is probably showing posttraumatic stress symptoms from her childhood and marriage."

The MMPI Caldwell report on Gary raised concerns about his anger and his ability to resolve childhood traumas. It indicated that should he act out his anger, he then would need to minimize or withhold it from the therapist. It also said that he would be slow to reveal "historical details." I noted that the psychologist's finding that he could control his impulses did not necessarily mean he was not dangerous, since abuse can be quite calculated.

The Abuse Scale on the Child Abuse Potential Inventory showed both parents to be within normal limits. Jean's score on the Rigidity Scale was slightly over the normal cutoff point and she tended to try to "fake good" on this inventory. Gary was above the normal cutoff point for the subscale "Problems with Self and Child." Milner (1986) cautions that assessment of abuse potential with this measure always needs to be supplemented with background and interview data.

PAST PHYSICAL FORCE AND NEGLECT OF CHILD

Gary admitted that when his daughter was still in diapers that he once spanked her hard enough to cause some red marks. I summarized Jean's reports of his apparent serious neglect of the child at least three times when she was older. For example, the child broke her jaw while under his care and Jean suspects he was intoxicated at the time. Jean reported that he refused to go to the hospital or to meet with the child protection worker who had been called into the case. Neither the parents nor any professional reported that Jean had struck the child.

EMOTIONAL ABUSE OF THE CHILD

This section of the report focused on the trauma that Gary caused the child by exposing her to violence against her mother. The child was present during one of the most violent episodes. The family court counselor noted that the child found her father's behavior to be scary and intimidating and that she talked about his anger often. As with other children in violent homes, this child feared for the death of her mother. To at least three different people she said, "Daddy is going to kill mommy."

The child would be at risk for more emotional abuse if Gary were to be abusive in a new relationship or continued his abuse with Jean even though they were separated. I presented statistics on the likelihood that either of these events would occur. Studies vary on the percentage that will reabuse, but they are clear that the men are more likely to abuse in a new relationship than the women are to be involved again in an abusive one.

The major concern over Jean's parenting was the possibility that she would be neglectful if she became severely depressed or relied too heavily on prescription tranquilizers. The chances of either of these happening was decreasing steadily over time. She was making progress in therapy and her physical distance from Gary was apparently alleviating these problems. Several people testified that she was more relaxed since living far away from him.

PROGRESS IN TREATMENT

This section described briefly what was known about each parent's treatment. Jean's ability to parent seemed to improve with supportive counseling, psychotropic medication, and distance from Gary. She had stopped all but one of the medications. Her self-esteem seemed quite high.

Gary appeared to be more accepting of treatment than he had been but continued to deny much of his aggression toward Jean. He seemed to rely on others' feedback to control his anger rather than on having developed internal controls. As with many other men who batter, he was frustrated with his job, feeling overqualified. However, he had not taken any steps to find a new job. A major concern was that he had not participated in any special programs for men who batter, in particular structured group programs that concentrate on lowering men's denial of abuse.

RECOMMENDATIONS

The final section of the report said:

> Although both parents had significant traumas in their childhoods, the strongest predictor of child abuse with these parents is Gary's history of aggression toward Jean. Gary has not taken full responsibility for his aggression and cannot empathize with Jean's fears. Of concern also is Gary's history of overly harsh discipline of the child. If he were to return to alcohol abuse, he would be at risk also for neglecting her needs.

I summarized the major points of the report and gave my opinion "to a reasonable degree of professional certainty" that the child should remain in the primary physical custody of her mother.

Jean and her attorney thought that Gary might become suicidal and/or homicidal if he lost the case. Gary's attorney and therapist were notified how they could contact Jean immediately if he should make a threat on her life. He was under financial strain for having spent many thousands of dollars on attorney's fees for custody hearings but he still seemed determined to keep fighting for custody. After all the reports were submitted, about two weeks before the trial, the case was settled. Gary agreed to have visitation only and further agreed to the proposed arrangements for visitation, vacations, and transportation. After a few months, surprisingly, Gary seemed accepting of the settlement and he and Jean were able to communicate directly to make arrangements for visitation. Such is not always the case and visitation centers may be needed.

CONCLUSION

Assessment of domestic violence cases is complicated by the reluctance of family members to reveal details of the abuse. However, sensitive interviewing techniques can lead to a fairly complete picture of the abuse and its aftermath. The most commonly used measure of family violence, the Conflict Tactics Scales, has limitations that can largely be overcome through modifications. Other measures of abuse have recently been developed but some of them have questionable validity or no evidence of validity.

Information gathered in the assessment process is needed for predicting severe dangerousness, screening clients from treatment, and evaluating treatment outcome. It can also be used to help overcome the biases encountered by victims who seek legal help. When assessment of particular cases is combined with findings from social science research, myths about domestic violence can be dispelled for judges, juries, and others. In this broadest of applications, information gathered in an assessment can educate society and advance social justice.

REFERENCES

Attala, J.M., Hudson, W.W., & McSweeney, M. (1994). A partial validation of two short-form partner abuse scales. *Women and Health, 21,* 125–139.

Beck, A.T., Ward, C.H., Mendelson, M., Mock, J., & Erbaugh, J. (1961). An inventory for measuring depression. *Archives of General Psychiatry, 4,* 53–63.

Berk, R.A., Berk, S., Loseke, D.R., & Rauma, D. (1983). Mutual combat and other family violence myths. In D. Finkelhor, R.J. Gelles, G.T. Hotaling, & M.A. Straus (Eds.), *The dark side of families: Current family violence research* (pp. 197–212). Newbury Park, CA: Sage.

Bernard, J.L., & Bernard, M.L (1984). The abusive male seeking treatment: Jekyll and Hyde. *Family Relations, 33,* 543–547.

Biaggio, M.K., & Maiuro, R.D. (1985). Recent advances in anger assessment. In C.D. Spielberger & J.N. Butcher (Eds.), *Advances in personality assessment* (pp. 71–111). Hillsdale, NJ: Erlbaum.

Blood, R.E., & Wolfe, D.M. (1960). *Husbands and wives.* Glencoe, IL: Free Press.

Blumenthal, M.D., Kahn, R.L., Andrews, F.M., & Head, K.B. (1972). *Justifying violence: Attitudes of American men.* Ann Arbor: University of Michigan Press.

Brekke, J.S. (1987). Detecting wife and child abuse in clinical settings. *Social Casework, 68,* 332–338.

Browne, A. (1987). *When battered women kill.* New York: Free Press.

Browning, J., & Dutton, D. (1986). Assessment of wife assault with the conflict tactics scale: Using couple data to quantify the differential reporting effect. *Journal of Marriage and the Family, 48,* 375–379.

Bulcroft, R.A., & Straus, M.A. (1975). *Validity of husband, wife, and child reports of conjugal violence and power.*

Buss, A.H., & Durkee, A. (1957). An inventory for assessing different kinds of hostility. *Journal of Clinical and Consulting Psychology, 21,* 343–349.

Campbell, D., Campbell, J., King, C., Parker, B., & Ryan, J. (1994). The reliability and factor structure of the index of spouse abuse with African-American women. *Violence and Victims, 9,* 259–274.

Campbell, J.C. (1995). Predicting homicide of and by battered women. In J.C. Campbell (Ed.), *Assessing dangerousness: Violence by sexual offenders, batterers, and child abusers.* Thousand Oaks, CA: Sage.

Campbell, J.C., & Lewandowski, L.A. (1997). Mental and physical health effects of intimate partner violence. *Psychiatric Clinics of North America, 20,* 353–374.

Cascardi, M., Langhinrichsen, J., & Vivian, D. (1992). Marital aggression: Impact, injury, and health correlates for husbands and wives. *Archives of Internal Medicine, 152,* 1178–1185.

Caulfield, M.B., & Riggs, D.S. (1992). The assessment of dating aggression: Empirical evaluation of the conflict tactics scale. *Journal of Interpersonal Violence, 7,* 549–558.

Chesler, P. (1987). *Mothers on trial: The battle for children and custody.* Seattle, WA: Seal Press.

Crowne, D.P., & Marlowe, D. (1964). *The approval motive: Studies in evaluative dependence.* New York: Wiley.

DeKeseredy, W.S. (1988). Woman abuse in dating relationships: The relevance of social support theory. *Journal of Family Violence, 3,* 1–14.

DeKeseredy, W.S., Saunders, D.G., Schwartz, M.D., & Alvi, S. (1997). The meanings and motives for women's use of violence in Canadian college dating relationships: Results from a national survey. *Sociological Spectrum, 17,* 199–222.

Demaris, A. (1989). Attrition in batterers' counseling: The role of social and demographic factors. *Social Service Review, 63,* 142–154.

Deschner, J.P. (1986, August). *Measuring family violence with the fighting methods inventory.* Paper presented at the 1986 annual convention of the American Psychological Association, Washington, DC.

Deschner, J.P., & McNeil, J.S. (1986). Results of anger control training for battering couples. *Journal of Family Violence, 1,* 111–120.

Dobash, R.E., & Dobash, R. (1979). *Violence against wives: A case against the patriarchy.* New York: Free Press.

Dutton, D.G. (1988a). *The domestic assault of women: Psychological and criminal justice perspectives.* Boston: Allyn & Bacon.

Dutton, D.G. (1988b). Profiling of wife assaulters: Preliminary evidence for a trimodal analysis. *Violence and Victims, 3,* 1, 5–29.

Dutton, M.A. (1992). *Empowering and healing the battered woman.* New York: Springer.

Edleson, J.L., & Brygger, M.P. (1986). Gender differences in self-reporting of battering incidences. *Family Relations, 35,* 377–382.

Elliott, F.A. (1977). The neurology of explosive rage: The dyscontrol syndrome. In M. Roy (Ed.), *Battered women* (pp. 98–109). New York: Van Nostrand.

Emery, R.E., & Wyer, M.M. (1987). Divorce mediation. *American Psychologist, 42,* 472–480.

Ewing, C.P., & Aubrey, M. (1987). Battered women and public opinion: Some realities about the myths. *Journal of Family Violence, 2,* 257–264.

Foa, E.B., Riggs, D.S., Dancu, C.V., & Rothbaum, B.O. (1993, October). Reliability and validity of a brief instrument for assessing post-traumatic stress disorder. *Journal of Traumatic Stress, 6*(4), 459–473.

Ganley, A.L. (1981). *Court-mandated counseling for men who batter.* Washington, DC: Center for Women's Policy Studies.

Gearan, P., & Rosenbaum, A. (1996). *Biological factors in relationship aggression. The psychology of adversity* (pp. 183–198). Amherst: University of Massachusetts Press.

Gefner, R., Rosenbaum, A., & Hughes, H. (1988). Research issues concerning family violence. In V.B. Van Hasselt, R.L. Morrison, A.S. Bellack, & M. Hersen (Eds.), *Handbook of family violence* (pp. 457–472). New York: Plenum Press.

Gondolf, E.W. (1987). Changing men who batter: A developmental model for integrated interventions. *Journal of Family Violence, 2,* 335–350.

Gondolf, E.W. (1988). Who are those guys? Toward a behavioral typology of batterers. *Violence and Victims, 3,* 187–204.

Gondolf, E.W. (1998, July). *Human subjects issues in batterer program evaluation.* Unpublished manuscript, Mid-Atlantic Addiction Training Institute, Indiana University of Pennsylvania.

Gottfredson, S.D., & Gottfredson, D.M. (1988). Violence prediction methods: Statistical and clinical strategies. *Violence and Victims, 3,* 303–324.

Hamberger, L.K., & Hastings, J.E. (1986). Personality correlates of men who abuse their partners: A cross-validation study. *Journal of Family Violence, 1,* 323–341.

Hamby, S.L., Poindexter, V.C., & Gray-Little, B. (1996). Four measures of partner violence: Construct similarity and classification differences. *Journal of Marriage & the Family, 58,* 127–139.

Harway, M., & Hansen, M. (1993). Therapist perceptions of family violence. In M. Hansen & M. Harway (Eds.), *Battering and family therapy: A feminist perspective* (pp. 42–53). Newbury Park, CA: Sage.

Holtzworth-Munroe, A., & Stuart, G.L. (1994). Typologies of male batterers: Three subtypes and the differences among them. *Psychological Bulletin, 116,* 476–497.

Horowitz, M., Wilner, N., & Alvarez, W. (1979). Impact of event scale: A measure of subjective stress. *Psychosomatic Medicine, 41,* 209–218.

Hotaling, G.T., & Sugarman, D.B. (1986). An analysis of risk markers in husband to wife violence: The current state of knowledge. *Violence and Victims, 1,* 101–124.

Hudson, W.W., & McIntosh, S.R. (1981). The assessment of spouse abuse: Two quantifiable dimensions. *Journal of Marriage and the Family, 11,* 873–888.

Jacobson, N., & Gottman, J. (1998). *When men batter women.* New York: Simon & Schuster.

Jouriles, E.N., & O'Leary, K.D. (1985). Interspousal reliability of reports of marital violence. *Journal of Consulting and Clinical Psychology, 53,* 419–421.

Kalichman, S.C. (1988). MMPI profiles of women and men convicted of domestic homicide. *Journal of Clinical Psychology, 4,* 847–853.

Kantor, G., Jasinski, J.L., & Aldarondo, E. (1994). Sociocultural status and incidence of marital violence in Hispanic families. *Violence and Victims, 9,* 207–222.

Kurz, D. (1993). Physical assaults by husbands: A major social problem. In R.J. Gelles & D.R. Loseke (Eds.), *Current controversies on family violence* (pp. 88–103). Thousand Oaks, CA: Sage.

Landenberger, K. (1993). Exploration of women's identity: Clinical approaches with abused women. *AHWONN's Clinical Issues, 4,* 378–384.

Lawrence, E., Heyman, R.E., & O'Leary, K.D. (1995). Correspondence between telephone and written assessments of physical violence in marriage. *Behavior Therapy, 26,* 671–680.

Lawrence, P.S. (1970). *The assessment and modification of assertive behavior.* (Doctoral dissertation in clinical psychology, Arizona State University). Ann Arbor, MI: University Microfilms International.

Levesque, D.A., Gelles, R.J., & Velicer, W.F. (1998, July). *Development and validation of a stages of change measure for battering men.* Paper presented at the conference Program Evaluation and Family Violence Research, University of New Hampshire.

Levy, B. (1991). *Dating violence: Young women in danger.* Seattle, WA: Seal Press.

Lewis, B.Y. (1983). The wife abuse inventory: A screening device for the identification of abused women. *Social Casework, 30,* 32–36.

Mantooth, C.M., Geffner, R., Franks, D., & Patrick, J. (1987). *Family preservation: A treatment manual for reducing couple violence.* Tyler: East Texas Crisis Center.

Margolin, G., John, R.S., & Gleberman, L. (1988). Affective responses to conflictual discussions in violent and nonviolent couples. *Journal of Consulting and Clinical Psychology, 56,* 24–33.

Marshall, L.L. (1992). Development of the severity of violence against women scales. *Journal of Family Violence, 7,* 103–121.

Mauger, P.A., Adkinson, D.R., & Simpson, D.G. (1979). *The interpersonal behavior survey manual.* Los Angeles: Western Psychological Services.

McNeely, R.L., & Robinson-Simpson, G. (1987). The truth about domestic violence: A falsely framed issue. *Social Work, 32,* 485–490.

McNeill, M. (1987). Domestic violence: The skeleton in Tarasoff's closet. In D.J. Sonkin (Ed.), *Domestic violence on trial: Psychological and legal dimensions of family violence* (pp. 197–217). New York: Springer.

Milner, J.S. (1986). *The child abuse potential inventory manual* (2nd ed.). Webster, NC: Psytec.

Milner, J.S., & Gold, R.G. (1986). Screening spouse abusers for child abuse potential. *Journal of Clinical Psychology, 42,* 169–172.

Monahan, J. (1981). *Predicting violent behavior: An assessment of clinical techniques.* Beverly Hills, CA: Sage.

Monahan, J. (1996). Violence prediction: The past twenty and the next twenty years. *Criminal Justice and Behavior, 23,* 107–119.

Murphy, C.M., & Baxter, V.A. (1997). Motivating batterers to change in the treatment context. *Journal of Interpersonal Violence, 12,* 607–619.

National Council of Juvenile and Family Court Judges. (1993). *Model code on domestic and family violence.* Reno, NV: National Council of Juvenile and Family Court Judges.

Neidig, P.H. (1986). The development and evaluation of a spouse abuse treatment program in a military setting. *Evaluation and Program Planning, 9,* 275–280.

Neidig, P.H., & Friedman, D.H. (1984). *Spouse abuse: A treatment program for couples.* Champaign, IL. Research Press.

Novaco, R.W. (1975). *Anger control: The development and evaluation of an experimental treatment.* Lexington, MA., Lexington Books.

O'Leary, K.D. (in press). Psychological abuse: A variable deserving critical attention in domestic violence. *Violence and Victims.*

O'Leary, K.D., & Curley, A.D. (1986). Assertion and family violence: Correlates of spouse abuse. *Journal of Marital and Family Therapy, 12,* 284–289.

O'Leary, K.D., Vivian, D., & Malone, J. (1992). Assessment of physical aggression against women in marriage: The need for multimodal assessment. *Behavioral Assessment, 14,* 5–14.

Parker, B., & Ulrich, Y. (1990). A protocol of safety: Research on abuse of women. *Nursing Research, 39,* 248–250.

Peters, S.D., Wyatt, G.E., & Finkelhor, D. (1986). Prevalence. In D. Finkelhor (Ed.), *Sourcebook on child sexual abuse.* Beverly Hills, CA: Sage.

Plichta, S.B. (1996). Violence and abuse: Implications for women's health. In M. Falk & K. Scott (Eds.), *Women's health: The commonwealth fund survey* (pp. 237–270). Baltimore: Johns Hopkins University Press.

Pokorny, A.D., Miller, B.A., Kaplan, H.B. (1972). The brief MAST: A shortened version of the Michigan alcoholism screening test. *American Journal of Psychiatry, 129,* 342–345.

Porter, S.J. (1986). Assessment: A vital process in the treatment of family violence. *Family Therapy, 13,* 105–112.

Poteat, G.M., Grossnickle, W.F., Cope, J., & Wynne, D.C. (1990). *Journal of Clinical Psychology, 46,* 828–834.

Radloff, L.S. (1977). The CES-D Scale: A self-report depression scale for research in the general population. *Applied Psychological Measurement, 1,* 385–401.

Rhodes, N.R. (1992). The assessment of spousal abuse: An alternate to the conflict tactics scale. In E.C. Viano (Ed.), *Intimate violence.* Washington, DC: Hemisphere.

Rodenburg, F.A., & Fantuzzo, J.W. (1993). The measure of wife abuse: Steps toward the development of a comprehensive assessment technique. *Journal of Family Violence, 8,* 203–229.

Rosewater, L.B. (1987). The clinical and courtroom application of battered women's personality assessment. In D. Sonkin (Ed.), *Domestic violence on trial* (pp. 86–96). New York: Springer.

Saunders, D.G. (1980). The police response to battered women: Predictors of officers' use of arrest, counseling, and minimal action (Doctoral dissertation, University of Wisconsin-Madison). *Dissertation Abstracts International, 40,* 6446A.

Saunders, D.G. (1982). Counseling the violent husband. In P.A. Keller & L.G. Ritt (Eds.), *Innovations in clinical practice: A source book* (Vol. 1, pp. 16–29). Sarasota, FL: Professional Resource Exchange.

Saunders, D.G. (1986). When battered women use violence: Husband abuse or self-defense? *Violence and Victims, 1,* 1, 47–60.

Saunders, D.G. (1988a). Issues in conducting treatment research with men who batter. In *Coping with family violence: Research and policy perspectives* (pp. 145–152). Beverly Hills, CA: Sage.

Saunders, D.G. (1988b). Other "truths" about domestic violence: A reply to McNeely and Robinson-Simpson. *Social Work, 33,* 179–183.

Saunders, D.G. (1989). *Who hits first and who hurts most? Evidence for the greater victimization of women.* Paper presented at the 41st annual meeting of the American Society of Criminology, Reno, NV.

Saunders, D.G. (1991a). *Child custody decisions in families experiencing woman abuse.* Manuscript submitted for publication.

Saunders, D.G. (1991b). Procedures for adjusting self-reports of violence for social desirability bias. *Journal of Interpersonal Violence, 6,* 336–344.

Saunders, D.G. (1993, November 29). *Recent trends in evaluating programs for men who batter.* Paper presented at the meeting "The Evaluation of Wife Batterers' Treatment Programs," Ministry of the Solicitor General of Canada, Ottawa, Ontario.

Saunders, D.G. (1994a). Child custody decisions in families experiencing woman abuse. *Social Work, 39,* 51–59.

Saunders, D.G. (1994b). Posttraumatic stress symptom profiles of battered women: A comparison of survivors in two settings. *Violence and Victims, 9,* 125–138.

Saunders, D.G. (1995). Predicting wife assault. In J.C. Campbell (Ed.), *Assessing dangerousness.* Thousand Oaks, CA: Sage.

Saunders, D.G. (1997). Feminist-cognitive-behavioral and process-psychodynamic treatments for men who batter: Interaction of abuser traits and treatment models. *Violence and Victims, 11,* 393–414.

Saunders, D.G. (1998).*Child custody and visitation decisions in domestic violence cases: Legal trends, research findings, and recommendations.* VAWnet, a project of the National Resource Center on Domestic Violence, http://www.vaw.umn.edu/Vawnet/custody/htm.

Saunders, D.G., & Browne, A. (in press). Domestic homicide. In R.T. Ammerman & M. Hersen (Eds.), *Case studies in family violence* (2nd ed.). New York: Plenum Press.

Saunders, D.G., & Hanusa, D.R. (1986). Cognitive-behavior treatment of men who batter: The short-term effect of group therapy. *Journal of Family Violence, 1,* 357–372.

Saunders, D.G., Lynch, A.E., Grayson, M., & Linz, D. (1987). The inventory of beliefs about wife beating. *Violence and Victims, 2,* 39–57.

Saunders, D.G., & Parker, J.C. (1989). Legal sanctions and treatment follow-through among men who batter: A multivariate analysis. *Social Work Research and Abstracts, 25,* 21–29.

Shepard, M.F., & Campbell, J.A. (1992). The abusive behavior inventory: A measure of psychological and physical abuse. *Journal of Interpersonal Violence, 7,* 291–305.

Shields, N.M., & Hanneke, C.R. (1983). Battered wives' reactions to marital rape. In D. Finkelhor, R.J. Gelles, G.T. Hotaling, & M.A. Straus (Eds.), *The dark side of families: Current family violence research* (pp. 132–148). Beverly Hills, CA: Sage.

Smith, M.D. (1989). Woman abuse: The case for surveys by telephone. *Journal of Interpersonal Violence, 4,* 80–98.

Smith, M.D. (1994). Enhancing the quality of survey data on violence against women: A feminist approach. *Gender & Society, 8,* 109–127.

Smith, P., Earp, J.A., & DeVellis, R. (1995). Measuring battering: Development of the women's experience with battering (WEB) scale. *Women's Health: Research on Gender, Behavior, and Policy, 1,* 272–288.

Sonkin, D.J. (1987). The assessment of court-mandated male batterers. In D.J. Sonkin (Ed.), *Domestic violence on trial* (pp. 174–198). New York: Springer.

Sonkin, D.J., & Ellison, J. (1986). The therapist's duty to protect victims of domestic violence: Where have we been and where are we going? *Violence and Victims, 1,* 205–214.

Sonkin, D.J., & Fazio, W. (1987). Domestic violence expert testimony in the prosecution of male batterers. In D.J. Sonkin (Ed.), *Domestic violence on trial* (pp. 218–236). New York: Springer.

Sonkin, D.J., Martin, D., & Walker, L.E.A. (1985). *The male batterer: A treatment approach.* New York: Springer.

Speilberger, C.D., Jacobs, G.A., Russell, S., & Crane, R.S. (1983). Assessment of anger: The state-trait anger scale. In J.N. Butcher & C.D. Speilberger (Ed.), *Advances in personality assessment* (Vol. 2, pp. 112–134). Hillsdale, NJ: Erlbaum.

Spence, J.T., & Helmreich, R.L. (1978). *Masculinity and femininity: Their psychological dimensions, correlates, and antecedents.* Austin: University of Texas.

Stacey, W.A., & Shupe, A. (1983). *The family secret: Domestic violence in America.* Boston: Beacon Press.

Stets, J., & Straus, M.A. (1990). Gender differences in reporting marital violence and its medical and psychological consequences. In M.A. Straus & R. Gelles (Eds.), *Physical violence in American families.* New Brunswick: Transaction Books.

Straus, M.A. (1983). Ordinary violence, child abuse, and wife beating: What do they have in common? In D. Finkelhor, R.J. Gelles, G.T. Hotaling, & M.A. Straus (Eds.), *The dark side of families: Current family violence research* (pp. 213–234). Newbury Park, CA: Sage.

Straus, M.A. (1990). The conflict tactics scales and its critics: An evaluation and new data on validity and reliability. In M.A. Straus & R.J. Gelles (Eds.), *Physical violence in American families: Risk factors and adaptations to violence in 8,145 families* (pp. 49–72). New Brunswick, NJ: Transaction Books.

Straus, M.A. (1993). Physical assaults by wives: A major social problem. In R.J. Gelles & D.R. Loseke (Eds.), *Current controversies on family violence* (pp. 67–87). Thousand Oaks, CA: Sage.

Straus, M.A., & Gelles, R.J. (1990). *Physical violence in American families.* New Brunswick, NJ: Transaction Books.

Straus, M.A., Gelles, R.J., & Steinmetz, S.K. (1980). *Behind closed doors: Violence in the American family.* New York: Doubleday/Anchor.

Straus, M.A., Hamby, S.L., Boney-McCoy, S., & Sugarman, D.B. (1996). The revised Conflict Tactics Scales (CTS2): Development and preliminary psychometric data. *Journal of Family Issues, 17,* 283–316.

Strube, M.J. (1988). The decision to leave an abusive relationship: Empirical evidence and theoretical issues. *Psychological Bulletin, 104,* 236–250.

Szinovacz, M. (1983). Using couple data as a methodological tool: The case of marital violence. *Journal of Marriage and the Family, 45,* 633–644.

Thyfault, R.K., Bennett, C.E., & Hirschhorn, R.B. (1987). Battered women in court: Jury and trial consultants and expert witnesses. In D.J. Sonkin (Ed.), *Domestic violence on trial* (pp. 71–85). New York: Springer.

Tjaden, P., & Thoennes, N. (1998). *Stalking in America: Findings from the national violence against women survey.* Washington, DC: National Institute of Justice.

Virkkunen, M., & Kallio, E. (1987). Low blood sugar in the glucose tolerance test and homicidal spouse abuse. *Aggressive Behavior, 13,* 59–66.

Walker, L.E.A. (1984). *The battered woman syndrome.* New York: Springer.

Walker, L.E.A., & Edwall, G.E. (1987). Domestic violence and determination of visitation and custody in divorce. In D.J. Sonkin (Ed.), *Domestic violence on trial: Psychological and legal dimensions of family violence* (pp. 127–154). New York: Springer.

Washburn, C., & Frieze, I.H. (1980, March). *Methodological issues in studying battered women.* Paper presented at the Annual Research Conference of the Association for Women in Psychology, Santa Monica, CA.

Weisz, A., Tolman, R., & Saunders, D.G. (1997). *Assessing the risk of severe domestic violence: The importance of survivors' predictions.* Manuscript under review. Wayne State University, School of Social Work.

White, G.L. (1977). The social psychology of romantic jealousy. *Dissertation Abstracts International, 37*(10), 5449-B.

Williams, O.J. (1998). Healing and confronting the African American male who batters. In R. Carrillo & J. Tello (Eds.), *Family violence and men of color.* New York: Springer.

Yoshihama, M., & Sorenson, S.B. (1994). Physical, sexual, and emotional abuse by male intimates: Experiences of women in Japan. *Violence and Victims, 9,* 63–78.

CHAPTER 13

Elder Abuse and Neglect

RONALD D. ADELMAN, MARK S. LACHS, and RISA BRECKMAN

MANY PEOPLE today are aware that being the elder of the family does not protect one against violence in the home. However, 20 years ago, when child and spouse abuse was becoming common knowledge, the public was not aware of elder abuse and neglect. Victims were isolated, shrouding their pain in silence. In the late 1970s, the reality of elder mistreatment emerged into public consciousness.

Initially, researchers, professionals, and policy makers tended to frame the phenomenon of elder mistreatment as a problem of caregiver stress. The victims were old and frail, requiring tremendous care, and the abusers, otherwise well-meaning family members, became abusive due to the burden of providing care without adequate resources, support, or guidance. Victim blaming was implicit in this framework, in that caregivers sometimes "have to" slap or hit frail, dependent, and relentlessly needy elders, not unlike the notion that husbands have no choice but to assault nagging wives or that parents have to beat rambunctious kids to keep them in line.

Our knowledge based on elder abuse and neglect has broadened over the past two decades. This chapter presents information on the profiles of victims and abusers, outlines the different forms of mistreatment, delineates risk factors and causation theories, provides information on the clinical assessment of this problem, and discusses legal considerations for clients and clinicians.

DESCRIPTION OF THE PROBLEM

Researchers at the University of New Hampshire's Family Research laboratory randomly selected 2,020 people aged 65 and over living on their own or with their families in the Boston metropolitan area. Findings showed an annual incidence rate of 32 people per 1,000 who experience physical or verbal abuse or neglect by family members (Pillemer & Finkelhor, 1988). Extrapolations from the study project 701,000 to 1.1 million elder mistreatment victims nationwide, a conservative estimate because this study did not examine all aspects of abuse (e.g., financial exploitation). Elder mistreatment, in this cross-sectional study, crossed all economic levels, and did not

271

correlate with race, religion, or educational background. The following subsections provide a more detailed description of family-mediated elder abuse and neglect.

Who Is Being Abused or Neglected?

Most definitions of elderly specify the age to be 65 years or older; this age was used by the Family Research Laboratory, and is commonly employed by programs serving the elderly, including many elder abuse programs. Otherwise, the victim may be competent or incompetent, healthy or frail, male or female. Although it was previously thought that most elder abuse victims were women, Pillemer and Finkelhor (1988) showed that men were the more frequent victims. The abuse inflicted by elderly husbands, however, was generally more severe than that inflicted by wives. Lachs and Pillemer (1995) propose a useful metaphor for conceptualizing elder abuse and neglect as a chronic disease. Like ongoing chronic illness, they characterize elder mistreatment as most often episodic and recurrent over time, rather than a onetime event of domestic violence.

Who Is Doing the Abusing or Neglecting?

Family-mediated abuse or neglect may be perpetrated by, among others, a spouse, child, grandchild, niece, nephew, or cousin. There may be more than one perpetrator. The University of New Hampshire study revealed that abuse is frequently committed by a spouse rather than an offspring. Spouses are not, however, intrinsically more likely than offspring to mistreat older people. The key variable appears to be that *abuse is most likely to be inflicted by the person with whom the victim lives.* In fact, elderly persons living alone experienced only about one-fourth of the mistreatment inflicted on those living with others (Pillemer & Finkelhor, 1988).

Where Is the Abuse or Neglect Occurring?

Family-mediated mistreatment usually occurs in the community: in the elderly person's own home, in a relative's home, or in a shared living arrangement. Mistreatment can also happen in an institution. Abusers may visit elderly relatives in a nursing home and abuse them there.

What Is the Pattern of Abuse or Neglect?

Although a onetime act of violence can be damaging, elder mistreatment is commonly characterized by a pattern of violence increasing in severity and incidence over time (Breckman & Adelman, 1988). Frequently, many different types of mistreatment coexist (e.g., physical abuse and financial exploitation).

What Types of Abuse or Neglect Are Occurring? Is the Mistreatment Intentional or Unintentional?

Although definitions of mistreatment vary widely, three types of abuse and neglect are generally recognized: psychological, physical, and financial. Both abuse and neglect can be intentional or unintentional (Breckman & Adelman, 1988). *Psychological abuse or neglect* induces mental and emotional distress in victims. Examples of psychological abuse include threatening remarks (e.g., "I am going to kill you," or "One of these days I'm going to poison your food and you won't know when"); ordering, harsh commands; infantilization; or isolating from others. Examples of psychological neglect include consistently disregarding or ignoring the older person's concerns. *Physical abuse or neglect* results in bodily harm to the victim. Examples of physical neglect include not providing adequate nourishment or not medicating properly.

The incidence of sexual abuse of older people may be higher than previously recognized. Benbow and Haddad emphasize the need to develop a careful definition of this form of abuse and focus on the development of ethical guidelines for consent when a cognitively impaired individual is participating in a sexual relationship (Benbow & Haddad, 1993).

Financial abuse or neglect refers to the misuse or theft of money, property, or material possessions or inattention to an older person's possessions or funds. Examples of financial abuse include stealing possessions or cash, or threatening the victim into handing over assets. An example of financial neglect is mismanaging the victim's money or assets.

In some cases, abusers deliberately abuse or neglect to cause harm; in other cases, the mistreatment is nondeliberate. Interventions vary according to the intent to harm. For example, mismedicating a relative because of poor understanding of the physician's directions may result in drug toxicity. This inadvertent mismedication by a caregiver could be classified as unintentional neglect. Clearer instructions can remedy this form of mistreatment. This circumstance is totally different from when the relative is intentionally neglectful, as, for example, when the relative leaves a severely demented older person alone for several days without supervision.

WHAT ARE THE POTENTIAL CAUSES AND RISK FACTORS OF ELDER MISTREATMENT?

Pillemer (1986) listed five potential risk factors that help to identify elder mistreatment: (1) psychopathology of the abuser, (2) external stress, (3) transgenerational violence, (4) dependency, and (5) social isolation.

PSYCHOPATHOLOGY OF THE ABUSER

Research suggests that psychopathology of the abuser is a major risk factor of mistreatment (Finkelhor & Pillemer, 1987; Wolf & Pillemer, 1989). Some abusers have had a series of hospitalizations for serious psychiatric disorders (e.g., schizophrenia and other psychoses). Many perpetrators abuse alcohol or other drugs. When an adult child has a mental illness requiring inpatient psychiatric assistance, the parents' home is often the discharge site of last resort. Out of concern that the patient will be homeless or have to stay in a shelter, or out of love or their own dependency needs, parents may agree to take the adult child back into their home.

EXTERNAL STRESS

Strauss, Gelles, and Steinmetz (1980) reported that financial problems, caregiving responsibilities, and other tensions may precipitate frustration and anger that can be expressed by some people through acts of abuse.

TRANSGENERATIONAL VIOLENCE

Violence can be a learned behavior, and it is widely believed that if the abusers were mistreated when they were children (perhaps by the person now being victimized, or by the victim's spouse, or by another relative), a spirit of retaliation, as a response to previous abuse, may be motivating current mistreatment. The mistreatment is considered to be a learned behavior in response to feelings of anger and frustration (see Wolf & Pillemer, 1989).

DEPENDENCY

Several studies have pointed out the financial dependency of the abuser on the victim (Hwalek, Sengstock, & Lawrence, 1984; Wolf, Godkin, & Pillemer, 1984). Abuse victims are not usually in need of care, but rather the abusers are more dependent on the victims (Pillemer & Finkelhor, 1988). In some cases, a mutual dependency exists. For example, the older person may be dependent on the abuser for socialization or for performing activities of daily living, whereas the abuser may be dependent on the victim for housing or money.

SOCIAL ISOLATION

Several studies have found that elder abuse victims have increased social isolation (Phillips, 1983; Pillemer, 1986). This isolation may provide increased opportunities for mistreatment. Furthermore, isolation works as a barrier to detection of such behavior.

ASSESSMENT APPROACHES

Assuming that a person has been identified as a victim of elder mistreatment, the clinician should observe and investigate the following factors: (1) the types, frequency, and severity of mistreatment; (2) the emotional, medical, cognitive, and functional status of the victim; and (3) the resources and supports available to the victim. This ongoing process of gathering and evaluating information typically overlaps with the intervention phase.

Tilden, Schmidt, Limandri, Chiodo, and Garland (1994) studied factors that influenced clinicians' approaches to victims of family violence. Through a mail survey, they examined experiences and attitudes toward family-mediated violence from the disciplines of dentistry, dental hygiene, medicine, nursing, psychology, and social work. One-third of subjects reported no educational exposure to issues concerning family violence, and about three-quarters of the subjects had no formal education in the topic of elder abuse. Those subjects with educational exposure to domestic violence had stronger suspicions of family violence; among all subjects, elder abuse was the least suspected form of mistreatment. Also, a significant number of respondees did not feel themselves to be responsible for dealing with issues of family violence. Interestingly, subjects in this study reported low confidence in the effectiveness of mandatory reporting laws and also reported low compliance with these laws.

Three determinants of how much information is gathered are the professional's role, the type of services the professional provides, and the amount of time the professional is involved with the client. For example, a health care provider in an emergency room, handling a crisis situation, attempts to quickly determine a victim's cognitive, emotional, and functional capacities, and tries to help the victim with immediate health and safety needs. A police officer responding to a 911 call makes a rapid determination as to the level of danger and types of crimes committed. As crisis interventionists, a primary function of these professionals is to gather and evaluate information to stabilize the situation. A community-based social worker, on the other hand, providing ongoing counseling, would have more time and opportunity to gather and evaluate in-depth information on the multiple factors affecting the mistreatment situation. If a crisis arises, however, this individual also would focus on the immediate safety and health needs of the victim. This professional's involvement would then continue beyond the crisis.

In many communities, interdisciplinary groups of professionals meet in case conferences to review and discuss complicated elder mistreatment cases. These groups frequently comprise representatives from health care, law enforcement, criminal justice, social service, and mental health systems. Case conferences enhance the possibility of a more thorough understanding and coordinated response to elder mistreatment cases, as each professional lends a specific perspective, expertise, and experience. It also provides a "support network" for multidisciplinary professionals who deal with elder abuse regularly, as this can be a demanding endeavor.

Comprehensiveness of the assessment is determined on a case-by-case basis. To ascertain a more accurate picture of the mistreatment, it is recommended that clinicians conduct private interviews with victims. Interviews should be structured so that the victim and family members(s) are interviewed individually (Quinn & Tomita, 1986).

Table 13.1 is an assessment chart originally developed for health care professionals working within hospitals. It has been used successfully by many different professionals

Table 13.1
Assessment of Elder Treatment: Issues and Considerations

Assessment Category	Assessment Issues	Assessment Interview (with patient and family member(s))
Access	• Victims and abusers may be reluctant to allow professional contact: Abusers may try to keep their actions "hidden" (e.g., threatening victims not to speak with outsiders). Victims may feel ashamed, protective of the abuser, fearful of not being believed; afraid of retaliation, abandonment, or institutionalization; or resigned to a situation they perceive as hopeless. • Attempts to gain access should be creatively repeated over a period of time, if necessary. Home Visits: • Professionals need to exercise caution as abusers may be abusive to nonfamily members.	• Where should the interview be conducted to afford the maximum amount of privacy? How can the interview be structured so that the patient and family member(s) are interviewed separately? • Is there a trusted person who can assist the professional in gaining access? Have other professionals previously gained access to members of the family? How? Home Visits: • Do the family members have a history of violence, mental illness, alcohol or drug abuse that may pose a threat to the professional's safety? If so, what precautionary steps need to be taken before contact?

(Continued)

Table 13.1   *(Continued)*

Assessment Category	Assessment Issues	Assessment Interview (with patient and family member(s))
Cognitive Status	• Unless declared legally incompetent, victims have a right to refuse professional contact and to remain in an abusive environment. • Many mistreated older persons develop debilitating responses to the victimization, such as confusion, memory loss, or cognitive impairment. These problems may be caused by depression, excessive fear, or anxiety.	• What is the patient's level of cognitive functioning? Is a referral for a comprehensive neuropsychological exam appropriate? Do family member(s) understand the patient's mental capabilities and appropriately interact with the patient? • Can the patient understand the risks and consequences of his or her decisions (e.g., remaining in an abusive environment)? Do family member(s) feel the patient has the ability to make appropriate lifestyle choices? • If cognitive impairment exists, is its onset recent or long-standing? Is it reversible or irreversible? Is the patient currently on any medication that can alter his or her cognitive functioning? Could it be related to victimization? How has the impairment affected the patient's relationship with others (e.g., more stress or greater dependency)?
Health Status	• Many victims of abuse are in relatively good health. Abuse victims and their nonabused counterparts have similar health-related problems. • Suspected victims may attempt to dismiss physical injuries as "accidental," stating, for example, that bruises/fractures (which were inflicted during a beating) resulted from a fall. • Abusers may prevent victims from receiving proper medical care to avoid discovery of abuse. • Professionals need to try to discriminate between physical signs and symptoms, which are a result of victimization (e.g., bruises inflicted by a beating), from age-related medical conditions (e.g., thin, wrinkled, dry, or fragile skin, which bruises easily). In some cases, both occur simultaneously.	• Does the patient have any medical problems (including loss of vision, hearing, mobility) which would limit self-protective ability in a crisis situation? • Is the patient's and family member(s)' explanation for the suspicious condition or injuries consistent with medical findings and concerns? Do the patient's current or past medical records contain information relevant to previous incidents of mistreatment (undetected or detected)? • Does the patient understand and appropriately utilize needed medical services, care, plans, and prescribed medications? If not, why? Does a family member interfere with patient's efforts to receive such care? If so, who interferes? • Have appropriate assessments been conducted to determine whether suspicious physical signs and symptoms are related to the patient's medical condition and/or mistreatment?

Table 13.1   *(Continued)*

Assessment Category	Assessment Issues	Assessment Interview (with patient and family member(s))
Functional Status	• Abusers who care for functionally dependent victims may appear frustrated, overwhelmed, guilty, or resentful of their responsibility. • Victims, whether or not functionally dependent, may be caregivers to the abusers. • Victims of neglect tend to require more home care than victims of abuse. • Abusers and victims may have unrealistic expectations of each other. • Abusers may not be the victims' primary caregivers. • Abusers may be resistant to allow outsiders to provide supportive services in the home.	• To what extent is the patient able to perform activities of daily living? If the patient requires help, who provides it? Why does this person help? How often? Does the patient regard this help as needed? Useful? Enough? How serious a problem is it for the patient if help is not provided when needed? Does it appear that a family member providing care does not have the desire, inclination, or resources to provide this care? • Is there evidence that the person providing care is doing so inadequately? Could other noncaregiving family members be acquiescing or actively participating in the mistreatment? • Is the patient receiving any supportive services (e.g., meals-on-wheels, home attendants)? If advisable, would the patient and family member(s) be willing to accept any (additional) supportive services? By whom? If not, why? Does a family member(s) refuse access to outsiders providing care in the home?
Living Arrangements	• Victims and abusers often live in the same household; often one is dependent on the other for housing.	• If patient and family member(s) live together, why? For how long? • Whose name is on the lease or deed? How are household expenses shared? • Is patient willing to consider alternative living arrangements for the suspected abusive family member(s) or self? If so, what kind?
Financial Status	• Abusers may be dependent on the victim for living and personal expenses. • Victims may have informally or legally given the abuser control over their income/assets. • Victims may have unmet care needs for financial reasons inconsistent with their financial ability.	• What are the patient's sources of income? Assets? Do the patient's finances contribute to family member's household expenses? If so, is this according to the patient's desires? • Who manages the patient's finances, why? For how long? How? Is this a legal or informal arrangement? How does the patient receive an account of transactions? • Is the patient unable or unwilling to purchase needed personal services? Why?

(Continued)

Table 13.1   *(Continued)*

Assessment Category	Assessment Issues	Assessment Interview (with patient and family member(s))
Social Support	• Victims are often socially isolated. • Abusers may attempt to limit and/or monitor victim's contacts with friends, other relatives, community/social groups, or professionals.	• Whom does a patient see during a typical day? What is the nature of these contacts? How does the patient perceive the quality of these contacts? • Is the patient satisfied with the extent and quality of his or her involvement with friends, neighbors, and outside activities? Is a family member preventing the patient's involvement with others? • Is the patient aware of supportive community services and crisis services? • How do the patient and family member(s) spend their time together (e.g., talking, activities)? Does the patient feel satisfied or dissatisfied with the relationship(s)?
Emotional/ Psychological Status	• Effects of victimization may include depression, fear, withdrawal, confusion, anxiety, low self-esteem, helplessness, shame, and guilt. • Observing victim's nonverbal behavior (e.g., no eye contact, expressionless face, body turned away from others) can be evidence of depression or anxiety. • Some abusers have a history of mental illness.	• How does the patient respond to the question, "Are you happy at home?" • Has the patient experienced any changes in mood, sleeping or eating patterns, weight loss? Could this be related to physical condition or medication? • Does the patient or family member have a history of mental illness? If so, how does it appear to affect their relationship?
Stresses	• Patterns of substance addiction and family violence exist in some mistreatment cases. • External factors such as unemployment, retirement, marriage/separation/divorce, residence change/household addition, death of someone close, and arrest, may create tension which may lead to mistreatment.	• What causes tension or conflict in the home? How does the patient attempt to resolve the conflict? Ask the patient to describe a recent family crisis. To whom does the patient turn for help? • Is there a history of family violence? • Does the patient and/or family member use alcohol excessively? Use illegal drugs? • Has there been a recent major event (e.g., retirement, death of someone close, etc.) which has altered the patient's lifestyle or emotional state? • Has the family member recently experienced problems with employment, relationships, finances, housing? How does this stress(es) affect the relationship with the patient? How does the family member cope with stress?

Table 13.1   *(Continued)*

Assessment Category	Assessment Issues	Assessment Interview (with patient and family member(s))
Abuse & Neglect Status: Frequency, Severity, Intent	• Mistreatment often increases in severity and frequency over time. • Several types of mistreatment may occur simultaneously (e.g., psychological abuse almost always accompanies physical abuse). • Denial of mistreatment by victims and abusers is common.	• When asking the patient more direct questions pertaining to mistreatment, first explain that such questions are routine because many families experience this problem but don't know where to turn for help. The following are examples of more direct questions that may be asked of patients, depending on the individual case: —Has anyone ever hurt you? —Has anyone ever touched you when you didn't want to be touched? —Has anyone ever forced you to do something against your will? —Has anyone ever taken anything that was your without permission? —Have you ever given anything away even though you really didn't want to? Why? —Dies anyone ever talk or yell at you in a way that makes you feel lousy or bad about yourself? —Are you afraid of anyone? —Has anyone ever threatened you? —Has anyone ever refused to help you take care of yourself when you needed help? • Explore each of the above affirmative responses further: How did (does) mistreatment occur? How often? Has mistreatment increased of changed over time? Explain. What precipitates mistreatment? Why does the patient think mistreatment occurs? Is the patient in danger as a result of the mistreatment? How serious is the danger? How serious are the consequences of mistreatment? Can the patient protect himself or herself? Does patient want to prevent mistreatment? How? If not, why? Have there been previous efforts to prevent mistreatment? If so, who helped? What happened? What would be different this time? What does the patient want to happen now?

Source: P. Ansell, and R.S. Breckman (1988). Assessment of Elder Mistreatment: Issues and Considerations. *Elder Mistreatment Guidelines for Health Care Professional: Detection and Intervention.* New York: Mt. Sinai/Victim Services Agency's Elder Abuse Project. Used with permission.

in nonhospital settings. This chart outlines assessment issues and interview guidelines as they relate to 10 different assessment categories: access, cognitive status, health status, functional status, living arrangements, financial status, social support, emotional/psychological status, stresses, and abuse and neglect status (Ansell & Breckman, 1988).

The clinician formulates intervention plans as the scope of the problem becomes clearer through the assessment process. As part of the assessment process, and to develop a solid intervention plan, it is important to consider what interventions have been made in the past, what worked and what did not, and why the victim may be interested in help now.

A comprehensive assessment should also seek to develop as clear a picture as possible of the characteristics of the abuser and the role he or she has in the older person's daily activities. The more the worker understands about the abuser and his or her relationship with the victim, the more likely it is that intervention plans will be responsive to the victim's circumstances. The following six questions are important to consider (Breckman & Adelman, 1988):

1. *Type of abuser.* Is the abuser or neglector experiencing caregiver stress? Does the abuser or neglector have malevolent motives? What motivated the mistreatment? Was the mistreatment intentional or unintentional? What proof exists?

2. *Type of mistreatment.* What mistreatment has occurred (physical, psychological, financial, neglect)?

3. *Severity and duration of mistreatment.* What damage has resulted from the mistreatment? How has this affected the victim? How has this affected the abuser's life? Over what period of time has the mistreatment occurred? Were there any intervals of time when mistreatment did not occur?

4. *Abuser acknowledgment of behavior and willingness to accept help.* Has the abuser admitted to any wrongdoing? Does the abuser minimize the seriousness of his or her actions? Does the abuser see a connection between his or her behavior and resulting harm? Does the abuser blame somebody else for problems (e.g., the victim, other household member)? Does the abuser blame problems on alcohol, loss of a job, a divorce, the death of a loved one? Does the abuser want help?

5. *Past and present interventions with the abuser.* What interventions have been tried before with the abuser? What helped, and why? What did not help and why? Does the abuser have a criminal record? If so, for what and when did the crime(s) occur? Does this record have any bearing on intervention plans? Is the abuser currently being assisted regarding the mistreatment problems?

6. *Safety risk to professionals in helping abuser.* Is the professional's safety compromised by helping the abuser? Is the abuse only directed to family and not outsiders? Does the worker's organization have a safety policy? Is it adequate? Will there be a safety issue for other workers engaged in the intervention plan (e.g., home attendants)?

Other issues to consider when assessing an abuser's service needs are the abuser's physical, mental, and functional status; the victim's desire to involve the abusing relative; organizational and professional responsibilities and capabilities; professional, victim, and family observations of the abuser; the availability of community resources/informal network; financial resources; and transportation. In general, the key to successful elder abuse intervention is a strategy similar to those employed in treating other "geriatric syndromes": creatively meeting unmet needs through a multidisciplinary effort that is tailored to the unique constellation of contributors and potential resources in each case.

LEGAL AND SYSTEMS CONSIDERATIONS

Several legal mechanisms can be employed to help victims of elder mistreatment. Laws differ from state to state, however, so this section discusses the options available, but does not address individual state laws.

MANDATORY REPORTING

One legislative response to elder mistreatment has been the passing of mandatory reporting laws. Mandatory reporting of elder abuse is required in the majority of states (Elder Abuse Project American Public Welfare Association & National Association of State Units on Aging, 1986). Mandatory reporting requires certain professional groups to report suspected adult abuse. The state then investigates and provides voluntary or involuntary adult protective services, depending on what information the investigation yields. Professionals are advised to become familiar with their state's mandatory reporting laws, as these have significant implications for intervention.

Five prominent controversial issues surround mandatory reporting of elder mistreatment. First, more than half of states with mandatory reporting use age as the determinant for who should be reported, sometimes specifying over 65 years,, and sometimes specifying 60 or 55 years (Elder Abuse Project American Public Welfare Association & National Association of State Units on aging, 1986). Thus, using "old age" as the screening criterion for which cases to report, has given mandatory reporting the reputation of being an ageist response to the larger problem of family violence against adults. Second, many elder mistreatment victims who are reported and investigated are competent adults, who understand the risks and consequences of their decisions, but choose to remain in abusive or neglectful environments. If there are services to be offered to the victim, professionals can let the victim know where to turn; if services are not available, then those investigating have nothing to offer either. In addition, mandatory reporting in these cases risks damaging the client-professional relationship based on trust and confidentiality. Third, although mandatory reporting can help those adults who are unable to understand the risks and consequences of their decisions and who are in imminent danger, it is possible to provide voluntary and involuntary assistance to judgmentally impaired adults without mandatory reporting, as is done in several states. Fourth, a positive development that has come from mandatory reporting is an increase of public awareness about the problem. This same public awareness campaign is possible, however, without mandatory reporting laws. Finally, victims often need a range of services (e.g., counseling, emergency housing, emergency money, lock replacement, court advocacy, crisis intervention, emergency police intervention, medical care). In most states, however, adequate money has not been allocated for the necessary provision of services when passing mandatory reporting laws, and ultimately these services are needed to develop a thorough and coordinated response to elder abuse and neglect.

ORDERS OF PROTECTION

Victims can try to obtain from court a restraining order that prohibits the abuser from engaging in certain behaviors (e.g., restraining the abuser from threatening or harassing the victim, and restricting the abuser from the victim's property). The order of protection is a signal to the abuser that society does not accept abusive behaviors. For some abusers, hearing from a judge that mistreatment will not be tolerated, and being threatened with jail, is enough to keep their behavior in check.

If the order of protection is violated, the abuser can be arrested on contempt of court charges, as well as for any criminal acts that were perpetrated. The goal is for the order of protection to discourage an abuser from continuing abusive behavior. Problems arise, however, if the abuser violates the order of protection. It then becomes necessary for the victim to call the police, have the abuser arrested on this violation (and perhaps additional charges), and follow through in court again. This is difficult for most victims, but extraordinarily difficult for ambivalent victims, those previously demoralized by the inadequacies of the police and criminal justice system to help, those unable to call for help, or those facing serious injury or death if they do call for help.

SUBSTITUTED JUDGMENTS

Reasons may arise to employ the services of friends, family, or professionals to manage financial affairs, both for individuals who are competent and those with judgmental impairments. Although substituted judgments are important mechanisms for protecting a person's estate or enabling someone to maintain a lifestyle, there is opportunity for exploitation. The following briefly describes the various types of substituted judgments (see Breckman & Adelman, 1988).

Power of attorney is a legal mechanism by which an individual, often feeling incapable of or inadequate in handling his or her own finances, can assign another to administer financial transactions. The power of attorney can be tailored to meet the specific needs of the individual (e.g., it can apply to one bank account, or to decisions involving real estate, stocks, and bonds). The individual selected for power of attorney is accountable only to the person requesting it. Therefore, a disadvantage of this legal mechanism is that if abuse occurs, nobody else would necessarily be cognizant of it.

Durable power of attorney is similar to power of attorney, but it takes effect only when persons authorizing its use lose the capacity to make decisions about their financial affairs.

A *representative payee* is an individual or organization appointed to manage a person's Social Security, veteran's pension, or railroad retirement benefits. Once this option is established, beneficiaries' wishes as to how to spend this money may not always be taken to account. The necessity for such an arrangement, therefore, and who is appointed representative payee, should be carefully considered.

Because of cognitive impairment, some individuals are no longer capable of managing their own finances. These individuals may be appointed a *conservator* or *guardian* by the court. This procedure is generally initiated by the family, a friend, or the state, although it may be initiated by a hospital or another institution where the person resides. The conservator has full responsibility for all financial matters relating to the ward's estate. Guardianship is even more expansive, as it includes responsibility for all financial and personal matters, including decisions concerning contracts, hospitalizations, and approaches to medical treatments. The comprehensive nature of conservatorship and guardianship leaves the ward vulnerable to mistreatment if those responsible for supervision are not honest and well meaning.

Laws concerning these substituted judgments differ from state to state. Workers assessing financial mistreatment may need to consult an accountant or attorney to determine whether financial mistreatment has occurred and to determine what steps, if any, can be taken to remedy the situation.

CASE ILLUSTRATION

Louise Frame is 84 years old and lives in her own co-op apartment in upper Manhattan. She was married briefly and has one daughter, Cheryl, who is now 50 years old. Cheryl has a long history of psychiatric illness and carries the diagnosis of chronic schizophrenia. She has had multiple psychiatric admissions and has been institutionalized for many years. Approximately one year ago, Cheryl was discharged from a psychiatric facility and Louise agreed to take her daughter in. For the first few months, all went well. Cheryl lived in the apartment, and mainly kept to herself but did help out with shopping and some light cleaning.

Over the past several years, Louise had developed congestive heart failure. The heart condition had been quite stable and Louise felt that she had excellent medical care and felt close to her internist. During the past 6 months, however, Louise's cardiac condition had deteriorated and she was hospitalized three times for exacerbations of congestive heart failure. Louise's physician questioned her about her compliance to the prescribed medication regimen and Louise stated that she was taking the medications religiously.

After the third hospitalization, the physician realized that Louise required help in the home—grocery shopping, housecleaning, and assistance to doctor appointments—as Louise stated that her daughter really was not able to help her adequately.

Home care workers performed all the necessary support tasks, and Louise, appreciative of their help, developed a warm and caring relationship with the workers. Although Cheryl lived in the apartment, she let the home care workers perform their jobs without interference.

But then, Louise started changing. The workers reported to their supervisor that she was slowly withdrawing. At first, she was less communicative. As time passed, she did not want to get out of bed, get dressed, or eat. The home care workers were concerned about this change and arranged for Louise to see her physician. The physician thought Louise was depressed, but Louise adamantly denied this and refused antidepressants and counseling.

On one occasion, a worker found Louise in tears after she was unable to pay the pharmacy delivery man the money due. The worker suspected that the daughter was stealing her money. The worker asked Cheryl about the missing money, at which point she flew into violent rage and ordered the worker out. The worker quickly called the police as she was worried about Louise. By the time the police arrived, Louise was holding her chest, appeared short of breath, and agreed to be taken by ambulance to the hospital.

In the emergency room, Louise was found to be back in congestive heart failure, and appropriate medications were initiated. Because Louise answered few questions and was quite tearful, a psychiatric consultation was obtained. The psychiatrist initially felt that Louise had a major depression, but thought her condition warranted further evaluation. Louise was admitted to the hospital for medical and psychiatric observation. When her physician entered her room with several residents, Louise asked to speak to him in private. She was tearful and confided to her physician that her daughter was stealing her money and therefore, she could not buy her medications regularly. Louise also stated that she was concerned that Cheryl was not taking the antipsychotic medications prescribed for her psychiatric illness. She begged her physician to keep this information confidential. She also told her physician about a lump in her right breast that she had recently noted.

The diagnosis from the psychiatric evaluation was major depression and Louise was started on antidepressant therapy. Because of the congestive heart failure, the physician's knowledge of financial abuse, and the psychiatrist's assessment, the patient could not be discharged home. Over the next several days, the social worker started an elder mistreatment assessment process. Also, her physician ordered tests to evaluate the breast lesion and determined that Louise had a localized breast cancer. The plans were to perform a lumpectomy and then radiation therapy.

The first area of assessment focused on Louise's cognitive status. The social worker learned from the home care workers that Louise's mental function was normal until three months prior to admission. It was clear that Louise's behavioral and cognitive changes occurred rather suddenly without any previous evidence of disorientation or confusion, all consistent with major depression.

Cheryl visited Louise frequently. Cheryl demanded to hear more about the prognosis of her mother's breast cancer. Cheryl became very agitated after speaking to the physician even when the doctor reassured Cheryl that the cancer can be easily treated. The floor nurses observed that she became more demanding of her mother (e.g., she insisted that Louise not slouch in bed and ordered Louise to share the hospital meals with her). Cheryl spoke in harsh, commanding tones with abrasive and offensive language. The daughter's behavior clearly was having a deleterious effect on Louise, who appeared frightened and agitated after the visits. At this time, her primary nurse noticed bilateral bruise marks on Louise's arms and suspected that Cheryl was mistreating her mother. When questioned about these marks, Louise looked away and did not speak.

The social worker spoke with Louise about Cheryl, attempting to understand Louise's thoughts and feelings about her daughter and to ascertain what had occurred in the home as well as in the hospital. Louise appeared concerned about Cheryl, admitted that she was not comfortable at home, but did not say that Cheryl mistreated her. When the physician reminded Louise of her prior confession, Louise denied that she had stated such a thing. She did say that her daughter had become "quirkier" since she was first discharged home from the psychiatric institution. The social worker tried to get clarification about what Louise meant, but Louise only sighed and, with seeming resignation, said, "I'm the only one left who looks after her. She has nobody else in this world. She can't look out for herself. I don't know what to do anymore." The social worker suggested to Louise that Cheryl might be in need of psychiatric help. Louise agreed that this was the case and she could not bring this subject up because it agitated her daughter. The social worker explored other social supports, and it appeared that Louise and Cheryl were isolated, without friends or family to assist them.

The social worker attempted to meet with Cheryl when she visited Louise but Cheryl refused to discuss her mother; she only expressed her fear about her mother's breast cancer, and then stormed away.

After Louise's heart condition was stabilized, she underwent lumpectomy and began radiation treatments. At this point, she was transferred to the psychiatric unit for observation, antidepressant therapy, and psychotherapy. Louise began to respond to the medication several weeks later. Her energy and appetite improved, and she was more responsive to therapy. In fact, Louise's depression had so improved that the psychiatric staff believed she could be treated successfully as an outpatient.

Therapy focused on Louise's plans for when she was to leave the psychiatric unit, and involved Louise's plans for safety. Louise admitted in therapy that Cheryl had become easily agitated, and that Cheryl grabbed her arms and shook her once. She also stated that Cheryl was completely focused on her breast cancer—even though the cancer was being treated, Cheryl did not seem to understand that effective treatment existed for this condition. Louise indicated that Cheryl had made the determination that Louise was dying from breast cancer and was angry with her mother for having developed this condition. In therapy, the issues that arose were Louise's guilt for abolishing her responsibility if she did not allow Cheryl in the home; shame about Cheryl's psychiatric condition and her own depression; and Louise's minimization of the danger she would face living with Cheryl, believing that she could stay out of Cheryl's way.

Louise understood that she would continue to require assistance at home and that most workers would be understandably reluctant to work in the home with Cheryl present.

The social worker approached this case with sensitivity and skill. Assessment issues included the emotional and psychological status of the victim and abuser, as well as the victim's functional and health status, financial status, social supports, living arrangements, types of mistreatment, safety issues, and the frequency and severity of mistreatment.

At this point, the psychiatric staff is planning for discharge. Louise is faced with several options, all with obvious disadvantages:

1. Louise could return home with home care (providing home care workers would be willing to do this), and hope that Cheryl does not hurt her (physically, emotionally, or financially) or cause problems with home care workers.
2. Louise could also go to court to try to obtain a restraining order, requiring Cheryl not to harass or harm Louise or the workers. Or Louise could return home and not allow Cheryl to live there, and try to get a restraining order restricting Cheryl from the property. Louise could also try to get the court to order Cheryl to obtain psychiatric care. It appears unlikely, however, that Louise would be receptive to options involving court at this point due to her guilt and shame.
3. Louise could sell or rent her home, and move into other housing, perhaps an adult home or senior housing. This, of course, would take time, and Louise would need to make interim plans (e.g., living in a month-to-month furnished apartment). The decision is Louise's, regardless of whether the staff believe it to be the safest.

For Louise, only a limited range of options is possible, however, it is important to realize that this is not always the case for victims of elder abuse and neglect. A considerable amount of support from medical, mental health, and social work system is essential to bring about optimal outcomes.

CONCLUSION

Although general knowledge about elder mistreatment serves as the foundation to guide the professional's overall work with victims, there is variation in the specific aspects of each elder mistreatment situation. Proper assessment requires the professional to have a good understanding of specific elements, which include evaluating and, if necessary, creatively approaching access difficulties; understanding the different types of mistreatment and recognizing that multiple forms of mistreatment may occur concurrently; evaluating the victim's health and functional status, living arrangements, financial status, social supports, and external stresses; understanding the victim's cognitive and emotional status; and evaluating the abuser's needs and care status. Gaining as much clarity as possible regarding all these elements of assessment is pivotal to devising an appropriate intervention plan, and also may have significant legal ramifications.

Assessment is an ongoing process that often involves the coordination of different professional disciplines and systems. The range and breadth of the assessment are influenced by the professional's own values, thoughts, and feelings about elder mistreatment, as well as time limitations and responsibilities.

REFERENCES

Ansell, P., & Breckman, R.S. (1988). *Assessment of elder mistreatment: Issues and considerations: Elder mistreatment guidelines for health care professional: Detection, assessment and intervention.* New York: Mt. Sinai/Victim Services Agency's Elder Abuse Project.

Benbow, S.M., & Haddad, P.M. (1993). Sexual abuse of the elderly mentally ill. *Postgraduate Medicine, 69,* 803–807.

Breckman, R.S., & Adelman, R.D. (1988). *Strategies for helping victims of elder mistreatment.* Newbury Park, CA: Sage.

Elder Abuse Project. American Public Welfare Association and National Association of State Units on Aging. (1986). *A comprehensive analysis of state policy and practice related to elder abuse.* Washington, DC: Author.

Finkelhor, D., & Pillemer, K.A. (1987). *Correlates of elder abuse: A case control study.* Paper presented at the third National Conference for Family Violence Researchers, Durham, NH.

Hwalek, M., Sengstock, M., & Lawrence, R. (1984, November). *Assessing the probability of abuse of the elderly.* Paper presented at the Annual Meeting of the Gerontological Society of America, San Antonio, TX.

Lachs, M.S., & Pillemer, K.A. (1995). Abuse and neglect of elderly persons. *New England Journal of Medicine, 332,* 437–443.

Pillemer, K.A. (1986). Risk factors in elder abuse: Results from a case-control study. In K.A. Pillemer & R. Wolf (Eds.), *Elder abuse: Conflict in the family* (pp. 239–263). Dover: Auburn House.

Pillemer, K.A., & Finkelhor, D. (1988). The prevalence of elder abuse: A random sample survey. *Gerontologist, 28,.51–57.*

Phillips, L.R. (1983). Abuse and neglect of the frail elderly at home: An exploration of theoretical relationships. *Journal of Advanced Nursing, 3,* 379–392.

Quinn, M.J., & Tomita, S. (1986). *Elder abuse and neglect.* New York: Springer.

Strauss, M.A., Gelles, R., & Steinmetz, S.K. (1980). *Behind closed doors: Violence in the family.* Garden City, NY: Anchor/Doubleday.

Tilden, V.P., Schmidt, T.A., Limandri, B.J., Chiodo, G.T., & Garland, M.J. (1994). Factors that influence clinicians' assessment and management of family violence. *American Journal of Public Health, 84,* 628–633.

Wolf, R., Godkin, M., & Pillemer, K.A. (1984). *Elder abuse and neglect: Report from the model projects.* Worcester: University of Massachusetts Medical Center, University Center on Aging.

Wolf, R., & Pillemer, K.A. (1989). *Helping elderly victims.* New York: Columbia University Press.

CHAPTER 14

Psychological Maltreatment
of Children

PAMELA M. BERLIN and JOAN I. VONDRA

PHYSICAL VIOLENCE in a family—even "behind closed doors" (Straus, Gelles, & Stein-metz, 1980)—can be a loud, attention-getting event. When injuries result, they may be noted by friends, neighbors, teachers, or service agents. And it is the *physical* evidence—broken furniture, black eyes, fractures, semen in a child—that is convincing to police, judges, and juries. But it is the *psychological* impact that warps lives, distorts relationships, fosters delinquency, and incurs lifelong costs in terms of special education, property repair or replacement, services for teen mothers, welfare for school dropouts, substance abuse programs, incarceration, and a host of other social services. Whether psychological harm takes place as a result of physical violence, sexual abuse, or emotional cruelty or unavailability, it leaves a legacy of individual maladjustment and interpersonal problems that is often passed down to another generation (see Youngblade & Belsky, 1990; Zeanah & Zeanah, 1989, for discussion of mechanisms). Of all the forms of child maltreatment examined in one study, it was parental "psychological unavailability"—a pattern of unresponsiveness, detachment, and lack of interest in the child—that resulted in the most compromised developmental and emotional functioning in early childhood (Egeland & Erickson, 1987). Young children who were verbally abused by hostile, rejecting mothers looked much like children who were physically abused—angry, noncompliant, and insecurely attached. Yet psychological maltreatment is among the least likely forms of maltreatment to be researched, it is least likely to convince a judge that child welfare is at stake, and it continues to receive no mention in child abuse laws in some states. Why is this?

The reasons are numerous and, to a certain extent, readily apparent. First, it can be significantly more difficult to document "clear and convincing" evidence of psychological injury resulting from parental behavior, as opposed to physical injury or sexual activity. Furthermore, psychological maltreatment is also present in cases of neglect—acts of omission rather than commission that generally occur over time and often take the form of an elusive behavioral pattern instead of a single, attention-grabbing event

(Brassard, Hart, & Hardy, 1993). Second, overburdened child protective service and juvenile court systems preclude the possibility of investigating and intervening in any but the most extreme and easily documentable cases of maltreatment. Third, the potential *number* of psychological maltreatment cases that occur in a wide cross-section of families is daunting. In addition, questions about family privacy and cultural diversity act as a powerful deterrent against "stirring up the muddy waters" of psychological maltreatment.

Each of these rationales provides a convincing argument against more extensive consideration of and attention to child psychological maltreatment. Nevertheless, the data we present in this chapter suggest that psychological maltreatment represents a core issue within child maltreatment and deserves special attention both in research and in practice. We provide the conceptual and empirical grounds for making this case, and suggest some practical strategies for—and implications of—incorporating psychological maltreatment into current intervention efforts.

DESCRIPTION OF THE PROBLEM

Psychological Maltreatment as a Core Issue

Garbarino (1980; Garbarino & Vondra, 1987) and others (Claussen & Crittenden, 1991; Navarre, 1987) have argued persuasively that psychological or emotional maltreatment is the underlying issue spanning every form of abuse and neglect. Extreme cases of physical abuse or neglect threaten the biological integrity of children. However, research indicates that on a day-to-day basis (and even during abusive episodes) it is more likely to be *psychological* maltreatment that undermines child functioning in the abusing or neglecting home. Physically maltreating mothers are more hostile, critical, and intrusive with their children, and less positive, supportive, and affectionate in everyday interactions (Crittenden, 1981, 1988; Lyons-Ruth, Connell, Zoll, & Stahl, 1987; Trickett & Susman, 1988; see Wolfe, 1985, for review). Physically neglecting mothers offer less supervision, cognitive stimulation, approval, affection, or emotional support on a day-to-day basis (Crittenden, 1988; Gaudin, Polansky, & Kilpatrick, 1992). All these behaviors are linked to poorer child functioning and development in studies of nonclinical families (Elder, Nguyen, & Caspi, 1985; Erickson, Sroufe, & Egeland, 1985; C. Patterson, Cohn, & Kao, 1989; see Maccoby & Martin, 1983, for review). Furthermore, although physical abuse and neglect need not accompany psychological maltreatment, it is questionable whether any form of abuse or neglect can occur in the absence of psychological maltreatment. In this case, it is the psychological integrity of the child that is jeopardized (Crittenden & Ainsworth, 1989; Rohner & Rohner, 1980).

What seems to matter most for a child's psychological development is the message that goes along with the abuse or neglect. Is it possible to bruise a child in anger without conveying the message, "Sometimes I really hate you" or "You are a no-good brat"? Can a parent leave a child dirty, cold, and alone without implying, "You aren't worth my attention"? Is a parent who seduces and/or sexually exploits his or her child not saying, "Your sexuality matters more than anything else" and "Power and sex are what love is all about"? Continually refusing a child's requests for help, denying a child warmth and emotional responsiveness, corrupting, exploiting, and isolating, are messages communicating to children what they are like, what they are worth, and what they can expect from others (Hart & Brassard, 1991). Research on parenting and on child maltreatment indicates that when such messages characterize the parent-child relationship, normal child development is compromised.

O'Hagan (1993) argued that it is the sustained, repetitive nature of the behavior that qualifies psychologically damaging interactions as "abuse." Whereas physical or sexual abuse can, theoretically, involve one or more isolated acts, by this definition, psychological abuse cannot. It is the physically noteworthy incidents that receive disproportionate attention, but it is the day-to-day inappropriate behaviors and emotional responses which seem to cause the lasting damage, even when accompanied by physical or sexual abuse.

Empirical work has begun to establish that emotional maltreatment does, in fact, threaten the psychological integrity of children, leading, in many cases, to significant and pervasive psychological dysfunction (Claussen & Crittenden, 1991; Egeland & Erickson, 1987; Egeland, Sroufe, & Erickson, 1983; Herrenkohl & Herrenkohl, 1981; Krugman & Krugman, 1984; McGee, Wolfe, & Wilson, 1997). The messages, "Nothing you do is good enough," "Your needs don't matter to me," and "Everyone is out to get you," take on serious consequences when they come from a significant parental or attachment figure, perhaps especially during childhood. Attachment theory and research attest to this.

According to attachment theory, children develop unconscious views of themselves and expectations of others based on their experiences of being nurtured and responded to from infancy (see Bretherton, 1985). When a mother (and presumably father) is observed to taunt, intrude on and/or frustrate, reject, or assume sexual overtones in speech or behavior toward an infant or young child, insecure attachment and maladaptive behavior patterns are the likeliest outcomes (Cicchetti & Barnett, 1991; Cicchetti & Olsen, 1990; Crittenden, 1988; Lyons-Ruth et al., 1987; Sroufe, Jacobvitz, Mangelsdorf, DeAngelo, & Ward, 1985). Threatening a toddler, teasing when he or she is distressed, not trying to comfort him or her after a fall, taking a toy with which the toddler is engaged, and demanding a show of affection from the child are behaviors in the laboratory and at home that have distinguished mothers whose children's attachment appears most troubled (Lyons-Ruth, Bronfman, & Parsons, in press; Schuengel, Bakermans-Kranenburg, & van IJzendoorn, 1997). Attachment insecurity is one of the few early prognostic indicators of subsequent child maladjustment (see Belsky & Nezworski, 1988; Toth & Cicchetti, 1996). Psychological maltreatment, in other words, attacks the very core of a young child's developmental foundations—his or her sense of self and of relationship security. Psychological maltreatment should therefore be considered a "core" issue in child maltreatment.

DEFINITIONAL ISSUES

Definitions of *psychological maltreatment* show as much variability as the acts that comprise it. The following constitute only a very select sample:

Mental injury by other than accidental means. (Virginia Code 16.1–228(A)(1), Supp. 1984)

Mental injury . . . under circumstances which indicate that the child's health or welfare is harmed or threatened thereby. (Public Law 93–247, 1974)

> Active, intentional berating, disparaging, or other abusive behavior toward the child which impacts upon the emotional well-being of the child; passive or passive/ aggressive inattention to the child's emotional needs . . . or emotional well-being. (American Humane Association, 1984)

> Sustained, repetitive, inappropriate behavior or emotional responses that inhibit legitimate and natural emotional expression and/or damage the creative and developmental potential of crucially important mental faculties and processes so as eventually to undermine the child's attempt to understand the world around her, confuse and/or frighten the child, and lead to a pervasive lack of confidence. (O'Hagan, 1993)

> Acts of omission or commission which are judged on the basis of a combination of community standards and professional expertise to be psychologically damaging. (Hart, Germain, & Brassard, 1983)

The key concern faced by child protective services and legal professionals is for carefully delineated definitions—particularly of *mental injury*—and illustrative examples. Without them, justification for governmental intervention is not adequately specified (Melton & Thompson, 1987). In the absence of federal standards, there is enormous diversity among states in providing such specification (Corson & Davidson, 1987; Garbarino, Guttmann, & Seeley, 1986; McMullen, 1992). Some states (e.g., Pennsylvania, Missouri, Virginia) never go beyond a reference to "mental injury" in their definition of child abuse and neglect. Others provide explicit descriptions of child conditions or behavior that may constitute evidence of emotional abuse or neglect (Arizona, New Hampshire, Wisconsin). For example, Wisconsin's child protective services statute specifies that mental injury has the following characteristics:

> Substantial harm to a child's psychological or intellectual functioning which may be evidenced by a substantial degree of certain characteristics of the child including, but not limited to, anxiety, depression, withdrawal, or outward aggressive behavior. "Mental harm" may be demonstrated by a substantial and observable change in behavior, emotional response, or cognition that is not within the normal range for the child's age and stage of development. (Wisconsin statute 948.04(2))

Still others do not recognize mental injury as child maltreatment unless it can be shown to have been caused by *physical* abuse or neglect (Delaware, New York, and Illinois). When mental injury *is* specified, states differ in terms of the role parents must play. Whereas failure to provide adequate care for emotional health is justification for intervention in some states, in others, parents must "inflict" mental injury or, in still others, "allow" it to occur. The inconsistency across state definitions and the general failure to be explicit in defining terms results in a host of problems at the legal and, ultimately, the service levels.

Although psychological maltreatment is arguably present in all forms of child maltreatment, and appears to be a potentiating factor (McGee et al., 1997), any definition of psychological maltreatment should allow distinctions to be made and comparisons to be drawn between psychological maltreatment and other forms of abuse and neglect. This permits investigation of the degree to which psychological maltreatment (1) occurs *in the absence of* other forms of maltreatment, and (2) *by itself* undermines child functioning and development.

Until researchers, protective service workers, lawyers and judges, and clinicians all have some understanding of the significance of psychologically harmful acts for current and future mental, social, and emotional development, effective policy cannot and will not be designed or implemented. The absence of this knowledge is a contributing factor to state definitions of abuse and neglect that make no reference to psychological maltreatment or mental injury. It also promotes protective service policies that allow any but the most extreme reports of psychological maltreatment to be screened out prior to investigation. Finally, it permits court custody decisions to be made that expose children to chronic and cumulative psychological maltreatment because professionals unversed in child development do not perceive "clear and convincing" evidence of current or impending damage (Tomkins et al., 1994).

However, such knowledge is not entirely lacking, as the growing body of research on parenting gives testimony. These studies are noted throughout the section on child assessment. A great deal more, however, remains to be done to clarify the concept of psychological maltreatment and its hypothesized effects.

Any discussion of psychological maltreatment in childhood requires consideration of the transaction between abusive parent behaviors and the strengths and vulnerabilities of an individual child at a particular phase of development (McGee & Wolfe, 1991). Developmental concerns play a primary role in determining whether a child's psychological needs are being addressed and whether psychological dysfunction is present. Both issues have relevance to definitions of and evidence for psychological maltreatment. A toddler who has difficulty separating from her parent for day care, who appears dependent with a day-care provider whom she clings to over relatively minor occurrences, who is easily agitated by new or challenging situations, and who cries easily when provoked by peers is far less likely to be considered a possible victim of psychological maltreatment than an 8-year-old who exhibits the same behaviors in the classroom. Similarly, a parent who keeps his children locked indoors except when accompanying them to the store, a park, or a relative's home may be viewed as conscientious and caring when his children are under 3 years of age, but abusive when his children are older than 10 years.

Child competencies (e.g., ability to separate, independence and autonomy, adaptive and peer skills) and child needs (e.g., constant supervision, verbal reasoning) change with age. So too must criteria for definitions and assessments. Changing assessment criteria are highlighted in the developmental approach adopted in the section on assessment strategies. The need for developmentally changing criteria in definitions is a corollary to the need for careful specification of what constitutes psychologically damaging acts and psychological injury to children.

A final concern relates to variation in community standards of "minimally adequate," let alone "optimal," child care. Because cultural differences exist in what is considered desirable and healthy child behavior and in what kinds of parental and familial treatment are appropriate, some degree of cultural sensitivity is needed in arriving at a definition of psychological maltreatment. This is especially evident when a criterion for establishing the presence of psychological maltreatment is "maladaptive" or "maladjusted" child behavior. Successful adaptation in one cultural milieu can require dramatically different behaviors than in another, as exemplified by U.S. subcultures as disparate as Amish farming communities, African American urban ghettos, Native American tribal reservations, Hispanic migrant worker groups, and rural White mining towns. These differences argue against adopting definitions mapped out by any one sociocultural group (e.g., White, urban professionals), but instead require that definitions evolve from joint efforts of individuals representing a wide range of social, cultural, and economic milieus.

On the other hand, there *are* fundamental developmental needs and goals common to all cultural groups that can and should form the basis for arriving at mutually agreed on definitions of psychological maltreatment. These have been summarized by Navarre (1987), and include (1) being and feeling valued; (2) feeling (potentially) competent; (3) seeing people as (potentially) responsive; (4) forming and maintaining positive relationships; (5) recognizing and responding to human emotions; (6) being able to learn, adapt, and problem-solve; and (7) seeing the world as something other than a hostile, threatening, and frightening place. As noted throughout this chapter, evidence of psychological maltreatment invariably relates to the impairment of one or more of these functions. Indeed, it is generally agreed that definitions must focus on *child impairment related to care* rather than variations in the care itself, since wide differences in child temperament and resiliency, familial and extrafamilial stresses and supports, alternative sources of care, and performance demands on the child will alter the developmental impact of particular behaviors and practices. The bottom-line question for definitional and intervention purposes is whether a child shows evidence of current or future dysfunction relating to the care received (but see Baily & Baily, 1986; McGee & Wolfe, 1991).

We conclude this discussion of definitional issues with a brief consideration of the distinct, often conflicting, definitional needs required for clinical versus legal intervention. What constitutes justifiable (coercive) intervention by the state obviously differs from what constitute appropriate standards of need for offering subsidized intervention services to children and families. Both differ, in turn, from what constitute appropriate standards of care in child institutional settings ranging from schools and day-care settings to juvenile "boot camps" and detention centers. At the same time, research on immediate and long-term effects of care in all these settings requires relatively more flexible standards and operational definitions than any of the aforementioned instances. In every case, more explicit, mutually agreed on, and widely accepted definitions of psychological maltreatment need to be developed. The following general guidelines are offered here (for a more extended discussion, see Cicchetti, 1991):

- *Legal definition.* Based on observable (psychological) damage to the child that can be related to the care received. Assessment requires measuring damage to the child, documenting parental mistreatment, and demonstrating failure on the part of caregivers to seek and participate in any professionally prescribed treatment plan.
- *Clinical definition.* Based on impending damage to the child, emphasizing predictable dysfunction. Assessment requires identifying developmentally and clinically significant patterns of child behavior predictive of subsequent maladjustment. Intervention requires parental cooperation.
- *Research definition.* Based on either observable patterns of family interaction *or* observable damage to the child, emphasizing the developmental needs of the child. Assessment requires identifying family interaction patterns that have been or can be related to disturbed child psychological functioning.

In the next section, assessment needs, strategies, and issues are presented that relate to these three broad agendas—legal intervention, clinical services, and research efforts. No single definition of psychological maltreatment is adopted to keep assessment concerns relevant to each agenda. Instead, assessment strategies focus more generally on failure to meet children's basic developmental needs. Supportive research is cited where such research exists.

ASSESSMENT APPROACHES

From the discussion of definitional issues, it should be apparent that different emphases exist across the legal, empirical, and clinical arenas regarding assessment of *risk* (defined in terms of parent or child functioning) versus *damage,* and of parental care versus child functioning. Whereas research and service programs tend to be more concerned with long-term developmental and familial outcomes and with the efficacy of prevention efforts, the legal and mandated service sectors must, necessarily, be more short term and crisis focused. Major attention is devoted in this section to assessment of injury to children—the core issue shared by all three arenas—but assessment of parental care and behavior is also given consideration.

The relative comparability of clinical and empirical perspectives on psychological maltreatment should not imply that there are notable connections or cross-fertilization even among the clinical and empirical literatures. Compartmentalization of work on child maltreatment within and across legal, clinical, and research communities impedes progress at many levels. In addition, an extreme dearth of empirical work on psychological maltreatment leaves unanswered important questions relating to definition, etiology, treatment, and outcome. Finally, lack of psychometric information on many of the measures used to assess child and familial functioning in cases of suspected maltreatment implies a need for concern about the reliability and validity of assessments.

With these caveats, and mindful of the need to take developmental considerations into account, the remainder of the section is devoted to the issues of identification and assessment of cases of child psychological maltreatment. Discussion of these issues is organized according to four developmental periods: infancy/toddlerhood, preschool and early school age, school age, and adolescence.

Infancy and Toddlerhood (Birth to 3 Years)

Perhaps more than at any other time in development, healthy growth and functioning in infancy are embedded in the environmental stresses and supports that shape parenting. This is due to the extreme dependency of the infant on parental care and, simultaneously, to the exclusivity of parental care as a healthy or undermining influence on development. The school-age child can seek out supportive adults in school and in the neighborhood and the adolescent may seek out empathic, often similarly situated peers. The infant or toddler, however, is considerably less capable of finding alternative ways to meet social, emotional, and/or intellectual needs. O'Hagan (1993) argued that, as a result, the younger the child, the easier it is to perpetrate emotional abuse and the more vulnerable the child is to the abuse. Furthermore, when psychological maltreatment begins very early, severe mistreatment tends to occur more frequently

(Ney, Fung, & Wickett, 1994). Thus, assessment of infant and toddler risk or damage requires special sensitivity to parental circumstances and care.

Even during pregnancy and the early postpartum period, it is possible to identify characteristics of mothers and their support systems that place infants at risk for psychologically damaging care. They include an unplanned or unwanted pregnancy, teen parenthood, failure to make provisions at home for the baby's arrival, evidence of disinterest on the part of the mother in her pregnancy or newborn, the absence of a stable intimate relationship, the perception of having few available supports, and maternal personality and psychological problems (Altemeier, O'Connor, Vietze, Sandler, & Sherrod, 1982; Brunnquell, Crichton, & Egeland, 1981; Coohey, 1996; Egeland & Brunnquell, 1979; Kempe & Kempe, 1978). These are *cumulative* risk indices for inadequate care and poor infant functioning that can often be easily assessed on the obstetric ward around the time of birth. Both Kempe and Kempe (1978) and Olds and Henderson (1989) used such indices as criteria for inclusion in intervention studies with demonstrated efficacy for improving parental care, child outcomes, and the risk of maltreatment. Several measures that, alone or together, have had some success in one or more research studies at discriminating already maltreating parents or parents who will later maltreat their young children are summarized in Table 14.1 (see R. Caldwell, Bogat, & Davidson, 1988 for discussion).

Psychologically abusive behaviors during mother-infant structured observations have also been associated with various forms of suspected and/or substantiated maltreatment as well as developmental impairment (Crittenden, 1988; Egeland & Sroufe, 1981; Lyons-Ruth et al., in press). These include (1) controlling play activities or other interactions in a way that ignores disinterest, discomfort, and other emotional signals of the infant; expressing anger/hostility or emotions that are opposite to those the infant shows (e.g., disinterest in infant curiosity, indifference to infant laughter; typical of mothers reported for abuse), and/or (2) appearing unresponsive to, uninterested in, and uncaring of infant activities and bids for attention, through words, affect, and behavior (typical of mothers reported for neglect). Examples of these behaviors are provided in Lyons-Ruth et al. (in press) and in O'Hagan (1993; Table 14.2). Due to the relatively wide margin of error when assessed across brief periods, their use for legal or clinical purposes may be limited and requires repeated observations over time.

Turning from parenting and its context to infant and toddler assessment, it is necessary, first, to be familiar with and knowledgeable of the developmental tasks of the period (see Table 14.2). When substantial delay or impairment is noted in the acquisition of any of these tasks, a close look at the home situation is warranted (see Greenspan, Nover, & Scheuer, 1987, for extended discussion of diagnostic assessment). Fraiberg (1980) provided several excellent descriptions of the use of a standardized infant developmental exam as an opportunity to observe both infant behavior and parent-infant interaction. Clinical observations of this sort can provide valuable information about the quality of relationship between parent and infant, as well as infant developmental status. More extended investigation is warranted when infants exhibit disinterest in the parent, are unable to get the parent to respond to their signals and needs during testing, or appear apathetic or ignorant regarding use of the test materials.

Formal assessment of the parent-infant relationship can be accomplished, in part, using the "Strange Situation" paradigm created by Ainsworth and Wittig (1969; Ainsworth, Blehar, Waters, & Wall, 1978). Greenspan and Lieberman (1988) suggested appropriate use of attachment assessments by trained clinicians. The wide

Table 14.1

Measures for Identifying Parents at Increased Risk of
Maltreating Infants and Children

Measure	Description	Supportive Research
Maternal Attitude Scale (Cohler, Weiss, & Grunebaum, 1970)	Maternal beliefs about child needs and parenting practices	Egeland & Brunnquell, 1979; Egeland & Sroufe, 1981
Adolescent Parenting Inventory (Bavolek, Kline, McLaughlin, & Publicover, 1979)	Adolescent beliefs about child needs and parenting practices	Bavolek, et al., 1979
Pregnancy Research Questionnaire (M. Schaefer & Manheimer, 1960)	Maternal reactions to pregnancy, maternal depression and dependency	Egeland & Brunnquell, 1979; Egeland & Sroufe, 1981
Maternal History Interview (Altemeier et al., 1979)	Feelings about pregnancy, social support, childrearing history, life stress, personality	Altemeier et al., 1979; Altemeier et al., 1982
Family Stress Checklist (Murphy, Orkow, & Nicola, 1985)	Parental experience of abuse, mental illness, psychosocial problems, and other risk factors	Murphy et al., 1985
Michigan Screening Profile of Parenting (Schneider, 1982)	Parent social support and family relations, expectations of child, coping skills	Gaines, Sandgrund, Green, & Power, 1978; Schneider, Helfer, & Hoffmeister, 1976
Child Abuse Potential Inventory (Milner, 1980)	Parental personality, social problems, views of self and child	Milner, Gold, Ayoub, & Jacewitz, 1984; Milner & Winberley, 1980
Maternal Characteristics Scale (Polansky, Borgman, & De Saix, 1972)	Maternal apathy/futility, impulsivity, verbal accessibility	Polansky et al., 1972; Polansky, Cabral, Magura, & Phillips, 1983
Personality Research Form (Jackson, 1967)	Parental aggression, defendence, impulsivity, succorance	Egeland & Brunnquell, 1979; Egeland & Sroufe, 1981
IPAT Anxiety Scale (Cattell & Scheier, 1963)	Anxiety	Egeland & Brunnquell, 1979; Egeland & Sroufe, 1981

margin of error in measurement and prediction using this technique requires that attachment data be used only *in conjunction with* other relevant clinical and standardized test information, including naturalistic observations of parent and infant, preferably in the home setting (see Fagot & Kavanagh, 1990). Attachment classification, particularly the "disorganized/disoriented" category, has been used to identify maltreated infants (Cicchetti & Barnett, 1991; Crittenden, 1988) and has been associated with subsequent child behavior problems and maladjustment up to age 7 years (see Lyons-Ruth, 1996).

Early play and peer behavior represent another source of information about child psychological well-being. Play themes have been related to maltreatment experiences in case studies of toddlers (Haynes-Seman & Hart, 1987) and unusually repetitive, stereotyped, disorganized, or passive play activities are indicators of psychological problems (Gould, 1972; Greenspan, 1981). Disturbances in play can be evaluated using

Table 14.2
Developmental Tasks of the Infancy/Toddlerhood Period

0–6 months	Acquiring some degree of regulation—through the support of caregivers—over bodily functions and states; learning to use caregivers to attain a comfortable state of physical and emotional arousal (stimulated to alertness, consoled to quiet, fed, moved, or changed to a state of physical comfort).
	Demonstrating interest in and curiosity about the world by gazing about and listening attentively.
	Exhibiting early social behaviors: smiling both indiscriminately at persons (before 4 months) and specifically at caregivers (after 4 months).
6–12 months	Developing a sense of unique interest in and trust of an attachment figure, learning to use a relationship for emotional closeness and for the security needed to separate and explore the unfamiliar.
	Becoming increasingly adept at communicating, first with gestures, then with single words (beginning around 12 months), a variety of needs, desires, and emotions.
	Demonstrating interest in and curiosity about the world by moving about and manipulating objects.
12–18 months	Beginning to incorporate pretend behaviors into play; increasing use of single words.
	Demonstrating interest in and curiosity about the world by increasingly independent physical exploration.
	Developing some attention span, goal-directedness, and persistence in effortful behavior.
18–24 months	Gaining a sense of emerging autonomy and initiative, and beginning to assert oneself as an independent (even willful) agent.
	Moving on to simple sentences and self-words to communicate needs, desires, and emotions.
24–36 months	Growing interest in peer activities and a beginning appreciation of "right" and "wrong" as dictated by adults.
	In conjunction with developing language skills, beginning to demonstrate some self-regulation in terms of waiting, sharing, and following rules . . . some of the time.

any of a number of published play scales, although all require specialized training (see C. Schaefer, Gitlin, & Sandgrund, 1991).

Increased problems with peers provide another indication that children may have troubled relations with parents. When paired with peer partners for activities, maltreated toddlers and preschoolers are more aggressive and resistant in response to both prosocial and aggressive peer behaviors (Howes & Eldredge, 1985). In a free play setting, on the other hand, they may exhibit greater social withdrawal (Hoffman-Plotkin & Twentyman, 1984). Several respected behavior rating scales with normative data on very young children include peer relation items (see Achenbach & Edelbrock, 1986; Harter & Pike, 1984; Quay, 1977; Quay & Peterson, 1967).

We conclude this section with a brief mention of physical problems having psychosocial origins. Research indicates that nonorganic failure to thrive—termed psychosocial dwarfism after age two—is an outcome, in part, of psychological maltreatment (see Batchelor & Kerslake, 1990; Chatoor & Egan, 1987; Green, Campbell, & David, 1984). Identifying characteristics of failure to thrive include weight and height below the third percentile or sudden loss in weight gain, feeding difficulties, lethargy and apathy, and in many cases, developmental delay or retardation. These infants engage in higher rates of self-comforting behavior and express more sadness, anger, distress, and/or disgust (Abramson, 1991). When treated in the hospital (with one-to-one nursing care) or removed to new homes, these youngsters typically show notable improvement. Both eating problems and growth hormone disturbance have been linked to emotional stress and disturbed mother-infant relationships (see Chatoor & Egan, 1987), findings that corroborate years of clinical observations. Cherniss, Pawl, and Fraiberg (1980) provided an extended case study of such an infant, her emotionally neglecting mother, and the course of intensive intervention (see also Wieder, Hollingsworth, Castellan, Hubert, & Lourie, 1987). Medical and clinical diagnosis should be undertaken in any suspected case of failure to thrive, with careful consideration of the relationship between infant and caregiver, including observations over an extended period of time (see O'Hagan, 1993).

PRESCHOOL AND THE EARLY SCHOOL YEARS (3 TO 7 YEARS)

Healthy development among youngsters of this age, although still highly dependent on family relations, reflects beginning autonomy from close and exclusive family bonds. Cognitive achievements during what Piaget termed the "Preoperational Period" of cognitive development allow the growing child to use fantasy in imaginative and self-enhancing ways to create a private world (but also to begin to distinguish fantasy from reality), to ask questions and seek the help of adults and peers outside the home, and to tackle rudimentary problems on his or her own.

Psychological maltreatment appears to stifle creative and effective mental functioning and problem solving. Several researchers have documented poor self-regulation and frustration tolerance during problem solving, cognitive limitations reflected in language and in perspective taking, and impaired curiosity and creativity among children experiencing different forms of maltreatment (Aber & Allen, 1987; Barahal, Waterman, & Martin, 1981; Erickson, Egeland, & Pianta, 1989; Hoffman-Plotkin & Twentyman, 1984). Often it is difficult to distinguish the poor cognitive functioning of maltreated children from that of socioeconomically impoverished comparison children, as both exhibit deficits associated with unstimulating, unresponsive, authoritarian home environments (Elmer, 1977; Vondra, Barnett, & Cicchetti, 1990). In each case, impaired cognitive functioning is the outcome of child-rearing conditions inadequate for normal child development.

Observations of parent and child working on challenging tasks together provide useful information about child functioning (*and* the relationship) to trained researchers or clinicians who have the expertise to note deviations from the norm. Many research studies rely on behavioral ratings made during such tasks to distinguish children experiencing better and poorer quality parenting (see Sroufe, 1983). In addition, developmental testing by qualified professionals can be invaluable for gaining a sense not only of the child's performance level, but also of his or her approach to cognitive challenges. The Stanford-Binet includes a facesheet with behavioral ratings that can be used to document impairments in attention span, affective expression, and/or motivational orientation observed during testing. Teacher reports of cognitive functioning, including language skills, problem-solving ability, possible learning disabilities, and classroom motivation, are important corroborative data that can be gathered using measures with appropriate norms. Examples would include selected "school readiness" measures (i.e., those with adequate psychometric and normative data) and the school performance section of behavior problem checklists such as the Child Behavior Checklist (Achenbach & Edelbrock, 1986). Documentation of a child's lack of skills necessary for school entry and schoolwork can represent important evidence contributing to a picture of compromised functioning.

Socially and emotionally, the child between ages 4 and 7 should be moving toward a balance between self-confident independence and appropriate reliance on adult assistance. Psychologically maltreated children, and maltreated children in general, are often strikingly impaired in this regard. The self-confidence that leads to excitement and enthusiasm during problem-solving is likely to be absent, and excessive dependency on adults is common (Egeland et al., 1983; Rohner & Rohner, 1980). However, when it comes to *parental* assistance, there may be help seeking on the part of the child, but little mutual affection and enjoyment. Among other things, Bousha and Twentyman (1984) reported that both abused and neglected children interacted less frequently with their mother at home than did comparison children.

Disciplinary problems are also to be expected. By definition, the psychologically maltreating parent does not provide the respect and affection that underlie effective discipline (see Baumrind, 1978, 1991). Noncompliance toward parents is a common finding in maltreated samples (Egeland & Sroufe, 1981; Egeland et al., 1983), but among young children, an almost obsessive compliance has also been noted (Crittenden, 1988; Kempe & Kempe, 1978). Rather than risk negative parental reactions, maltreated children may also assume an attitude of "pseudo" independence, appearing unconcerned about or actively denying their own emotional needs (Miller, 1981). Controlling or "caretaking" behavior toward parents is another characteristic of some emotionally exploitative parent-child relationships; parents may "spousify" their children by relying on them to meet their own emotional needs (Cassidy, 1988; Main & Cassidy, 1988). A higher than average number of tantrums that persist into the preschool and early school years is another indication of child maladjustment stemming from psychologically distressing home life.

Assessment of many of these behaviors, particularly in the company of parents, requires behavioral observations by trained professionals (O'Hagan, 1993). Parental report, although potentially biased and unreliable, may provide supplementary evidence of dysfunction. Indeed, maltreating parents tend to report a clinical frequency of behavior problems in their children, and are likely to be especially sensitive to antagonistic, disruptive, and other aversive behaviors that act as stressors (Aragona & Eyberg, 1981; Kadushin & Martin, 1981). Behavior problem checklists with norms for parental report may therefore be useful in assessment. Furthermore, teachers and staff in day-care and preschool/school settings can obviously provide valuable information, based on their experiences interacting both with the target child and other children. Dependency, noncompliance, and poor control of negative emotions are all potential symptoms of maltreatment that teachers are well qualified to note.

Symptoms indicative of poor self-confidence, low self-esteem, and a negative self-concept, however, may be expressed only indirectly, either through withdrawal or through acting-out behavior. Prior to the age of 7 or 8, it is unclear how effectively children can recognize and voice global feelings of worthlessness or inadequacy on standard self-report measures (see Harter, 1982, 1983). Indeed, recent data on abused and psychiatric samples of children suggest that both may, in fact, exaggerate their competencies and social acceptance on self-report measures (Vondra et al., 1990; Zimet & Farley, 1986). These findings have been interpreted in terms of both delayed cognitive development and defensive processes. In at least one study, more negative self-perceptions among (female) physically or sexually abused elementary school-children emerged only on a projective measure designed to capture unconscious responses, but not on a standard self-report measure (Stovall & Craig, 1990). For preschoolers and early school-age children, then, self-esteem may best be assessed through a combination of teacher and clinician observations, as opposed to self-report measures.

Difficulty establishing and maintaining peer relations can also be a symptom of troubled parent-child relations stemming from psychological maltreatment. In fact, given the linkages documented between parent-child relations and developing peer relations (Fagot & Kavanagh, 1990; Park & Waters, 1989; Sroufe & Fleeson, 1986, 1988), this may be one of the key areas of functioning to note disturbance. Social withdrawal and isolation have been observed among children experiencing various forms of maltreatment (Hoffman-Plotkin & Twentyman, 1984; J. Kaufman & Cicchetti, 1989). Children who have been maltreated appear to possess fewer social skills and to exhibit less prosocial behavior with peers than do comparison children, perhaps especially in structured (as opposed to free play) settings (George & Main, 1979, 1980; Howes & Eldredge, 1985).

Peer sociometrics, in which classmates name their most and least favorite play partners during individual interviews, have proven validity in research on peer relations. Specific measures have been reviewed by Berndt (1984), Hymel (1983), and Ladd (1985). However, the cumbersome procedures required to obtain peer sociometrics make reliance on teacher report measures more practical, although not necessarily as accurate. Discussion of the relative usefulness of a variety of teacher report measures appears in Hymel and Rubin (1985) and Ledingham and Younger (1985).

Physical problems with possible psychosocial origins requiring attention at this age include not only psychosocial dwarfism (e.g., Silverton, 1982), but also enuresis and encopresis (McCarthy, 1979), and habit disorders such as thumb-sucking, rocking, and head-banging. After ruling out organic factors through medical examination and history, notice should be taken of circumstances in the home that may have had a bearing on the emergence and maintenance of these problems. Stressful events and circumstances can provoke a variety of physical symptoms in children and/or behavioral regression (e.g., bed-wetting, thumb-sucking), as research has documented (see Rutter, 1981).

Throughout this section, there has been little mention of the child as a direct *informant* regarding either self-perceptions and self-functioning or parental behavior. Even young children can provide valuable information about their own experiences directly through behavior and words (see Garbarino & Stott, 1989). Children often provide key information during informal, spontaneous comments or observations that alert caregivers' or teachers' notice. Indications that a child fears going home or fears a parent should certainly be taken seriously and carefully pursued. Among young children, though, direct questioning may not be effective unless carried out by a skilled and experienced individual familiar to the child, and, at all ages, inquiry must be sensitive to the emotional nees and cognitive level of the child. In addition to direct questioning, it is useful to use more indirect assessment methods such as a narrative story stem technique to elicit information about family experiences and conflicts. Buchsbaum, Toth, Clyman, Cicchetti, and Emde (1992) stress that while maltreated preschoolers may indicate verbally that their relationship with their mother is fine, their narratives elaborate themes of neglect, punitiveness, and rejection. Garbarino and Stott (1989) provided extended consideration of the issues involved in using children as information sources that is pertinent to this discussion.

Before proceeding to the middle school years, mention should be made of two specific forms of psychological maltreatment that may be especially relevant for children of preschool and early school age. The first is maltreatment arising from an abusive spousal relationship, when emotional and/or physical abuse of one parent is carried out in the presence of children. A growing literature cites numerous child adjustment problems that can be linked to this terrifying experience (Christopoulos et al., 1987; Jaffe, Wolfe, & Wilson, 1990), although spouse abuse is an important risk condition for compromised parenting and physical forms of child maltreatment. Preliminary evidence suggests that child problems are not as severe as those among children who are battered themselves, but substantial in relation to children from nonviolent homes (Jaffe et al., 1990; Kenning, Merchant, & Tomkins, 1991). Many child symptoms associated with spousal violence are discernible in the classroom setting, where distractibility, inattentiveness, academic problems and, at the more extreme end, separation anxiety and school phobia are likely to be noticed by teachers (see Tomkins et al., 1994). When young children observe spouse abuse, there is neither adequate cognitive sophistication to "make sense of" and distance oneself from, nor outside peer or adult relations to buffer the consequent psychological distress and vulnerability. Data linking childhood observations of spouse abuse in the home with involvement in exploitative heterosexual relationships later in adolescence and adulthood (Gwartney-Gibbs, Stockard, & Bohmer, 1987; Kalmuss, 1984; see Tomkins et al., 1994) testify to the long-term consequences of this form of child psychological maltreatment. A parental self-report measure of spousal conflict that has proven successful in research is the *Conflict Tactics Scale* (Straus et al., 1980), which includes items relating to physical and emotional abuse. On the other hand, the *Family Behavior Survey* (Jouriles et al., 1991) is one of the few instruments that specifically requests information about the frequency of spousal arguments witnessed by the child. Information about spousal violence is obviously difficult to obtain without reliance on parental report, although careful child interviews by trained clinicians may provide preliminary documentation. National survey data collected by Tomkins and his colleagues from social service administrators and providers suggest that "speaking only to battered mothers and not to the children will result in many children slipping through the cracks" (p. 171). Since estimates of the number of children who witness physical or even sexual abuse of their mother reach three million a year, this is probably not an insignificant number.

A second form of psychological maltreatment, significantly less frequent in occurrence, is a medical phenomenon termed Munchausen syndrome by proxy. In this case, parents involve children more directly in their own psychopathology by imagining—and in some cases of infants or very young children, by inflicting—child physical ailments ranging from apnea (irregular breathing) and diarrhea to cardiorespiratory arrest (Chan, Salcedo, Atkins, & Ruley, 1986; K. Kaufman, Coury, Pickrel, & McCleery, 1989; Palmer & Yoshimura, 1984). Although physical abuse is implicated when symptoms are inflicted through behaviors such as partial suffocation and administration of ipecac, psychological maltreatment occurs when children are old enough to experience the forgery of symptoms and exploitation of medical attention and technology as missocialization. Psychological maltreatment is also implicit in repeated parental efforts to encourage unnecessary child examination and testing by medical personnel. What has been interpreted in terms of parental needs for attention, often among parents with a history of feigning medical problems and/or using mental health services, means for children repeated trips to clinics, hospitals, and private practices for problems imagined or exaggerated beyond any basis in reality. The phenomenon occurs often enough that medical personnel recommend specific education for community professionals dealing with children of all ages (K. Kaufman et al., 1989).

MIDDLE SCHOOL AGE (8 TO 11 YEARS)

Professionals in a variety of disciplines agree that children in this age period may be the most *professionally* neglected when it comes to child abuse and neglect, particularly in the case of psychological maltreatment. By the middle school years, children have acquired a degree of cognitive sophistication that warns them to keep family troubles private, and that aids them in developing stratagems for accomplishing this. Fear of family dissolution, separation from parent(s), and/or parental reprisal are powerful motives to avoid disclosure even to trusted individuals. Obvious symptoms in the failure-to-thrive infant or regressed preschooler are less obvious in the mistreated schoolchild. Efforts to take refuge in sexual relationships, substance abuse, and other forms of delinquent behavior may not yet have emerged (although delinquent problems are increasingly visible among children under age 15 years). Extremes in physical condition and behavioral outcomes may be least apparent during the primary school years, when family problems may also be most actively and successfully disguised or hidden.

In the absence of physical conditions detectable to medical professionals and behavioral extremes that bring youth to the attention of school staff, neighborhood officials, or the police, it becomes more important than ever to have a solid knowledge of behavioral and developmental norms to distinguish signs of disturbance that may result from psychological maltreatment. Development during this period, however, is in many ways a consolidation and expansion of abilities and skills that emerged more dramatically during previous developmental stages. Thus, it can be even more difficult to decide when behavioral differences or deviations represent anomalies that will disappear with time versus symptoms of underlying disturbance.

Across middle childhood, language and problem-solving skills allow children to negotiate more effectively with adults and peers, to reason in a logical (although not necessarily thorough) manner, and to regulate their own behavior to a degree not possible earlier in development. However, these cognitive achievements do not emerge independently of social and emotional functioning which, themselves, appear particularly vulnerable to the effects of maltreatment. Regardless of whether cognitive and socioemotional functioning were compromised earlier in development by psychological maltreatment or not until middle childhood, there are likely to be social and emotional consequences that may further undermine cognitive functioning.

As Belsky (1984) argued in the case of parenting, unless an individual is relatively free from psychological issues and from emotional distress, it is unlikely that person will be able to "decenter" enough from his or her own problems to attend to the needs and cues of others. In the case of psychologically abused or neglected children, problems with self-esteem and self-confidence, dependence/independence, and closeness and intimacy—all hypothesized outcomes of disturbed attachment relations—will likely interfere with peer and adult relations and, ultimately, with adaptation to school and society. Social and emotional issues can interfere with effective language skills, self-regulation, attention and persistence, and problem-solving. Deficits in cognitive functioning among maltreated children may take the form of inabilities to concentrate, control, and regulate one's own behavior, take the perspectives of others, and use other cognitive skills important for adapting to social and academic life.

To the extent that maltreatment is long-standing, the combination of developmental problems may result in grade retention or in placement in a special "learning disabled" or "socioemotionally disturbed" classroom. As Broadhurst (1984) noted, "The behavior of emotionally maltreated and emotionally disturbed children is similar" (p. 19). Numerous studies note a disproportionate amount of retention and placement among maltreated and failure-to-thrive samples (e.g., Hufton & Oates, 1977; Vondra, Barnett, & Cicchetti, 1989). Within a normal classroom, difficulties performing up to expectations, getting along with peers, and negotiating class rules and requirements may all be signs of disturbance stemming from maltreatment and psychological stress at home (Downey & Walker, 1989). The most frequent source of child maltreatment reports is educators (16% of all reports, National Center on Child Abuse and Neglect [NCCAN], 1995). As with preschoolers, it is critical to incorporate teacher reports within any assessment plan, both in terms of academic progress and classroom adaptation.

Reports from teachers or other adults who work with the child on a regular basis (e.g., a Big Brother/Sister, a scout leader, church youth guides, recreation center staff) can also provide critical information about social and emotional functioning. As during the preschool years, developmental issues revolve around self-regulation and peer relations. Behavioral and emotional extremes in these and related areas of functioning are relevant. Generally, behavior problems observed during the preschool and school years—and those that typify maltreated children (see Broadhurst, 1984)—fall into one of two patterns: (1) internalizing problems that involve overcontrol of emotional expression such as anxiety, depression, and somatic complaints; and (2) externalizing problems that involve undercontrol of emotional expression such as conduct problems, hyperactivity, and antisocial behaviors. Girls, in particular, are at risk for internalizing problems, and if psychological abuse or neglect increases during these years, they may develop significant adolescent adjustment problems. Boys, on the other hand, are at greater risk for externalizing disorders (Wolfe & McGee, 1994). Ratings on behavior problem checklists by adults familiar with the child can be compared with age norms to detect abnormal levels of difficulty/maladjustment. Particular behaviors that have been highlighted in descriptions of psychologically maltreated schoolchildren include extreme passivity and compliance, hysteria and obsessions, phobias, depression, and attempted suicide in the internalizing category, and destructiveness, cruelty, lying or stealing, aggressiveness, and extreme demandingness in the externalizing category (Broadhurst, 1984; Crittenden, Claussen, & Sugarman, 1994).

As in the preschool years, peer relations can be assessed by teachers/youth group leaders, or rated by classmates or other peers. Since emotionally maltreated children display distortions in relationships of varying degrees of severity, it is significant to note that peer rejection during the elementary and middle school years, particularly among boys who are aggressive, is a marker for later school dropout and/or juvenile delinquency (see Asher & Coie, 1990; Crittenden et al., 1994). In addition, extremely shy or withdrawn behavior among girls, perhaps indicating the absence of any intimate peer relationships, has been identified in some studies as a risk factor for subsequent mental health problems. Thus, peer rejection represents an important link between psychological maltreatment and developmental psychopathology.

A critical difference between assessment of preschool and school-age children is the availability of standardized diagnostic interviews for use with children over 7 or 8 years old. In particular, the Child Assessment Schedule (CAS; Hodges, Kline, Fitch, McKnew, & Cytryn, 1981; Hodges, McKnew, Cytryn, Stern, & Kline, 1982) gathers information from a child interview for classification of child psychopathology according to the American Psychiatric Association's *Diagnostic and Statistical Manual of Mental Disorders,* 3rd edition *(DSM-III).* When used by professionals with clinical training in interviewing and scoring, the CAS has demonstrated reliability and validity in identifying children with clinically defined behavior problems. Also useful is the Schedule for Affective Disorders and Schizophrenia for School-age Children (Kiddie-SADS; Orvaschel & Puig-Antich, 1987), a well-respected clinical interview measure of childhood depression and schizophrenia.

Interviewing school-age children as a direct source of information about possible psychological maltreatment is less constrained by child cognitive limitations than is interviewing younger children. Still, the tendency of school-age children to think in concrete terms on the basis of immediate circumstances requires that the interviewer be knowledgeable about child development and experienced in child interviews. Increased defensiveness about revealing family "secrets," denial and repression (Miller, 1986), and issues about trust and mistrust (often justifiable) demand a high degree of clinical expertise as well. The reader is again referred to Garbarino and Stott (1989) for further consideration of these issues.

When, at any age, significant child problems have been identified, there must also be evidence of psychological maltreatment if that diagnosis is to be made. It is not possible to map out any one, or even several, sequence(s) of contact and inquiry that will suit all of the situations in which such a need arises, nor is it our purpose to do so. It is worthwhile, nevertheless, to identify instruments that have been used to evaluate parental practices and the quality of the home environment. Several have been summarized by Garbarino and his colleagues (1986). Some of these measures, and others, are presented in Table 14.3.

At all times, choice of instrument(s) and/or rater(s) must depend on the particular needs and circumstances of the case. It seems obvious, but worth reiterating, that multiple perspectives provide richer, fuller descriptions than any single perspective, no matter how objective. Just as multiple assessments of child functioning from multiple sources may be critical for founding a case, so too may multiple perspectives on parental care be essential for documenting it.

The measures described in Table 14.3 provide opportunities to gather corroborating evidence of child-rearing practices and conditions that may be psychologically abusive. The perspective we adopt is that psychologically abusive practices are reflected not only in specific parental behaviors, but also in the overall home environment. As Egeland and Erickson (1987) note:

> Abuse should not be viewed only as an isolated incident, but as an environment. . . . We
> have found that in addition to overt abuse and neglect, the homes of many of these children

Table 14.3
Measures for Assessing Parental Care

Measure	Respondents	Authors
Parental Acceptance-Rejection Questionnaire	Parents Children/Adolescents	Rohner & Rohner, 1980
Adolescent Abuse Inventory	Parents Adolescents	Sebes, 1986; see also Garbarino, 1989
Conflict Tactics Scales (Verbal Aggression Scale)	Parents	Straus, 1990; see also Vissing, Straus, Gelles, & Harrop, 1991
Family Experiences Questionnaire	Adolescents	Briere & Runtz, 1988; Briere & Runtz, 1989
Childhood Level of Living Scale	Trained Observer	Polansky, Borgman, & De Saix, 1972; Polansky, Cabral, Magura, & Phillips, 1983
Child Well-Being Scales	Trained Observer	Magura & Moses, 1986; see also Gaudin, Polansky, & Kilpatrick, 1992
Home Observation for Measurement of the Environment (HOME) Inventory	Trained Observer	B. Caldwell & Bradley, 1984; Rosario, Salzinger, Feldman, & Hammer, 1987
Psychological Maltreatment Scale	Trained Observer	Taylor, Underwood, Thomas, & Franklin, 1988

> are characterized by chaos, disruption, and disorganization. Drug and alcohol abuse are common, the mothers often are physically abused, and, in general, the homes provide a very aversive environment for raising the children. (pp. 115–116)

In other words, psychologically abusive child care includes behaviors *and* circumstances, maintained over time by parents or guardians, that actively undermine children's psychological development. Chronic spouse abuse, deprivation of stimulation, failure to supervise or to enforce minimal behavioral limits, fabrication of child medical symptoms, and emotional dependency on the child thus qualify for psychological maltreatment as much as repeated parental threats, degradation, and belittlement. Measures in Table 14.3 represent an effort to capture this variety.

ADOLESCENCE (12 TO 18 YEARS)

Developmental tasks across adolescence focus on physical, psychological, and emotional preparation for the roles, responsibilities, and independence of adulthood. Increased power for the adolescent accrues within the family with the emergence of adultlike cognitive, social, and physical capabilities. Adolescents can argue logically about the way things could or should be; they can turn to the support and example set by an expanding field of significant others; they have the physical strength to resist physical discipline or coercion; and they can exercise real options to leave the home situation, either temporarily or permanently. It is not surprising, then, that adolescence is a period of increased conflict with parents and of increased maltreatment.

The National Incidence Study of Child Abuse and Neglect (1982) reported a dispro-portionate number of adolescents (12–17 years), relative to their representation in the national population, who had been maltreated. As parents struggle to deal with adoles-cent excesses and the striving for autonomy, it is particularly easy for parenting to become abusive or neglectful. Control, frustration, anger, disapproval, and disengage-ment can all become extreme under the circumstances, to the point that adolescent psy-chological functioning is undermined and developmental progress is jeopardized.

Psychological maltreatment during adolescence—whether it begins then or contin-ues from an earlier period—is especially likely to *produce* behavioral extremes as well. The physical and psychological changes of adolescence themselves foster emotional and behavioral extremes, but adolescents also have more opportunities to demonstrate extreme behavior than do younger children, in part as a result of emerging adultlike ca-pabilities. Thus, the adolescent may be especially vulnerable to damage and loss of self-esteem, the very hallmark of psychological maltreatment. Unlike younger chil-dren, however, the adolescent is more likely to attempt escape through drugs, sexual promiscuity/delinquent behavior, or suicide, all of which are less viable options for children. The arena for misbehavior also increases, with the relative freedom and ex-panding social world of the adolescent. As a consequence, the disobedience and defi-ance of the 9-year-old at home or in school may, during adolescence, be acted out against community and society in delinquent acts.

At the same time, by adolescence, maltreatment may be a long-term, cumulative ex-perience that builds to a crescendo when the adolescent gains new perspectives and initiative. To the extent that the adolescent is also less dependent on family bonds, ado-lescents may feel less compulsion to hide family problems and preserve family intact-ness. The result may be a new willingness to share information with sympathetic others. When considered in conjunction with the relative cognitive sophistication of the adolescent, it becomes more appropriate to utilize standardized self-report mea-sures of symptoms and experiences for assessment.

Research indicates that psychological maltreatment has unique links with self-reported low self-esteem in adolescence. Briere and Runtz (1990) discriminated be-tween female undergraduates who reported psychological maltreatment and those who reported other forms of abuse and neglect (before age 15) using items that tap severe self-criticism, guilt, and perceived undeservingness. In their view, general measures of self-esteem may be less effective in capturing the particular self-concept issues asso-ciated with psychological maltreatment than measures designed specifically for that purpose. Items on their own scale include the following:

1. Sometimes I call myself "dirty" names in my head.
2. I don't enjoy looking in a mirror.
3. Sometimes I feel that people like me more for what I look like or what I can offer sexually than who I really am inside.
4. I often feel guilty about things I have done.
5. I often feel contaminated.
6. Sometimes I feel that I don't deserve to live.
7. I like myself most of the time. (reverse scored)

Consistent with other studies of maltreatment during adolescence, these re-searchers noted that reported psychological maltreatment was associated with shame, anxiety, depression, somatic complaints, dissociation, and suicidal ideation among the young women in their sample (Briere & Runtz, 1988; Hoglund & Nicholas, 1995). In their study of adolescents, Wolfe and McGee (1994) found that girls' poor adjustment was generally a function of neglect and nonphysical forms of abuse. In terms of personality and ego functioning, then, it seems important to include a questionnaire or assessment of depression (e.g., Beck Depression Inventory, Schedule of Affective Disorders and Schizophrenia), with special attention to items pertaining to suicide.

Other problems associated with psychological maltreatment during adolescence are encompassed within the broad rubric of "delinquent behaviors." Conduct problems within and outside school, antisocial behavior, and criminal behavior are associated with inconsistent parental discipline, parental neglect, gross lack of supervision, and family dysfunction (see Loeber & Dishion, 1983; G. Patterson & Stouthamer-Loeber, 1984). Retrospective data indicate that a high percentage of delinquents were abused or neglected earlier (Lewis, Mallouh, & Webb, 1989). In at least one study, self-reported delinquent behaviors among high school students were associated with reports of emotional abuse and neglect, but not with reports of physical abuse (Brown, 1984). Other studies indicate that when both physical and emotional abuse are experienced, hostility and anger become even stronger. Cumulative forms of abuse may lead to greater adjustment difficulties (Hoglund & Nicholas, 1995; Wolfe & McGee, 1994). Garbarino (1989; Garbarino, Wilson, & Garbarino, 1986) and others cited data indicating that a majority of adolescent runaways and prostitutes experienced parental physical, sexual, and/or psychological maltreatment, ultimately leading to their departure from home.

In many cases, evidence of earlier disturbance is available from reports of school adjustment problems, school failure, and/or problems with peers (Parker & Asher, 1987). In most cases, parent-child and parent-adolescent relationship problems have been ongoing. Thus, although psychological abuse or neglect by parents may have been long-standing, and behavior problems noted earlier, not until adolescence do the behavioral consequences of maltreatment become extreme enough to demand both attention and intervention.

Assessment of maltreatment during adolescence can and should be accomplished by gathering information from multiple sources. Several of the measures in Table 14.3 were designed for completion by children or adolescents, who should certainly be questioned about family circumstances and parental behavior. It is important to focus attention on adolescents' appraisals of their own maltreatment histories since this is a time when synthesis of moral, cognitive, and interpersonal experience occurs at more conscious levels. Because adolescence presents opportunities to renegotiate relationship issues and foster identity formation, supporting adolescent awareness of how maltreatment undermines perceptions of self and family can be critical for the youth's subsequent development (McGee et al., 1997). Although external validation is also important, reports by parents and other observers may misrepresent interactions or exclude important information about less frequently occurring events. Furthermore, maltreatment during adolescence may reflect developmental and interpersonal processes within a dysfunctional family system that victimize the adolescent more subtly and indirectly than any individual parental acts. The clinical case studies described by both Minuchin (1974) and Haley (1980) illustrate this.

Significant adolescent pathology (delinquency, mental illness, somatic symptoms) can evolve from parental and familial efforts to preserve marital or other family relations from disruption due to conflict, mental illness, or substance abuse. O'Hagan (1993) described as one indication of psychological maltreatment inappropriate reliance on adolescent family members—even by health professionals—to care and take responsibility for adult family members with mental health problems. However, no family member would necessarily report specific behaviors that, in and of themselves, appear to constitute psychological abuse or neglect. Indeed, maltreatment is denied by the use of other clinical labels, as Garbarino (1989) noted:

> Adolescent maltreatment tends to be associated with problematic acting-out behavior of the teenager or dysfunction within the family, and to be dealt with as such by agencies other than protective services. These cases may be buried under labels of "dysfunctional families," "school adjustment problems," "running away,""acting out," or "marital problems" even when there is no apparent difference in the level of abuse experienced. (p. 698)

In cases where general family dysfunction is indicated, trained clinicians should conduct evaluations through family interviews and observations. Psychological maltreatment in these cases may be diagnosed on the basis of symptomatic adolescent behavior that can be directly linked to dysfunction in the family system.

A specific concern in adolescence is psychological maltreatment by parents reacting to knowledge or evidence that their adolescent is homosexual or bisexual. Martin (1996) noted convincing data that this is a problem of no small proportions with powerful effects on adolescent behavior and adjustment. These data include the higher rate of psychological abuse among homosexual and bisexual youth (especially those from ethnic minority families) as opposed to heterosexual youth, estimates that one out of every four homosexual or bisexual youth is forced to leave home due to conflict over his or her sexual orientation and that some 60% of homosexual youth abuse alcohol or drugs, the finding that a disproportionate number of homeless youth and young prostitutes (especially male) are homosexual or bisexual and that homosexual and bisexual youth represent almost one third of the nation's completed suicides. Her review of legal data indicated that "when faced with . . . harassment of queer youth, the most common response of courts is to ignore the abuse" (Martin, 1996, p. 179). She attributed this, in part to "the discretion and lack of guidance given to courts in determining the existence of emotional abuse" (p. 192), recommending a model statutory provision against emotional abuse specifying that endangering a child's emotional health constitutes such abuse and offering guidance on recognizing abuse without relying on "demonstrable harm." In the next section, legal issues are considered more generally and in relation to broader systems issues that act as barriers to serving psychologically maltreated children and youth.

LEGAL AND SYSTEMS CONSIDERATIONS

The beginning and end point for consideration of psychological maltreatment as a legal issue is the difficulty of proving "beyond a reasonable doubt" that child psychological dysfunction (1) both exists and jeopardizes future development, (2) is caused by parental care, and (3) will continue indefinitely as a result of parental refusal to seek help (for self or child). Cases involving psychological maltreatment alone (i.e., not co-occurring with physical or sexual abuse/neglect) are significantly less likely than cases involving other forms or combined forms of child maltreatment to be referred to Child Protective Services (CPS) (American Humane Association, 1988). They are also less likely to be accepted for investigation by CPS; they are certainly less likely to result in any legal action involving parental rights, and they rarely conclude with removal of the child from his or her home or with court-mandated intervention, even though most states now have provisions for doing so (Melton & Davidson, 1987). The reasons have been noted or alluded to earlier, but bear further mention.

CPS caseloads are excessive. Reporting of child maltreatment in general increased dramatically (331% from 1976 to 1993—NCCAN, 1995), and although it has leveled off in recent years, adequate investigation of those cases places an enormous burden on already overworked caseworkers. To the extent that physical and sexual maltreatment *also* represent psychological maltreatment, these cases demand top priority. At the same time, no commonly accepted, well-specified definitions of psychological maltreatment and injury exist either within or across most states. Evidence of psychological injury, already difficult to document reliably for a courtroom, may or may not be accepted as adequate justification for governmental intervention depending on the idiosyncracies of state law, the expertise of court officials in dealing with developmental and family issues, and judicial attitudes about child versus family needs and rights.

From the perspective of Child Protective Services, child dysfunction suspected to be the result of parental psychological maltreatment is typically better served through the mental health system than through CPS. Psychological maltreatment is, in many cases, not yet a legally defensible construct that can be used either to coerce parents into treatment (for themselves or their children) or to remove children from their care. Although a few model programs exist for case management by an interdisciplinary team representing *both* CPS and mental health services, these are few and far between (see Rosewater, 1989).

When children are identified as showing deviant, delayed, and/or disturbed behavior that may be related to parental care, parents should be invited to share in and discuss the situation (see Garbarino & Stott, 1989). In some instances, temporary family stress (e.g., a separation, job loss, or death) may be responsible or there may be special circumstances operating that require specific responses. When indicated, children should be referred for evaluation, and appropriate support services for children and parents should be recommended. Parental cooperation and participation are voluntary, however, so success depends largely on how parents are approached, how well contacts and services are coordinated, and how parents respond to each of them (Fraiberg, 1980; O'Hagan, 1993).

In many cases, this scenario entails a working relation between child care or educational settings and mental health agencies and service providers. Day care and school personnel can play a vital role in identifying, referring, and even serving children in need. Increasingly, schools *are* offering program models for linking children and families with relevant services both within school and in the broader community (Behrman, 1992; Davies, 1995). School-based programs that teach about domestic violence can educate staff as well as children about the effects of witnessing spousal violence and about appropriate intervention (Jaffe, 1991). In-service training for teachers and child-care providers about identifying and documenting suspected psychological (and other forms of) maltreatment and, equally important, dealing with the child and parents involved, may be a crucial first step toward connecting a family to services. For the present, cooperative efforts by child care, educational, and mental health facilities may be the most effective strategy for dealing with cases of psychological maltreatment. Frequently, however, legal and political agendas at the local and/or state level neither support nor encourage such collaborative efforts. Establishing such priorities and setting up incentives for serving children's needs collaboratively is a much needed start.

When there is evidence of serious, significant, or protracted harm to the child inflicted or allowed to occur by the child's parents, the case should be turned over to child protective services. In regard to cases referred to CPS, Corson and Davidson (1987) suggested the following guidelines for staff workers:

> Certainly, any pervasively bizarre or exaggerated behavior or statements of the child should be cause for the worker to secure a comprehensive mental health evaluation for the child. Likewise, where the worker has information which suggests that the child has been the victim of repetitive parental terrorizing, rejection, severe isolation . . . or morally corrupting and degrading acts, a complete professional evaluation is certainly called for. (p. 199)

This is the route required for seeking court-ordered therapy or removal of the child from the home (ordinarily on a temporary basis). Corson and Davidson argued, furthermore, that when parents agree to professionally recommended therapy, CPS intervention should be voluntary only and no court action should be initiated. It is only when parents refuse therapy or there appears to be continued harm or threat of harm to the child's psychological well-being that court action may be most appropriate. Success in the legal sense, however, is difficult to secure, and often requires that evidence meet "grave threat" (to child) standards. Dean (1979) made the following recommendations for agencies and caseworkers seeking court action:

> Contact the Juvenile Court and establish agreement on definitions and guidelines for court referrals; document the abuse and its negative impact on the child; use expert eye witnesses such as psychologists and psychiatrists; determine what other interventions have been attempted and what results were achieved. (p. 18)

Those with experience bringing such cases to court agree that an emphasis on *dire* consequences to child functioning and imminent threat of permanent injury, stated in explicit, nontechnical terms, is critical. Diagnosis of a *DSM-IV* mental disorder by a qualified psychologist or psychiatrist can also play an important role in a court ruling. Finally, cases that involve accompanying physical symptoms (failure-to-thrive, psychosocial dwarfism, physical injury) are generally considered more persuasive to court officials (Martin, 1996).

From these observations, it is clear that there must be cooperative working relations between CPS staff and mental health service providers for evaluating the extent of psychological damage that may be linked to parental care. There must also be working relations with court attorneys and child court advocates to ascertain, first, whether existing evidence is adequate to make a case and, second, what other evidence may be necessary to secure a favorable ruling. Because, once again, there is likely to be enormous variability across states, communities, and judges, collaboration within and across local agencies and professionals is likely to play an important role in successful adjudication.

There is consensus both within and outside the legal system that psychological mal-treatment has not been adequately defined or operationalized from a legal standpoint, and that this inadequacy has important implications for current efforts to protect chil-dren from harm. Although at least three different model standards for state child abuse and neglect statutes have been developed (American Bar Association Juvenile Justice Standards Project, 1980; U.S. Department of Justice, 1980; Whiting, 1976), there re-mains little agreement about appropriate justification for state intervention. At pres-ent, then, from a service perspective, psychological maltreatment must be considered primarily a mental health issue rather than a legal issue, with intervention efforts founded on voluntary parental participation and cooperation.

This circumstance gives added importance to the role of community organizations serving children—whether day-care centers, well-baby clinics, youth centers, or schools—as potential partners to mental health services in helping to bring support and resources to children and families. There remains a critical need to inform those work-ing with children in community settings *and* those serving children and families in legal settings about basic developmental and clinical issues relating to child maltreat-ment. This includes not only recognizing child and family symptomatology, but know-ing how to work with the family constructively and supportively toward a mental health referral. Although much applied research remains to be done (see Melton & Thompson, 1987), the developmental significance of psychological maltreatment is in-creasingly clear through research efforts. Awareness and understanding of the consid-erable and long-lasting impact of psychological maltreatment on the developing child are fundamental educational goals still to be realized in legal and in community settings.

CASE ILLUSTRATIONS

CASE 1: INFANT

Brianna is an 11-month-old infant who first came to the attention of staff at the com-munity medical clinic when her mother brought her in for immunizations required by a community college day-care center. Brianna's 19-year-old mother, Donna, enrolled in a nurses' training program after being informed that her welfare benefits would soon cease. Day-care services were provided by the community college as part of the local back-to-work program in which Donna was enrolled. In the clinic waiting room, Bri-anna sat on the floor in the toy corner, examining the toys with great solemnity. Al-though occasionally looking over to her mother, she made no attempt to engage her in any interaction and never expressed any pleasure or fun. Other children entered the play area for toys, but Brianna avoided eye contact and withdrew to the corner with a single toy. Donna sat three rows away looking at a magazine and listening to music with headphones on.

When Brianna's name was announced, Donna picked her up abruptly, took the toy away, and carried the startled child into the nurse practitioner's office. There was no greeting or affect of any kind exchanged between mother and baby. Donna handled Brianna roughly while undressing her, with the comment, "Hey, cut it out," although there was little struggle on Brianna's part. When the nurse approached her, Brianna re-garded her warily, but did not protest being picked up. She felt stiff and neither smiled nor babbled in response to the nurse's repeated efforts to engage her. As the nurse did a brief, developmental exam, it became apparent that cognitive and motor milestones were delayed, and it appeared that her social development was seriously impaired. Brianna was only in the third percentile for height and weight and, in general, appeared more like an 8-month-old than an infant nearly a year old. When the nurse inquired about Brianna's last well-baby visit, Donna shrugged and looked away.

Noting Donna's apparent disinterest and the lack of emotional connection between mother and baby, the nurse gently inquired about the supports available to Donna in caring for Brianna. Donna was brusque and stated flatly that she took care of Brianna herself and did not need anyone's help. Not surprised by this rebuff, the nurse continued her checkup and suggested that Donna must have a hard time getting her own needs met when she spent all her time with Brianna. She focused her soft-spoken comments and questions around Donna's efforts to care for the two of them and Donna's ability to get things done the way she wanted. Working slowly and deliberately, the nurse gave Brianna back to Donna to finish dressing and asked her about Brianna's behavior. Shortly afterward, she noted aloud that things must be tough for both mother and baby, and expressed her concern about the well-being of each of them. With caring for Donna's needs interwoven in her comments and questions, the nurse described her specific worries about Brianna and her appreciation for Donna's wish that Brianna be as healthy and capable as she could be. The nurse described services at the clinic and the day-care center to support Donna in doing a good job as a solo parent and to help Brianna catch up in growth and understanding. Since the clinic had an outreach facility at the community college, various intervention services (possible counseling for Donna, a young mothers' support group, and a mother-baby group) could be provided in conjunction with Brianna's day care and Donna's school program. The nurse gently encouraged Donna to think about her own needs for emotional support as well as Brianna's growth and development needs. She offered Donna contact information for two programs and promised to call her about the programs and possible participation in the next day or two.

The nurse was able to use her consulting hour two days later to talk further with Donna about her needs as a caring mother and Brianna's needs to catch up on her growth and development. She contacted both programs to let them know of Donna's (mild) interest, with permission from Donna for them to contact her about possible participation. She followed up this contact with two more phone calls over the next few weeks, always supporting Donna in her motivation to get the best care for Brianna, always listening and questioning with care and respect for Donna's efforts. Thanks, in large part, to the quality of her initial contacts with Donna, both mother and child could be engaged by staff from the intervention programs and enrolled in therapy. Although early psychological harm was apparent and could be linked to the quality of the mother-child relationship, this case was not severe enough to warrant intervention by child protective services and would certainly not have prompted any legal action. Assistance to mother and child depended wholly on the ability of professional staff to help what turned out to be an angry, defended mother acknowledge need on her own part and the part of her child.

CASE 2: SCHOOL-AGE CHILD

Mike is an 8-year-old in the third grade of a private school for gifted children. Despite intelligence considerably above average, Mike has been described as hyperactive, unable to sustain learning activities, very demanding of both teachers' and classmates' attention, and aggressive when it is not forthcoming. After a variety of unsuccessful classroom interventions on the part of his first- and second-grade teachers, the school determined that Mike would not continue in third grade unless his parents, Gary and Carol, were able to make a commitment to an ongoing, multipronged effort to address Mike's needs.

The school psychologist conducted psychoeducational testing with Mike and interviewed Gary and Carol over the course of two meetings that had to be rescheduled several times due to their multiple professional and social commitments. Gary is a corporate attorney who travels extensively as part of his work, and Carol is an anesthesiologist. Both work full time and often have evening commitments as well. After-school child care for Mike and his siblings (ages 6 and 10) is provided by a string of neighborhood adolescent babysitters. When the psychologist asked Gary to describe his relationship with Mike, Gary erupted into anger and insisted that it had no bearing on the school's failure to control Mike. He insisted that Mike was perfectly easy to control at home since Gary ran a "tight ship" and considered himself a stern disciplinarian; the hyperactivity and aggression shown at school must be the result of a "too permissive" atmosphere. Carol became tearful at this point and said that she knew it was their fault, that neither of them really knew anything about raising children. She admitted that Mike's older brother was on medication for depression, and that his younger sister was beginning to behave like Mike at school. Gary continued to rage, both at his wife for admitting they could possibly be at fault and at the psychologist for allowing Mike's difficulties to continue into third grade.

The school recommended a referral to a child psychiatrist for a medication evaluation and individual therapy for Mike. Family therapy was also strongly recommended. Special care was taken to consider the long-term consequences of Mike's problem behavior and to emphasize the role that family and school played in setting Mike on a more adaptive course. For a period of time, Mike's behavior worsened as his parents struggled to come to terms with the school's recommendation. Family therapy eventually began and, increasingly, it became obvious that the parents' problematic marriage contributed to Mike's difficulties and lack of improvement. After four months, Gary and Carol separated and Carol became increasingly instrumental and effective in addressing her children's need for structure, involvement, and warmth. She reduced her schedule and social commitments, employed a competent housekeeper, and actively worked with the school and Mike's therapist to establish a behavioral program. By the end of third grade, Mike was doing better at school and, in general, appeared less needy, far less angry, and better organized. Family therapy continued, with Mike meeting separately with each parent.

CONCLUSION

The case illustrations highlight some of the ambiguities in determining what constitutes psychological maltreatment, how best to intervene without legal coercion, and which ways are most effective for utilizing multiple community agencies to foster parental involvement in remedial efforts. With respect to the issue of definition, there continues to be little agreement about the particular acts that constitute psychological maltreatment, the extent to which parental intent must be established, and the kind of evidence that can be used to document maltreatment. On the other hand, developmental research is gradually building a case for the significant long-term harm that accompanies psychological abuse and neglect, and there is widespread recognition that demonstrable "mental injury"—of the sort discussed in this chapter—is the bedrock on which such cases must rest.

Given the definitional problems still to be resolved, it remains unlikely that the majority of cases of psychological maltreatment will result in legal action or in legally mandated intervention. This places special onus on community institutions and agencies to identify children in need, to help parents recognize when intervention could be helpful, and to assist both children and parents in gaining the services that would support their current and future functioning.

Education and training for *all* professionals having regular contact with parents and children—in identifying possible cases, and in initiating and following up a referral—may prove the most effective strategy for helping children and families toward healthier functioning. Education and training for legal professionals—in understanding children's developmental needs and in recognizing conditions that place a child in developmental jeopardy—may be the best protection against further harm to children. Both must take place if there is to be progress in dealing with the largely unaddressed problem of psychological maltreatment. And progress must be made if children's psychological health and development are valued as societal priorities.

REFERENCES

Aber, J., & Allen, J. (1987). Effects of maltreatment on young children's socioemotional development: An attachment theory perspective. *Developmental Psychology, 23,* 406–414.

Abramson, L. (1991). Facial expression in failure-to-thrive and normal infants: Implications for their capacity to engage the world. *Merrill-Palmer Quarterly, 37,* 159–182.

Achenbach, T.M., & Edelbrock, C.S. (1986). *Manual for the Teacher's Report Form and Teacher Version of the Child Behavior Profile.* Burlington: Department of Child Psychiatry, University of Vermont.

Ainsworth, M.D.S., Blehar, M.C., Waters, E., & Wall, S. (1978). *Patterns of attachment.* Hillsdale, NJ: Erlbaum.

Ainsworth, M.D.S., & Wittig, B.A. (1969). Attachment and the exploratory behavior of one-year-olds in a strange situation. In B.M. Foss (Ed.), *Determinants of infant behavior* (Vol. 4, pp. 111–136). London: Methuen.

Altemeier, W.A., O'Connor, S., Vietze, P.M., Sandler, H.M., & Sherrod, K.B. (1982). Antecedents of child abuse. *Journal of Pediatrics, 100,* 823–829.

Altemeier, W.A., Vietze, P.M., Sherrod, K.A., Sandler, H.M., Falsey, S., & O'Connor, S.M. (1979). Prediction of child maltreatment during pregnancy. *Journal of the American Academy of Child Psychiatry, 18,* 201.

American Bar Association Juvenile Justice Standards Project. (1980). *Standards relating to abuse and neglect* (Standard 2.1c). Cambridge, MA: Ballinger.

American Humane Association. (1984). *Trends in child abuse and neglect: A national perspective.* Denver, CO: Author.

American Humane Association. (1988). *Highlights of official child neglect and abuse reporting, 1986.* Denver, CO: Author.

Aragona, J.A., & Eyberg, S.M. (1981). Neglected children: Mothers' report of child behavior problems and observed verbal behavior. *Child Development, 52,* 596–602.

Asher, S.R., & Coie, J. (1990). *Peer rejection in childhood.* New York: Cambridge University Press.

Baily, T.F., & Baily, W.H. (1986). *Operational definitions of child emotional maltreatment.* Augusta: Maine Department of Human Services.

Barahal, R.M., Waterman, J., & Martin, H.P. (1981). The social cognitive development of abused children. *Journal of Consulting and Clinical Psychology, 49,* 508–516.

Batchelor, J., & Kerslake, A. (1990). *Failure to find failure to thrive.* London: Whiting and Birch.

Baumrind, D. (1978). Parental disciplinary patterns and social competence in children. *Youth and Society, 9,* 239–276.

Baumrind, D. (1991). The influence of parenting style on adolescent competence and substance use. *Journal of Early Adolescence, 11,* 56–95.

Bavolek, S.J., Kline, D.F., McLaughlin, J.A., & Publicover, P.R. (1979). *Development of the Adolescent Parenting Inventory (API): Identification of high risk adolescents prior to parenthood.* Logan: Department of Special Education, Utah State University.

Behrman, R.E. (Ed.). (1992). The future of children. *School-Linked Services, 2,* 1.

Belsky, J. (1984). The determinants of parenting: A process model. *Child Development, 55,* 83–96.

Belsky, J., & Nezworski, T. (Eds.). (1988). *Clinical implications of attachment.* Hillsdale, NJ: Erlbaum.

Berndt, T.J. (1984). Sociometric, social-cognitive, and behavioral measures for the study of friendship and popularity. In T. Field, J.L. Roopnarine, & M. Segal (Eds.), *Friendships in normal and handicapped children* (pp. 31–52). Norwood, NJ: ABLEX.

Bousha, D., & Twentyman, C. (1984). Abusing, neglectful, and comparison mother-child interactional style: Naturalistic observations in the home setting. *Journal of Abnormal Psychology, 93,* 106–114.

Brassard, M.R., Hart, S.N., & Hardy, D.B. (1993). The psychological maltreatment rating scales. *Child Abuse & Neglect, 17,* 715–729.

Bretherton, I. (1985). Attachment theory: Retrospect and prospect. In I. Bretherton & E. Waters (Eds.), Growing points in attachment theory and research. *Monographs of the Society for Research in Child Development, 50*(1/2, Serial No. 209), 3–38.

Briere, J., & Runtz, M. (1988). Multivariate correlates of childhood psychological and physical maltreatment among university women. *Child Abuse & Neglect, 12,* 331–341.

Briere, J., & Runtz, M. (1989). The Trauma Symptom Checklist (TSC-33): Early data on a new scale. *Journal of Interpersonal Violence, 4,* 151–163.

Briere, J., & Runtz, M. (1990). Differential adult symptomatology associated with three types of child abuse histories. *Child Abuse & Neglect, 14,* 357–364.

Broadhurst, D.D. (1984). *The educator's role in the prevention and treatment of child abuse and neglect.* Washington, DC: National Center on Child Abuse and Neglect, U.S. Department of Health and Human Services.

Brown, S.E. (1984). Social class, child maltreatment, and delinquent behavior. *Criminology, 22,* 259–278.

Brunnquell, D., Crichton, L., & Egeland, B. (1981). Maternal personality and attitude in disturbances of childrearing. *American Journal of Orthopsychiatry, 51,* 680–691.

Buchsbaum, H.R., Toth, S.L., Clyman, R.B., Cicchetti, D., & Emde, R.N. (1992). The use of narrative story stem technique with maltreated children: Implications for theory and practice. *Development and Psychopathology, 4,* 603–625.

Caldwell, B., & Bradley, R. (1984). *Home Observation for Measurement of the Environment.* Little Rock: University of Arkansas.

Caldwell, R.A., Bogat, G.A., & Davidson, W.S. (1988). The assessment of child abuse potential and the prevention of child abuse and neglect: A policy analysis. *American Journal of Community Psychology, 16,* 609–624.

Cassidy, J. (1988). Child-mother attachment and the self in six-year-olds. *Child Development, 59,* 121–134.

Cattell, R.B., & Scheier, I.H. (1963). *Handbook for the IPAT anxiety scale* (2nd ed.). Champaign, IL: Institute of Personality and Ability Testing.

Chan, D., Salcedo, J., Atkins, D., & Ruley, E. (1986). Munchausen syndrome by proxy: A review and case study. *Journal of Pediatric Psychology, 11,* 71–80.

Chatoor, I., & Egan, J. (1987). Etiology and diagnosis of failure to thrive and growth disorders in infants and children. In J.D. Noshpitz (Ed.), *Basic handbook of child psychiatry: Advances and new directions* (Vol. 5). New York: Basic Books.

Cherniss, D.S., Pawl, J., & Fraiberg, S. (1980). Nina: Developmental guidance and supportive treatment for a failure to thrive infant and her adolescent mother. In S. Fraiberg (Ed.), *Clinical studies in infant mental health* (pp. 103–140). New York: Basic Books.

Christopoulos, C., Cohn, D.A., Shaw, D.S., Joyce, S., Sullivan-Hanson, J., Kraft, S., & Emery, R.E. (1987). Children of abused women: I. Adjustment at time of shelter residence. *Journal of Marriage and the Family, 49,* 611–619.

Cicchetti, D. (1991). Defining psychological maltreatment: Reflections and future directions [Special issue]. *Development and Psychopathology: Defining Psychological Maltreatment, 3,* 1–2.

Cicchetti, D., & Barnett, D. (1991). Attachment organization in maltreated preschoolers. *Development and Psychopathology, 4,* 397–411.

Cicchetti, D., & Olsen, K. (1990). The developmental psychopathology of child maltreatment. In M. Lewis & S. Miller (Eds.), *Handbook of developmental psychopathology.* New York: Plenum Press.

Claussen, A.H., & Crittenden, P.M. (1991). Psychological maltreatment: Relations among types of maltreatment. *Child Abuse & Neglect, 15,* 5–18.

Cohler, B., Weiss, J., & Grunebaum, H. (1970). Child care attitudes and emotional disturbance among mothers of young children. *Genetic Psychology Monographs, 82,* 3–47.

Coohey, C. (1996). Child maltreatment: Testing the social isolation hypothesis. *Child Abuse & Neglect, 20,* 241–254.

Corson, J., & Davidson, H. (1987). Emotional abuse and the law. In M.R. Brassard, R. Germain, & S.N. Hart (Eds.), *Psychological maltreatment of children and youth* (pp. 185–202). New York: Pergamon Press.

Crittenden, P.M. (1981). Abusing neglecting problematic and adequate dyads: Differentiating by patterns of interaction. *Merrill-Palmer Quarterly, 27,* 201–218.

Crittenden, P.M. (1988). Relationships at risk. In J. Belsky & T. Nezworski (Eds.), *Clinical implications of attachment* (pp. 136–174). Hillsdale, NJ: Erlbaum.

Crittenden, P.M., & Ainsworth, M.D.S. (1989). Attachment and child abuse. In D. Cicchetti & V. Carlson (Eds.), *Child maltreatment: Research and theory on the consequences of abuse and neglect* (pp. 432–463). New York: Cambridge University Press.

Crittenden, P.M., Claussen, A.H., & Sugarman, D.B. (1994). Physical and psychological maltreatment in middle childhood and adolescence. *Development and Psychopathology, 6,* 145–164.

Davies, D. (1995). Commentary: Collaboration and family empowerment as strategies to achieve comprehensive services. In L.C. Rigby, M.C. Reynolds, & M.C. Wang (Eds.), *School-community connections: Exploring issues for research and practice* (pp. 267–280). San Francisco: Jossey-Bass.

Dean, D. (1979). Emotional abuse of children. *Children Today, 8,* 18–20.

Downey, G., & Walker, E. (1989). Social cognition and adjustment in children at risk for psychopathology. *Developmental Psychology, 25,* 835–845.

Egeland, B., Breitenbucher, M., Dodds, M., Pastor, D., & Rosenberg, D.M. (1978). *Life event scale scoring manual.* Unpublished manuscript, University of Minnesota.

Egeland, B., Breitenbucher, M., & Rosenberg, D. (1980). Prospective study of the significance of life stress in the etiology of child abuse. *Journal of Consulting and Clinical Psychology, 48,* 195–205.

Egeland, B., & Brunnquell, D. (1979). An at-risk approach to the study of child abuse. *Journal of the American Academy of Child Psychiatry, 18,* 219–235.

Egeland, B., & Erickson, M.F. (1987). Psychologically unavailable caregiving. In M.R. Brassard, R. Germain, & S.N. Hart (Eds.), *Psychological maltreatment of children and youth* (pp. 110–120). New York: Pergamon Press.

Egeland, B., & Sroufe, L.A. (1981). Developmental sequelae of maltreatment in infancy. In R. Rizley & D. Cicchetti (Eds.), *New directions for child development: Developmental perspectives on child maltreatment* (pp. 77–92). San Francisco: Jossey-Bass.

Egeland, B., Sroufe, L.A., & Erickson, M. (1983). The developmental consequence of different patterns of maltreatment. *Child Abuse & Neglect, 1,* 459–469.

Elder, G.H., Jr., Nguyen, T.V., & Caspi, A. (1985). Linking family hardship to children's lives. *Child Development, 56,* 361–375.

Elmer, E. (1977). A follow-up study of traumatized children. *Pediatrics, 59,* 273–279.

Erickson, M.F., Egeland, B., & Pianta, R. (1989). The effects of maltreatment on the development of young children. In D. Cicchetti & V. Carlson (Eds.), *Child maltreatment: Theory and research on the causes and consequences of child abuse and neglect* (pp. 647–784). New York: Cambridge University Press.

Erickson, M.F., Sroufe, L.A., & Egeland, B. (1985). The relationship between quality of attachment and behavior problems in preschool in a high-risk sample. In I. Bretherton & E. Waters (Eds.), Growing points in attachment theory and research. *Monographs of the Society for Research in Child Development, 50*(1/2, Serial No. 209), 147–166.

Fagot, B.I., & Kavanagh, K. (1990). The prediction of antisocial behavior from avoidant attachment classifications. *Child Development, 61,* 864–873.

Fraiberg, S. (Ed.). (1980). *Clinical studies in infant mental health.* New York: Basic Books.

Gaines, R., Sandgrund, A., Green, A.H., & Power, E. (1978). Etiological factors in child maltreatment: A multivariate study of abusing, neglecting, and normal mothers. *Journal of Abnormal Psychology, 87*(5), 531–540.

Garbarino, J. (1980). Defining emotional maltreatment: The message is the meaning. *Journal of Psychiatric Treatment and Evaluation, 2,* 105–110.

Garbarino, J. (1989). Troubled youth, troubled families: The dynamics of adolescent maltreatment. In D. Cicchetti & V. Carlson (Eds.), *Child maltreatment: Theory and research on the causes and consequences of child abuse and neglect* (pp. 685–706). New York: Cambridge University Press.

Garbarino, J., Guttmann, E., & Seeley, J. (1986). *The psychologically battered child: Strategies for identification, assessment, and intervention.* San Francisco: Jossey-Bass.

Garbarino, J., & Stott, F.M. (1989). *What children can tell us.* San Francisco: Jossey-Bass.

Garbarino, J., & Vondra, J. (1987). Psychological maltreatment: Issues and perspectives. In M.R. Brassard, R. Germain, & S.N. Hart (Eds.), *Psychological maltreatment of children and youth* (pp. 24–44). New York: Wiley-Interscience.

Garbarino, J., Wilson, J., & Garbarino, A.C. (1986). The adolescent runaway. In J. Garbarino, C.J. Schellenbach, J.M. Sebes, & Associates (Eds.), *Troubled youth, troubled families* (pp. 41–54). New York: Aldine.

Gaudin, J.M., Jr., Polansky, N.A., & Kilpatrick, A.C. (1992). The Child Well-Being Scales: A field trial. *Child Welfare, 71,* 319–328.

George, C., & Main, M. (1979). Social interactions of young abused children: Approach, avoidance, and aggression. *Child Development, 50,* 306–318.

George, C., & Main, M. (1980). Abused children: Their rejection of peers and caregivers. In T. Field (Ed.), *High-risk infants and children: Adult and peer interactions.* New York: Academic Press.

Gould, R. (1972). *Child studies through fantasy: Cognitive-affective patterns in development.* New York: Quadrangle Books.

Green, W.H., Campbell, M., & David, R. (1984). Psychosocial dwarfism: A critical review of the evidence. *Journal of the American Academy of Child Psychiatry, 23,* 39–48.

Greenspan, S.I. (1981). *Psychopathology and adaptation in infancy and early childhood: Principles of clinical diagnosis and preventive intervention.* New York: International Universities Press.

Greenspan, S.I., & Lieberman, A.F. (1988). A clinical approach to attachment. In J. Belsky & T. Nezworski (Eds.), *Clinical implications of attachment* (pp. 387–414). Hillsdale, NJ: Erlbaum.

Greenspan, S.I., Nover, R.A., & Scheuer, A.Q. (1987). A developmental diagnostic approach for infants, young children, and their families. In S. Greenspan, S. Wieder, R. Nover, A. Lieberman, R. Lourie, & M. Robinson (Eds.), *Infants in multirisk families* (pp. 431–498). Madison, CT: International Universities Press.

Gwartney-Gibbs, P., Stockard, J., & Bohmer, S. (1987). Learning courtship aggression: The influence of parents, peers, and personal experiences. *Family Relations, 36,* 276–282.

Haley, J. (1980). *Leaving home: The therapy of disturbed young people.* New York: McGraw-Hill.

Hart, S., Germain, B., & Brassard, M. (Eds.). (1983). *Proceedings summary of the International Conference on Psychological Abuse of Children and Youth.* Indiana University, Office for the Study of the Psychological Rights of the Child.

Hart, S.N., & Brassard, M.R. (1991). Psychological maltreatment: Progress achieved. *Development and Psychopathology, 13,* 61–70.

Harter, S. (1982). The perceived competence scale for children. *Child Development, 53,* 87–97.

Harter, S. (1983). Developmental perspectives on the self system. In P.H. Mussen (Ed.), *Handbook of child psychology* (Vol. 4, pp. 275–385). New York: Wiley.

Harter, S., & Pike, R. (1984). The pictorial scale of perceived competence and social acceptance for young children. *Child Development, 55,* 1969–1982.

Haynes-Seman, C., & Hart, J.S. (1987). Doll play of failure to thrive toddlers: Clues to infant experience. *Zero to Three, Bulletin of the National Center for Clinical Infant Programs, 7*(4), 10–13.

Herrenkohl, R.C., & Herrenkohl, E.C. (1981). Some antecedents and consequences of child maltreatment. In R. Rizley & D. Cicchetti (Eds.), *New directions for child maltreatment: Developmental perspectives in child maltreatment.* San Francisco: Jossey-Bass.

Hodges, K.K., Kline, J., Fitch, P., McKnew, D., & Cytryn, L. (1981). The Child Assessment Schedule: A diagnostic interview for research and clinical use. *Catalog of Selected Documents in Psychology, 11,* 56.

Hodges, K.K., McKnew, D., Cytryn, L., Stern, L., & Kline, J. (1982). The Child Assessment Schedule (CAS) diagnostic interview: A report on reliability and validity. *Journal of the American Academy of Child Psychiatry, 21,* 468–473.

Hoffman-Plotkin, D., & Twentyman, C.T. (1984). A multimodal assessment of behavioral and cognitive deficits in abused and neglected preschoolers. *Child Development, 55,* 794–802.

Hoglund, C.L., & Nicholas, K.B. (1995). Shame, guilt, and anger in college students exposed to abusive family environments. *Journal of Family Violence, 10,* 141–155.

Howes, C., & Eldredge, R. (1985). Responses of abused, neglected, and non-maltreated children to behaviors of their peers. *Journal of Applied Developmental Psychology, 6,* 261–270.

Hufton, I.W., & Oates, R.K. (1977). Nonorganic failure to thrive: A long-term follow-up. *Pediatrics, 59,* 73–77.

Hymel, S. (1983). Preschool children's peer relations: Issues in sociometric assessment. *Merrill-Palmer Quarterly, 29,* 237–260.

Hymel, S., & Rubin, K.H. (1985). Children with peer relationship and social skills problems: Conceptual, methodological, and developmental issues. In G.J. Whitehurst (Ed.), *Annals of child development* (Vol. 2, pp. 251–297). Greenwich, CT: JAI Press.

Jackson, D.H. (1967). *Personality Research Form manual.* New York: Research Psychologists Press.

Jaffe, P.G. (1991). Child witnesses of woman abuse: How can schools respond? *Response to Victimazation of Women and Children, 14,* 12.

Jaffe, P.G., Wolfe, D.A., & Wilson, S.K. (1990). *Children of battered women.* Newbury Park, CA: Sage.

Jouriles, E.N., Murphy, C.M., Farris, A.M., Smith, D.A., Richters, J.E., & Waters, E. (1991). Marital adjustment, parental disagreements about childrearing, and behavior problems in boys: Increasing the specificity of the marital assessment. *Child Development, 62,* 1424–1433.

Kadushin, A., & Martin, J.A. (1981). *Child abuse: An interactional event.* New York: Columbia University Press.

Kalmuss, D. (1984). The intergenerational transmission of marital aggression. *Journal of Marriage and the Family, 46,* 11–19.

Kaufman, J., & Cicchetti, D. (1989). Effects of maltreatment on school-age children's socioemotional development: Assessments in a day-camp setting. *Developmental Psychology, 25,* 516–524.

Kaufman, K.L., Coury, D., Pickrel, E., & McCleery, J. (1989). Munchausen syndrome by proxy: A survey of professionals' knowledge. *Child Abuse & Neglect, 13,* 141–147.

Kempe, R.S., & Kempe, C.H. (1978). *Child abuse.* Cambridge, MA: Harvard University Press.

Kenning, M., Merchant, A., & Tomkins, A. (1991). Research on the effects of witnessing parental battering: Clinical and legal policy implications. In M. Steinman (Ed.), *Woman battering: Policy responses.* Cincinnati, OH: Anderson.

Krugman, R.D., & Krugman, M.K. (1984). Emotional abuse in the classroom. *American Journal of Diseases of Children, 138,* 284–286.

Ladd, G.W. (1985). Documenting the effects of social skills training with children: Process and outcome assessment. In B. Schneider, K. Rubin, & J. Ledingham (Eds.), *Children's peer relations: Issues in assessment and intervention* (pp. 243–271). New York: Springer-Verlag.

Ledingham, J.E., & Younger, A.J. (1985). The influence of evaluator on assessments of children's social skills. In B. Schneider, K. Rubin, & J. Ledingham (Eds.), *Children's peer relations: Issues in assessment and intervention* (pp. 111–124). New York: Springer-Verlag.

Lewis, D.O., Mallouh, C., & Webb, V. (1989). Child abuse, delinquency, and violent criminality. In D. Cicchetti & V. Carlson (Eds.), *Child maltreatment: Theory and research on the causes and consequences of child abuse and neglect* (pp. 707–721). New York: Cambridge University Press.

Loeber, R., & Dishion, T. (1983). Early predictors of male delinquency: A review. *Psychological Bulletin, 94,* 168–199.

Lyons-Ruth, K. (1996). Attachment relationships among children with aggressive behavior problems: The role of disorganized early attachment patterns. *Journal of Consulting and Clinical Psychology, 64,* 64–73.

Lyons-Ruth, K., Bronfman, E., & Parsons, E. (in press). Maternal frightened, frightening, or atypical behavior and disorganized infant attachment patterns. In J. Vondra & D. Barnett (Eds.), Atypical attachment in infancy and early childhood. *Monographs of the Society for Research and Child Development.*

Lyons-Ruth, K., Connell, D.B., Zoll, D., & Stahl, J. (1987). Infants at social risk: Relations among infant maltreatment, maternal behavior, and infant attachment behavior. *Developmental Psychology, 23,* 223–232.

Maccoby, E.E., & Martin, J. (1983). Socialization in the context of the family: Parent-child interaction. In E.M. Hetherington (Ed.), *Handbook of child psychology: Socialization, personality, and social development* (Vol. 4, pp. 1–101). New York: Wiley.

Magura, S., & Moses, B.S. (1986). *Outcome measures for child welfare service.* Washington, DC: Child Welfare League of America.

Main, M., & Cassidy, J. (1988). Categories of response to reunion with the parent at age six: Predictable from infant attachment classifications and stable over a one-month period. *Developmental Psychology, 24,* 415–426.

Martin, S.R. (1996). A child's right to be gay: Addressing the emotional maltreatment of queer youth. *Hastings Law Journal, 48,* 167–195.

McCarthy, D. (1979). Recognition of signs of emotional deprivation: A form of child abuse. *Child Abuse & Neglect, 3,* 423–428.

McGee. R.A., & Wolfe, D.A. (1991). Psychological maltreatment: Toward an operational definition. *Development and Psychopathology, 3,* 3–18.

McGee, R.A., Wolfe, D.A., & Wilson, S.K. (1997). Multiple maltreatment experiences and adolescent behavior problems: Adolescents' perspectives. *Development and Psychopathology, 9,* 131–149.

McMullen, J.G. (1992). The inherent limitations of after-the-fact statutes dealing with the emotional and sexual maltreatment of children. *Drake Law Review, 41,* 483–510.

Melton, G.B., & Davidson, H.A. (1987). Child protection and society: When should the state intervene? *American Psychologist, 42*(2), 172–175.

Melton, G.B., & Thompson, R.A. (1987). Legislative approaches to psychological maltreatment: A social policy analysis. In M.R. Brassard, R. Germain, & S.N. Hart (Eds.), *Psychological maltreatment of children and youth* (pp. 203–216). New York: Pergamon Press.

Miller, A. (1981). *The drama of the gifted child.* New York: Basic Books.

Miller, A. (1986). *Thou shalt not be aware: Society's betrayal of the child.* New York: Farrar, Straus, & Giroux.

Milner, J.S. (1980). *The child abuse potential inventory: Manual.* Webster, NC: Psytec.

Milner, J.S., Gold, R., Ayoub, C., & Jacewitz, M. (1984). Predictive validity of the child abuse potential inventory. *Journal of Consulting and Clinical Psychology, 52,* 879–884.

Milner, J.S., & Winberley, R.C. (1980). Prediction and explanation of child abuse. *Journal of Clinical Psychology, 36,* 875–884.

Minuchin, S. (1974). *Families and family therapy.* Cambridge, MA: Harvard University Press.

Murphy, S., Orkow, B., & Nicola, R.M. (1985). Prenatal prediction of child abuse and neglect: A prospective study. *Child Abuse & Neglect, 9,* 225–235.

National Center on Child Abuse and Neglect (NCCAN). (1982). *The national study of the incidence and severity of child abuse and neglect.* Washington, DC: U.S. Government Printing Office.

National Center on Child Abuse and Neglect (NCCAN), U.S. Department of Health and Human Services. (1983). *Child protection: A guide for state legislation.* Washington, DC: U.S. Government Printing Office.

National Center on Child Abuse and Neglect (NCCAN), U.S. Department of Health and Human Services. (1995). *Child maltreatment 1993: Reports from the states to the national center on child abuse and neglect.* Washington, DC: U.S. Government Printing Office.

Navarre, E.L. (1987). Psychological maltreatment: The core component of child abuse. In M.R. Brassard, R. Germain, & S.N. Hart (Eds.), *Psychological maltreatment of children and youth* (pp. 45–56). New York: Pergamon Press.

Ney, P.G., Fung, T., & Wickett, A.R. (1994). The worst combinations of child abuse and neglect. *Child Abuse & Neglect, 18,* 705–714.

O'Hagan, K. (1993). *Emotional and psychological abuse of children.* Toronto: University of Toronto Press.

Olds, D.L., & Henderson, C.R. (1989). The prevention of maltreatment. In D. Cicchetti & V. Carlson (Eds.), *Child maltreatment: Theory and research on the causes and consequences of maltreatment.* New York: Cambridge University Press.

Orvaschel, H., & Puig-Antich, J. (1987). *Schedule for Affective Disorder and Schizophrenia for School-Age Children* (KIDDIE-SADS). Pittsburgh: Western Psychiatric Institute and Clinic.

Palmer, A., & Yoshimura, G. (1984). Munchausen syndrome by proxy. *Journal of the American Academy of Child Psychiatry, 23,* 503–508.

Park, K.A., & Waters, E. (1989). Security of attachment and preschool friendships. *Child Development, 60,* 1076–1081.

Parker, J.G., & Asher, S.R. (1987). Peer relations and later personal adjustment: Are low-accepted children at risk? *Psychological Bulletin, 102*(3), 357–389.

Patterson, C.J., Cohn, D.A., & Kao, B.T. (1989). Maternal warmth as a protective factor against risks associated with peer rejection among children. *Development and Psychopathology, 1,* 21–38.

Patterson, G.R., & Stouthamer-Loeber, M. (1984). The correlation of family management practices and delinquency. *Child Development, 55,* 1299–1307.

Polansky, N.A., Borgman, R., & De Saix, C. (1972). *Roots of futility.* San Francisco: Jossey-Bass.

Polansky, N.A., Cabral, R.J., Magura, S., & Phillips, M.H. (1983). Comparative norms for the childhood level of living scale. *Journal of Social Service Research, 6,* 45–56.

Public Law 93-247. (1974). Child Abuse, Prevention, and Treatment Act of 1974. USC 5101.

Quay, H.C. (1977). Measuring dimensions of deviant behavior: The Behavior Problem Checklist. *Journal of Abnormal Child Psychology, 5,* 277–287.

Quay, H.C., & Peterson, D.R. (1967). *Behavior problem checklist.* Urbana: Children's Research Center, University of Illinois.

Rohner, R.P., & Rohner, E.C. (1980). Antecedents and consequences of parental rejection: A theory of emotional abuse. *Child Abuse & Neglect, 4,* 189–198.

Rosario, M., Salzinger, S., Feldman, R., & Hammer, M. (1987). *Home environments of physically abused and control school-age children.* Paper presented at the Biennial Meeting of the Society for Research in Child Development, Baltimore.

Rosewater, A. (1989). *Getting systems working together for youth in state care.* Workshop, Children's Defense Fund Conference.

Rutter, M. (1981). Stress, coping, and development: Some issues and some questions. *Journal of Child Psychology and Psychiatry, 22,* 323–356.

Schaefer, C.E., Gitlin, K., & Sandgrund, A. (Eds.). (1991). *Play diagnosis and assessment.* New York: Wiley.

Schaefer, M.S., & Manheimer, H. (1960). *Dimensions of perinatal adjustment.* Paper presented at the Eastern Psychological Association, New York.

Schneider, C.J. (1982). The Michigan screening profile of parenting. In R.M. Starr (Ed.), *Child abuse prediction: Policy implications* (pp. 157–174). Cambridge, MA: Ballinger.

Schneider, C.J., Helfer, R.E., & Hoffmeister, J.K. (1976). A predictive screening questionnaire for potential problems in mother-child interaction. In R. Helfer & C. Kempe (Eds.), *Child abuse and neglect: The family and the community* (pp. 393–407). Cambridge, MA: Ballinger.

Schuengel, D., Bakermans-Kranenburg, M.J., & van IJzendoorn, M.H. (1997). *Attachment and loss: Frightening maternal behavior linking unresolved loss and disorganized infant attachment.* Manuscript under review, Leiden University.

Sebes, J.M. (1986). Defining high risk. In J. Garbarino, C.J. Schellenbach, J. Sebes, & Associates (Eds.), *Troubled youth, troubled families* (pp. 83–120). New York: Aldine.

Silverton, R. (1982). Social work perspective on psychosocial dwarfism. *Social Work in Health Care, 7,* 1–14.

Sroufe, L.A. (1983). Infant-caregiver attachment and patterns of adaptation in preschool: The roots of maladaptation and competence. In M. Perlmutter (Ed.), *Minnesota Symposia on Child Psychology* (Vol. 16, pp. 41–81). Hillsdale, NJ: Erlbaum.

Sroufe, L.A., & Fleeson, J. (1986). Attachment and the construction of relationships. In W. Hartup & Z. Rubin (Eds.), *Relationships and development* (pp. 51–71). Hillsdale, NJ: Erlbaum.

Sroufe, L.A., & Fleeson, J. (1988). The coherence of family relationships. In R.A. Hinde & J. Stevenson-Hinde (Eds.), *Relationships within families: Mutual influences* (pp. 27–47). Oxford, England: Clarendon Press.

Sroufe, L.A., Jacobvitz, D., Mangelsdorf, S., DeAngelo, E., & Ward, M.J. (1985). Generational boundary dissolution between mothers and their preschool children: A relationship systems approach. *Child Development, 56,* 317–325.

Stovall, G., & Craig, R.J. (1990). Mental representations of physically and sexually abused latency-aged females. *Child Abuse & Neglect, 14,* 233–242.

Straus, M.A. (1990). The Conflict Tactics Scales and its critics: An evaluation and new data on validity and reliability. In M. Straus & R.J. Gelles (Eds.), *Physical violence in American families.* New Brunswick, NJ: Transaction.

Straus, M.A., Gelles, R.J., & Steinmetz, S.K. (1980). *Behind closed doors: Violence in the American family.* New York: Anchor Press.

Taylor, J., Underwood, C., Thomas, L., & Franklin, A. (1988). Measuring psychological maltreatment of infants and toddlers. In R.L. Jones (Ed.), *Tests and measures for black populations.* Berkeley, CA: Cobb & Henry.

Tomkins, A.J., Mohamed, S., Steinman, M., Macolini, R.M., Kenning, M.K., & Afrank, J. (1994). The plight of children who witness woman battering: Psychological knowledge and policy implications. *Law and Psychology Review, 18,* 137–186.

Toth, S.L., & Cicchetti, D. (1996). Patterns of relatedness, depressive symptomatology, and perceived competence in maltreated children. *Journal of Consulting and Clinical Psychology, 64,* 32–41.

Trickett, P.K., & Susman, E.J. (1988). Parental perceptions of childrearing practices in physically abusive and nonabusive families. *Developmental Psychology, 24,* 270–276.

U.S. Department of Justice, Office of Juvenile Justice and Delinquency Prevention. (1980). *Standards for the administration of juvenile justice and delinquency prevention* (Standard 3.113e). Washington, DC: U.S. Government Printing Office.

Vissing, Y.M., Straus, M.A., Gelles, R.J., & Harrop, J.W. (1991). Verbal aggression by parents and psychosocial problems of children. *Child Abuse & Neglect, 15,* 223–238.

Vondra, J., Barnett, D., & Cicchetti, D. (1989). Perceived and actual competence among maltreated and comparison school children. *Development and Psychopathology, 1,* 237–255.

Vondra, J., Barnett, D., & Cicchetti, D. (1990). Self-concept, motivation, and competence among preschoolers from maltreating and comparison families. *Child Abuse & Neglect, 14,* 525–540.

Whiting, L. (1976). Defining emotional neglect: A community workshop looks at neglected children. *Children Today, 5,* 2–5.

Wieder, S., Hollingsworth, E.L., Castellan, J.M., Hubert, J., & Lourie, R.S. (1987). Another baby, another chance: Madeline and Anita. In S. Greenspan, S. Wieder, R. Nover, A. Lieberman, R. Lourie, & M. Robinson (Eds.), *Infants in multirisk families* (pp. 189–328). Madison, CT: International Universities Press.

Wolfe, D.A. (1985). Child-abusive parents: An empirical review and analysis. *Psychological Monographs, 97,* 462–482.

Wolfe, D.A., & McGee, R.A. (1994). Dimensions of child maltreatment and their relationship to adolescent development. *Development and Psychopathology, 6,* 165–181.

Youngblade, L.M., & Belsky, J. (1990). The social and emotional consequences of child maltreatment. In R. Ammerman & M. Hersen (Eds.), *Children at risk: An evaluation of factors contributing to child abuse and neglect* (pp. 109–146). New York: Plenum Press.

Zeanah, C.H., & Zeanah, P.D. (1989). Intergenerational transmission of maltreatment. *Psychiatry, 52,* 177–196.

Zimet, S.G., & Farley, G.K. (1986). Four perspectives on the competence and self-esteem of emotionally disturbed children beginning day treatment. *Journal of the American Academy of Child Psychiatry, 25,* 76–83.

CHAPTER 15

Psychological Maltreatment of Women

RICHARD M. TOLMAN, DANIEL ROSEN, and GILLIAN CARA WOOD

INCREASED INTEREST in psychological maltreatment as a form of abuse, and advances in measurement have resulted in new understanding of the nature and effects of psychological maltreatment on adult well-being. Moving beyond descriptions in the popular press and the handful of articles of the past decade, recent studies converge with similar findings: psychological maltreatment is a common, harmful form of abuse. Women experiencing this form of abuse report it to be damaging, and often more painful for them than physical abuse. Psychological maltreatment may accompany other forms of family violence but has harmful effects even when not paired with these forms of violence. Practitioners need to skillfully assess psychological maltreatment to effectively intervene with those who experience and perpetrate this form of abuse.

DESCRIPTION OF THE PROBLEM

DEFINING PSYCHOLOGICAL MALTREATMENT

Broadly construed, psychological maltreatment can be any behavior that is harmful or intended to be harmful to the well-being of a spouse. Given that some pain and lack of cooperation in relationships characterizes the human condition, and is present to some degree in all relationships, a definition of psychological maltreatment includes any kind of harmful behavior would be clinically useless. The critical clinical question of concern here is when does negative behavior in relationships constitute a pattern of maltreatment?

The growing literature on psychological maltreatment suggests that it may be useful to construe such maltreatment on a continuum. On the one end are isolated hurtful behaviors that may occur in any relationship: withdrawing momentarily, listening

The authors are grateful to Julie Field, J.D., Robert Pickus, J.D., Barbara Hart, J.D., and the National Center for Women and Family Law for their generous help on the legal section of this chapter and Sarah Shatz for her help on other portions of the chapter.

unempathically, speaking sharply in anger. On the other end of the continuum is pervasive, one-sided, severe psychological torture paralleling intentional brainwashing and mistreatment of prisoners of war.

Andersen, Boulette, and Schwartz (1991) construe the concept of psychological maltreatment as a form of mind control. They argue that any relationship that involves covert strategies of psychological coercion or regulation over individual freedoms is maladaptive. While not proposing a specific assessment instrument, they suggest that presence of totalism which characterizes mind-controlling relationships can be assessed by counting the number and severity of psychologically coercive features and deception present in the system. The list of these features include verbal or physical dominance early in the courtship or marriage, isolation or imprisonment to some degree, guilt induction to promote victim self-blame, hope-instilling by contingent expressions of love, fear arousal, maintenance and escalation to terror, promotion of powerlessness and helplessness, pathological expressions of jealousy, required secrecy and enforced loyalty and self-denunciation. Couples may vary in the number of features, severity, and duration of these features. Whether a particular couple exhibits a significant array of these features becomes the critical and difficult assessment task.

Several methods of categorizing psychological maltreatment have been developed. A frequently used typology is the Power and Control Wheel (Pence & Paymar, 1993), which describes eight forms of psychological maltreatment, including coercion, intimidation, emotional abuse, isolation, minimization/blame/denial, misuse of children, abuse of male privilege, and economic abuse. These forms of psychological maltreatment increase men's control over their partners. Physical and sexual assault reinforce the power of these other tactics. Dutton and Starzomski (1997) found that dimensions of the Wheel were intercorrelated and suggest that this supports the view that the forms of abuse constitute a syndrome of abuse and control.

Marshall (1994) identified 42 different types of psychological abuse. While most authors have emphasized the connections between physical violence and psychological maltreatment, Marshall suggests that psychological maltreatment can exist independently of violence. In contrast to the Duluth model previously described, Marshall argues that psychological maltreatment may not necessarily be used in an overtly controlling or dominating manner. These issues are explored later in this chapter.

RELATIONSHIP OF PHYSICAL AND PSYCHOLOGICAL MALTREATMENT

Physical abuse is almost always accompanied by some form of psychological maltreatment. Theoretically, psychological maltreatment can be viewed as functionally equivalent to physical abuse, (i.e., functions to establish dominance and control over the other) (Tolman & Edleson, 1989).

There is evidence that psychological maltreatment often precedes physical abuse in relationships. Murphy and O'Leary (1989), studying the etiology of partner violence in newly married couples, found that psychological aggression was a precursor to physical aggression.

A strict separation of psychological maltreatment from physical maltreatment may be illusory, as even physical abuse has aspects of psychological maltreatment. In addition to the physical pain and intimidation a woman may feel when her husband slaps her in front of her child, she may also feel humiliated, embarrassed, and demeaned.

The latter feelings may even be the more harmful and debilitating effects of his physically abusive behavior.

INTENSITY AND FREQUENCY

The intensity and frequency of negative behaviors must be considered in defining what constitutes a pattern of psychological maltreatment. Occasional yelling or swearing for instance, may be readily tolerated in a relationship, while frequent instances of screaming and obscene insults may not. However, as with physical abuse, it is important not to trivialize the impact of certain behaviors just because they occur infrequently or appear to be low in intensity to the practitioner.

COMBINATION OF TYPES OF MALTREATMENT

The combination of various forms of psychological maltreatment must also be considered. Verbal degradation paired with social isolation and economic deprivation is likely to be more powerful than verbal abuse alone. Likewise, support and maltreatment should not be viewed as a single bipolar continuum, but rather as a distinct continuum (Gurley, 1989). The combination of support and maltreatment may interact in unexplored ways. High levels of support may either mitigate or intensify the impact of maltreating behaviors. Presence of support from one's partner may buffer the impact of abuse received from that same person. However, it also may increase the negative emotional impact on the victim because it increases the sense of betrayal and confusion felt by the victim of such abuse.

INTENT

Straus, Sweet, and Vissing (1989) point out the divergence in importance of intent in definitions of psychological maltreatment. Some authors focus on the aggressive acts of spouse or parent as the defining criterion; others focus on injury or harm suffered by the spouse or child. In practice, it is difficult to use a judgment of intent in assessing psychological maltreatment. Couples will vary in their descriptions of the same events and very often disagree as to the intent. In assessment, practitioners generally must consider the topography of the act itself (e.g., made an economic threat) and the harm it does (i.e., what the victim reports about the impact of the behavior, for example, she felt frightened and backed down from her request) more strongly than the perpetrator's account of his intent in the incident, which is usually favorably presented.

Marshall (1996) emphasizes the complexity of assessing intent in defining psychological maltreatment. Even when negative intent is absent or not perceived, a behavior may have aversive effects and be considered maltreatment. She argues that "soft-spoken" abuse can include subtle messages which overtly express concern but covertly undermine a partner's well-being.

RECIPROCITY

An exchange of painful behaviors is likely to be present in a relationship. In accounts of their interaction, couples will often punctuate sequences of exchanges of negative behavior differently. Generally, abusive men present their abusive behavior as resulting from their partner's inappropriate behavior or abusive behavior toward them. The practitioner may easily be pulled into the male partner's construction of himself as a helpless victim in the relationship, who responds abusively only out of frustration with an impossibly behaving spouse. However, the key here is to consider the combination or constellation of factors (i.e., isolation, physical abuse, access to economic resources) that may make more potent and impactful symmetrically exchanged behaviors, such as yelling, put-downs, and emotional, verbal, or sexual withdrawal. Important here is physical abuse, which makes implicit threats of further abuse salient in any subsequent tense or conflict-laden situation. No one can deny the pain in being called a hateful name by one's partner, or by being put down in one's sexual or other abilities. But when those acts are accompanied by the implicit or explicit threat of physical abuse, they are likely to be more damaging. When power is unequally distributed in a relationship, the more powerful partner has more access to control via abusive behaviors.

The previous discussion is not meant to imply that only men are abusive in relationships. Rather, it is argued that men, by virtue of their greater economic power, status, and ability to use or threaten intimidating physical force in relationships, are more likely to be the perpetrators of damaging abuse. The author's clinical experience has been in working with men who are primary abusers of their female partners. Therefore, this chapter reflects that focus.

EFFECTS OF PSYCHOLOGICAL MALTREATMENT

Research on psychological maltreatment supports the contention that psychological maltreatment is in itself harmful. Victims of physical maltreatment have reported that psychological maltreatment itself may be more harmful than the physical abuse they suffer. For example, Follingstad, Rutledge, Berg, Hause, and Polek (1990) interviewed 234 women about their experiences with physical and psychological aggression. Almost three-quarters of the women (72%) rated emotional abuse as having a worse impact on them than physical abuse.

A growing number of studies have examined the effects of psychological maltreatment on measures of individual and relationship variables. Straus et al. (1989) reported findings from a general population survey indicating that regardless of the presence of physical abuse, the more verbal aggression a woman experiences from her spouse the greater the probability that she will be depressed. Tolman and Bhosley (1991) interviewed women one year after their male partners had been involved in group treatment for battering and found that psychological maltreatment was a powerful predictor of the women's psychosocial problems, whether or not the men had reabused their partners physically. Marshall (1994) found few significant differences in psychological symptoms, measured by the SCL-90-R, among women experiencing little or no violence, moderate violence, or severe violence. In a sample of battered and nonbattered women, Tolman and Stoops (1997) found that psychological abuse predicted women's psychological symptoms and relationship dissatisfaction. Arias and Pape (1999) found that even after controlling for physical abuse, psychological abuse was a significant predictor of both PTSD symptomatology and intentions to leave partners permanently. In a study of batterers and their partners, Jacobson, Gottman, Gortner, Berns, and Shortt (1999) found that at 2-year follow-up, emotional abuse predicted marital dissolution but physical abuse did not. In a sample of sheltered and non-sheltered battered women, Sackett and Saunders (1999) found that psychological abuse contributed to depression and low self-esteem, independent of physical abuse.

ASSESSMENT APPROACHES

Categories of Maltreatment

While not exhaustive, the following section lists several major categories of psychological maltreatment with examples of each. In trying to categorize psychological maltreatment, it becomes clear that a behavior may have more than one type of impact and that there is a great deal of overlap and interconnections between the categories listed. For example, a verbal put-down in front of others could fall into several of the following categories. Most obviously, it is degrading to be insulted in front of other people. The same behavior may contribute to isolation because a victim of such verbal abuse may want to avoid social situations in which such abuse may recur. The put-down may create fear, because it signals that physical abuse may follow. The put-down may be a technique for enforcing a trivial demand made by the abuser. The clinical utility of the categories listed here must not be judged by their precision or exclusivity, but rather their ability to provide guidance in assessing psychological maltreatment in a relationship.

Creation of Fear

Fear may be induced in many ways. The most obvious form involves physical threats. The man may make extreme terroristic threats, such as threatening to kill the woman, her children, family, or friends, or permanently disfigure her. He may brandish weapons or confine her for hours under threat of harm. On the other hand, physical threats may be much more implicit; a frightening look or stance, or agitated mood that puts her in fear of physical harm. Actually, data from factor analyses of the Conflict Tactics Scale (Straus, 1979) to be discussed supports placement of physical threats as physical rather than psychological abuse. Threats to hit and threats with a weapon both load more strongly on a physical abuse factor than on a factor with other psychological maltreatment items (Barling, O'Leary, Jouriles, Vivian, & MacEwen, 1987). As stated previously, rigid distinctions between physical and psychological abuse may be misplaced, but the legal considerations discussed later in this chapter make distinguishing between threatened abuse and actual physical abuse more important.

Nonphysical threats take many forms. An abusive man may threaten to take away the children, to place his partner in a mental institution, or to deny her financial support to gain her compliance. He may threaten to leave her or have an affair. He may threaten to reveal secrets about her or to humiliate her in public. These psychological threats reinforce obedience. Because often some other threats have actually been carried out, these threats can effectively promote anxiety and terror.

Isolation

Isolating behavior can take many forms. A man may leave only a small amount of gas in the car or closely monitor the amount of miles a woman drives during the day to restrict her activities. He may prohibit her from having friends over to the apartment. Isolation can take more subtle forms, such as putting down her friends, or making fun of her family. He may be rude or threatening to people who come over, making it uncomfortable for his partner to maintain relationships with others. He may refuse to go to joint social events or family gatherings. Isolation may also include controlling the flow of information, by requiring that secrets be kept within the family, or limiting information coming into the family. The effect of these behaviors is that the woman's contact with the outside world is limited. Often such isolation increases over time, as her resources and sense of competence in the outside world become increasingly diminished.

Monopolization

Monopolization refers to behaviors that make the abuser the psychological center of the victim's perceptions. An abusive man may be intrusive by interrupting his partner's activities: for example, by harassing her at work or constantly telephoning her. He may intrude or interfere with her friendships. He can disrupt or deprive her of private time or her possessions. He may demand her involvement in his interests only. He may be excessively possessive of her and her time. He may monitor her whereabouts constantly and demand that she account for how she uses her time. Coupled with isolation and behaviors that exhaust her physically and emotionally (e.g., depriving her of sleep and food, terroristic threats), extreme monopolization creates a totalistic state similar to that experienced by prisoners of war being brainwashed by their captors (Andersen et al., 1991).

Economic Abuse

Economic abuse may appear in a variety of forms. A woman may have access to adequate financial resources to fulfill household responsibilities, but her partner may exclude her from important financial decisions that affect her and her family. He may deny her access to cash, checking accounts, or credit cards, limiting her autonomy and forcing her to ask him for each dollar she spends. He may misuse or misappropriate the family's funds, creating extreme financial hardship. The impact of economic abuse may isolate her, deny her self-improvement opportunities, or demean her. It may heighten her anxiety about providing basic needs for herself and her children.

Degradation

Degrading behaviors make someone feel less competent, less adequate, or even less human. Extreme degrading behavior may take the form of having her perform sexual acts in front of other people, including her children. He may force her to eat from a bowl on the floor, or make her beg for some essential like food or going to the bathroom. Other more common forms of humiliation and degradation include verbal abuse in front of others, insults, name-calling, put-downs, and criticism of someone's abilities.

Rigid Sex Role Expectations/Trivial Requests

Often, psychologically maltreating men demand compliance with trivial demands that frequently correspond to rigid sex-role expectations. As NiCarthy (1986) points out, these demands may leave a woman feeling like an incompetent child or a servant. For example, he expects her to perform household chores flawlessly and forces her to account for the time she spends on all activities. He may intrude on her work or leisure-time to demand that she do something for him. Demands that fit sex rigid sex role expectations may be sexual; he may expect her to have sex when she does not desire it, or to take part in sexual acts she does not want to perform.

Psychological Destabilization

Psychological destabilization denotes acts that leave the victim unclear as to the validity of her own perceptions. This may be brought about by lying, manipulation, or other deliberate attempts to confuse the victim. An abuser may deny his actions or blame his partner for his abusive behavior or his angry moods. He may lie about his whereabouts or activities and then accuse her of overreacting when she confronts him. He may hide her possessions and deny any knowledge of their whereabouts. Whereas isolated deceptions may not in themselves result in shaking a partner's confidence in her perception of reality, pervasive efforts combined with other forms of maltreatment may have such an effect.

Emotional or Interpersonal Withdrawal

Psychological maltreatment may be passive rather than active; that is, positive and supportive behaviors generally expected in a relationship may be withdrawn or withheld. Such withdrawal may be complete, by leaving the relationship for long periods of time with no explanation. A man may remain physically present but give his partner the silent treatment, ignore her, or show insensitivity to her emotional and sexual needs. One man in a treatment group told the other men, "She was pregnant and asked me for a glass of water. I told her to get it herself, I wasn't going to pamper her just because she was having a kid. She still had two legs." He may not confide in her or share difficulties outside the relationship. He may deny her companionship. The same man who denied his partner a glass of water while pregnant also told the group: "I never go out with her—it's just not my way. I don't enjoy it. She's always on me to go out to a restaurant or a movie, but it just wouldn't be me." Other forms of passive maltreatment include not living up to commitments made in the relationship, and not appreciating the accomplishments, interests, or contributions of one's partner.

Contingent Expressions of Love

The previously described categories, range from overt infliction of psychological harm to passive denial of expected supports. A potent and theoretically important category of psychological maltreatment concerns acts that on their face appear to be positive. What makes such acts psychological maltreatment is that they are only delivered in the context of compliance with the abuser's demands. In addition, these occasional indulgences further disturb the victim's psychological equilibrium.

ASSESSMENT APPROACHES

Concurrent Physical Abuse

As discussed, psychological maltreatment often occurs in combination with physical violence. Because of the immediate life-threatening and dramatic nature of physical abuse, a concern for psychological dimensions of abuse may be obscured. This constitutes a clinical error for several reasons. Physical abuse may diminish or cease during treatment but psychological maltreatment may not. In some cases, psychological maltreatment may even intensify following the cessation of physical abuse. Therefore, it is important to get a baseline of the degree of psychological maltreatment and to signal to clients the practitioner's concern for the full range of abusive behavior. When treating a man who batters his wife, inclusion of psychological maltreatment in the assessment process helps to define the need for his attention to his full repertoire of abusive behavior. Assessment of the types of abusive behavior a man uses will guide intervention goals, as different change strategies may be directed at various types of abusive behavior.

Women experiencing abuse need to have their full experience validated. Women may feel relieved to know that someone understands and can name the mystifying array of abusive behaviors her partner has directed at her. Helping a battered woman to recognize the range of abusive behaviors she has experienced can enable her to assess whether remaining in the relationship is a good idea.

RELIABILITY OF SELF-REPORT

The assessment of behavior in relationships raises several methodological issues. First, the behaviors of interest generally occur in contexts that cannot be observed by the practitioner. Second, reliable assessment of behavior depends on interobserver agreement, in the case of marital therapy, two members of a conflictual couple. Therefore, assessment of behavior largely depends on the self-report of each partner of activities that occur outside the intervention setting. However, research tends to indicate that spouses are generally not good observers of their own or their partner's behavior (Christensen, 1987). Because assessment of psychological maltreatment depends on reports by distressed couples about levels of displeasing events, one can expect that self-reports of psychological maltreatment will be plagued by these issues of reliability. Research has corroborated widespread clinical reports that men who batter deny and minimize their abusive behavior (Edleson & Brygger, 1986; O'Leary & Arias, 1988; Szinovacz, 1983). Edleson and Brygger found that men's reports at intake were less reliable than those after treatment when compared with their partners' reports. While most studies primarily focused on physical abuse, Straus et al. (1989) found that men in the general population were more likely than women to minimize reports of psychological maltreatment. Tolman (1989) documented that men who batter minimized their reports of psychological maltreatment at intake, compared with their partner's reports. While men as a group revealed a higher degree of agreement with their partners about behaviors such as yelling, swearing, and name-calling, they were not as forthcoming in reports of other types of psychological maltreatment.

A more recent study by Moffit et al. (1997), however, did not find large discrepancies in reporting by men or women. Participants in the study were young couples recruited from the community as part of a longitudinal study of relationships. Perpetrators of abusive behavior, whether they were men or women, tended to slightly underreport their behavior compared with victims' reports. Agreement was low for specific items, but higher when using aggregates (based on variety reports) and higher measurement error was adjusted using latent structure methods.

However, there are several cautions in generalizing this study to clinical populations. Nonclinical cases may not be burdened by denial processes that characterize abusers. The low rate of abuse in the general population may overemphasize intracouple agreement due to relatively low rates of socially undesirable behavior. Agreement is likely to be high when abuse has not occurred, as was the case in the Edleson and Brygger study (1986) described in this section.

PARTNER REPORTS

A man's denial and minimization necessitates involvement of both partners in the assessment. When abusive men come to treatment separately, their partners need to be involved. However, involvement should not be in conjoint sessions. Conjoint sessions may endanger a victim of physical abuse in a number of ways. First, a woman will not be able to disclose information about abuse or controversial issues in treatment without fear of retaliation by the partner. In addition, conjoint work gives an implicit, if not explicit, message that both partners share responsibility for the abusive behavior. Therefore, safety dictates getting information from partners of abusive men in separate sessions or through telephone contact.

In evaluating a woman's report of maltreatment, it is important to remember that she may also minimize the extent of abuse she has experienced. Sometimes such minimization may be because she is fearful of what the partner will do to her if she discloses the extent of the abuse, but it may also be because of her self-protective mechanisms (e.g., to reduce her anxiety). Therefore, early reports of maltreatment levels may be revised as she becomes more trusting or less fearful of the consequences of disclosing the full extent of her partner's maltreating behavior.

Counterclaims of Maltreatment

When confronted with their abusive behavior, physical or psychological, abusive men often counter with claims that they too are abused by or mistreated by their partners. As discussed, there is often an exchange of maltreating behavior in a relationship. But at the start of the man's treatment, it is counterproductive to focus assessment extensively on mutual issues. Although his reports of the mutual abuse can be heard empathically, attention to that must be deferred until it can be safely addressed. This is some time after the practitioner is assured that physical violence has ceased and the man has tools with which to maintain nonviolence. Therefore, finetuned assessment of exchange of problematic relationship behaviors is deferred to a later stage of treatment, and preliminary assessment focuses primarily on his behavior.

Measurement Approaches

Checklists

The Conflict Tactics Scale (CTS; Straus, 1979) has been widely used in research studies and in programs for both assessment and evaluation purposes. In its original form, the CTS contains only a limited number of items addressing nonphysical or psychological abuse. Six items have been used to measure what Straus et al. (1989) refer to as verbal/symbolic aggression: (1) insulted or swore at him/her, (2) sulked and/or refused to talk about it, (3) stomped out of the house or yard, (4) did or said something to spite him/her, (5) threatened to hit him/her or throw something at him/her, and (6) threw or smashed or hit or kicked something.

The items are at best a very limited sample of types of symbolic and verbal aggression. Several variations of the Conflict Tactics Scale have appeared in the literature (see, e.g., Brekke, 1987), increasing somewhat the number of items addressing psychological maltreatment. These expanded measures generally have not been subjected to additional examination of their reliability or validity. A revised conflict tactics scale has been developed by Straus, Hamby, Boney-McCoy, and Sugarman (1996) and includes an expanded eight-item scale of psychological aggression. The psychological aggression scale has good internal reliability (alpha = .79).

Although the CTS, even in its expanded form, may not be useful for fine-grained analysis of psychological maltreatment, it may be useful as a broad screening tool, to identify the potential presence of physical and psychological maltreatment.

The Partner Abuse Inventory (Hudson, 1990) is a modification of the earlier Inventory of Spouse Abuse (ISA; Hudson & McIntosh, 1981) that assesses both physical and nonphysical abuse. The Nonphysical Abuse includes a broad sample of psychologically maltreating behavior. Therefore, the PAI-NP provides information not just about the presence of psychological maltreatment but also about the specific forms it takes in the relationship being assessed. The internal consistency of PAI-NP is high (alpha > .90). In a partial validation study (Attala, Hudson, & McSweeney, 1994), battered women in a shelter scored significantly higher than a comparison group of nonbattered nurses.

The Spouse Specific Aggression Scale (O'Leary & Curley, 1986) is a scale of 29 items that assess psychological aggression in relationships. The scale has a parallel 29-item scale measuring assertion in relationships, the Spouse Specific Assertion Scale. The scales have good internal consistency reliability. Physically abusive men reported more psychological aggression toward their partners than did nonphysically abusive men who were dissatisfied with their relationships and men who were satisfied with their relationships. In a more recent study, spouse specific aggression scores differentiated batterers in counseling from nonabusive men (Rathus, O'Leary, & Meyer, 1996). The items are worded so that they can be used for reporting on psychological aggression by either partner.

The Psychological Maltreatment of Women Inventory (PMWI, Tolman, 1989) is a 58-item scale that includes a broader sample of behaviors than does the CTS or ISA. The PMWI has parallel forms for men and women to fill out. Similar in format to the ISA, the PMWI asks clients to report on the relative frequency of each behavior. Two factor analytically derived subscales measure dominance-isolation and verbal-emotional abuse with high reliability (alpha > .90) for both women and men reporters. The PMWI subscales successfully differentiated among battered women, relationship distressed but nonbattered women, and women in nondistressed relationships (Tolman, 1999).

The PMWI also has a short form which contains 14 items reflecting both subscales of the longer PMWI. The short form subscales also have good internal consistency (dominance-isolation, alpha = .88; verbal-emotional, alpha = .92). Battered women scored significantly higher than relationship distress and nonbattered women, as well as relationship-satisfied women (Tolman, 1999).

A 10 item short form for measuring psychological maltreatment in adolescent dating relationships (PMWI-A) has now been developed. The 10-item scale has items representing both factors, and both subscales had good internal consistency reliability (.77 for males, .81 for females) in a study of high school students (Callahan, 1998).

Monitoring Measures

Monitoring measures are often used on an ongoing basis in the treatment of abusive men. Ongoing measurement provides additional information as denial and minimization subside during the intervention process, and also provide critical information about safety throughout the course of intervention.

Critical incident logs require men to monitor instances in which they use coercive or abusive behaviors (Pence, 1989; Sonkin, Martin, & Walker, 1985). These logs can be a source of information about use of psychological maltreatment. Because men tend not to be forthcoming about their abusive behavior early at intake, ongoing assessment of this form is an important aspect of the intervention process.

In addition to rendering information about the abusive behavior, such logs also yield important information about antecedents and consequences of the abusive behavior.

Ongoing monitoring by female partners can be used in a similar fashion to check on the reliability of men's reports, and to provide critical safety information.

A general marital therapy monitoring measure that may have application for assessment of psychological maltreatment is the Daily Checklist of Marital Activities (DCMA; Broderick, 1980). The DCMA is a 109-item checklist of behaviors that spouses may engage in on daily basis. Clients are instructed to rate whether each of the 109 behaviors has occurred per day, and then to rate how pleasant or unpleasant that behavior was for them. Because the DCMA lists a large number of negative behaviors (54 of the 109 items), it may provide a basis for assessing the presence of psychological maltreatment. A high number of negative items, especially if directed by one member of the relationship toward the other, provides a basis for determining that psychological maltreatment is occurring. Use of such a monitoring measure may be supplemented by other questionnaire and interview techniques.

Observational Measures

Generally, observational measures are impractical in a clinical setting. Even in research settings, attempts to assess relationship behavior via direct observation are infrequent. One scale for assessing marital interaction is the Marital Interaction Coding System (MICS) (Hops, Wills, Patterson, & Weiss, 1972). The MICS has several categories that assess behaviors relevant to psychological maltreatment, including put-down, turn-off, and criticize. Although the coding system can rate some dimensions of behavior relevant to psychological maltreatment, it deals only with behaviors that are observable during a brief, contrived encounter. Assessment is possible only of molecular rather than molar sequences of behavior. Despite these problems, such a measure may be useful in discriminating abusive from nonabusive couples. As Margolin, John, and Gleberman (1988) demonstrated, the MICS can discriminate between physically abusive, verbally abusive, and nonabusive couples.

Psychological maltreatment has implications in several areas of law, including family law, criminal law, and tort law. Practitioners should be aware that each individual state determines the rules of each of these bodies of law; as a result, the status of women making claims based on psychological treatment also varies from state to state.

LEGAL AND SYSTEMS CONSIDERATIONS

The legal implications of psychological maltreatment remain largely unexplored. However, there are implications of psychological maltreatment in various aspects of the legal system, and several emerging areas in which psychological maltreatment may become relevant.

Grounds for Divorce

All states now have some type of no-fault divorce, which greatly decreases the significance of demonstrating psychological maltreatment to obtain a divorce decree. Some states, however, are considering bills that would repeal no-fault divorce in certain circumstances. Other states offer fault-based divorce as an alternative to no-fault divorce. Standards for obtaining divorce on this basis vary from state to state: some require the plaintiff to show "mental cruelty," others require a showing of "habitual cruel and inhuman treatment." In *Rakestraw v. Rakestraw* (1998 Miss. App. LEXIS

159) judgment for divorce was affirmed, despite "no confirmation that he ever struck his wife," where:

> Beyond the lack of monetary aid and resulting hardships, William refused entirely to assist with household chores . . . withheld emotional support from Rebecca as well as their daughters . . . [h]e frequently belittled Rebecca before family and friends by referring to her as "stupid" or "ignorant" . . . was prone to throwing household items about during what might best be described as temper tantrums. (pp. 73–74)

MARITAL TORTS

A tort is a "civil" (as opposed to "criminal") wrong: that is, where an individual has been harmed by another individual, the person harmed may sue "in tort" for damages incurred by the behavior of the other. Examples include medical malpractice, or reckless driving that causes injury to another. Until recently, the doctrine of "interspousal immunity" precluded women from suing their husbands for damages arising out of the marital relationship. Today, however, most states today have abolished interspousal immunity; others have abolished the immunity for intentional torts (including intentional infliction of emotional distress); a minority of states allow spouses to sue one another in tort only after the marriage has been dissolved.

The most important causes of action available to women who have experienced psychological abuse are negligent and intentional infliction of emotional harm. Courts have long allowed individuals to sue in tort for negligent or intentional infliction of emotional harm. With abolition of the interspousal immunity bar between spouses, women whose husbands have psychologically abused them may now have recourse to a remedy under this tort. In *Massey v. Massey* (1991), the court found in favor of the plaintiff on her claim of emotional distress and awarded her $362,000. The court there rejected Mr. Massey's claim that "absent a finding of physical injury, a cause of action for infliction of emotional distress may not be asserted in a divorce suit." A second Texas case, *Twyman v. Twyman* (1990), found that a woman had made out a claim for negligent infliction of emotional harm where:

> William knew of Sheila's previous violent rape and her inability to emotionally "handle" participation in sexual bondage activities, he repeatedly conditioned the continuance of their marriage upon such activities, participated in sexual bondage activities with extramarital partners, cruelly described such partners and experiences to her, pressured her to engage in conduct she found distasteful, and exposed their 10-year-old-son to graphic depictions of sexual bondage acts.

CUSTODY

Child custody laws vary from state to state, but most require the court to make custody decisions in light of the best interest of the child. At least 38 states have adopted laws making domestic violence a relevant factor in custody decisions (ABA, 1994). On May 7, 1996, Massachusetts became the first state with a judicially created requirement that each court consider the impact of domestic violence on children before awarding custody to an abuser. Although this is hopeful, the case at issue involved both physical and psychological abuse, and it is unclear whether a showing of psychological abuse alone would enter the court's considerations. In other states, as well, where domestic violence may be considered, the definition of abuse is generally very narrow, and does not encompass psychological as distinguished from physical maltreatment, except in the narrow context of placing the abused parent in a reasonable fear of immediate serious bodily injury.

Although statutes may not mandate consideration of psychological maltreatment in determining custody, generally a judge has broad discretion in determining what is in the best interests of a child in a particular case. Judges can, if they choose, consider psychological maltreatment of one or the other parent to be relevant because it bears on the character and fitness of the maltreating parent.

Criminal Defense

Battered woman syndrome is now widely recognized as a scientific evidence, admissible in criminal defense trials so long as the expert is qualified and the evidence is relevant to the fact pattern at hand. This evidence has been introduced on behalf of battered defendants in two contexts: to show duress and to show self-defense. Although the battered woman syndrome generally is thought of as applying to those individuals who have been victims of recurrent physical abuse, the syndrome actually refers to a psychological condition that can result from psychological maltreatment alone. Nonetheless, most courts require a showing of physical abuse.

Self-Defense

Criminal law varies from state to state, but one of two self-defense regimens is in place in every state. Most states require a two-part showing for a defendant to plead self-defense: (1) a subjective belief or fear that at the time of the killing, the defendant believed herself to be in imminent danger of death or serious bodily injury, and that lethal force was necessary to prevent that harm; (2) a showing that this subjective belief was objectively reasonable, that is, a reasonable person would have drawn the same subjective conclusion in those circumstances. A minority of states require only the subjective showing. It is unlikely that a psychologically abused defendant could make this showing on evidence of psychological abuse alone, and to date, no court has allowed purely psychological abuse to constitute a basis for such a defense.

Duress

Psychological abuse may also help an abused defendant make a showing of "duress" as a defense to crimes other than homicide (for which this defense is not available). For example, given the existence of persuasive psychological maltreatment, a woman may be convinced to commit welfare fraud, rob a bank, or commit some other crime at her partner's insistence. Typically, the defendant is required to show three elements: (1) that the abuser placed the defendant in fear of immediate or imminent danger of death or severe bodily harm; (2) that the defendant's fear that the abuser would carry out his threat was well-founded; (3) that the defendant honestly believed that the only way to avoid this harm was to commit the crime that the abuser wanted her to commit. As with self-defense, this threshold is difficult to meet with evidence of psychological abuse alone. However, the defense also covers threats of immediate family, and so an abuser's threats to harm or kidnap a defendant's child—a common form of psychological abuse—would most likely meet the requirements of this defense.

ORDERS FOR PROTECTION

Protection statutes vary from county to county, requiring different showings by abused women in different counties or municipalities. Most statutes expressly permit an order on the basis of assault without battery. "Assault" consists of placing another in fear of physical injury, not actually causing the injury. As a result, threat of injury alone constitutes sufficient evidence for an order of protection to be issued. In some jurisdictions, other forms of psychological abuse (aside from threats) may also meet the threshold required to obtain an order of protection. In Pennsylvania, for example, the domestic violence law contains a section entitled "false imprisonment," which means depriving someone of his or her liberty. If a woman is so fearful that she does not leave her house, or so constrained by the demands of her partner that she is not able to go to school or work, she can get a protection order. She can be issued such an order, even if physical abuse has not occurred. Some other states have similar provisions.

SUMMARY

Assessment of psychological maltreatment may have implications in the legal arena. As our methods for determining existence of psychological maltreatment in a relationship become more refined, it is likely that much information will be utilized by the legal system. Practitioners working with cases of abuse must become increasingly sensitive in dealing with the legal issues if they are to serve their clients with full competence.

CASE ILLUSTRATION

Diane is a 19-year-old unmarried mother who recently came to an adolescent health clinic that provides medical care and mental health services to teenagers and their children. Diane was referred to the clinic's social worker for assessment when she reported to the attending physician that she was confused about her current relationship and felt that she felt "trapped" by her boyfriend. She reported that she had recently begun living with Zack, the father of her baby, after having broken up for nearly 2 months. During the interim she and the baby had lived with her parents and younger brother. The last grade of school Diane had completed was the 11th grade, and she has not been in school in several years.

Diane and Zack met while she was working at a local retail store in the managers' training program. She told how he bought a shirt a day for a week before he got up the nerve to ask her out. Their relationship initially was very exciting for Diane. Zack told her how he was finishing up college and had several job offers lined up. He would buy Diane many expensive gifts, take her out for dinner, and always seemed to have money.

Diane described how she was overwhelmed by his generosity and enjoyed spending time with him. She had rented her own apartment and he would come over frequently to spend the night. They began having intercourse soon after they met. Initially, Zack had used condoms, but he stopped, claiming that they were taking away from the experience. When Diane told him that she wanted him to use condoms or go on birth control herself, he would sulk, claiming that she did not trust him and love him. She would relent and they began to regularly have unprotected sex.

Two months into the relationship Diane became pregnant. She described Zack as happy about the news, but she was concerned that a baby at this point in her life would thwart her plans to return to school to obtain her high school diploma. When she began to discuss having an abortion with Zack, he became very upset and told Diane that he would leave her if she brought up the issue again. Diane dropped the idea of an abortion and became involved in her pregnancy.

Zack moved in with Diane shortly after she became pregnant. After they began living together, he convinced her to stop working while she was pregnant. Diane had saved money from her years of working and she signed Zack onto her checking account so that he would have money for school. Zack would take Diane's car most days, claiming that he was going to class and many nights would not come home, telling Diane that he was at the library studying. When Zack was around, he was moody and had a short temper. Diane described how he would get angry at her for not having the apartment clean or making his food the way he liked it. If she did something to displease him, he would withdraw and not talk to her. Diane believed that she was helping Zack through a difficult time in school and attributed his behavior to the stress he was under at school. Diane lived far from public transportation and became lonely and depressed.

One night when Zack had failed to come home a friend of Diane's called to invite her to a party. Her friends came to pick her up and when she returned later that night, Zack was home and furious that she had left without telling him where she was going. When she told him that she had just been out with friends, he flew into a rage, slapped her in the face, and accused her of cheating on him. He stormed out of the apartment and did not return for three days. Diane was seven months pregnant at the time and terrified that Zack would not return and she would have to raise the baby by herself. When Zack returned, he told her that he would not be able to remain with her if he could not trust her. Diane promised him that she would not leave without telling him where she was going and whom she would be with.

As her pregnancy progressed, she began to notice that Zack was more critical of her friends calling them "low-lifes who were on AFDC who would not work and needed to get a job." Diane described how Zack's jealousy made him extremely suspicious of her friends. She commented that before she got together with Zack many of her friends were male. If she were to go somewhere with one of these friends, he would start fights with them or call them up to argue. Diane reported that Zack accused her of having sex with her male friends. His jealousy had an extremely isolating effect on Diane and she ended up pulling away from her friends so that Zack would not get upset.

Diane noticed a distinct change in their relationship after the baby was born. She described how Zack's use of alcohol increased after the baby's arrival. She gave the baby her last name which produced a serious fight. He began to act as if the baby were not his and would deny that he was the father when asked. During this time, one of Diane's friends had called to tell her that she had seen Zack in a local bar with another woman the previous night. Zack had told Diane that he was at the library studying and when she confronted him he told her that he had dropped out six months ago because of her constant nagging and that her frigidity and lack of concern for her appearance had driven him to see other women.

As Diane began to think about ending the relationship, Zack threatened to hurt himself if she ever left him. He made vague threats of driving his car off a nearby cliff. Diane was scared by his threats and blamed the problems in their relationship on herself. Diane reflected on how poorly she felt about herself. She felt that she had no way out of the relationship. She was exhausted from being up with the baby all night and had no money for child care or transportation. Zack was around less and less and began to talk down to her and criticize her for the slightest mistakes that she made.

Diane described how she would need to beg him for money for diapers and other necessities for the baby. This led to more arguments and eventually Zack stopped coming home at all. He called Diane and told her that he had met someone else who was not crazy like she was and he did not want to be with her anymore. Two weeks later, Diane was evicted from her apartment and owed three months' back rent. With no money and no place to go, she was forced to move back with her parents.

Diane's parents were religious and they were upset with her for not being married to the baby's father. When Diane attempted to explain how Zack had behaved, her parents would tell her she was being selfish and not thinking about what it would be like for her son to grow up without a father. She rarely spoke with her parents and they told her they needed to know when she was moving out.

Six weeks after Zack left her, he appeared at her parents house and told her that he would give her another chance to be a good girlfriend. Having no where else to go, Diane left her parents' house and moved in with Zack who was staying at a friend's trailer.

While Diane had denied at the assessment that she was being physically abused by Zack, use of a structured checklist revealed that Zack used occasional force toward her in the form of pushing and slapping. It was also revealed that Zack would force Diane to have sex. Diane reported that she had never needed to seek medical treatment for the slaps, but had begun drinking more regularly to help calm her nerves.

As a result of Diane's involvement at the adolescent health clinic, the social worker was able to schedule individual therapy sessions for Diane to deal with her depression, low self-esteem, and use of alcohol. Because Zack would object to this type of action, the social worker arranged for the counseling sessions to coincide in conjunction with the baby's visits to the clinic.

The goal of the individual counseling was to get Diane to the point where she would be able to join one of the clinic's adolescent mothers groups. Such groups are structured to deal with a wide range of abuse that exists in adolescent relationships. These specially designed groups are oriented to empower the participants. The intervention relies on the ability of the practitioner not only to affirm the experience of the battered adolescent, but to help restore her self-image, evaluate why she is in the relationship, and explore options and resources that are available to her. The goal of the intervention is not to reunite (or separate) the couple, but rather to focus on Diane's empowerment and safety.

Utilizing the adolescent version of the Psychological Maltreatment Women's Index (PMWI-A) helped illustrate the forms of psychological maltreatment that occur in the context of this relationship. In Diane's case, Zack became controlling early on in their relationship making the decisions regarding contraception and what to do about an unintended pregnancy. Using a combination of guilt and threats of leaving Diane, Zack was able to get what he wanted without including Diane in the decision process.

As the relationship progressed, Zack was able to control more of Diane's daily life and was successful in cutting her off from outside social networks. Zack convinced Diane to stop working early on in her pregnancy and used her car leaving her isolated at home and far from outside resources. Zack's mood was erratic and Diane never knew what to expect and she found that little things like the cleanliness of the apartment or the preparation of his dinner would anger him.

Zack's jealousy of Diane increased as he became more physically violent with Diane. Her attempts to maintain friendships resulted in Zack slapping Diane and leaving her alone without transportation for several days. Zack also began arguing and fighting with Diane's friends ensuring that they would not want to be around.

Arrival of their baby only increased the level of stress in the relationship. Zack's use of alcohol increased making his behavior more unpredictable; it became clear that he was dating other women and lying about attending school. He blamed all his problems on Diane, and when she mentioned the need to end the relationship, he threatened to hurt himself.

Diane's situation was exacerbated because Zack had access to her checking account, she lacked social support from her own family, and she increased her use of alcohol to cope with the situation. Although she was able to leave the relationship for nearly a month and a half, this was because Zack had left her. When he returned, she reentered the relationship. A successful intervention must address the many forms of maltreatment that Zack uses to control Diane.

CONCLUSION

Awareness of the damaging effects of psychological maltreatment in relationships is growing. Practitioners must be better prepared to identify and treat the victims and perpetrators of psychological maltreatment. Psychological maltreatment is difficult to define, and such lack of adequate definition limits the practitioner's attempts to properly address the problem. This chapter has attempted to define the problem and to identify tools for the practitioner to use to aid in clinical assessment of psychological maltreatment. Barriers to effective assessment have been identified, and some suggestions for addressing these barriers have been presented.

We have become more sophisticated and sensitive to family violence in all its forms in recent years. Psychological maltreatment is likely to receive increased attention from the courts, in both civil and criminal contexts. Hopefully, the increased attention being directed to the problem of psychological maltreatment will result in a rapid and fruitful expansion of knowledge about this problem.

REFERENCES

Andersen, S.M., Boulette, T.R., & Schwartz, A.H. (1991). Psychological maltreatment of spouses. In R.T. Ammerman & M. Hersen (Eds.), *Case studies in family violence* (pp. 293–328). New York: Plenum Press.

Arias, I., & Pape, K.T. (1999). Defining psychological abuse in intimate relationships: multiple perspectives. *Journal of Emotional Abuse: Violence and Victims, 14*(1).

Attala, J., Hudson, W.W., & McSweeney, M. (1994). A partial validation of two short-form partner abuse scales. *Women & Health, 21,* 125–139.

Barling, J., O'Leary, K.D., Jouriles, E.N., Vivian, D., & MacEwen, K.E. (1987). Factor similarity of the conflict tactics scales across samples, spouses, and sites: Issues and implications. *Journal of Family Violence, 2,* 37–54.

Brekke, J.S. (1987). Detecting wife and child abuse in clinical settings. *Social Casework, 68,* 332–338.

Broderick, J.E. (1980). *Attitudinal and behavioral components of marital satisfaction.* Unpublished doctoral dissertation, State University of New York at Stony Brook.

Callahan, M.R. (1998). *Adolescent dating violence victimization, coping and psychological well-being.* Unpublished doctoral dissertation, University of Michigan, Ann Arbor.

Christensen, A. (1987). Assessment of behavior. In K.D. O'Leary (Ed.), *Assessment of marital discord* (pp. 13–57). Hillsdale, NJ: Erlbaum.

Dutton, D.G., & Starzomski, A.J. (1997). Personality predictors of the Minnesota power and control wheel. *Journal of Interpersonal Violence, 12,* 70–82.

Edleson, J., & Brygger, M. (1986). Gender differences in reporting of battering incidents. *Family Relations, 35,* 377–382.

Follingstad, D.R., Rutledge, L.L., Berg, B.J., Hause, E.S., & Polek, D.S. (1990). The role of emotional abuse in physically abusive relationships. *Journal of Family Violence, 5,* 107–120.

Gurley, D. (1989, January). *Understanding the mixed roles of social support and social obstruction in recovery from child abuse.* Paper presented at the Responses to Family Violence Research Conference, West Lafayette, IN.

Hops, J., Wills, T.A., Patterson, G.R., & Weiss, R.L. (1972). *Marital interaction coding system.* Eugene: University of Oregon and Oregon Research Institute.

Hudson, W.W.(1990). *Partner abuse scale: Physical.* Tempe, AZ: Walmyr.

Hudson, W.W., & McIntosh, S.R. (1981). The assessment of spouse abuse: Two quantifiable dimensions. *Journal of Marriage and the Family, 43,* 873–885.

Jacobson, N.S., Gottman, J.M., Gortner, E., Berns, S., & Shortt, J.W. (1999). Psychological factors in the longitudinal course of battering: When do the couples split up? When does the abuse decrease? *Violence and Victims, 14*(1).

Margolin, G., John, R., & Gleberman, L. (1988). Affective responses to conflictual discussions in violent and nonviolent couples. *Journal of Consulting and Clinical Psychology, 56,* 24–33.

Marshall, L.L. (1994). Physical and psychological abuse. In W.R. Cupach & B.H. Spitzberg (Eds.), *The dark side of interpersonal communication* (pp. 281–311). Hillsdale, NJ: Erlbaum.

Marshall, L.L. (1996). Psychological abuse of women: Six distinct clusters. *Journal of Family Violence, 11,* 379–409.

Moffit, T.E., Caspi, A., Krueger, R.F., Magdol, L., Margolin, G., Silva, P.A., & Sydney, R. (1997). Do partners agree about abuse in their relationship? A psychometric evaluation of interpartner agreement. *Psychological Assessment, 9,* 47–56.

Murphy, C., & O'Leary, K.D. (1989). Psychological aggression predicts physical aggression in early marriage. *Journal of Consulting and Clinical Psychology, 57,* 579–582.

NiCarthy, G. (1986). *Getting free: A handbook for women in abusive relationships.* Seattle, WA: Seal Press.

O'Leary, K.D., & Arias, I. (1988). Assessing agreement of reports of spouse abuse. In G.T. Hotaling, D. Finkelhor, J.T. Kirkpatrick, & M.A. Straus (Eds.), *Family abuse and its consequences: New directions in research* (pp. 218–227), Newbury Park, CA: Sage.

O'Leary, K.D., & Curley, A.D. (1986). Assertion and family violence: Correlates of spouse abuse. *Journal of Marital and Family Therapy, 12,* 281–289.

Pence, E. (1989). Batterer programs: Shifting from community collusion to community confrontation. In P.L. Caesar & L.K. Hamberger (Eds.), *Treating men who batter: Theory, practice and programs* (pp. 24–50). New York: Springer.

Pence, E., & Paymar, M. (1993). *Education groups for men who batter.* New York: Springer.

Rathus, J.H., & O'Leary, K.D. (1997). Spouse-specific dependency: Scale development. *Journal of Family Violence, 12,* 159–168.

Rathus, J.H., O'Leary, K.D., & Meyer, S.L. (1996). *Attachment, proximity control, and wife abuse.* Unpublished manuscript, University at Stony Brook, Stony Brook, NY.

Sackett, L.A., & Saunders, D.G., (1999). The impact of different forms of psychological abuse on battered women. *Violence and Victims, 14*(1).

Sonkin, D., Martin, D., & Walker, L. (1985). *The male batterer.* New York: Springer.

Stets, J.E. (1990). Verbal and physical aggression in marriage. *Journal of Marriage and the Family, 52,* 501–514.

Straus, M. (1979). Measuring intrafamilial conflict and violence: The conflict tactics (CT) scale. *Journal of Marriage and the Family, 45,* 75–88.

Straus, M.A., Hamby, S.L., Boney-McCoy, S., & Sugarman, D.B. (1996). The revised conflict tactics scales. *Journal of Family Issues, 17,* 283–316.

Straus, M.A., Sweet, S., & Vissing, Y.M. (1989, November). *Verbal aggression against spouses and children in a nationally representative sample of American families.* Paper presented at the annual meeting of the Speech Communication Association, San Francisco.

Szinovacz, M. (1983). Using couple data as a methodological tool: The case of marital violence. *Journal of Marriage and the Family, 45,* 633–644.

Tolman, R.M. (1989). The initial development of a measure of psychological maltreatment of women by their male partners. *Violence and Victims, 4,* 159–178.

Tolman, R.M. (1999). The validation of the psychological maltreatment of women inventory: Preliminary report. *Violence and Victims, 14*(1).

Tolman, R.M., & Bhosley, G. (1991). The outcome of participation in a shelter sponsored program for men who batter. In D. Knudsen & J. Miller (Eds.), *Abused and battered: Social and legal responses to family violence* (pp. 113–122). New York: Aldine de Gruyter.

Tolman, R.M., & Edleson, J.L. (1989). Cognitive-behavioral intervention with men who batter. In B.A. Thyer (Ed.), *Behavioral family therapy* (pp. 169–190). Springfield, IL: Thomas.

Tolman, R.M., & Stoops, C. (1997, July). *The impact of psychological maltreatment on women's well-being and relationship satisfaction.* Paper presented at the 5th International Family Violence Research Conference, Durham, NH.

PART FOUR

SPECIAL ISSUES

CHAPTER 16

Child Witnesses of Domestic Violence

MARLIES SUDERMANN and PETER G. JAFFE

UNTIL RECENTLY, children who witnessed violence in their family were not considered to be the victims of violence. Without the obvious physical contact and wounds from child abuse, these children were ignored as a highly vulnerable population. There is now sufficient evidence and research to confirm that children who observe violence are the unintended or indirect victims of such behavior. A growing body of literature (e.g., Jaffe, Wolfe, & Wilson, 1990; Peled, Jaffe, & Edleson, 1995) supports the long-standing reports from women's shelters that children who witness family violence are frequently traumatized, and almost invariably show effects of the witnessed violence. This violence and the likely consequences make these children the victims of psychological maltreatment, and if the violence is not stopped, they can be considered in need of protection (Echlin & Marshall, 1995).

This chapter considers this special population of vulnerable children by first describing the problem and then outlining several assessment approaches to identify the scope of the children's adjustment difficulties. Special legal and child protection issues are explored and illustrated with a case study. For the purpose of this chapter, the term *marital violence* is replaced by the term *wife assault*. The overwhelming majority (95%) of instances of marital violence involve women as victims and men as perpetrators, according to police and court reports (Dutton, 1988). Although women do behave violently, this violence in the marital situation is most often defensive in intent. Women also instill fear in their husbands far less often in their husbands than in the reverse situation. Given the extensive nature of violence against women in our society and the historical perspective of denying the problem or blaming the victim, marital violence is a misleading term in the present context.

DESCRIPTION OF THE PROBLEM

Research studies conducted over the past 20 years make it increasingly difficult for society to ignore the pressing social and legal problem of family violence and wife assault. Straus and Gelles (1986), in a well-conducted, large-scale survey, found that severe husband-to-wife violence occurred in 11.3% of American homes. The American Medical Association (AMA, 1992) has published data indicating that American women were four times more likely to be physically injured at the hands of their own partner than injured in a motor vehicle accident, and that marital violence was in fact the leading cause of physical injury to American women.

In Canadian studies, similar findings have been reported by Statistics Canada, a well-respected national research agency. A random telephone survey found that one in four women between the ages of 18 and 65 had experienced violence at the hands of a current or past marital partner. Of those women who were experiencing violence in a current marriage, 34% had felt at some point their lives were in danger. Children were reported to witness violence in many cases of severe violence (Statistics Canada, 1994). Despite a common misconception that wife abuse mostly occurs out of the view of children, in fact children witness or are aware of the majority of violent incidents. Estimates of what proportion of violent incidents are witnessed or overheard by children and teens vary from 40% (Bard, 1970) to 80% (Sinclair, 1985). Children often witness or overhear more violence than their parents estimate, and children sometimes try to intervene or are in the middle of the violence, in the case of infants or toddlers. Sometimes children try to get out of harm's way, and are not successful. They are often afraid to go for help, because of the code of secrecy which the abuser has often conveyed to all family members around the violence. Children can be the victims of retribution by the abuser if they tell. Children are at increased risk of themselves being physically abused and sexually abused in homes where there is wife assault, and the increased risks are only now being studied. Sometimes children, especially older male children and teens, wish to or try to harm the abuser (sometimes their father), and some do carry out this wish. Every year women are murdered by their abusive male partners or husband, and children also witness a significant proportion of these murders (Crawford & Gartner, 1992). Sometimes the abuser or his family members obtain custody of the children afterward.

Clinical and empirical investigations have repeatedly shown that children who witness wife abuse are likely to demonstrate emotional and behavior problems, and social and school adjustment difficulties (Fantuzzo & Lindquist, 1989; Hughes, 1988; Jaffe et al., 1990). Children who witness severe and repeated violence are likely to develop severe distress and difficulty in their emotional adjustment and behavioral, social, and school development. Documentation of the problems experienced by children who are witnesses to woman abuse initially came from battered women's shelters (Hughes, 1982; Layzer, Goodson, & deLange, 1985; McKay, 1987; Pressman, Cameron, & Rothery, 1989; D. Wolfe, Jaffe, Wilson, & Zak, 1985). Problems noted included externalizing aggressive/destructive behavior) problems, including aggression to siblings and peers, noncompliance with adults and rules, destructiveness, and generalized anger and irritability. Internalizing (emotional) problems were also noted in children in women's shelters, including sadness, withdrawal, fear, anxiety, and somatic complaints.

Other studies have shown that children who witness woman abuse are frequently hampered in their social and school development (Pepler, Moore, Mae, & Kates, 1989;

Randolf & Talamo, 1997). Children who are witnessing violence or who have done so in the past may be preoccupied with this issue, and have difficulty concentrating on school learning tasks. Their social development may be hampered because they are too sad, anxious, or preoccupied to participate; or their tendency to use aggressive strategies in interpersonal problem solving may make them unpopular and rejected.

We believe that these effects on children are not only due to witnessing discrete acts of violence against their mothers; the effect of living in a climate of fear and uncertainty should not be underestimated. When violence can break out precipitously and capriciously, children (as well as their mothers) are living a life of extreme anxiety and tension. This alone must have an effect on children and can produce the somatic complaints, anxiety, irritability, difficulty concentrating on normal developmental activities, withdrawal, and outbursts of aggression which are typical of children from woman abusing environments. Also important to recognize is the impact of verbal abuse and emotional oppression, which typically accompany physical abuse. These factors also contribute to emotional and behavioral maladjustment in no small measure. Also, it is not surprising that many children from these environments learn coercive and aggressive interaction patterns, and learn to disrespect females, if male, and to have low self-esteem, if female.

Another important factor in effects on children of living in a home where there is woman abuse is that their mother's ability and availability to parent will be reduced by the time and energy she must devote to dealing with her own psychological and physical trauma, and in ensuring the safety of the children. A mother who is physically injured, extremely stressed, tense, who has been isolated from family and community supports by the abuser, and who must deal with practical realities like deciding whether to leave, moving, and seeking legal and community assistance, is in a situation where her time and energies are obviously drained from normal activities such as child care and self-care. It is not surprising that some women who are abused experience full-blown depression, which may further impair their energy to parent. Very often, they are called on to be heroic mothers who still parent amazingly well under severe strains, but the strains and demands take their toll.

POSTTRAUMATIC STRESS DISORDER

Recent studies have shown that many children who witness woman abuse suffer from posttraumatic stress disorder (PTSD). The definition of posttraumatic stress disorder, according to the *Diagnostic and Statistical Manual of Mental Disorders,* fourth edition (*DSM-IV;* American Psychiatric Association, 1994b) includes the following: the person has been exposed to an event involving actual or threatened death or serious injury, or a threat to the physical integrity of the self or others; and the person's response involved acute fear, helplessness, or horror; or in the case of children, agitated or disorganized behavior. In addition, the event is reexperienced (e.g., through nightmares, intrusive remembering of the event in response to cues that remind the person of the event); there is persistent avoidance of stimuli that remind the person of the event; and there are persistent symptoms of increased arousal, such as difficulty falling asleep, irritability, outbursts of anger, difficulty concentrating, hypervigilance and exaggerated startle response (American Psychiatric Association, 1994a). Lehmann (1997) found that 56% of a sample of children in women's shelters met the full criteria for PTSD, while the majority of the remaining children showed some symptoms associated with this disorder. Both Terr (1991) and the current authors have suggested that while the conceptualization of PTSD has been developed with the concept of persons who experience an overwhelming traumatic event, children who witness violence in the home are often exposed to a more chronic and long-lasting form of violence, which Terr has termed Type II trauma. Many children who are exposed to woman abuse in their homes may never have known a calm, peaceful environment, even from their earliest childhood or infancy, and thus their development and reactions are differently and more chronically affected than those children who experience a single traumatic event against a background of a peaceful and supportive environment.

WITNESSING WOMAN ABUSE AND OTHER FORMS OF VIOLENCE AND TRAUMA

Clinical observation in our practice suggests strongly that children who have experienced the trauma of war and also experience woman abuse are at greatly increased risk behaviorally and developmentally. We would also observe that many children witness extrafamilial forms of woman abuse in the course of war. Osofsky, Wewers, Hann, and Fick (1993), while studying children living in violent urban neighborhoods in the United States, found serendipitously that children who were exposed to family violence had the worst mental health outcomes. Other studies have shown that children who experience both physical child abuse and witness woman abuse in the home have even worse difficulties and maladjustment than children who only experience one of these traumas (Sternberg et al., 1993).

A recent qualitative study by Berman (1998) compared the experiences and perspectives of children and youth who had experienced the trauma of war and those who had witnessed woman abuse. The results indicated that the experiences of those witnessing woman abuse in their family had perhaps even more devastating experience because they did not have any safe and supportive place or time of reference with which to contrast the traumatic experiences, while those experiencing war trauma could view it as an aberration compared with the safety and security of their family and prewar community. Thus, while children growing up in violent homes have been compared with children growing up in a war zone, children from violent homes may be, psychologically even worse off in some ways.

PHYSICAL AND SEXUAL ABUSE IN HOMES WHERE CHILDREN WITNESS WOMAN ABUSE

Children are at greatly increased risk of physical child abuse in homes where they witness woman abuse. Different studies have given different estimates, but most agree that there is at least a 30% to 40% overlap for experiencing physical child abuse in a home where there is woman abuse (Hughes, Parkinson, & Vargo, 1989; Straus, Gelles, & Steinmetz, 1980). Far fewer studies include child sexual abuse, but clinical experience and findings from studies of families of child sexual abuse victims show that there is often a significant overlap between child sexual abuse and woman abuse (Sas, Cunningham, & Hurley, 1995). Often, after a woman separates from an abusive male partner and there is unsupervised child visitation to that parent, there is an increased risk of child physical and sexual abuse due to the anger, emotional upset, and lessened oversight by the mother.

CHILD WITNESSES OF WOMAN ABUSE WHO ARE MISDIAGNOSED WITH ATTENTION-DEFICIT/HYPERACTIVITY DISORDER

Children who witness woman abuse are, in our experience, and in that of many battered woman's shelter children's advocates, frequently misdiagnosed with attention-deficit/hyperactivity disorder. This is because clinicians who are seeing these children in family practice or children's mental health centers do not ask about or recognize the problem and experiences of witnessing woman abuse. The externalizing (conduct) problems, irritability, difficulty concentrating and preoccupations of children associated with witnessing woman abuse are frequently confused with symptoms of children whose primary problems are attentional in nature.

SYMPTOMS OF WITNESSING WOMAN ABUSE AT DIFFERENT DEVELOPMENTAL LEVELS

Prenatal

Woman abuse often takes place during a woman's pregnancy (McFarlane, Parker, Soeken, & Bullock, 1992). The results can be stress and injury to the fetus, as well as miscarriage or death of the fetus.

Infancy

Infants are often literally in the middle of physical abuse, because of the time they spend in their mother's arms or near her. Infants are sometimes hit by blows when in their mother's arms, or are thrown or abducted as a tactic by the abuser. Even very young infants have been shown to react with severe physiological distress at witnessing conflict between their mother and other persons as shown by measures of heart rate, galvanic skin response, and behavioral observations (Cummings & Davies, 1994). In addition, a mother who is being emotionally and physically abused is not receiving the support and environment she needs to devote herself to the intense, responsive care an infant needs (Jaffe, Wolfe, Wilson, & Zak, 1986). Many women who are abused experience symptoms of depression (Hilberman & Munson, 1978), and depression is one of the worst predictors of maternal functioning. When women are depressed and abused, and seek medical help, they are often medicated without appropriate attention being given to the abuse situation (Tearmann Society for Battered Women, 1988).

Behavioral manifestations in infants who are witnessing woman abuse include prolonged crying, irritability, difficulty sleeping, and disruption in eating and play/exploration (which are crucial for optimal development). A result can be failure to thrive; in extreme cases, an infant simply does not gain weight, drops off weight percentile curves, or even loses weight. Failure-to-thrive infants are at risk of dying or having severe and long-lasting impairment in brain function due to malnutrition.

Toddlers and Preschoolers

Preschoolers who witness violence typically experience poor health, poor sleeping habits, and excessive screaming or crying (Alessi & Hearn, 1984; Davidson, 1978; Hughes, 1986; Layzer et al., 1985). They have been described as having problems related to weight and eating patterns (Layzer et al., 1985), enuresis (Hughes, 1986), and somatic complaints (Hilberman & Munson, 1978). Older preschoolers begin to evidence difficulty relating to other children and adults (Layzer et al., 1985). Cummings and colleagues' (Cummings, 1987; Cummings, Iannotti, & Zahn-Waxler, 1985) studies of toddlers and preschool children show that these children tend to have two reactions when verbal conflict is actually occurring: they go from playing happily to stopping play and returning to their mothers. Other toddlers become aggressive in response to hearing conflict and start throwing toys or aggressing against peers or siblings.

School-Age or Latency-Age Children

School-age children who are witnessing woman abuse typically show elevated levels of internalizing and externalizing behavior problems, compared with demographically matched controls (D. Wolfe et al., 1985). Violence-exposed boys tend to show greater externalizing and internalizing problems than their peers not exposed to violence, whereas girls tend to exhibit internalizing problems only (Jaffe, Wolfe, Wilson, & Slusczarzck, 1986). School-age children also demonstrate increasing difficulty in peer relationships, often marked by excessive aggression and hostility (Alessi & Hearn, 1984). Aggressive and hostile behaviors are reported more for males than females (Rosenbaum & O'Leary, 1981; D. Wolfe et al., 1985; D. Wolfe, Zak, Wilson, & Jaffe, 1986). These children also evidence a number of school-related problems including erratic attendance, poor achievement, poor concentration, and school phobias (Carlson, 1984; Hughes, 1986). School-age children often continue to display problems with enuresis, nightmares, insomnia, and somatic complaints (Hughes, 1986). Sometimes there is school refusal, as the child is too overwhelmed to face the additional challenges of school. Other times, children who do well in school and have a supportive environment there like to spend as much time as possible at school, arriving early and leaving late. School-age children who witness violence also have been described as secretive, withdrawn, clingy and overly dependent; these differences may be sex specific, as they appear to typify school-age girls more than their male counterparts (Hughes, 1982, 1986). Researchers have found that gender difference in adjustment difficulties begin at the age when children enter school (Jaffe, Wolfe, Wilson, & Slusczarzck, 1986) and intensify as they enter adolescence (Carlson, 1984; Cassady, Allen, Lyon, & McGeehan, 1987; Hughes, 1986; Jaffe, Wolfe, Wilson, & Slusczarzck, 1986).

Adolescents

Included among the adjustment problems demonstrated most often by adolescent witnesses of wife assault are hostility, aggression, running away from home (Jaffe et al., 1990), projection of blame onto others, anxiety, somatic complaints (Alessi & Hearn, 1984), and withdrawn and suicidal behaviors (Hughes, 1986). As they get older, adolescent boys are more inclined to identify with their father and become abusive and violent in their own relationships with girls and women, including their mother, sisters, or girlfriend (Barnett, Pittman, Ragan, & Salus, 1980; Carlson, 1984; Jaffe et al., 1990). Adolescent girls are also more likely to become future victims of violence in their dating and marital relationships (Jaffe et al., 1990). This latter effect is not because these girls are choosing violent partners, but if they do encounter a violent male partner, they are less likely to leave the relationship, perhaps because they view the violent behavior as less aberrant and may feel that this is part and parcel of adult marital or dating relationships.

School adjustment is also adversely affected in adolescents, with dropping out of school or underachieving being two very common outcomes. Sometimes adolescent girls stay home from school to assist their mother with care of younger siblings, on occasions when the mother has been abused. Frequently school is simply not a priority due to the emotional and behavioral turmoil engendered by the witnessing of woman abuse. In our clinical experience, many street youth have had the experience of witnessing woman abuse.

Subtle Symptoms

In addition to the emotional, behavioral and developmental difficulties previously outlined, children who witness violence exhibit subtle symptoms of witnessing violence. Subtle symptoms can be classified into three major areas: (1) responses and attitudes about conflict resolution, (2) assigning responsibility for violence, and (3) knowledge and skills in dealing with violent incidents. Many children who have witnessed woman abuse believe that violence is a justifiable response to interpersonal conflict, given certain conditions. They may feel that the victim is to blame for violence, because they have heard their father, stepfather, or other male figure say to their mother, "It's your fault, you never do what I say" or "If you didn't mess everything up we wouldn't have these problems," or similarly blame the victim for their (the perpetrator's) violence. Children often internalize these messages and come to blame their mother for the violence.

Very often, younger children blame themselves for the violence, or for some occurrences, especially if the violence has been preceded by an argument over child rearing or by comments by the male perpetrator about the woman's "failure" to "keep the children in line." Younger children are also less able than older children to reason about cause and effect and to recognize situational nuances and cues. Thus, for example, the child who left his or her bicycle in the driveway, annoying their father, may feel responsible for an episode of violence toward their mother which occurs in proximity to this event. Younger children's developmental tendency to be egocentric in their thinking also contributes to this pattern of self-blame. Both younger and older children may try to intervene and stop the violence, and in so doing, become physically injured themselves.

Older children may blame their mother for the violence partly because of societal tendencies toward victim-blaming in woman abuse (e.g., "Why didn't she leave?"), and partly because it is safer to take their anger out on their mother than on the potentially violent father or male figure.

These children are also learning that "might makes right," and this is reflected in their greater acceptance of interpersonal violence in solving peer conflicts (Marshall, Miller, Miller-Hewitt, Sudermann, & Watson, 1995). They are more likely to feel that verbal insults and put-downs are justification for physical retaliation, and they may be able to generate far fewer nonviolent conflict-resolution strategies than their peers from nonviolent homes.

They are also learning very skewed messages about gender roles. Very old-fashioned and stereotyped, male-dominant beliefs about who should be in control in relationships are typical in children and youth who have witnessed woman abuse. This is sometimes evident at school in terms of disrespect toward female teachers by male and female children. Sometimes, especially in boys, a generalized disrespect for authority develops; it is not a coincidence that witnessing woman abuse is very prevalent in young offender populations, as well as in adult offenders.

Finally, it was mentioned that child witnesses of woman abuse must develop (often ineffectively) an atypical repertoire of safety skills. These children often require basic knowledge and skills to handle an emergency that is not covered in a school course on fire, accident, and traffic safety (Jaffe et al., 1990). When a violent outbreak occurs, these children must assess the lethality or seriousness of the situation and determine an appropriate action plan. However, calling the police and enlisting the help of neighbors, or extended family and friends, are actions that conflict with the code of secrecy about family affairs that perpetrators of woman abuse often engender and enforce in their children. Thus, these children are put into a very conflicted and anxious state of mind in the midst of an emergency situation.

MODERATING DETERMINANTS OF PSYCHOSOCIAL IMPACT

It has been posited that a number of factors, such as severity of violence witnessed, duration of witnessing, and compensatory factors such as a supportive relationship with the mother or other family members, and strengths such as school or social skills, would affect the severity of violence witnessing effects that a particular child would experience (Jaffe & Sudermann, 1995). Additional variables that might affect the outcome of witnessing violence include age of the child at onset and stopping of the violence, and availability of emergency services to assist with dealing with violence. While few studies have systematically addressed these issues, Lehmann (1997) reported that a longer duration of witnessing violence (4 years or more), more than one violent perpetrator (in sequence), and greater frequency of violent acts witnessed, all increased the negative effects of witnessing violence (in terms of PTSD symptomatology). Younger children also seemed to be affected more than older children, although age at onset of the violence was not reported and may be an important variable. Lehmann also found that the older children and teens might be engaging in some denial around their symptoms, in a self-protective manner.

LONG-TERM EFFECTS

Long-term effects on children who have witnessed woman abuse have not been well studied in a prospective manner, and most studies of child witnesses of woman abuse have employed shelter samples, although many women who are abused do not use a shelter. However, the presence of many men and women in the adult prison population who have witnessed woman abuse while growing up is one indicator of the severity of the long-term effects. More study is needed in this area. One finding that has consistently been found in retrospective studies is that men who abuse their female partners have a much higher rate of witnessing woman abuse than men who do not engage in abuse (Hotaling & Sugarman, 1986; Kalmuss, 1984; O'Leary, Malone, & Tyree, 1994; Straus et al., 1980).

ASSESSMENT APPROACHES

The effects of witnessing woman abuse on children are serious and broad-ranging. Therefore, assessment approaches must also be comprehensive. Often the first area to address with a child or adolescent who has witnessed violence is breaking the code of secrecy around the problems, and developing a safety plan because it is often not a given that the violence they are experiencing has ended. These activities must be accomplished before further assessment takes place. Issues to address with children include telling them that violence is not their fault, that it is right to seek help for the problem, and that they are not responsible for stopping the violence. Keeping themselves safe is the first priority, followed by accessing help to stop the violence against their mother. Keeping out of the violence, knowledge of community emergency response numbers, and identifying adults who will help in an emergency and safe places to go are of prime importance. We find that safety plans are best developed with the child's mother, if at all possible.

Another priority in assessing children and adolescents exposed to woman abuse is to ask about the occurrence of physical child abuse and child sexual abuse, and if these are present, to involve the normal investigative and child protection/reporting criteria in response. Occurrence of child maltreatment during the children's visits with their father should be assessed if he was the woman abuser.

After the screening for safety planning and child physical and sexual abuse are completed, the person who assesses a child who has witnessed violence should address a wide range of areas: emotional problems, behavioral problems, posttraumatic stress disorder, school and social adjustment, conflict resolution skills, and attitudes and beliefs about violence against others, gender roles, and family violence. Also very important are social and environmental disruptions in children's lives as an effect of the violence on the children's primary caregivers, their mothers. Coping skills and strengths in the child's caregivers and family system are also important to address.

BUILDING RAPPORT AND BREAKING THE CODE OF SECRECY

As mentioned, children from violent homes are often imbued with a "code of secrecy" that has been ingrained over a long period of time. They may have been punished for telling family business to outsiders, or threatened with being cut off from the family if they tell. They may not be used to interacting with nonfamily members in extended family networks or community organizations. Therefore, the therapist's first tasks are to build rapport with the child and to dispel the code of secrecy. Two invaluable aids in this endeavor are to enlist the support of the mother, if possible, and to have good information beforehand as to what happened in the family with regard to violence. It is essential, in interviewing children who have witnessed violence, to have as good an idea as possible about what has happened, so that the child does not feel that they are the one who is "telling," and so that the child does not have to recount every detail if this is difficult for them (Arroyo & Eth, 1995).

In assessing children and adolescents who have witnessed wife assault, it is important to give them a measure of control in the interviews. They have often experienced abusive control from the abuser, and in overcoming their problems, it is important to empower them. This can often be done through asking the child to decide on things such as where to sit, whether they feel more comfortable if they can color or draw during the interview, when to have breaks, and what order to talk about things. The child may not be ready to talk about details of the abuse in the first interview, and if this is attempted, a lot of "I don't know" and "I forget" responses may be forthcoming from the child. These are often protecting the child who is using avoidance defenses, and may also be appropriate responses for the child who is deciding whether the interviewer is a trustworthy, supportive person. Therefore, multiple interviews are best. If the assessor has the support of the mother (or the foster mother or child protective services worker, in the case of children who are in care), the child will have "permission" to talk. Even with this assistance, the child may be entrenched in a pattern of denial and minimization that have formed part of his or her coping style for a long time.

Sometimes it is easier for children to talk after they have attended a group for children who have witnessed violence, where they have learned to break their silence, and where they have learned that other children have these experiences too, and it is not their fault. Children are mostly ashamed and embarrassed to come from a family where there is violence and dysfunction, and if formal assessment instruments are given before good rapport is developed, or before the code of secrecy is broken, the responses obtained may reflect denial rather than an accurate picture.

The severity of violence witnessed by children can range from verbal abuse and occasional pushing, holding, or slapping, to frequent physical abuse, assault with weapons, sexual assault in front of children, and even murder. Physical violence is almost always accompanied by verbal and emotional abuse, including belittling of mothers, limiting and controlling their movements, and restricting access to social supports. Thus, not only physical abuse, but also emotional and verbal abuse should be considered when duration and severity of the abuse are assessed. Administering to mothers a standardized instrument, such as the Conflict Tactics Scale (Straus, 1979) or other similar questionnaire can be useful in this regard. For a similar purpose, Lehmann and Wolfe (1992) have developed a 13-item questionnaire called the History of Violence Witnessed by Child Questionnaire. For each item, frequency, duration, and the types of exposure (hearing, seeing, trying to intervene) are measured.

A social history of the child and family is also important to obtain, including such additional items as number of abusive partners the child has been exposed to, number of family moves, and reasons for these, number of school changes, and changes in principal caregivers. Developmental history, including milestones related to walking, talking, and school progress are also useful to obtain and to correlate with the onset of violence witnessing. For example, if a child had difficulty with weight gain in infancy, it is possible that this failure to thrive related to a very violent period in the mother's victimization.

In terms of psychological assessment, instruments related to emotional and behavior problems are administered. The assessor may wish to begin with questionnaires completed by the mother, other caregivers and teachers, such as the Child Behavior Checklist (Achenbach & Edelbrock, 1983). The Children's Depression Inventory is useful for assessing suicidal tendencies in children and younger teens. For adolescents, self-report instruments such as the Personality Inventory for Youth (Lachar & Gruber, 1995) or the Youth Self Report Form (Achenbach, 1991) are useful in obtaining a picture of overall adjustment. Specific areas such as anxiety and aggression can further be assessed with more specialized instruments.

Specific instruments to assess trauma and its impact are then used. For example, the Trauma Symptom Checklist for Children (TSCC, TSCC-A; Briere, 1996), with or without the items on sexual abuse, is appropriate for detecting posttraumatic stress symptoms. This instrument is a self-report measure for children aged 8 to 16 years. It measures anxiety, depression, anger, under- and overarousal, dissociation and, in the TSCC, sexual concerns. The TSCC-A leaves out the items relating to sexual abuse. The items on dissociation and under- and overarousal are very relevant to children who have witnessed woman abuse. The standardization sample of over 3,000 children includes children and youth who have experienced woman abuse, and some specific profiles for these children are included in the manual.

Another instrument geared to posttraumatic stress symptoms is the Children Impact of Traumatic Events Scale Family Violence Form (CITES-FVF; V. Wolfe & Lehmann, 1992). In addition to 25 items addressing trauma symptoms, the CITES-FVF measures attributions of dangerous world, personal vulnerability, and self-blame/guilt.

If there are school problems, obtaining a copy of school report cards is important. The child may need an assessment of learning ability and learning disabilities, and school achievement should also be assessed with formal instruments to check for discrepancies between school achievement and academic ability.

Many communities are running educational and treatment groups for children exposed to woman abuse (Marshall et al., 1995; Peled & Davis, 1995). To assess children's starting point and later progress with respect to issues addressed in these groups, a questionnaire to measure relevant issues has been developed (Sudermann, Marshall, Miller-Hewitt, Miller, & Watson, 1993). This questionnaire addresses attitudes and beliefs about violence against women, children intervening in woman abuse in the home, the use of violence to resolve interpersonal conflict, non-violent conflict resolution, knowledge of safety plans, and community emergency and counseling resources, among other issues. For older teens, a questionnaire entitled the London Family Court Clinic Questionnaire on Violence in Relationships (Jaffe, Sudermann, & Reitzel, 1989; Jaffe, Sudermann, Reitzel, & Killip, 1992) may be useful with regard to assessing attitudes and beliefs around woman abuse in general, as well as dating violence.

The Child Witness to Violence Interview (Jaffe et al., 1990) is an interview for assessing children who have witnessed woman abuse. This interview format covers attitudes and responses to anger by the child, safety skills, and attitudes around responsibility to violence.

CAREGIVERS AND THE SOCIAL ENVIRONMENT

A significant proportion of the adjustment problems of children who witness wife assault is likely mediated through the effects of wife assault on their mothers (D. Wolfe et al., 1985). Wolfe et al. found that measures of maternal health, stress, negative life events, and socioeconomic status were significantly related to child behavior problems in a sample of families where woman abuse had occurred. It is easy to understand that parenting is undermined in woman who are (1) being abused physically and verbally, (2) having to cope with repeated crises, (3) experiencing major economic and social dislocations when leaving the abusive situation, and (4) subjected to continued harassment and conflict after the separation. Also, social and economic disruptions that often occur along with woman abuse impact directly on the children. Typically it is the woman and children who must leave familiar surroundings, community, school, and network of friends to flee violence. Sometimes they cannot even take their most prized toy, stuffed animal, or clothes, for fear of alerting their father to their departure. These circumstances often continue for a long time, as the mother is unable to obtain possession of the matrimonial home, or fears that doing so would be too dangerous. These circumstances further compound the adjustment for children, who must start over in a new school and make new friends. Thus, these circumstances of social and physical upheaval should be taken into account in assessing a child witness to marital violence.

Finally, factors that offset the negative influences of witnessing women assault are very important and must be taken into account. Protective factors may include one or more of the following: intelligence, school achievement, good peer relationships, social skills, skills in sports and extracurricular activities, and a warm and nurturing relationship with at least one adult (Rae-Grant, Thomas, Offord, & Boyle, 1989; Rutter, 1979).

LEGAL AND SYSTEMS CONSIDERATIONS

Children who witness their mothers being assaulted by their fathers frequently find themselves involved in the legal system. Several roles may evolve that require special consideration in both civil and criminal proceedings:

1. The child as a delinquent youth whose behavior problems are strongly linked to the violence witnessed.
2. The child in need of protection as a result of witnessing violence.
3. The child involved in a custody or access dispute where exposure to violence may be a central theme.
4. The child as an actual witness in court proceedings related to assault charges against the father.

Each of these areas requires a great deal of coordination by professionals in the justice, mental health and social service systems. Battered women and their children may find a confusing and overwhelming maze of programs, policies, and legislation as they cope with the aftermath of violence. The child's role in each of these legal matters is described in general terms in the following subsections. Specific legislation varies from one state (or province) to another, and interpretations may be a function of local practice and available resources.

DELINQUENT YOUTH

Adolescents who witness violence may exhibit externalizing symptoms that include assaultive behavior, suicide attempts, and running away from home (Jaffe et al., 1990). One consistent finding in the literature appears to be the link between dangerous behavior and witnessing violence at home. For example, Lewis, Shanok, Pincus, and Glaser (1979) conducted a study on violent behavior in a population of incarcerated juvenile offenders. Offenders with the highest level of current violent behavior and violent offenses were four times more likely to have witnessed violence at home than were offenders in the least violent group. An important consideration of this factor exists at the level of police intervention, court assessment, and court disposition. Police officers, as the only 24-hour fully mobile social service, have a unique opportunity to intervene in breaking the intergenerational cycle of violence (Jaffe, Finlay, & Wolfe, 1984). Many crisis calls to police involving the conduct problems of these children relate to the imitation of violence witnessed at home. If charges are made, then juvenile court judges may require comprehensive clinical assessments to help them understand the etiology of a young person's violent behavior (Jaffe, Leschied, Sas, & Austin, 1985). When such behavior is clearly linked to the impact of witnessing violence at home, specialized services will be required to address this issue. Incarceration or community supervision, without any attempt to help offenders deal with attitudes and behavior learned in the home environment, may be futile.

One avenue to provide services is to offer groups in juvenile custodial facilities for child witnesses of woman abuse. In our experience, there is a very high incidence in such facilities of children who have witnessed woman abuse, and the issue will be relevant to a high proportion of inmates/residents. Bentley has successfully run such groups, following a modified version of the groups process described in Loosley, Bentley, Rabenstein, and Sudermann (1997). Bentley notes that an important issue with groups for juvenile offenders who are also witnesses of woman abuse is to make the group environment voluntary and nurturing.

CHILDREN IN NEED OF PROTECTION

Are children who observe their fathers assaulting their mothers in need of protection? From the perspective of an overburdened child protection worker who is struggling with a caseload of physical and sexual abuse victims, the answer may be no. From the perspective of a shelter for battered women staff member who is hesitant to report "witnessing violence" as child abuse for fear of revictimizing the battered women through threats of losing her children, the answer may also be no. However, careful consideration needs to be given to the plight of children who observe violence. Their daily reality includes fear for their mother's safety and the ever-looming danger of becoming "caught in the crossfire" (Roy, 1988). The link between observation of violence and serious emotional and behavioral problems is now very well established. A persuasive argument can be made that these children are experiencing serious threats to their social and emotional development, and are at risk of developing behavioral disorders as well.

Some jurisdictions have included witnessing family violence in their child protection statutes, with mixed results. Some American jurisdictions have followed an approach of holding the mother accountable for "failure to protect" their children if they do not leave an abusive partner, because the child protection system has leverage mainly over the mother, and also because of failure to focus on the issue of responsibility for the violence and working to empower the mother through effective assistance to her. Other jurisdictions have enacted legislation that focuses on children who witness violence as children who are being emotionally abused and neglected, as in Alberta, Canada (Echlin & Marshall, 1995; Echlin & Osthoff, in press). However, statistics on the outcome of this legislation are difficult to collect, with cases of children witnessing woman abuse lumped together within the general category of emotional abuse and neglect. The answer may lie in fostering more collaboration and coordination between child protection, police/court criminal proceedings charging the offender, and supportive services by women's advocates and shelters. Training for all of the staff in child protective services about the dynamics of woman abuse, and overcoming the gulf of mistrust that exists in some areas between child protective services and women's advocates, is very important. While empowering and protecting women who are abused is overall the most effective way to protect children who witness abuse, there are also some extreme cases, where children who witness violence must be removed from their families, due to imminent danger to their physical and emotional health through staying in the situation, and the nonviability of other solutions. In our clinical experience, these extreme cases usually occur when there are multiple risk factors and dangers to the children, including other forms of abuse and neglect, in addition to witnessing woman abuse.

CHILDREN IN CUSTODY DISPUTES

Violence in marriages often leads to separations and in some cases the initiation of custody and access (visitation) disputes. These disputes may lead to complex legal proceedings in which the court is faced with conflicting allegations and concerns over parents' abilities and/or children's best interest. Children who witness such violence raise a special dilemma for the court. A mother's lawyer may argue that her victimization eliminates the father from consideration as a custodial parent. A father's lawyer may argue that the alleged incidents of wife assault have nothing to do with his role as of a father. These disputes lead to special consideration for child witnesses. Children's wishes and best interests in custody disputes must be considered in the context of this violence. It would be difficult to argue that fathers who have directed emotional and physical abuse "only" to their partners can be appropriate role models and facilitate a positive relationship for the children with their mother. Fathers who abuse the children's mother should also be considered as committing emotional abuse toward the children, given the extreme distress and long-lasting emotional and behavioral problems caused by this behavior. Judges and assessors in these matters should hold the perpetrators of the violence accountable for its effects on children, rather than focusing on the mother's "failure to protect," which we contend is a form of victim blaming.

Often women are afraid to bring forward issues of woman abuse and child abuse in the context of a custody and access dispute because they are afraid the court will not be sympathetic, and will view them as vengeful and untruthful, or at the least, the "unfriendly parent" who will not promote access. On the other hand, if they do not mention abuse, they are guilty of "failure to protect" (Echlin & Osthoff, in press). Serious concerns have been expressed about gender bias in this area, which has limited the courts' understanding of the issues involved (Chesler, 1986; Walker, 1989).

Careful consideration needs to be given to the current popularity of mediation in resolving these custody disputes. This process involves a neutral third party who encourages parents to cooperate in developing a postseparation parenting arrangement. However, mediation is inappropriate for marriages characterized by violence. A woman who has been terrorized for many years cannot be expected to negotiate as an equal party in many instances (Jaffe et al., 1990; Walker & Edwall, 1987). It may even be unsafe for the woman to be in the same building with her former partner, as he may use the opportunity to harass or stalk her, or find out where she is living (if this information has been withheld for safety reasons). However, the choice of mediation is sometimes made by women who have been abused, and if they feel the process empowers them and is safe, this should be their choice, without coercion from anyone. The mediator must be well apprised of woman abuse issues and be prepared to stop the process if power imbalances and implied threats are impinging on the mediation.

Another related issue is the practice of promoting consideration in some jurisdictions of joint custody. While joint custody may be the ideal in the case of a nonconflictual divorce, the presumption of joint custody can be very harmful in cases where there has been woman abuse. Child access to the noncustodial parent must also be very carefully considered when there has been woman abuse. A recent study by the Nova Scotia Law Reform Commission of 1,157 woman abuse cases found that over 80% of the accused received probation sentences if convicted, and of these, 40% broke probation, about half of these being reassaults. Twenty-four percent of reassaults took place on the occasion of court ordered child visitation or access. Even when there is not an out-and-out physical reassault, the abuser can use child exchanges as the occasion to verbally harass and threaten his ex-partner, and to keep track of her whereabouts. Sometimes the harassment is overt, and sometimes it is fairly subtle. A significant proportion of woman abusers also physically and/or sexually abuse their children and stepchildren. For these reasons, access must be very carefully considered. Sometimes it may be best to use supervised access centers, or supervised exchange points. Sometimes, access may simply not be in the children's best interests until the abuser has been treated for the abuse, and has learned to take responsibility for stopping his abusive behavior.

CHILDREN AS WITNESSES

When children are the only witnesses to serious incidents of violence in their home, they may have to testify in court about their observations. However, most of these incidents are never reported to the police (Dutton, 1988), and when charges are made, children are rarely called except in cases of homicides or severe assaults (Dobash, 1977). Children have significant barriers to successfully telling their stories in court. The courtroom is an adult setting dominated by professionals with little understanding of child development and little sensitivity to translate language and proceedings to the child's age-appropriate level. Aside from these barriers, children also face the emotional trauma of reliving a painful and overwhelming life event. In these matters, they are forced to reveal information that will most likely be damaging to the wellbeing of their father. Although there may be of a supportive prosecutor, the long-term consequences of such testimony in the family system may be divisive. In any event, the court may not trust the memories of children because of their age (Goodman & Rosenberg, 1987).

Recent developments in the court system have suggested a growing sensitivity to children's roles as credible witnesses. Aside from educating judges and lawyers about these issues, specialized services have been created to help prepare children for court. These preparation programs focus on helping children to cope with their anxiety and fears about being on the witness stand and on helping educate children about their role in the court process, as well as the roles of judges, prosecutors, defense lawyers and juries (Hurley, Sas, & Wilson, 1988).

CASE ILLUSTRATION

Tom and Marie had been married for about 12 years and had three children, a son, Mike, aged 12, and two girls, Jane, age 9, and Beth, age 7. Tom owned his own small business, and Marie had begun working part time as a secretary, after being away from the workforce for a few years to care for the children. Tom tended to make most of the decisions in the family, and almost from the beginning of the marriage had been very critical and emotionally abusive toward Marie. He called her names and put her down in front of the children. Tom tended to favor Mike over Jane and Beth, and spent a lot of time with Mike in sports-related activities. Mike was a very good hockey and soccer player for his age, and his dad often coached his teams and attended many of his games over the years. The girls tended not to get much attention from their father, and were close to their mother.

There had been intermittent occasions of physical violence by Tom toward Marie throughout the marriage, and this increased in severity in the past few years. Tom was usually somewhat sorry afterward, although he often cited pressures at work, and claimed that Marie also was at fault for disagreeing with him. After a particularly severe incident of physical violence, in which Marie sustained cracked ribs and bruises about the head, and which the children witnessed, police were called by a neighbor, and officers attended and took Marie to hospital, and called relatives to come and get the children. Marie went to stay briefly in a women's shelter, and then moved in with relatives, together with the children. Tom threatened that he would get custody of the children, unless she decided to return. Tom was charged, and was awaiting trial. The police report was detailed, but did not include information about the whereabouts of the children during the incident. All three children actually witnessed the incident. Tom hired a lawyer, who dealt with the criminal matter, and obtained a referral for a family law lawyer. Marie applied for legal aid, but was very worried about the outcome of the custody matter, even though she had done the majority of child care for all three children. She did not have the financial resources to get a place for her and the children to live in the same neighborhood where the children went to school.

The couple and their children were referred to a psychologist for an assessment of child custody and access. During the assessment, it became clear that Mike was a very angry and confused adolescent. He was still doing well in his sports, but at school he was getting into increasing difficulty with his behavior. He got into several fights with other boys, and his attitude toward teachers was very disrespectful, especially toward his female homeroom teacher. Mike's marks were slipping badly, and he was tending to hang out with other boys who got into trouble. He had a great deal of trouble talking about his feelings about the separation, but tended to say his mother could end the problems by going back to his father. He stated a firm wish to live with his father, if his parents weren't going to get back together. He stated that his father and he had more interests in common than he and his mother. He also did not think that his mother would have enough money to pay for his hockey registration and equipment, if he were to live with her.

The two girls were also experiencing some difficulties around the time of the separation. Jane was doing well in school, but had developed some perfectionistic tendencies, and seemed to her teacher to be very anxious and startled easily. She was becoming more withdrawn, and tended to avoid becoming involved in new activities offered after school, citing the need to get home and help watch her younger sister. In the assessment, she could talk about her feelings of sadness and grief about the troubles in her family, and her biggest wish was for a "normal" family, with no violence. She generally felt that she did not want her mother and father to get back together, because the violence might start again, but at times she fantasized about her parents reuniting. She could describe, in the most vivid detail of all the children or adults in the family, the incident of violence, and she often thought about this incident while she was supposed to be working on seatwork at school, or at other times such as when she was falling asleep at night. She at first said that she did not want to go on access visits to her father, because he spent most of the time either taking them to her brother's hockey games, or he would spend time with his friends, and would leave Jane to look after her sister. She also complained that her father and his friends drank a lot and said bad things about her mother. After the access visits, her mother sometimes asked her how things had gone, but she was afraid to complain to her mother. Instead she made up excuses not to go on access visits, looking for invitations to stay with friends, or saying she had too much homework. She wished to live with her mother.

In clinical observation and assessment it appeared that Jane was becoming somewhat parentified in her role with her mother, in that she was very attuned to her mother's needs, was taken into mother's confidence a great deal, and was expected to help her mother with child care for her sister, as her brother often got into fights with both girls, if he was left to babysit.

Beth, the 7-year-old, had experienced some nightmares about the violent incident which resulted in the separation, but during the assessment, made it clear that she did not feel comfortable talking about it. She was afraid that her father would be "mad" if she talked about what happened. She admitted to being afraid that her father would find out and punish her if she talked about the violence. Socially she was getting along well at school, but the teacher had found that she did not work well on her own, and tended to daydream and needed much extra encouragement in order to learn new concepts.

Beth would not talk much about the access visits. She only said they were "Okay, as long as Jane comes too." She did say that dad spent most of his time with Mike. She did mention that dad sometimes rented fun movies for the girls, and they sometimes got to stay up late, so the visits with dad were sometimes fun, in her view.

During the course of the assessment, Marie reported that she was coming to her wit's end in parenting Mike, and was considering if she should let Tom have custody of Mike, although she really felt it would be better if all three children stayed with her. Mike had become increasingly noncompliant, angry and defiant, and one day, while riding in the back of the family van behind her (while she was driving), he had stabbed a pen knife through the back of her seat from behind. While she was not injured, the incident had shaken her confidence in her ability to manage Mike, and she also did not know if her own nerves could stand the strain of dealing with this type of situation much longer. With the assistance of the psychologist, she was able to have Mike assessed and admitted for short-term residential care at a children's mental health center. Mike was angry at being admitted, but with treatment focusing on the needs of children who have witnessed family violence/woman abuse, he was able to make gains quickly. Marie also took part in a parenting group that provided parent-to-parent support as well as professional input on techniques for parenting teenagers. She began to feel more empowered to deal with both her children's feelings, and their discipline.

On one occasion, an incident occurred while Beth was involved in a church confirmation ceremony. Tom attended the event, as did Marie, Jane, and Mike. Despite his assurances during the assessment, that he never was violent toward Marie, except possibly in a defensive manner (holding her arms so she could not hit him), Tom picked an argument with Marie in the church lobby, and in front of the children and several adult witnesses, slapped Marie in the face. After this incident, Marie mentioned that Tom had been insulting her and threatening her during times in which he picked up and dropped off the children for access.

After this, Tom voluntarily stopped having access with the children, on the advice of his lawyer, and this coincided with Mike being at the treatment center. The girls had mixed feelings about this. On the one hand, they were relieved that they did not have to listen to their father's threats and putdowns directed toward their mother, and they mentioned that their father also put down their mother during the access visits. On the other hand, they felt this was a further proof of their father not caring about them, since when Mike was not available for access, their father did not bother to pick them up.

It was recommended in the custody and access assessment that Marie be awarded custody of all three children, on the grounds that she was in any case closer to the girls, and that Mike was being very adversely affected by his father's example of violence against women. Mike was headed toward conflict with the law as a juvenile offender and bully as a result of modeling his father's behavior, and as a result of his volatile feelings from witnessing the abuse being expressed as anger toward teachers and peers. It was recommended that Tom attend a batterer's treatment program which emphasized that abusive men take responsibility for their violence. It was recommended that access to the children be resumed in a supervised setting, for a few hours a week, while Mike and Tom underwent treatment. After that, a review was recommended to reevaluate the issue of access. It was recommended that a supervised or neutral access transfer point might need to continue to be in place, even if access became unsupervised. Mike improved a great deal during three months' treatment in a residential facility, and he adjusted well at school. He continued to have periodic anger and aggression outbursts with his sisters and peers, but these were now within limits that the school and Marie were able to handle. It was also recommended that Marie attempt to shield Jane from the role of confidante to mother, and use her less for child care. It was emphasized in the assessment that Jane needed to be more sheltered from adult information about the divorce, and more free to involve herself in school and peer activities as she felt able. Play therapy was recommended for Beth, the 7-year-old, who was having trouble expressing her feelings about the violence and the separations, and art therapy was recommended for Jane, the 10-year-old. Both girls showed signs of low self-esteem, as they perceived that Mike was favored by their father during access visits. Nevertheless, their school and peer adjustment improved in the year following the separation.

In a court hearing on custody and access, Marie was awarded interim custody of all three children. However, a review of custody and access was recommended, after Mike's treatment course, and prior to final determination of child custody.

COMMENT

This case illustrates that there are serious emotional and behavioral consequences for children and adolescents in witnessing marital violence, and that children's wishes are not always a good indicator of what is best in terms of their postseparation placement. It is common for preteen and adolescent boys to begin imitating the father's violent behavior, and to begin to use verbal and physical violence toward their mother and siblings and peers. This case also illustrates that child access pickup and dropoff are prime times for renewed verbal and sometimes physical abuse by the abuse perpetrator. Often children are subjected to hearing further put-downs of their mother by their father when they are on access visits. Women are sometimes reluctant to report these events, when they have no adult witnesses, as they do not want to be seen as impeding access, lest they anger the abuser further, or be seen as the "unfriendly parent" in the court proceedings. Sometimes a neutral, public place for pickup and dropoff is helpful, some people successfully use the homes of supportive grandparents, relatives, or friends, and others need the services of a supervised access center. This case also illustrates that mental health treatment is often needed for children who are experiencing the deleterious effects of witnessing their mother being abused.

Assessors in these matters need to be aware that violence does not always end with separation, but in fact may grow more serious and take on different forms through conflicts over child custody or visitation. It is important for assessors to have a thorough knowledge about domestic violence including the impact of violence on victims and child witnesses. Although this case illustrates a relatively positive outcome, there are many situations where abused women and children's needs are not recognized or resources are not available to adequately address safety and treatment issues.

CONCLUSION

It is important to envision the many changes to our legal, social service, and health systems that will be necessary to eliminate or greatly reduce the incidence and ameliorate the impact on children witnessing woman abuse. It is equally important to change public attitudes about woman abuse, and children who are exposed to it, because without public knowledge and concern about these issues, it is very difficult to implement lasting changes in public service and legal systems.

One of the most important endeavors is professional and public education about woman abuse, its effects on children, and the substrate of gender inequality that allows woman abuse to continue. Woman abuse and the effect on children should be included as a core topic for professional schools in law, social work, psychology, medicine, nursing, teaching, public health, education, and any other professions in the health, law and social service fields. In-service education, particularly for current leaders in these fields, is also very important.

Legislative and procedural changes are needed in legal areas such as consequences for perpetrators, handling of parole violations, treatment for perpetrators, restraining orders, and other safety measures for abused women. Legislative and practice changes are also needed in the area of child custody and access, to make perpetrating woman abuse a relevant and important risk factor in assessing parenting capacity and access rights. In child protective services, the emphasis needs to be changed from focusing on "failure to protect" by mothers, to focusing on the responsibility of the abuser, and the empowerment of nonabusive women. Greater cooperation between child protective services workers and violence against women workers needs to be implemented. There need to be outreach services for women and mothers, in particular, who are too disadvantaged, isolated, abused, depressed, or burdened with child care, to attend appointments at out-of-home services.

Children's mental health providers and family therapists, as well as nurses, family physicians, obstetricians, and pediatricians as well as other medical personnel, need to ask screening questions about woman abuse and family violence at intake and on an ongoing basis. These service providers must build better bridges to violence against women's services as well as child protective services.

Two other very important areas are community coordination of services and community accountability. Without regular coordination and the relationships between agencies and between service providers that are built through coordination, there will be narrow forms of service with many gaps.

Finally, prevention is very important. In terms of primary prevention, provision of knowledge to children and youth is a very promising area (Jaffe, Sudermann, Reitzel,

& Killip, 1992; Sudermann & Jaffe, 1997). Programs such as A.S.A.P. (A School-Based Anti-violence Program; Sudermann, Jaffe, & Schieck, 1996) give children and youth the information they need to reach out for help if they are witnessing abuse at home, being abused, or if they are starting to get into abusive dating relationships. They can learn skills for violence-free conflict resolution, and the values that promote gender and cultural equity. Also important in terms of secondary prevention is outreach through provision of information to primary health care and community centers, so that women and children who are experiencing violence can obtain help early on. Also, for those children and youth who are at high risk of repeating the pattern of violence (because they have witnessed violence), secondary prevention programs such as groups for children who have witnessed violence (e.g., D. Wolfe et al., 1997) are promising.

REFERENCES

Achenbach, T.M. (1991). *Youth self report.* Vermont: University Associates in Psychiatry.

Achenbach, T.M., & Edelbrock, C.S. (1983). *Manual for the child behavior checklist and revised child behavior profile.* Burlington, VT: University Associates in Psychiatry.

Alessi, J.J., & Hearn, K. (1984). Group treatment of children in shelters for battered women. In A.R. Roberts (Ed.), *Battered women and their families* (pp. 49–61). New York: Springer.

American Medical Association. (1992). Violence against women. *Journal of the American Medical Association, 267,* 107–112.

American Psychiatric Association. (1994). *Diagnostic and statistical manual of mental disorders* (4th ed.). Washington, DC: Author.

Arroyo, W., & Eth, S. (1995). Assessment following violence-witnessing trauma. In E. Peled, P.G. Jaffe, & J.L. Edleson (Eds.), *Ending the cycle of violence: Community responses to children of battered women* (pp. 27–42). Thousand Oaks, CA: Sage.

Bard, M. (1970). Role of law enforcement in the helping system. In J. Monahan (Ed.), *Community mental health and the criminal justice system* (pp. 99–109). Elmsford, NJ: Pergamon Press.

Barnett, E.R., Pittman, C.B., Ragan, C.K., & Salus, M.K. (1980). *Family violence: Intervention strategies* (DHHS Publication No. OHDS 80-30258). Washington, DC: U.S. Government Printing Office.

Berman, H. (in press). The relevance of narrative research with children who witness war and children who witness woman abuse. In R. Geffner, P.G. Jaffe, & M. Sudermann (Eds.), *Children exposed to family violence: Current issues in research intervention, prevention and policy development.* Florida: Haworth Press.

Briere, J. (1996). *Trauma symptom checklist for children.* San Antonio, TX: The Psychological Corporation/Harcourt Brace.

Carlson, B.E. (1984). Children's observations of inter-parental violence. In A.R. Roberts (Ed.), *Battered women and their families* (pp. 147–167). New York: Springer.

Cassady, L., Allen, B., Lyon, E., & McGeehan, D. (1987). *The child-focused intervention program. Treatment and program evaluation for children in a battered women's shelter.* Paper presented at the third National Family Violence Researchers' Conference, Durham, NH.

Chesler, P. (1986). *Mothers on trial: The battle for children and custody.* Seattle, WA: Seal Press.

Crawford, M., & Gartner, R. (1992). *Woman killing: Intimate femicide in Ontario 1974–1990.* Toronto, ON: Women We Honour Action Committee.

Cummings, E.M. (1987). Coping with background anger in early childhood. *Child Development, 58,* 976–984.

Cummings, E.M., & Davies, P.T. (1994). *Children and marital conflict.* New York: Guilford Press.

Cummings, E.M., Iannotti, R.J., & Zahn-Waxler, C. (1985). Influence of conflict between adults on the emotions and aggression of young children. *Developmental Psychology, 21,* 495–507.

Cummings, N., & Mooney, A. (1988). Child protective workers and battered women's advocates: A strategy for family violence intervention. *Response, 11,* 4–9.

Davidson, T. (1978). *Conjugal crime: Understanding and changing the wife beating pattern.* New York: Harthorne.

Dobash, R.E. (1977). *The relationship between violence directed at women and violence directed at children within the family setting.* London, ON: House of Commons, Select Committee on Violence in the Family.

Dutton, D.G. (1988). *The domestic assault of women: Psychological and criminal justice perspectives.* Toronto, ON: Allyn & Bacon.

Echlin, C., & Marshall, L. (1995). Child protection services for children of battered woman: Practice and controversy. In E. Peled, P.G. Jaffe, & J.L. Edleson (Eds.), *Ending the cycle of violence: Community responses to children of battered women.* Thousand Oaks, CA: Sage.

Echlin, C., & Osthoff, B. (in press). Child protection workers and battered woman's advocates working together to end violence against women and children. In R. Geffner, P.G. Jaffe, & M. Sudermann (Eds.), *Children exposed to family violence: Current issues in research intervention, prevention and policy development.* Florida: Haworth Press.

Fantuzzo, J.W., & Lindquist, U.C. (1989). The effects of observing conjugal violence on children: A review and analysis of research methodology. *Journal of Family Violence, 4,* 77–94.

Ganley, A.L., Schechter, S., & Carter, J. (1996). *Domestic violence: A national curriculum for children's protective services.* San Francisco, CA: Family Violence Prevention Fund.

Goodman, G.S., & Rosenberg, M.S. (1987). The child witness to family violence: Clinical and legal considerations. In D. Sonkin (Ed.), *Domestic violence on trial* (pp. 97–126). New York: Springer.

Head, S. (1988). *A study of attitudes and behavior in dating relationships with special reference to the use of force.* Unpublished report, Board of Education for the City of Scarborough, Ontario.

Hotaling, G.T., & Sugarman, D.B. (1986). An analysis of risk markers in husband to wife violence: The current state of knowledge. *Violence and Victims, 1,* 101–124.

Hughes, H.M. (1982). Brief interventions with children in a battered women's shelter: A model preventive program. *Family Relations, 31,* 495–502.

Hughes, H.M. (1986). Research with children in shelters: Implications for clinical services. *Children Today.*

Hughes, H.M. (1988). Psychological and behavioral correlates of family violence in child witnesses and victims. *American Journal of Orthopsychiatry, 58,* 77–90.

Hughes, H.M., Parkinson, D.L., & Vargo, M.S. (1989). Witnessing spouse abuse and experiencing physical abuse: A double whammy. *Journal of Family Violence, 4,* 197–209.

Hurley, P., Sas, L., & Wilson, S. (1988). Empowering children for abuse litigations. *Preventing Sexual Abuse, 1,* 8–12.

Jaffe, P., Austin, G., Leschied, A., & Sas, L. (1981). Critical issues in the development of custody and access dispute resolution services. *Canadian Journal of Behavioral Science, 19,* 405–417.

Jaffe, P., Finlay, J., & Wolfe, D. (1984). Evaluating the impact of a specialized civilian family crisis unit within a police force on the resolution of family conflicts. *Journal of Preventive Psychiatry, 2,* 63–73.

Jaffe, P.G., & Geffner, B. (1998). *Child custody disputes and domestic violence: Critical issues for mental health, social service and legal professionals. Children exposed to marital violence.* Washington, DC: American Psychological Association.

Jaffe, P.G., Leschied, A.W., Sas, L., & Austin, G. (1985). A model for the provision of clinical assessment and service brokerage for young offenders: The London family court clinic. *Canadian Psychologist, 26,* 54–61.

Jaffe, P.G., & Sudermann, M. (1995). Child witnesses of woman abuse: Research and community responses. In S. Stith & M.A. Straus (Eds.), *Understanding partner violence: Prevalence, causes, consequences and solutions* (pp. 232–254). Minneapolis, MN: National Council on Family Relations.

Jaffe, P.G., Sudermann, M., & Reitzel, D. (1989). *The London family court clinic questionnaire on violence in relationships.* London, ON: London Family Court Clinic.

Jaffe, P.G., Sudermann, M., & Reitzel, D. (1992). Working with children and adolescents to end the cycle of violence: A social learning approach to intervention and prevention programs. In R. DeV. Peters, R.J. McMahon, & V.L. Quinsey (Eds.), *Aggression and violence throughout the life span* (pp. 129–146). Newbury Park, CA: Sage.

Jaffe, P.G., Sudermann, M., Reitzel, D., & Killip, S. (1992). An evaluation of a secondary school primary prevention programme on violence in relationships. *Violence and Victims, 7,* 129–146.

Jaffe, P.G., Wolfe, D.A., & Wilson, S. (1990). *Children of battered women.* Newbury Park, CA: Sage.

Jaffe, P.G., Wolfe, D.A., Wilson, S., & Slusczarzck, M. (1986). Similarities in behavior and social maladjustment among child victims and witnesses to family violence. *American Journal of Orthopsychiatry, 56,* 142–146.

Jaffe, P.G., Wolfe, D.A., Wilson, S., & Zak, L. (1986). Emotional and physical health problems of battered women. *Canadian Journal of Psychiatry, 31,* 625–629.

Kalmuss, D.S. (1984). The intergenerational transmission of marital aggression. *Journal of Marriage and the Family, 46,* 11–19.

Kovacs, M. (1981). Rating scales to assess depression in school-aged children. *Acta Paedopsychiatrica, 46,* 305–315.

Lachar, D., & Gruber, C. (1995). *Personality inventory for youth.* Los Angeles: Western Psychological Services.

Layzer, J.I., Goodson, B.D., & deLange, C. (1985). Children in shelters. *Response, 9,* 2–5.

Lehmann, P. (1997). The development of posttraumatic stress disorder (PTSD) in a sample of child witnesses to mother assault. *Journal of Family Violence, 12,* 241–257.

Lehmann, P., & Wolfe, V.V. (1992). *History of violence witnessed by child questionnaire.* Unpublished questionnaire. London, ON: Madame Vanier Children's Services.

Lewis, D.O., Shanok, S.S., Pincus, J.H., & Glaser, G.H. (1979). Violent juvenile delinquents: Psychiatric, neurological, psychological, and abuse factors. *Journal of the American Academy of Child Psychiatry, 18,* 307–319.

Loosley, S., Bentley, L., Rabenstein, S., & Sudermann, M. (1997). *Group treatment for children who witness woman abuse.* London, ON: Community Group Treatment Programme.

Marshall, L., Miller, N., Miller-Hewitt, S., Sudermann, M., & Watson, L. (1995). *Evaluation of groups for children who have witnessed violence.* London, ON: London Family Court Clinic and Centre for Research on Violence Against Women and Children.

Marshall, L.L., & Rose, P. (1990). Premarital violence: The impact of family or origin violence, stress and reciprocity. *Violence and Victims, 5,* 51–64.

McFarlane, J., Parker, B., Soeken, K., & Bullock, L. (1992). Assessing for abuse during pregnancy: Severity and frequency of injuries associated entry into prenatal care. *Journal of the American Medical Association, 267,* 3176–3178.

McKay, E.J. (1987). *Children of battered women.* Paper presented at the third National Family Violence Researchers' Conference, Durham, NH.

Moore, T.E., & Pepler, D. (1989, August). *Domestic violence and children's psychosocial development: Exploring the linkage.* Paper presented at the American Psychological Association Annual Meeting, New Orleans.

Nova Scotia Law Reform Commission. (1995). *Ending domestic violence in Nova Scotia.* Halifax, NS: Author.

O'Leary, K.D. (1988). Physical aggression between spouses: A social learning perspective. In V.B. Van Hasselt, R.L. Morrison, A.S. Bellack, & M. Hersen (Eds.), *Handbook of family violence* (pp. 109–130). New York: Plenum Press.

O'Leary, K.D., Malone, J., & Tyree, A. (1994). Physical aggression in early marriage: Pre relationship and relationship effects. *Journal of Consulting and Clinical Psychology, 62,* 594–602.

Osofsky, J.D., Wewers, S., Hann, D.M., & Fick, A.C. (1993). Chronic community violence: What is happening to our children. In D. Reiss, J.E. Richters, M. Radke-Yarrow, & D. Scharff (Eds.), *Children and violence* (pp. 1–24). New York: Guilford Press.

Peled, E., & Edleson, J.L. (1995). Process and outcome in small groups for children of battered women. In E. Peled, P.G. Jaffe, & J.L. Edleson (Eds.), *Ending the cycle of violence: Community responses to children of battered women* (pp. 77–96). Thousand Oaks, CA: Sage.

Peled, E., Jaffe, P.G., & Edleson, J.L. (1995). *Ending the cycle of violence: Community responses to children of battered women.* Thousand Oaks, CA: Sage.

Pepler, D., Moore, T.E., Mae, R., & Kates, M. (1989). The effects of exposure to family violence on children: New directions for research and intervention. In G. Cameron & M. Rothery (Eds.), *Family violence and neglect: Innovative interventions* (pp. 41–73). Hillsdale, NJ: Erlbaum.

Pressman, B., Cameron, G., & Rothery, M. (1989). *Intervening with assaulted women: Current theory, research and practice.* Hillsdale, NJ: Erlbaum.

Rae-Grant, N., Thomas, B.H., Offord, D.R., & Boyle, M.H. (1989). Risk protective factors, and the prevalence of behavior and emotional disorders in children and adolescents. *Journal of the American Academy of Child and Adolescent Psychiatry, 28,* 262–268.

Randolf, M., & Talamo, Y. (1997). *Multi-method evaluation of children who witness domestic violence.* Poster presented at the second International Conference on Children Exposed to Domestic Violence, London, Ontario.

Rosenbaum, A., & O'Leary, K.D. (1981). Children: The unintended victims of marital violence. *American Journal of Orthopsychiatry, 51,* 692–699.

Roy, M. (1988). *Children in the crossfire.* Deerfield Beach, FL: Health Communications.

Rutter, M. (1979). Protective factors in children's responses to stress and disadvantage. In M.W. Kent & J.E. Rolf (Eds.), *Primary prevention of psychopathy: Promoting social competence and coping in children* (Vol. 3, pp. 49–74). Hanover, NH: University Press of New England.

Sas, L., Cunningham, A.H., & Hurley, P. (1995). *Tipping the balance to tell the secret: Public discovery of child sexual abuse.* London, ON, Canada: London Family Court Clinic.

Sinclair, D. (1985). *Understanding wife assault: A training manual for counsellors and advocates.* Toronto: Ontario Government Bookstore.

Statistics Canada, Canadian Centre for Justice Statistics (1994, March). Wife assault: The findings of a national survey. *Juristat Service Bulletin, 14,* ISSN #: 0715-271-x.

Sternberg, K.L., Lamb, M.E., Greenbaum, C., Cicchetti, D., Dawud, S., Cortes, R.M., Krispin, O., & Lorey, F. (1993). Effects of domestic violence on children's behavior problems and depression. *Developmental Psychology, 29,* 44–52.

Straus, M.A. (1979). Measuring intra-family conflict and violence. The conflict tactics (CT) scales. *Journal of Marriage and the Family, 41,* 75–87.

Straus, M.A., & Gelles, R.J. (1986). Societal change and change in family violence from 1975 to 1985 as revealed in two national surveys. *Journal of Marriage and the Family, 48,* 465–479.

Straus, M.A., Gelles, R.J., & Steinmetz, S. (1980). *Behind closed doors: Violence in the American family.* Garden City, NY: Doubleday.

Sudermann, M., & Jaffe, P.G. (1997). Children and youth who witness violence: New directions in interventions and prevention. In D.A. Wolfe, R.J. McMahon, & R. DeV. Peters (Eds.), *Child abuse: New direction in prevention and treatment across the lifespan.* Thousand Oaks, CA: Sage.

Sudermann, M., Jaffe, P.G., & Hastings, E. (1995). Prevention programs in secondary schools. In E. Peled, P. Jaffe, & J. Edleson (Eds.), *Ending the cycle of violence: Community responses to children of battered women* (pp. 255–274). Thousand Oaks, CA: Sage.

Sudermann, M., Jaffe, P.G., & Schieck, E. (1996). *A.S.A.P.: A school-based anti- violence programme* (1996 ed.). London, ON: London Family Court Clinic.

Sudermann, M., Marshall, L., Miller, N., & Miller-Hewitt, S. (1995). *Children's questionnaire for groups for children who have witnessed violence.* Unpublished document. London, ON: London Family Court Clinic.

Tearmann Society for Battered Women. (1988). *Medical services or disservice?: An exploratory study of wife assault victims' in health care delivery settings.* New Glasgow, NS: Author.

Terr, L. (1991). Childhood traumas: An outline and overview. *American Journal of Psychiatry, 140,* 10–20.

Walker, L.E. (1989). Psychology and violence against women. *American Psychologist, 44,* 695–702.

Walker, L.E., & Edwall, G.E. (1987). Domestic violence and determination of visitation and custody in divorce. In D.J. Sonkin (Ed.), *Domestic violence on trial: Psychological and legal dimensions of family violence* (pp. 127–152). New York: Springer.

Wolfe, D.A., Jaffe, P., Wilson, S., & Zak, L. (1985). Children of battered women: The relation of child behaviour to family violence and maternal stress. *Journal of Consulting and Clinical Psychology, 53,* 657–665.

Wolfe, D.A., Wekerle, C., Reitzel-Jaffe, D., Grasley, C., Pittman, A.L., & MacEachran, A. (1997). Interrupting the cycle of violence: Empowering youth to promote healthy relationships. In D.A. Wolfe, R.J. McMahon, & R. DeV. Peters (Eds.), *Child abuse: New directions in prevention and treatment across the life span* (pp. 10–39). Thousand Oaks, CA: Sage.

Wolfe, D.A., Zak, L., Wilson, S., & Jaffe, P. (1986). Child witnesses to violence between parents: Critical issues in behavioral and social adjustment. *Journal of Abnormal Child Psychology, 14,* 95–104.

Wolfe, V.V., & Lehmann, P.J. (1992). *The children's impact of traumatic events scale–Family violence version.* Unpublished assessment instrument. London, ON: Children's Hospital of Western Ontario.

Young v. Young, 14 R.F.L. (3rd) 222 (N.B.Q.B. 1986).

CHAPTER 17

Adolescent Perpetrators
of Sexual Abuse

WILLIAM D. MURPHY and I. JACQUELINE PAGE

A REVIEW of sex offender programs across the country in 1978 (Brecher, 1978) found only one program focusing on juveniles. By 1994, there were 1,000 such programs identified in a national survey (Freeman-Longo, Bird, Stevenson, & Fiske, 1995). There has been a similar increase in publications (Barbaree, Hudson, & Seto, 1993), although the quality of the literature (Weinrott, 1996) has probably not kept pace with the proliferation of programs. The explosion in treatment programs is probably related to many issues.

One is the recognition that juveniles commit a large number of sexual crimes (Murphy, Haynes, & Page, 1992; Weinrott, 1996), and that a number of adult offenders began their offending career as adolescents (Abel & Rouleau, 1990). In addition, the National Task Force on Juvenile Sexual Offending has been effective (National Council on Juvenile and Family Court Judges, 1993) in encouraging development of treatment programs and encouraging both professionals and the public to recognize the seriousness of this problem.

For professionals working with adolescents and for the legal system, there has at least been some shift from an early stance that appeared to minimize the problems of juvenile sexual offending (Atcheson & Williams, 1954) to recognizing its seriousness. However, there has also been a proliferation of clinical approaches and treatment assumptions (National Council on Juvenile and Family Court Judges, 1993) that may go beyond current empirical knowledge. The tendency within the field has been to treat the juvenile offender as a "junior adult perpetrator" without recognition of developmental differences. At the same time, 19 states have passed legislation that subject adolescents to registration and/or community notification (Matson & Lieb, 1997). These laws do not take into account potential differences between adult and adolescent sex offenders (Association for the Treatment of Sexual Abusers [ATSA] Position Statement, 1997).

367

Societal concerns about juvenile crime in general, and sexual abuse specifically, put pressure on those in the field to provide adequate assessment for this population. Assessment is important to determine risk and to determine those interventions that are likely to reduce risk. This chapter attempts to provide a balance between our current knowledge of this population, the current accepted standards for assessment, and limitations of our assessment process.

DESCRIPTION OF THE PROBLEM

Because of the limitations, not all the data related to adolescent sexual offenders can be reviewed. Fortunately, there are a number of recent reviews (Barbaree, Marshall, & Hudson, 1993; Becker & Hunter, 1997; Murphy et al., 1992; Vizard, Monck, & Misch, 1995; Weinrott, 1996). In this section, we attempt to highlight specific issues in this population related to assessment.

DEFINITION

Legally, definitions of adolescent sex offenders can vary from state to state and country to country (Bala & Schwartz, 1993), including the age at which a youth can be held legally accountable for an offense. Because of variability in laws, most clinicians have adopted clinical definitions. Ryan, Lane, Davis, and Isaac (1987) define the juvenile sex offender as a youth from puberty to legal age who commits any sexual act with a person of any age against the victim's will, without consent, or in an aggressive or threatening manner. Most clinicians define an age difference of 4 to 5 years between the offender and victim as an indication of abuse regardless of the physical or verbal coercion applied. From a clinical standpoint, it is important to attempt to delineate potential power differences, developmental differences, or differences in emotional stability that would make it difficult for an individual to give informed consent. At times, clinical definitions of sexually abusive behavior may not meet legal criteria for sexual offenses. On the other hand, at times state statutes may specify age differences, such as 2 to 3 years, that most clinicians would not consider to constitute sexually abusive behavior. Although it is important that clinicians be aware of legal definitions of abuse in their jurisdictions, it is equally important that they be aware of the clinical definitions of abuse, which is what is targeted in assessment and treatment programs.

SCOPE OF THE PROBLEM

Weinrott (1996) has outlined the different approaches for determining incidence or prevalence rates. These can vary from victimization surveys, review of Child Protective Services records, and use of law enforcement records. Each produce different estimates of prevalence and incidence. Within the United States, it is estimated that adolescents commit 30% to 50% of child molestations, and 18% to 20% of rapes (Barbaree, Hudson, et al., 1993; Murphy et al., 1992; Weinrott, 1996). Very similar data have also been reported for the United Kingdom (Vizard et al., 1995).

CHARACTERISTICS

Like adult offenders, adolescent offenders show a wide range of deviant sexual behaviors, including rape, child molestation, exhibitionism, obscene phone calling, voyeurism, etc. (Barbaree, Marshall, et al., 1993). In general, if hands-off offenses are excluded, victims of adolescent offenders are most often children (Fehrenbach, Smith, Monastersky, Deisher, 1986; Ryan, Miyoshi, Metzner, Krugman, & Fryer, 1996). The types of sexual behavior displayed by the adolescent tend to vary from study to study. However, it should be recognized that many adolescent offenders engage in very intrusive behaviors, including penetration, and a significant number do use significant verbal threats and physical force (Ryan et al., 1996). In addition, many of these offenders show fairly high rates of other delinquent behaviors (Ryan et al., 1996; Weinrott, 1996).

In general, the majority of victims are females. However, when one looks at only those subsets of offenders who abuse children, the ratio of male to female victims becomes much more equal (Barbaree, Hudson, et al., 1993; Murphy et al., 1992). In general, as with adult offenders most victims are known to the offender (Fehrenbach et al., 1986).

There have been multiple attempts to look at specific excesses or deficits. The majority of these could be defined as non-sex-offender specific and primarily suggest variability in the population (Weinrott, 1996). Many studies indicate significant family dysfunction, history of social/behavioral problems, and history of academic problems, but it is not clear that the adolescent offender is different from other diagnostic groups (Murphy et al., 1992; Weinrott, 1996). Rather than repeating reviews of those specific areas, our focus in this chapter is on potential overlap of the juvenile sex offender with two other populations. Questions arise as to whether this population really differs from generalized delinquents and whether sexual and physical abuse is the etiology for the adolescent sex offender.

DELINQUENCY

Descriptive data in this population suggest rates of generalized delinquency in the 40% range for this population (Weinrott, 1996). Using structured psychiatric interviews, Kavoussi, Kaplan, and Becker (1988), in an inner-city sample, found that the most frequent diagnosis in their group was conduct disorder (48%). However, Bruinsma (1995), in a sample of offenders from the Netherlands found that only 10% were given conduct disorder diagnoses, including attention deficit disorder.

There have been a number of studies comparing the juvenile sex offender to delinquent criminals. Lewis, Shanok, and Pincus (1979) did not find differences between the juvenile sex offender and the violent, juvenile non-sex offender, but did find differences between these two groups and nonviolent delinquents (Lewis, Shanok, & Pincus, 1981). The data was primarily based on clinical ratings, and the use of more objective data found little differences at least in neuropsychological function between these three groups (Tarter, Hegedus, Alterman, & Katz-Garris, 1983). Truscott (1993) found no differences between incarcerated adolescent sex offenders, violent offenders, and property offenders on the MMPI. Jacobs, Kennedy, and Meyer (1997) found few differences between adolescent sex offenders and adolescent non-sex offender delinquents on IQ, academic achievement, MMPI, and the Hare Psychopath Checklist.

Spaccarelli, Bowden, Coatsworth, and Kim (1997) looked at official records and collected self-report data from offenders regarding violent offenses and sex offenses. As might be expected, it was found that there were many subjects not identified as sex offenders who had committed sexual offenses, and there were a number of subjects who had not been identified as engaging in violent behavior who self-reported such. When subjects were divided not only on official but also on self-report records, it was found that there was little difference between the sex offenders and the violent offenders. There were differences, as in other studies, between adolescent sex offenders and what they label their less-violent offenders. Compared with less-violent offenders, the adolescent sex offender group had been exposed to more severe physical abuse and domestic violence, held attitudes accepting sexual and physical violence, and were more likely to use aggressive and control strategies in response to stress.

Other studies report mixed results finding both similarities and differences (Blaske, Borduin, Henggeler, & Mann, 1989; Ford & Linney, 1995; Hastings, Anderson, & Hemphill, 1997; Katz, 1990; Kempton & Forehand, 1992; Monto, Zgourides, & Harris, 1998; Van Ness, 1984). These studies have shown that adolescent rapists showed more anger deficits than general juvenile delinquents, had lower self-esteem, were perceived by their mothers as having more neurotic symptoms and poor peer relationships, showed less bonding with their peers, actually showed fewer internalizing behaviors compared with other delinquents, and showed more general global maladjustment. Conduct-disordered youth were also found to be higher than adolescent child molesters on socialized aggression, aggressive coping, avoidance coping, and unexpectedly coping by engaging in sexual behavior.

The preceding data present a very mixed picture and the results may vary based on several factors. These include the type of sample (incarcerated versus outpatient), the nature of the sex offense (child molesters vs. rapists vs. mixed offenders), and specific measures used. In addition, as the Spaccarelli et al. study clearly indicates, there is overlap between these groups. What the data do indicate is that there is a great deal of heterogeneity in the adolescent sex offender group. It would appear that there are subsets of juvenile sex offenders who differ very little from a general delinquent population and sexual offending represents another delinquent/violent behavior. It also appears that there are subsets of juvenile sex offenders who are quite different from the delinquent population and who may require different interventions.

ABUSE HISTORY

From an etiological standpoint, history of abuse has been posited as causative of sexual offending. However, data to support this is mixed. Histories of sexual abuse vary from sample to sample and vary depending on the type of offenders. As pointed out by Weinrott (1996) and Cooper, Murphy, and Haynes (1996), rate of victimization varies from a low of 20% to highs in the 50% to 60% range. Similarly, physical abuse rates also vary greatly between 13% and 40% (Weinrott, 1996). There are exceptions such as Lewis et al. (1979) who reported rates as high as 76%, although very similar rates were seen in violent, non-sex offenders. Benoit & Kennedy, (1992) found no differences in sexual or physical abuse rates between adolescent sex offenders and aggressive and nonaggressive delinquent offenders. Brannon, Larson, and Doggett (1989) report a sexual victimization rate of 70% for a group of 63 incarcerated adolescents of which only 11 were incarcerated for sex offending.

Within the sex offender group, there are also factors that seem to relate to the rate of abuse reported. Worling (1995a) reviews studies reporting abuse rates classified by whether these were collected pretreatment or during posttreatment. Those studies that have collected abuse data pre-treatment report an average rate of 22% while those who report abuse post-treatment had rates of 52%. This could reflect increased honesty as trust developed within a treatment relationship, but it cannot be ruled out that offenders may be presenting experiences that justify their behavior.

Sexual abuse also appeared to differ significantly in terms of the age and sex of the victim. Offenders against children seem to have higher rates of personal abuse than those who offend against peers (Ford & Linney, 1995), although this may only be true for the subset of child molesters who molest young males (Cooper et al., 1996; Worling, 1995a, 1995b). Also sexual abuse rates seem to be much higher in those engaging in hands-on offenses versus hands-off offenses (Fehrenbach et al., 1986).

Although there is variability, adolescent sex offenders as a group appear to have experienced more physical and sexual abuse than would be expected in a nonclinical population. However, there also appears to be a great deal of heterogeneity, and the most consistent finding is for those who molest young males. This is also true for adult offenders (Hanson & Slater, 1988). There is increasing evidence that regardless of the etiological role that sexual abuse has in the development of sex offending, those individuals who have been sexually abused differ significantly from those who have not been abused. Abused adolescent sex offenders tend to have an earlier onset, to have more victims and to have male victims compared with nonabused adolescent sex offenders (Becker & Stein, 1991; Cooper et al., 1996; Kaufman, Hilliker, & Daleiden, 1996; Richardson, Kelly, Bhate, & Graham, 1997). Abused subjects appear to display more psychological difficulties (Becker, Kaplan, Tenke, & Tartaglini, 1991; Cooper et al., 1996) and to display more deviant sexual arousal patterns (Becker, Hunter, Stein, & Kaplan, 1989).

What is currently lacking in the field, both in terms of guiding research but also in terms of clinical application, is some type of classification/typology system that would allow the study of more homogeneous groups. Work in this area is very limited (Knight & Prentky, 1993; Weinrott, 1996), and until we have better ability to classify and type offenders, it will be necessary to assess a wide variety of characteristics in this group to do adequate treatment planning and risk prediction.

ASSESSMENT APPROACHES

NATURE OF THE ASSESSMENT PROCESS

The evaluator's role in the assessment of the adolescent sex offender requires a focus not only on the adolescent and his treatment needs but also his risk to the community. Therefore, assessment does not just focus on the adolescent but also his risk to potential victims in the community.

Because the guidelines place community safety first (ATSA, 1997), mental health professionals may at times have to reevaluate their general decision-making process, especially in terms of level of placements for children and adolescents. Community safety takes precedence over the least restrictive environment; in making the decision, the evaluator is focusing not only on the intensity and types of treatment needed, but also on what types of external controls are available to assist in maintaining community safety. For example, levels of probation supervision available, use of house arrest, and electronic monitoring, where available may allow lower levels of placements.

Adolescent offenders and their families may be very resistant to evaluation. Many of these offenders will be court mandated and will be in denial of the offense, as will the family. Accordingly, adequate assessment requires information from sources other than the offender and the family. Every attempt must be made to obtain school records, police reports, victim statements, juvenile court records, and records of past treatment. Becker and Hunter (1993) compared adolescent self-reports with reports of the referral sources and found significant differences, especially in terms of level of violence. For example, 42% of the adolescents reported no violence in the offense, whereas this is true in only 8% of the information received from referral sources. Twenty-five percent of the adolescents reported physical violence, 61% of the data from the referral sources indicated physical violence. Similarly, Emerick and Dutton (1993) compared adolescents' reports with collateral statements and confirmation polygraph testing. The data clearly indicated that when subjects were polygraphed, they reported more victims, higher levels of force, and more intrusiveness in the offense, even compared with collateral reports.

Without some alternative sources of information, offenders will many times minimize the nature of their abuse experience, will minimize the number of victims, and the amount of violence. Because of the resistance of some families and adolescents, assessments may need to be completed over several sessions. During the assessment process, direct confrontational approaches about discrepancies are not likely to be productive. Our experience is that when discrepancy exists between the offenders/ families' report and other statements, families can be approached in one of two ways. The first is a nonjudgmental request for assistance from the family in clarifying discrepancies. A second approach is to explore with the family what the meaning would be to them or what their fears would be if the collateral information were true. At times, evaluators seem to mistakenly believe that it is "their job" to get the truth. In reality, the purpose of the evaluation is for the offender to provide information, but the responsibility should be on the offender. It should also be recognized that the "whole truth" will not be obtained during the initial assessment process. Much of the information around details of the offense and other offending behaviors tends to emerge during the treatment process.

ASSESSMENT MODEL

Evaluation of adult and adolescent sex offenders has historically followed a cognitive/behavioral/relapse prevention model (Becker & Hunter, 1997; Murphy et al., 1992). Table 17.1 outlines assessment areas that are considered sex-offender specific and should be part of the overall assessment of adolescent sex offenders. In addition, there is usually an assessment of general factors, such as overall psychopathology,

Table 17.1
Areas of Offender Specific Assessment

Nature and Extensiveness of Offending
Level of Denial
Cognitive Distortions
Victim Empathy
Risk Factors
Social/Sexual Competence
Sexual Knowledge/Experience
Deviant Sexual Arousal
Personal Abuse

delinquency, intellectual/academic status, and family functioning. Although most adolescent sex offender programs tend to follow this assessment model and the specific areas of assessment tend to be linked to treatment, there has not been any clear evidence that changes in these factors actually relate to overall treatment outcome.

Assessment usually begins with an attempt to determine the nature of offender behavior, extensiveness and intrusiveness of the behavior, and length of time the behavior has been occurring. It is important to determine to the extent possible types of sex-offending behavior or other inappropriate behaviors that the offender has engaged in apart from the referral offense. Related to this is a determination of the degree of violence used in the offense. From this information, the clinician is trying to determine how set the offender's deviant pattern may be, how much planning the person used in the offense, and how compulsive is the behavioral pattern. The evaluation is also determining whether there is a rather limited or rather narrow sexual interest pattern or whether the adolescent is engaging in multiple deviant behaviors that may be more difficult to control in outpatient settings.

The next three factors in Table 17.1 (Level of Denial, Cognitive Distortions, and Victim Empathy) can in some ways be viewed as a continuum. Offenders and families, when initially entering evaluation, are generally all in some level of denial. They may be in total denial stating that the offense never occurred. More often, however, the offenders may be admitting to certain aspects of the offense, but engaging in cognitive distortions and minimizations that they use to excuse their behaviors. These can vary from stating, "I only touched her," "it only happened once"; to placing blame on the victim, by stating that "she was asking for it," "she or he didn't say no"; or placing blame on psychological factors, such as "I did it because I was abused," "I was angry." Also included in this general category of cognitive distortions are more general societal attitudes that may be supportive of sexually violent behavior, such as acceptance of rape myths or adversarial sexual beliefs (Burt, 1980).

Finally, within this continuum, victim empathy can be seen as the opposite end of denial in that the offender admits all of the behaviors and recognizes the impact the offending behavior has on the individual. In fact, although victim empathy is frequently mentioned as a treatment target, the reality is that within the adult literature there is not strong support for generalized empathy deficits in sexual offenders (Hanson & Scott, 1995). There has been little research using standardized assessment of empathy deficits in adolescents and the study that does exist does not find a difference between adolescent sex offenders and other offenders (Monto et al., 1998). Therefore, the empathy deficits many times referred to may be secondary to cognitive distortions used by offenders. That is, one cannot recognize the harm being done if one is projecting blame on the victims or on other external factors.

Understanding level of denial and degree of distortions is important in overall treatment planning. Offenders and families who totally deny their offense may be difficult to treat on an outpatient basis because it is difficult to monitor their behavior. If the offender and family are failing to admit to abusive behavior, they are unlikely to admit to any type of risk situation or other problems that would allow one to safely intervene in the community. In addition, the more extreme the distortions, the more difficult it is for the offender to take responsibility for himself and therefore more difficult for him to make changes that he may need to make. For example, if offenders can convince themselves that the responsibility is the child's, then they may be less likely to avoid situations where children congregate or to avoid contact with children.

A part of the assessment process, but also what becomes part of the treatment process, is to identifying those factors that place the offender at risk. Most sexual offenses do not occur impulsively or spontaneously, and there may be external situations or internal states that increase the offender's risk to offend (Gray & Pithers, 1993). As part of the initial assessment, an attempt is made to identify the process by which the offender chooses and grooms victims, and explore feeling states and stressors that may be linked to the offenses. At times, however, this is more difficult to establish initially because of offenders' denial and distortions. Therefore, although one attempts to establish these factors, the full picture does not emerge until treatment has progressed past some of the denial and distortions. However, to the extent that one can establish certain factors that increase risk, one can make specific recommendations for monitoring. For example, one can clearly identify high-risk situations in the community that the offender who abuses young children needs to avoid.

Deviant sexual arousal has been a mainstay in theorizing about adult sex offenders and is a factor related to recidivism (Hanson & Bussière, 1996). Although there is much more limited data on this factor with adolescent offenders, attempts to determine the adolescent's sexual attraction pattern is still an important part of treatment. Offenders with more established deviant arousal patterns, such as set attraction to children, will need specialized treatment interventions.

As part of the overall assessment, there also is an attempt to assess the offender's overall social competence and general sexual knowledge, functioning, and experience. There is no clear evidence that adolescent sexual offenders are any more deficit in these areas than adolescents presenting with other mental health issues (Murphy et al., 1992; Weinrott, 1996). However, to the extent that there may be certain psychological factors that place offenders at risk, such as anger, depression, and poor heterosocial skills, it is important to determine the overall level of the offender's social competence. For an offender who has difficulty managing anger, and anger seems to be related to offending patterns, then specific anger management training will be necessary. In addition, offenders who have primary involvement with young children, need to establish appropriate peer social relationships and at some point sexual relationships. Finally, most programs try to assess the offender's history of personal abuse, and this issue was detailed in a previous section. It is not clear that being a victim of sexual abuse is a direct cause of abusive behavior, but it does seem evident from the literature that those offenders who have been abused may have more significant problems and may need more intensive treatment.

In addition to the sex offender specific variable, it is essential to assess general psychological/academic functioning. Any specific intellectual deficits or learning disabilities may have an impact on treatment. For those offenders with specific learning disabilities or lower IQ, programs may need to be adjusted to fit their needs. Since much of the treatment of sex offenders is cognitively oriented, such treatment may require major adjustments for some offenders.

Similarly, although there is no one personality type or one type of psychopathology in offenders, understanding of other behavioral problems may be important for treatment planning and determining overall risk. The offender who engages in externalizing behaviors may be very difficult to manage on an outpatient basis and may need a different structure than one whose symptom pattern is more internalizing. In addition, the offender with significant alcohol and drug problems may require specific treatment in that area prior to sex offender specific treatment. Offenders with specific psychiatric diagnoses, such as Major Depression or Attention Deficit Disorder, may need pharmacological interventions. The assessment in this area is based generally on clinical interviews, and standard psychometric instruments, such as MMPI-A, Child Behavior Checklist, Millon Adolescent Personality Inventory, and standardized IQ measures. These measures can be helpful for their stated purpose. However, evaluators should not believe that there is a profile that is specific to the adolescent offender.

Again, as with assessment of general psychological functioning, assessment of the family of the adolescent sex offender is required. In terms of risk, for an offender to be maintained in the community, a support system must be involved in treatment. Although many families begin with some distortions, those in total denial or who are extremely hostile and maintain that stand are not going to provide the support necessary to appropriately monitor behavior. In addition, those families that are organized very chaotically, with significant criminal behavior and delinquent behavior among the family members, may not be able to provide the structure necessary for community-based treatment. Families who have had knowledge of the abuse in the past and have attempted to cover it up must also be assessed very closely in terms of their ability to monitor.

When the abuse is within family, those families are many times torn between support for the victim and the offender. At times, there may be a tendency for the family to want to have the victim and offender share blame, feeling that the victim should have told about the abuse. Often this is a treatment issue and needs to be assessed early. What is important is that the family is willing to recognize the need to protect the victim from the offender and to accept that the offender may have to leave the home and have no contact with the victim for some period of time. Also, in family assessment, it is important to try to determine whether other members of the family, including the parents, have been sexually abused, and how disclosure of sexual abuse within the current family situation is impacting the parents. One can see a variety of reactions that will require different interventions. On one hand, a mother or father may state that he or she has been sexually abused but that it did not have any major impact. Similarly they may feel that the current abuse is "minor" in nature as compared to their own abuse and therefore minimize the impact of the abuse on the current victim. Disclosure of abuse may rekindle feelings about their own abuse, such as depression or posttraumatic stress disorder symptoms, which make it very difficult for the parent to function. In such cases, it is important to see that the parent receives adequate treatment as rapidly as possible. Finally, one may see extreme anger at the offender and total rejection. In such cases, it may be necessary to discontinue contact between the family and the offender to allow family members time to explore their own feelings.

SEX OFFENDER SPECIFIC INSTRUMENTS

In general, a limited number of instruments are specifically designed for the assessment of adolescent sex offenders. As noted, assessment in areas such as social competence, sexual knowledge, general psychological functioning/psychopathology, and family functioning, includes instruments that are used in general clinical assessment. In addition, a major portion of assessment is based on the clinical interview, which we will outline first, followed by the instruments available for specific areas.

Clinical Interview

It should be noted that in this context, the social/sexual history refers to all information collected from the patient, family, and collateral sources. Because most clinicians are experienced in collecting general social histories in adolescents, we will not focus on social aspect of the history but outline areas to be covered in Table 17.2. In general, the psychosexual history is geared to developing an understanding of the adolescent's development, history of adaptive and maladaptive behaviors throughout his life, general family relationships, general excesses and deficits, and any medical or psychiatric factors that will affect treatment. Some clinicians will have less experience in collecting sexual histories, especially sexual histories from adolescents. Again, general areas of inquiry are included in Table 17.1. One attempts to collect a history about "normal" sexual development, potential nondeviant sexual problems, and very specific information regarding the deviant sexual behavior. Generally, adolescents like adults, may at times become embarrassed and anxious when providing sexual histories. It is important for the interviewers to remain matter-of-fact, themselves not appearing embarrassed, and to clearly let the adolescents know that many people find it difficult to provide such intimate information. There are actually few data on collecting sexual histories in adolescents in general, and adolescent offenders specifically. Kaplan, Becker, and Tenke (1991) provide evidence that those adolescent offenders who have been victims of physical or sexual abuse have a slight preference for female interviewers, and they recommend that programs have both genders available for interviewing.

It is generally helpful that the sexual history come later in the overall interviewing process with the social history. It is easier to begin with what may be less personal information, such as information about sexual education, and questions regarding general sexual knowledge. It is important to explore the offender's masturbatory history and the types of fantasies used, since offenders who are using deviant fantasies will be reinforcing their offending pattern.

Most adolescents will not voluntarily disclose the scope of their sexual offending behavior without some specific questioning. Generally, one begins with offenses for which they have been referred, trying to detail the nature of those behaviors. The interviewer can then proceed, asking about other sexual behaviors, and then becoming more direct, asking about specific deviant sexual behaviors. Many adolescents may not report any behaviors at their own initiative. When youth are specifically asked, however, it is surprising what they will report. The interviewer should attempt to determine if any specific factors seem to increase the offender's risk to offend and to look at the types of cognitions he uses to justify such behavior.

Assessment of Sexual Attraction/Arousal

In addition to what one obtains in an interview by self-report, basically three approaches to the assessment of sexual arousal have been used with adolescents: Adolescent Sexual Interest Card Sort, Multiphasic Sex Inventory, and psychophysiological assessment of sexual arousal. Within the adult offender area, the psychophysiological assessment of sexual arousal has been a mainstay of the offender assessment process. For the adolescent sex offender, there is much more limited data. There are no data available comparing adolescent offenders with either normal or other populations. In addition, the ethical standards of the Association for the Treatment of Sexual Abusers (ATSA, 1997) suggest that arousal measures should not be used on those

Table 17.2
Social/Sexual History of the Psychosexual Assessment

PSYCHOSOCIAL HISTORY

- Demographics
- Current Emotional Functioning
- Current Maladaptive/Problem Behaviors
- History of Emotional/Behavioral/Substance Abuse Problems
- History of Aggression/Violence
- Treatment History (When, Why, Where, Length, Outcome)
- Medication History
- Medical/Physical Problems
- Legal History/Court Involvement
- School (Grade, Special Education Needs, Problems, Failed)
- Estimate of Cognitive Functioning
- Childhood History (Developmental, Medical, Significant Events)
- Victimization (Physical, Sexual, Emotional)
- Family (Constellation, Functioning/Circumstances, Involvement)
- Relationship with Family Members
- Family Social/Cultural Factors
- Leisure/Recreational Activities (Hobbies, Peer Relations, Interests)

SEXUAL HISTORY

- Sex Education/Sexual Knowledge
- Attitudes Toward Sexuality (Including Family's Attitude)
- Attitudes Toward Women/Sex Role Stereotyping
- First Sexual Experience
- Masturbatory History
- Fantasy Content
- History of Consenting Sexual Relationships
- History of Sexual Dysfunction
- Feelings Regarding Sexual Adequacy or Inadequacy

DEVIANT SEXUAL HISTORY

- Types of Deviation
- Specific Behaviors Engaged In (Including Length of Time Engaged In)
- Deviant Masturbatory Fantasies (Frequency and Percent)
- Deviant Behavior (Frequency, Period of Time, Antecedents, Consequences, Coercion Used, Force Used)
- Perception of Victim's Reaction/Victim Empathy
- Mode of Offense
- Role of Substance Abuse in Offense
- Grooming
- Risk Factors
- Distortions/Minimizations/Rape Supportive Attitudes

adolescents younger than age 14 unless one has Institutional Review Board type of approval.

For adolescent offenders, the vast majority of data are from the research group of Becker and Hunter. Findings indicate fairly good test-retest reliability (Becker, Hunter, Goodwin, Kaplan, & Martinez, 1992). In addition, adolescents do not seem to show high levels of responding to all stimuli and generally show a range of arousal responses in the lab (Becker, Stein, Kaplan, & Cunningham-Rathner, 1992). However, there are some indications that arousal measures are negatively correlated with age, and younger subjects may show more responding (Kaemingk, Koselka, Becker, & Kaplan, 1995).

In terms of relationships to offender/offense characteristics, Becker, Kaplan, and Tenke (1992) found higher rates of deviant arousal in those subjects who had been abused versus nonabused subjects. However, this may only be true for those who have male victims (Becker et al., 1989). Hunter, Goodwin, and Becker (1994) also found higher levels of deviant arousal in those subjects with male victims only; however, they also found that on a number of other variables there was less correspondence between measured arousal and offense histories. Arousal measures have also been shown to change with specific behavioral treatments aimed at reducing deviant sexual arousal (Hunter & Goodwin, 1992; Hunter & Santos, 1990; Weinrott, Riggan, & Frothingham, 1997).

The Adolescent Sexual Interest Card Sort is a second potential measure of deviant sexual arousal. The card sort is a 64-item self-report instrument that requires subjects to rate on a 5-point scale degree of sexual arousal the thoughts of engaging in a variety of sexual behaviors. Hunter, Becker, and Kaplan (1995) found that 60 of the 64 items had significant test-retest reliability, and the item clusters had good internal consistency. However, when correlated with arousal measures within the same sexual category, significant correlations were found on 4 of 14 items. Weinrott et al. (1997) found that the card sort was significantly influenced by denial and minimizations, which is a major limitation of this self-report measure.

A final standardized instrument that is used to estimate sexual attraction is the Multiphasic Sex Inventory—Juvenile Form (Nichols & Molinder, 1984). However, it is not clear that this test has been standardized on adolescents and seems to represent the adult version with some questions rewritten. The Multiphasic Sex Inventory is a multi-scale measure that includes measure of sex offenses, such as child molestation, rape, exhibitionism, and other paraphilias, in addition to providing scales related to sexual obsessions, cognitive distortions, and justifications. The scales related to child molestation, rape, and exhibitionism are arranged such that one could infer that those who score higher for engaging in more deviant sexual behavior may be more attracted to that behavior.

In general, although assessment of sexual arousal is frequently used both with adult and juvenile programs, we have rather limited data with adolescent offenders. The most consistent finding is increased deviant arousal among those who molest young males and those who have been sexually abused. Further data are needed to look at whether arousal measures separate out other categories of offenders. In addition, although arousal measures with adolescents may be used in treatment planning, it should be recognized that there is really no normative data. Arousal measures should not be used to make statements about likelihood of having committed an offense, and at this point cannot be used to predict any future behavior.

Cognitive Distortions

The assessment of cognitive distortions and rape supportive attitudes has been a mainstay of the adult offender area (Milner, Murphy, Valle, & Tolliver, 1998). Within the adult area, scales have been developed to assess these concepts. However, again there are limited scales in the adolescent offender area. The Adolescent Cognition Scale (Hunter, Becker, Kaplan, & Goodwin, 1991), the Cognitive Distortions and Immaturity Scale, and Justifications Scale of the Multiphasic Sex Inventory (Nichols & Molinder, 1984) are the primary tools. The Adolescent Cognition Scale was found to have poor test-retest reliability and did not discriminate between groups of juvenile offenders and youth without a history of sexual perpetration (Hunter et al., 1991). It also seemed to be influenced by social desirability.

Scales measuring cognitive distortions on the Multiphasic Sex Inventory have some reliability and validity within the adult offender population (Milner et al., 1998). However, it is not clear that they have been validated on adolescent populations. Although many programs use scales, such as Rape Myth Acceptance, Sexual Stereotyping, and Adversarial Sexual Beliefs (Burt, 1980), no studies have tested these scales specifically with adolescents or have compared adolescent sex offenders with other populations.

Modus Operandi Scale

A recently developed test that is sex offender specific and has some reliability and validity data associated with it is the sex offender modus operandi scale, developed by Kaufman and colleagues (Kaufman et al., 1996; Kaufman, Wallace, Johnson, & Reeder, 1995). This scale, which has both adult and adolescent versions, is divided into two primary sections. The first gathers general demographic information and the offender's criminal and personal history. The second portion assesses specific aspects of the offender's modus operandi that include targeting/selecting victims, gaining victim's trust, gaining victim's compliance with sexual activity, maintaining victim's silence after the onset of the sexual crime. The scale has relatively good internal consistency, and data are beginning to support its validity (Kaufman et al., 1995, 1996). Although in the early stages of development, the scale may be of value in objectively assessing the grooming process and to some extent assessing specific risk factors. However, it is not in widespread clinical use at this time.

Risk Assessment

When asked to evaluate adolescent sex offenders, especially in the preadjudication or postadjudication phase, the major question is risk for reoffense and secondarily the level of structured placement necessary. Although far from perfect, there has been a significant amount of work in the adult sex offender area regarding prediction of both violent and sexual reoffending (Hanson & Bussière, 1996; Rice & Harris, 1997). The data indicate that factors such as male victim, unrelated victim, histories of previous sexual and nonsexual crimes, psychopathy, age of offender, and deviant sexual arousal measured physiologically are predictive of reoffending, at least in child molesters. These data also clearly indicate that actuarial measures are better than clinical judgment (Rice & Harris, 1995). There is much more limited data among adolescent sex offenders. Early on, Groth, Hobson, Lucey, and St. Pierre (1981) outlined clinical factors that potentially relate to sex reoffending. These include such issues as no force within the offense, no bizarre or ritualistic behaviors, first offense, no chronic antisocial or violent behavior, no evidence of severe psychopathology, the offender acknowledging the offense, and the offender having social and psychological resources and external support within the community. Monastersky and Smith (1985) also describe a very extensive checklist that classifies subjects into low, moderate, and high risk. Although many treatment providers still follow the general procedures outlined by Groth et al. and Monastersky and Smith, there has been little empirical data to validate these factors.

Smith and Monastersky (1986) investigated some of these criteria in a group of 112 male juvenile offenders. Approximately 50% were found to be non-reoffenders, 34% were nonsexual reoffenders, and 14% were found to be sexual reoffenders. In general, the staff's clinical judgment was not significantly associated with reoffending and there was a tendency to overpredict reoffenses. Stepwise multiple discrimination identified seven variables including unhealthy sexual attitudes, referral offense being rape, clinical rating of low, moderate, or high risk, number of siblings living with offender, evidence of depression or negative self-esteem, willingness to explore offense nondefensively, and history of physical or sexual abuse that was predictive of reoffense. The overall classification rate was only 62.5%, and generally there was a great deal of overlap between groups. A concern with this study is that the variables may not replicate. Also, there are concerns about cross-validation.

Schram, Milloy, and Rowe (1991) followed 197 male juvenile sex offenders in Washington and found that truancy history, thinking errors or cognitive distortions, and prior sexual offenses were related to sexual reoffending. They also found that non-reoffenders were rated by clinicians as having less deviant sexual arousal. These factors are somewhat similar to those in the adult literature to the extent that truancy history may in general be related to delinquency or general antisocial tendencies, and prior sexual offenses and deviant sexual arousal are factors in the adult literature that have been related to reoffending. However, deviant sexual arousal was clinically rated and may be difficult to replicate.

In general, we are lacking empirical data at this point in time that would allow use of actuarial methods to predict adolescent sex offender recidivism and to assist therefore in determining level of treatment. Until further data are available, we are left to using clinical variables that have been outlined in addition to drawing somewhat on the adult literature. It would appear that issues related to general delinquent behavior, previous sexual offending, deviant sexual arousal and attitudes should be given significant weight in determining overall risk.

The second aspect of risk assessment is to determine when an individual has progressed through treatment and can be discharged from that program. Table 17.3 outlines factors that many times are considered in determining progression of treatment. A number of these are related to general behavioral problems, such as general antisocial behavior, poor school performance, continued poor interpersonal skills, and the presence of addictive behavior. It is assumed that individuals making poor decisions in one aspect of their life are more likely to make unhealthy decisions in the sex offending area. Other factors are more related to progression through sex offender specific treatment, such as denial, continued distortions, failure to apply relapse plan, deviant sexual arousal, and lack of family support or system involvement. In addition, individuals who tend to engage in compulsive sexual behavior, such as compulsive masturbation, or who within the treatment program continue to show inappropriate sexualized

Table 17.3
Risk Assessment within Treatment

- Compulsive or Inappropriate Sexual Behavior
- Continued Denial
- Continued Evidence of Cognitive Distortions/Criminal Thinking/Rape Supportive Attitudes
- Continued Failure to Apply Relapse Prevention Plan and/or Being in High Risk Situations
- Continued Deviant Sexual Arousal
- Continued Antisocial/Oppositional Behavior
- Poor School/Work Performance
- Continued Nonsexual Victimization
- Continued Sexualized Behavior, Violating Boundaries, Staring at Body Parts, Inappropriate Sexual Comments
- Continued Poor Interpersonal Skills
- Lack of Family/Support System Involvement
- Addictive Behaviors

behavior, such as inappropriate comments to staff and continued violation of boundaries, would appear to have difficulty controlling sexuality well and to be at risk for offending behavior. Most programs also focus on whether the offender continues various forms of nonsexual victimization. This can range from aggressive nonsexual behavior to verbal, cruel comments to other peers.

LEGAL AND SYSTEMS CONSIDERATIONS

Those working in the area of evaluation and treatment of adolescent sex offenders are part of a broader system dealing with the problem of sexual violence. The system includes law enforcement, child protective services, victim services, parole and probation, and juvenile/family court. The first issue that needs to be addressed is the role of the offender evaluator in this system. A mental health professional working with the adolescent sex offender must maintain relationships with these systems for adequate assessment to occur. Information is needed from many of these systems, and for adequate treatment to occur, these systems are often involved in the monitoring and supervision, a part of treatment. At the same time, those involved with adolescent sex offenders must recognize their limitation and recognize that they are not law enforcement, juvenile court, or probation or parole. The role of the adolescent offender specialists is to use their knowledge to inform other systems of overall risk and treatment needs. It is not the job of mental health professionals to investigate sexual abuse allegations or to make criminal justice sanction recommendations.

REFERRAL QUESTION

An important consideration in offender assessment is the specific referral questions (Zussman, 1989). Although many questions can be asked, there are five specific questions the evaluator will most often be asked to address: (1) risk for reoffending and level of placement, (2) specific treatment needs, (3) removal from the home, (4) whether the individual fits the profile of a sexual offender, (5) whether the individual is ready for discharge from a program.

As outlined earlier, we have a general assessment model for assessing this population and clinical approaches to risk assessment and determination of treatment progress. We are lacking in some instances clear empirical support for specific measures. However, even with these limitations, mental health professionals can provide some assistance to the court as to level of placement, treatment needs, and release. Following the assessment process, one can identify excesses and deficits with the offender. The evaluation can provide data related to not only sex offender specific treatment needs but collateral treatment needs, such as alcohol and drug treatment, psychopharmacological treatment, and education remediation. It is also possible to provide information to other systems regarding general reoffense risk and treatment progress. In making such recommendations, the evaluator needs to state the limitations of our knowledge in this area and not attempt to overpredict. An important aspect of risk assessment is to outline not only those factors that appear to relate to the offender's risk, but also the external control that will be necessary to minimize risk. Following a relapse prevention model (Gray & Pithers, 1993), in addition to the focus on prediction, there should be an attempt to design an environment where offending is less likely to occur. It is important to communicate to systems that risk is not a static factor but is a dynamic factor that can change as the offender's environmental situation and psychological state changes.

Many times the offender evaluator may be asked about whether the offender needs to be removed from the home. It is generally accepted within the field that if the offender has victimized within the home, he needs to be removed from it at least initially (National Council on Juvenile and Family Court Judges, 1993). In situations where there are no victims in the home, recommendations about removal from the home are based on factors related to general risk assessment and the type of structure that can be put in place to avoid reoffending. If the offender has a long history of sex-offending behavior, shows other high-risk characteristics, and if the family refuses to cooperate, then an out-of-home placement will probably be required.

The final question that is many times asked, at times by the court and at times by defense attorneys, is whether an individual fits the profile of a sex offender. Underlying this question is basically a question of guilt or innocence. This is a question that the mental health professional should not attempt to address, as we currently have no data that would allow us to address such questions. Murphy and Peters (1992) have outlined limitations of profiling. The literature on adolescent sex offenders indicate heterogeneity, and there is no one specific profile of sex offenders. In addition, determining whether someone has or has not committed a sex offense can only be based on adequate child protective services and police investigation. Guilt and innocence are legal determinations, and there are no psychological or behavioral science approaches that really bear on these questions.

CONFIDENTIALITY AND INFORMED CONSENT

Adolescent offenders and their families should be asked to sign informed consent that outlines the assessment procedure as well as limits on confidentiality. Adolescent offenders, in most situations, will not be seen in a situation where they can be promised confidentiality. It is our policy for both the adolescent and the legal guardian to sign the consent for evaluation. However, one working in this area must recognize that at times families have little choice but to participate in the evaluation. In many instances, if the family refuses to participate in an evaluation, the courts may increase the consequences the offender is facing. There is no easy answer, and this problem is inherent in forensic situations. It is important to be sensitive to this issue and where possible, if the family feels uncomfortable with the evaluation process being offered, consider alternative providers for treatment. However, they should not be allowed to "escape" to a provider who has no knowledge of the area.

CASE ILLUSTRATION

Social History

Dan, a 15-year-old adolescent, was referred for evaluation and treatment by the local juvenile court. He had been charged with the attempted rape and physical attack of his 63-year-old female neighbor.

Dan has lived with his father since he was approximately 7 years of age. His parents were not married but did live together until approximately 1983. His mother moved out of state approximately one year after his father received custody of Dan in 1988. She did not see Dan again until he was arrested on the current charges and placed in detention. His mother has a long history of drug abuse and possible involvement in prostitution, although she is drug-free at this time. The mother did have custody for approximately two years, and it is not clear what Dan was exposed to during that period. Dan perceives that his relationship with his mother is positive, although he has only seen her once in the past 9 years. He does talk to her by phone approximately twice a month.

Dan's father has been investigated for physical abuse of the boy on at least two occasions, with the most recent known investigation being when Dan was age 12. He and his father are very competitive with one another and have difficulty relating except through competition. There is a strong push by the father for Dan to be involved in athletics. In general, the father stresses traditional and stereotyped male behavior and values.

Dan denies any significant reaction to his parents' situation, although his father reports that Dan became enuretic and withdrawn after the final separation. Dan is described as striving to make himself appear more important than others or as having more than others, with this pattern increased at the time of the separation. Currently, the pattern appears to be displayed as a sense of entitlement. Dan continues to experience problems with enuresis.

Educationally, he is on grade level with average grades. There is no history of learning disabilities. Reports of peer relations were mixed. Dan appears to have friends, but the father also reports that he has conflict with teammates. There is no history of arrest for previous sexual offenses or nonsexual offenses.

Sexual History

Dan reports that his first sexual experience was when he was in kindergarten when he and a female peer went in coat room and fondled each other. He notes that he always knew about sex and that "it came to me naturally." Dan states that he did not receive any formal sex education, but does remember reading *Our Bodies, Ourselves* when he was 11 years of age. This is the same age that he reports beginning to masturbate. He currently reports that when he masturbates 25% of his fantasies are of rape and 5% are of males. Dan reports no sexual involvement with males or females his age and denies a history of sexual abuse.

INAPPROPRIATE/DEVIANT SEXUAL HISTORY

Dan's history of inappropriate/deviant sexual behavior began when he was in kindergarten, at which time he reports he would rub on other children when they were sleeping. In the first or second grade, he began grabbing girls and this pattern continued into high school. By his own report, he has grabbed approximately 150 to 200 females and has sexually harassed one teacher. In addition, Dan has engaged in window peeping since the seventh grade. He has engaged in inappropriate sexual behavior toward his father's significant other, including stealing her underwear and using it to masturbate, peeping on her, and touching her while she was asleep. He has made 1–900 calls totaling $1,000, and has made extensive use of sexually explicit material including stealing material from his father. The present offense involved breaking into a woman's home, removing all his clothes and grabbing her around the neck when she came out of a bathroom. He admits to thoughts of killing her so she could not identify him. However, she was able to engage him in conversation and avoided the rape.

TEST RESULTS

In addition to clinical interviewing, testing was used to assess deviant behaviors and attitudes, intellectual functioning, social skills, attitudes toward women and aggression, personality, and a specific assessment of sexual arousal patterns. Dan was found to be functioning in the average range of intelligence. Personality testing revealed that he tends to be self-centered and seeks immediate gratification. He distrusts others, which significantly impacts his peer relations and interactions. Dan is an angry adolescent who approaches the world with a hostile stance and has the potential for significant physical aggressive behavior. In addition, he can be passive-aggressive and stubborn. On scales measuring attitudes toward women and aggression, he tended to accept violence as a way to solve problems and held a number of adversarial sexual beliefs. That is, he tends to see relationships between males and females as basically being adversarial with one out to get the other. The Multiphasic Sex Inventory revealed that he tends to be sexually obsessed, and he described a number of paraphilias, including fetishism, voyeurism, and obscene phone calls, and admitted to fantasies involving bondage and discipline. He also engages in a number of distortions to justify his behavior and takes a "victim stance." That is, he tends to see himself as being mistreated and uses this to justify his behavior. Assessment of his sexual arousal pattern showed a pattern that reflected a high level of deviant sexual arousal. He responded to a variety of stimuli including aggressive sexual stimuli.

IMPLICATIONS

Based on the information obtained, it is evident that Dan is in need of sex offender specific treatment within a structured, secure environment due to the level of risk that he presents. He is a dangerous offender who has displayed inappropriate and aggressive sexual behaviors since approximately the age of 5. His has a very deviant arousal pattern and engages in numerous distortions that dismiss both his responsibility for the offenses and the impact on his victims. In addition, some exploration of Dan's attitudes toward women and relationship will be needed.

His tendency to be self-centered and disregard the feelings and rights of others combined with his hostile attitude and negative perception of women intensifies the situation. In addition, the family dynamics present in this case are a confounding variable. His father is very controlling and, while he verbally states that Dan's behaviors are wrong, he provides mixed messages in regard to treatment. Significant work will be needed as to his father's attitudes and messages that he gives Dan. While Dan has only seen his mother once in the past 9 years, the impact of his early childhood days with her will need to be explored. Dan was reportedly exposed to questionable lifestyles during the time he was living with her, and explorations of his perception of her and his memories of that time may be beneficial in the overall course of treatment.

He has a very deviant sexual arousal pattern and also displays personality traits that indicate a degree of impulsiveness. He currently continues to utilize aggression in his sexual fantasies. He will need specific treatment aimed at reducing/assisting him to control his deviant urges and fantasies.

CONCLUSION

Adolescent sex offenders represent a significant social problem, and data clearly indicate that they are responsible for a significant amount of the sexual abuse that occurs in our society. There is increased awareness of the problem of this group, and there have been increased attempts to address these offenders. Clinical approaches have at times not had the level of empirical support desired. However, we cannot wait to address this problem until all the "data are in." Adolescent offenders engage in many deviant sexual behaviors, some of which are intrusive with the use of physical force. Data clearly indicate that this is a heterogeneous population with multiple needs. Systems are needed to better classify offenders.

Assessment of this group has generally followed a cognitive behavioral model, with assessment approaches and at time instruments "borrowed" from the adult offender literature. The field is in need of instruments that are sex offender specific for adolescents. However, until we have such instruments, we need to use those approaches that have at least some support, even if this is with adults (given the dangerousness of this population). It is important, however, that clinicians integrate specific sexual assessments with knowledge of adolescent development and psychopathology in interpreting and making recommendations.

A final pressing empirical area relates to actuarial approaches to recidivism prediction in this population. A major question is risk to reoffend and level of placement needed. We are forced to answer this question many times using clinical judgment and variables derived from adult populations. In the next 10 years, we hope to see more data related to adolescents.

REFERENCES

Abel, G.G., & Rouleau, J.L. (1990). The nature and extent of sexual assault. In W.L. Marshall, D.R. Laws, & H.E. Barbaree (Eds.), *Handbook of sexual assault: Issues, theories, and treatment of the offender* (pp. 9–21). New York: Plenum Press.

Association for the Treatment of Sexual Abusers. (1997). *Position on the effective legal management of juvenile sexual offenders*. Beaverton, OR: Author.

Atcheson, J.D., & Williams, D.C. (1954). A study of juvenile sex offenders. *American Journal of Psychiatry, 111,* 366–370.

Bala, N., & Schwartz, I. (1993). Legal responses to the juvenile sex offender. In H.E. Barbaree, W.L. Marshall, & S.M. Hudson (Eds.), *The juvenile sex offender* (pp. 25–44). New York: Guilford Press.

Barbaree, H.E., Hudson, S.M., & Seto, M.C. (1993). Sexual assault in society: The role of the juvenile sex offender. In H.E. Barbaree, W.L. Marshall, & S.M. Hudson (Eds.), *The juvenile sex offender* (pp. 1–24). New York: Guilford Press.

Barbaree, H.E., Marshall, W.L., & Hudson, S.M. (Eds.). (1993). *The juvenile sex offender*. New York: Guilford Press.

Becker, J.V., & Hunter, J.A. (1993). Aggressive sex offenders. *Child and Adolescent Psychiatric Clinics of North America, 2,* 477–487.

Becker, J.V., & Hunter, J.A. (1997). Understanding and treating child and adolescent sexual offenders. In T.H. Ollendick & R.J. Prinz (Eds.), *Advances in clinical child psychology* (Vol. 19, pp. 177–197). New York: Plenum Press.

Becker, J.V., Hunter, J.A., Goodwin, D., Kaplan, M.S., & Martinez, D. (1992). Test-retest reliability of audio-taped phallometric stimuli with adolescent sex offenders. *Annals of Sex Research, 5,* 45–51.

Becker, J.V., Hunter, J.A., Stein, R.M., & Kaplan, M.S. (1989). Factors associated with erection in adolescent sex offenders. *Journal of Psychopathology and Behavioral Sciences, 11,* 353–362.

Becker, J.V., Kaplan, M.S., & Tenke, C.E. (1992). The relationship of abuse history, denial and erectile response profiles of adolescent sexual perpetrators. *Behavior Therapy, 23,* 87–97.

Becker, J.V., Kaplan, M.S., Tenke, C.E., & Tartaglini, A. (1991). The incidence of depressive symptomatology in juvenile sex offenders with a history of abuse. *Child Abuse and Neglect, 15,* 531–536.

Becker, J.V., & Stein, R.M. (1991). Is sexual erotica associated with sexual deviance in adolescent males? *International Journal of Law and Psychiatry, 14,* 85–95.

Becker, J.V., Stein, R.M., Kaplan, M.S., & Cunningham-Rathner, J. (1992). Erection response characteristics of adolescent sex offenders. *Annals of Sex Research, 5,* 81–86.

Benoit, J.L., & Kennedy, W.A. (1992). The abuse history of male adolescent sex offenders. *Journal of Interpersonal Violence, 7,* 543–548.

Blaske, D.M., Borduin, C.M., Henggeler, S.W., & Mann, B.J. (1989). Individual, family, and peer characteristics of adolescent sex offenders and assaultive offenders. *Developmental Psychology, 25,* 846–855.

Brannon, J.M., Larson, B., & Doggett, M. (1989). The extent and origins of sexual molestation and abuse among incarcerated adolescent males. *International Journal of Offender Therapy and Comparative Criminology, 33,* 161–171.

Brecher, E.M. (1978). *Treatment programs for sex offenders*. Washington, DC: National Institute of Law Enforcement and Criminal Justice.

Bruinsma, F. (1995). Immediate assessment of adolescent sex offenders seen at the police station. *International Journal of Offender Therapy and Comparative Criminology, 39,* 307–316.

Burt, M.R. (1980). Cultural myths and supports for rape. *Journal of Personality and Social Psychology, 38,* 217–230.

Cooper, C.L., Murphy, W.D., & Haynes, M.R. (1996). Characteristics of abused and nonabused adolescent sexual offenders. *Sexual Abuse: A Journal of Research and Treatment, 8,* 105–119.

Emerick, R.L., & Dutton, W.A. (1993). The effect of polygraphy on the self report of adolescent sex offenders: Implications for risk assessment. *Annals of Sex Research, 6,* 83–103.

Fehrenbach, P.A., Smith, W., Monastersky, C., & Deisher, R.W. (1986). Adolescent sexual offenders: Offender and offense characteristics. *American Journal of Orthopsychiatry, 56,* 225–233.

Ford, M.E., & Linney, J.A. (1995). Comparative analysis of juvenile sexual offenders, violent nonsexual offenders, and status offenders. *Journal of Interpersonal Violence, 10,* 56–70.

Freeman-Longo, R.E., Bird, S., Stevenson, W.F., & Fiske, J.A. (1995). *1994 nationwide survey of treatment programs and models.* Brandon, VT: Safer Society.

Gray, A.S., & Pithers, W.D. (1993). Relapse prevention with sexually aggressive adolescents and children: Expanding treatment and supervision. In H.E. Barbaree, W.L. Marshall, & S.M. Hudson (Eds.), *The juvenile sex offender* (pp. 289–319). New York: Guilford Press.

Groth, A.N., Hobson, W.F., Lucey, K.P., & St. Pierre, J. (1981). Juvenile sexual offenders: Guidelines for treatment. *International Journal of Offender Therapy and Comparative Criminology, 25,* 265–272.

Hanson, R.K., & Bussière, M.T. (1996). *Predictors of sexual offender recidivism: A meta-analysis* (User Report No. 1996-04). Ottawa: Department of the Solicitor General of Canada.

Hanson, R.K., & Scott, H. (1995). Assessing perspective-taking among sexual offenders, non-sexual criminals, and nonoffenders. *Sexual Abuse: A Journal of Research and Treatment, 7,* 259–277.

Hanson, R.K., & Slater, S. (1988). Sexual victimization in the history of sexual abusers: A review. *Annals of Sex Research, 1,* 485–499.

Hastings, T., Anderson, S.J., & Hemphill, P. (1997). Comparisons of daily stress, coping, problem behavior, and cognitive distortions in adolescent sexual offenders and conduct-disordered youth. *Sexual Abuse: A Journal of Research and Treatment, 9,* 29–42.

Hunter, J.A., Becker, J.V., & Kaplan, M.S. (1995). The adolescent sexual interest card sort: Test-retest reliability and concurrent validity in relation to phallometric assessment. *Archives of Sexual Behavior, 24,* 555–561.

Hunter, J.A., Becker, J.V., Kaplan, M.S., & Goodwin, D.W. (1991). Reliability and discriminative utility of the adolescent cognitions scale for juvenile sexual offenders. *Annals of Sex Research, 4,* 281–286.

Hunter, J.A., & Goodwin, D.W. (1992). The clinical utility of satiation therapy with juvenile sexual offenders: Variations and efficacy. *Annals of Sex Research, 5,* 71–80.

Hunter, J.A., Goodwin, D.W., & Becker, J.V. (1994). The relationship between phallometrically measured deviant sexual arousal and clinical characteristics in juvenile sexual offenders. *Behaviour Research and Therapy, 32,* 533–538.

Hunter, J.A., & Santos, D.R. (1990). The use of specialized cognitive-behavioral therapies in the treatment of adolescent sexual offenders. *International Journal of Offender Therapy and Comparative Criminology, 34,* 239–247.

Jacobs, W.L., Kennedy, W.A., & Meyer, J.B. (1997). Juvenile delinquents: A between-group comparison study of sexual and nonsexual offenders. *Sexual Abuse: A Journal of Research and Treatment, 9,* 201–217.

Kaemingk, K.L., Koselka, M., Becker, J.V., & Kaplan, M.S. (1995). Age and adolescent sexual offender arousal. *Sexual Abuse: A Journal of Research and Treatment, 7,* 249–257.

Kaplan, M.S., Becker, J.V., & Tenke, C.E. (1991). Influence of abuse history on male adolescent self-reported comfort with interviewer guide. *Journal of Interpersonal Violence, 6,* 3–11.

Katz, R.C. (1990). Psychosocial adjustment in adolescent child molesters. *Child Abuse and Neglect, 14,* 567–575.

Kaufman, K.L., Hilliker, D.R., & Daleiden, E.L. (1996). Subgroup differences in the modus operandi of adolescent sexual offenders. *Child Maltreatment, 1,* 17–24.

Kaufman, K.L., Wallace, A.M., Johnson, C.F., & Reeder, M.L. (1995). Comparing female and male perpetrators' modus operandi: Victims' reports of sexual abuse. *Journal of Interpersonal Violence, 10,* 322–333.

Kavoussi, R.J., Kaplan, M., & Becker, J.V. (1988). Psychiatric diagnoses in adolescent sex offenders. *Journal of American Academy of Child and Adolescent Psychiatry, 27,* 241–243.

Kempton, T., & Forehand, R. (1992). Juvenile sex offenders: Similar to, or different from, other incarcerated delinquent offenders? *Behaviour Research and Therapy, 30,* 533–536.

Knight, R.A., & Prentky, R.A. (1993). Exploring characteristics for classifying juvenile sex offenders. In H.E. Barbaree, W.L. Marshall, & S.M. Hudson (Eds.), *The juvenile sex offender* (pp. 45–83). New York: Guilford Press.

Lewis, D.O., Shanok, S.S., & Pincus, J.H. (1979). Juvenile male sexual assaulters. *American Journal of Psychiatry, 136,* 1194–1196.

Lewis, D.O., Shanok, S.S., & Pincus, J.H. (1981). Juvenile male sexual assaulters: Psychiatric, neurological, psychoeducational, and abuse factors. In D.O. Lewis (Ed.), *Vulnerabilities to delinquency* (pp. 89–105). Jamaica, NY: Spectrum.

Matson, S., & Lieb, R. (1997, October). *Megan's law: A review of state and federal legislation.* Olympia, WA: Washington State Institute for Public Policy.

Milner, J.S., Murphy, W.D., Valle, L., & Tolliver, R.M. (1998). Assessment issues in child abuse evaluations. In J.R. Lutzker (Ed.), *Handbook of child abuse research and treatment* (pp. 75–115). New York: Plenum Press.

Monastersky, C., & Smith, W. (1985). Juvenile sexual offenders: A family systems paradigm. In E.M. Otey & G.D. Ryan (Eds.), *Adolescent sex offenders: Issues in research and treatment* (pp. 164–183). Rockville, MD: U.S. Department of Health and Human Services.

Monto, M., Zgourides, G., & Harris, R. (1998). Empathy, self-esteem, and the adolescent sexual offender. *Sexual Abuse: A Journal of Research and Treatment, 10,* 127–140.

Murphy, W.D., Haynes, M.R., & Page, I.J. (1992). Adolescent sex offenders. In W. O'Donohue & J.H. Geer (Eds.), *The sexual abuse of children: Clinical issues* (Vol. 2, pp. 394–429). Hillsdale, NJ: Erlbaum.

Murphy, W.D., & Peters, J.M. (1992). Profiling child sexual abusers: Psychological considerations. *Criminal Justice and Behavior, 19,* 24–37.

National Council on Juvenile and Family Court Judges. (1993). The revised report from the National Task Force on Juvenile Sexual Offending, 1993, of the National Adolescent Perpetrator Network. *Juvenile and Family Court Journal, 44,* 1–120.

Nichols, H.R., & Molinder, I. (1984). *Multiphasic sex inventory manual.* Tacoma, WA: Authors.

Rice, M.E., & Harris, G.T. (1995). Violent recidivism: Assessing predictive validity. *Journal of Consulting and Clinical Psychology, 63,* 737–748.

Rice, M.E., & Harris, G.T. (1997). Cross-validation and extension of the violence risk appraisal guide for child molesters and rapists. *Law and Human Behavior, 21,* 231–241.

Richardson, G., Kelly, T.P., Bhate, S.R., & Graham, F. (1997). Group differences in abuser and abuse characteristics in a British sample of sexually abusive adolescents. *Sexual Abuse: A Journal of Research and Treatment, 9,* 239–257.

Ryan, G., Lane, S., Davis, J., & Isaac, C. (1987). Juvenile sex offenders: Development and correlation. Child abuse and neglect [Special issue]. *Child Abuse and Neglect, 11,* 385–395.

Ryan, G., Miyoshi, T.J., Metzner, J.L., Krugman, R.D., & Fryer, G.E. (1996). Trends in a national sample of sexually abusing youths. *Journal of the American Academy of Child and Adolescent Psychiatry, 35,* 17–25.

Schram, D.D., Milloy, C.D., & Rowe, W.E. (1991). *Juvenile sex offenders: A follow-up study of reoffense behavior.* Seattle: Washington State Institute for Public Policy.

Smith, W.R., & Monastersky, C. (1986). Assessing juvenile sexual offenders' risk for reoffending. *Criminal Justice and Behavior, 13,* 115–140.

Spaccarelli, S., Bowden, B., Coatsworth, J.D., & Kim, S. (1997). Psychosocial correlates of male sexual aggression in a chronic delinquent sample. *Criminal Justice and Behavior, 24,* 71–95.

Tarter, R.E., Hegedus, A.M., Alterman, A.I., & Katz-Garris, L. (1983). Cognitive capacities of juvenile violent, nonviolent, and sexual offenders. *Journal of Nervous and Mental Disease, 171,* 564–567.

Truscott, D. (1993). Adolescent offenders: Comparison for sexual, violent, and property offences. *Psychological Reports, 73,* 657–658.

Van Ness, S.R. (1984). Rape as instrumental violence: A study of youth offenders. *Journal of Offender Counseling, Services, and Rehabilitation, 9,* 161–170.

Vizard, E., Monck, E., & Misch, P. (1995). Child and adolescent sex abuse perpetrators: A review of the research literature. *Journal of Child Psychology and Psychiatry, 36,* 731–756.

Weinrott, M.R. (1996). *Juvenile sexual aggression: A critical review.* Boulder, CO: Center for the Study and Prevention of Violence.

Weinrott, M.R., Riggan, M., & Frothingham, S. (1997). Reducing deviant arousal in juvenile sex offenders using vicarious sensitization. *Journal of Interpersonal Violence, 12,* 704–728.

Worling, J.R. (1995a). Adolescent sex offenders against females: Differences based on the age of their victims. *International Journal of Offender Therapy and Comparative Criminology, 39,* 276–293.

Worling, J.R. (1995b). Sexual abuse histories of adolescent male sex offenders: Differences on the basis of the age and gender of their victims. *Journal of Abnormal Psychology, 105,* 610–613.

Zussman, R. (1989). Forensic evaluation of the adolescent sex offender. *Forensic Reports, 2,* 25–45.

CHAPTER 18

Adult Survivors of Sexual Abuse

STEVEN N. GOLD and LAURA S. BROWN

WHETHER CLINICAL or forensic in nature, assessment of adult survivors of childhood sexual abuse (CSA) is frequently a complex task that presents a range of challenges not routinely encountered in general psychological practice. The heterogeneity of this group, as well as the frequency with which persons with this history present to treatment require, however, that clinicians become skilled in the task. Competency in evaluating this clientele unquestionably entails development of specialized knowledge and skills. Familiarity with topics such as psychological trauma, interpersonal violence and abuse, posttraumatic stress, and dissociative symptomatology is required. Areas needed for expertise in working with survivors of CSA are not well covered in most graduate psychology training programs (Alpert & Paulson, 1990; Feldman-Summers & Pope, 1994; MacFarlane & Waterman, 1986; Pope & Feldman-Summers, 1992).

Beyond mastery of these specialty areas, effectiveness in assessing survivors necessitates a thorough understanding of intricate conceptual controversies that emerged very soon after clinicians and researchers began to systematically study childhood sexual abuse and its long-term impact on adaptive functioning. These hotly debated topics touch on issues and processes fundamental to psychological theory, research, and practice. They include matters such as (1) what constitutes a trauma, and how traumatic events differ from stressful events in general (Shalev, 1996); (2) the nature of recall and forgetting, particularly for traumatic events (Loftus, 1993; Pope, 1996); (3) questions of how CSA is or is not a risk factor for adult psychopathology (Beitchman, Zucker, Hood, daCosta, & Ackman, 1991; Kendall-Tackett, Williams, & Finkelhor, 1993); (4) the potential for therapists to iatrogenically induce false memories, impaired functioning, and emotional distress (Ofshe & Waters, 1994); (5) whether clinicians have responsibility for seeking corroborative evidence for memories of abuse, even in clinical, nonforensic situations (Yapko, 1994); and (6) whether psychological practice should be legislatively restricted to empirically validated methods (Hinnefeld & Newman, 1997; Truth and Responsibility in Mental Health Practices Act, 1995).

This is an area into which a prudent practitioner will not want to tread without extensive knowledge. The reader is therefore cautioned that the space limitations of this chapter make it crucial that this be considered an introduction to assessing survivors, rather than a comprehensive treatment of the subject. Reading is not sufficient preparation in this area, and should be accompanied by formal instruction and supervision (Courtois, 1997; Gold, 1997; Pope & Brown, 1996). Additionally, a general knowledge of trauma assessment provides a helpful, if not indispensable, foundation for developing skills at the assessment of survivors of CSA (Briere, 1997).

DESCRIPTION OF THE PROBLEM

CHILDHOOD SEXUAL ABUSE

Due to variations in methodology and sampling, a wide range of estimates exists in the literature as to the incidence and prevalence of childhood sexual abuse. Problems in obtaining responses that are not likely to be strongly affected by factors that would encourage either underreporting or overreporting are difficult to surmount. There are also disagreements about definitions of CSA, with some research including noncontact abuse, such as being exposed to or photographed for pornography and other studies including only contact abuse. However, it is generally agreed that the most accurate estimate is that approximately one-third of all girls and one-sixth of all boys have been subjected to some form of CSA, broadly defined, by the time they reach their 18th birthday (Salter, 1995).

Although these figures suggest a disturbingly high prevalence of CSA, it is important to appreciate that a much smaller subgroup of survivors is likely to come to the attention of clinical and forensic psychologists. There is considerable empirical evidence that survivors who present for clinical services tend to have CSA histories that differ appreciably from those in the general population. CSA reported by a substantial proportion of survivors in nonclinical samples consists of a single incident (Briere & Runtz, 1988; Finkelhor, Hotaling, Lewis, & Smith, 1990; Russell, 1986) and may include a noncontact experience. In contrast, several studies in clinical settings found on average CSA of over 5 years' duration that frequently has included penetration and other overstimulating or frightening contact with the perpetrator (G. Anderson, Yasenik, & Ross, 1993; Briere & Conte, 1993; Gold, Hughes, & Swingle, 1996). This suggests that impairment of sufficient scope to motivate an individual to seek psychological services is most likely to be seen in survivors with a history of more severe and longer lasting CSA.

More pertinent prevalence data, therefore, can be found in the literature investigating the proportion of individuals in clinical samples with a history of CSA. The currently available data suggest that an appreciably greater percentage of CSA is found in clinical than in nonclinical populations. The majority of women psychiatric inpatients (Bryer, Nelson, Miller, & Krol, 1987; Jacobson & Richardson, 1987), women psychiatric emergency room patients (Briere, Woo, McRea, Foltz, & Sitzman, 1997; Briere & Zaidi, 1989), and women in outpatient settings (Lipschitz, Kaplan, Sorkenn, Chorney, & Asnis, 1996) report a CSA history. Such a history is also overrepresented among patients with psychosomatic presentations, such as chronic pelvic pain or irritable bowel syndrome (Walker et al., 1988; Walker, Katon, Roy-Byrne, Jemlka, & Russo, 1993). When one considers that on average this population reports much more extensive CSA than that in the general population, implications of these findings have powerful impact on clinicians' diagnostic hypotheses. These data underscore the caution that some degree of familiarity with CSA trauma and its sequelae is required for effective functioning in a general clinical setting. Even if one does not intend to specialize in treatment of CSA survivors, one can reasonably assume that this group will be encountered in clinical practice (Pope & Tabachnik, 1995).

Sequelae of Abuse

There is a fairly sizable research literature on the long-term effects of childhood sexual abuse, and several diagnostic syndromes that have regularly been observed among survivors of CSA. Probably the diagnostic category most commonly associated with CSA both in the clinical literature and in the minds of many practitioners is posttraumatic stress disorder (PTSD). Symptoms comprising PTSD are grouped in the *DSM-IV* (American Psychiatric Association [APA], 1994) into three major categories: (1) reexperiencing of the traumatic event (e.g., in the form of intrusive recollections, dreams, and flashbacks); (2) avoidance of reminders of the trauma and numbing of responsiveness; and (3) arousal (e.g., as reflected by insomnia, hypervigilance, and irritability). PTSD has been found to be prevalent in survivors of a wide range of traumatic experiences, including childhood sexual abuse (van der Kolk, Weisaeth, & van der Hart, 1996).

However, as Finkelhor (1990) has pointed out, many CSA survivors do not meet criteria for a diagnosis of PTSD, and in several respects this syndrome does not adequately capture the range and scope of reactions routinely observed among survivors. The concept of a trauma as encoded in the *DSM* criteria does not adequately capture the complexity of the experience of CSA. While the experience of CSA is frequently traumatic, it is also confusing and overstimulating, and frequently occurs in a complex relational matrix where a perpetrator is simultaneously a loved source of dependency needs and a feared source of abuse (Freyd, 1996). Largely in response to observations such as these, Judith Herman (1992a, 1992b) has proposed establishment of a new diagnostic category: complex PTSD (CD). The CD diagnosis captures many of the difficulties commonly manifested by survivors of extensive CSA that are not regularly encountered among survivors of single-event trauma. These include problems such as dissociative symptoms (e.g., amnesia, depersonalization); somatization (e.g., chronic pain, conversion symptoms); impaired regulation of affect and impulses (e.g., self-destructive behavior, suicidal preoccupation); negative self-perception (e.g., shame, ineffectiveness, feeling damaged); impaired capacity for interpersonal relations (e.g., inability to trust, revictimization); and disrupted sense of meaning (e.g., loss of sustaining beliefs, hopelessness). Findings of empirical investigation of sexual and physical abuse survivors are consistent with the contention that CD subsumes but is more extensive than PTSD (Roth, Newman, Pelcovitz, van der Kolk, & Mandel, 1997).

The constellation of symptoms comprising the CD diagnosis highlights the pervasive range of impairments beyond PTSD that can potentially be related to an extensive CSA history. Depressed mood and associated depressive symptoms are common (Browne & Finkelhor, 1986; McGrath, Keita, Strickland, & Russo, 1990). Dissociative features, often extensive enough to meet criteria for diagnoses ranging from Dissociative Amnesia to Dissociative Identity Disorder (i.e., multiple personality disorder), may occur (Kluft, 1990). CSA survivors may manifest anxiety disorders other than PTSD, such as Agoraphobia, Panic Disorder, Social Phobia, or Obsessive Compulsive Disorder. Somatoform Disorders, such as Conversion Disorder or Pain Disorder, may be present. A variety of addictive and compulsive syndromes, often developed in an attempt to manage disruptive levels of distress, such as alcoholism, substance abuse, eating disorders, compulsive gambling, compulsive spending, and compulsive sexual activity, may coexist with other disorders. Sufficient criteria may be met to warrant the diagnosis of *DSM* Axis II disorders, most commonly and notably Borderline Personality Disorder (Herman, Perry, & van der Kolk, 1989; cf. the difficulty modulating affect and impulse, impaired self-perception, and impaired capacity for relatedness in CD).

A diverse scope of symptoms and diagnoses, therefore, may be observed among survivors and may be (but will not always be) etiologically related to their childhood abuse. However, as emphasized in this chapter, many aspects of CSA survivors' experience beyond their symptoms need to be encompassed by a productive assessment. Often the temptation in assessment is to focus the evaluation primarily on identifying symptoms and arriving at diagnoses. Effective evaluation of CSA survivors requires that the investigator not restrict assessment to the survivor's history of CSA and current symptomatology. Such an approach will result in a product of limited clinical or forensic utility.

ASSESSMENT APPROACHES

ESTABLISHING RAPPORT

Discussions of rapport are more commonly associated with treatment than with assessment. Nevertheless, a premature focus on information gathering to the relative exclusion of explicitly attending to establishing a collaborative working relationship with the examinee can drastically limit the extent and quality of data obtained. Although this is certainly true in any assessment situation, it is especially the case when evaluating CSA survivors. The experience of CSA and, often, other forms of abuse frequently engenders a deep-seated sense of wariness and mistrust of others, particularly those in authority (McCann, Pearlman, Sakheim, & Abrahamson, 1988). These coercive interpersonal experiences often teach survivors that the best tactic for resisting situations is passive compliance, giving the appearance of cooperation while limiting their involvement to superficial, rote responses. The type of material elicited in such a situation is of minimal value in conducting a substantive assessment.

Consequently, it is imperative that the evaluator expressly attend to developing and maintaining a respectful and collaborative working relationship with the survivor. Particular care needs to be exerted to create an atmosphere that maximizes a sense of safety and security in the examinee. The more successfully this is accomplished, the more likely it is that the information provided by the survivor will be accurate, rich, and pertinent to the concerns that the assessment is designed to address.

The central method for accomplishing these ends may, initially, seem paradoxical: the objectives of the assessment are most likely to be attained by placing much of the control, direction, and pacing of the evaluation process in the hands of the examinee. This approach will be successful to the degree that it is executed not as a strategy, but out of a genuine understanding that empowering the survivor is the most likely means of conducting an accurate and productive evaluation. Conversely, overly forceful or rigid tactics can only be expected to lead the survivor to shut down, withdraw, counterattack, or provide material that is severely limited in depth and substance.

Important information can be gained by observing how the survivor handles the opportunity to direct the interview. Does the examinee remain reticent to provide an account of the abuse? If so, what do his or her comments and style of presentation suggest about the reason for this hesitancy? Is the capacity to relate information impaired by dissociation, numbing, or other possible symptomatic manifestations that in turn can be noted as an aspect of the assessment? What countertransferential reactions are elicited in the interviewer by the survivor's response?

MAINTAINING CONCEPTUAL CLARITY

A core concept in approaching the assessment of a CSA survivor is that evaluators must exercise caution in conceptualizing direct causal connections between CSA and limitations in functioning in adulthood, in contrast to identifying CSA as a risk factor. A risk factor raises likelihood; it does not constitute a cause. Despite some early and less-than-scholarly accounts that contended a set of symptoms exists that is pathonomonic for CSA (see, e.g., Blume, 1990, pp. xvi–xxi) the more general early as well as recent consensus is that this is not the case (Alpert, Brown, & Courtois, 1996; Briere, 1996; Pope & Brown, 1996). Because CSA is such a complex and unique experience, cutting across developmental stages and constituting a range of contact and noncontact acts in a variety of social and interpersonal contexts, no one experience of CSA presents the same meaning and potentials for sequelae as any other such experience. Survivors of CSA present with a wide range of difficulties that vary with such factors as age of exposure, length of exposure, type of abuse, and relationship with abuser, as well as the presence or absence of cofactors of both risk and resilience. Some of these problems, such as disturbed patterns of sexual functioning, may be directly traceable to survivors' experiences of sexual exploitation and violation (Briere & Runtz, 1990; Browne & Finkelhor, 1986). Other commonly observed impairments may result from factors that may have occurred in conjunction with childhood molestation, such as parental neglect, rather than being a direct consequence of sexual abuse (Beitchman et al., 1991; Browne & Finkelhor, 1986; Nash, Hulsey, Sexton, Harralson, & Lambert, 1993).

Still other difficulties may be seen in survivors who are in no way related, either directly or indirectly, to the abuse: for instance, bipolar disorder. One cannot presume that every problem in adjustment manifested by a particular survivor is a consequence of CSA. It is always possible that a factor other than sexual abuse may be the source of a given problem, although some recent data (Briere, 1997) argue that even in the presence of other forms of child maltreatment, CSA stands out as the most powerful predictor of severe adult psychopathology. While it may seem obvious that CSA is not the primum causum, in actual practice, once a client is identified as a survivor, it is easy to fall into the fallacy of overgeneralization, assuming that any and all presenting complaints are attributable to that individual's abuse history.

It will not be sufficient, therefore, to simply assess the forms and magnitude of pathology manifested by the survivor, or the duration and types of molestation to which she or he was subjected. The meaning of the experience, both at the time and in the present, and the social context in which that meaning was formed, will also be extremely important to understand in making sense of possible impacts of CSA on a given individual. In both clinical and forensic situations, it will usually be pertinent to differentiate the degree to which current distress and problems in functioning are attributable to CSA, and the extent to which they may be related to other causal factors.

Clinically, this will be useful in terms of focusing treatment. Forensically, such differentiation becomes important in assigning causality and possible damages.

This intricate issue is further complicated because for most adult survivors the events comprising their CSA occurred years, or, very often, decades prior to the assessment. This considerable gap in time introduces to the evaluation the ambiguities of memory for remote events, encoded at a much earlier level of cognitive development, under emotionally traumatic or confusing circumstances. Additionally, changes in the survivor's appraisal of the meaning of the CSA experience potentially change the nature and type of symptoms manifested, so that the presentation of a given individual may change as those appraisals change (e.g., from "it wasn't so bad" to "it was catastrophic"). Finally, the developmental traumas incurred as a result of the CSA may have themselves, in turn, led to other problems of personality functioning that appear linked to the CSA, but may primarily be a referred problem from the original source of distress. Thus, for example, many survivors of severe CSA engage in self-inflicted violence, such as cutting or burning themselves (Briere, 1996). However, this self-harm appears not to be a direct result of CSA, but a flawed coping strategy for dealing with more direct results, such as intrusive thoughts or overpowering affects.

How, then, in evaluating CSA survivors, can the evaluator guard against subscribing to the fallacy that any difficulties manifested by them must be attributable to their experiences of childhood molestation? Recognizing the necessity of avoiding succumbing to this faulty line of reasoning helps bring into focus a more productive approach to assessing survivors. This strategy entails conceiving the evaluation process as consisting of the examination of a set of four interrelated questions:

1. What is the nature and degree of difficulties currently presented?
2. What is the duration and intensity of CSA reported, and in what interpersonal context did it occur?
3. To what extent can each of the current difficulties be deduced to be directly or indirectly attributable to the CSA described?
4. In addition to CSA, what other factors might be contributing to, or more adequately account for, each of the current difficulties?

In the case of a clinical assessment, the evaluator will often also want to explicitly consider a fifth question:

5. What strengths and resources exist that can be employed to help ameliorate or resolve each of the current difficulties?

In every evaluation instance, the relative importance of each of these questions, particularly the first two, may vary. In most clinical situations, the primary concern is likely to be on question 1: the areas and scope of impairment. In contrast, in many forensic evaluations, particularly those where a survivor is suing or bringing criminal charges against an alleged perpetrator, the requirement will be equally strong to vigorously pursue and explore all possible alternative etiological hypotheses prior to assigning weight to the CSA. This may be so even when there is clear corroboration that such abuse occurred. Whether an evaluation is clinical or forensic, the relative emphasis on symptomatology or on the credibility of the description of CSA should not be allowed to obscure attention to the issue encapsulated in question 3: the degree to which a feasible connection between historical abuse and contemporary difficulties can be deduced from the assessment data gathered to address the first two questions.

ASSESSING CURRENT DIFFICULTIES

In both clinical and forensic settings, although especially in the latter, precision of assessment and improved reliability and validity may be obtained through the use of psychometric instruments and structured or semistructured interviews. As with any assessment question, psychometric instruments must be chosen that are reliable and valid for assessment of the questions at hand. Additionally, more general psychometric instruments may be utilized when there are available data regarding responses of CSA survivors on the particular instrument.

One psychological test, the Trauma Symptom Inventory (TSI; Briere, 1995), has been developed specifically for the assessment of the entire complex range of post-trauma phenomena. It is both age- and race-normed, and provides validity and clinical scales. Because it was created with a focus on survivors of repetitive interpersonal trauma, it is a valid test for the assessment of CSA sequelae. Briere's interpretive manual that accompanies the test provides common post-CSA response configurations on the TSI, although he, too, is cautious in avoiding overgeneralizations.

Research on the response of CSA and other interpersonal violence survivors on the MMPI and MMPI-2 is currently available in sufficient quantity (Dutton, 1992; Engles, Moisan, & Harris, 1994; Goldwater & Duffy, 1990; Lundberg-Love, Marmion, Ford, Geffner, & Peacock, 1992; Rosewater, 1985a, 1985b) to allow for cautious inclusion of this instrument in a standard assessment clinically, and to argue strongly for its inclusion forensically. However, extreme caution must be used in employment of computerized MMPI and MMPI-2 interpretations when CSA is at issue, since none of the currently available versions factor in such a history. Buchanan, Mazzeo, Grzegorek, Romas, and Fitzgerald (1998) have recently presented data indicating that such computer-generated narratives are explicitly lacking in validity in cases where sexual victimization is present in a history. Consequently, use of the MMPI or MMPI-2 as a component of evaluating CSA should be done for the more general development of a picture of problems in functioning, unless the evaluator is familiar with the specific research on response patterns in the victimization context.

Although some research is now available on response patterns of single-incident trauma survivors on the Rorschach (Levin, 1993), insufficient data are available to argue for its inclusion in a standard CSA assessment protocol. Given that there are apocryphal notions about Rorschach response patterns of CSA survivors (see Pope, Butcher, & Seelen, 1993, for examples of this sort of psychometric stereotype), as well as the highly subjective nature of the scoring and interpretation of this test and other projective instruments (Gann, 1995), it may be best left out of a standard protocol.

Existing standardized tests alone are obviously not adequate in providing a comprehensive and relevant database for productively assessing CSA survivors. Clinicians and forensic evaluators are encouraged to develop standard or semistandardized interview schedules for use in all assessments with CSA survivors, incorporating the suggestions made earlier in this chapter about the importance of assessing the full range of risk factors, so as to ensure coverage and questions about that range, not simply CSA. A semistructured interview that allows for survivor-directed changes in timing, pacing, and order of questions may be the best choice, allowing for enhanced reliability of assessment while empowering the survivor to take charge of the affect-laden aspects of the interview. In the following sections, we describe topics that should be included in such a semistructured interview.

ASSESSING DYSFUNCTIONAL COPING STRATEGIES

One of the hallmarks of CSA in the clinical population is that survivors often present with a range of dysfunctional coping strategies. Such strategies frequently reflect the nature and meaning of the abuse experience for the survivors, and represent attempts to modulate affect, engage in self-soothing, and reduce anxiety, as well as to numb and distance from the event.

Some such strategies are extremely blatant to mental health professionals. These include self-inflicted violence, such as nonlethal cutting, burning, head-banging or other self-abuse; the compulsive use of alcohol, nicotine, or other drugs, food, or sexual behavior; and self-deprecating styles of relating. Other such strategies are somewhat more subtle, but equally important to assess. For example, compulsive overwork, disguised as productivity or devotion to a job, frequently becomes a highly socially-valued, and thus difficult to escape, strategy for numbing of affect among some survivors of CSA.

Assessment should inquire into the range of coping strategies. Open-ended questions, such as "What kinds of things have you done to help yourself feel better/less overwhelmed?" may assist the survivor in disclosing some of the more subtle forms of dysfunctional coping. Normalizing statements can also make it possible for the survivor to feel sufficient decrease in shame to be able to disclose more stigmatized forms of coping. Statements such as "Many people who have experiences like yours cope with their feelings in ways that are hard to talk about, or that other people often don't understand. Do you think you might have done any of that sort of thing?" However, assessors should be cautioned that frequently survivors in treatment may wait months or years to trust a therapist sufficiently with the knowledge of self-inflicted violence. In a forensic context, therefore, it is possible that a survivor will underreport such a coping strategy, due to the time-limited nature of forensic assessment. In such circumstances, a thorough review of prior medical and mental health records may elicit this sort of information, and in turn offer a less shame-inducing way for an evaluator to bring up the topic, (e.g., "I notice that you frequently go to the ER for 'accidents.' I wonder if maybe you're coping with feelings by hurting yourself").

ASSESSING ABUSE HISTORY

To examine the possible relationship between current difficulties and past CSA experiences, the evaluator will want to obtain information about the duration and scope of CSA the survivor has endured. This, however, raises a sensitive dilemma. Accessing such information carries risk for substantial exacerbation of symptomatology and distress (Gold & Brown, 1997). Failure to approach this material with care and caution can elicit intrusive flashbacks, recollections, nightmares, and thoughts about the abuse, precipitously increase anxiety, compromise adaptive coping skills, and augment reliance on self-destructive and self-mutative strategies for managing distress.

This does not mean that the evaluator must avoid discussion of the particulars of the CSA entirely. It does indicate, however, that this is an area in which it is particularly important to allow the examinee to direct the pace, sequence, and timing of exploration. Informed consent to the process must explicitly detail the risks of participating, and the evaluator should assess with the survivor what his or her coping and self-care strategies will be should assessment evoke painful symptoms (Pope & Brown, 1996). The more the survivor perceives him- or herself to be in control of discussion of the abuse, the more productive and less damaging the process of disclosure is likely to be. Nevertheless, the evaluator needs to be familiar with methods of deescalating intrusive symptoms in the event that exploration of CSA experiences inadvertently triggers flashbacks or anxiety (Gold & Brown, 1997). The client must be assured of the right to stop the process, take breaks, switch the focus, and otherwise titrate both affect and the flow of information. The evaluator must be certain that only necessary questions are asked, so that intrusions into privacy are kept to an absolute minimum.

In gauging how much detail is needed regarding the survivor's CSA experiences, the examiner must be clear about the purpose of obtaining an account of the abuse. Collecting information about the fine details of the abuse is not an end in itself. In most assessment situations its purpose is provide sufficient information to allow the evaluator to deduce how and to what extent the client's symptoms may be related to her or his CSA history. Keeping this aim in mind will provide a useful criterion against which to determine the nature and scope of information that is required for a particular evaluation.

Compounding the intricacies of this aspect of the evaluation are the problems of fragmentary memory for abuse. The controversy about recovered memories has centered almost exclusively on recollections of CSA (Loftus, 1993; Pope, 1996). However, there is extensive evidence that incomplete recall has been observed in a broad range of trauma survivors (Elliott, 1997), including combat veterans (Karon & Widener, 1997) and rape victims (Coons, Bowman, Pellow, & Schneider, 1989). Recognition that recollection of traumatic experiences is often disrupted by the hyper- and hypoarousal of trauma exposure is codified in the *DSM* criteria for diagnosing posttraumatic stress disorder. "Inability to recall an important aspect of the trauma (psychogenic amnesia)" (p. 250) has been among the formal criteria for diagnosing PTSD since the publication of the *DSM III-R* (American Psychiatric Association, 1987), which predates onset of the recovered memory controversy by at least 5 years. Moreover, an expanding body of empirical studies indicate that anywhere from 20% to 60% of CSA survivors report incomplete memory for abuse even when there is clear corroboration that abuse occurred (see, e.g., Briere & Conte, 1993; Herman & Schatzow, 1987; Loftus, Polonsky, & Fullilove, 1994; Williams, 1994, 1996).

One implication of this finding is that information obtained about survivors' CSA will often be incomplete at initial assessment. This may be the case even in instances where the survivor herself or himself believes that full memory for the abuse has been maintained (Gold, Hughes, & Hohnecker, 1992). Overly brief inquiry about CSA experiences, or a failure to return to a potentially incomplete history can, therefore, easily leave the examiner with a misleading impression of how thorough or specific is the examinee's retention of his or her abuse experiences. In any case, assessors must be reconciled to the fact that in evaluating abuse survivors, they will at times have to rely on an account of CSA that is disjointed and sketchy. Evaluators need to create a flexible and at times somewhat lengthy timeline for the completion of such an evaluation, meeting the survivor at his or her level of capacity to report. A further complication in assessing CSA history is the issue of completeness and clarity of self-report. It is ironic, given our current level of knowledge of the base rates of CSA in the general population, that this aspect of personal history continues to be subjected to greater scrutiny than almost any other sort of self-report. Yet, the complex nature of CSA means that it may be encoded and retrieved from memory with somewhat differing degrees of accuracy than are other, less loaded events, such as parental alcoholism or childhood illness. Instances exist in which survivors are unsure about the accuracy of their own abuse memories, even those continuously held. This uncertainty is partly due to the disconnected nature of their abuse recollections, in part a consequence of the disincentives for believing that the CSA actually occurred, and attributable as well as to the remoteness in time of the events involved. CSA survivors frequently want to downplay the significance of what has been done to them, or may feel guilt or shame out of imagined complicity with their abuse. All these factors may contribute to self-doubt.

The same factors that cause survivors to question their recollections may lead evaluators to doubt the veracity of the survivors' depiction of their CSA history, and historically the mental health field has tended to display such doubt, at times in the face of physical evidence of abuse. Additionally, some types of severe and sadistic CSA, such as those in the histories of child pornography survivors, are so horrific that even seasoned trauma experts may wish to deny or downplay the possibility that such accounts depict real events. Furthermore, there are circumstances in forensic settings that could potentially constitute inducements for examinees to malinger or fabricate simply because of the demand characteristics of forensic assessment. To date, however, there are no empirical studies that establish a base rate of malingering or deception in the forensic CSA population above or beyond usual forensic concerns about such factors.

How can the evaluator begin to untangle the various factors that may bolster or detract from the clarity and precision of reported CSA memories? One key aspect is exercising particular care and precision in the wording used in interviewing about abuse memories so that potentially suggestive questioning is avoided. Open-ended questions that do not assume that a CSA survivor has encoded the experience as abuse, followed by more precise behaviorally worded inquiries for the purpose of clarification are the preferred strategy to pursue. Thus, an evaluator may begin with such questions as "Was there a time in your childhood when someone said or did something sexual with you that felt uncomfortable in some way?" If there are questions of continuity of recall, an evaluator might begin by asking, "Is what you are telling me now something that you have always had knowledge of? If not, please tell me how you became aware of what you know now." These forms of questions allow the survivor to identify what happened and to decide what to label abuse, to define and describe his or her own experience of knowing and unknowing rather than fit it into predetermined categories of remembering and forgetting.

A related approach to assessing the accuracy of CSA memories is to phrase follow-up questions in concrete, behavioral terms rather than in generalities. It is more useful to ask what specific aspects of the abuse are available now and whether they were accessible previously. Asking about particulars, such as who the abuse perpetrator was, how old the survivor was when the abuse began and stopped, whether anyone was ever told or found out about the abuse while it was occurring, and what specific sexual acts took place, is a useful approach for two reasons. First, the more specific the nature of the question, the less ambiguous the response is likely to be. Second, narrow, direct, factual questions such as these are less likely to elicit distress and intrusive symptoms than open-ended requests for a narrative account of incidents.

To be consistent with the client-directed approach to assessment advocated here, however, the examiner must preface a direct line of questioning such as this. We strongly recommend that the evaluator alert the survivor that she or he is about to ask specific questions about CSA. In doing so, it is useful to explicitly encourage him or her to let the examiner know whether there are questions she or he does not wish to answer. It may be helpful to offer to a survivor the opportunity to respond "yes" or "no" to a list of standard questions about types of abuse, such as, "Did anyone ever put his penis in your mouth?" This reduces the pressure on the survivor to narrate painful materials more readily evoked by general queries such as "What things did person X do?"

Employing a client-directed approach is particularly important because many survivors have developed, as a consequence of their CSA experiences, a stance of passive acquiescence in response to authority. Rather than express their hesitancy to address CSA material, therefore, they are likely to persist in responding despite emergence of discomfort and intrusive symptoms, or to persevere while shutting down emotionally and withdrawing interpersonally. By allowing this compliant response to occur, the evaluator permits the collaborative relationship with the examinee to be disrupted, potentially restricting the quantity and quality of data obtained throughout the remainder of the assessment. Conversely, by offering less emotionally challenging strategies for the survivor to talk about the experience, the evaluator conveys care and allows for trust to build, which in turn is likely to improve the quality of information shared in the assessment process.

ASSESSING THE CSA CONTEXT

In addition to gathering information about the CSA itself, it will often be important to examine the larger context in which the abuse occurred. Related factors—such as degree of social support, responses to disclosure or discovery of CSA, and adjustment prior to the onset of CSA—may attenuate or exacerbate the pernicious impact of the abuse. Investigation of the interpersonal and social context in which CSA occurred is therefore an essential part of making sense of the extent of its enduring repercussions.

To the extent that it is possible, therefore, the examiner will want to ascertain what life was like for the survivor before the onset of the abuse. How stable, dependable, and predictable was the family environment and the larger community in which the family resided? How emotionally responsive and supportive were the examinee's primary caretakers? Were there individuals outside the immediate family—friends, neighbors, teachers, extended family members—to whom the survivor was attached and who may have exerted an appreciable influence on his or her self-concept and sense of well-being?

How did things change after the onset of CSA? What does the survivor recall about its immediate impact? Did academic, athletic, or social functioning change once the abuse started? Did performance suffer in these areas? Did withdrawal from any of these pursuits occur? Conversely, did the survivor escape into excessive involvement in any of these spheres of activity? Were symptoms of anxiety or depression present? Was there the emergence of other behavior changes—alcohol or drug abuse, self-mutilation or suicidal gestures, anger outbursts, aggressive behavior—which may have signaled that something was wrong? If so, were these changes noticed by significant adults? How did they respond? Was the survivor aware at the time of covictims? If so, what was the effect of that knowledge? Did the survivor make attempts to report the abuse? If so, what happened in response to those attempts? Did anyone find out about the CSA without being told? In either case, what was the response? Was it perceived as well-intentioned, malevolent, apathetic? Was its impact helpful, destructive, or negligible? What did the examinee conclude from the responsiveness or indifference of primary caretakers? How might those conclusions have affected his or her perceptions and beliefs in an enduring way?

The relevancy of lines of questioning such as these may not be as readily obvious to the examiner as investigation of the particulars of the abuse itself, yet these are the factors that can make all the difference in the impact of the CSA experience. It is easy to forget that although CSA may consist of discontinuous and destabilizing events, it can also be congruent with an ongoing surrounding atmosphere of emotional rejection, neglect, and coercive control that potentates the harmfulness of the CSA. Conversely (although not commonly), a child may be experiencing many positive life factors in parallel to an experience of sexual abuse, especially when a perpetrator is extrafamilial. In any case, CSA occurs in the larger context of the child's life and social network. Without an appreciation of the nature of that context, the meaning and consequences of the events comprising the examinee's CSA experiences cannot be adequately assessed and understood. In many instances, on careful assessment of the larger childhood life context in which the abuse occurred, the examiner will find that the CSA is one manifestation of a much more pervasive picture. One may find, for example, a larger atmosphere of chaos and conflict among family members, emotional neglect, or frank rejection and contempt for the survivor in childhood. More concretely, features such as physical violence between the parents, chronic substance abuse by parents, or physical neglect or physical abuse of the survivor and of the survivor's siblings will be found to characterize the family of origin environment. In such cases, there will be many factors in addition to CSA that may account for the survivor's current difficulties as well as or better than the sexual abuse, or that may have exacerbated the harmful effects of the CSA in some manner.

ASSESSING STRENGTHS AND RESOURCES

While the general context in which CSA occurs may appreciably intensify its adverse impact, it can also have the opposite effect. A generally supportive home environment, particularly one in which the survivor as a child felt safe enough to reveal the abuse to a parent or other trusted adult, and in which that adult saw to it that the abuse stopped, may greatly attenuate the negative consequences of CSA. At least in clinical populations, this seems to rarely have been the case (Briere, 1996). However, we have observed clinically that the existence of a supportive relationship in childhood, even with someone outside the immediate family to whom abuse was not necessarily disclosed, can considerably bolster the survivor's adaptive capacity. Self-described "Thrivers" tend to report that such positive connections with supportive others made the difference in their capacity to cope as well as to later utilize psychotherapy and other resources in adulthood (L. Anderson, 1995; Morrow & Smith, 1995). This finding is consistent with other research on resilient children (Masten, Best, & Garmezy, 1991), underscoring the importance of assessing for the presence of resources in the survivor's childhood as well as in the present, since these factors may improve prognosis and capacity to benefit from psychotherapy.

In the face of the extraordinary stressor of CSA, the greater the survivor's social and personal resources, the better equipped he or she will be to manage the sequelae of CSA in particular and the strains of day-to-day living in general. The more such assets are available to the survivor on which to draw, the more likely the person is to resolve the abuse and overcome its long-term debilitating effects. Thorough assessment of the CSA survivor, therefore, will entail exploration of past and current life circumstances and inner capabilities that can be employed in the process of recovery.

LEGAL AND SYSTEMS CONSIDERATIONS

Forensic assessment in general calls for a somewhat different mind-set than clinical assessment. Typically, a forensic evaluator has specific questions that arise from the legal matter at hand, and has the task, not of helping the client, but of preparing to inform triers of fact of information that will assist in arriving at legal judgments in a courtroom setting. This lends a particular focus to a forensic evaluation that is unnecessary and even counterproductive in a clinical assessment, as well as a level of questioning and skepticism that would undermine the development of trust necessary for psychotherapy. Additionally, in any forensic evaluation, the assessor must be continuously testing and challenging alternative hypotheses, including the hypothesis that the person evaluated is malingering symptoms or degree of distress, or consciously or nonconsciously deceiving the assessor. Because forensic assessment itself constitutes a specialized skill-set, this section will restrict itself to addressing additional special considerations arising from forensic assessment of CSA survivors. Readers with an interest in the field of forensic assessment are referred to Weiner and Hess (1987).

Potentially, any forensic assessor may encounter a CSA survivor in a context where CSA is not the focus of the legal matter. CSA survivors may also have been the targets of racial discrimination in the workplace, or passengers in a car hit by a drunk driver, or be in a contested child custody matter, or be charged with theft. Some evidence would suggest that plaintiffs in certain kinds of cases (e.g., sexual harassment, see Buchanan et al., 1998 for a discussion of this question) are more likely than not to have a history of CSA because the adult exposure to stress is so aggravating to underlying CSA sequelae (Briere, 1997).

However, since the middle 1980s, some survivors have litigated in civil courts against their alleged perpetrators, making their CSA experience central to the forensic evaluative process (L. Brown, 1995). It is this sort of case that is the focus of this section. There are several typical scenarios in such cases:

1. A survivor with continuous recall brings suit before the age of majority. In these cases, the actual CSA is likely to have occurred relatively recently.
2. A survivor with continuous recall brings suit in adulthood after becoming aware that the always-recalled abuse is likely to have been a cause of his or her emotional and behavioral difficulties. Such "delayed understanding" lawsuits are explicitly permitted under the laws of 27 states (Pope & Brown, 1996), and can frequently be brought under existing case law in other jurisdictions.
3. A survivor experiences delayed recall of sexual abuse and brings suit. These so-called repressed memory lawsuits are also explicitly permitted in 27 states, but

have been less successful in gaining standing in some of the other jurisdictions where they are not written into law.

4. A survivor experiences a delayed recall and makes a report of the crime to the police for purposes of obtaining victims' compensation funds. In an extremely small number of these cases, criminal charges are filed against the alleged perpetrator.

In the first three of these instances, the forensic evaluator is charged with the task of determining whether there are damages arising from the sexual abuse. In the second instance, the evaluator must also inquire into the nature of the delayed understanding of always-recalled abuse, although most statutes do not require the determination of a date certain, but allow for the process of an unfolding of understanding. In the third case, especially since the onset of the debate over delayed recall in 1992, the evaluator is charged with assessing, to the degree possible, the reality of what the plaintiff says that he or she recalls. In the fourth case, it is very difficult to characterize what the task of a forensic expert might be, given the rarity of these cases, but it is likely to contain some elements of all the tasks inherent in evaluation for purposes of civil litigation.

In any forensic matter, reliance on the self-report of the interviewee is considered substandard practice, given the demand characteristics inherent in the situation. All forensic examiners will pursue evidence to either corroborate or refute their hypotheses. No consensus exists as to what sort of evidence is considered good-quality corroboration for a self-report of CSA; the authors are aware of cases in which a written confession by an alleged perpetrator was considered noncorroborative when recanted after conviction (Wright, 1994). However, forensic evaluators should consider the following in seeking to confirm or refute the survivor's self-report:

- Reports of covictims.
- Autobiographical materials generated by the survivor concurrent with the time that abuse is alleged to have occurred, such as diary or journal entries, poetry, or artwork.
- School and childhood medical records.
- Reports of peers of the survivor. It appears to be not uncommon that the sexually abused child comments to peers in ways that only become remarkable to the peer when adulthood is reached. We have anecdotal evidence of a number of survivors being told by childhood acquaintances that the survivor had said something about the abuse to the peer, even in instances where the survivor did not go on to have continuous recollection into adulthood.
- Where available, information about the sexual history of the alleged perpetrator. While, for example, the purchase or use of child pornography does not absolutely predict that a person will engage in contact child sexual abuse, it may be seen as a likely risk factor, given that it constitutes a noncontact abuse of the children in the print or video medium.

Forensic evaluators cannot comment as to credibility or truthfulness, since those matters are within the purview of the triers of fact, the jury and judge. However, the evaluator can assist the decision makers immeasurably by a careful assessment of all data that supports or refutes alternative hypotheses, including the hypothesis that CSA probably did occur, or that CSA, known to have occurred, probably did have certain negative sequelae. As with clinical assessment, a rush to either fix on or fixedly exclude the hypothesis of CSA, or for that matter any one hypothesis, will especially badly serve the triers of fact.

If an issue at trial is the delayed recall of the CSA, it is incumbent on the evaluator to inquire into both the experience of recall and possible sources of suggestion and source contamination. While there is no "right way" for a person to experience a delayed recall of CSA, evaluators should be especially cautious of recollections occurring in highly suggestive contexts. Examples of the latter include groups primarily composed of CSA survivors that also contain individuals who suspect having been abused but who have no conscious recollection of CSA at the time of joining, when the plaintiff is one of those not-yet-remembered persons. In such an instance, group dynamics may encourage a person to identify as a survivor or overinterpret certain symptoms as evidence of a CSA history. Empirical evidence suggests that being in therapy per se is an extremely uncommon trigger event for delayed recall (Elliott & Briere, 1995). However, if a survivor does begin recall in the context of participating in psychotherapy, inquiry should be made regarding the therapist's stance about CSA, response to disclosures, and techniques used in treatment. While no empirical evidence exists that any particular approach to therapy raises a risk of erroneous report of CSA (Olio, 1996; Pope & Brown, 1996), some individual therapists apparently engage in tactics such as insisting that a client must have been abused because of manifesting a particular symptom pattern. Delayed recalls arising in the context of this sort of marginal practice must be viewed with great caution and suspicion.

The evaluator must also explore other suggestive influences. These include, but are not limited to, frequent viewing of media discussions of CSA, viewing of pornography, reading first-person accounts of CSA or fiction (e.g., *A Thousand Acres;* Smiley, 1991) in which CSA and its delayed recall are thematic, and so on. Anecdotal experience suggests that many survivors who have delayed recall are highly avoidant of this sort of material, and will frequently trace the onset of intrusive recall to involuntary exposure to this sort of memory cueing, or to other, less obvious sensory cues. However, if the survivor identifies having repeated exposures to a highly suggestive environment, then again, caution must be used in supporting a hypothesis that the events recalled in this fashion are likely to have occurred, absent other strong corroborative material.

Familiarity and plausibility of CSA are also factors to assess with regard to delayed recall. Pezdek and Roe (1994) have demonstrated empirically that suggestions are much less likely to be taken when the event in question is unfamiliar to the person. If the plaintiff operates in a social context where discussion of CSA is common, or where there is great familiarity with CSA as a phenomenon, this adds to potential openness to suggestion, although to what degree is not known. Conversely, the person who had a strong belief prior to recall that "our sort of people do not sexually abuse children" is less likely to have taken on a suggestion of abuse.

The evaluator in this situation must also be prepared to testify as to the controversy recently generated over the phenomenon of delayed recall. This is a tremendously intricate issue in its own right. We therefore refer the reader to Pope and Brown (1996) and to D. Brown, Scheflin, and Hammond (1997) for extensive reviews of this literature.

CASE ILLUSTRATION

Susan was a 35-year-old Caucasian heterosexual woman from a lower-middle-class family, working as a retail clerk, who self-referred for evaluation because she had recently begun to, in her words, "have painful thoughts about things I think happened with my uncle when I was little." Susan reported that she had a history of problematic relationships with men, including a number of episodes of sexual coercion by dates and acquaintances, and was currently in no intimate relationship and uncertain that she wanted to pursue one. She held a master's degree in the humanities, but had never worked in her field. She described herself as always having been unhappy; she had gone through a period of out-of-control use of drugs and alcohol in her early and middle 20s, stopping when she received a citation for DUI three years prior to presenting to treatment. She did report close relationships with a few long-time women friends. Her work performance was good and she got high marks for her dedication to her job.

Susan reported that in the 6 months prior to seeking evaluation, she had begun to have distressing dreams in which she felt menaced by her uncle. She stated that she had always "felt funny," uncomfortable, and frightened around him. She described him as a verbally abusive, hard-drinking man who was frequently in her childhood home because he was her mother's favorite brother, and often served the role of a father figure in the absence of Susan's own father, who had divorced Susan's mother when Susan was 3 years old. Susan indicated that her uncle, George, frequently resided with her, her mother, and older brother for long periods, or would stay over at the house when he was not formally living there.

Susan explained that what she perceived to be a cueing or triggering event to these dreams was the disclosure to her by a close woman friend of the latter's history of CSA. She remembers telling her friend that at least she did not have that to deal with in her own past, then went home and began dreaming of her Uncle George. In the month prior to presenting for evaluation she had begun to have intrusive images of him lying on top of her, and of his penis in her mouth. Susan told the evaluator on initial intake that she did not want to believe that any of her intrusive images were real. She suggested that she might simply be going crazy, and requested that the evaluator assess that question to assist her in determining what course of treatment to pursue.

Susan's self-presentation certainly is rich in red flags regarding a possible history of CSA. Consequently, the first step the evaluator needed to take to ensure the most open-minded assessment possible was to consider possible differential diagnoses as well as differential etiologies, and to inform Susan that this was the approach to be taken. The evaluator requested that Susan read and sign an informed consent to the evaluation process. The consent form explained what would be asked, what tests might be used, and informed Susan of her rights to question the evaluator, stop the process at any time with no penalties, and asked to whom she would like the results of the assessment to be given. She was also informed of her confidentiality rights and any mandatory reporting requirements that might affect those. Susan and the evaluator discussed the form, and the evaluator made as certain as possible that Susan felt fully informed and at ease with signing the consent.

The evaluator also discussed with Susan how she felt about talking to him, a man. He suggested that if she wanted to have a woman do the assessment, he would be glad to facilitate that process. Susan reported that simply being asked as to her preference and given room to express it was helpful to her. She reported that she had indeed been somewhat uneasy when she found that she had been assigned to a male intake person. She said that she needed to know that the evaluator would not touch her, and would not come any closer in the room than he already was, which was across from her by a distance of about six feet. She said that it helped that he looked nothing like her uncle, but that she had already been feeling some very uncomfortable feelings being stuck in a room with a man. The evaluator asked her if she wanted to change where she was sitting, and again reminded her that if she wanted to leave at any time or take a break, that he would support her in that. He noted this information as a part of the overall assessment, and then explained to Susan that he would be asking her some questions, that they would probably feel very personal and intrusive at times, and that he would only ask what was clinically necessary. He again reminded her that she could refuse to answer any question or ask to come back to a question later.

The evaluator then began to take Susan through a semistructured interview that focused on both risk factor exposures and resiliency factors. He began by focusing on resiliency factors, already having the information that Susan was highly educated. He asked her about school performance, favorite subjects, and teachers she had liked, and explained to her that it was important that he know her strengths and skills, and that she know that he saw her entire self, not just her troubles. This strategy was helpful in creating an atmosphere of greater trust and comfort for her, since school had been her "savior" as she put it, and talking about school proved to be the easiest type of self-disclosure in which she could engage. This strategy by the evaluator illustrates the importance, in assessing CSA survivors, of not allowing the question of trauma exposure to become so paramount to the assessment process that strategies for integrating containment and relationship-building are left out of an interview or made less than secondary.

Not until their second meeting did the evaluator begin to bring up the topic of possible trauma exposures. Again working from the semistructured interview format, he asked Susan to describe painful or difficult experiences that had happened before she started school, while in elementary school, in secondary school, and postsecondary school. Since school was a positive and well-recalled aspect of Susan's life, he used this as an anchor for her to place the time, and thus her age and developmental stage, of certain life occurrences. The evaluator learned that Susan's family had a history of alcoholism on her mother's side, but no other family histories of mental illness; that her physical health had been good in childhood, and that her mother had been caring, although struggled greatly with poverty and job uncertainty. Uncle George had frequently been left alone with Susan and her brother while her mother worked. The evaluator also learned that Susan did not exhibit symptoms suggestive of an obsessive-compulsive disorder or other anxiety disorders, an important consideration in making a differential diagnosis.

Susan went on to report that she was continuing to have intrusive images and states that the evaluator coded as "flashbacks" of George having sexual contacts with her. She reported that she tried hard not to think about these images and experiences, but that they continued to come to her unbidden. She reported that she felt as if she were several different ages in the various images, ranging from about 5 to 9 years old. She reported realizing that she had always been sickened by the smell of the particular men's cologne used by her uncle. She also had found herself alternately attracted to and repelled by men who were, like him, of a particular build and body type (commenting to the evaluator at that point how glad she was that he did not resemble this type of man). She denied reading or watching visual media about sexual abuse. In fact, she reported that several friends of hers had tried to get her to go to a movie about sexual abuse. Not only had she said no, but found herself sitting in the dark crying and shaking; this had happened about a year before the onset of her first intrusive images.

The evaluator administered several psychometric instruments to Susan. These included a MMPI-2, a Trauma Symptom Inventory (TSI), a Beck Depression Inventory, and a brief cognitive screening test. On the MMPI-2, Susan had a valid profile, with an elevated F scale. She had elevations on scales 2, 4, 6, and 8, with a distinctive "V" shape between scales 4, 5, and 6. Subscales of 8 indicating thought disorder were not elevated, however, nor was the Bizarre Mentation content scale, which assisted the evaluator in coming to rule out the presence of psychotic process in Susan. Research on victims of violence (Dutton, 1992; Rosewater, 1985) suggests that this pattern of response is consistent with, although not pathognomic of, a history of exposure to interpersonal violence. On the TSI, Susan again obtained a valid profile. She was positive for critical items indicating thoughts of self-harm. Her scales were elevated on the following clinical scales; Dissociation, Defensive Avoidance, Intrusive Experience, Disturbed Sexual Behavior, Impaired Self-Reference, and Tension-Reducing Behavior. This pattern is consistent with individuals who have experienced repetitive exposure to trauma, particularly in childhood, since the last three scales indicate changes to personality and coping styles in response to repeated trauma exposures. On the Beck, Susan scored within the depressed range. On the cognitive screen, evidence was present of problems with concentration, although abstraction was still functioning well, indicating that Susan's higher education and apparent intelligence were not significantly impaired by her distress.

The findings of this evaluation suggested that a hypothesis that Susan might have been sexually abused and was now experiencing a delayed recall was a reasonable one. Other hypotheses that the evaluator considered were not as strongly supported. There was little other trauma exposure in childhood, and even adult coercive sexual experiences had been emotionally coercive, rather than physically violent. Susan was not obsessive-compulsive, arguing against the notion that her intrusive images were obsessive thoughts. There was an absence of evidence for thought disorder or psychotic processes, suggesting no impairment in reality testing. George had been alone with Susan for extended periods of time during the ages at which she recalled abuse happening; the nature of his relationship to her mother, who was Susan's primary parent, would have made it difficult to disclose, or to contain conscious knowing (see Freyd, 1996) of events of sexual abuse by him. Even with this relatively stronger support for the sexual abuse hypothesis, the evaluator was careful to simply let Susan know that this was a better hypothesis, but not necessarily "the truth." He was able to reassure her that she was not crazy, however, and that she might want to consider psychotherapy that would assist her in making sense of her current experiences. At no time did he suggest to her that she fit any sort of pattern or protocol for survivors of sexual abuse. He also suggested that she obtain a medication evaluation from her primary care physician, or a psychiatrist or nurse practitioner, to consider antidepressant medication.

CONCLUSION

Effective assessment of adult survivors of childhood sexual abuse requires specialized knowledge and skills. Competent evaluation of survivors entails thorough familiarity with topics not routinely addressed in detail in most graduate training programs. This includes areas such as psychological trauma, posttraumatic stress disorder, complex PTSD, violence and victimization, the long-term debilitating effects of abuse, and the nature of memory in general and of recall of traumatic events in particular. Extensive experiences of abuse and coercion often result in a restricted interpersonal repertory, frequently characterized by a combination of pervasive mistrust, hypervigilance, unassertiveness, and passive compliance. This interpersonal stance constitutes an exceptional test of the examiner's interpersonal skill and flexibility. Without taking the time to help the examinee establish an adequate level of comfort, security, and trust, little useful information will be obtained. The evaluator must, therefore, develop a collaborative working relationship with the survivor by allowing her or him to take the lead in directing and pacing the assessment process. An overly forceful approach is most likely to lead the survivor to withdraw and become increasingly uncooperative, or to passively comply by producing material that is extremely restricted in depth and substance.

Most standardized psychological tests have not been empirically validated for application to CSA survivors. One of the few instruments specifically developed for use with such a population is Briere's (1995) Trauma Symptom Inventory. Evaluators need to develop standard or semistructured interview schedules to assess for the presence of common sequelae to CSA not adequately covered in existing standardized measures.

Regardless of the data collection methods used, comprehensive assessment of CSA survivors necessitates that the evaluation not be limited to exploration of symptoms and syndromes. Whether the evaluation is clinical or forensic, the examiner will ultimately want to be able to deduce the extent to which current difficulties can be attributed to CSA experiences. Rather than assuming that survivors' problems can all be traced to CSA, the assessor will need to gather enough data about both CSA experiences and psychological problems to appraise whether a logical causal relationship between them can reasonably be inferred.

A major segment of the evaluation, therefore, will center on the nature, extent, and duration of the abuse experienced. However, exploration of this area raises the risk of eliciting intrusive recollection of abuse trauma and significantly intensifying distress. Consequently, it is particularly imperative that this material be approached in a manner that places as much control as possible in the hands of the examinee. In addition, asking specific, behavioral, closed-ended questions about the abuse is much less likely to trigger discomfort and intrusive recall than requesting an open-ended narrative account. Due to the frequently fragmentary nature of recollection of abuse trauma, it is especially important that inquiries be presented in a way that avoids leading and suggestive phrasing.

Areas beyond current impairment and CSA history will need to be covered to sufficiently evaluate the possible relationship between them. Elements of the broader life context in which the abuse occurs—such as level of interpersonal support, reactions to discovery or disclosure of CSA, and adjustment prior to CSA onset—can appreciably ameliorate its adverse long-term consequences. Conversely, and much more commonly, a general atmosphere of neglect, rejection, chaos, and conflict in the social milieu of survivors will greatly aggravate the impact of CSA. Similarly, extensive exploration of survivor strengths and his or her personal and interpersonal resources is an essential component of the assessment process. The more such assets exist, the greater the capacity to resolve the abuse and overcome its long-term debilitating effects.

REFERENCES

Alpert, J.L., Brown, L.S., & Courtois, C.A. (1996). Symptomatic clients and memories of childhood abuse: What the trauma and child sexual abuse literature tells us. In J. Alpert, L.S. Brown, S.J. Ceci, C.A. Courtois, E.F. Loftus, & P.A. Ornstein (Eds.), *Final report of the working group on investigation of memories of childhood abuse* (pp. 15–105). Washington, DC: American Psychological Association.

Alpert, J.L., & Paulson, A. (1990). Graduate-level education and training in child sexual abuse. *Professional Psychology: Research and Practice, 21,* 366–371.

American Psychiatric Association. (1987). *Diagnostic and statistical manual of mental disorders* (3rd ed., Rev.). Washington, DC: Author.

American Psychiatric Association. (1994). *Diagnostic and statistical manual of mental disorders* (4th ed.). Washington, DC: Author.

Anderson, G., Yasenik, L., & Ross, C.A. (1993). Dissociative experiences and disorders among women who identify themselves as sexual abuse survivors. *Child Abuse & Neglect, 17,* 677–686.

Anderson, L.R. (1995, August). *Resources used and problems faced by successful survivors of sexual abuse.* Poster session presented at the 103rd annual convention of the American Psychological Association, New York.

Beitchman, J., Zucker, K., Hood, J., daCosta, G., & Ackman, D. (1991). A review of the short-term effects of childhood sexual abuse. *Child Abuse & Neglect, 16,* 101–118.

Blume, E.S. (1990). *Secret survivors: Uncovering incest and its aftereffects in women.* New York: Wiley.

Briere, J.N. (1995). *Trauma symptom inventory.* Odessa, FL: Psychological Assessment Resources.

Briere, J.N. (1996). *Therapy for adults molested as children* (Rev. 2nd ed.). New York: Springer.

Briere, J.N. (1997). *Psychological assessment of adult posttraumatic states.* Washington, DC: American Psychological Association.

Briere, J.N., & Conte, J. (1993). Self-reported amnesia for adults molested as children. *Journal of Traumatic Stress, 6,* 21–31.

Briere, J.N., & Runtz, M. (1988). Symptomatology associated with childhood sexual victimization in a nonclinical adult sample. *Child Abuse & Neglect, 12,* 51–59.

Briere, J.N., & Runtz, M. (1990). Differential adult symptomatology associated with three types of child abuse histories. *Child Abuse & Neglect, 14,* 357–364.

Briere, J.N., Woo, R., McRae, B., Foltz, J., & Sitzman, R. (1997). Lifetime victimization history, demographics, and clinical status in female psychiatric emergency room patients. *Journal of Nervous and Mental Disease, 185,* 95–101.

Briere, J.N., & Zaidi, L.Y. (1989). Sexual abuse histories and sequelae in female psychiatric emergency room patients. *American Journal of Psychiatry, 146,* 1602–1606.

Brown, D., Scheflin, A., & Hammond, C. (1997). *Memory, trauma, treatment and the law.* New York: Norton.

Brown, L.S. (1995). The therapy client as plaintiff: Clinical and legal issues for the treating therapist. In J.L. Alpert (Ed.), *Sexual abuse recalled: Treating trauma in the era of the recovered memory debate* (pp. 311–336). Northvale, NJ: Jason Aronson.

Browne, A., & Finkelhor, D. (1986). Impact of child sexual abuse: A review of the research. *Psychological Bulletin, 99,* 66–77.

Bryer, J.B., Nelson, B.A., Miller, J.B., & Krol, P.A. (1987). Childhood sexual and physical abuse as factors in adult psychiatric illness. *American Journal of Psychiatry, 144,* 1426–1430.

Buchanan, N.T., Mazzeo, S.E., Grzegorek, J., Romas, A.M., & Fitzgerald, L.F. (1998, August). *Use of computerized MMPI-2 in sexual harassment litigation: A time to use your head instead of the formula.* Paper presented at the 106th annual convention of the American Psychological Association, San Francisco.

Coons, P.M., Bowman, E.S., Pellow, T.A., & Schneider, P. (1989). Post-traumatic aspects of the treatment of sexual abuse and incest. *Psychiatric Clinics of North America, 12,* 325–335.

Courtois, C.A. (1997, August). *Invited address: 1996 award for distinguished contributions to applied psychology as a professional practice.* Paper presented at the American Psychological Association Annual Convention, Chicago.

Dutton, M.A. (1992). *Empowering and healing the battered woman.* New York: Springer.

Elliott, D.M. (1997). Traumatic events: Prevalence and delayed recall in the general population. *Journal of Consulting and Clinical Psychology, 65,* 811–820.

Elliott, D.M., & Briere, J. (1995). Posttraumatic stress associated with delayed recall of sexual abuse: A general population study. *Journal of Traumatic Stress, 8,* 629–647.

Engles, M.L., Moisan, D., & Harris, R. (1994). MMPI indices of childhood trauma among 110 female outpatients. *Journal of Personality Assessment, 63,* 135–147.

Feldman-Summers, S., & Pope, K.S. (1994). The experience of "forgetting" childhood abuse: A national survey of psychologists. *Journal of Consulting and Clinical Psychology, 62,* 636–639.

Finkelhor, D. (1990). Early and long-term effects of child sexual abuse: An update. *Professional Psychology: Research and Practice, 21,* 325–330.

Finkelhor, D., Hotaling, G., Lewis, I.A., & Smith, C. (1990). Sexual abuse in a national survey of adult men and women: Prevalence, characteristics, and risk factors. *Child Abuse & Neglect, 14,* 19–28.

Freyd, J.J. (1996). *Betrayal trauma theory: The logic of forgetting childhood abuse.* Cambridge, MA: Harvard University Press.

Gann, M. (1995). The Rorschach and other projective methods. In J. Ziskin (Ed.), *Coping with psychiatric and psychological testimony* (5th ed., pp. 823–884). Los Angeles: Law and Psychology Press.

Gold, S.N. (1997). Training professional psychologists to treat survivors of childhood sexual abuse. *Psychotherapy, 34,* 365–374.

Gold, S.N., & Brown, L.S. (1997). Therapeutic responses to delayed recall: Beyond recovered memory. *Psychotherapy, 34,* 182–191.

Gold, S.N., Hughes, D.M., & Hohnecker, L. (1992). Degrees of repression of sexual abuse memories. *American Psychologist, 49,* 441–442.

Gold, S.N., Hughes, D.M., & Swingle, J.M. (1996). Characteristics of childhood sexual abuse among female survivors in therapy. *Child Abuse & Neglect, 20,* 323–335.

Goldwater, L., & Duffy, J.F. (1990). Use of MMPI to uncover histories of childhood abuse in adult female psychiatric patients. *Journal of Clinical Psychology, 46,* 392–398.

Herman, J.L. (1992a). Complex PTSD: A syndrome in survivors of prolonged and repeated trauma. *Journal of Traumatic Stress, 5,* 377–391.

Herman, J.L. (1992b). *Trauma and recovery: The aftermath of violence—from domestic abuse to political terror.* New York: Basic Books.

Herman, J.L., Perry, J.C., & van der Kolk, B.A. (1989). Childhood trauma in borderline personality disorder. *American Journal of Psychiatry, 146,* 490–495.

Herman, J.L., & Schatzow, E. (1987). Recovery and verification of memories of childhood sexual trauma. *Psychoanalytic Psychology, 4,* 1–14.

Hinnefeld, B., & Newman, R. (1997). Analysis of the truth and responsibility in mental health practices act and similar proposals. *Professional Psychology: Research and Practice, 28,* 537–543.

Jacobson, A., & Richardson, B. (1987). Assault experiences of 100 psychiatric patients: Evidence of the need for routine inquiry. 138th Annual Meeting of the American Psychiatric Association, (1985, Dallas, TX). *American Journal of Psychiatry, 144,* 908–913.

Karon, B.P., & Widener, A.J. (1997). Repressed memories and World War II: Lest we forget! *Professional Psychology: Research and Practice, 28,* 338–340.

Kendall-Tacket, K., Williams, L.M., & Finkelhor, D. (1993). Impact of sexual abuse on children: A review and synthesis of recent empirical studies. *Psychological Bulletin, 113,* 164–180.

Kluft, R.P. (Ed.). (1990). *Incest-related syndromes of adult psychopathology* (pp. 263–288). Washington, DC: American Psychiatric Press.

Levin, P. (1993). Assessing PTSD with the Rorschach projective technique. In J. Wilson & B. Raphael (Eds.), *International handbook of traumatic stress* (pp. 189–200). New York: Plenum Press.

Lipschitz, D.S., Kaplan, M.L., Sorkenn, J., Chorney, P., & Asnis, G.M. (1996). Childhood abuse, adult assault, and dissociation. *Comprehensive Psychiatry, 37,* 261–266.

Loftus, E.F. (1993). The reality of repressed memories. *American Psychologist, 48,* 518–537.

Loftus, E.F., Polonsky, S., & Fullilove, M.T. (1994). Memories of childhood sexual abuse: Remembering and repressing. *Psychology of Women Quarterly, 18,* 67–84.

Lundberg-Love, P.K., Marmion, S., Ford, K., Geffner, R., & Peacock, L. (1992). The long-term consequences of childhood incest and victimization upon adult women's psychology symptomatology. *Journal of Child Sexual Abuse, 1,* 81–102.

MacFarlane, F., & Waterman, J. (1986). *Sexual abuse of the young child.* New York: Guilford Press.

Masten, A.S., Best, K.M., & Garmezy, N. (1991). Resilience and development: Contributions from the study of children who overcame adversity. *Development and Psychology, 2,* 425–444.

McCann, L., Pearlman, L.A., Sakheim, D.K., & Abrahamson, D.J. (1988). Assessment and treatment of the adult survivor of childhood sexual abuse within a schema framework. In S.M. Sgroi (Ed.), *Vulnerable populations: Evaluation and treatment of sexually abused children and adult survivors* (Vol. 1, pp. 77–101). New York: Lexington Books.

McGrath, E., Keita, G.P., Strickland, B.R., & Russo, N.F. (Eds.). (1990). *Women and depression: Risk factors and treatment.* Washington, DC: American Psychological Association.

Morrow, S.L., & Smith, M.L. (1995). Constructions of survival and coping by women who have survived childhood sexual abuse. *Journal of Consulting and Clinical Psychology, 42,* 23–44.

Nash, M.R., Hulsey, T.L., Sexton, M.C., Harralson, T.L., & Lambert, W. (1993). Long-term sequelae of childhood sexual abuse: Perceived family environment, psychopathology, and dissociation. *Journal of Consulting and Clinical Psychology, 61,* 276–283.

Ofshe, R., & Waters, E. (1994). *Making monsters: False memories, psychotherapy, and sexual hysteria.* New York: Scribner & Sons.

Olio, K. (1996). Are 25% of clinicians using potentially risky therapeutic practices? A review of the logic and methodology of the Poole, Lindsay et al. study. *Journal of Psychiatry and Law, 24,* 277–298.

Pezdek, K., & Roe, C. (1994). Memory for childhood events: How suggestible is it? *Consciousness and Cognition, 3,* 374–387.

Pope, K.S. (1996). Memory, abuse, and science: Questioning claims about the false memory syndrome epidemic. *American Psychologist, 51,* 957–974.

Pope, K.S., & Brown, L.S. (1996). *Recovered memories of abuse: Assessment, therapy forensics.* Washington, DC: American Psychological Association.

Pope, K.S., Butcher, J.N., & Seelen, J. (1993). *The MMPI, MMPI-2, & MMPI-A in court: A practical guide for expert witnesses and attorneys.* Washington, DC: American Psychological Association.

Pope, K.S., & Feldman-Summers, S. (1992). National survey of psychologists' sexual and physical abuse history and their evaluation of training and competence in these areas. *Professional Psychology: Research and Practice, 23,* 353–341.

Pope, K.S., & Tabachnick, B.G. (1995). Recovered memories of abuse among therapy patients: A national survey. *Ethics & Behavior, 5,* 237–248.

Rosewater, L.B. (1985a). Feminist interpretation of traditional testing. In L.B. Rosewater & L.E.A. Walker (Eds.), *Handbook of feminist therapy: Women's issues in psychotherapy* (pp. 266–273). New York: Springer.

Rosewater, L.B. (1985b). Schizophrenic, borderline, or battered. In L.B. Rosewater & L.E.A. Walker (Eds.), *Handbook of feminist therapy: Women's issues in psychotherapy* (pp. 215–225). New York: Springer.

Roth, S., Newman, E., Pelcovitz, D., van der Kolk, B., & Mandel, F.S. (1997). Complex PTSD in victims exposed to sexual and physical abuse: Results from the *DSM-IV* field trial for posttraumatic stress disorder. *Journal of Traumatic Stress, 10,* 539–555.

Russell, D. (1986). *The secret trauma: Incest in the lives of girls and women.* New York: Basic Books.

Salter, A. (1995). *Transforming trauma: A guide to understanding and treating adult survivors of child sexual abuse.* Thousand Oaks, CA: Sage.

Shalev, A.Y. (1996). Stress versus traumatic stress: From acute homeostatic to chronic psychopathology. In B.A. van der Kolk, A.C. McFarlane, & L. Weisareth (Eds.), *Traumatic stress: The effects of overwhelming experience on mind, body, and society* (pp. 77–101). New York: Guilford Press.

Smiley, J. (1991). *A thousand acres.* New York: Knopf.

Truth and Responsibility in Mental Health Practices Act. (1995). State of New Hampshire H.B. 236 to amend New Hampshire Rev. Stat. Ann. 330-A to add a new 330-A.28.

van der Kolk, B.A., Weisaeth, L., & van der Hart, O. (1996). History of trauma in psychiatry. In B.A. van der Kolk, A.C. McFarlane, & L. Weisareth (Eds.), *Traumatic stress: The effects of overwhelming experience on mind, body, and society* (pp. 47–74). New York: Guilford Press.

Walker, E.A., Katon, W.J., Harop-Griffiths, J., Holm, L., Russo, J., & Hickok, L.R. (1988). Relationship of chronic pelvic pain to psychiatric diagnoses and childhood sexual abuse. *American Journal of Psychiatry, 146,* 75–80.

Walker, E.A., Katon, W.J., Roy-Byrne, P.P., Jemlka, R.P., & Russo, J. (1993). Histories of sexual victimization in patients with irritable bowel syndrome or inflammatory bowel disease. *American Journal of Psychiatry, 150,* 1502–1506.

Weiner, I.B., & Hess, A.K. (Eds.). (1987). Handbook of forensic psychology. New York: Wiley Interscience.

Williams, L.M. (1994). Recall of childhood trauma: A prospective study of women's memories of childhood sexual abuse. *Journal of Consulting and Clinical Psychology, 62,* 1167–1176.

Williams, L.M. (1996). Recovered memories of abuse in women with documented child victimization histories. *Journal of Traumatic Stress, 8,* 649–673.

Wright, L. (1994). *Remembering Satan: A case of recovered memory and the shattering of an American family.* New York: Knopf.

Yapko, M. (1994). *Suggestions of abuse: True and false memories of childhood sexual trauma.* New York: Simon & Schuster.

Author Index

Abel, G.E., 65
Abel, G.G., 367
Aber, J., 297
Abidin, R.R., 136, 139, 148, 164, 173
Abrahamson, D.J., 393
Abramson, L., 297
Achenbach, T., 134, 166, 189, 230, 296, 298, 352
Ackman, D., 390, 394
Adams, D., 28, 30
Adams, J.A., 224, 229
Adelman, H.S., 54
Adelman, R.D., 271, 272, 280, 282
Adkinson, D.R., 255
Afrank, J., 291, 300
Ageton, S.S., 212
Agnew, R., 103
Ainsworth, M.D.S., 288, 294
Alessi, J.J., 347, 348
Alexander, J.F., 25
Aljazireh, L., 214, 215
Allen, B., 348
Allen, J., 133, 297
Allgier, E.R., 212
Alpert, J.L., 65, 390, 394
Altemeier, W.A., 294, 295
Alterman, A.I., 369
Alvarez, W., 257
Alvi, S., 116, 249
Aman, C., 215, 216
Amaya-Jackson, L., 216
Ammerman, R.T., 3, 4, 6, 7, 128, 130, 131, 132, 161
Anderson, G., 15, 167, 391

Anderson, L.R., 401
Anderson, S.J., 370
Anderson, S.M., 323, 327
Andrews, F.M., 255
Andrews, L.K., 230
Anglin, K., 139
Ansell, P., 279, 280
Appelbaum, P.S., 41
Aragona, J.A., 298
Araji, S., 185
Arguedas, C.C., 77, 78
Arias, I., 33, 34, 325, 329
Arrowood, A.A., 190
Arroyo, W., 214, 351
Ash, P., 144, 145
Asher, S.R., 303, 306
Asnis, G.M., 391
Atcheson, J.D., 367
Atkins, D., 300
Atkins, M., 3, 10, 12, 216, 230
Atkinson, L., 145
Attala, J., 250, 331
Aubrey, M., 259
August, R.L., 236
Austin, G., 354
Azar, S.T., 48, 50, 51, 53, 63, 64, 65, 66, 133, 137, 147, 159, 161, 165, 166, 167, 168

Babcock, J., 38
Bachman, R., 107, 108, 109, 114, 115, 116, 118
Baily, T.F., 292
Baily, W.H., 292

413

Bakermans-Kranenburg, M.J., 289
Bala, N., 368
Baldwin, A., 12
Baldwin, C., 12
Baldwin, L.M., 63
Balla, D.A., 14
Barahal, R.M., 297
Barbaree, H.E., 65, 367, 368, 369
Bard, M., 344
Barling, J., 33, 326
Barnett, D., 171, 289, 295, 297, 299, 302
Barnett, E.R., 348
Baron, L., 185
Barth, K.L., 224
Barth, R.P., 221
Batchelor, J., 297
Baumrind, D., 298
Bavolek, S.J., 133, 136, 295
Baxter, V.A., 248
Bays, J., 188, 189, 200
Beach, S.R.H., 34
Beatty, S.B., 139
Becerra, R.M., 49, 56, 94
Beck, A.T., 167, 171, 230, 255
Becker, J.V., 65, 368, 369, 371, 372, 376,
    378, 379
Behrman, R.E., 308
Beitchman, J., 390, 394
Belden, L., 212
Bellack, A.S., 131
Belsky, J., 4, 11, 63, 128, 129, 167, 287, 289,
    301
Benbow, S.M., 273
Benedek, E.P., 61, 222, 229
Benefield, R.G., 26
Benjet, C.L., 48, 51, 53, 64, 65, 161
Benoit, J.L., 370
Berg, B.J., 325
Berger, A.M., 94, 102
Beriama, A., 3, 10, 12
Berk, R.A., 249
Berk, S., 249
Berkowitz, S., 65
Berlin, P.M., 287
Berlinger, L., 188, 189, 200
Berman, H., 346
Bernard, J.L., 256
Bernard, M.L., 256
Berndt, T.J., 299
Berns, S., 325
Bersoff, D.N., 51
Berstein, A.C., 197

Besbarov, D.J., 56
Besharov, D.J., 128, 132, 142
Bess, B.H., 61
Bessmer, J., 134, 165
Best, K.M., 401
Bhate, S.R., 371
Bhatt, B., 221
Bhosley, G., 325
Biaggio, M.K., 254
Bigelow, K.M., 127, 128, 131, 150, 158, 161,
    162, 165, 166, 167, 171, 174, 178
BigFoot, S.S., 65
Billings, L.L., 65
Binder, J.L., 24
Bird, S., 367
Bisanz, J., 215
Bishop, D.S., 63
Black, M., 159, 160
Blackman, J., 92, 93
Blake, D.D., 230, 237
Blake, E.T., 224
Blakemore, P., 120
Blanchard, E.B., 65
Blashfield, R.K., 13
Blaske, D.M., 370
Blau, T.H., 53
Blehar, M.C., 294
Blick, L.C., 201
Blume, E.S., 394
Blumenthal, M.D., 255
Blush, G., 196
Boat, B., 199, 201, 214, 215, 228
Bochnak, E., 74, 75, 77, 81
Bogat, G.A., 65, 294
Bohmer, S., 300
Bolocofsky, D.N., 52
Boney-McCoy, S., 32, 97, 139, 245, 246, 248,
    249, 330
Bonner, B.L., 130, 131
Bonner, B-L., 65
Borduin, C.M., 370
Borgman, R., 295
Bornstein, G.K., 215
Borodin, E.S., 24
Boruch, R., 3, 10, 12
Bottoms, B.L., 215, 216
Boulette, T.R., 323, 327
Bourne, R., 94
Bousha, D., 298
Boussy, C.A., 20
Bowden, B., 369
Bowman, E.S., 398

Boyle, M.H., 354
Bradley, A., 61, 187
Bradley, R., 4, 166, 304
Brannon, J.M., 370
Brant, J., 56
Brassard, M., 3, 288, 289, 290
Braunling-McMorrow, D.B., 136
Braunling-Morrow, D., 165
Breckman, R.S., 271, 272, 279, 280, 282
Brekke, J.S., 245, 330
Bresee, P., 61
Bretherton, I., 289
Briere, J., 34, 304, 305, 306, 352, 391, 394, 395, 396, 398, 401, 402, 404, 408
Broadhurst, D.D., 12, 100, 104, 211, 302
Broderick, J.E., 332
Brody, N., 16
Brodzinsky, D.M., 161, 168
Bronfman, E., 289, 294
Brookoff, D., 35
Brooks, C.M., 50
Brosig, C.L., 140
Broughton, D., 189
Brown, A.L., 214, 215
Brown, D., 404
Brown, L.S., 390, 391, 394, 397, 398, 402, 404
Brown, P.D., 24
Brown, S.E., 306
Browne, A., 4, 40, 78, 81, 82, 110, 185, 244, 253, 259, 392, 394
Browning, J., 246
Bruck, M., 54, 61, 62, 186, 198, 202
Brunner, J.F., 139
Brunnquell, D., 294, 295
Bryer, J.B., 391
Brygger, M., 246, 247, 329
Buchanan, N.T., 396, 402
Budd, K.S., 48, 63, 161, 162
Bulcroft, R.A., 246
Bulkley, J.A., 169, 170
Bullock, L., 347
Bumby, K.M., 140, 142
Bunshaft, D., 64
Burdick, N., 17
Burgdorf, K., 56
Burgess, A.W., 108
Burnaam, M.A., 97
Burt, M.R., 212
Bush, B.A., 161
Buss, A.H., 254
Bussiere, M.T., 374, 379

Butcher, J.N., 132, 133, 145, 396
Butler, S., 145

Cabral, R.J., 295, 304
Caesar, P.L., 26
Caffaro, J., 198
Caldwell, B., 166, 304
Caldwell, R.A., 65, 294
Callaghan, M., 237
Callahan, M.R., 331
Cameron, G., 344
Campbell, D., 252
Campbell, J., 252
Campbell, J.A., 251
Campbell, J.C., 244, 246, 257
Campbell, M., 297
Campbell, R.V., 161
Campis, L.K., 138
Cantos, A.L., 29, 41
Capaidi, D.M., 29, 38, 39
Card, J.A., 184
Carlson, B.E., 348
Carlson, C.I., 139
Carroll, N.E., 212
Carter, A.S., 228
Cascardi, M., 31, 35, 37, 40, 246
Caspi, A., 288, 329
Cassady, L., 348
Cassidy, D.J., 214, 215
Cassidy, J., 298
Cassisi, J.E., 131
Castellan, J.M., 297
Cattell, R.B., 295
Caulfield, M.B., 245
Cavallero, L., 48, 51, 64, 65
Cavanaugh, J., 187, 191, 193, 194
Cazenave, N.A., 117
Ceci, S.J., 54, 61, 62, 186, 198, 202, 214, 215, 216
Chaffin, M., 187
Champion, M.A., 215
Chan, D., 300
Chandler, R.M., 140, 142
Chatoor, I., 297
Cherniss, D.S., 297
Chesler, P., 261, 356
Chilamkurti, C., 131
Chiodo, G.T., 274
Chorney, P., 391
Christensen, A., 329
Christopher, J.S., 127, 129, 137
Christopoulos, C., 300

Cicchetti, D., 4, 11, 13, 14, 16, 18, 128, 129, 142, 143, 171, 228, 289, 292, 295, 297, 299, 300, 302, 346
Clark, J., 171
Clark, L.A., 16, 17
Claussen, A.H., 158, 159, 288, 289, 302, 303
Clayton, R.N., 224
Coates, C.L., 38
Coatsworth, J.D., 369
Coffman, S., 28
Cohen, S., 138, 167
Cohler, B., 295
Cohn, D.A., 288, 300
Coie, J., 303
Coll, C., 17
Collins, C., 228
Columbus, M., 133
Colvin, A., 166
Comerly, S., 227
Conaway, L.P., 127, 129, 130, 131, 137, 168
Conerly, S., 196
Conn-Caffaro, A., 198
Connell, D.B., 288, 289
Conte, J., 188, 193, 195, 199, 391, 398
Contrath, T.B., 224
Coohey, C., 294
Coolahan, K., 17
Coons, P.M., 398
Cope, J., 250
Cornell, C.P., 103
Corson, J., 290, 309
Cortes, R.M., 346
Corwin, D.L., 188, 189, 200
Courtois, C.A., 391, 394
Coury, D., 300, 301
Cox, A., 96
CoyleCoolahan, K., 171
Coyne, J., 136, 147
Cozby, P.C., 93
Craig, R.J., 299
Crane, R.S., 137, 254
Crawford, M., 344
Crichton, L., 294
Crittenden, P.M., 158, 159, 288, 289, 294, 295, 298, 302, 303
Crnic, K., 17
Crocker, P.L., 74, 76, 84
Cromwell, R.L., 13
Cronbach, L.J., 17
Crosby, L., 29, 38, 39
Crowell, N.A., 108
Crowne, D.P., 253

Cummings, E.M., 347, 348
Cunningham, A.H., 346
Cunningham-Rathner, J., 378
Curley, A.D., 32, 255, 331
Cytryn, L., 303

Dachman, R.S., 165
DaCosta, G., 390, 394
Dadds, M.A., 165, 174
Dahlstrom, W.G., 132, 133, 145
Daleiden, E.L., 371, 379
Daly, M., 112
Damon, L., 184, 189, 194
Dancu, C.V., 257
Daro, D., 157
David, R., 297
Davidson, H., 290, 308, 309
Davidson, T., 347
Davidson, W.S., 65, 294
Davies, D., 308
Davies, P.T., 347
Davis, J., 353, 368
Davis, T.C., 212
Dawud, S., 346
Dawud-Noursi, S., 19
Day, B.T., 168
Dean, D., 309
DeAngelo, E., 289
Deblinger, E., 216, 230
Deisher, R.W., 369, 371
DeKeseredy, W.S., 116, 249, 256
DeLange, C., 344, 347
Delgado, L.E., 174
DeLoache, J.S., 214, 215
Demaris, A., 253
DeoGaudioWeiss, A., 171
DePanfilis, D., 167
DePaola, L., 15, 167
Derezotes, D.S., 141
Derogatis, L.R., 132, 147, 163
DeRoma, V.M., 164
De Saix, C., 295
Deschner, J.P., 251, 258
DeVellis, R., 257
DeVoe, E., 201
De Young, M., 195
DiBlasio, F.A., 157
DiClemente, C.C., 26
DiClemente, R.J., 95, 98
Dietrich, K.N., 136
Dingwall, R., 92
Dishion, T., 134, 306

Dixon, F., 216, 230
Dobash, R., 249
Dobash, R.E., 27, 38, 112, 249, 357
Dobash, R.P., 27, 38, 112
Doctor, R.M., 158, 161, 165, 167, 171, 174, 178
Doggett, M., 370
Domon, L., 227
Donaldson, M., 214, 215
Downey, G., 301
Doyle, C., 161
Droegemueller, W., 157, 169
Dubowitz, H., 159, 160, 161
Duffy, J.F., 396
Dumas, J.E., 138
Durfee, M., 224, 227
Durkee, A., 254
Dutton, D., 35, 246, 255, 323, 343, 357
Dutton, M.A., 248, 257, 258, 396, 407
D'Zurilla, T.J., 138

Earp, J.A., 257
East, P.L., 136
Echlin, C., 343, 355, 356
Eddleman, J., 136, 165
Eddy, J.M., 139
Edelbrock, C., 166, 189, 296, 298, 352
Edelson, J., 323, 329, 343
Edleson, J.L., 246, 247
Edmunds, C.N., 119
Edwall, G.E., 356
Edwards, B., 160, 168
Edwards, D., 134, 165
Edwards, L.A., 133
Egan, J., 297
Egeland, B., 157, 158, 159, 287, 288, 289, 294, 295, 297, 298, 303
Egston, C., 228
Ehrensaft, M.K., 31
Elder, G.H. Jr., 288
Eldredge, R., 296, 299
Elliott, D.M., 398, 404
Elliott, F.A., 256
Elliott, S.N., 140
Ellis, J.T., 140
Ellison, J., 252
Elmer, E., 297
Emery, R.E., 65, 93, 96, 102, 259, 300
England, P., 62
Engles, M.L., 396
Enos, F.W., 224
Ensom, R., 218

Epstein, N., 63, 135
Erbaugh, J., 255
Erickson, M., 157, 158, 159, 287, 288, 289, 297, 298, 303
Esplin, P.W., 214, 215, 228
Estes, A., 134, 139
Eth, S., 62, 214, 351
Everett, D., 224
Everson, M.D., 199, 201, 214, 215, 228
Everstein, D., 27
Everstein, L., 27
Ewigman, B., 134, 135, 160, 161
Ewing, C.P., 259
Eyberg, S.M., 134, 148, 165, 166, 298

Fagot, B.I., 295, 299
Faigman, D.L., 40
Fairbanks, L., 214, 216
Faller, K., 169, 193, 194, 201
Falsey, S., 295
Famularo, R., 64
Fantuzzo, J., 3, 7, 10, 12, 15, 17, 18, 19, 20, 48, 131, 167, 171, 251, 344
Farley, G.K., 299
Farris, A.M., 300
Faust, D., 49, 52, 145
Fazio, W., 80, 260
Fehrenbach, P.A., 369, 371
Feldbau, S., 24, 37
Feldman, R., 304
Feldmans-Summers, S., 390
Feldmeth, J., 190
Felice, M.E., 136
Feller, J.N., 169, 170
Felsman, J.K., 140
Fenton, T., 64
Fernandez, A., 39
Ferraro, K.J., 34
Feshbach, N.D., 135, 136
Fick, A.C., 346
Field, J., 322
Finkel, M.R., 224
Finkelhor, D., 95, 97, 102, 120, 170, 185, 189, 211, 212, 217, 218, 221, 228, 236, 245, 271, 272, 273, 274, 390, 391, 392, 394
Finlay, J., 354
Fiora-Gormally, N., 76, 77, 78, 85
Firestone, P., 218
Fischler, R.S., 54
Fiske, J.A., 367
Fitch, P., 303

Fitzgerald, L.F., 396, 402
Flannery, P.J., 212
Fleeson, J., 299
Fleischman, M.J., 64
Flynn, J.M., 134, 148
Foa, E., 216, 230, 257
Fogarty, L., 188, 193, 195, 199
Foley, M.A., 214
Folkman, S., 138, 168
Follingstad, D.R., 325
Foltz, J., 391
Ford, K., 396
Ford, M.E., 370, 371
Forehand, R., 134, 165, 370
Forman, B.D., 228
Foster, S.L., 17, 18, 137
Fox, R.A., 162, 163
Foy, D., 39, 187
Fraiberg, S., 294, 297, 308
Francis, J.M., 17
Franklin, A., 304
Franks, D., 254
Fraser, B., 50, 169
Frederick, C., 214, 216
Freeman-Longo, R.E., 367
Freidman, W.J., 214
Fremorrow, W.J., 214, 215
Freyd, J.J., 392, 407
Friedman, D.H., 27, 29, 254
Friedman, V.M., 190
Friedrich, W., 189
Frieze, I.H., 82, 248
Fritz, G.S., 95
Fromuth, M.E., 95
Frothingham, S., 378
Fryer, G.E., 369
Fuhrman, T., 137
Fuhrmann, G., 48, 51, 64, 65
Fullilove, M.T., 398
Fullmer, A., 214
Fung, T., 294
Futa, K.T., 140, 142

Gable, S., 159, 160, 161
Gaines, R., 295
Galvin, M.R., 4
Gangley, A.L., 81
Ganley, A., 27, 254, 255
Gann, M., 396
Garbarino, A.C., 306
Garbarino, J., 56, 94, 130, 167, 288, 290,
     299, 300, 303, 304, 306, 307, 308

Garcia, J., 215
Gardner, R., 190
Garland, M.J., 274
Garmezy, N., 401
Gartner, R., 344
Gaudin, J.M., 164
Gaudin, J.M. Jr., 288, 304
Gearan, P., 256
Geddie, L.F., 65
Geffner, R., 93, 254, 396
Gefner, R., 245
Geiselman, R.S., 215
Gellen, M.I., 38
Gellert, G.A., 224
Gelles, R., 3, 33, 73, 92, 94, 95, 96, 103, 108,
     111, 112, 243, 244, 245, 246, 247, 248,
     249, 254, 255, 273, 287, 300, 304, 344,
     346, 350
George, C., 299
Germain, B., 290
Gershater, R.M., 161
Gershater-Molko, R.M., 157
Gibbens, T.C., 62
Gidycz, C.A., 34, 212
Gil, D.G., 92, 97, 99
Gilbert, M.T., 160
Gilbert, N., 221
Gilkerson, L., 17
Giller, E.L., 216
Gillespie, C.K., 74, 77, 78, 80, 81, 85
Gillian, G., 94
Gioglio, G., 120
Giovanonni, J.M., 49, 56, 94
Gitlin, K., 296
Glaser, D., 228
Glaser, G.H., 354
Glaser, J.B., 224
Gleason, W.J., 39
Gleberman, L., 258, 332
Glutting, J.J., 16
Godkin, M., 274
Goh, D.S., 187, 191, 193, 194
Gold, P.E., 214
Gold, R.G., 256
Gold, S.N., 390, 391, 397, 398
Goldfried, M.R., 24
Golding, J.M., 97, 229
Goldstein, D., 37
Goldstein, M.Z., 3, 7
Goldwater, L., 396
Gondolf, E.W., 247, 252, 253
Gonzales, L., 61

Goodman, G., 61, 62, 197, 202, 214, 215, 216, 229, 231, 357
Goodman-Delabunty, J., 51
Goodson, B.D., 344, 347
Goodwin, D., 378, 379
Goodwin, J., 195
Gordon, B.N., 214, 215
Gordon, M., 54, 75
Gordon, R.A., 132
Gorsuch, R.L., 17, 18
Gortner, E., 325
Gottfredson, D.M., 252
Gottfredson, S.D., 252
Gottman, J., 38, 258, 325
Gould, R., 295
Grace, N., 140
Graham, F., 371
Graham, J.R., 132, 133, 145
Graham, P., 92
Grambsch, P., 189
Grasley, C., 362
Graves, H.C.B., 224
Gray, A.S., 374, 382
Gray, J., 218, 219, 226
Gray-Little, B., 245, 251
Grayson, M., 255
Green, A.H., 295
Green, L.F., 17
Green, W.H., 297
Greenbaum, C., 346
Greene, B.F., 127, 128, 131, 150, 158, 161, 162, 165, 166, 167, 170
Greenspan, S.I., 294, 295
Gries, L.T., 187, 191, 193, 194
Grisso, T., 48, 51, 52, 53, 63, 64, 65, 66
Grossman, H.J., 13
Grossnickle, W.F., 250
Grotevant, H.D., 139
Groth, A.N., 379
Gruber, C., 352
Gruber, E., 95, 98
Grunebaum, H., 295
Grzegorek, J., 396, 402
Gurainick, M., 17
Gurley, D., 324
Guttmann, E., 130, 290, 303
Guyer, M.J., 144, 145
Gwartney-Gibbs, P., 300

Haddad, P.M., 273
Haggarty, D.J., 50, 52
Haith, M.M., 229

Haley, J., 306
Hall, E.R., 212
Hall, N.W., 127
Hally, C., 162
Hamberger, L.K., 24, 35, 37, 38, 256
Hamby, S.L., 32, 139, 245, 246, 248, 249, 251, 330
Hamilton, J., 228
Hammer, M., 304
Hammerschlag, M.R., 224
Hammond, C., 404
Hampton, G., 17
Hampton, R.L., 99
Hann, D.M., 346
Hans, V.P., 51
Hansen, D.J., 4, 127, 129, 130, 131, 132, 136, 137, 138, 140, 141, 142, 147, 150, 160, 162, 164, 168
Hansen, I., 65
Hanson, R.K., 371, 373, 374, 379
Hanusa, D.R., 254, 255
Hardy, D.B., 3, 288
Harkness, W.L., 212
Harop-Griffiths, J., 391
Harper, K., 224, 229
Harralson, T.L., 394
Harris, G.T., 379
Harris, R., 370, 373, 396
Harrold, M., 161
Harrop, J.W., 304
Hart, B., 322
Hart, J.S., 295
Hart, S., 3, 288, 289, 290
Harter, S., 230, 296, 299
Hartman, A., 167
Hastings, J.E., 24, 35, 37, 38, 256
Hastings, T., 370
Haugaard, J.J., 91, 93, 94, 95, 96, 99, 102
Hause, E.S., 325
Haynes, M.R., 367, 368, 369, 372, 374
Haynes, S.N., 17, 18
Haynes-Seman, C., 295
Head, K.B., 255
Hearn, K., 347, 348
Hecht, D.B., 129, 130, 131, 137, 141
Hegedus, A.M., 369
Heger, A.H., 189
Heinze, M.C., 48, 65
Hekimian, E., 137, 166, 168
Helfer, R.E., 295
Heller, K., 138, 167
Helmreich, R.L., 255

Hembrooke, H., 61
Hemphill, P., 370
Henderson, C.R., 294
Henggeler, S.W., 65, 370
Hennessy, K., 142, 143
Henry, D., 230, 237
Herman, J.L., 392, 393, 398
Herrenkohl, E.C., 289
Herrenkohl, R.C., 289
Hersen, M., 3, 4, 6, 7, 131, 132
Hershkowitz, I., 214, 215, 228
Herzberger, S., 140
Hess, A.K., 402
Hess, P., 65
Hevman, R.E., 35
Hewitt, S., 189, 190, 201
Heyman, R.E., 27, 30, 33, 37, 139, 247
Hibbard, R.A., 191, 195
Hickok, L.R., 391
Hillard, J.R., 39
Hilliker, D.R., 371, 379
Hinnefeld, B., 390
Hirsch, R.A., 51, 52
Hoagwood, K., 11, 12
Hoberman, H.M., 138, 167
Hobson, W.F., 379
Hodges, K.K., 303
Hoekelman, R.T., 195
Hoffman, R.A., 38
Hoffman-Plotkin, D., 296, 297, 299
Hoffmeister, J.K., 295
Hoge, S.K., 52, 53
Hoglund, C.L., 306
Hohnecker, L., 398
Holden, G.W., 133
Holdsworth, M.J., 48, 63, 161, 162
Hollingsworth, E.L., 297
Holm, L., 391
Holmbeck, G.N., 137
Holtzworth-Munroe, A., 25, 139, 244, 252, 256
Hood, E., 145
Hood, J., 390, 394
Hops, J., 332
Horowitz, M., 257
Hosokawa, M.C., 134, 135
Hotaling, G., 211, 236, 244, 256, 258, 350, 391
Housecamp, B.M., 39
Howe, A.C., 140
Howes, C., 296, 299

Hubert, J., 297
Hudson, S.M., 367, 368, 369
Hudson, W.W., 250, 331
Huffman, M.L.C., 214, 215, 216
Hufton, I.W., 302
Hughes, D.M., 391, 398
Hughes, H., 93, 245, 344, 346, 347
Huguley, S., 103
Hulsey, T.L., 394
Hunter, J.A., 368, 371, 372, 378, 379
Hurley, P., 346, 357
Hurvis, S., 171
Hutchinson, G., 25
Hutchinson, M.A., 81
Huynen, K.B., 165
Hwalek, M., 274
Hymel, S., 299

Iannotti, R.J., 348
Ingram, D.L., 224
Isaac, C., 368

Jackson, D.H., 295
Jacobs, G., 137
Jacobs, W.L., 369
Jacobson, A., 391
Jacobson, N., 38, 41, 258, 325
Jacobvitz, D., 289
Jaffe, P., 227, 300, 308, 343, 344, 347, 348, 350, 353, 354, 356, 361, 362
James, D.P.H., 218, 219, 226
Jampole, L., 228
Jason, M.J., 224
Jemlka, R.P., 391
Jenkins, R., 17
Jennings, K.T., 198
Jensen, B.L., 38
Jensen, P.S., 11, 12
Jensen, R.F., 56
Johannson, M.A., 29
John, R., 258, 332
Johnson, C.F., 379
Johnson, J.H., 136
Johnson, M.K., 214
Johnson, M.P., 30
Jones, A., 77
Jones, D., 61, 62, 185, 187, 190, 199
Jones, M., 38
Jordan, S.B., 77, 78
Jouriles, E.N., 93, 246, 300, 326
Joyce, S., 300

Kadushin, A., 298
Kaemingk, K.L., 378
Kaemmer, B., 132, 133, 145
Kahn, R.L., 255
Kalichman, S.C., 128, 132, 140, 142, 253
Kallio, E., 253
Kalmuss, D., 300, 350
Kamarck, T., 138, 167
Kanda, M.B., 223
Kanner, A.D., 136, 147
Kantor, G.K., 35, 36
Kao, B.T., 288
Kaplan, H.B., 255
Kaplan, M., 369
Kaplan, M.G., 136
Kaplan, M.L., 391
Kaplan, M.S., 371, 376, 378, 379
Karon, B.P., 398
Kaslow, F., 41
Kates, M., 344
Katon, W.J., 391
Katz, B., 212
Katz, R.C., 370
Katz, S.M., 228
Katz-Garris, L., 369
Kaufman, J., 299
Kaufman, K.L., 65, 130, 131, 132, 252, 300,
    301, 371, 379
Kaufman, K.S., 163
Kavanagh, K., 295, 299
Kavoussi, R.J., 369
Kazdin, A.E., 168
Keenan, J.M., 215
Keita, G.P., 392
Kelley, M.L., 140
Kelly, J.A., 128, 129, 138, 140
Kelly, L., 34
Kelly, R., 61, 187
Kelly, T.P., 371
Kempe, C.H., 157, 169, 300, 301
Kempe, R.S., 300, 301
Kempton, T., 370
Kendall-Tackett, K.A., 218, 228, 390
Kennedy, W.A., 369, 370
Kenning, M., 291, 300
Kerslake, A., 297
Kessler, M.L., 127, 128, 131, 150, 158, 161,
    162, 165, 167, 171, 174, 178
Kilili, S., 161, 162, 170
Killip, S., 353, 361
Kilpatrick, A.C., 164, 288, 304

Kilpatrick, D.G., 119
Kim, S., 369
Kimmel, D.C., 138
King, C., 252
King, G.A., 135
Kinports, K., 76, 78, 79
Kinscherff, R., 64
Kirker, W.S., 215
Kivlahan, C., 160
Klatt, H.J., 13
Kline, D.F., 295
Kline, J., 303
Klingman, L.R., 212
Kluft, R.P., 392
Knapp, S.J., 54
Knight, R.A., 371
Knodson, S., 224, 229
Knutson, J.F., 93, 94, 102
Koelling, R., 215
Koeppl, G.K., 228
Kolko, D.J., 128, 130, 138, 141, 168
Koocher, G.P., 7
Kopper, B.A., 227
Koselka, M., 378
Koss, M.P., 34, 212
Kovacs, M., 230
Koverola, C., 160, 168, 187, 189
Kraft, S., 300
Kramer, D.G., 224
Krasner, W., 212
Krauss, E., 74, 75, 77, 81
Krebs, S., 196, 200
Kriegler, J.A., 230, 237
Krispin, O., 346
Krol, P.A., 391
Krueger, R.F., 329
Krugman, M.K., 289
Krugman, R.D., 289, 369
Kubany, E.S., 17, 18
Kuhl, A.F., 38
Kuiper, N.A., 215

Lachar, D., 352
Lachs, M.S., 271, 272
Lamb, M.E., 19, 214, 215, 228, 346
Lamb, S., 226
Lambert, L., 15, 167
Lambert, N.M., 14
Lambert, W., 394
Lamberty, G., 17
Land, C., 160

Landenberger, K., 257
Lane, S., 368
Lang, A.R., 227
Lang, R., 189
Langhinrichsen, J., 31, 37, 246
Lanyon, R.I., 49, 64
Larson, B., 370
Larus, D.M., 214, 215
LaTaillade, J.J., 38
Launius, M.H., 38
Lauretti, A., 63, 64, 65, 66, 159
Lawrence, E., 40, 247
Lawrence, P.S., 255
Lawrence, R., 274
Laws, D.R., 65
Lawson, L., 187
Layzer, J.I., 344, 347
Lazarus, R.S., 136, 138, 147, 168
Le, P.T., 140, 142
Ledingham, J.E., 133, 299
Lee, A., 118
Lehmann, P., 345, 350, 352
Leichter, D., 4
Leippe, M.R., 214, 229
Leivenluft, R.F., 50, 52
Leonard, K.E., 36
Leong, D.J., 38
Leschied, A.W., 354
Leske, G., 138, 167
Letourneau, C., 135
Leventhal, J.M., 228
Levesque, D.A., 254
Levin, P., 396
Levy, B., 243
Levy, R., 49
Lewandowski, L.A., 257
Lewis, B.Y., 250
Lewis, D.O., 4, 306, 354, 369, 370
Lewis, I.A., 211, 236, 391
Libai, D., 61
Lieb, R., 367
Lieberman, A.F., 294
Ligezinsky, M., 218
Limandri, B.J., 274
Limber, S., 61, 142, 143, 144, 145
Lindholm, K.J., 99
Lindquist, U.C., 344
Lindsey, M., 38
Linney, J.A., 370, 371
Linton, M., 215
Linz, D., 255
Lipschitz, D.S., 391

Litwins, N., 134
Locke, H.J., 138
Lodico, M.A., 95, 98
Loding, B., 63, 64, 65, 66
Loeber, R., 306
Loftus, E.F., 390, 398
Lohr, J.M., 35, 37
Long, S., 227
Lorey, F., 346
Loseke, D.R., 249
Lourie, R.S., 297
Lowe, T., 229
Loyd, B.H., 164
Lubetski, M.J., 4, 6
Lucey, K.P., 379
Lundberg-Love, P.K., 396
Lundquist, L.M., 131, 137, 140, 141, 142
Lusk, R., 189
Luster, T., 12
Lutz, M.N., 10
Lutzker, J.R., 127, 128, 130, 131, 132, 136,
    150, 157, 158, 160, 161, 162, 165, 166,
    167, 171, 174, 178
Lutzker, S.Z., 136, 165
Lyman, R.D., 138
Lyna, P.R., 224
Lynch, A.E., 255
Lynch, M., 11, 16, 18, 128, 129
Lyon, E., 348
Lyon, T., 186
Lyons-Ruth, K., 288, 289, 294, 295

MacEachran, A., 362
MacEwen, K.E., 326
MacFarlane, F., 390
MacFarlane, K., 190, 196, 200, 227
MacMillan, V.M., 127, 131, 132, 136, 137,
    138, 140, 150, 160, 162, 164, 168
Macolini, R.M., 291, 300
Macpherson, S., 74, 75, 77, 78, 80, 81, 82,
    84
MacWhinney, B., 215
Mae, R., 344
Magdol, L., 329
Magnatta, M., 145
Magura, S., 163, 295, 304
Main, M., 298, 299
Maiuro, R.D., 254
Malcoe, L.H., 118
Malinoski-Rummell, R., 4, 130, 131
Mallouh, C., 306
Malone, J., 31, 33, 41, 247, 350

Mandel, F.S., 392
Mandel, U., 166
Mangelsdorf, S., 289
Manheimer, H., 295
Manion, I., 160, 168, 218
Manly, J.T., 171
Mann, B.J., 370
Mantooth, C.M., 254
Manz, P., 17, 19
March, J.S., 216
Marcus, S., 3, 10, 12
Margolin, G., 258, 329, 332
Marlowe, D., 253
Marmion, S., 396
Marshall, L., 251, 323, 324, 325, 343, 349, 353, 355
Marshall, W.L., 65, 368, 369
Martin, D., 33, 34, 246, 254, 331
Martin, H.P., 297
Martin, J.A., 298
Martin, S.R., 307, 309
Martinez, C.R. Jr., 18, 19
Martino, T., 15, 167
Mash, E.H., 64
Mash, E.J., 131
Mason, J.W., 216
Masten, A.S., 401
Matarazzo, J.D., 51, 52
Matson, S., 367
Matthews, K.L., 136
Mauger, P.A., 255
Mayhew, D., 215
Mazzeo, S.E., 396, 402
Mazzuacco, M., 132
McAdoo, H., 12, 17
McArthur, C., 13, 14
McCann, L., 393
McCarthy, D., 299
McCleery, J., 300, 301
McCord, J., 187
McCord, L., 61
McCormak, W.M., 224
McCormick, A., 28
McCurdy, D., 157
McCurdy, K., 171
McDermott, P., 10, 13, 14, 16, 17, 19
McEachran, A., 6, 127, 128, 129, 131, 132, 150
McFarlane, A.C., 216
McFarlane, J., 347
McGee, R.A., 289, 290, 291, 292, 306
McGeehan, D., 348

McGimpsev, B.J., 158, 167
McGimsey, J.F., 165
McGrath, E., 392
McGraw, J.M., 61, 187, 199
McIntosh, S.R., 250, 331
McIntyre, J., 218
McKay, E.J., 344
McKnew, D., 303
McLaughlin, J.A., 295
McLeer, S.V., 210, 216, 230, 237
McMahon, M., 27
McMahon, R., 134, 139, 165
McMillian, M.H., 50, 52
McMullen, J.G., 290
McNeely, R.L., 244
McNeil, J.S., 258
McNeill, M., 259
McQuiston, M., 185, 190
McRae, B., 391
McSweeney, M., 250, 331
Meddin, B.J., 65
Meehl, P.E., 13, 14, 17
Megson, D.A., 165
Mehm, J.G., 94, 102
Mehrabian, A., 135
Melton, G.B., 49, 50, 51, 52, 54, 61, 62, 66, 142, 143, 144, 145, 290, 308, 310
Mendelson, M., 255
Mendez, J., 18, 19
Menzies, R.J., 64
Merchant, A., 300
Merikangas, K.R., 39
Mermelstein, R., 138, 167
Merriam, K., 28
Merry, S.N., 230
Messick, S., 16, 17, 19
Metzner, J.L., 369
Meyer, J.B., 369
Meyer, L.C., 212
Meyer, S.L., 26, 28, 33, 331
Meyers, L.E.B., 188, 189, 200
Michelli, J., 229
Mickey, M.R., 219
Miller, A., 298, 303
Miller, B.A., 255
Miller, B.S., 214, 229
Miller, C.M., 214, 215
Miller, J.B., 391
Miller, J.K., 54
Miller, N., 349, 353
Miller, W.R., 26
Miller-Hewitt, S., 349, 353

Milloy, C.D., 380
Milner, J.S., 6, 64, 131, 132, 144, 148, 162,
    163, 256, 261, 295, 379
Minuchin, S., 306
Misch, P., 368
Mishkin, B., 50, 52
Mitchell, M.S., 170, 171
Miyoshi, T.J., 369
Mock, J., 255
Moffit, T.E., 329
Mohamed, S., 291, 300
Mohr, W., 20
Moisan, D., 396
Molinder, I., 378, 379
Monahan, J., 64, 252, 253, 259
Monane, M., 4
Monastersky, C., 369, 371, 380
Monck, E., 368
Montgomery, J., 118
Monto, M., 370, 373
Moore, T.E., 344
Moore, W.E., 51
Moran, P.B., 214, 229
Morgan, M.H., 190
Morrow, S.L., 401
Morse, S.J., 49, 50
Moses, B.S., 163, 304
Moskowitz, D.S., 133
Mulder, M.R., 193
Muram, D., 184, 189
Murphy, C., 24, 26, 28, 29, 30, 33, 34, 35,
    36, 248, 300, 323
Murphy, S., 295
Murphy, W.D., 162, 367, 368, 369, 372, 374,
    379, 382
Murray, M.C., 216
Myers, J., 49, 197
Mynatt, C.R., 212

Nader, K., 214, 216, 230, 237
Nash, M.R., 394
Navarre, E.L., 288
Neidig, P., 27, 29, 30, 33, 37, 41, 254
Nelson, B., 169, 391
Nelson, K., 214, 215
Newcomb, K., 134, 165
Newman, E., 230, 237, 392
Newman, R., 390
Ney, P.G., 294
Nezu, A.M., 138
Nezworski, T., 289
Nguyen, T.V., 288

NiCarthy, G., 28, 327
Nicholas, K.B., 56, 306
Nichols, H.R., 378, 379
Nicola, R.M., 295
Noble, L.D., 228
Norcross, J.C., 26
Novaco, R.W., 254, 255
Nover, R.A., 294
Nunez, F., 214

Oates, R.K., 302
O'Connor, S., 294, 295
O'Dell, S.L., 134, 148
O'Farrell, T.J., 29, 30, 36
Offord, D.R., 354
O'Hagan, K., 289, 290, 293, 294, 297, 298,
    307, 308
Okazaki, S., 17, 18
Oldershaw, L., 135
Olds, D.L., 294
O'Leary, K.D., 24, 26, 27, 28, 29, 30, 31, 32,
    33, 34, 35, 36, 37, 39, 41, 93, 244, 246,
    247, 255, 323, 326, 329, 331, 348, 350
Olio, K., 404
Oliver, M., 61
Oliveri, M.K., 187
Olson, D., 41
Olson, R.L., 136, 137, 160, 164
Orkow, B., 295
Orr, S., 214
Orstein, P.A., 214, 215
Orvaschel, H., 229, 230, 303
Osofsky, J.D., 346
Osthoff, B., 355, 356
O'Toole, R., 56

Packer, L.S., 61
Padian, N., 229
Page, I.J., 367, 368, 369, 372, 374
Pagelow, M.D., 56
Pallotta, G.M., 137
Palmer, A., 300
Palmer, S.E., 65
Palotta, G.M., 168
Pan, H.S., 37
Pape, K.T., 325
Paradise, J.E., 224
Park, K.A., 299
Parker, B., 214, 215, 247, 252, 347
Parker, J.C., 254
Parker, J.G., 306
Parkinson, D.L., 346

Parks, J., 39
Parrish, J., 73, 79, 84
Parrot, A., 212, 227
Parsons, E., 289, 294
Partridge, I.M., 95
Patrick, J., 254
Patterson, C.J., 288
Patterson, G.R., 306, 332
Pawl, J., 297
Paymar, M., 251, 323
Peacock, L., 396
Pearlman, L.A., 393
Peck, G.Q., 212
Pelcovitz, D., 392
Peled, E., 343, 353
Pellow, T.A., 398
Pence, E., 27, 251, 323, 331
Pepler, D., 344
Perkins, K.A., 94, 102
Perlmutter, B.F., 139
Perry, B.D., 216
Perry, J.C., 393
Perry, N.W., 50
Pesce, C., 40
Peters, J.M., 382
Peters, S.D., 185, 245
Peterson, D.R., 296
Peterson, L., 134, 135, 159, 160, 161
Petrila, J., 49, 50, 51, 52, 66, 142, 143, 144, 145
Pezdek, K., 404
Phillips, L.R., 274
Phillips, M.H., 295, 304
Pianta, R., 157, 297
Pickrel, E., 300, 301
Pickus, R., 322
Pillemer, K., 120, 271, 272, 273, 274
Pincus, J.H., 354, 369, 370
Pirog-Good, J., 24
Pithers, W.D., 374, 382
Pitman, R.K., 214
Pittman, A.L., 362
Pittman, C.B., 348
Plichta, S.B., 243
Poindexter, V.C., 245, 251
Pokorny, A.D., 255
Polansky, N.A., 162, 164, 288, 295, 304
Polansky, N.F., 162
Polek, D.S., 325
Polonsky, S., 398
Pope, K.S., 390, 391, 392, 394, 396, 398, 402, 404

Port, L., 62
Porter, S.J., 245
Portwood, S.G., 170, 171
Poteat, G.M., 250
Pouquette, C.L., 159
Power, E., 295
Poythress, N.G., 49, 50, 51, 52, 66, 142, 143, 144, 145
Prado, L., 62
Prentice-Dunn, S., 138
Prentky, R.A., 371
Pressman, B., 344
Prince, J., 62
Prochaska, J.O., 26
Procidano, M., 138, 167
Ptacek, J., 34
Publicover, P.R., 295
Puig-Antich, J., 303
Pullybank, J., 215
Pynoos, R., 62, 214, 216, 230, 237

Quas, J., 214, 216
Quay, H.C., 296
Quinn, M.J., 275
Quinton, D., 96

Racusin, R.J., 140
Rada, R.T., 195
Radloff, L.S., 257
Rae-Grant, N., 354
Ragan, C.K., 348
Ralphe, D., 216, 230
Randolf, M., 345
Rathus, J.H., 331
Raue, P.J., 24
Rauma, D., 249
Reed, R.S., 214, 231
Reeder, M.L., 379
Regehr, C., 226
Reichard, R.D., 221
Reiss, A.J. Jr., 107
Reitzel, D., 353, 361
Reitzel-Jaffe, D., 362
Rekedal, S., 228
Renier, A., 228
Reppucci, N.D., 93, 94, 95, 99, 170, 171
Revilla, J., 224, 229
Reynolds, C.R., 230
Rhodes, N.R., 247, 249, 250
Ricci, L.R., 224
Rice, J.M., 160, 161
Rice, M.E., 379

Richard, D.C.S., 17, 18
Richardson, B., 391
Richardson, G., 371
Richmond, B.O., 230
Richters, J.E., 300
Ridolfi, K., 78, 80, 82, 84
Riggan, M., 378
Riggs, D.S., 34, 35, 245, 257
Rigler, D., 128
Rizley, R., 129
Robey, A., 37, 38
Robin, A.L., 133, 137
Robinson, D.R., 137, 166, 168
Robinson, E., 134, 165
Robinson-Simpson, G., 244
Rockwell, L.A., 224
Rodenburg, F.A., 251
Rodham, H., 49
Roe, C., 404
Roe, R., 169, 170
Roehling, P.V., 133
Roesch, R.G., 51
Rogers, C., 24, 135
Rogers, E.S., 138, 167
Rogers, T.B., 215
Roghmann, K., 195
Rohner, E.C., 288, 298, 304
Rohner, R.P., 288, 298, 304
Rohrbeck, C.A., 133, 147, 166
Rollin, B.E., 92
Rollnick, S., 26
Romanczyk, A., 214, 229
Romas, A.M., 396, 402
Roosa, M., 15
Rosa, J., 188, 193, 195, 199
Rosario, M., 304
Roscoe, B., 170
Rose, M., 210
Rosen, D., 322
Rosenbaum, A., 33, 37, 41, 93, 245, 256, 348
Rosenberg, M.S., 357
Rosenstein, P., 135, 136
Rosenwald, R.J., 37, 38
Rosewater, A., 308
Rosewater, L.B., 34, 77, 83, 261, 396, 407
Ross, A.W., 134, 148, 166
Ross, C.A., 391
Ross, D.F., 214, 229
Ross, K., 196
Roth, J.A., 107
Roth, S., 392
Rothbaum, B.O., 257

Rothery, M., 344
Rouleau, J.L., 367
Rowe, W.E., 380
Roy, M., 355
Roy-Byrne, P.P., 391
Rubin, B.L., 50, 52
Rubin, G.B., 141
Rubin, K.H., 299
Rudy, L., 62, 215, 216
Ruggiero, K., 216, 230
Ruley, E., 300
Rummell, R.M., 140
Runtz, M., 34, 304, 305, 306, 391, 394
Rusby, J.C., 134
Rushe, R.H., 38
Russ, D.F., 214
Russel, R., 51
Russel, S., 137
Russell, D., 34, 95, 97, 103, 210, 211, 254, 391
Russo, J., 391
Russo, N.F., 392
Rutledge, L.L., 325
Rutter, M., 91, 96, 299
Ryan, G., 368, 369
Ryan, J., 252
Rychtarik, R.G., 26

Sackett, L.A., 325
Sagatun, I.J., 61
Sahd, D., 195
Sakheim, D.K., 393
Salcedo, J., 300
Salter, A., 391
Saltzman, L.E., 108, 109, 114, 115, 118
Salus, M.K., 348
Salzinger, S., 304
Sameroff, A.J., 12
Samra, J., 228
Sanders, J.D., 25
Sanders, M.R., 165, 174
Sandgrund, A., 295, 296
Sandler, H.M., 294, 295
Sandler, I.N., 15
Santos, D.R., 378
Sarason, I.G., 136
Sariola, H., 168
Sas, L., 62, 346, 354, 357
Sattler, J.M., 14
Saunders, D.G., 4, 112, 116, 243, 244, 245, 247, 248, 249, 251, 252, 253, 254, 255, 256, 257, 258, 259, 325

Saunders, E.J., 50
Sauzier, M., 217
Saywitz, K.J., 188, 189, 193, 194, 197, 200, 202, 215
Schaefer, B.A., 14
Schaefer, C., 136, 147
Schaefer, C.E., 296
Schaefer, C.J., 295
Schatzow, E., 398
Scheflin, A., 404
Scheier, I.H., 295
Schetky, D.H., 61, 222, 229
Scheuer, A.Q., 294
Schieck, E., 362
Schlee, K.A., 35, 40
Schmidt, T.A., 274
Schneider, C.J., 295
Schneider, E.M., 75, 77, 78, 80, 83
Schneider, P., 398
Schonfeld, D.J., 228
Schoof, M., 39
Schram, D.D., 380
Schuengel, D., 289
Schulte, A., 216
Schultz, G.L., 141
Schumacher, J., 36
Schwartz, A.H., 323, 327
Schwartz, I., 368
Schwartz, M.D., 116, 249
Schwartz-Kenney, B.M., 214, 215
Schwartzman, A.E., 133
Scott, C., 215
Scott, H., 373
Sebes, J.M., 304
Sedlak, A.J., 12, 65, 100, 104, 211
Sedlar, G., 127, 137, 147
Seelen, J., 396
Seeley, J., 130, 290, 303
Seifer, R., 12
Selzer, M.L., 133
Senchak, M., 36
Sengstock, M., 274
Sensabaugh, G.F., 224
Sepejak, D.S., 64
Seto, M.C., 367, 368, 369
Sexton, M.C., 394
Seymour, A.K., 119
Sgroi, S., 184, 186, 192, 193, 227
Shalev, A., 214, 390
Shanok, S.S., 354, 369, 370
Shapiro, E.R., 62
Shatz, S., 322

Shaw, D.S., 300
Shen, H., 117
Shepard, M.F., 251
Sherrod, K.B., 294, 295
Shor, D.P., 228
Shortt, J.W, 38
Shortt, J.W., 325
Shubin, C.I., 224
Shupe, A., 250
Sieck, W.R., 4, 6
Siegel, B.R., 167
Siegel, J.M., 97, 136, 137
Silva, F., 16, 17
Silva, P.A., 329
Silver, H.K., 157, 169
Silverman, F.N., 157, 169
Silverton, R., 299
Simkins, L., 228
Simpson, D.G., 255
Sinclair, D., 344
Sitzman, R., 391
Sivan, A.B., 195
Siven, A.B., 228
Skinner, H.A., 133
Slater, S., 371
Slobogin, C., 49, 50, 51, 52, 66, 142, 143, 144, 145
Slusczarzck, M., 348
Small, M.A., 54, 61, 62
Smiley, J., 404
Smith, C., 117, 211, 236, 391
Smith, D.A., 29, 39, 41, 300
Smith, M.D., 247
Smith, M.L., 401
Smith, P., 257
Smith, S.R., 49
Smith, T.W., 25
Smith, W., 369, 371, 380
Snell, J.E., 37, 38
Snow, B., 61, 187
Snowden, L.R., 141
Soeken, K., 347
Soler, E., 73
Sonkin, D., 33, 34, 80, 81, 244, 246, 252, 254, 260, 331
Sorenson, E., 188, 193, 195, 199
Sorenson, S.B., 117, 252
Sorenson, S.G., 97
Sorenson, T., 61, 187
Sorkenn, J., 391
Southwick, S.M., 216
Soysa, C.K., 48

Spaccarelli, S., 15, 369
Spanier, G.B., 138
Sparrow, S.S., 14
Spence, J.T., 255
Spielberger, C.D., 137, 230, 254
Spieth, L.E., 127, 129, 140
Spinetta, J.J., 128
Spivak, G., 64
Sroufe, L.A., 288, 289, 294, 295, 297, 298, 299
Stacey, W.A., 250
Stahl, J., 288, 289
Starr, R.H., 92, 136, 159, 160, 161
Starr, S.D., 50
Starzomski, A.J., 323
Stearns, G.B., 61
Steele, B.F., 157, 169
Steer, R.A., 167, 171
Stein, J.A., 97
Stein, R.M., 371, 378
Steinberg, A., 214
Steinman, M., 291, 300
Steinmetz, S., 33, 73, 94, 96, 103, 244, 248, 249, 273, 287, 300, 304, 346, 350
Stellwagen, L.D., 62
Stern, L., 303
Stern, P., 169, 170
Sternberg, K.J., 19, 141, 214, 215, 228
Sternberg, K.L., 346
Sternberg, S., 74, 75, 77, 78, 80, 81, 82, 84
Stets, J., 24, 29, 30, 244
Stevenson, W.F., 367
Stockard, J., 300
Stoll, K., 95
Stone, M., 38
Stoops, C., 325
Storment, J.M., 212
Stormo, K.J., 227
Stott, D.H., 17
Stott, F., 17, 299, 300, 303, 308
Stouthamer-Loeber, M., 306
Stovall, G., 299
St. Pierre, J., 379
Straaus, M.A., 108, 112, 117
Strain, P., 17
Straus, M., 3, 6, 29, 30, 32, 33, 35, 36, 73, 94, 96, 108, 111, 112, 117, 139, 243, 244, 245, 246, 247, 248, 249, 255, 287, 300, 304, 324, 325, 326, 329, 330, 344, 346, 350
Strauss, J.S., 13
Strauss, M.A., 273

Strickland, B.R., 392
Stritake, W.G.K., 227
Stromberg, C.D., 50, 52
Strube, M.J., 259
Strupp, H.H., 24
Stuart, G.L., 244, 252, 256
Sudermann, M., 343, 349, 350, 353, 355, 361, 362
Sue, D., 141
Sue, S., 17, 18
Sugarman, D.B., 32, 139, 244, 245, 246, 248, 249, 256, 258, 302, 303, 330, 350
Sullivan, R., 221
Sullivan-Hanson, J., 300
Summers, K.J., 139
Summit, R., 187
Susman, E.J., 288
Sutton, S., 15, 167
Sweet, S., 324, 325, 329, 330
Swenson, C.C., 158, 165, 167, 174, 178
Swingle, J.M., 391
Sydney, R., 329
Szinovacz, M., 246, 247, 329
Szykula, S.A., 64

Tabachnick, B.G., 392
Talamo, Y., 345
Tarler-Beniolo, L., 134, 148
Tartaglini, A., 371
Tarter, R.E., 369
Taub, E.P., 62
Taylor, B., 116
Taylor, J., 304
Taylor, L., 54
Tebano-Micci, A., 228
Tellegen, A., 132, 133, 145
Tenke, C.E., 371, 376, 378
Tennen, H., 140
Teply, L.L., 50
Terdal, L.G., 131
Terr, L., 214, 346
Tertinger, D.S., 166
Thoennes, N., 121, 201
Thomas, B.H., 354
Thomas, L., 304
Thompson, R.A., 167, 290, 310
Thyfault, R.K., 73, 75, 78, 80, 81, 82, 260
Tiedeman, D.V., 13, 14
Tighe, E., 18, 19
Tilden, V.P., 274
Tisheiman, A.C., 137, 168
Tjaden, P., 121, 201

Tobey, A.E., 214, 216
Toglia, M.P., 214
Tohen, M., 91
Tolliver, R.M., 162, 379
Tolman, A.O., 139
Tolman, R., 32, 253, 322, 323, 325, 329, 331
Tomita, S., 275
Tomkins, A., 291, 300
Tonigan, J.S., 26
Toth, S., 4, 11, 13, 142, 143, 289, 300
Touchette, P.E., 161
Touliatos, J., 139
Tracy, E.M., 167
Trickett, P.K., 288
Trilling, H.R., 50, 52
Tsuang, M.T., 91
Tsui, P., 141
Turbett, J.P., 56
Tuteur, J.M., 134, 135
Tutty, L.M., 29
Twentyman, C., 48, 64, 137, 166, 168, 296, 297, 298, 299
Tyree, A., 33, 41, 350

Ulrich, Y., 247
Underwood, C., 304
Upchurch, D.M., 117
Uutela, A., 168

Valle, L., 162, 379
Vandercreek, L., 54
Van Der Hart, O., 214, 392
Van Der Kolk, B., 214, 392, 393
Van Der Veen, F., 138
VanHasselt, V.B., 4, 6, 7, 127, 128, 131, 132, 150, 161, 162
Van IJzendoorn, M.H., 289
Van Ness, S.R., 370
Van Scoyk, S., 218, 219, 226
Vargo, M.S., 346
Vazquez, G.H., 17
Velicier, W.F., 254
Vera, T.Y., 159
Vicary, J.R., 212
Vietze, P.M., 294, 295
Virkkunen, M., 253
Vissing, Y.M., 304, 324, 325, 329, 330
Vivian, D., 31, 33, 36, 37, 41, 246, 247, 326
Vizard, E., 368
Vondra, J., 63, 167, 287, 288, 297, 299, 302
Vrij, A., 193

Wagner, N.N., 95
Wahler, R.G., 138, 147, 167
Walker, C.E., 65, 130, 131, 132, 163
Walker, E., 301, 391
Walker, H., 17
Walker, L., 33, 34, 40, 81, 82, 246, 247, 251, 254, 257, 258, 331, 356
Wall, S., 294
Wallace, A.M., 379
Wallace, K.M., 138
Wallen, J., 237
Walters, G.C., 135
Waltz, J., 38
Wang, K., 81
Ward, C.H., 255
Ward, M.J., 289
Warner, J.E., 140, 142
Warner-Rogers, J.E., 127, 129, 130, 131, 137, 140, 141
Warshaw, C., 212
Washburn, C., 248
Wasik, B., 17
Waterman, J., 61, 187, 189, 194, 227, 297, 390
Waters, E., 294, 299, 300
Watkins, M.W., 13
Watson, D., 16, 17
Watson, L., 349, 353
Watson-Perczel, M., 158, 167
Weather, S., 230, 237
Webb, M.E., 165
Webb, V., 306
Weber, M.K., 228
Webster, C.D., 64
Wechsler, D., 147
Weiner, I.B., 402
Weinrott, M.R., 367, 368, 369, 370, 371, 374, 378
Weisaeth, L., 392
Weiss, A., 12, 17
Weiss, J., 295
Weiss, R.L., 139, 332
Weiss, R.V., 14
Weissman, M.M., 229
Weisz, A., 253
Weithorn, L.A., 61
Wekerle, C., 65, 362
Wells, G., 218
Wells, S.J., 56
West, C.G., 39
Westman, J.C., 222
Wettstein, R.M., 41

Wewers, S., 346
Whitcomb, D., 62, 199
White, G.L., 255
White, S.T., 224
Whitehead, T.M., 61
Whiteside-Mansell, L., 4
Whiting, L., 310
Whittaker, J.K., 167
Wickett, A.R., 294
Widener, A.J., 398
Wieder, S., 297
Wilcox, B.L., 50
Wiley, D., 74, 75, 77, 78, 80, 81, 82, 84
Wiley, R., 99
Williams, C.L., 132, 145
Williams, D.C., 367
Williams, D.H., 92
Williams, K.R., 110
Williams, L., 185, 189, 212, 217, 218, 221, 228, 390, 398
Williams, O.J., 254
Wills, T.A., 332
Wilner, N., 257
Wilson, J., 306
Wilson, M., 112
Wilson, R.K., 289, 290, 306
Wilson, S., 227, 300, 343, 344, 347, 348, 350, 353, 354, 356, 357
Winberley, R.C., 295
Wisniewski, N., 34
Wissow, L.S., 7
Wittig, B.A., 294
Wolf, E.D.A., 227
Wolf, R., 273, 274
Wolfe, D., 6, 51, 64, 65, 127, 128, 129, 130, 131, 132, 137, 140, 142, 150, 168, 288, 289, 290, 291, 292, 300, 302, 306, 343, 344, 347, 348, 350, 353, 354, 356, 362
Wolfe, V.H., 189
Wolfe, V.V., 352, 353

Wolkind, S., 92
Woo, R., 391
Wood, G.C., 322
Wood, J., 61, 187
Wright, L., 403
Wurr, C.J., 95
Wyatt, G.E., 95, 97, 103, 185, 219, 245
Wyer, M.M., 259
Wynne, D.C., 250

Yapko, M., 390
Yasenik, L., 391
Yehuda, R., 216
Yoshihama, M., 252
Yoshimura, G., 300
Youngblade, L.M., 287
Younger, A.J., 299
Yuille, J.C., 228
Yule, B., 96

Zahner, G., 91
Zahn-Waxler, C., 348
Zaidi, L.Y., 391
Zak, L., 344, 347, 348, 353, 354
Zayas, L.H., 141
Zeanah, C.H., 287
Zeanah, P.D., 287
Zellman, G.L., 56, 169
Zgourides, G., 370, 373
Zigler, E., 127
Zimet, S.G., 299
Ziskin, J., 49, 52, 145
Zoll, D., 288, 289
Zollinger, T.W., 191
Zoltek-Jick, R.R., 61
Zucker, K., 390, 394
Zuravin, S., 64, 157, 158, 159, 160
Zussman, R., 381
Zweben, A., 26

Subject Index

Abusive Behavior Observation Checklist, 248

Adjustment Scales for Children and Adolescents (ASCA), 14

Adolescent Abuse Inventory, 304

Adolescent Cognition Scale, 379

Adolescent Parenting Inventory, 295

Adolescent perpetrators of sexual abuse, 367–389
  assessment approaches, 371–381
    assessment model, 372–381
    nature of, 371–372
  case illustration, 383–385
  description of the problem, 368–371
  legal and systems considerations, 381–383

Adolescents. *See* Adolescent perpetrators of sexual abuse; Legal and systems issues of family violence and children

Adolescent sexual interest card sort, 376, 378

Adult-Adolescent Parent Inventory (AAPI), 133

Adults. *See* Clinical issues and partner violence assessment; Epidemiology of intimate partner violence and adults; Legal and systems issues of family violence and adults

Adult survivors of sexual abuse, 390–411
  assessment approaches, 393–402
    areas of assessment 396–402
    establishing rapport, 393–394
    maintaining conceptual clarity, 394–396
  case illustration, 405–407

description of the problem, 391–393
legal and systems considerations, 402–404

Adversarial sexual beliefs, 379

Alcohol abuse, 35–37

American Academy of Child and Adolescent Psychiatry, 224, 227, 228, 229

American Academy of Pediatrics, 222, 224

American Bar Association, 50

American bar association juvenile justice standards project, 310

American Humane Association, 290, 308

American Medical Association, 344

American Professional Society on Abused Children (APSAC), 190, 191, 204

Amnesty international, 257

Anatomical dolls, 204

Assessment issues: an overview:
  content considerations, 6–7
  legal and systems considerations, 7
  methodological and psychometric considerations, 5–6
  practical considerations, 4–5

Attitudes toward women scale, 255

Audio-videotaping, 199–200

Battered Child Syndrome, 157

Battered Woman Syndrome, 40, 75–76, 81

Beck Depression Inventory (BDI), 37, 167, 171, 173, 178, 255, 257, 306, 407

Behavioral coding, 165

Behavioral coding system, 134

Borderline Personality Disorder, 38

Bureau of Justice, 113, 212

Buss-Durkee Hostility Inventory, 254

California Professional Society on the Abuse
of Children (CAPSAC), 202
California wellness foundation (TCWF), 157
Campbell's Danger Assessment Index, 253
CES-D Depression Scale, 257
Checklist for living environments to assess
neglect (CLEAN), 167
Child Abuse and Neglect Interview Schedule,
132
Child Abuse and Neglect Interview
Schedule-Revised (CANIS-R), 6
Child Abuse Potential Inventory (CAPI), 6,
132, 144, 147–148, 163, 173, 262, 295
Child Assessment Schedule (CAS), 303
Child Behavior Checklist (CBCL), 134, 166,
189, 204, 230, 298, 352, 375
Child Depression Inventory (CDI), 230
Childhood Level of Living Scale (CLLS),
162, 304
Child Manifest Anxiety Scale-Revised
(CMAS-R), 230
Child neglect, 157–183
assessment approaches, 161–169
case illustration, 171–178
description of the problem, 158–161
legal and systems considerations, 169–171
Child physical abuse, 127–156
assessment approaches, 131–141
case illustration, 145–150
description of the problem, 127–131
legal and systems considerations,
141–145
practical issues in assessment, 139–141
Child protective services (CPS), 15, 57, 60,
63, 139–140, 142, 144–146, 149–150,
169, 308, 368
Children. See Child neglect; Child physical
abuse; Child witnesses of domestic
violence; Clinical issues of family
violence and child assessment;
Epidemiology of family violence and
children; Extrafamilial child sexual
abuse; Incest in young children; Legal
and systems issues of family violence
and children; Psychological
maltreatment of children
Children impact of traumatic events scale
family violence form (CITES-FVF),
353
Children's Depression Inventory, 352
Children's memory. See Incest in young
children

Child Sexual Abuse Legitimacy Scale, 190
Child Sexual Behavior Inventory, 189
Child Well-Being Scales, 163, 304
Child witnesses of domestic violence,
344–360
assessment approaches, 350–354
case illustration, 357–360
description of the problem, 344–350
legal and systems considerations,
354–357 (see also Legal and systems
issues of family violence and
children)
misdiagnosis of child witnesses, 347
symptoms of child witnesses, 347–350
at different developmental levels,
347–349
long-term effects, 350
moderating determinants of
psychosocial impact, 350
subtle symptoms, 349–350
Clinical issues of family violence and child
assessment, 10–23
measurement issues, 11–15
multidemensionality, 12–13
multivariate risk, 12
nomothesis, 13–15
quality of measurement, 15–20
consequential validity, 19–20
construct validity, 16–17
contextual relevence, 18–19
cultural validity, 17–18
Clinical issues and partner violence
assessment, 24–47
assessment techniques, 32–34
co-occurrence of psychological problems
and, 35–39
determination of violence as a primary or
secondary target, 30
diagnostic debates and, 39–42
ethical issues, 42
frequency, severity, and chronicity of,
26–27
minimization and denial of abuse, 34–35
population, 27–29
purpose and goals of, 24–32
recommendations, 30–32
Clinician administered PTSD scale-child and
adolescent version (CAPS-C), 230
Cognitive distortions and immaturity scale,
379
Committee on family violence of the national
institute of mental health, 108

Community interaction checklist, 138, 147, 167

Conflict Tactics Scale (CTS), 6, 32, 103, 111, 112, 116, 121, 139, 245–253, 300, 330, 352

Conflict Tactics Scale-Revised (CTS-R), 32–34

Daily checklist of marital activities, 332

Denver developmental screening test, 194

Department of child and family services (DCFS), 171

Department of children's services, 205–206

Departments of public health and human services, 20

Depression, 37

Diagnostic and Statistical Manual of Mental Disorders, 13, 39–41, 43, 258, 345, 392, 393, 398

Difficult child scale, 173

Drug abuse screening test, 133

Dyadic Adjustment Scale (DAS), 138–139

Dyadic Parent-Child Interaction Coding System, 165

Dyadic Parent-Child Interaction Coding System II (DPICS-II), 134

Eco map, 167

Elder abuse and neglect, 271–286
    assessment approaches, 274–281
        characteristics of the abuser, 280–281
        issues and considerations, 275–280
    description of the problem, 271–274
        demographics of abuse, 272
    legal and systems considerations, 281–283

Elderly. *See* Elder abuse and neglect; Epidemiology of intimate partner violence and adults

Epidemiology of family violence and children, 91–106
    children as aggressors, 103–104
    children as victims, 96–103
    definitional issues, 93–95
    values and epidemiology, 92–93

Epidemiology of intimate partner violence and adults, 107–123
    definition of terms, 108
    elder abuse, 120–121
    fatal violence, 109–110
    gender and violence, 116–117
    nonfatal violence, 110–115
    sexual violence, 118–120

Extrafamilial child sexual abuse, 210–242
    assessment of impact on the child, 222–224
        medical assessment, 222–224
    assessment of impact of extrafamilial sexual abuse, 224–231
        information sources, 225
        standardized instruments for assessing psychopathology, 230
        tasks of assessment, 225
        tasks for meeting with child, 229
        tasks for meeting with parents/caretakers, 227
    case illustration of, 234–236
    description of the problem, 210–212
    detection and disclosure of, 216–220
        children's concerns, 219
        parent/family beliefs and myths, 219
    investigation of, 220–222
    legal considerations, 231–234
    overview of assessment, 213–216
        developmental issues and, 213–216

Eyberg Child Behavior Inventory (ECBI), 134, 148, 150, 166, 173

Family behavior survey, 300

Family beliefs inventory, 133

Family experiences questionnaire, 304

Family stress checklist, 295

Federal Bureau of Investigations (FBI), 107, 109

Francine Hughes, 77

Frye test, 52, 60

Hare psychopath checklist, 369

Harris-Lingoes, 133

Hassles scale, 147

Head start, 17, 20

History of violence witnesses by child questionnaire, 352

Home Accident Prevention Inventory (HAPI), 166–167, 173

Home observation for measurement of the environment (HOME) inventory, 166, 304

Home Simulation Assessment (HAS), 136, 164

Impact of event scale, 257

Incest in young children, 184–208
    assessment approaches, 188–189
    assessment by developmental age, 196–199

Incest in young children *(Continued)*
  case illustration, 204–206
  description of the problem, 185–188
    coercian in, 186
    developmental limitations of the child,
      188
    disclosure of, 185–186
    family support of disclosure, 187–188
    fear and threat in, 186
    guilt and shame, 186
    retraction, 187
  eight to eleven-years, 197–198
  five to seven-years, 197
  interviewing considerations, 198–199
  legal and systems considerations, 199–204
    anatomical dolls, 204
    assessment issues, 200
    children's testimonial competence, 203
    custody disputes, 201–202
    false allegations, 201
    leading questions and suggestibility, 202
    memory, 202–203
    role of evaluator, 204
  under five years of age, 196–197
Index of social network strength, 167
Index of spouse abuse, 252
Insanity defense. *See* Legal Issues and
Institute of medicine, 226
Intermittent Explosive Disorder (IED),
  41–42
Interpersonal process code, 134
Interpersonal support evaluation list, 138,
  167
Inventory of spouse abuse, 331
IPAT anxiety scale, 295
Issues checklist (IC), 137

Knowledge of behavioral principles as
  applied to children (KBPAC), 134, 147

Lamb warning, 53
Legal and systems issues of family violence
  and adults, 73–87
  admissibility of expert testimony, 78–81
  presentation at trial, 81–84
  defense strategies, 75–78
  overview of, 74–75
Legal and systems issues of family violence
  and children, 48–72
  general legal issues, 49–54
    basic legal terms and distinctions,
      52–54

investigation and prosecution, 54–66
  adolescent testimony, 61–62 *(see also*
      Adolescent perpetrators of sexual
      abuse)
  child testimony, 61–62
  competency to stand trial, 62
  mental health professionals and, 54–66
Life experiences survey, 136

Marital Adjustment Scale (MAS), 138
Marital Interaction Coding System (MICS),
  139, 332
Marlowe-Crowne Social Desirability Scale,
  253, 256
Maternal attitude scale, 295
Maternal characteristics scale, 295
Maternal history interview, 295
Maternal Observation Matrix (MOM), 134,
  135
Measure of wife abuse, 251
Mehrabian and epstein emotional empathy
  scale, 135
Michigan alcohol screening test, 133, 255
Michigan screening profile of parenting, 295
Millon Adolescent Personality Inventory,
  375
Millon Clinical Multiaxial Inventory, 38,
  256
Minnesota Multiphasic Personality Inventory
  (MMPI), 34, 38, 64, 83), 132–133, 147,
  253, 256, 262, 369, 375, 396, 407
Mother-child interaction scale (MCIS), 135
Multidimensional anger inventory, 137
Multiphasic sex inventory, 376, 378, 379
Multiphasic sex inventory-juvenile form, 378

National Academy of Science Report, 67
National Center for Child Abuse and Neglect
  (NCCAN), 98–101, 104, 128–130, 140,
  143
National Council of Juvenile & Family Court
  Judges, 261
National Crime Victimization Survey
  (NCVS), 108, 112–119
National family violence survey, 108, 111
National Institute of Justice and the Center
  for Disease Control and Prevention,
  121
National Institute of Mental Health, 111
National Institute on Drug Abuse, 119, 133
National survey of youth (1972), 103,
National women's study, 119–120

Novaco's anger index, 254
Nova Scotia law reform commission, 356

Ohio state psychological association, 41

Parental acceptance-rejection questionnaire, 304
Parental Anger Inventory (PAI), 137, 147, 150, 164
Parental distress scale, 173
Parental locus of control scale, 138
Parental Stress Index Short Form (PSI/SF), 164
Parent Behavior Checklist (PBC), 163, 173
Parent child distress scale, 173
Parenting alliance inventory, 139
Parenting stress index, 136, 150, 173
Parent interview and assessment guide, 132
Parent opinion questionnaire, 133, 147, 150, 166
Parent/partner empathy scale, 135, 136
Parent problem solving instrument, 168
Parent problem solving measurement, 168
Partner abuse inventory, 331
Penn Interactive Peer Play Scale (PIPPS), 19
Perceived Competence Scale for Children (PCSC), 230
Perceived social support questionnaire, 138, 167
Personality disorders, 37–39
Personality inventory for youth, 352
Personality research form, 295
Planned Activities Training (PAT), 165, 174
Posttraumatic stress disorder (PTSD), 39–41, 187, 216, 230, 237, 325, 345, 346, 350, 392
Power and control wheel, 323
Pregnancy research questionnaire, 295
Problem-solving self-monitoring form, 138
Project safecare, 172, 178
Project 12-ways, 172
Psychological maltreatment of children, 287–321
  assessment approaches, 293–307
    adolescence (12 to 18 years), 304–307
    infancy and toddlerhood (birth to 3), 293–297
    middle school age (8 to 11 years), 301–304
    preschool and early school years (3 to 7 years), 297–301

case illustrations, 310–312
description of the problem, 288–293
  core issues, 288–289
  definitional issues, 289–293
legal and systems considerations, 307–310
Psychological maltreatment scale, 304
Psychological maltreatment of women, 322–340
  assessment approaches, 328–332
  case illustration, 335–338
  categories of maltreatment, 326–328
  description of the problem, 322–325
  legal and systems considerations, 332–335
Psychological maltreatment of women inventory (PMWI), 331
Psychological maltreatment of women scale, 32

Rape myth acceptance, 379

Schedule for Affective Disorders and Schizophrenia for School-Age Children (SADS), 303, 306
Sexual abuse. *See* Adolescent perpetrators of sexual abuse; Adult survivors of sexual abuse; Epidemiology of family violence and children; Epidemiology of intimate partner violence and adults; Extrafamilial child sexual abuse; Incest in young children
Sexually abused child syndrome, 61
Sexual stereotyping, 379
Sixth Amendment, 61
Social network map, 167
Social problem solving inventory, 138
Social Skills Rating System (SSRS), 19
Social Support Scale For Children (SSSC), 230
Spouse specific aggression scale, 32
Spouse specific assertion scale, 331
Standards for educational and psychological testing, 17
State-Trait Anger Scale (STAS), 137, 254
State-Trait Anxiety Inventory for Children (STAIC), 230
Study of child abuse and neglect (NIS-3), 12
Supplementary homicide reports (SHR), 109, 117
Symptom-checklist-90-revised, 132, 147, 163

Teacher report form of the child behavior checklist (TRF-CBCL), 230

Termination of parental rights (TPR), 63, 66
The Burning Bed, 77
Third national incidence study of child abuse and neglect (NIS-3), 129–130
Trauma Symptom Inventory (TSI), 396, 407–408
Trauma symptoms checklist for children, 352

Uniform crime reporting (UCR), 107, 109
U.S. Advisory Board on Child Abuse and Neglect (ABCAN), 101–102, 104
U.S. Bureau of the Census, 113
U.S. Department of Justice, 310

Veterans Administration, 36
Violence against women act, 73

Ways of coping checklist-revised, 138, 168
Wechsler Adult Intelligence Scale-III (WAIS-III), 147
Woman battering, 243–270
    assessment approaches, 244–256
        assessment of violent behavior, 245–247
        interviewing methods, 247–252
        offender characteristics, 252–256
    case illustration, 260–264
    description of the problem, 243–244
    legal and systems considerations, 258–260
    survivors' stages of change, 256–258
Women. *See* Psychological maltreatment of women; Woman battering

Youth self report form, 352